READINGS
IN
MARKETING
MANAGEMENT

READINGS
IN
MARKETING
MANAGEMENT

Edited by

PHILIP KOTLER
Northwestern University

KEITH K. COX
University of Houston

PRENTICE-HALL, INC.   ENGLEWOOD CLIFFS, N.J.

PRENTICE-HALL INTERNATIONAL, INC., London
PRENTICE-HALL OF AUSTRALIA, PTY. LTD., Sydney
PRENTICE-HALL OF CANADA, LTD., Toronto
PRENTICE-HALL OF INDIA PRIVATE LIMITED, New Delhi
PRENTICE-HALL OF JAPAN, INC., Tokyo

CONTENTS

PART **2**

ANALYZING MARKETING OPPORTUNITIES

PART 5

CONTROLLING THE MARKETING EFFORT

SECTION A
MARKETING CONTROL

Introduction

Marketing is a fantastically varied discipline. We were reminded of this in trying to assemble a useful collection of readings that would appeal to students and practitioners of marketing management. Our first attempt at developing a well-rounded collection of readings resulted in over 150 excellent pieces—far too many for any one book. It became clear that we would have to painfully prune the collection.

Our first principle was to choose those readings that were of obvious interest to the marketing manager rather than to the specialist or technician in marketing research, advertising, or sales management.

Our second principle was to select articles that ranged over many types of marketing situations—consumer, industrial, distributor, services, government, and international. This was done to avoid a common tendency to overemphasize consumer marketing situations. In fact, we even added some articles that go beyond traditional product service marketing, articles dealing with the marketing of organizations, persons, places, and ideas.

Our third principle was to select many articles that deal with real marketing situations treated analytically. We wanted to avoid textbook-like explanations, devoid of illustration and application, and to give instead analyses of situations facing such companies as Procter & Gamble, Raytheon Corporation, Ford Motor Company, Zenith, du Pont, McKinsey and Company, and so on. Articles were chosen that provided anecdotal material for their intrinsic reading interest and backed this up with the derivation of important concepts in marketing.

Our fourth principle was to pick out articles that illustrated the best in modern marketing analysis and management, particularly as derived from the use of behavioral and quantitative concepts. Hopefully these articles will increase the appreciation of readers as to the potency of these scientific perspectives in aiding effective marketing performance.

Our fifth principle was to blend classic articles representing the finest statement of certain marketing problems and principles with several recent articles that open new analytical pathways. The collection shows the continued growth of fine analysis in the emerging science of marketing management.

These five principles eventually led to the choice of thirty-six excellent articles. These articles were then arranged in a way to emphasize awareness of the marketing-management process. The book is divided into six major parts that parallel this process, starting with conceptualizing marketing management and proceeding through analyzing marketing opportunities, organizing for marketing, planning the marketing program, controlling the marketing effort, and extending the marketing idea. Each part in turn is subdivided into logical sections, featuring articles on each subject that provide a basis for edification and discussion.

Since there were numerous good articles that could not be included due to the length of the book, we are providing a selected bibliography of additional articles at the end of each of the six parts.

Philip Kotler
Northwestern University

Keith K. Cox
University of Houston

READINGS
IN
MARKETING
MANAGEMENT

CONCEPTUALIZING MARKETING MANAGEMENT

The study of marketing management should begin with an overview of the basic systems and concepts that guide marketing behavior. Levitt (pp. 3–14) suggests that markets should be examined from the viewpoint of value satisfactions of the buyer. These can be achieved through "product augmentation," which is what businessmen add to the factory output to give it greater customer appeal. Forrester (pp. 15–24) concludes this part by construction of a model to represent the dynamics of market and company interactions. The linkages between market and company form feedback loops that can produce sales growth or decline.

THE CONCEPT OF MARKETING

1

Improving Sales through Product Augmentation

THEODORE LEVITT
Harvard University

People don't buy products; they buy the expectation of benefits. Yet narrow production-minded executives and most economic theorists are resolutely attached to the idea that goods have intrinsic properties. A loaf of bread is presumed to be quite obviously something different from a diamond. Each is somehow viewed as having inherent characteristics rather than as conveying benefits on buyers. This accounts in the business world for pricing policies based one-sidedly on costs.

PEOPLE DON'T BUY PRODUCTS

Physics long ago abandoned the notion that things have intrinsic or inherent characteristics. It is time that we do the same in business. *People spend their money not for goods and services, but to get the value satisfactions they believe are bestowed by what they are buying.*

The marketing view demands the active recognition of a new kind of competition that is in galloping ascendance in the world today. This is *the competition of product augmentation:* not competition between what companies produce in their factories, but *between what they add to their factory output in the form of packaging, services, advertising, customer advice, financing, delivery arrangements, warehousing, and other things that people value.*

Reprinted with permission from *European Business*, April, 1969, pp. 5–12.

When the outputs of competing factories are essentially identical and their prices the same, the conversion of an indifferent prospect into a solid customer requires a special effort. Whether the product is cold rolled steel or hot cross buns, whether accountancy or delicacies, competitive effectiveness increasingly demands that the successful seller offer his prospect and his customer more than the generic product itself. He must surround his generic product with a cluster of value satisfactions that differentiates his total offering from his competitors'. He must provide a total proposition, the content of which exceeds what comes out at the end of the assembly line.

CASES: COSMETICS, COMPUTERS, FERTILIZERS

Take *cosmetics*. In America it is an industry with 1967 factory sales of over three billion dollars. Yet in 1967 not a single American woman bought a single penny's worth of cosmetics. Charles Revson, the entrepreneurial genius who built Revlon into the thriving enterprise it is today, has said, "In the factory we make cosmetics. In the store we sell hope." Women use cosmetics, but they don't buy them; they buy hope. Mr. Revson has built his magnificent edifice on the correct understanding of human drives. He knows that chastity is the rarest of sexual aberrations.

"Hope" is the extra plus—the special promise of customer-satisfying benefits—that gives cosmetics their special appeal. It is not with the generic product that Revlon addresses itself to the consumer, but with the special promise of differentiating glamour, personal fulfillment, and sex appeal. What is important is not so much what Revlon puts inside the compact as the ideas put inside the customer's head by luxurious packaging and imaginative advertising.

Pressure valves, polypropylene and screw machines cannot be similarly glamorized, nor does glamor itself attract any solvent customers for screw machines. But hope does—the buyer's hope that in choosing your company's screw machines, he has made a safer and better choice. Of course, the customer expects quality equipment and competitive prices. He expects on-time delivery. But successful companies increasingly find it pays to give the customer more—to supply him with extras he was not himself aware he wanted. Having been offered these extras, the customer finds them beneficial and therefore prefers doing business with the company that supplies them. *By augmenting their generic products with unsolicited extras that produce extra customer benefits*, the seller produces for himself extra customers.

In recent years, *computer manufacturers* have been especially active in augmenting their products with application aids, programming services, information-systems advice, and training programs for their customers. These services are so important for sales success that it has become perfectly clear that the computer manufacturer with the biggest share of the market is not necessarily the one whose computers are always the best or the cheapest. Success and leadership have gone to the company with the best total package of customer-satisfying and therefore customer-getting values. The most important part of this package turns out to be something quite profoundly different from the computer hardware itself. It is the so-called peripheral services and aids with which the generic product is so effectively surrounded.

Computers are not distinctive in their capacity to lend themselves to this kind of service augmentation. It works with perhaps even greater force for the most mundane commodities. Take *fertilizer*. The International Minerals and Chemical Corporation sells a prosaic mix of fertilizer ingredients—phosphate, superphosphate, and potash—very much more successfully than its competitors. It does well not because its prices are lower, its delivery more reliable, or its salesmen quicker at grabbing the luncheon check. It succeeds so well because it has carefully analyzed the over-all business problems of its prospects and then has done something imaginative about its findings. It provides its customers with free business consultancy services as part of its total product package. As a result, it has given its prospects a special set of reasons for prefering to do business with IMC rather than with its competitors. IMC does not offer a better product, but it offers a *different* product—a product with new and superior benefits for its users.

THE PRODUCT IS NOT THE MESSAGE

For years, almost instinctively, consumer goods manufacturers have recognized that the generic product is perhaps the least important part of the product itself. In clothing, it is not dresses one sells, but fashion. In retailing—the retail store—it is often atmosphere, or selection, or speed of service, or delivery that matters more than the quality of the products themselves. In *cigarettes* the point reaches its most extraordinary extreme. Only a particularly prudish observer can fail to come to any conclusion other than that American cigarette companies literally sell only one product—sex. Even the "low-tar-and-nicotine" brands embellish their television ads with suggestive scenes of sexual prowess and allurement. The most successful of all American campaigns in over thirty years is pure sex —the Marlboro Country ads. The rugged outdoor simplicity of the American frontiersman appeals to the male animal for what it implies about his virility. It suggests a powerful masculinity undiluted by contaminating urban softness. And it appeals to the female just as effectively by implying that a woman who smokes Marlboros is an uninhibited primitive of irresistible attraction.

It is not too wild to suggest that the *large retail department store* should view itself as being in show business. The customer goes there as much to be titillated and entertained as to buy what is displayed. She goes to have her senses heightened and her spirits elevated. Indeed, unless her senses are properly titillated and her spirits lifted, she certainly will not buy, or buy in the desired quantity. It is relevant that the producer of the magnificent lighting effects of the original Broadway production of *My Fair Lady* received so many offers from large retailers that he established a successful lighting consulting firm.

The necessity of creating the proper buying atmosphere, of producing properly promising packaging, and of offering sufficiently appropriate customer services is so obvious to today's businessman that he is largely unaware that he is responding to that necessity. Yet to do these things well, he must be aware of the fact that he is doing them at all. Any number of companies, upon being told of International Minerals and Chemical's customer consulting services, will respond with impressive examples of how they have done the same sorts of things for various customers. They may indeed have done the same sorts of things, but they have not done the same thing. They have helped customers on an *ad hoc* basis when a particular salesman has taken the initiative, when a particular prospect actually requested the help, when a particular customer was in visible trouble. That is all very well. The point is that IMC does it on an organized, fully-budgeted, continuously programmed basis. It has men with the full-time responsibility of analyzing its prospects' and customers' problems for the purpose of constantly producing product augmentations designed to help with these problems and hence help give customers special reasons for dealing with IMC. As a consequence, IMC has created within its vast organization a powerfully prevailing culture in which the customer is viewed not as the object of a military encounter—to be targeted, banged away at, gotten the big guns out for—but as an entity with problems that he is trying to solve and in whose solution IMC should participate.

THE PROBLEM OF DEFINING THE PROBLEM

The marketing concept views the customers' purchasing activities as being problem-solving activities. This view of what the consumer does can have a profound effect on how the supplier or seller conducts his affairs. It affects more than how he does business and how much business he does. It affects what business he tries to do and what his product line should be. *By looking at what the customer is actually trying to do, the seller will see that his problem as a seller is quite different from what is usually assumed.* Only after he defines his problem properly can the seller decide what is proper for him to to. Never is this necessity more urgent than when competition is most severe. The most severe kind of competition is warfare. It is not surprising therefore that war strategy has so often focused so carefully on a prior definition of the specific problem at hand. Since one gets few second chances, it is essential that the first succeed.

Incorrect definition of the problem—or incorrect statements of the objective—can produce similarly incorrect conclusions about the appropriateness of a given strategy in business. A current example is the burgeoning *demand for aid to the aged* that has been generated by life-sustaining drugs and *Medicare**. The ratio of elderly people in hospitals is rising. At the same time the demand for nursing homes is booming in part because of drugs and Medicare, and in part because of the great availability of retirement pensions and the rising independence of adult

* Medical care for the aged, a bill passed by the U.S. Congress in 1968.

children who don't want aging and ailing parents to live with them. A superficial look suggests great commercial opportunities in hospitals and nursing homes. Such opportunities do indeed exist, but they are exaggerated. A more analytical look shows that many hospital beds are occupied by post-operative patients who are too well to require hospital care and too well to require nursing-home confinement. What they require is convalescent care—a transition facility between in-patient surgery at hospitals and ultimate nursing-home confinement. The availability of such transitionary convalescent centers would greatly relieve pressures on hospitals and greatly enhance the dignity of patients who are too well for terminal nursing-home residence. Recognition of precisely this problem has created companies like Extendicare, Inc., and American Medicorp, Inc., which provide convalescent home services while many others are still busily building terminal nursing homes.

This is a case of companies whose careful examination of the full range of conditions to which they addressed themselves resulted in a product-line activity that, in effect, altered the business into which they might otherwise have gone. Serving hospitals or running terminal nursing homes is quite different from running convalescent centers.

And supplementing a factory-produced product with services is quite different from running a factory, and it is different from the usual way of selling the product.

THE CLASSIC EXAMPLE OF AMERICAN AIRLINES

A classic example is the work of American Airlines during its early efforts at promoting air freight. The motivation was obvious. Airplanes carried people all day long and half through the night. But from midnight until dawn these costly but highly mobile fixed assets remained idle. Searching for new uses, American sought out the Distributor Products Division of the Raytheon Corporation as a possible air cargo customer. The DP Division supplied transistors and vacuum tubes to distributors who resold largely to small radio and television repair shops throughout the nation. It had five warehouses supplied from a single factory warehouse near Boston.

American studied Raytheon's distribution operations in infinite detail. The result was a proposal to eliminate all five field warehouses and supply distributors directly by overnight air cargo. American proposed that all daily orders be assembled at the factory each night, picked up by American at the plant, and transported by air cargo overnight to fourteen break-bulk locations throughout the nation. From there common carrier truckers would deliver the orders immediately to distributors.

But American did not stop there, leaving it to Raytheon to work out the details. American enlisted the help of the Freiden Company and Western Union. Together the three companies designed an elaborate automatic data transmissions system with feeder terminals in the field and print-out readers at the plant. Electronically transmitted orders were received by a computer at the plant and automatically converted into shipping invoices, slotted into shipping schedules, and fed into inventory control and production schedules. The net result was that Raytheon received a systems proposal that was so complete and persuasive in every detail that it became easy for Raytheon to take a decision in favor of air cargo.

What was American Airlines' product? To say that it was air cargo is to miss the point. It was the provision of that fashionable commodity, *a system.* Air freight alone was a minor, and by itself insufficient, element of the system. American surrounded this particular element, the generic product, with a cluster of augmented benefits that became the deciding variables in the transaction. The product was not air cargo; it was a fully-integrated, automated, and complete communications-distribution system.

American might have stopped with the mere proposal to substitute air cargo for the warehouses. It might have said simply that communications and teleprinters and computers and trucking were not its business and that it knew nothing about such things. But it systematically and conscientiously did more. It arranged to do the whole task that was needed to solve Raytheon's problem. As a consequence, it created a customer where none existed—where the customer was not even aware that he was a prospect.

THE NEW COMPETITION: HIDDEN COMPETITION

This is today's hidden competition, the nongeneric component of the product.

In the case of industrial goods and services, it is particularly prevalent in the relations between large companies whose customers are relatively small and fragmented, or whose competences are limited. This is not the visible competition between televised toothpastes or headline-getting competition between giant suppliers of aero-space systems to NASA. It is the new competition of product augmentation.

Take *the construction industry.* Life used to be enormously uncomplicated for manufacturers of construction materials. They simply supplied boards or beams or tiles and let somebody else worry about assembling them. But as new materials and new producers generated new competition, one manufacturer after another has been forced into strange and complex new business—not only to protect traditional markets but to help produce new ones.

Aluminium Company of America not only makes construction extrusions, but finances the skyscrapers that use them; Armstrong Cork manufactures not only ceiling tiles, but also integrated lighting systems; and Weyerhaeuser Company, the nation's largest lumber producer, has developed perhaps one of the most elaborate and fully encompassing "products" with which to compete in the residential housing field—the Registered Home program. This program attempts to shore up the position of its dealers against the inroads of big-tract home builders and housing component makers, who often bypass dealers and buy lumber directly from competing manufacturers. Weyerhaeuser correctly believes there is a continuing and sizeable market for the output of the small builder, but that he needs help of a kind he often is incapable of providing himself. As a consequence, Weyerhaeuser has gotten deeply involved not only in selling the lumber but in pushing sales of the houses themselves and everything that goes with them: architect's plans, financing, sales training, merchandising aids, and color-coordinated interiors.

What Weyerhaeuser is trying to do is put its dealer into home construction, or at least into producing and supplying prefabricated components to custom home building. Working through local mortgage houses, Weyerhaeuser offers to make funds available to dealers and mortgage companies from national sources. Weyerhaeuser guarantees the top 15% of the mortgage and gives a twenty-year written warranty to the home buyer on all lumber it supplies to a new house. This is considered a potent argument to a generation accustomed to warping doors and sticking windows. In return, the dealer commits himself to buy all lumber for Registered Homes from Weyerhaeuser.

While this is an example of an extremely complex form of product augmentation, some are much simpler and more venerable. The Campbell Soup Company has for years offered management-training programs for retail food store owners and management-level employees. The Pillsbury Company offers its Creative Marketing Service International to small retailers. Under this program, retailers pay for otherwise costly merchandising services from Pillsbury, but it costs no money. They pay with points earned from the purchase of Pillsbury products. W. R. Grace & Co. offers a complete package of ten key services to the customers of its various plastics. Butler Buildings pays the cost of consulting studies designed to make dealer operations more effective. General Electric has created a considerable incentive for multi-brand dealers to push GE major appliances with its Major Appliance Marketing Program. The dealer carries only floor samples and does nothing more than complete the selling transaction. Then GE takes over, drawing the appliance out of its own warehouse, delivering it to the buyer, installing and demonstrating and, where needed, servicing it. United Van Lines, the moving and storage company, offers a free detailed community information service for its prospective movers.

The new competition is costly but inescapable. In a world of highly undifferentiated generic products, there is an inevitable shift to new forms of competition. This shift clearly requires an analysis of customer and consumer needs that extends beyond the generic product itself. And since it is not really the generic product that people buy, but the benefits it bestows, then to think of "the product" in terms more encompassing than in the past is not only competitively wise but ontologically sound. *It is the benefits that are the product.*

SURVIVAL PROBLEMS FOR SMALL BUSINESS

Because this new competition is costly, it creates *survival problems for the small members of industries dominated by large firms.* It is to be expected, therefore, that survival for the small firm will increasingly take the form of carving out highly specialized niches in markets that the large think-big firms have not yet organized themselves to reach, or indeed cannot reach.

In the major appliance field, Gibson and Speed Queen have done exactly that. Faced with the thriving aggressiveness of mass-merchandising stores that sell well-known major appliances at relatively rock-bottom prices, major department stores have difficulty in making an impression on the community of being low-priced sellers. Their cost structures generally prevent them from selling these highly advertised commodities at competitively low prices. Speed Queen and Gibson have helped them to make a competitive, low-price impression. They have chosen not to compete with the major producers either on advertising volume or in the same distribution outlets; they offer their appliances almost exclusively to large metropolitan department stores at highly attractive prices. These stores use their own reputations and local advertising power to promote these brands, thus enabling their stores to make an impact as low-price sellers of major appliances while giving otherwise obscure brands the benefit of the stores' reputations.

While large companies can do more for their distributors and dealers and thereby outsell their small competitors, the small recipients of these services from large suppliers become more competitive because of these services. Thus, Du Pont systematically makes cost analysts available to fabricators of its plastics. Large fabricators have their own analysts and don't need Du Pont. The small ones do, and get the benefit of the nation's largest plastic producer. But Du Pont's customer service activities extend far beyond this. They include making available to its customers at out-of-pocket-costs its own internally developed training programs, including training even of lathe operators.

The F. W. Means Co., the Chicago-based linen supply firm, has a free interior decorating service for the restaurants that use its linens and uniforms. But not all ancillary supplier services come for free. Distillers Corporation-Seagrams, Ltd., offers to its 450 independent wholesalers the services of its Distributor Consulting Service at a standard fee—$60 a day per consultant. The rate is less than half the fee of outside consulting firms, but the service is felt to be equal in quality. The consultants are given full independence. Typical jobs run to $10,000, but have been as high as $15,000. The service takes on almost any job: warehousing, computer installation, truck routing, administrative procedures, market studies, compensation.

HIDDEN ATTRIBUTES CAN HAVE A POWER OF LIFE OR DEATH OVER THE SUCCESS OF A PRODUCT

The examples of the augmented products cited above have in common a single attribute: they contain features that produce results—a competitive plus. These key features, the features that distinguish these products from those of competitors, are invariably external to the generic products in the old-fashioned terms of which we are in the habit of defining industries.

In some cases the things with which a product is surrounded are so visibly important to its success that we thoughtlessly take their importance for granted. Their significance is totally overlooked. Quick examples are clothing (it is style and color that is bought, not shelter or coverage), cosmetics (images and packaging, not chemicals) even cars (styling, size, comfort, accessories, not transportation).

With some "products" the surrounding attributes have a virtual life or death power over the success of the product, yet we are seldom aware of it. For example, one survey suggests that people think of airlines as selling seats on planes going from X to Y. The product is viewed as sit-down rapid transit between airports. Yet if the airlines viewed that as their product, they would die. Their product has a powerful and deciding hidden attribute—the supporting software reservation services.

The consequences of a breakdown in an airline's reservations system would be as revenue-destructive as the breakdown of the airplanes themselves. A product is something that is capable of producing revenue. When an airline seat cannot produce revenue because the computerized reservations system has broken down, it becomes painfully clear that the reservations system is a central part of the airline's product.

A product therefore consists of all its attributes that produce solvent customers. By this standard, it can be said without excessive stretching that the *Edsel automobile* was not a product. It did not produce enough customers. But the Edsel's magnificent failure demonstrates the importance of yet another vital nongeneric aspect of product attributes. *This is the element of excitement.*

Excitement is a fragile and abstract commodity not likely to attract the serious attention of solid executives schooled in the arcane arts of finance, law and manufacturing. Yet it is as crucial for new-product success in cars, computers, and cutting tools as in cosmetics.

Edsel's fatal failure was in major part a failure to sustain the excitement which extensive pre-introduction promotion had produced.

Nothing sells itself, not even the most venerable and tantalizing of all commodities—sex. It has to be embellished, elaborated, amplified, *enriched, perfumed, styled, corseted, colored and cosmeticized.* If even sex needs that kind of doctoring, no experienced male can conceivably argue that other things don't. No purchasing decision for any product, no matter how sophisticated its engineering or critically crucial its economics, is ever made that exclusively by the strict determinism of the slide rule.

The issue is a simple one—*what is the relative importance of slide rule versus the human rule?* The argument made here is that the latter is more important, even in selling slide rules, than is generally conceded, or than sellers are generally aware, and that the ingredient of excitement and other embellishments should to this extent be viewed as characteristics of the products themselves. They must be viewed as part of the essential characteristics built into the product from the beginning.

SELL EXCITEMENT

Even the most prosaic products with no relation to life or death require the sustaining ingredient of excitement. That is one reason that there is such a booming demand for the services of companies who stage elaborate show-biz *sales meetings and business conventions.* One of the most successful practitioners of this approach is Anthony E. Cascino of International Minerals and Chemical, the fertilizer company. Says he, "It is not just that a sales meeting imparts information; it must also provide inspiration and enthusiasm. Even the most revolutionary marketing approach will suffer if it lacks emotion and empathy. Salesmen need excitement and stimulation, and a sales meeting should provide the atmosphere through which these characteristics can be generated."[1]

The way a generic product is engineered and positioned affects the ultimate consumer. *But it can be used to engage the enthusiasm and energy of the middlemen who handle it through the distribution chain.* Francis C. Rooney, Melville Shoes' effervescent and solidly businesslike president, says flatly, "People no longer buy shoes to keep their feet warm and dry. They buy them because of the way the shoes make them feel—masculine, feminine, rugged, different, sophisticated, young, glamorous, 'in.' Buying shoes has become an emotional experience. Our business now is selling excitement rather than shoes."

Three factors combine to emphasize the accelerating necessity to build excitement into the very core of business activity. *One* is that we live in a society in which so many people have so many more things and so much more money than they need to sustain life at some reasonable level of amenities. *Second* is that there is so little to set one generic customer or industrial product off from another. And *third* is the inevitable routinization of man's daily task, whether in business, at home, or at play. In such a world, combined with product standardization and far-above-subsistence living, it is not surprising that man responds eagerly to the fascinating *shock of the unexpected.*

The adult searches for and needs excitement, the felicitous injection into his life of benignly unexpected events. That is why *excitement will increasingly,* in spite and perhaps because of computers and management science, *become a powerful ingredient in business success.* The man, the company, the product that denies this most in practice will suffer most in the market.

SYSTEMS SELLING

It is fashionable to talk about systems selling. The term originated in fact with the buyer. It meant awarding a package contract to companies who could design, engineer, build, assemble and service the complete

---

[1] Anthony E. Cascino, "Organizational Implications of the Marketing Concept," in *Managerial Marketing,* as quoted by William Lazer and Eugene J. Kelley (Homewood, Ill.: Richard D. Irwin, Inc., 1962, rev. ed.), p. 373.

package; examples are numerous, such as in refineries, dams or major weapons. *The package is the system.* The growing complexity of products that have elaborate inter-industry characteristics has made systems buying a necessity. Computers must be tied into communications networks, warehouses tied into computers and transportation networks.

One of the best examples is *Litton Industries.* To call this company a "conglomerate" is to mistake the apparent structure for the operating substance. Litton's acquisition activity is a process of creating under a single roof the competence to provide customers with an integrated mix of benefits they might otherwise have to buy separately on the open market. Litton is creating a new "product," a product system.

Similarly, *International Minerals and Chemical Corporation* offers a "service system"; the service system achieves the ultimate of total integration. It sells a system while the system sells both itself and a service . . . Let us look at IMC's farm management program to its direct farm customers.

The program is called M.O.R.E., Mathematically Optimized Resource Employment. It sells better farm management and simultaneously uses a system to sell farm fertilizer. IMC's computer keeps on file a great deal of information about a cooperating farmer's operation—the size of his farm, the type of service, what crops he has been planting, what yields he has been getting, what equipment and personnel he has, as well as current market prices and weather data. With all this, IMC can supply a computerized scientific farm management service designed to make more profit for the farmer through proper and balanced use of IMC fertilizer nutrients and other agricultural chemicals.

Each farmer on the M.O.R.E. program gets a new operating plan each fall, updated to correspond to price trends and weather predictions and government farm programs. Working with the specific data of each farm, the computer provides the farmer with a series of alternative plans, including estimates of both crop and money yields for different combinations or fertilizer usage and crops. If all or part of a farm is rented and sharecropped, the computer even divides plans into profits goals for landlord and operator. The computer will also provide each farmer with personalized advice on such questions as: should I buy or lease additional land? What is a reasonable price for the land? Should I put some former "land-bank" lands back into use? Should I try a new crop? Should I delay planting because of the moisture content of the subsoil? Should I buy a new truck, or is it a bigger unloader that I really need?

IMC's M.O.R.E. helps the farmer become a more successful farmer and hence a bigger and more loyal customer for IMC's farm chemicals. These chemicals account for about 70% of IMC's sales of over $300 million annually. *What, therefore, is IMC's product?* To call it farm fertilizers is to mistake visible appearances for customer-satisfying essences. The farmer on the M.O.R.E. program is viewed as a chemical processor whose outputs are not just food and fiber, but celluloses, carbohydrates, proteins, and oils—all processed chemicals. His inputs are a variety of capital, land, labor, as well as certain chemical raw materials such as fertilizers, lime, and pesticides. The farmer is viewed as a producer of processed chemicals whose operation should be as carefully calculated as are those of other producers of processed chemicals. IMC has designed a package to enable the farmer to make decisions not about how much or what kind of fertilizer he should employ, but how to run his processing business more effectively.

That is M.O.R.E.'s product—that is the system, the system that practically sells itself to the one-section farmer (640 acres) who uses about $25,000 worth of crop chemicals a year.

Systems selling involves the creation of an augmented product that enables the customer to do business more easily with the supplier.

CONCLUSIONS

We live in an age when we must think more differently than ever about what a product or service is. It is not so much the basic, generic, central thing we are selling that counts, but the whole cluster of value satisfactions with which we surround it. It does little or no good to make a better mousetrap when "betterness" now has a new, more subtle meaning; and that is where modern marketing comes in. *Modern marketing consists of orienting a company toward trying to find out what at any time the customer will define "betterness" to mean.* This requires the entire company to be more effectively organized and oriented towards fulfilling the customer-getting requirements implied by that definition.

THE MARKETING SYSTEM

2

Modeling of Market and Company Interactions

JAY W. FORRESTER
Massachusetts Institute of Technology

All of you in marketing recognize that many linkages connect a company to its market. Some of these linkages are tangible like the flow of orders toward the company and the counterflow of product to the customer. Other linkages are obvious like the sales effort and advertising expended to communicate with the market. But many linkages are subtle and tenuous like those that carry customer attitudes and needs back to the decision-making points in the company.

But recognizing these linkages between company and market does not mean that one can see clearly the time-varying responses caused by interactions between them. It is in the interplay of forces caused by these interacting linkages that we find the causes of company and product growth and conversely find the influences which can cause stagnation and decline.

These company-market linkages form networks of feedback loops. In these loops an action by the company causes a response in the market which in turn produces the information on which decisions are based to control future company actions. The dynamic behavior of these feedback loops is poorly understood and contains many surprises.

The complexity of these interactions is far too great for analytical solution using conventional mathematical approaches. With trivial exceptions, mathematics deals only with linear systems. Yet some of the most

Reprinted with permission from *Marketing and Economic Development,* ed. Peter D. Bennett, published by the American Marketing Association, Fall, 1965, pp. 353–64. 15

important behavior mechanisms in marketing depend for their very existence on nonlinear relationships. The only effective tool for understanding nonlinear, multiple-loop, feedback systems is the construction of a model that permits simulation of the behavior relationships which we perceive within the company and market.

The construction of models to represent market dynamics is now possible. The problem is not, as often supposed, the need for more empirical data. The pace of progress will be set entirely by the availability of investigators who understand the kinds of factors that are important in feedback system behavior and who can conceptually structure the presently available information and data.

Some of the linkages between a company and market appear in Figure 1. The company uses incoming information from the market as the basis for generating the outputs from company to market. These outputs generated by the company include price and the quality of products and services. Another output from the company is delivery delay which reflects the relationship between incoming order rate and production capability. Product suitability reflects the adequacy of new product development and the degree of perception by the company of market needs. Sales effort is a result of the company's resource allocation policies.

In the opposite direction from market to company, there is, of course, a flow of orders and payments. But there are also other important information streams. These might be defined in a variety of ways. One useful structuring of information from the market to the company is in terms of reflections of those linkages which the company projects to the market. The company should be interested in the market reactions toward price, quality, delivery delay, and product suitability.

Starting from Figure 1, to construct a dynamic simulation model requires that we define the responses that we believe exist in the two separate sectors—the company and the market. In each sector the task is to take the incoming inputs as a basis for generating the outputs. Within the company the time delays and policy interactions must be represented which convert market information into the outputs of price, quality, delivery delay, product suitability, sales effort, and product flow. Within the market the characteristics must be conceptualized and defined which we believe react to the inputs from the company and generate a stream of orders as well as the sources of information flowing to the company. This means that the model represents our operational knowledge about the management processes in the company and the customer processes in the market.

Figure 1 implies the futility of attempting to teach marketing as an isolated corporate function. In the corporation, marketing shares with the area of management information systems the characteristic that it depends on an unusually high number of linkages to other parts of the business system. It is not self-sufficient. By contrast, production is a more self-contained corporate function. I feel that this high degree of interconnectedness in marketing explains many of the difficulties encountered in attempting to teach the subject. Marketing can not be successfully isolated from its dynamic interactions with other company functions.

FIGURE 1: COMPANY-MARKET LINKAGES

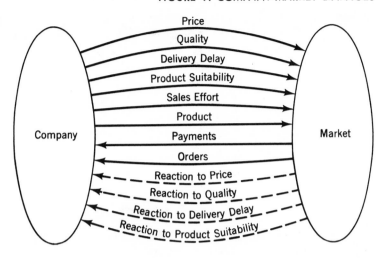

In Figure 1 we see implied many of the simpler feedback loops in the system. Company activities to generate quality lead to an actual product quality that produces a market reaction to quality and an information return to the company about the reaction to quality which is one of the inputs to the future management of quality. Likewise, a loop connects company price policy through prices to the market and back through the reaction of the market to price. But the system is not a collection of separate and isolated loops controlling the separate company outputs. There are many important cross couplings. For example, a policy which reduces price can reduce the payment stream and thereby company profits so that pressure is brought on the activities controlling quality which then may lower the quality output from the company and in time cause a decrease in market orders. The feedback loops connecting company and market have many devious interconnections. The dynamic interactions within these loops can defeat our attempts at intuitive judgment about system behavior.

Some of the feedback loops between company and market are so-called "negative feedback loops" which attempt to adjust system operation toward some reference goal. Other loops are "positive feedback" in character and these latter account for the processes of growth and decline.

Figure 2 shows an example of a positive feedback loop involved in the growth of a new product. The sales effort operating at some sales effectiveness produces a sales rate. The sales effectiveness is a reflection of the desirability of the product and is a measure of the ease with which it can be sold. The sales rate generates revenue. A part of the revenue becomes available in the sales budget to support future sales effort. If the sales effectiveness is high enough and the fraction of revenue going to the sales budget is large enough, then a given sales effort will produce a sales rate and budget higher than necessary to sustain the initial sales effort. Under

FIGURE 2: POSITIVE FEEDBACK IN SALES GROWTH

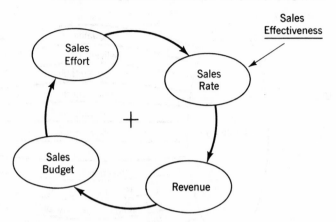

these favorable circumstances, sales effort leads to a growing sales budget which then supports an increasing sales effort. The regenerative growth process continues until something within the loop, perhaps the sales effectiveness, changes in an unfavorable direction. The rapidity of growth depends on the coefficients in the system such as the sales effectiveness and the fraction of revenue going to the support of sales effort. The rapidity of growth is also directly influenced by the delays around the loop. Because of the market delays, the sales rate lags behind the corresponding sales effort; because of manufacturing and invoice collection delays, the revenue lags behind the sales rate; because of the corporate budgeting procedures, the sales budget lags behind the incoming revenue; and because of the time to locate and train salesmen, the sales effort lags behind the budget. Other conditions being equal, the rate of sales growth will be doubled if the delays around this positive feedback loop can be reduced to half.

Conversely, a positive feedback loop can show degenerative decline. In the example of Figure 2, if the sales effectiveness is low, the sales effort may not support its own sales budget leading to a future reduction in sales effort that further reduces sales. Positive feedback loops can exhibit either growth or decay. By contrast, negative feedback loops tend to adjust activity toward a reference goal but in the attempt they often produce fluctuation.

Figure 3 shows a negative feedback loop coupling sales rate, order backlog, delivery delay, and sales effectiveness. In this diagram it is assumed that sales effort remains constant. The relationship between order backlog and sales rate depends on the production capacity characteristics of the company. For illustration, assume that the production capacity is constant and the sales effort is more than adequate to create the corresponding sales rate if delivery delay is short. Under these circumstances, sales rate will exceed production capacity and the order backlog will increase. The increase in the order backlog will continue until the resulting increase in delivery delay becomes sufficient that some customers become unwilling to wait for delivery. As the delivery delay becomes longer, the

FIGURE 3: NEGATIVE FEEDBACK LIMITING SALES

product becomes less attractive and the product becomes less easy to sell. This means that, as delivery delay increases, the sales effectiveness declines until sales rate falls to the production capability. This negative feedback loop is at work in any market situation where delivery delays are long enough to be of concern to the customer. A negative feedback loop as shown in Figure 3 can exhibit instability. There are delays at each point in the loop. The sales rate does not respond immediately to changes in delivery delay because many of the orders under negotiation are already committed and cannot be redirected. Order backlog is an accumulation over time of discrepancies between the sales rate and the production capacity and backlog lags behind a change in sales rate. Delivery delay here represents the delay recognized by the market and this lags behind the true delay as indicated by the order backlog. These delays, coupled with the other characteristics of the loop, can lead to overcorrection. A sales rate which is too high goes unrecognized until the backlog builds up and until the delivery delay is recognized. By this time delivery delay is excessive and leads to a reduction in sales rate below the production capacity. Then, order backlog declines unduly before the low delivery delay is recognized and sales again rise.

An important part of the negative feedback loop of Figure 3 is the nonlinear relationship between delivery delay and sales effectiveness as shown in Figure 4. Sales effectiveness is a maximum when delivery is zero. For very small delivery delays (measured in seconds for a drugstore item and up to months for a digital computer) there is no reduction of sales as delivery delay increases. However, with longer delivery delays, a region of steep slope is encountered where the delay is sufficient to discourage a progressively larger fraction of customers. For still longer delays, the curve levels out as it approaches zero sales effectiveness, representing the fact that a few customers find the product particularly suitable and are willing to plan ahead and wait unusually long.

FIGURE 4: NONLINEAR RELATIONSHIP

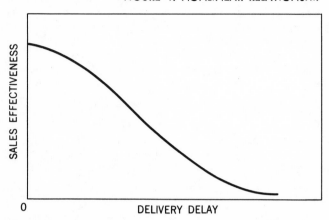

Now what would happen in a coupled company and market system involving the two control loops of Figures 2 and 3? These are shown interconnected in Figure 5. Here, if we assume that only a limited production capacity is available, the positive feedback loop will regenerate a rising rate of sales until the production capacity limit is reached. When the production rate no longer increases with sales, the negative loop would show an increasing delivery delay and this would produce a declining sales effectiveness to limit further growth. This process of growth limitation is commonly encountered in many subtle ways in new product situations. A new product may enjoy adequate production as long as it does not encroach seriously on established products. As the new product grows, it may find increasing difficulty in competing for available capacity. Capacity limitation is often not recognized because its effect can occur even before the plant facilities are operating at maximum output. As the plant begins to reach its full capacity, flexibility is lost and orders for special variations in the product cause congestion and confusion. Average delivery delay increases even though it appears that the manufacturing capacity is still not fully occupied. Any situation where order backlogs are long enough to be viewed unfavorably by customers implies that this negative feedback loop is active in partially suppressing sales. Figure 5 can be recognized as an extremely simplified subset of the possible interactions contained in Figure 1. Even in this severely simplified form of Figure 5, the implied system behavior can not be intuitively estimated as one contemplates changing the many factors within the two coupled loops.

The growth behavior of the double-loop system under one set of system conditions is shown in Figure 6. The figure is taken from a simulation run using "industrial dynamics" methods[1] and the DYNAMO compiler[2] for simulating the model. Growth in sales rate occurs during the first 60

[1] Forrester, J. W., *Industrial Dynamics,* Cambridge, Mass., M.I.T. Press, 1961.
[2] Pugh, A. L., III; *DYNAMO User's Manual,* 2nd ed. Cambridge, Mass., M.I.T. Press, 1963.

FIGURE 5: COUPLED NEGATIVE AND POSITIVE FEEDBACK LOOPS

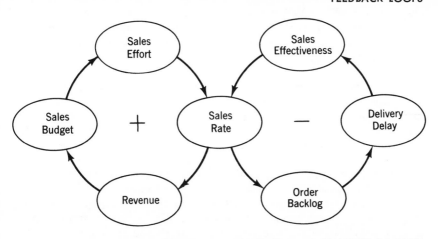

FIGURE 6: GROWTH AND STAGNATION IN SALES

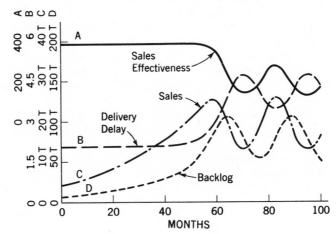

months. Thereafter sales tend to fluctuate because the production capacity limit has been reached. During the early period of growth, sales effectiveness remains constant and high while at the same time the delivery delay remains constant and low. As the sales rate begins to approach the production capacity, the delivery delay increases and the sales effectiveness falls. After month 60, the system fluctuates because of the characteristics of the negative feedback loop in which readjustments within the loop are delayed and instability occurs on either side of the equilibrium position.

The major characteristics of Figure 6—the rapidity of early growth and the fluctuation during the stagnation period—depend on the parameters and the time delays in the two loops. The positive feedback loop of Figure 2 is the primary determinant of the growth phase shown in Figure

6; and the negative feedback loop in Figure 3 is the primary determinant of the behavior after sales growth has been arrested by reaching the production capacity. In Figure 6 we see a transition from positive feedback loop behavior to negative loop behavior which is triggered by the nonlinear characteristics represented in the production capacity and the sales effectiveness.

In Figures 5 and 6, the cessation of sales growth could not be forestalled by improved or expanded marketing activities. A larger fraction of revenue devoted to sales effort would only cause the delivery delay to increase further and drive down the sales effectiveness to still lower values. Similar interactions, within the multiple channels of the far greater complexity of real-life situations, can invalidate marketing decisions by the inner workings of the market-company system.

It is sufficient to say that any marketing decision considered by itself is apt to become a victim of other interacting factors.

When one examines a model of the interactions between company and market, he discovers many mechanisms which can cause limitation in sales and stagnation in growth. In fact, one should reverse the common query, "How can I increase sales?" A better question is "How should one limit sales?" It is clear that one must limit sales. If the product has the highest quality, immediate delivery, the most suitable design, the widest distribution, the best salesmen, and the lowest price, sales will exceed the physical or financial capability of the company.

The oversimplified economic view suggests that price is the mechanism which balances supply and demand. But as a practical matter this is not true. There is no way to determine a price which will cause exact balance between supply and demand. Price is established on the basis of manufacturing cost, past traditions, competitors' prices, or in response to financial pressures on the company. If the price is set lower than the economic equilibrium value, then other influences must share the burden of limiting orders. The first effect will usually be a rise in delivery delay to make the product less attractive. After a period of long deliveries, the company may grow careless and allow quality to decline so that the lower quality contributes to limiting sales. The company profitability is, however, very sensitive to the balance of factors at work in the limitation of sales. As more of the burden is shifted to long delivery delay, lower quality, obsolete design, and unskilled salesmen, the price must be correspondingly lowered to maintain sales. Profit margins fall and create financial pressures which cause further deterioration in the product characteristics of interest to the customer. A degenerative spiral can then develop with lower quality forcing lower prices which exert financial pressure and further reduce quality.

Returning to Figure 1 we see a number of information channels flowing from market to company carrying information about market reactions to company performance. These information channels are of the utmost importance in determining the kinds of decisions made within the company. Yet these information channels are subject to many ills. The quality of an information channel can be measured in several ways—by its persuasiveness, delay, bias, distortion, error, and cross-talk.

An information channel usually shows greater persuasiveness and influence on the decision-making processes as it deals with short-term factors and as it deals with information which is easily measured. Information is more persuasive when the method of measurement is well known and widely accepted. For example, inventory information is highly persuasive since it appears monthly on the balance sheet measured to five decimal places (even though it may not be truly meaningful even in the first decimal place). By contrast, information indicating what the customers think of the company's product quality lacks persuasiveness because it is difficult to measure and hard to define. Oftentimes the most important information is the least persuasive.

Delay represents the time it takes information to travel along a channel. Information delays can be very long. For example, there can easily be a five-year delay between the quality actually produced in a product and the reputation for quality which is prevalent in the market. The time taken to judge quality is partly controlled by the natural life of the product. A meaningful measure of quality in an electric refrigerator can only be made if one waits through the normal life of the refrigerator. Even after quality is observed directly by a user, further delays are encountered before this reputation is transmitted to potential customers who have not been users.

Bias is the offset in an information channel where the perceived information deviates consistently from the true conditions. One often sees bias in a company's belief about the degree to which customers are satisfied. The company wants to believe it is doing well. Favorable reports bolster the self image and are remembered and circulated. Unfavorable reports are dismissed as exceptions or as unfortunate accidents.

Distortion is a deviation between the input and output of an information channel which is a function of the nature of the information itself. Distortion is sometimes intentional as in an averaging process. Averaging of sales data suppresses short-term fluctuation while allowing longer term deviations to be transmitted. The fidelity of the process therefore depends on the periodicity of the information being transmitted.

Error refers to random deviations and mistakes in an information channel. More effort is expended in reducing error than in reducing any of the other types of information deficiencies. Yet of the six types of information degradation, error is probably least important in affecting the feedback systems that couple a company to its market.

Cross-talk is a term borrowed from telephone usage and represents the tendency of information to be transposed from one channel to another. Transposition of the meaning of information is conspicuously evident in the channels flowing from market to company. There is a tendency for all customer dissatisfaction to take the form of indicating that the price is too high. This can happen at many points in the information channels. Price is too high for the low quality, or price is too high for the poor delivery, or price is too high for the discourteous salesmen. But the qualification is lost and only the reference to price is transmitted. Suppose that the customer is dissatisfied with the performance of his last purchase. He has decided not to buy again. When the salesman appears, the socially acceptable and most expeditious reason for not buying is to say that the price is too high. That is a value judgment which the salesman can not effectively counter. Were the customer to complain of quality, the salesman might offer to send a service engineer or he might explain how quality control at the factory has been improved. Or he might offer to take back the equipment for repair. But, if the customer wants none of these and wants not to be bothered, he says the price is too high. Suppose, however, that the customer does complain about the low quality and the obsolete design. Will the salesman risk the wrath of the development department and the factory by carrying these complaints back to the home plant? Probably not. He will simply report that the price is too high. But suppose that the salesman has courage to press complaints of an obsolete product. What will the management do to restore falling sales? It may well reduce price because it knows how to accomplish that, whereas a redesign is uncertain and far in the future.

From simulation of the information channels and decision-making policies that create the company–market system one can learn much about the behavior which in real life is so baffling. Interactions are complex. The human mind is not well adapted to intuitively estimating the behavior of complex feedback linkages. Marketing is a function which can not exist by itself. It is intimately coupled to production, capital investment policies, product design, and the company's educational programs. As one makes changes in a particular set of market linkages he may simply create greater difficulties in another area. It is only through knowledge of the entire system that successful coupling between company and market can be achieved.

SELECTED BIBLIOGRAPHY
for
PART 1

BOULDING, KENNETH. "General Systems Theory—The Skeleton of Science," *Management Science*. April, 1956, pp. 197–208.

BUZZELL, ROBERT. "Is Marketing a Science?," *Harvard Business Review*. January–February, 1963, pp. 32ff.

DRUCKER, PETER. "The Shame of Marketing," *Marketing/Communications*. August, 1969, pp. 60–64.

FORRESTER, JAY. "Advertising: A Problem in Industrial Dynamics," *Harvard Business Review*. March–April, 1959, pp. 100–110.

KEITH, ROBERT. "The Marketing Revolution," *Journal of Marketing*. January, 1960, pp. 35–38.

LEVITT, THEODORE. "Marketing Myopia," *Harvard Business Review*. July–August, 1960, pp. 45–56.

SIMMONDS, KENNETH. "Removing the Chains from Product Strategy," *Journal of Management Studies*. February, 1968, pp. 29–40.

ANALYZING MARKETING OPPORTUNITIES

The four areas covered in analyzing present and future marketing opportunities are the marketing environment, buyer behavior, market segmentation, and market measurement. Kahn (pp. 26–41) predicts some substantive changes in society by the year 2000, which will mean new threats and new marketing opportunities for the business firm. Adler (pp. 42–56) looks at the implications to marketing of basic changes in social and cultural values of consumers, especially of the younger consumers. Howard and Sheth (pp. 57–79) develop perhaps the most sophisticated theory of buyer behavior available today. In the Sales Management article (pp. 80–89), the more specialized area of industrial-buyer behavior is examined in depth. Yankelovich (pp. 90–102) shows that most markets are far from homogeneous. Segmentation of markets into meaningful subgroups can be the basis of effective marketing strategy. Finally, two articles look at forecasting and measurement problems in marketing. Hummel (pp. 103–110) demonstrates how the Standard Industrial Classification System can help locate new prospects in industrial marketing. Cross (pp. 111–117) describes an interesting application of the operations-research approach to forecasting and planning the introduction of a new method of gasoline retailing.

THE MARKETING ENVIRONMENT

3

The Next
Thirty-three
Years

HERMAN KAHN
Hudson Institute

What I am going to try to do this afternoon is just leaf through a study we have just finished; it is not really a study, the subtitle of the book is *A Framework for Speculation on the Next Thirty-three Years* and we take that dead seriously. We expect to bring out two more books by the end of next year and then to sit down and start a study. So what you are getting is more catharsis than study, to get it out of the system so that we can do something serious. I though I would just give you a list of the reasons why we do these kinds of studies (see Figure 1, especially number 6).

PRE-INDUSTRIAL SOCIETIES

After about ten thousand years man learned to scratch the soil and that was called agriculture. That was important because cities followed—civilization, civic life, living in cities. We had a number of different civilizations, always being characterized by the phrase "pre-industrial." Now, that lumps together a lot of different things. That lumps together a 3,000-year-old civilization in China, say, with the tribal society in Africa. You know, it is not the kind of adjective that you would normally use, but there are a lot of different kinds of people who are included in that term "pre-industrial." In many ways the characteristic of pre-industrial

FIGURE 1: WHY STUDY THE YEAR 2000?

1. "Playful" speculation
2. Context for five- to ten-year "policy research" studies
3. May make practical ten- to twenty-year "policy research" studies
4. Direct guidance (or even proper perspective) to "arms control" and "power politics" policies
5. Proper perspective for many developmental and evolutionary-type issues
6. The end of the second millennium A.D. may be a most important historical transition point
   A. Effective end of pre-industrial culture
   B. Onset of post-industrial culture
   C. Precursor of (almost) post-economic culture

societies, the most interesting for my purpose this afternoon, is that their gross national product per capita, i.e., the amount of goods and services they produced, lay between $50 and $200. That is, we know of no society which ever got above $200—or at least for very long—and we know of no society that got below $50. You know, you get hungry.

If you want to ask yourselves what the typical pre-industrial society was like, look at Indonesia today: one hundred million people, about the size of the Roman Empire, or the Han Empire of the Chinese, and about the same GNP per capita. You can think of that $50 to $200 as normality, i.e., the normal state of civilized man, and one of the things that seems to happen—today about 60 per cent of the world lives in such societies. Now, some of them are impressive. The Chinese have better nuclear weapons than the French, but they are still a pre-industrial society because by and large they live that way.

The end of this century should see the end of pre-industrial societies. If things go reasonably smoothly, less than 10 per cent of the world's population will be pre-industrial. That is an achievement, one of the greatest achievements known to mankind, and it will be a little bit like the United States, they will discover poverty. In some sense, when problems are beginning to vanish they get more intense, and it is quite clear that the end of poverty, worldwide poverty, will be one of the big issues by the end of the twentieth century.

Now, as you know, about 200 years ago we broke out of the $200 box. Let me define: say, $500 to $2,000, in other words, a factor of ten more, is industrial society. $50 to $200 is pre-industrial. Such an industrial society was Western Europe just after the War, Eastern Europe today and the more advanced parts of Latin America. These are industrial societies. You know what they look like.

POST-INDUSTRIAL SOCIETY

Let me go another factor of ten, $5,000 to $20,000 per capita, and let me call that post-industrial (see Figure 2). What does a post-industrial society look like? We are not sure, but the United States is beginning to look like one and we will be one within the next ten, twenty, thirty, or forty years. Many people believe that the change from industrial to post-industrial may be as significant in man's affairs as the change from hunting to agriculture, from pre-industrial to industrial. We are suggesting that in the next thirty to thirty-five years, forty years, you will have to add a third incident to those two incidents I mentioned. You add a big factor. In addition, things are going very fast today. It may be one hundred years to arrive at something you might call post-economic.

FIGURE 2: THE POST-INDUSTRIAL
(OR POST-MASS CONSUMPTION) SOCIETY

1. Per capita income about fifty times the pre-industrial
2. Most "economic" activities are tertiary and quaternary (service-oriented), rather than primary or secondary (production-oriented)
3. Business firms no longer the major source of innovation
4. There may be more "consentives" (vs. "marketives")
5. Effective floor on income and welfare
6. Efficiency no longer primary
7. Market plays diminished role compared to public sector and "social accounts"
8. Widespread "cybernation"
9. "Small world"
10. Typical "doubling time" between three and thirty years
11. Learning society
12. Rapid improvement in educational institutions and techniques
13. Erosion (in middle class) of work-oriented, achievement-oriented, advancement-oriented values
14. Erosion of "national interest" values
15. Sensate, secular, humanist, perhaps self-indulgent criteria become central

Now, a good deal of what you read today about the so-called post-industrial society would fit better into post-economic. After all, you are talking about incomes of $5,000 to $20,000 per capita, that is, an average income of about $25,000 per family to $50,000 per family. It is big, but many people are familiar with such incomes. There are very few of you, say, who are familiar with incomes of $50,000 to $200,000 per capita, that is, roughly, $250,000 to half a million dollars per family; that begins to get outside your ken. That is a different world and if that is what the factors either made or are making, it is a very odd world.

I won't bother talking about this post-economic world. It may never come and if it comes I have very little feel for it, so we are not going to try to think about it. I do want to distinguish between the post-industrial and the post-economic.

The post-industrial is interesting because we are going into it right now. Things that are happening today are things you think of as very characteristic of such a society.

Figure 3 gives a quick glimpse of what the last third of the twentieth century looks like to us. If you are at all familiar with the first and second thirds, you will notice, as the subtitle says, "apolitical and surprise-free." Now, originally, and in our book, we still call this a projection, not a prediction. We mean by this that we put in all the theories we had—that is why it is surprise-free. In other words, if everything goes according to your expectations, then it is not a surprise. Then we said, "The most surprising thing that could occur is to have no surprise," and therefore the most surprising thing that can happen is for the thing to come out like Figure 2. That was certainly our position for about a year and a half to two years.

FIGURE 3: FINAL THIRD
OF THE TWENTIETH CENTURY

(Relatively Apolitical and Surprise-Free Projection)
1. Continuation of basic, long-term "multifold trend"
2. Emergence of "post-industrial" culture
3. Worldwide capability for modern technology
4. Very small world: increasing need for regional or worldwide "zoning" ordinances: for control of arms, technology, pollution, trade, transportation, population, resource utilization, and the like
5. High (1 to 10 per cent) growth rates in GNP per capita
6. Increasing emphasis on "meaning and purpose"
7. Much turmoil in the "new" and possibly in the industrializing nations
8. Some possibility for sustained "nativist," messianic, or other mass movements
9. Second rise of Japan (to being potentially, nominally, or perhaps actually, the third largest power)
10. Some further rise of Europe and China
11. Emergence of new intermediate powers, such as Brazil, Mexico, Pakistan, Indonesia, East Germany, and Egypt
12. Some decline (relative) of the U.S. and the U.S.S.R.
13. A possible absence of stark "life-and-death" political and economic issues in the old nations

Unlike the rest of the staff of the Hudson Institute, I am beginning to take that somewhat more seriously and I would like to call it now a prediction rather than a projection. . .

Basically, the world looks relatively peaceful to me and to many of my colleagues. As a matter of fact, at least for the next ten or twenty years, maybe the next thirty or forty. Let me give you a couple of examples of what I mean:

If you had, say, gone to the Peace Conference in 1815 and asked people, "What do you expect?" they would have said, "Twenty-five more years of worldwide revolution, civil war, tyranny, etc." What they got was a hundred years of relative peace and it came as a shock because they just weren't used to that idea in 1830 or 1838. It was not what they expected and, furthermore, the big event—the rise of Prussia—was really unexpected and changed everything.

I am suggesting that a similar thing is occurring today. Everybody is sitting around and waiting for the sword to drop, you know, and in fact it is relatively peaceful. Now, you can tell me, correctly, we are involved in a large war—half a million troops—and it is not so peaceful, but it is relatively peaceful compared to expectations.

You know the phrase "la belle époque"? It is a European phrase and it refers to the period 1901 to 1913, "the good era." Many historians challenge that phrase on the ground that nobody ever used it before 1914 and therefore it is Auld Lang Syne, it is wishful thinking, it is romancing, and not a serious thing. Let me make a suggestion to you: We have just passed through another "belle époque" from 1952 to 1967. In the history of the world there is no such period of worldwide growth, relative peace, worldwide prosperity. It is hard to find one country which has not doubled its gross national product during that period and most countries increased it by much more. That is a very impressive period. . .

The suggestion is that rather than ending with 1914, maybe "la belle époque" will continue for another twenty-five or thirty years and then maybe there will be a 1914.

People have always told me, "You are giving a very optimistic talk, or discussion," and I look at them and my jaw drops. I am suggesting 1914 will come again. That is not an optimistic statement. I don't really believe that, I just don't know, but I am suggesting at least ten, twenty, or thirty years of worldwide sustained growth, growth of peace, growth of prosperity.

There is what we call the multiple trend, which is listed in Figure 4. This is basically a trend in Western society, which is now worldwide, which has been going on for about seven, eight, or nine centuries. I am going to make a daring extrapolation and I am going to say that what has been going on for seven, eight, or nine centuries will continue for thirty-three years. It is a little more courageous than it sounds. There have been a lot of ebbs and flows in those nine centuries. What I am suggesting is that we will be in a flow period and not an ebb.

Now, if you are taking a microscopic look, the ebb and flow doesn't mean much to you, but if you are caught up in one of these ebbs and flows, like the revolution in Russia or Hitler in Germany—it can be left

FIGURE 4: THERE IS A BASIC LONG-TERM MULTIFOLD TREND TOWARD:

1. Increasingly sensate (empirical, this-worldly, secular, humanistic, pragmatic, utilitarian, contractual, epicurean or hedonistic, and the like) cultures
2. Bourgeois, bureaucratic, "meritocratic," democratic (and nationalistic?) elites
3. Accumulation of scientific and technological knowledge
4. Institutionalization of change, especially research, development, innovation, and diffusion
5. Worldwide industrialization and modernization
6. Increasing affluence and (recently) leisure
7. Population growth
8. Urbanization and (soon) the growth of megalopolises
9. Decreasing importance of primary and (recently) secondary occupations
10. Literacy and education
11. Increasing capability for mass destruction
12. Increasing tempo of change
13. Increasing universality of the multifold trend

or right, it makes no difference—you notice it; it is not just a ripple. But from our point of view, that is just a ripple. I am going to suggest that the next thirty-three years will be a flow, that they will flow in tune with this 800-, 900-, 1,000-year old trend, but what is most important as far as I am concerned is this notion of an increasingly sensate society.

To some degree advertising is probably the second or third most sensate of man's activities.

I won't bother spending any time on the other issues there, except for Number 10, the increasing literacy and education. One of the points I am going to make is the increasingly important role of the intellectual, the man who deals with ideas. For whatever it is worth, people include the advertising profession as intellectuals—and that is a mistake on both parts. You people deal with ideas to make a living, artistic or complex ideas.

The intellectual has certain problems. We have a phrase we use in the Institute called "trained incapacity," the kind of ability to overlook things which comes only with a Ph.D. from a good university. It runs a gamut of things. For example, sometimes people have trouble telling the difference between night and day, a sort of twilight zone problem. How do you draw a line? They have trouble distinguishing between night and day. Sometimes people confuse night and noon because of twilight zone problems—that takes an I.Q. of 200! You can't do it at a lesser I.Q. You get confused.

There are some more important notions here. There used to be a Congressman in New York City who was an expert on prices, who did not know that the average American bought his car at a discount. Now, nobody had ever done a study of this, so how could you know? I assume this guy paid retail for his car, or paid less. He was that kind of a person.

Let me give you another kind of example of this: you know the term "book learning"? It is a vulgar expression but it is filled with meaning. It tries to make the point that if a man has learned everything in carefully formulated lectures on carefully formulated issues, which are documented, on which there has been a study, he may not be able to receive the kind of information that much of the world is wrong. For example, go up to any expert in any area in any university and ask him, say, "Did you predict the revolution? Do you remember when Khrushchev fell? Why didn't you predict it?" The answer always is, "That great expert Khrushchev couldn't tell. How could I?" Quite a good answer.

One of the guys at the Hudson Institute used to run an engineering firm in the Far East and twice he pulled his guys out before the revolution. He also had a beautiful false alarm rate; he never pulled them out when there was no revolution, and I asked him, "How could you do it? How did you know?" And he said, "Everybody knew, the taxi driver, the porter, everybody except the Government and the American Embassy." It is a little bit like a man whose wife is running around. He is not the first to know, or the second. He is the last to know. And you only find out about it when there is documentation, that is, when the divorce papers have been filed. You are the last to the last—and that is very late.

I am making this point—as I say, I am an intellectual myself, you know, and I have some of these problems, though less than my colleagues —because the world I am going to describe is an intellectual world and one which somehow must be treated intellectually, and that is one of the ways in which it is disaster-prone.

Let me just continue the point. Let me start with this basic idea of a sensate trend. Now, the easiest way to describe it is to look at the fine arts (see Figures 5 and 6).

What I am going to do over here is to use the language of the philosophers of history, even though I don't accept their theories—like people in the United States use the language of Freud but nobody in the United

FIGURE 5:

Ideational Art	Idealistic or Integrated Art
Transcendental	Mixed Style
Supersensory	Heroic
Religious	Noble
Symbolic	Uplifting
Allegoric	Sublime
Static	Patriotic
Worshipful	Moralistic
Anonymous	Beautified
Traditional	Flattering
Immanent	Educational

FIGURE 6:

Sensate Art	Late Sensate Art
Worldly	Underworldly
Naturalistic	Protest
Realistic	Revolt
Visual	Overripe
Illusionistic	Extreme
Everyday	Sensation Seeking
Amusing	Titillating
Interesting	Depraved
Erotic	Faddish
Satirical	Violently Novel
Novel	Exhibitionistic
Eclectic	Debased
Syncretic	Vulgar
Fashionable	Ugly
Superb Technique	Debunking
Impressionistic	Nihilistic
Materialistic	Pornographic
Commercial	Sarcastic
Professional	Sadistic

States accepts Freud's theories. He believed in original sin and no American believes in original sin, no American I know.

I use the term "ideational." That describes a culture which is bound up with an important idea, generally a religious idea. If you want two examples that you may be familiar with, there is seventh and sixth century Greece, or Western Europe, say, from the fifth century to the tenth century. There is no piece of literature which has come down to us from the medieval period—this particular part of the medieval period—which refers to human happiness. It was not an important issue. This gives you an idea of what that culture was like. They had no perspective, by the way, in their paintings, not because they didn't understand about perspective—they weren't interested. A painting was an act of worship. God didn't have to have little lines to help Him look at things, you know, He can see the whole. If you look at cathedrals built in that period, you find that they are technologically beyond our capabilities. That is an interesting point. You couldn't build one of them today and if you ask why, it's because they generally took about 250 years to finish. Does anybody here want to start a 250-year project? Well, you understand, that is only a moment to God, but it is a long time to a sensate culture, which this is.

The next thing we call ideational or integrated is patriotic art, poster art, socialist realism—Shakespeare in England, Renaissance Italy, any Strategic Air Command base, if you have ever been on one. Any group—the New Left has this kind of art now—any group that is trying to get something done—inspirational art—very square—nobody has the patience to be caught dead with it today.

Sensate art (Figure 6) is your business. A good Hollywood movie or a good ad is sensate. It appeals to the superficialities, you know, to the appearance of things. I will give you in a moment some other descriptions of sensate. Some of it is called late sensate art, or post-sensate: the kind of thing you find in the East Village, modern art generally. Psychedelic art plays part of that—dreams, sensation-seeking, titillating, sadist, erotic novels, exhibitionist, and so on.

Now, there is no question that fine arts today are post-sensate, or late sensate, and your own ads are following that same tradition and the question immediately arises, "Is this important or unimportant?" Does it make any difference? Do you remember Khrushchev tried to shut down the Modern Art exhibition in Moscow and he got into an argument with the artists? He said, "Twenty years ago we would have sent you to Siberia." And the artists said, "Those days are gone forever," and everybody clapped. It shows you the power of this kind of art. Is it or is it not important, this trend in the fine arts? I don't know. Nobody else does, but every philosopher of history argues that if you look at the various aspects of a society, the fine arts is the leading sector. That is, either it drags the rest with it or, more likely, it expresses tendencies within the culture. In other words, it is a symptom, not a cause.

I would argue that this is too easy. I would call it a conjecture. For whatever it is worth, the ten people who were taken seriously in this field all came up with the same conclusion, that as the fine arts go, so goes the rest of the culture. It is the leading sector.

We could examine three systems of truth (see Figures 7 and 8).

FIGURE 7: THREE SYSTEMS OF TRUTH*

Ideational	Sensate	Late Sensate
Revealed	Empirical	Cynical
Charismatic	Pragmatic	Disillusioned
Certain	Operational	Nihilistic
Dogmatic	Practical	Chaotic
Mystic	Worldly	Blasé
Intuitive	Scientific	Transient
Infallible	Skeptical	Superficial
Religious	Tentative	Weary
Supersensory	Fallible	Sophistic
Unworldly	Sensory	Formalistic
Salvational	Materialistic	Atheistic
Spiritual	Mechanistic	Trivial
Absolute	Relativistic	Changeable
Supernatural	Agnostic	Meaningless
Moral	Instrumental	Alienated
Emotional	Empirically, or	Expedient
Mythic	Logically	Absolutely
	Verifiable	Relativistic

* See e.g., Sorokin, *Social & Cultural Dynamics*, Vol. 1, especially pp. 84–91.

FIGURE 8: ONE COULD ALSO CONTRAST THE IDEATIONAL, INTEGRATED (IDEALISTIC), AND SENSATE SYSTEMS OF:

Fine Arts	Family Relationships
Performing Arts	Civic Relationships
Architecture	Literature
Truth	Ethics
Music	Education
Law	Government
Economics	Etc.

Ideational truth is the kind of truth you get from God, integrated with and mixed up with that of sensate. . . .

Late sensate truth I would argue, is the most important thing that is going on in the world today—and a good deal of our study revolves around such issues. They have a bad characteristic: they can never be decided. You could spend ten years studying them and you don't know much more than you did when you started.

Let me make a quick comment about Number 13, an absence of life-and-death political and economic issues (Figure 3).

I was in Israel about a year and a half ago and it is a rather interesting country. Israel is a country run by the Ashkenazic Jews, who are European Jews. Most of the population are Oriental Jews, a different kind, and there is a good deal of friction between the Oriental and the Ashkenazic Jews. But the Ashkenazic Jews run the country and that is going to be the culture. Once in a while an Oriental Jew will come up to an Ashkenazic Jew and say, "I don't want the European culture. I am going to drop out." The Ashkenazic Jew always answers, "There are a hundred million Arabs." The Oriental Jew thinks for about three seconds and says, "Where is the electrical engineering school?" We call that reality testing.

Now, it is different in the United States. Even economics is different, but if you check in Cambridge Square or here in the East Village, or Haight-Ashbury, you will find that the various kids who live in that area claim to get along on about $10 a week, $500 a year. If you check, that is exactly what SNCC and CORE pay their people. Roughly speaking, it is the mode income nowadays. It is the "in" thing to do, to live on $10 a week.

If you also check with the Post Office, you will find that they are willing to pay night work, minimum salary, at about $500 a month. Now, you have got to be a little bit articulate, you know, you have to be literate to work in the Post Office, but you don't have to be washed—at least not at night—or clean shaven. They are very permissive at night.

FIGURE 9: ONE HUNDRED TECHNICAL INNOVATIONS VERY LIKELY IN THE LAST THIRD OF THE TWENTIETH CENTURY

1. Multiple applications of lasers and masers for sensing, measuring, communication, cutting, heating, welding, power transmission, illumination, destructive (defensive), and other purposes
2. Extreme high-strength and/or high-temperature structural materials
3. New or improved superperformance fabrics (papers, fibers, and plastics)
4. New or improved materials for equipment and appliances (plastics, glasses, alloys, ceramics, intermetallics, and cermets)
5. New airborne vehicles (ground-effect machines, VTOL and STOL, super-helicopters, giant and/or supersonic jets)
6. Extensive commercial application of shaped-charged explosives
7. More reliable and longer-range weather forecasting
8. Intensive and/or extensive expansion of tropical agriculture and forestry
9. New sources of power for fixed installations (e.g., magnetohydrodynamic, thermionic and thermoelectric, and radioactivity)
10. New sources of power for ground transportation (storage battery, fuel cell, propulsion (or support) by electromagnetic fields, jet engine, turbine, and the like)
11. Extensive and intensive worldwide use of high altitude cameras for mapping, prospecting, census, land use, and geological investigations
12. New methods of water transportation (such as large submarines, flexible and special purpose "container ships," or more extensive use of large automated single-purpose bulk cargo ships)

13. Major reduction in hereditary and congenital defects
14. Extensive use of cyborg techniques (mechanical aids or substitutes for human organs, senses, limbs, or other components)
15. New techniques for preserving or improving the environment
16. Relatively effective appetite and weight control
17. New techniques and institutions for adult education
18. New and useful plant and animal species
19. Human "hibernation" for short periods (hours or days) for medical purposes
20. Inexpensive design and procurement of "one of a kind" items through use of computerized analysis and automated production
21. Controlled and/or supereffective relaxation and sleep
22. More sophisticated architectural engineering (e.g., geodesic domes, "fancy" stressed shells, pressurized skins, and esoteric materials)
23. New or improved uses of the oceans (mining, extraction of minerals, controlled "farming," source of energy, and the like)
24. Three-dimensional photography, illustrations, movies, and television
25. Automated or more mechanized housekeeping and home maintenance
26. Widespread use of nuclear reactors for power
27. Use of nuclear explosives for excavation and mining, generation of power, creation of high-temperature–high-pressure environments, and/or as a source of neutrons or other radiation
28. General use of automation and cybernation in management and production
29. Extensive and intensive centralization (or automatic interconnection) of current and past personal and business information in high-speed data processors
30. Other new and possibly pervasive techniques for surveillance, monitoring, and control of individuals and organizations
31. Some control of weather and/or climate
32. Other (permanent or temporary) changes—or experiments—with the overall environment (e.g., the "permanent" increase in C_{14} and temporary creation of other radioactivity by nuclear explosions, the increasing generation of CO in the atmosphere, projects Starfire, West Ford, and Storm Fury)
33. New and more reliable "educational" and propaganda techniques for affecting human behavior—public and private
34. Practical use of direct electronic communication with and stimulation of the brain
35. Human hibernation for relatively extensive periods (months to years)
36. Cheap and widely available central war weapons and weapon systems
37. New and relatively effective counterinsurgency techniques (and perhaps also insurgency techniques)
38. New techniques for very cheap, convenient, and reliable birth control
39. New, more varied, and more reliable drugs for control of fatigue, relaxation, alertness, mood, personality, perceptions, fantasies, and other psychobiological states
40. Capability to choose the sex of unborn children
41. Improved capability to "change" sex of children and/or adults
42. Other genetic control and/or influence over the "basic constitution" of an individual
43. New techniques and institutions for the education of children
44. General and substantial increase in life expectancy, postponement of aging,

and limited rejuvenation
45. Generally acceptable and competitive synthetic foods and beverages (e.g., carbohydrates, fats, proteins, enzymes, vitamins, coffee, tea, cocoa, and alcoholic liquor)
46. "High quality" medical care for undeveloped areas (e.g., use of medical aides and technicians, referral hospitals, broad spectrum antibiotics, and artificial blood plasma)
47. Design and extensive use of responsive and supercontrolled environments for private and public use (for pleasurable, educational, and vocational purposes)
48. Physically nonharmful methods of overindulging
49. Simple techniques for extensive and "permanent" cosmetological changes (features, "figures," perhaps complexion and even skin color, and even physique)
50. More extensive use of transplantation of human organs
51. Permanent manned satellite and lunar installations—interplanetary travel
52. Application of space life systems or similar techniques to terrestrial installations
53. Permanent inhabited undersea installations and perhaps even colonies
54. Automated grocery and department stores
55. Extensive use of robots and machines "slaved" to humans
56. New uses of underground "tunnels" for private and public transportation and other purposes
57. Automated universal (real time) credit, audit and banking systems
58. Chemical methods for improving memory and learning
59. Greater use of underground buildings
60. New and improved materials and equipment for buildings and interiors (e.g., variable transmission glass, heating and cooling by thermoelectric effect, and electroluminescent and phosphorescent lighting)
61. Widespread use of cryogenics
62. Improved chemical control of some mental illnesses and some aspects of senility
63. Mechanical and chemical methods for improving human analytical ability more or less directly
64. Inexpensive and rapid techniques for making tunnels and underground cavities in earth and/or rock
65. Major improvements in earth moving and construction equipment generally
66. New techniques for keeping physically fit and/or acquiring physical skills
67. Commercial extraction of oil from shale
68. Recoverable boosters for economic space launching
69. Individual flying platforms
70. Simple inexpensive home video recording and playing
71. Inexpensive high-capacity, worldwide, regional, and local (home and business) communication (perhaps using satellites, lasers, and light pipes)
72. Practical home and business use of "wired" video communication for both telephone and TV (possibly including retrieval of taped material from libraries or other sources) and rapid transmission and reception of facsimiles (possibly including news, library material, commercial announcements, instantaneous mail delivery, other printouts, and so on)
73. Practical large-scale desalinization

74. Pervasive business use of computers for the storage, processing, and retrieval of information
75. Shared-time (public and interconnected?) computers generally available to home and business on a metered basis
76. Other widespread use of computers for intellectual and professional assistance (translation, teaching, literature search, medical diagnosis, traffic control, crime detection, computation, design, analysis, and to some degree as intellectual collaborator generally)
77. General availability of inexpensive transuranic and other esoteric elements
78. Space defense systems
79. Inexpensive and reasonably effective ground-based BMD
80. Very low-cost buildings for home and business use
81. Personal "pagers" (perhaps even two-way pocket phones) and other personal electronic equipment for communication, computing, and data processing program
82. Direct broadcasts from satellites to home receivers
83. Inexpensive (less than $20), long lasting, very small battery operated TV receivers.
84. Home computers to "run" household and communicate with outside world
85. Maintenance-free, longlife electronic and other equipment
86. Home education via video and computerized and programmed learning
87. Stimulated and planned and perhaps programmed dreams
88. Inexpensive (less than one cent a page), rapid high-quality black and white reproduction; followed by color and high-detailed photography reproduction—perhaps for home as well as office use
89. Widespread use of improved fluid amplifiers
90. Conference TV (both closed circuit and public communication system)
91. Flexible penology without necessarily using prisons (by use of modern methods of surveillance, monitoring, and control)
92. Common use of (longlived?) individual power source for lights, appliances, and machines
93. Inexpensive worldwide transportation of humans and cargo
94. Inexpensive road-free (and facility-free) transportation
95. New methods for rapid language teaching
96. Extensive genetic control for plants and animals
97. New biological and chemical methods to identify, trace, incapacitate, or annoy people for police and military uses
98. New and possibly very simple methods for lethal biological and chemical warfare
99. Artificial moons and other methods for lighting large areas at night
100. Extensive use of "biological processes" in the extraction and processing of minerals

That means that if you are living in a pad with eleven other people, you can take turns. Each one works a month and you have got it made for the year and you are living well, despite the fact that you are paying high prices for things like LSD. Now, you have got to pay, I gather, a dollar or two, or five dollars, because the Feds got into the act. But I want to give you a sense of the extreme cheapness of living.

Freud once made a very perceptive comment—he made many—and I will paraphrase it, I don't remember his exact words. He said: "To most people the only touch with reality is the long arm of the job. Take away the requirements of earning a living and they immediately lose their minds." I would like to change that to the long arm of the job and the requirements of national security. I would argue that one of the most characteristic things about the United States for the next ten to twenty or thirty years is going to be that this particular type of reality testing will not be available to the average American. That is, no matter how foolish he is, how stupid he is, even in foreign policy, even in national defense, even in economics, he ain't going to go hungry and there will not be any Chinese Communists walking around San Francisco, so it doesn't make much difference at that level what you do.

It may be different thirty years later or forty years later, but not in the short and medium run, and that makes a good deal of difference to the fellow making the run.

Let me make a quick comment about the post-industrial culture. I was going to discuss technology—Number 3 in Figure 3.

There are about a hundred people who study this post-industrial culture around the world. They disagree on almost everything but on one thing they are all agreed: intellectuals run this society. Now, this is just the kind of thing you would expect the intellectuals to agree on, and one can make arguments pro and con. What are this issues? What are the facts at issue? And I wanted to discuss that. Let me actually skip it, though, because I do want to hit two other issues and we are running out of time.

In Figure 9 I list one hundred items we call technological innovations, all of which are almost certain to occur before the end of the century. These are the sure things, not the exciting things, but the sure-shot things. I would bet you twenty to one on any one of them and I will take your money, not for the year 2000 but the year 1980 for most of those things. (But see also Figures 10 and 11.)

Now I arranged the list in a funny way. First of all I didn't bother arranging it so it is eclectic and disorganized. The first twenty-five are things which are more or less unambiguously good things. . . .

The next twenty-five are serious things. I mean by that you would just as soon they did happen in many cases. They are very controversial. There is one I happen to be very amused by, so I would like to just mention it. It is Number 34, "Direct Communication Geared to Stimulation of the Brain." This is the kind of thing you guys are in, but you are very indirect. Let me give you an idea of the possibilities. You have probably heard of them, but let me elaborate a little bit on it and then I will terminate this lecture.

PLEASURE CENTERS

It turns out that you can communicate direct with the human brain in all kinds of ways. You can stimulate memories, you can imprint things,

FIGURE 10: SOME LESS LIKELY BUT IMPORTANT POSSIBILITIES

1. "True" artificial intelligence
2. Practical use of sustained fusion to produce neutrons and/or energy
3. Artificial growth of new limbs and organs (either in situ or for later transplantation)
4. Room temperature superconductors
5. Major use of rockets for commercial or private transportation (either terrestrial or extraterrestrial)
6. Effective chemical or biological treatment for most mental illnesses
7. Almost complete control of marginal changes in heredity
8. Suspended animation (for years or centuries)
9. Practical materials with nearly "theoretical limit" strength
10. Conversion of mammals (humans?) to fluid breathers
11. Direct input into human memory banks
12. Direct augmentation of human mental capacity by the mechanical or electrical interconnection of the brain with a computer
13. Major rejuvenation and/or significant extension of vigor and life span—say 100 to 150 years
14. Chemical or biological control of character or intelligence
15. Automated highways
16. Extensive use of moving sidewalks for local transportation
17. Substantial manned lunar or planetary installations
18. Electric power available for less than .3 mill per kilowatt hour
19. Verification of some extrasensory phenomena
20. Planetary engineering
21. Modification of the solar system
22. Practical laboratory conception and nurturing of animal (human?) foetuses
23. Production of a drug equivalent to Huxley's soma
24. A technological equivalent of telepathy
25. Some direct control of individual thought processes

FIGURE 11: TEN FAR-OUT POSSIBILITIES

1. Life expectancy extended to substantially more than 150 years (immortality)
2. Almost complete genetic control (but still homo sapiens)
3. Major modification of human species (no longer homo sapiens)
4. Antigravity (or practical use of gravity waves)*
5. Interstellar travel
6. Electric power available for less than .03 mill per kw hour
7. Practical and routine use of extrasensory phenomena
8. Laboratory creation of artificial live plants and animals
9. Lifetime immunization against practically all diseases
10. Substantial lunar or planetary bases or colonies

* As usually envisaged this would make possible a perpetual motion machine and therefore the creation of energy out of nothing. We do not envisage this as even a far-out possibility, but include antigravity, even though it annoys some physicist friends, as an example of some totally new use of basic phenomena or the seeming violation of a basic law.

maybe, even, but what these fellows have done today has to do with the stimulation of the pleasure centers. The rats are the most thoroughly investigated here. Let me tell you about the rat experiment. You can take a rat, wire his pleasure center to a button and give it its choice between pressing the button, and food, sex, water, or rest. If it is given its own choice it will invariably press the button 5,000 times an hour, for hour after hour. If you make it take a little food, a little rest, a little water, it leads a longer life than the control rat and as far as we can see a happy one. Okay? My picture of the future!

A lot of us Americans get their pleasure centers—and we have got a number of them—wired to a console on their chest, with a lot of buttons. Now, you wouldn't want to play your own buttons, that would be depraved, so you find somebody—and I am prudish, I hope it is the opposite sex—and you play each other's buttons. I can see it going now. Have you ever tried one and four together? Well, you have got my picture of the future.

4

Cashing-in on the Cop-out:
Cultural Change
and Marketing Potential

LEE ADLER
RCA

Late one night in March, 1967, three disconsolate young men were sipping coffee and pondering their futures. They had had enough of conventional middle-class values, nine-to-five jobs, and wearing ties. They wanted to drop out. They discussed going to Morocco, living in a commune in Pennsylvania, and other hippie life styles. But how to earn a minimum of "bread" to finance their departure from the larger society? Aware of the mod clothing revolution, the young men decided to go it one better by opening a really "funky" clothing store for both sexes. They rented a loft on Lexington Avenue in New York, bought some surplus World War I U.S. Army jackets for 50 cents apiece, and opened for business.

Today, three years later, The Different Drummer is running at an annual sales volume of over $1,500,000. The firm has expanded its square footage some fourfold. It has created a national franchise plan; the first four stores are now open. It is receiving weekly inquiries from retail chains and textile firms as to its interest in being acquired. There is personal irony in this story for Todd Merer, president and former criminal lawyer, and his two associates, erstwhile schoolteacher and importer, respectively, for instead of dropping out they find they have really dropped in. They experience all the pressures of any other business man-

From *Business Horizons*, February, 1970, pp. 19–30. Copyright, 1970 by the Foundation for the School of Business, at Indiana University. Reprinted with permission.

agement. They work long hours and, inevitably, they are drawn into the vortex of conventional commercial life.

The story of The Different Drummer holds a profound message for marketing. The message is that the moral, social, and cultural value system changes occurring today entail the most sweeping and grave consequences for every sector of the marketing front—strategy formulation, new product development, advertising, distribution, and marketing research. These consequences can be problems or they can be opportunities, depending on whether marketers are alert to what is happening in their environments, and what they do about it.

Several difficulties complicate assessment of the situation. One is the common tendency to link serious, deeply rooted change to the generation gap and to equate it with fads and fashions. Sooner or later, it is assumed, these changes will go the way of the green eyeshade and the hula hoop, and things will be as before. A second difficulty lies in the very nature of these changes: they are elusive and hard to define, and their practical effects are often indirect. A third obstacle lies in the nature of the marketing executive. He is likely to become resentful and unyielding in the face of shifting values, rather than acknowledging and capitalizing on them. Young folks may just have something when they decide not to trust anyone over 30.

On the other hand, we should not go to the opposite extreme and regard the current scene as altogether unique. Values always ride a pendulum. Hedonism gives way to Puritanism and, in the fullness of time, hedonism returns. American society has assimilated many changes similar to today's. The emancipation of woman, for example, had countless effects on marketing. Better education allowed them to join the work force, and they were able to add to disposable income. Smoking became acceptable. Fashions were modified. In the 1920's, for instance, our attitudes toward modesty changed, thereby destroying the market for veils.

An army of social psychologists, economists, political scientists, educators, religious leaders, and journalists is chronicling the texture and weave of American life. I will not pretend to duplicate their efforts, but it will be useful to trace briefly the origin, development, and expressions of value change as a foundation for considering their significance for marketing.

OVERVIEW: YESTERDAY AND TODAY

Consideration of some of the basic beliefs that activated the nineteenth century will help to provide perspective on what is happening to our culture in the late twentieth century: mankind will reach the millennium through hard work; progress comes through free enterprise and individual effort; competence sets the only limit to a man's upward mobility in a mobile society; education is eminently worthwhile, for it frees the sons of the working class and resuscitates the immigrant; and accumulation of material goods is a noble endeavor.

In addition, families were large, which provided a sense of belonging and security; life styles were influenced by Puritanism, which took a basically dour attitude toward pleasure, and the Protestant ethic, which emphasized hard work, productivity, and problem-solving; and life for most people was difficult and focused primarily on satisfying creature needs.

The twentieth century view of the character of the nineteenth century American is partly true and partly myth, but it is of value to us for the counterpart it provides with our current self-image. Some of the principal characteristics of the nineteenth century figure were self-reliance, an unquestioning belief in his self-virtue, a profound sense of purpose, optimism, and a feeling of personal power.

We all recognize the one fundamental force that is generating the shifts in today's society: high technology, as seen in electronic communications media, the computer, automation, and nuclear power. The effects of these technological advances are awesomely widespread. They include an explosion in the mass media; an information revolution; extraordinary affluence, which is related to, produces, and is in turn affected by a rising education level, enhanced tastes, and a sharpening of the critical faculty; a sharp increase in urban disintegration; life in the shadow of a nuclear holocaust; a marked improvement in technology's power to reshape man and his environment (the promise of artificial organs, manipulation of the weather, undersea life, and so on); a velocity of change so great as to constitute a difference in kind rather than merely of degree; an enormously more intricate society; and increasingly intense confrontations between conflicting viewpoints.

These forces, interacting among each other, are generating greater acceptance of modifications in basic values. To repeat, these are *not* just changes among the lunatic fringe, minority groups, or the alienated. I would classify the following factors as particularly vital:

—A questioning of materialistic pursuits at the peak of our affluence
—Increasing pressure for social justice
—A decline in respect for authority and the law
—A belief in the rightness of militancy and confrontation
—A love of novelty
—A passion for style and format paralleled by a loss of interest in content.

These social convulsions stimulate each other to further convulsions, phenomena that include dropping out, psychic malaise, estrangement from institutional authority, social protest, minority group uprisings, role reversals (for example, the old emulating the young), new communications modes, greater assertion of individuality, increased use of drugs, a sharp rise in violence, and greater sexual freedom.

THE NEW CONSUMER

This social upheaval is molding a new American consumer. Because society is in transition, it is impossible to define this consumer precisely; indeed, one of his characteristics is a permanent state of change. We can, however, discern some of his salient qualities. These qualities are most often associated with the young, but they are also to be found among the young in spirit. For one thing, those who have the new state of mind do not change when they reach their thirtieth birthdays. Moreover, the typical reexamination of life's basic purpose, meaning, and direction that psychologists report among people in their forties is resulting in the acceptance of these newer values among the middle-aged. In addition, the near-veneration with which the larger society treats the young promotes the adoption of their views by the older half of the population.

I would list the following as crucial consumer characteristics and behavioral traits from a marketing standpoint:

—A more keenly etched sense of self
—More cynicism, disbelief, and questioning
—Complex needs for self-definition, purpose, love, esteem, a sense of belonging, and esthetic satisfaction
—Greater intelligence, sharper wit
—Lessened inhibition
—A passion for personal involvement
—Jaded capacity to receive
—Responsiveness to multimedia presentations
—Susceptibility to apparent paradox
—Tolerance for individual deviations from traditional standards of behavior, dress, and taste
—A greater sense of community among the young as a separate subculture, which cuts across social and economic class lines
—Emphasis on immediate short-term gratifications, and an associated discounting of the future in terms of planning and saving
—An acceptance of, if not positive liking for, impermanence.

IMPLICATIONS FOR MARKETING

The effects of these dramatic changes color the whole spectrum of marketing. Some factors bear on over-all marketing strategy; other implications affect individual line-and-staff functions.

For example, market segmentation in terms of customer wants and needs has been increasingly accepted as a strategy superior to producer segmentation or demographic segmentation. Now the growing tendency to cater to individual tastes, supported by a hedonistic philosophy and the disposable income to finance it, is inevitably leading to ever greater market segmentation. If the product design policy of The Different Drummer was carried to its logical extreme, no two garments would be alike.

The growing concern for social justice and for protecting the individual in an ever more crowded, impersonal, and intricate world has become the foundation for a countervailing force: the consumer movement. The Food and Drug Administration and other regulatory bodies have adopted tougher government controls. Ralph Nader has attacked, successively, the automotive industry, tire manufacturers, excessive fat in frankfurters, and inadequacies in baby foods. Note that he attracts an army of college graduates as zealous as crusaders to help his cause: young people who are not rushing to find executive trainee slots in industry. Even housewives have picketed supermarkets to protest high prices.

Increasingly, industry itself is yielding to these values. "The modern definition of corporate social responsibility," said Robert J. Keith, board chairman, Pillsbury Company, at the 1968 annual meeting, "holds us to larger and more positive standards. In today's world, we are expected to make significant contributions to nothing less than the quality of life, and to do so in the context of growing expectation of quality."*

After a study of the psychology and sociology of American women, Pillsbury announced that it would "change its approach to product development to meet the needs of this generation," modify existing products, and communicate differently.

"The old ideas of Ann Pillsbury will disappear and a new direct relationship with consumers will emerge. And our advertising will be developed with their interests and tastes specifically in mind . . . we will search for some media systems of our own through which to provide these homemakers with the type of knowledge they require. The research will extend our work in publishing to more than recipe books. It means our labels will contain new and different types of information than we now display."

In a related development, there is new respect for the black man as a consumer, expressed by the rising number of advertising agencies, marketing research programs, and media devoted to the black segment of our population. This awareness has introduced black manikins in store windows, Afro styling, and changes in product design.

The role of style reflects growing sophistication, a refinement of esthetic sensitivity, and a desire for self-enhancement. Style now means not just the cut of a garment or the color of a slip cover, but style of life as well, whether it be casual or elegant, offbeat bohemian or formal and proper. Whatever the style is, it tends to be carried out in a unified way —in apparel, home furnishings, books, entertainment, and food. And it seeks to be gracious and positive. This is leading to smarter styling: to product lines linked by a "look" expressed in color, design, and pattern; to integrated department store merchandising of products that are used together (for example, cooking and tablewares for gourmet dining such as chafing dishes, serving trays, and ice buckets, items formerly scattered in at least three different departments).

Implications for Marketing Intelligence

A logical point of departure in analyzing the impact of cultural change on marketing is the marketing intelligence function, for it bears the responsibility of identifying, measuring, interpreting, and reporting on what is going on in the larger society. I am deliberately using the term "marketing intelligence" rather than "marketing research" because the former embraces a broader scope using all the tools and methods avail-

* *Advertising Age,* September 16, 1968, p. 1.

able, whereas marketing research is often linked with a narrow, mechanical recording of the past. Indeed, the very breadth and speed of social and cultural developments is hastening the growth of marketing intelligence systems.

One of the principal specifics of this evaluation is the emergence of environmental scanning as a discipline for analyzing and weighing the future impact of change. Using both secondary and primary sources of data, scanning systems—like radar—examine the environment on a periodic if not continuous basis. The marketing intelligence man is not content to study only the current market of his company or client; he analyzes the total environment using the disciplines of the social anthropologist, politician, priest, economist, and psychologist. He has also learned to examine the effect of value system evolution on neighboring and distant industries, both here and abroad, and to integrate raw facts from a wide variety of sources in anticipating competitive forays, newly emerging hazards, or unexplored opportunities.

Deeply concerned with the implications of electronic media for journalism, a Chicago newspaper conducted an in-depth study. The investigation, utilizing detailed personal interviews of readers and nonreaders, established that most people no longer rely on newspapers for a straightforward presentation of the news; this they get from television. Rather, they now look to the newspaper for background orientation, analysis, and interpretation. As a result, to be responsive to the needs of its readers, the paper revised its editorial content and direction, as well as its format, and sharply reversed the slump in its circulation.

In another instance, the environmental scanning unit of a major consumer goods producer examined the possible effects of the changing quality of urban life on their business. After trying many correlations they found one of considerable significance: once urban congestion passed a certain point, there was a sharp rise in demand for the company's disposable packages and a decline in demand for reusable containers. Corresponding shifts occurred in preferences for the firm's package sizes. These findings, as measured in terms of population density, led to changes in the packaging mix, in distribution policies, and in local advertising content. In turn, this created better relationships with the company's retailers, fostered a happier selling climate for the sales force and, ultimately, contributed to an improved sales picture in the largest metropolitan areas.

In the mid-1960's, Paul Young, the junior-wear buyer at J. C. Penney Company, assessed both U.S. and foreign developments and noted the trend toward mod apparel among teen-age girls in England. He sensed its potential appeal in the United States for young people anxious to express their individuality, to declare symbolic war on their elders, and to wear "badges" that would permit in-group members to recognize each other. He left Penney and set up Paraphernalia, with the backing of Puritan Sportswear. He brought over Mary Quant from England and in October, 1965, opened the first outlet with dancing girls in the windows. Paraphernalia is now a franchise organization of some sixty-five stores nationwide with retail sales of some $4,600,000 a year.

One of the general consequences of the weakened hold of the hair-shirt mentality of Puritanism is a desire for greater comfort. As a society, we are increasingly coming to feel that it is not sinful to be comfortable. This, in turn, is leading to improved design in everything from furniture to can openers to women's undergarments.

In my opinion, the acceleration of value changes also calls for a new look at qualitative research methods. What are the tensions and conflicts deep within the consumer as he hurdles the tremendous psychological gulfs separating conformity from individuality, the concept of original sin from a life of pleasure, a belief that only work is moral from the enjoyment of huge amounts of leisure time? How do we capture the inner thoughts of persons struggling to find life's meaning and to define the proper mission of the individual—now that it is no longer simply earning one's daily bread, and now that the entire middle class is becoming a class of philosophers? What are the consequences of these interior monologues on consumer behavior?

Psychological research in particular merits reexamination for its potential, in the hands of sensitive, perceptive practitioners, for detecting the often subtle shifts in values and attitudes that are not as discernible by quantitative methods. (This is not to reject the latter but rather to suggest the more widespread use of a tandem approach.)

A famous motivation research study of the early 1950's found that women felt guilty about using cake mixes because they did not contribute much to the success of the cake. They felt they were somehow cheating their families. A study completed in mid-1969 for a group of food and appliance manufacturers has found that now women want to get out of the kitchen as quickly as possible. Their desire to feed their families well has not lessened, but they are prepared to trust manufacturers of convenience foods and see no reason to take twenty minutes to do what can be done as well in two. These, and related findings in women's fundamental attitudes toward being in the kitchen, appliances, foods, their role as food preparers and servers have sweeping consequences for new product development, appliance design, kitchen layout, and in what marketers say about these products to make them harmonize with these new values.

A deeper probing of the motivations underlying the nonconformist revolution in apparel suggests a powerful role for escapism. Strikingly different clothes permit role playing or "disguising" of self. It is this urge that also explains the sharp growth of sales of wigs and falls for women and even for weekend beards and sideburns for men.

Implications for Developing New Products and Services

The obvious imperative for marketers wishing to be attuned to the times is to audit their current and proposed lines of products and services and to build in satisfaction of the complex needs and desires of the new consumer. The entire financial services industry is an example of an industry that has redesigned its offerings to appeal to the new consumer. The industry realized that most consumers are trapped between two poles. On the one hand, they seek immediate gratification and resist postponement of pleasure; on the other, they are aware of the need to provide for future financial requirements. The second need is sharpened by the intensified importance society attaches to education and by a somewhat newer value, the desire to retire early and to enjoy retirement.

Having identified these values through ongoing marketing research, sponsored by the Institute of Life Insurance, the life insurance industry has retailored its offerings. Over and above the basic death benefit, life insurance policies now stress the plus values of providing for the education of children, for retirement, and "rainy day" savings. To help provide adequate retirement funds, insurance is being marketed increasingly in packages with equities such as mutual funds.

The over-all direction of the systems approach to financial services is toward family financial planning and the sale of services to fulfill those plans. The ultimate vision is of a package that would include: forecasting income over the life-span of the household based on education and occupation; budgeting expenditures and savings against current and anticipated income; scheduling the acquisition of major items (house, car, boat, or second home) and planning for major expenditures (foreign travel, for example); planning investments, including amount, kind, timing, and risk; retirement planning; and estate planning. The extension of these plans would involve budget worksheets and normative data; continuing counsel on the budget as well as on the use of credit, tax factors, insurance coverages, accounting, and banking services; receipt and disbursement of funds; and arrangements for mortgage financing or loans.

In addition to insurance companies, the commercial banks, savings banks and finance companies are all taking steps in this direction. Chemical Bank introduced its Money Minder service in 1969. By coding each check issued, the customer is able to obtain a monthly and year-to-date report on expenditures by expense category. The system provides budget control and handy data for tax computations. The AIMS Group is a New York-based financial counseling firm specializing in the needs of upper-income men, which recommends and arranges for real estate investments, tax shelter purchases such as oil exploration participations, insurance, estate planning, and related services. A financial field "conglomerate" is planning to sell packages consisting of executive loans and investment in undeveloped real estate and insurance.

An interesting offshoot in the financial services area reflects still another cultural trend: the growing appreciation for things esthetic. To capitalize on this development, a New York organization is setting up a fine arts mutual fund, which will operate exactly like other mutual funds except that paintings and sculpture will replace stocks and bonds. A committee of experts—museum curators, critics, and dealers—will make the selections and counsel on price. Owners of shares in the funds will have to agree to a substantial minimum investment and to a phased deferment of sales of shares, if required, to prevent forced sales of holdings. Lest the fund be accused of utter crassness, shareholders will enjoy the art in their offices or homes on a rotating basis while awaiting long-term capital appreciation.

The art world itself, where it used to take a generation, if not a century, for major movements to evolve, has undergone a transformation. Art vogues have changed from abstract expressionism to pop art, to op art, to minimal, process, and concept art, all within a dozen years and at an accelerating velocity. "Everyone is famous for fifteen minutes," said Andy Warhol.

The love of novelty and style and a swift pace of change are turning an improbable array of products into fashion items. Utilitarian objects like cooking pots now blossom in fashion colors and patterns and, with teak handles, are now elegant enough to serve from. Lathes and milling machines are now not only functional but attractively designed.

Significant role reversals create a market for new clothing items. Sexual differences, for example, are being obliterated in terms of mutual responsibilities, mores, and behavior; hence, we see long-haired males using more toiletries and even cosmetics such as body lotions, moisturizers, and skin conditioners. They are willing to wear "female-styled" clothes such as shirts with ruffles or garments in bright colors made of velvets, velours, and voile, while females sport bell-bottomed slacks, boots, and buckskin jackets. We see his-and-hers matched outfits, and pastel-colored shoes have appeared in such men's shoe chains as French Shriner and Florsheim.

Another development is that the concept of impermanence is more acceptable in our society. The Puritan ethic forbade wastefulness; one did not, for example, discard things until they were thoroughly worn out. Today, however, assisted by technological advances in newer materials and fabrication methods, and by affluence, the disposables "industry" (its state is too primeval, diffuse, and chaotic for it to be a proper industry) is undergoing a boom of vast proportions. One segment of the field, the market for nonwoven fabrics, is expected to soar from an estimated $400,000,000 in sales in 1966 to over $1,300,000,000 in 1975. When Scott Paper Company first offered paper dresses in 1966 as a promotion at $1.25 each, the firm, to its astonishment, sold over 500,000 units. Nonwoven fabrics are now used in a myriad of products—surgeon's gowns, operating room drapes, bath mats, wipes, panties, tablecloths, work uniforms, bed underpads, diapers, coasters, bartenders' and waiters' jackets, rainwear, and so on.

The desire for social equality and the effort to integrate minority groups into the larger society has had an impact on marketing. Afro-styled clothing is featured in many stores, and "soul food"—ham hocks, candied yams, collard greens, and black-eyed peas—may be ordered in some good restaurants, and even in a popular-priced food chain, Horn & Hardart. It does not seem unreasonable to forecast that food manufacturers will soon have packaged and frozen soul food on supermarket shelves alongside Chinese, Mexican, and Italian specialties.

Implications for Distribution

To reach the markets created by value system changes, the marketer may be able to use established channels, but it is possible that he will have to hack his own route to market. For example, Paraphernalia began to sell its women's apparel to department stores to expand distribution quickly beyond its first owned store. But the firm found that department stores were unsatisfactory because their impersonal vastness created the wrong ambience. What young people wanted was their own exclusive buying environment. This prompted Paraphernalia to refine its own retail concepts to provide an intimate, friendly setting, featuring the posters, rock-and-roll music, and lights favored by its target segment—young women who wanted a place to socialize where few aged ladies over 30 would venture.

The Different Drummer has gone even further, violating many of the rules of retailing in the process. They opened for business in a second-story loft; they dared to go uptown rather than to their "natural" location in Greenwich Village. They hired inexperienced ghetto teen-agers as salespeople. Their staff is a haven for drop-outs, including the son of an ambassador and the daughter of a millionaire investment banker. Characteristic of their unique tone is the preamble to their proposal addressed to prospective franchisees:

"If a man doesn't keep pace with his companion, perhaps it is because he hears the sound of a different drummer."—Henry Thoreau

In the complex and tension-filled atmosphere of modern society, existing within Thoreau's meaning may often be wishful thinking. To be able to do so and at the same time gain material rewards, is not always the easiest of things. For us, The Different Drummer has become such an oasis. Will it be yours?

The tempo of the times and the demand for ease and convenience are supporting the phenomenal growth of the "fast food" business. International Industries, Beverly Hills, is one of many examples. The company sold its first International House of Pancakes franchise in 1960. It soon recognized that its real marketing future lay not in pancakes but in franchising systems. In the succeeding nine years, the company grew to a network of franchised fast food outlets, including Copper Penny Restaurants, Orange Julius of America, Will Wright Ice Cream Shoppes, and the Original House of Pies.

The remarkable renaissance of boutiques is a result of the search for ways to reach the new consumer with new types of goods. Within department stores, the boutique tends to cluster goods around a "look," specific usage occasions, or a theme. It is this approach that has led to gourmet shops, patio-living boutiques, "unisex" shops, and similar reorganizations of traditional retailing patterns. Independent boutiques are mushrooming as well; the Paperhanger in Washington, which deals only in paper fabric products, is a good example. On the industrial front, the perfection of nonwoven disposables is stimulating changes in established modes of distribution. The roles, product lines, and competitive positions of industrial launderers, linen supply houses, wholesale paper merchants and rag dealers are in the process of transition as they compete for the market for paper wipes, towels, and work clothes.

The emergence of new markets has required the creation of entirely new distribution patterns. National Student Marketing Corporation is registering extraordinary volume gains with its unique ways of promoting, selling, and moving goods to students who arrange for and publicize the showing of such "campy" films as W. C. Fields and Laurel and Hardy. Special commercials of equally campy tone and fiercely honest content are interspersed between the films, and samples of sales literature are distributed. The goods advertised can be purchased at the film shows, college bookstores, from the campus representatives, or by mail order.

Implications for Advertising and Promotion

The implications of the new values are clear for advertising. The under-30 generation loathes sham and hypocrisy; they respect the truth; they resent excesses of earnestness; and they cannot abide pomposity. "Tell it like it is" is the touchstone.

This attitude has generated a new communications mode, the put-on, which bears on the effectiveness of marketing communications. While the put-on superficially resembles practical jokes, irony, and hoax, it is really none of these. The put-on is actually a product of the credibility gap, the inability to accept what is seen as pretentious, dishonest mouthings of vested interests. In effect, the put-on is a vague, ambiguous, hostile, oblique communication in which we cannot be sure of what the speaker really means unless one is really "where it's happening, baby."

Communicating memorably and persuasively with the new consumer clearly calls for new approaches in copy and art. Successful advertising and promotion include indirect, allusive, low key appeals; shorter messages; more experimentation with nonlinear presentations of information (cool, ambiguous, involving); more wit, honesty, verve, self-deprecation, irreverence (but not irrelevance); crisp, contemporary design in formats, packages, physical facilities; greater utilization of mixed media, especially audio-visual modes; blending of the real and the absurd; faster pace; and cautious use of the more ephemeral elements of today's under-thirties subculture (rock-and-roll music, psychedelic art, and high color).

A magazine advertisement prepared by McCann-Erickson, Inc., for General Motors Opel Kadett is one example of the new advertising. A provocative-looking young girl stands next to the car; the headline reads, "Buick introduces automobiles to light your fire." To those familiar with a rock-and-roll group known as The Doors and their song, "Light My Fire," the sexual metaphor is overt. McCann-Erickson researched the headline among over-thirties. It was found to be "not offensive" to those who knew what it meant and, obviously, would not offend those who did not know what it meant. The significance of this should not be overlooked: it seems possible to segment messages even in mass media in ways not previously feasible.

Ten years ago, most product advertising consisted of fairly straightforward, sometimes ponderous, presentations of product features. Five years ago, product sell had become grimly fanciful; Alka-Seltzer's television commercials, for example, showed a stomach tortured by excessive consumption. In contrast, a recent Alka-Seltzer commercial prepared by Jack Tinker & Partners reflects the characteristics of today's advertising in its campy tone and fast cuts. The commercial lightly takes advantage of the rebellious spirit of the day and resentment of authority by showing a prison dining room demonstration against bad food. Most of the time is used to show the convicts banging their tin cups on the tables. Not a word is spoken until the end of the spot, when the convicts begin to chant, "Alka-Seltzer! Alka-Seltzer! Alka-Seltzer!"

The International Coffee Organization reaches its prime target—young people, 17 to 25—through youth-oriented radio stations, college magazines, and the college editions of magazines. The advertising, prepared also by McCann-Erickson, is low key and amiable, full of allusions to the concerns of young people. One magazine ad, for instance, shows a hirsute rock-and-roll group. In the background an M.P. has his hand on the drummer's shoulder. The headline asks, "Another group is after your drummer?" Visually, this ad would immediately "turn off" the older generation—so much so that they might even miss the point, the concern that young people have about going into the army.

The radio spots for this advertiser capitalize on the absurd and the irreverent. The copy approach enables the agency to offer real facts about brewing a good cup of coffee and, by being self-deprecating, catches listeners off-guard, thereby allowing the message to get through. Here is a typical 60-second spot:

HE: You know, Karen, I used to think you were really a freaky girl—learning how to yodel, running off to Tibet for Labor Day weekend.

SHE: Everybody has their little outs, Walter.

HE: But you were such a homebody making this coffee—measuring just the right amounts of coffee and water.

SHE: There is only one correct grind for every coffee-maker.

HE: Karen, I think underneath that chrome leotard you're probably a very sweet girl. I mean, you made a full three-quarter pot for just the two of us.

SHE: One must make at least three-quarters of a pot, Walter, or coffee has no soul.

HE: But what really got me was your insisting on cold water to start the brewing.

SHE: Any guru can tell you good coffee has to start with cold water.

HE: Karen, the coffee is really delicious. Could you stop standing on your head long enough to have some with me?

ANNOUNCER: It makes you think. And things happen over it. So next time you have something to think about or talk over, do it over a cup of coffee, the Think Drink.

The poster craze of the late 1960's illustrates the new attitude toward advertising, the blending of art and advertising in one medium, how companies (even big, staid ones) can capitalize on this movement, and the appeal of disposability. The trend began with the success of giant blowups of Humphrey Bogart, W. C. Fields, and other pop culture heroes. The vivid, psychedelic posters became art objects. Subsequently, commercial posters were republished, and campy commercial posters were hung in the home. General Motors published a Day-Glo poster of a wild bird for the Pontiac Firebird; Humble Oil Company incorporated its tiger into a poster captioned "I need you now." Alka-Seltzer pokes gentle fun at American food tastes with a poster showing a hamburger on a bed of ketchup-drenched French fries and a caption printed red, white, and blue, reading simply, "Alka-Seltzer."

These are only a handful of examples of hundreds. Before switching to its new theme, the Coca-Cola Company had asked prominent personalities and rock-and-roll groups to take the basic music of "Things Go Better with Coke" and score and sing it in their own style and beat and even in their own words. Fifty-three versions of the basic commercial were created; ten years ago, or even five years ago, this would have been heresy. Self-deprecation abounds in advertising; in one superb example, Benson & Hedges cigarettes poke fun at their extra length. Vignettes and fast cuts are popular, reflecting the enormously successful mode of "Laugh-In."

Emerging attitudes also permit the advertising of newer product categories. The new openness about sex, the stress on individual decisions (as opposed to being told what to do by the church), the social value of being able to "do more" for fewer children—all of these factors underlie the acceptance of birth control products and their advertisement in reputable women's magazines and mass magazines. Similarly, the new climate has made it possible to promote vaginal spray deodorants not only in print but on television. This product category is growing so fast one can hardly count the individual brands; together they have created an estimated $15 million market in two years.

Implications for Packaging

No sector of the marketing front is unaffected by the impact of the cultural revolution; packaging, too, should be reexamined in the light of value change. Flexnit Company, New York, for example, completed a research study on packaging concepts that one would not even have dared to do ten years ago. The objective of the study was to determine how far the company could go in presenting nudity in its girdle and brassiere packages. Flexnit found that in today's climate they could go as far as they liked in depicting unclad women so long as nudity was logically a part of the situation (for example, a woman stepping out of the shower and starting to dress) and not erotic in intent. The only other limitations were to stop short of showing hair and to avoid showing women in unnatural or awkward poses. Incidentally, nudity seems to be more acceptable in the Midwest and South than in the Northeast.

Implications for Corporate Policies

The rising tide of social outrage; the deepening concern with truth in advertising, in lending, in packaging; the push for greater assurance of beneficial products, notably in cigarettes and drugs; the desire to help the downtrodden—all of these pressures act on the corporation to accept more social responsibility. The key point for our thesis, apart from the obvious moral issue involved, is that making a contribution to the larger society is not necessarily the opposite of profit making. As a matter of fact, today's values create new marketing opportunities. Put in its most cynical form, the formula would read: today's altruism is tomorrow's self-interest.

Many of these programs are in housing and finance. To make a dent in the urgent problems of housing in ghettos, Celanese Corporation and American Standard, Inc., recently joined in a variant of the so-called "turnkey" approach. The two firms organized Construction for Progress, Inc., and in a gentlemen's agreement with New York City's Housing Authority, erected a six-story, 66-family, low-income apartment building in East Harlem. The private developer was able to put up the building in only 40 percent of the time that the official body, hampered by many bureaucratic restrictions, would have needed. Upon completion, the Housing Authority bought the building for $1,200,000, giving the developer a return of between 3 percent and 4 percent on his investment.

In a comparable arrangement, the New York Bank for Savings and the Bowery Savings Bank jointly initiated a series of turnkey rehabilitations of new housing projects in Harlem. The New York Bank for Savings is also one of the leaders in supplying mortgage money for industrial plants being built in the Flatlands industrial park in Brooklyn to create job opportunities in nearby ghetto areas. Aluminum Company of America, through a subsidiary, Alcoa Properties, Inc., now owns and operates eleven urban development projects in seven cities. Two offshoots are building turnkey, low-rent projects in Monroe, Mich., and Pittsburgh.

There are other ways of being a useful corporate citizen. Xerox Corporation has sponsored a series of television shows dealing honestly with controversial social issues. Clairol is training underprivileged black girls in Washington as beauty parlor operators. Mind, Inc., a subsidiary of CPC International, Inc., has developed programmed learning techniques to provide minimum reading, writing, arithmetic, and typing skills to enhance the employability of the underprivileged.

PRACTICAL APPLICATIONS

What should a marketer do about the kinds of social, moral, cultural, and psychological value system changes that have been discussed? How can he identify practically and act on changes that are relevant to his business?

One industry is tracking cultural and social change and then applying its lessons to all aspects of marketing. The Motion Picture Association commissioned a large national probability sample study of movie-goers, utilizing both quantitative and qualitative information-gathering approaches. The study confirmed the appropriateness of product changes to meet the tastes of the changing market. In particular, movies treating such lively topics as sexual freedom and individuality in a bold, honest, open manner are well accepted by the key market segment—younger people. The industry, having the right product, seeks the right distribution channels: intimate theaters in suburban shopping centers and in university towns, and quasi-art theaters.

Similarly, the industry is remodeling its promotional strategies. The traditional ballyhoo, the claims of "colossal," "gigantic," and "stupendous" are yielding to subtler copy. Concurrently, there has been an increase in the use of specialized media: for example, student newspapers, surfacing "underground" publications such as *The Village Voice* in New York, and the college editions of magazines like *Time*.

For some marketers, adapting to the times is a simple process. Salada discovered that younger people regard tea as a weak beverage enjoyed only by little old ladies. To reverse this image, Salada developed a new spot television campaign. One ID opens with a close-up of a grandmother's face, wrinkled and bespectacled. The next frame gives a full view of her—attired in black leather jacket and pants and leaning against a motorcycle.

In other cases, cross-currents in our social climate pose grave moral and practical problems for marketers. Aware of the increase in violent crime, a major manufacturer, for instance, designed a nonlethal cigarette lighter-like device for personal self-defense. The device would spray a Mace-like gas and a nonwashable dye, and would include a siren to summon the police. But negative considerations intruded, and the firm commissioned a qualitative research study using focused group interviews with various demographic segments, including whites and blacks, to test the product concept. The firm decided not to market it for several reasons. Arming the population might aggravate rather than ease social tensions and escalate verbal arguments. Finally, they realized that the promotion to sell the device would have to appeal to fear, and they were opposed to this as a copy platform.

The value changes now taking place in our society should not be dismissed as ephemeral, nor should they be ignored by all but social psychologists. Rather, marketers should be aware of their profound implications for product development, for selling and distribution methods, and for advertising and promotional approaches. Assessment of these changes may lead to defensive program, at the least, and the more aggressive firm will recognize a vast potential in the wants of the new consumer motivated by different values.

Margaret Mead has observed that today's adults are like the immigrants of several generations ago. They are unfamiliar with current mores and behavior patterns and they cannot understand the language, for they have not grown up in a universe of television, cybernetics, space travel, and the new math. But as marketers, today's adults are going to have to learn the new language; if they don't, they may get left behind.

MARKETS AND BUYER BEHAVIOR

5

A Theory
of Buyer
Behavior

JOHN A. HOWARD
Columbia University

JAGDISH N. SHETH
University of Illinois

The usual purpose of a theory is to explain empirical phenomena. The empirical phenomenon which we want to explain is the buying behavior of individuals over a period of time. More specifically, our theory is an attempt to explain the *brand choice* behavior of the buyer. We assume that brand choice is not random but systematic, and the task we have undertaken in developing this theory is to formulate a structure that enables us to view it as a system.

To elaborate on our assumption: First, we assume that buying behavior is rational in the sense that it is within the buyer's "bounded rationality";[1] that is, his behavior is rational within the limits of his cognitive and learning capacities and within the constraint of limited information. Second, we are attempting to build a positive theory and not a normative theory. Third, if brand choice behavior is assumed to be systematic, then it can be observed in certain standard ways. Later on, we describe a series of measures of the buyer's buying behavior generally labeled purchase behavior, attitude toward a brand, comprehension of the brand, attention to impinging stimuli, and intention to buy a brand. Fourth, if behavior is systematic, it is caused by some event—a stimulus—either in the buyer or in the buyer's environment. This event or stimulus is the input to the

---

[1] J. G. March and H. A. Simon, *Organizations* (New York: Wiley and Sons, 1958).

system, and purchase behavior is the output. What we must describe then, is what goes on between the input and the output.

A SUMMARY OF THE THEORY

Much buying behavior is more or less repetitive, and the buyer establishes purchase cycles for various products which determine how often he will buy. For some products, such as durable appliances, this cycle is lengthy and purchase is infrequent. For many other products, such as food and personal-care items, the purchase cycle is short and purchase is frequent. Confronted by repetitive brand-choice decisions, the consumer simplifies his task by storing relevant information and establishing a routine in his decision process. Therefore our theory must identify the elements of his decision process, observe the changes that occur in them over time as a result of their repetitive nature, and show how a combination of decision elements affects search processes and the incorporation of information from the buyer's commercial and social environment.

The elements of a buyer's brand-choice decision are (1) a set of motives, (2) several alternative courses of action, and (3) decision mediators by which the motives are matched with the alternatives. Motives are specific to a product class, and reflect the underlying needs of the buyer. The alternatives are the various brands that have the potential of satisfying the buyer's motives.

There are three important notions involved in the definition of alternatives as brands. First, the several brands which become alternatives to the buyer need not belong to the same product class *as defined by the industry*. For example, a person may see Sanka coffee, Ovaltine, and Tetley's tea as three alternatives to satisfy his motives related to beverage consumption. He also may see only two alternatives, such as coffee and beer, both belonging to physically dissimilar product classes. Second, the brands which are alternatives of the buyer's choice decision are generally small in number, collectively called his "evoked set." The evoked set is only a fraction of the brands he is aware of, and a still smaller fraction of the total number of brands actually on the market. Third, any two consumers may have quite different alternatives in their evoked sets.

Decision mediators are the set of rules that the buyer employs to match his motives and his means of satisfying those motives. They serve the function of ordering and structuring the buyer's motives, and then ordering and structuring the various brands based on their potential to satisfy these ordered motives. Decision mediators develop by the buyer's process of learning about the buying situation. They are therefore influenced by information from the buyer's environment, and even more importantly by the actual experience of purchasing and consuming the brand.

When the buyer is just beginning to purchase a product class, he lacks experience; he does not have a set of decision mediators for that product class. To develop them, he *actively seeks information* from his commercial and social environments. The information he actively seeks, or accidentally receives, is subjected to perceptual processes, which not only limit his intake of information (magnitude of information is affected) but modify it to suit his frame of reference (quality of information is affected). These modifications are significant in that they distort the neat "marketing-stimulus–consumer-response" relation.

Along with his active search for information, the buyer may to some extent generalize from similar past experience. Such generalization may be due to the physical similarity of a new product class to an old product class. For example, during initial purchases of whiskey, a buyer may generalize from his experiences in buying gin. Generalization can also occur when two product classes are physically dissimilar, but have a common meaning deriving from a company brand name. For example, a buyer might generalize from his experience in buying a refrigerator or range to his first purchase of a dishwasher.

Whatever the source, the buyer develops sufficient decision mediators to enable him to choose a brand which seems to have the best potential for satisfying his motives. If the brand proves satisfactory, the potential of that brand to satisfy his motives for subsequent purchases is increased, and the probability of his buying that brand again is likewise increased. With repeated satisfactory purchases of one or more brands, the buyer is likely to manifest a routine decision process in which the sequential steps in buying are so well structured that an event which triggers the process may also complete it. Routine purchasing implies that decision mediators are well established, and that the buyer has strong brand preferences.

The phase of repetitive decision making in which the buyer reduces the complexity of a buying situation with the help of information and experience is called "the psychology of simplification." The more the buyer simplifies his environment, the less is his tendency to engage in active search behavior. The environmental stimuli related to the purchase situation become more meaningful and less ambiguous. Furthermore, the buyer establishes more cognitive consistency among brands as he moves toward routine response, and the incoming information is then screened with regard to its magnitude and quality. He becomes less attentive to stimuli which do not fit his cognitive structure, and he distorts these stimuli when they are forced upon him. These implied mechanisms explain a phenomenon for which there is growing evidence (cf. the work of John Dollard of Yale University): people can be exposed to a television commercial but not perceive it.

A surprising phenomenon occurs in the case of frequently purchased products, such as food and personal-care items. The buyer, after establishing a routine decision process, may begin to feel bored with such repetitive decision making. He may also become satiated, even with a preferred brand. In both cases, he may feel that all existing alternatives—including the preferred brand—are unacceptable, which generates a desire to *complicate* the buying situation by considering new brands. This process can be called "the psychology of complication." Ultimately the buyer identifies a new brand, and begins again to simplify. Thus the continuing process of buying frequently purchased items develops a cycle of information seeking that goes from simplification to complication and back again.

Determining the intensity of a buyer's information-seeking effort at a point in time is obviously important to the marketing manager. For example, if he knows that a substantial group of buyers are at a level of routine decision making where they feel satiated or bored, he can introduce a new brand or innovation which might provide the needed source of change. Similarly, if buyers are engaged in extensive brand-choice problem solving, they are likely to actively seek information. The mass media may therefore prove very effective in communicating information about a brand.

Any theory of human behavior must account for individual differences. However, in order to identify the invariant relations of human behavior, at least under field conditions, it is often necessary to hold interpersonal variability constant by taking into account mediating variables and so classify individuals into homogeneous subgroups. The marketing manager is also interested in differentiated masses of buyers. He wants to understand and separate individual differences so that he can classify or segment the total market in terms of these differences. If we can understand the psychology of the individual buyer, we may achieve this classification.

Depending on the internal state of the buyer, a given stimulus may result in a given response. For example, one buyer who urgently needs a product may respond to an ad for a brand in that product class by buying it; another buyer who does not need the product may simply notice the ad and store the information; a third buyer may ignore the ad altogether. A construct such as "level of motivation" will then explain divergent reactions to the same stimulus. Alternatively, two buyers may both urgently need a product, but they buy two different brands. This can be explained by another construct: "predisposition toward a brand."

ELEMENTS OF THE THEORY

Figure 1 represents our theory of buyer behavior. The central rectangular box isolates the various internal variables and processes which, taken together, show the state of the buyer. The inputs to the rectangular box are stimuli from the marketing and social environments. The outputs are a variety of responses which the buyer is likely to manifest, based on the interaction between the stimuli and his internal state.

Besides the inputs and outputs, there are a set of seven influences which affect the variables in the rectangular box.[2] These variables appear at the

---

[2] Terminology is difficult in a problem area that cuts across both economics and psychology, because each discipline has often defined its terms differently from the other. We find the economist's definitions of "exogenous," vs. "endogenous," and "theory" vs. "model" more useful than those of the psychologist. The psychologist's distinction of hypothetical constructs and intervening variables, however, provides a helpful breakdown of endogenous variables. Finally, for the sake of exposition, we have often not clearly distinguished here between the theory and its empirical counterparts. Although this practice encourages certain ambiguities, and we lay ourselves open to the charge of reifying our theory, we believe that it simplifies the exposition.

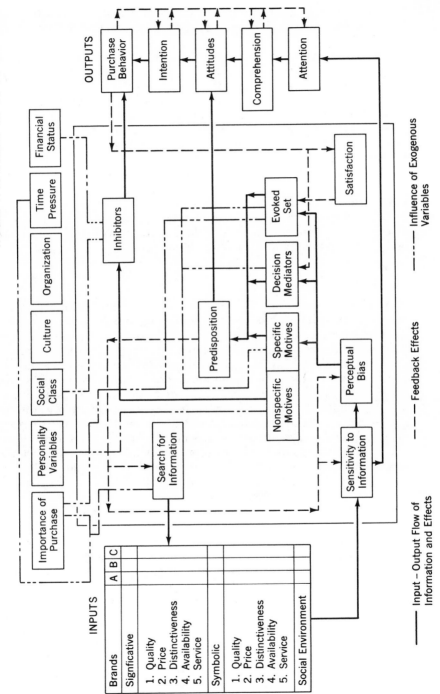

FIGURE 1: A THEORY OF BUYER BEHAVIOR

top of the diagram and are labeled "exogenous" variables. Their function is to provide a means of adjusting for the interpersonal differences discussed above.

The variables within the rectangular box are hypothetical constructs, which serve the role of endogenous variables in the sense that changes in them are explained, but they are something less than endogenous variables in that they are not well defined and are not observable. Their values are inferred from relations among the output intervening variables.

Several of the exogenous variables such as personality, social class, and culture have traditionally been treated as endogenous variables. We believe that they affect more specific variables, and that, by conceiving their effect via the hypothetical constructs, we can better understand their role.

Our theory of buyer behavior has four major components: stimulus variables, response variables, hypothetical constructs, and exogenous variables. We will elaborate on each of these components below, in terms of both their substance and their interrelationships.

Stimulus Input Variables

At any point in time, the hypothetical constructs which reflect the buyer's internal state are affected by numerous stimuli from his environment. This environment is classified as either commercial or social. The commercial environment consists of the marketing activities of various firms, by which they attempt to communicate to the buyer. From the buyer's point of view, these communications basically come via either the brand objects themselves or some linguistic or pictorial representation of brand attributes. If brand elements such as price, quality, service, distinctiveness, or availability are communicated through brand objects (significates), the stimuli are defined and classified as *significative* stimuli. If, on the other hand, brand attributes represented by linguistic or pictorial symbols are communicated via mass media, billboards, catalogs, salesmen, etc., the stimuli from these commercial sources are classified as *symbolic* stimuli. We view the marketing mix as the optimum allocation of funds between the two major channels of communication to the buyer—significative and symbolic.

Each commercial input variable is hypothesized to be multivariate. The five major dimensions of a brand—price, quality, distinctiveness, availability, and service—probably summarize the various attributes. The same dimensions are present in both the significative and symbolic communication that becomes the input stimuli for the buyer. However, certain dimensions may be more appropriately conveyed by significative rather than symbolic communication, and vice versa. For example, price is easily communicated by both channels; shape may best be communicated by two-dimensional pictures rather than verbal communication. Finally, size may not be easily communicated by any symbolic representation: the physical product (significate) may be necessary.

The third stimulus input variable is the information that the buyer's social environment provides for a purchase decision. The most obvious example is word-of-mouth communication.

The inputs to the buyer's mental state from the three major categories of stimuli are processed and stored through their interaction with a series of hypothetical constructs. The buyer may react to these stimuli immediately, or later.

Hypothetical Constructs

Our hypothetical constructs and their interrelationships are the result of an integration of Hull's[3] learning theory, Osgood's[4] congnitive theory, and Berlyne's[5] theory of exploratory behavior, along with other ideas.

These constructs fall into two classes: (1) those having to do with perception, and (2) those having to do with learning. Perceptual constructs serve the function of information processing; learning constructs serve the function of concept formation. It is interesting that, after years of experience in advertising, Reeves[6] arrived at a very similar classification: his "penetration" is analogous to perceptual variables, and his "unique selling propositions" are analogous to learning variables. We will first describe learning constructs, since they are the major components of decision making; the perceptual constructs which serve the important role of obtaining and processing information are more complex, and will be described later.

Learning Constructs. The learning constructs are labeled (1) motives —specific and nonspecific, (2) brand-potential of the evoked set, (3) decision mediators, (4) predisposition toward brands, (5) inhibitors, and (6) satisfaction with the purchase of a brand.

Motive is impetus to action. The buyer is motivated by expectation or anticipation, based on learning from the outcome of past purchase of a brand in his evoked set. Motives or goals may be thought of as constituting a means-end chain, and hence as being general or specific, depending upon their position in the chain.

The specific motives—lower level motives in the means-end chain—are very closely anchored to the attributes of a product class; in this way they become purchase criteria. Examples of specific motives are those for buying a dietary product—low calories, nutrition, taste, and value. Similarly, the specific motives in buying an air conditioner might be durability, quietness, cooling power, and design.

Very often, several specific motives are nothing more than indicators of some underlying, more general motive; that is, some motive that is

3 C. L. Hall, *Principles of Behavior* (New York: Appleton-Century-Crofts, 1943); and C. L. Hull, *A Behavior System* (New Haven: Yale University Press, 1952).

4 C. E. Osgood, G. J. Suci, and P. H. Tannenbaum, *Measurement of Meaning* (Urbana: University of Illinois Press, 1957).

5 D. E. Berlyne, "Motivational Problems Raised by Exploratory and Epistemic Behavior," in *Psychology: A Study of a Science*, Vol. 5, ed. S. Koch (New York: McGraw-Hill, 1963).

6 R. Reeves, *Reality in Advertising* (New York: Knopf, 1961).

higher in the means-end chain. In the foregoing example, the specific motives of nutrition and low calories might be indicators of the common motive of good health.

Motives also serve the important function of raising the buyer's general motivational state, thereby rousing him to pay attention to environmental stimuli. Probable examples of nonspecific motives are anxiety and fear, the personality variables of authoritarianism, exhibitionism, and aggressiveness, and the social motives of power, status, and prestige. Although they are nonspecific, they are not innate but learned, mostly as a result of acculturation. The nonspecific motives also possess a hierarchy within themselves. For example, anxiety is considered to be the source of another motive, that of the need for money Brown.[7]

Brand potential of the evoked set is a second learning construct. A buyer who is familiar with a product class has an evoked set of alternatives to satisfy his motives. The elements of his evoked set are some of the brands that make up the product class. This concept is important because the brands in a buyer's evoked set constitute competition for the seller.

A brand is, of course, a class concept, like many other objects or things. The buyer attaches a *word* to this concept—a label or brand name. The brand name conveys certain meanings, including its potential to satisfy his motives. In an advanced economy with relatively careful quality controls, the buyer is generally assured that any one brand object is like another. If quality controls are not adequate, the buyer will probably not summarize the potential of a brand in one word or label, but instead divide it into subclasses.

Various brands in the buyer's evoked set will generally satisfy his goal structure differently. One brand may possess such strong potential that it is an ideal brand for the buyer. Another brand may satisfy his motives barely enough to be part of his evoked set. Through a learning process, the buyer obtains and stores knowledge of each brand's potential, and then ranks them in order of their potential to satisfy his wants. The evoked set, in short, is a set of alternatives to be evaluated. Predisposition represents the buyer's preference ranking of them.

Decision mediators, a third learning construct, are the buyer's mental rules for matching alternatives with motives and ranking them in terms of their want-satisfying capacity. As mental rules, they exhibit reasoning, wherein the cognitive elements related to alternatives and motives are structured. In addition, decision mediators also contain a set of criteria by which the buyer denotatively discriminates between the brands he views as being in a product class, and those brands that are not. The words he uses to describe these criteria are the words he thinks with and finds easy to remember. These criteria are important to the manufacturer, because if he knows them he can deliberately build into his product and its promotion those characteristics which will differentiate his brand from competing brands.

Decision mediators thus represent enduring cognitive rules established

---

[7] J. S. Brown, *The Motivation of Behavior* (New York: McGraw-Hill, 1961).

by the process of learning, and their function is to establish meaningful and congruent relations among brands, so that the buyer can manifest goal-directed behavior. In view of the fact that decision mediators are learned, principles of learning become crucial in understanding their development and change over time.

There are two broad sources of learning: (1) actual experience, and (2) information. Actual experience can be with either the *same* buying situation in the past, or with a *similar* buying situation. The latter is generally labeled "generalization." Similarly, information as a source of learning can come from either the buyer's commercial or his social environment. Later, we will elaborate on each of these sources of learning.

Predisposition, a fourth construct, is the summary effect of the previous three constructs. It refers to the buyer's preference toward brands in his evoked set. It is, in fact, an aggregate index expressed in attitudes, which in turn can be measured by attitude scales. It might be visualized as the "place" where brands in the evoked set are compared with the mediator's choice criteria, to yield a judgment on the relative contribution of the brands to the buyer's motives. This judgment includes not only an estimate of the value of the brand, but also an estimate of the confidence with which the buyer holds that position. This uncertainty aspect of predisposition can be called "brand ambiguity," in that the more confidently he holds it, the less ambiguous the connotative meaning of the brand is to him and the more likely he is to buy it.[8]

Inhibitors, the fifth learning construct, are forces in the environment which create important disruptive influences on the actual purchase of a brand, even when the buyer has reasoned out that that brand will best satisfy his motives. In other words, when the buyer is motivated to buy the product class and is predisposed to buy a particular brand, he may not buy it because certain environmental forces inhibit the purchase act and prevent him from satisfying his preferences.

We postulate at least four types of inhibitors. They are (1) a high price for the brand, (2) lack of availability of the brand, (3) time pressure on the buyer, and (4) the buyer's financial status. The first two are part of the environmental stimuli, and therefore they are part of the input system. The last two come from the two exogenous variables of the same name. Temporary barriers to the purchase of a brand may also be created by social constraints emanating from other exogenous variables.

An essential feature of all inhibitors is that they are *not internalized* by the buyer, because their occurrence is random and strictly situational. However, for a given buyer, some inhibitors may persist systematically over time. If they persist long enough, the buyer is likely to incorporate them as part of his decision mediators, thus permitting them to affect the mental structure of his alternatives and motives. An example of such internalization might be the consequences of the constant time pressure a housewife faces because she has taken a job. Continuation of the time

---

[8] G. S. Day, "Buyer Attitudes and Brand Choice Behavior," Unpublished Ph.D. dissertation, Columbia University, 1967.

pressure may alter her evoked set as well as her motive structure. Convenience and time saving become important motives, and her evoked set may come to include time-saving brands, such as instant coffee. Similarly, a brand may be withdrawn by a company because of its stage in the product life cycle. The permanent unavailability of that brand will be learned and internalized by buyers, and they will remove that brand from their evoked sets.

Satisfaction, the last of the learning constructs, refers to the degree of congruence between the actual consequences of purchase and consumption of a brand, and what was expected from it by the buyer at the time of purchase. If the actual outcomes are judged by the buyer to be *better than or equal to* the expected, the buyer will feel satisfied; that is,

$$\text{actual consequences} \geqslant \text{expected consequences.}$$

If, on the other hand, the actual outcomes are judged to be *less than* what he expected, the buyer will feel dissatisfied; that is,

$$\text{actual consequences} < \text{expected consequences.}$$

Satisfaction or dissatisfaction with a brand can be with any one of its different attributes. If the brand proves to be more satisfactory than the buyer expected, the attractiveness of the brand will be enhanced. If it proves less satisfactory than he expected, its attractiveness will diminish. Satisfaction, therefore, affects the ranking of brands in the evoked set for the next buying decision.

We also think that, if a brand purchase proves completely unsatisfactory, the buyer will *remove* the brand from his evoked set. In other words, he will not consider it for future purchases. If the brand has proved extremely satisfactory, the buyer will retain *only* the purchased brand in his evoked set; other brands will have close to zero probability of consideration. In short, *extreme* outcomes are likely to affect the *number* of brands in the evoked set, and reasonable discrepancies between actual and expected outcomes will affect the *ranking* of the brands in the evoked set.

Relations among Learning Constructs. Several important notions underlie the concept of predisposition toward a brand and its related variables. The simplest way to describe them is to state that we may classify a decision process as either "extensive problem solving," "limited problem solving," or "routine response behavior," depending on the strength of predisposition toward brands. In the early phases of buying, the buyer does not yet have well-developed decision mediators; specifically, his product-class concept is not well formed and his predisposition is low. As he acquires information and gains experience in buying and consuming a brand, his decision mediators become firm and his predisposition toward that brand is generally high.

In extensive problem solving, predisposition toward a brand is low. None of the brands are sufficiently discriminated on the basis of their decision-mediator criteria for the buyer to show preference for any one brand. At this stage of decision making, brand ambiguity is high, and the buyer actively seeks information from his environment. The more extensive the search for information, the greater is *latency of response*—the time interval between initiation of a decision and its completion. Similarly, deliberation or reasoning is high, since the buyer lacks a well-defined product-class concept—the denotative aspect of his decision mediators. He is also likely to consider many brands as part of his evoked set, and stimuli coming from the commercial environment are less likely to trigger an immediate purchase reaction.

When predisposition toward brands is moderate, the buyer's decision process is one of limited problem solving. Brand ambiguity still exists, since he is not able to discriminate and compare brands to develop a preference for one brand over others. He is likely to seek information, but not to the extent he does for extensive problem solving. More importantly, he seeks information to compare and discriminate various brands more on a relative basis than to compare them absolutely. He thinks and deliberates, since his predispositions are only tentatively defined. His evoked set consists of a small number of brands, and he has about the same degree of preference for each of them.

In routine response behavior, the buyer has accumulated sufficient experience and information to eliminate brand ambiguity, and he has a high level of predisposition toward one or two brands in his evoked set. He is unlikely to actively seek information from the environment, since such information is not needed. Also, insofar as he does admit information, it will tend to be that which supports his current choice. Very often, this congruent information will act as a "triggering cue" to motivate him to manifest purchase behavior.

Much impulse purchase behavior is really the outcome of a strong predisposition and a facilitating commercial stimulus, such as a store display. The buyer's evoked set consists of a few brands, toward which he is highly predisposed. However, he will have greater preference toward one or two brands in his evoked set than toward the others.

As mentioned earlier, predisposition is an aggregate index of how well a brand conforms to the choice criteria contained in a decision mediator. Thus, any changes in these criteria as a result of learning from experience or information imply some change in predisposition. The greater the learning, the stronger is predisposition toward brands in the evoked set. The exact nature of learning will be described later, when we discuss the dynamics of buying behavior. However, there are two other issues which need some attention here.

First, although our focus is on brand choice behavior, the buyer also simplifies the total sequence of behavior necessary to make a purchase—i.e. going to the store, looking at products, paying at the counter, etc.—by reducing the number of steps and ordering them in a definite sequence. The greater is his predisposition, the more will be his simplification of total buying behavior, and therefore the more routine will be his purchase behavior.

Second, if the purchase cycle is very long, as is the case for automobiles and other durable appliances, the buyer may develop firm decision mediators and yet manifest exploratory behavior to a marked degree at each purchase decision, because (1) market conditions invariably change and the buyer may find past experience insufficient, and (2) his decision mediators have become fuzzy, through lack of use and the resultant forgetting.

Perceptual Constructs. Another set of constructs serves the function of procuring and processing information relevant to a purchase decision. As mentioned earlier, information can come from any one of the three stimulus inputs—significative commercial stimuli, symbolic commercial stimuli, and social stimuli. Here we will describe only the constructs; their use by the buyer will be explained when we discuss the dynamics of buying behavior. The perceptual constructs in Figure 1 are (1) sensitivity to information, (2) perceptual bias, and (3) search for information.

A perceptual phenomenon implies either ignoring a physical event which could be a stimulus, seeing it attentively, or sometimes imagining what is not present in reality. All perceptual phenomena create some change in the quantity or quality of objective information.

Sensitivity to information refers to the opening and closing of sensory receptors which control the intake of information. The manifestation of this phenomenon is generally called "perceptual vigilance" (paying attention or "perceptual defense" (ignoring information). Sensitivity to information therefore serves primarily as a gatekeeper for information entering the buyer's nervous system, thus controlling the quantity of information input.

Sensitivity to information is a function of two variables, according to Berlyne.[9] One is the degree of stimulus ambiguity. If a stimulus to which the buyer is exposed is very familiar or too simple, its ambiguity is low and the buyer will not pay attention—unless he is predisposed to such information from past learning. Furthermore, if stimulus ambiguity continues to be low, the buyer feels a sense of monotony and actively seeks other information—he can be said to *complicate* his environment. If the stimulus is so complex and ambiguous that the buyer finds it hard to comprehend, he will ignore it by resorting to perceptual defense. Only if the stimulus is moderately ambiguous will the buyer be motivated to pay attention and freely absorb objective information about the brand under consideration.

In response to a single communication, the buyer at first may find the information complex and ambiguous and tend to ignore it. As the information continues to enter his nervous system, he may find it really to be at the medium level of ambiguity, and pay attention. As the process of communication progresses and he pays continuing attention, he may find the information too simple and look for more complex information.

The second variable which governs sensitivity to information is the buyer's predisposition toward the brand which is the subject of that information. The buyer learns to attach connotative meanings to a brand and to the symbols which stand for the brand. Thus, both the *source* of com-

---

[9] D. E. Berlyne, op. cit.

munication and the *content* of communication, as well as the brand itself, can come to have meaning for him. For example, he may have learned in the past to associate *low* credibility with commercial sources and *high* credibility with social sources. Similarly, he may attach connotations of quality to certain attributes of the brand, such as package, color, flavor, and taste. These connotations are part of his predisposition toward the brand.

Predisposition thus acts as a feedback in Figure 1, governing sensitivity to information, and, in turn, the intake of further information. This feedback is his degree of interest. The more pertinent to the brand is the information, the more likely the buyer is to open up his receptors and pay attention to it. Similarly, the more pertinent the source, the greater the attention the buyer is likely to give the communication.

Perceptual bias is the second perceptual construct. The buyer not only selectively attends to information, but he may actually distort it, once it enters his nervous system. In other words, the quality of information can be altered by the buyer. He may distort the cognitive elements contained in information to make them congruent with his own frame of reference, as determined by the amount of information he has already stored. Theories of cognitive consistency have been developed[10] to explain how this congruency is established and what its consequences are, in terms of the distortion of information that might be expected. Most qualitative change in information occurs as a result of feedback from various decision components, such as motives, the evoked set, and decision mediators. These relations are too complex, however, to describe in this summary.

The perceptual phenomena described above are likely to be less operative if information is received from the buyer's social environment. This is so because (1) the source of social information (such as a friend) is likely to be favorably regarded by the buyer, and (2) the information itself is modified by the social environment (the friend) so that it conforms to the needs of the buyer; therefore, distorted reception and further modification is less likely.

Search for information is the third perceptual construct. During the total buying phase, which extends over time and involves several repeat purchases of a product class, there are times when the buyer *actively* seeks information. It is very important to distinguish times when he passively receives information from occasions when he actively seeks it. We believe that perceptual bias is less operative in the latter instance, and that a commercial communication at that stage has, therefore, a high probability of influencing the buyer.

Active seeking of information occurs when the buyer senses ambiguity of brand meaning in his evoked set. As we saw earlier, this happens in the extensive problem-solving and limited problem-solving phases of the decision process. Ambiguity of brand meaning exists because the buyer is not certain of the purchase outcome of each brand. In other words, he has not

10 S. Feldman, ed., *Cognitive Consistency: Motivational Antecedents and Behavioral Consequences* (Academic Press, 1966); and M. Fishbein. ed., *Readings in Attitude Theory and Measurement* (New York: Wiley and Sons, 1967).

yet learned enough about alternatives to establish an expectancy of brand potential that will satisfy his motives. This type of brand ambiguity is generally confined to initial buying of that brand.

However, ambiguity may exist despite knowledge of relative brand potential. This ambiguity rests in the buyer's inability to discriminate between alternatives. The buyer may be unable to discriminate because his motives are not well structured: he does not know how to order them. He may then seek information to resolve conflict among goals—a resolution implied in his learning of the appropriate product-class aspect of decision mediators, as discussed earlier.

There is yet another stage of buying behavior in which the buyer is likely to seek information. It is when the buyer has established a routine decision process, but he is so familiar and satiated with repeat buying that he feels bored. Then all the existing alternatives in his evoked set, including the more preferred brand, become unacceptable to him. He seeks change or variety in that buying situation. In order to obtain this change, he actively searches for information on other alternatives (brands) that he never considered before. At this stage, he is particularly receptive to any information about new brands. This explains large advertising budgets in a highly stable industry, a phenomenon which has long baffled both the critics and defenders of advertising. New products on the market and buyer forgetfulness are not plausible explanations.

Response Variables

The complexity of buyer behavior extends beyond our hypothetical constructs. Just as there is a variety of inputs, there is also a variety of buyer responses, which become relevant for different areas of marketing strategy. The wide variety of consumer responses can be easily appreciated in the diversity of measures used to evaluate advertising effectiveness. We have attempted to classify and order this diversity of buyer responses in terms of output variables. Most of our output variables are directly related to some, but not other constructs. Each output variable serves different purposes, both in marketing practice and in fundamental research.

Attention. Attention is related to sensitivity to information. It is a buyer response that indicates the magnitude of his information intake. Attention is measured continuously during the time interval that the buyer is receiving information. There are several psycho-physiological methods of quantifying the degree of attention a buyer pays to a message. Awareness is not an appropriate measure, because it is a stock concept, not a flow concept.

Comprehension. Comprehension refers to the store of knowledge about a brand that the buyer possesses at any point in time. This knowledge can vary from simple awareness of a single brand's existence to a complete description of the attributes of a brand. It reflects the denotative meaning of the brand. In that sense it is strictly cognitive, and not included in the motivational aspects of behavior. Simply stated, it is a description of the common denotative elements of the brand in words with which the buyer communicates, thinks, and remembers. Some of the standard measures of advertising effectiveness such as awareness, aided or unaided recall, and recognition may capture different aspects of the buyer's knowledge of a brand.

Attitude toward a Brand. Attitude toward a brand is the buyer's evaluation of the brand's potential to satisfy his motives. It therefore includes the connotative aspects of the brand concept; it contains those aspects of the brand which are relevant to the buyer's goals. Attitude is directly related to predisposition, consisting of both the evaluation of a brand in terms of the decision-mediator criteria of choice, and the confidence with which that evaluation is held.

Intention to Buy. Intention to buy is the buyer's forecast of which brand he will buy. It includes not only the buyer's predisposition toward a brand, but also a forecast of inhibitors. Intention to buy has been used extensively in predicting the purchases of durable goods, with some recent refinements in terms of the buyer's confidence in his own forecast; however, these studies are in terms of broadly defined product classes.[11] We may characterize intention to buy as a response short of actual purchase behavior.

Purchase Behavior. Purchase behavior is the overt manifestation of the buyer's predisposition, in conjunction with any inhibitors that may be present. It differs from attitude to the extent that inhibitors are taken into consideration; and it differs from intention to the extent that it is actual behavior, which the buyer only forecasted in his intention.

What becomes a part of a company's sales, or what the consumer records in a diary as a panel member, is only the terminal act in the sequence of shopping and buying. Very often, it is useful to observe the complete movement of the buyer from his home to the store and his purchase in the store. Yoell,[12] for example, presents several case histories showing that time-and-motion study of consumer purchase behavior has useful marketing implications.

We think that, at times, it may be helpful to go so far as to incorporate the act of consumption into the definition of purchase behavior. We have, for example, used a technique for investigating decision making in which the buyer verbally describes the sequential pattern of his purchase and consumption behavior in a given buying situation. Out of this description, we have obtained a "flow chart" of sequential decision making which reveals the number and structure of the decision rules the buyer employs.

Several characteristics of purchase behavior become useful if we observe the buyer in a repetitive buying situation. These include the incidence of buying a brand, the quantity bought, and the purchase cycle. Several stochastic models of brand loyalty, for example, have been developed.[13] Similarly, we could take the magnitude purchased and compare light

---

[11] T. F. Juster, *Anticipations and Purchases: An Analysis of Consumer Behavior* (Princeton University Press, 1964).

[12] W. A. Yoell. "Science of Advertising through Behaviorism," unpublished paper, 1965.

[13] J. N. Sheth, "A Review of Buyer Behavior," *Management Review* (August 1967), B718–B756.

buyers with heavy buyers to determine if heavy buyers are more loyal buyers.

The Interrelationships of Response Variables. In Figure 1 the five response variables are ordered to create a hierarchy, similar to the variety of hierarchies used in practice, such as AIDA (attention, interest, desire, and action); to the Lavidge and Steiner[14] hierarchy of advertising effectiveness; as well as to the different mental states a person is alleged by anthropologists and sociologists to pass through when he adopts an innovation.[15] There are, however, some important differences which we believe will clarify certain conceptual and methodological issues raised by Palda[16] and others.

First, a response variable called "attention" has been added, which is crucial because it indicates whether or not a communication is received by the buyer. Second, several different aspects of the cognitive realm of behavior, such as awareness, recall, and recognition, are lumped into one category called "comprehension," to suggest that they are all varying indicators of the buyer's storage of information about a brand. In this way we obtain leverage for understanding buyer innovation. Third, attitude is defined to include its affective and conative aspects, since any attempt to establish causal relations between attitude and behavior must take into account the motivational aspects of attitude. Furthermore, the perceptual and the preference maps of the buyer with respect to brands are separated into "comprehension" and "attitude," respectively. Fourth, another variable, "intention to buy," is added, because properly defined and measured intentions for several product classes in both durable and semidurable goods have proved useful. To the extent that intention incorporates a buyer's forecast of his inhibitors, it might form a basis for marketing strategy designed to remove the inhibitors before actual purchase behavior is manifested.

Finally, and most important, we have incorporated several feedback effects which were described when the hypothetical constructs were discussed. We will now show the relations as direct connections among response variables—although these "outside" relations are merely the reflection of relations among the hypothetical constructs. For example, purchase behavior via satisfaction involves consequences that affect decision mediators and brand potential in the evoked set; any change in mediators and brand potential constitutes a change in predisposition. Attitude is related to predisposition, and therefore it can change in the period from pre-purchase to post-purchase. By incorporating this feedback, we are opening the way to resolving the question of whether attitude causes purchase behavior, or purchase behavior causes attitude. Over a period of time the relation is interdependent, each affecting the other. Similarly, we have a feedback from "attitude" to "comprehension" and

[14] R. J. Lavidge and G. A. Steiner, "A Model for Predictive Measurements of Advertising Effectiveness," *Journal of Marketing* (October 1961), pp. 59–62.

[15] E. M. Rogers, *Diffusions of Innovations* (New York: The Free Press, 1962).

[16] K. S. Palda, "The Hypothesis of a Hierarchy of Effects: A Partial Evaluation," *Journal of Marketing Research* (February 1966), pp. 13–24.

"attention," the rationale for which was given when perceptual constructs were described.

THE DYNAMICS OF BUYING BEHAVIOR

We will now explain the changes in hypothetical constructs which occur as a result of learning. Learning constructs are, of course, directly involved in the change that we label "learning." Since some learning constructs indirectly govern perceptual constructs by way of feedback, there is also an indirect effect on the learning constructs themselves. As mentioned earlier, decision mediators, which structure motives and the evoked set, can be learned from two broad sources, (1) past experience, and (2) information. Past experience can be further classified as deriving from buying a specified product or buying a similar product. Similarly, information can come from the buyer's commercial environment or his social environment; if the source is commercial, the information may be significative or symbolic.

We will look at development and change in learning constructs as due to (1) generalization from similar buying situations, (2) repeat buying of the same product class, and (3) information.

Generalization from Similar Purchase Situations

Some decision mediators are often similar across product classes because many motives are common to a wide variety of purchasing activities. For example, a buyer may satisfy his health motive by buying many different product classes. Similarly, he may buy many product classes at the same place; this very often leads to spatial or contiguous generalization. The capacity to generalize allows the buyer to exercise great flexibility in adapting his purchase behavior to the myriad of varying market conditions he faces.

Generalization refers to the transfer of responses from past situations to new situations which are similar, based on the relevance of stimuli. It saves the buyer time and effort otherwise spent in seeking information to resolve the uncertainty inevitable in a new situation. Generalization can occur at any one of the several levels of purchase activity, but we are primarily interested in the generalization of those decision mediators which involve only *brand-choice* behavior, in contrast to choice of store or choice of time and day for shopping.

Two kinds of brand generalization should be distinguished. First, there is *stimulus generalization,* in which the buyer—who has associated a brand purchase with a decision mediator (product class)—associates with the same decision mediator a new brand similar to the old one. For example, suppose a buyer has a decision mediator which calls for the purchase of *double-edged* shaving blades. His purchase response may then be transferred to a new brand of *stainless steel* double-edged blades via the same decision mediator. He may further refine his decision mediator to associate his purchase behavior with only one brand of new stainless steel blades, rather than with all.

Stimulus generalization can occur, not only when two brands are physically similar, but also when two brands are physically dissimilar but possess the same meaning. This is called *semantic generalization*. It is likely to occur when a radically new product is introduced by a company with which the buyer has had satisfactory past experience. The buyer can generalize via the company image. This is especially true of durable appliances, where a brand name is common to different products.

Second, there is *response generalization*, in which the buyer generalizes an *old response* to a *new response*, given the *same stimulus*. It can occur when the buyer, after reading an ad for brand A, goes to the store to buy it, but finds brand B, which is similar to brand A, and switches. In the same fashion, a buyer may "move up" the quality ladder for a particular make of automobile. Finally, he might buy *larger* packages of the same brand product.

Just as we find semantic *stimulus* generalization, we also find semantic *response* generalization. For example, a buyer who is motivated to purchase low-calorie food may generalize his response from skim milk to diet cola.

Repeat Purchase Experiences

Another source of change in learning constructs is the repeated purchase of the same product class over a period of time. In Figure 1 the purchase of a brand involves two types of feedback, one affecting decision mediators and the other affecting brand potential of the evoked set. First, the experience of buying, with all its cognitive aspects of memory, reasoning, etc., has a learning effect on decision mediators. This occurs irrespective of which specific brand the buyer chooses in any one purchase decision, because decision mediators, like motives, are product-specific and not limited to any one brand. Hence, every purchase has an incremental effect in more firmly establishing decision mediators. This is easy to visualize if we remember that buying behavior is a series of mental and motor steps; the actual choice is only its terminal act.

Purchase of a brand creates certain satisfactions for the buyer which he compares with his evaluation of the brand's potential. If the buyer is satisfied, the potential of the brand is enhanced, increasing the probability of repeat purchase. If he is dissatisfied, the potential of the brand is diminished, and the probability of repeat purchase is reduced. Hence the second feedback, from purchase behavior to satisfaction, changes the attractiveness of the brand purchased.

If there are no inhibitory forces influencing the buyer, he will continue to buy a brand which proves satisfactory. In the initial stages of decision making, he may show some tendency to oscillate between brands in order to formulate his decision mediators. In other words, he may learn by trial and error at first, then settle on a brand, and thereafter buy it with such regularity as to suggest that he is brand loyal. However, unless a product involves high purchase risk, there is a time limit on this brand loyalty: he may become bored with his preferred brand and look for something new.

Information as a Source of Learning

The third major means by which learning constructs are changed is information received from (1) the buyer's commercial environment, consisting of advertising, promotion, salesmanship, and retail shelf display; and (2) his social environment, consisting of his family, friends, reference groups, and social class.

We will first describe the influence of information as if perceptual constructs were absent. In other words, we will assume that the buyer receives information with perfect fidelity, as it exists in the environment. Also, we will discuss separately information received from commercial and social environments.

The Commercial Environment. A company communicates its offerings to buyers either by the physical brand itself (significates), or by symbols (pictorial or linguistic) which represent the brand. Significative and symbolic communication are the two major means of interaction between sellers and buyers.

Figure 1 shows the influence of information on motives, decision mediators, the evoked set, and inhibitors. We believe that the influence of commercial information on motives (specific and nonspecific) is limited. The main effect is primarily to *intensify* whatever motives the buyer has, rather than to create new ones. For example, a physical display of the brand may intensify his motives above the threshold level, which, combined with strong predisposition, can result in impulse (unplanned) purchase. A similar reaction is possible when an ad creates sufficient intensity of motive to provide an impetus for the buyer to go to the store. A second way to influence motives is to show the *perceived instrumentality* of the brand, and thereby make it a part of the buyer's defined set of alternatives.

Finally, to a very limited extent, marketing stimuli may change the *content of motives.* This, we believe, is rare. The general conception among both marketing men and laymen is that marketing stimuli do change the buyer's motives. However, on a closer examination it would appear that what is changed is the *intensity* of those motives already provided by the buyer's social environment. Many dormant or latent motives may become stimulated. The secret of success very often lies in identifying the change in motives created by social change and intensifying them, as seems to be the case in the advertising projection of youthfulness for many buying situations.

Marketing stimuli are important in determining and changing the buyer's evoked set. Commercial information tells him of the existence of brands (awareness), their identifying characteristics (comprehension plus brand name), and their relevance to the satisfaction of his needs (decision mediator).

Marketing stimuli are also important in creating and changing the buyer's decision mediators. They become important sources for *creating* (learning) decision mediators when the buyer has no prior experience to rely upon. In other words, when he is in the extensive-problem-solving (EPS) stage, it is marketing and social stimuli which are his important sources of learning. Similarly, when the buyer actively seeks information because all existing alternatives are unacceptable to him, marketing stimuli become important in *changing* his decision mediators.

Finally, marketing stimuli can unwittingly create inhibitors. For example, a company's efforts to emphasize a price-quality association may result in a high-price inhibition in the mind of the buyer. Similarly, in emphasizing the details of usage and consumption of a product, marketing communication might perhaps create inhibition related to time pressure.

The Social Environment. The social environment of the buyer—family, friends, and reference groups—is another major source of information influencing his buying behavior. Most social input is likely to be symbolic (linguistic), although at times a friend may show the physical product to the buyer.

Information from the social environment also affects the four learning constructs: motives, decision mediators, the evoked set, and inhibitors. However, the effect on these constructs in different than that of the commercial environment. First, information about brands is considerably modified by the social environment before it reaches the buyer. Most of the modifications are likely to be in adding connotative meanings to brands and their attributes, and in the effects of such perceptual variables as sensitivity to information and perceptual bias.

Second, the buyer's social environment will probably strongly influence the content of his motives, and his ordering of them to establish a goal structure. Several research studies have concentrated on such influences (Bourne;[17] Bush and London;[18] Gruen;[19] Laird;[20] Katz and Lazarsfeld.[21])

Third, the buyer's social environment may also affect his evoked set. This is particularly true when he lacks experience. Furthermore, if the product class is important to the buyer, and he is not technically competent or he is uncertain in evaluating the consequences of the brand for his needs, he may rely more on the social than on the marketing environment for information. This is well documented by several studies using the perceived risk hypothesis.[22]

Information-Processing Effects

As we have said, distortion of stimuli by the perceptual constructs—sensitivity to information, perceptual bias, and search for information—

[17] F. S. Bourne, "Group Influence in Marketing," *Some Applications of Behavioral Research*, ed. R. Lickert and S. P. Hayes (Paris: UNESCO. 1957), pp. 208–224.

[18] G. Bush and P. London, "On the Disappearance of Knickers: Hypothesis for the Functional Analysis of Clothing," *Journal of Social Psychology* (1960). pp. 359–366.

[19] W. Gruen, "Preference for New Products and Its Relationship to Different Measures of Conformity, *Journal of Applied Psychology* (December 1960), pp. 361–366.

[20] D. A. Laird, "Customers are Hard to Change," *Personnel Journal* (1950), pp. 402–405.

[21] E. Katz and P. Lazarsfeld, *Personal Influence* (Glencoe, Illinois: The Free Press, 1955).

[22] R. A. Bauer, "Consumer Behavior as Risk Taking," in *Proceedings of American Marketing Association* (1960), pp. 389–398; R. A. Bauer and L. H. Wortzel, "Doctor's Choice: The Physician and His Sources of Information About Drugs," *Journal of Marketing Research* (February 1966), pp. 40–47; and D. F. Cox. "The Measurement of Information Value: A Study in Consumer Decision-Making," *Proceedings of American Marketing Association* (December 1962), pp. 413–421.

is likely to be much greater for marketing stimuli than for social stimuli. This is so essentially because the buyer attaches greater credibility—competence and trust—to social sources, and because of the ease of two-way communication in social situations. Similarly, the buyer may more actively seek information from his social environment, particularly evaluative information. Thus, the foregoing discussion of the commercial and social environments must be qualified by the perceptual effects inevitable in any information processing.

EXOGENOUS VARIABLES

As mentioned earlier, there are several influences operating on the buyer's decisions which we treat as exogenous; that is, we do not explain their formation and change. Many of these influences come from the buyer's social environment, and we wish to separate those effects of his environment which have occurred in the past and are not related to a specific decision, from those which are current and do directly affect the decisions that occur while the buyer is being observed. The inputs that occur during the observation period provide information to the buyer to help his current decision making. Past influences are already embedded in the values of the perceptual and learning constructs. These exogenous variables are particularly appropriate as market-segmenting variables, because they are causally linked to purchase.

Strictly speaking, there is no need for exogenous variables, since in the social sciences these forces are traditionally left to *ceteris paribus*. We will bring them out explicitly, however, for the sake of research design, so that a researcher may control or take into account the individual differences among buyers that are due to past influence. Incorporating the effects of these exogenous variables reduces the unexplained variance, or error in estimation, which it is particularly essential to control under field conditions. Figure 1 presents a set of exogenous variables which we believe provide the control essential to obtaining satisfactory predictive relations between the inputs and outputs of the system.

Importance of purchase refers to differential degrees of ego-involvement in or commitment to different product classes. It is therefore an entity which must be carefully examined in inter-product studies. Importance of purchase will influence the size of the evoked set and the magnitude of the search for information. For example, the more important the product class, the larger is the evoked set.[23]

Time Pressure is a current exogenous variable and therefore specific to a decision situation. When a buyer feels pressed for time, because of any of several environmental influences, he must allocate his time among alternative uses. In this process a reallocation unfavorable to purchasing activity can occur. Time pressure will create inhibition, as mentioned earlier. It will also unfavorably affect the search for information.

Financial Status refers to the constraint a buyer may feel because he lacks financial resources. This can affect his purchase behavior by creating

23 J. A. Howard and C. G. Moore, "A Descriptive Model of the Purchasing Function," unpublished paper, 1963.

a barrier (inhibitor) to purchasing the most preferred brand. For example, a buyer may want to purchase an expensive foreign car, but lacking sufficient financial resource, he will settle for a low-priced American model.

Personality Traits are such variables as self-confidence, self-esteem, authoritarianism, and anxiety, which have been researched to identify individual differences. These individual differences are "topic free" and therefore supposedly exert their effect across product classes. We believe their effect is felt on (1) nonspecific motives and (2) the evoked set. For example, the more anxious a person, the greater his motivational arousal; dominant personalities are more likely (by a small margin) to buy a Ford instead of a Chevrolet; the more authoritarian a person, the narrower the category width of his evoked set.

Social and Organizational Setting involves the group, a higher level of social organization than the individual. It includes informal social organization, such as family and reference groups, which is relevant for *consumer behavior;* and formal organization, which constitutes much of the environment for *industrial purchasing.* Organizational variables are those of small group interaction, such as power, status, and authority. We believe that the underlying processes of intergroup conflict in both industrial and consumer buying behavior are in principle very similar, and that the differences are largely due to the formal nature of industrial activity. Organization, both formal and social, is a crucial variable because it influences most of the learning constructs.

Social Class involves a still higher level of social organization, the social aggregate. Several indices are available to classify people socially. Perhaps the most common index is Warner's classification. Social class mediates the relation between input and output by influencing (1) specific motives, (2) decision mediators, (3) the evoked set, and (4) inhibitors. The latter influence is important, particularly in the adoption of innovations.

Culture provides a more comprehensive social framework than social class. It consists of patterns of behavior, symbols, ideas, and their attached values. Culture will influence motives, decision mediators, and inhibitors.

CONCLUSIONS

In the preceding pages we have summarized a theory of buyer brand choice. It is complex, but we strongly believe that complexity is essential to an adequate description of buying behavior.

We hope that our theory will provide new insights into past empirical data, and guide future research by instilling coherence and unity into current research, which now tends to be atomistic and unrelated. Models can be constructed of the relations between the output intervening variables, and a splendid beginning along these lines has been carried out by Day.[24] Also, as the hypothetical constructs are explored, elements of the constructs will be broken out and better defined, so that these elements can be invested with the operational status of intervening variables.

[24] G. S. Day, op. cit.

McClelland's work with achievement, for example, has shown how this transformation can occur with motive. In this way our theory suggests specific programs of research.

We are vigorously pursuing a large research program aimed at testing the validity of this theory. The research was designed in terms of the variables specified by the theory, and our preliminary results lead us to believe that it was fruitful to use the theory in this way. Because it specifies a number of relationships, it has clearly been useful in interpreting preliminary findings. Above all, it is a great aid in communication among the researchers and with the companies involved.

Finally, a number of new ideas are set forth in the theory, but we would like to call attention to three in particular. The concept of evoked set provides a means of reducing the noise in many analyses of buying behavior. The product class concept offers a new dimension for incorporating many of the complexities of innovation, and especially for integrating systematically the idea of innovation into a framework of psychological constructs. Anthropologists and sociologists have been generally content to deal with peripheral variables and to omit the psychological constructs which link the peripheral variables to behavior. The habit-perception cycle in which perception and habit respond inversely offers hope for explaining, to a great extent, the phenomenon which has long baffled both critics and defenders of advertising: large advertising expenditures in a stable market, where, on the surface, it would seem that buyers are already sated with information.

6

Industrial Marketing: All Eyes Are on the Buyer

Sales Management

Though many industrial marketing men cling to the idea that their chief function is to mount an onslaught aimed at "making the sale," this type of thinking is rapidly going out of style. The increasing complexity of industrial procurement makes it no longer realistic to regard each purchase as an isolated event that "just happens." Both buyers and sellers are concerned with building long-term relationships that will allow them to exchange technical information and do business over a span of several years. For the most part, marketing literature tends to depict this romance as a one-way process that depends for its success on the initiative of the marketer, but the fact is that buyers are equally concerned with staying on good terms with suppliers. Indeed, many purchasing managers see their most important job as that of maintaining the company's reputation as a good customer. Why? Because this is the best way they can make sure their company will receive prompt service and, perhaps more important, have continuous access to the design and inventive skills of its suppliers. For this reason, marketers should view their part in the purchasing process as much more than writing up orders. "Companies don't make purchases," says Dr. Charles S. Goodman, of the Wharton School of Finance and Commerce. "They establish relationships."

The relationships amount to more than a game of corporate gin rummy between the salesman on one hand and the purchasing agent on the

 Reprinted with permission from *Sales Management*, October 15, 1967, pp. 71–78.

other. More commonly, buying and selling among big industrial concerns are performed by teams composed of specialists in every aspect of business from production to cost accounting. Under this system, the role of the marketing department, and especially of the industrial sales force, is primarily one of bringing about the best possible communications between the two teams. First, the marketer must respond to concrete requirements of the buying organization and endeavor to do his best to persuade the potential customer that his company is best equipped to help the buying organization achieve its goals. For the successful marketer, however, this basic task is no more than a starting point. Effective communication attempts to anticipate—and even to precipitate—forthcoming changes in customer requirements in order to direct them into channels advantageous to the marketer.

So fundamental is this idea to success in modern industrial marketing that the authors of the Marketing Science Institute's (MSI) survey of industrial buying go so far as to recommend that the entire marketing effort of a company be based on a thorough analysis of buyer behavior. Not only does such an analysis entail the use of the same psychological and communications theories that formed the basis for MSI's study of personal selling but it has direct implications for everyday marketing strategy. For instance, while the term "market segmentation" is conventionally applied to differentiating among buyers on the basis of, say, their needs for a certain product or their preference for high-priced or low-priced goods, MSI points out that markets may also be segmented according to the circumstances in which buyers enter the market. Thus, a marketing organization may be expected to develop teams of specialists to deal with potential customers who are in the process of developing a new product and are seeking technical assistance (the "new task" situation). Or, individual salesmen may make a career out of persuading noncustomers that they should forsake their current suppliers and switch to his company (a case of an "out" supplier trying to bring about a "modified rebuy").

Not only is the particular buying situation of critical importance to marketing managers but they must be aware of the various tactics that are best suited for different stages in the buying process and of the wide variation in information requirements among members of the buying team (called "buying influences" by MSI). Since their position in an organization gives each of the buying influences a formal stake in the outcome, each one views purchasing from his own peculiar vantage point. Design and development engineers try to minimize the risks of making an error and "play it safe." Yet the designs and specifications that come from them greatly influence the procurements that follow because the way they state their requirements eliminates from consideration many suppliers who would otherwise be qualified.

Marketing men in the buying company tend to look at purchasing as a means of enhancing the salability of their own products. Manufacturing people favor simple items that make the production job as inexpensive and trouble-free as possible. Research and development men are

BLUEPRINT OF A BUYING SITUATION

BUYPHASES	BUYCLASSES		
	New Task	Modified Rebuy	Straight Rebuy
1. Anticipation or recognition of a problem (need) and a general solution			
2. Determination of characteristics and quantity of needed item			
3. Description of characteristics and quantity of needed item			
4. Search for and qualification of potential sources			
5. Aquisition and analysis of proposals			
6. Evaluation of proposals and selection of supplier(s)			
7. Selection of an order routine			
8. Performance feedback and evaluation			

The BUYGRID Model shows that industrial purchasing does not consist of a single act but of eight separate events that occur in sequence. An important part of the marketer's job is to provide members of the buying center with the right information at the right time.

frequently overlooked but are important because they set the broad criteria within which the other technical decision-makers operate and provide clues as to what the company's requirements will be in the future.

In a few cases, all of the buying decisions may be made by general management, though its role is usually more limited. After management recognizes the original need, it sets broad criteria and policies and delegates the buying decisions to lower levels. When the original recognition of the need comes from lower levels, management generally plays no role in the procurement process; although it may veto whatever happens at any point. The purchasing agent performs a number of specialized activities that vary in importance among companies and buying situations. Regardless of his formal strength in a given situation, however, the purchasing agent is usually able to help or hurt, significantly, the chances of any supplier.

Understanding complex industrial buying processes requires a framework for analyzing the various buying situations and how they emerge

HOW THE DECISION-MAKING PROCESS VARIES WITH EACH BUYCLASS

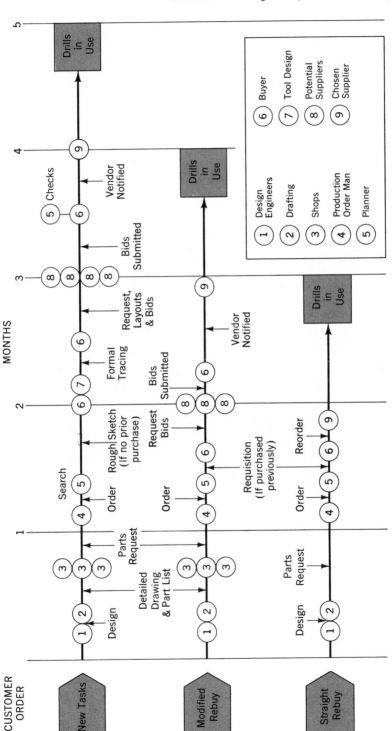

Until the buyer (6) begins his search for a supplier, the three types of buying situations are essentially the same, as these critical-path diagrams demonstrate. From that point on, however, the process of purchasing a product, in this case a special drill, varies markedly. A new task may entail policy questions and special studies, while a straight rebuy is nearly automatic.

84

AN EDUCATED GUESS AS TO WHAT HAPPENS INSIDE THE BLACK BOX

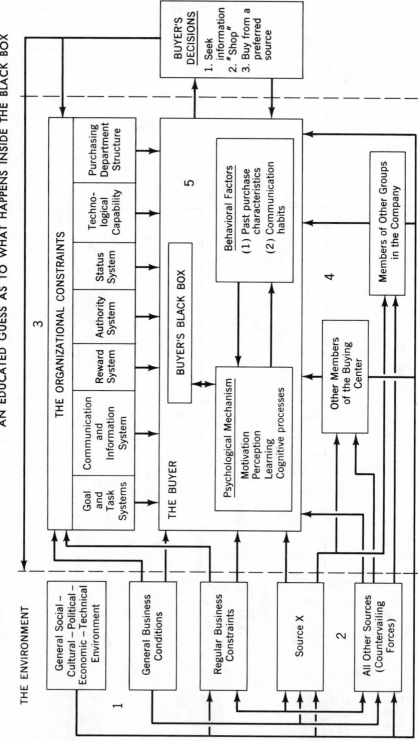

from the continuous process of problem-solving and decision-making that goes on within the buying offices of a large corporation. Usually, transactions are classified in one of three ways: market segment or class of trade reached; product or service marketed; or end-use of the product. MSI suggests that these classifications should be supplemented by a fourth system that takes into consideration the particular selling techniques required for each phase of the buying process. MSI's answer is the BUY-GRID framework.

Using this system, all buying situations may be divided into "buy-classes" according to the newness of the problem. Thus the "new task" situation is one that has never occurred before and consequently requires the buyer to learn much about an area in which he has had little experience. In contrast, the "straight rebuy" pertains to a recurring requirement that is filled by the same supplier as a matter of routine. The "modified rebuy" occurs when a company decides to consider other suppliers for a product that it has previously bought on a straight rebuy basis. Obviously, the marketer's tactics must be tailored to each situation, especially the amount and type of information he provides to the purchasing decision-makers, who are likely to pump him dry in a new task situation, and turn him off when they're considering a straight rebuy.

The procurement process itself may be broken down into eight "buy-phases," as shown on the lefthand side of the chart. Together these form a sort of chain reaction. Once the process gets under way, it will move from one phase to the next until the purchase is made or the deal is called off. Depicting the process as eight decision points—all of which are subject to influence by marketers—underlines the importance of directing the

---

Too frequently, marketers make the mistake of assuming that just because their potential customer is a battle-hardened businessman, he is motivated primarily by the laws of economic behavior. The fact is that despite his apparent preoccupation with specifications and schematics, the industrial buyer is more human than marketing men realize.

Marketing Science Institute devotes a special section of its report to allied research by Dr. Yoram Wind, of the Wharton School, where he points out that industrial buying decisions made by human beings as members of an organization, may be depicted as emanating from the buyer's mind, which is subject to external stimuli (see diagram above). Because no one is sure what goes on inside a person's psyche, or "black box," behavioral scientists have resorted to educated guessing. By discovering the statistical relation between the information that enters the black box and the decisions that result, it is possible to predict with some degree of accuracy how a person will behave under certain circumstances. Thus, Dr. Wind maintains that it is possible to size up a buyer by analyzing the five sets of variables that influence his decisions:

1. Environmental variables, which are of three types:
   a. General variables affecting the value system of the people of the given society.
   b. General business conditions.
   c. Regular business constraints.

2. Inputs from suppliers. These are generally of two types: those supporting source X and those supporting the competitors of source X.

3. Organizational variables. The effect of these variables on the behavior of organization members has been widely recognized by behavioral scientists but almost entirely neglected by marketing experts.

4. Interpersonal influences of other members of the organization.

5. The buyer's own characteristics, especially his psychological mechanisms and behavioral characteristics, which serve as the principal processors between the inputs to which he is subject and his responses.

THE BUYER'S DILEMMA: HOW FAR DOES IT PAY TO SEARCH?

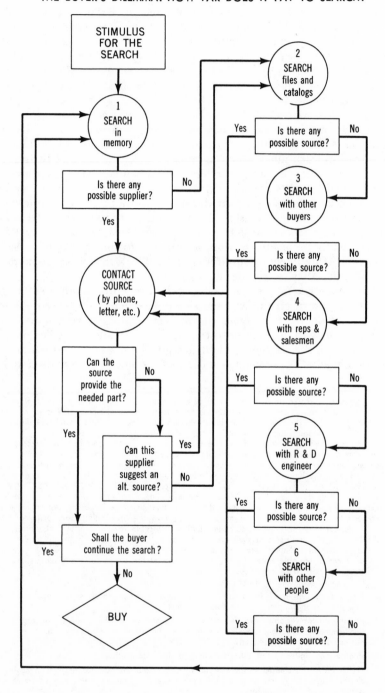

sales effort at the entire chain of events instead of treating the sale as an isolated moment of truth that happens independently of the other events. As the process unfolds, there occurs a "creeping commitment" on the part of the buyer, which gradually narrows the field of potential suppliers. Thus, in most cases, it is difficult for a vendor to enter the buying process during the late phases with any hope of success.

In studying the BUYGRID matrix, it becomes apparent that the most intricate buying situations will fall in the upper lefthand corner of the chart; that is, in the early stages of a new task assignment. It is here that management makes its most difficult decisions and where, in many instances, it welcomes the advice of suppliers. But this is by no means the first stage at which an alert marketer can influence the buying process. Something must set off the chain reaction to begin with, and, while that stimulus may come from within the buying organization, it frequently comes from a member of the selling team who anticipates or, better still, precipitates a need for a product or service within the purchasing company.

The BUYGRID framework not only helps the marketer to visualize the decision-making process but helps identify a number of decision points at which he can assist the buying company by providing technical data and advice. This assistance can significantly influence the trend of the process in a way that is favorable to the marketer's company. The critical-path analyses show how these decision points vary among the three buy-classes.

Perhaps most important, the BUYGRID matrix illustrates the tremendous responsibility of the industrial salesman as a communicator. Order-taking is the least important part of his job. He is the communications arm of his company, constantly mediating between representatives of seller and buyer and ferreting out critical decision points. It is he who must provide meaningful data to decision-makers on the buying team, be they engineers or purchasing agents, and at just the right time. In short, his judgment, or lack of it, can win or lose a contract for his company at any point in the procurement process.

The BUYGRID framework is particularly useful because it focuses directly on the basic nature of the customer's requirements. However, to put this abstract idea of "understanding buyer behavior" into action, it may be helpful for the industrial marketing manager to have in mind a

---

Selling to a large industrial concern is like trying to hit a moving target because members of the buying center are continually looking for ideas and products that will solve specific production problems. As the diagram shows, the buyer's search generally follows a predictable pattern, taking the simplest route and venturing into unknown territory only when familiar sources fail to produce the desired solution. However, each buyer has his own search habits that reflect his training and experience, personal hopes, and the foibles of his particular organization.

Buyers are subject to two conflicting forces: On the one hand, time pressure tends to minimize search activities and to restrict them to the immediate neighborhood. On the other, most opportunities for a buyer to distinguish himself require extensive search. Thus, once a search is under way, the buyer will weigh carefully the anticipated rewards against the cost in effort and money.

profile of the buying habits, patterns, and influences of each major customer or potential customer. Although a profile will not enable the marketer to predict precisely the identity of all buying influences, it can be of great value in providing the marketing staff with a reasonably explicit blueprint of the customer's buying processes. Constructing a profile of the buying organization forces the marketing manager and the sales staff to think through, define intelligibly, and render useful to others their subjective experiences with a particular firm and its key decision-makers. By maintaining these profiles, the accumulated knowledge and experience about a customer can be systematically organized, and companies may be categorized according to the type of buying situation that most frequently emerges within them. Many customers are likely to buy particular goods and services on a rebuy basis. The marketer of standard parts and components, subassemblies, chemicals, or commodities is not likely to face many new task situations unless he creates a new market or develops a new product. By contrast, a marketer of machine tools, engineering services, aerospace, or computer-communication systems may find that most of his customers are in a new task situation each time they buy or lease.

Whatever the task faced by the marketer, his customer profiles should specify distinguishing elements about each customer's requirements as he is confronted with the three different buying situations. The marketer should be able to answer questions such as: In what proportion are the different types of buying situations likely to arise in this company? How will each situation be handled inside the buying company once it arises? Who are the major buying influences likely to be? Under what conditions is each buying influence likely to play a key role in the product-supplier selection process? What information is of major importance to each buying influence? Answers to these questions can be of great help to the seller in directing his search and retrieval of information and in programming the elements of his marketing.

If the marketing effort is to service the various decision points in the customer's buying process, it must be organized accordingly. Such an approach seeks to use specialists in the marketing organization in the most effective way while retaining the flexibility needed to reckon with the fact that the next opportunity, perhaps even with the same customer, may entail a different buying situation.

One possible application of this approach is to have customer contacts made by an "account executive," or customer's man, who coordinates the various aspects of the marketer's program and represents his organization in all buying influences within the customer company. As various customer problems and requirements arise, this customer's man can call upon specialists from his own company. The marketer's team should be composed of problem-defining, problem-solving, technical, negotiating, and servicing personnel. Each specialist is charged with maintaining close, personal relationships with his counterparts at a variety of organizational levels in the customer organization. Within this group of specialists, appropriate individuals can be consulted as particular problems arise.

Occasionally, they may travel together to meet representatives of the customer company.

Just as there is a growing recognition among industrial marketers that diversity in advertising (by type of influences, for example) is useful, this may be extended to other elements of the marketing mix. Personal communications tasks, for instance, can be handled most effectively by salesmen who sell best in particular types of customer buying situations. Many companies already build specialization into the allocation of their marketing effort in other ways. Certain salesmen may be specialized in both training and assignment, handling lines or products different from those of other salesmen. They may be differentiated according to type of account, in turn reflecting differences in customers' applications or in the types of services needed. Salesmen may be "specialists" in geographic areas. Technical representatives or applications engineers have specialized functions when compared to regular salesmen. The MSI study strongly suggests that salesmen can also profitably "specialize" according to the type of buying situation, the nature of the customer's needs, and the resources of the marketing organization.

Of course, even with the best of marketing plans, the industrial salesman frequently comes up against situations that try his patience. This is especially true when he attempts to capture an account that is routinely handled by a competitor on a straight rebuy basis—obviously a common occurrence in everyday selling. The more a buyer "knows" about a given component, the less he needs to rely on the seller's guarantee or reputation for quality. Consequently, an aspiring supplier is faced not only with possible commitments between a potential buyer and a competitor but with the fact that the buyer is convinced that he "knows" everything he needs to know about the product in question. Under these circumstances, the salesman's role is essentially educational. Even if he has a superior product, he will have a difficult time seeing a buyer who is confidently committed to a supplier and has turned his attention to more pressing problems. Few salesmen are capable of achieving change in the face of such a routine purchasing procedure, primarily because they are deliberately trained to behave in a routine manner themselves. But in this situation, a routine selling job will get the salesman nowhere. Unless he can patiently study the customer's requirements one by one and gradually get his prospect to reexamine his needs, the salesman is likely to be little more than a nuisance.

MARKET SEGMENTATION

7

New Criteria
for Market
Segmentation

DANIEL YANKELOVICH

Daniel Yankelovich and Associates

The director of marketing in a large company is confronted by some of the most difficult problems in the history of U.S. industry. To assist him, the information revolution of the past decade puts at his disposal a vast array of techniques, facts, and figures. But without a way to master this information, he can easily be overwhelmed by the reports that flow in to him incessantly from marketing research, economic forecasts, cost analyses, and sales breakdowns. He must have more than mere access to mountains of data. He must himself bring to bear a method of analysis that cuts through the detail to focus sharply on new opportunities.

In this article, I shall propose such a method. It is called *segmentation analysis*. It is based on the proposition that once you discover the most useful ways of segmenting a market, you have produced the beginnings of a sound marketing strategy.

UNIQUE ADVANTAGES

Segmentation analysis has developed out of several key premises:

1. In today's economy, each brand appears to sell effectively to only certain segments of any market and not to the whole market.
2. Sound marketing objectives depend on knowledge of how segments which

produce the most customers for a company's brands differ in requirements and susceptibilities from the segments which produce the largest number of customers for competitive brands.
3. Traditional demographic methods of market segmentation do not usually provide this knowledge. Analyses of market segments by age, sex, geography, and income level are not likely to provide as much direction for marketing strategy as management requires.

Once the marketing director does discover the most pragmatically useful way of segmenting his market, it becomes a new standard for almost all his evaluations. He will use it to appraise competitive strengths and vulnerabilities, to plan his product line, to determine his advertising and selling strategy, and to set precise marketing objectives against which performance can later be measured. Specifically, segmentation analysis helps him to—

1. Direct the appropriate amounts of promotional attention and money to the most potentially profitable segments of his market.
2. Design a product line that truly parallels the demands of the market instead of one that bulks in some areas and ignores or scants other potentially quite profitable segments.
3. Catch the first sign of a major trend in a swiftly changing market and thus give him time to prepare to take advantage of it.
4. Determine the appeals that will be most effective in his company's advertising; and, where several different appeals are significantly effective, quantify the segments of the market responsive to each.
5. Choose advertising media more wisely and determine the proportion of budget that should be allocated to each medium in the light of anticipated impact.
6. Correct the timing of advertising and promotional efforts so that they are massed in the weeks, months, and seasons when selling resistance is least and responsiveness is likely to be at its maximum.
7. Understand otherwise seemingly meaningless demographic market information and apply it in scores of new and effective ways.

These advantages hold in the case of both packaged goods and hard goods, and for commercial and industrial products as well as consumer products.

Guides to Strategy

Segmentation analysis cuts through the data facing a marketing director when he tries to set targets based on markets as a whole, or when he relies primarily on demographic breakdowns. It is a systematic approach that permits the marketing planner to pick the strategically most important segmentations and then to design brands, products, packages, communications, and marketing strategies around them. It infinitely simplifies the setting of objectives.

In the following sections we shall consider nondemographic ways of segmenting markets. These ways dramatize the point that finding marketing opportunities by depending solely on demographic breakdowns is like trying to win a national election by relying only on the information in a census. A modern census contains useful data, but it identifies neither the crucial issues of an election, nor those groups whose voting habits are still fluid, nor the needs, values, and attitudes that influence how those groups will vote. This kind of information, rather than census-type data, is the kind that wins elections—and markets.

Consider, for example, companies like Procter & Gamble, General Motors, or American Tobacco, whose multiple brands sell against one another and must, every day, win new elections in the marketplace.

These companies sell to the whole market, not by offering one brand that appeals to all people, but by covering the different segments with multiple brands. How can they prevent these brands from cannibalizing each other? How can they avoid surrendering opportunities to competitors by failing to provide brands that appeal to all important segments? In neither automobiles, soaps, nor cigarettes do demographic analyses reveal to the manufacturer what products to make or what products to sell to what segments of the market. Obviously, some modes of segmentation other than demographic are needed to explain why brands which differ so little nevertheless find their own niches in the market, each one appealing to a different segment.

The point at issue is not that demographic segmentation should be disregarded, but rather that it should be regarded as only one among many possible ways of analyzing markets. In fact, the key requirement of segmentation analysis is that the marketing director should never assume in advance that any one method of segmentation is the best. His first job should be to muster all probable segmentation and *then* choose the most meaningful ones to work with. This approach is analogous to that used in research in the physical sciences, where the hypothesis that best seems to explain the phenomena under investigation is the one chosen for working purposes.

TEN MARKETS

In the following discussion we shall take ten markets for consumer and industrial products and see how they are affected by seven different modes of nondemographic segmentation. The products and modes are shown schematically in Figure 1. Of course, these segments are not the only ones important in business. The seven I have picked are only *examples* of how segmentation analysis can enlarge the scope and depth of a marketer's thinking.

Watches

In this first case we deal with a relatively simple mode of segmentation analysis. The most productive way of analyzing the market for watches turns out to be segmentation by *value*. This approach discloses three distinct segments, each representing a different value attributed to watches by each of three different groups of consumers:

1. *People who want to pay the lowest possible price for any watch that works reasonably well.* If the watch fails after six months or a year, they will throw it out and replace it.
2. *People who value watches for their long life, good workmanship, good material, and good styling.* They are willing to pay for these product qualities.
3. *People who look not only for useful product features but also for meaningful emotional qualities.* The most important consideration in this segment is that the watch should suitably symbolize an important occasion. Consequently, fine styling, a well known brand name, the recommendation of the jeweler, and a gold or diamond case are highly valued.

In 1962, my research shows, the watch market divided quantitatively as follows:

Approximately 23% of the buyers bought for lowest price (value segment #1).
Another 46% bought for durability and general product quality (value segment #2).
And 31% bought watches as symbols of some important occasion (value segment #3).

Defining and quantifying such segments is helpful in marketing planning—especially if a watch company's product happens to appeal mostly to one segment or if the line straddles the three segments, failing to appeal effectively to any. Without such an understanding, the demographic characteristics of the market are most confusing. It turns out, for example, that the most expensive watches are being bought by people with both the highest and the lowest incomes. On the other hand, some upper-income consumers are no longer buying costly watches, but are buying cheap, well-styled watches to throw away when they require servicing. Other upper-income consumers, however, continue to buy fine, expensive watches for suitable occasions.

Timex's Timely Tactics. The planning implications in value segmentation are very broad for the industry. For one thing, many of the better watch companies in the years between 1957 and 1962 were inadvertently focusing exclusively on the third segment described—the 31% of the market that bought a watch only as a gift on important occasions—thus leaving the bulk of the market open to attack and exploitation.

The U.S. Time Company took advantage of this opening and established a very strong position among the more than two-thirds of America's watch buyers in the first two segments. Its new low-price watch, the Timex, had obvious appeal for the first segment, and it catered to the second segment as well. At that time, higher-price watches were making the disastrous mistake in their advertising of equating product quality with water-proof and shock-resistant features. The Timex also offered these low-cost features, at lower prices, thus striking at a vulnerable area which the competition itself created. When Timex pressed its attack, it was able within a few years to claim that "Timex sells more watches than any other watch company in the world."

Even the *timing* of Timex's watch advertising was involved. Much of the third segment was buying watches only during the Christmas season,

FIGURE 1: EXAMPLE OF SEGMENTATION IN
DIFFERENT INDUSTRIES

Market	Mode of Segmentation						
	Value	Susceptibility to Change	Purpose	Aesthetic Concepts	Attitudes	Individualized Needs	Self-Confidence
Watches	✓						
Automobiles	✓	✓		✓			
Perfumes			✓				
Bathing Soaps			✓				
Hair Care			✓	✓		✓	
Other Packaged Goods	✓						
Retail Soft Goods	✓						
Adding Machines	✓		✓				
Computers		✓			✓		✓
Light Trucks		✓					✓

and so most of Timex's competitors concentrated their advertising in November and December. But since buying by the other two segments went on all the time, Timex advertised all year-round, getting exclusive attention ten months of the year.

Thus, nondemographic segmentation in the watch industry has directly affected almost every phase of marketing, including the composition of the product line. Major watch companies know that they must plan product line, pricing, advertising, and distribution within the framework of the three basic value segments of this market.

Automobiles

The nondemographic segmentation of the automobile market is more complex than that of the watch market. The segments crisscross, forming intricate patterns. Their dynamics must be seen clearly before automobile sales can be understood.

Segmentation analysis leads to at least three different ways of classifying the automobile market along nondemographic lines, all of which are important to marketing planning.

Value Segmentation. The first mode of segmentation can be compared to that in the watch market—a threefold division along lines which represent how different people look at the meaning of *value* in an automobile:

1. *People who buy cars primarily for economy.* Many of these become owners of the Ford Falcon, Rambler American, and Chevrolet. They are less loyal to any make than the other segments, but go where the biggest savings are to be found.
2. *People who want to buy the best product they can find for their money.* These prospects emphasize values such as body quality, reliability, durability, economy of operation, and ease of upkeep. Rambler and Volkswagen have been successful because so many people in this segment were dissatisfied.
3. *People interested in "personal enhancement" (a more accurate description than "prestige").* A handsomely styled Pontiac or Thunderbird does a great deal for the owner's ego, even though the car may not serve as a status symbol. Although the value of an automobile as a status symbol has declined, the personal satisfaction in owning a fine car has not lessened for this segment of the market. It is interesting that while both watches and cars have declined in status value, they have retained *self-enhancement* value for large portions of the market.

Markets can change so swiftly, and the size of key segments can shift so rapidly, that great sensitivity is required to catch a trend in time to capitalize on it. In the automobile market, the biggest change in recent years has been the growth in segment two—the number of people oriented to strict product value. Only a few years ago, the bulk of the market was made up of the other segments, but now the product-value segment is probably the largest. Some automobile companies did not respond to this shift in the size of these market segments in time to maintain their share of the market.

Aesthetic Concepts. A second way of segmenting the automobile market is by differences in *style* preferences. For example, most automobile buyers tell you that they like "expensive looking" cars. To some people, however, "expensive looking" means a great deal of chrome and ornamentation, while to others it means the very opposite—clean, conservative lines, lacking much chrome or ornamentation.

Unfortunately, the same *words* are used by consumers to describe diametrically opposed style concepts. Data that quantify buyers according to their aesthetic *responses*—their differing conceptions of what constitutes a good-looking car—are among the most useful an automobile company can possess.

The importance of aesthetic segmentation can be pointed up by this example:

When Ford changed from its 1959 styling to its 1960 styling, the change did not seem to be a radical one from the viewpoint of formal design. But, because it ran contrary to the special style expectations of a large group of loyal Ford buyers, it constituted a dramatic and unwelcome change to them. This essential segment was not prepared for the change, and the results were apparent in sales.

Susceptibility to Change. A third and indispensable method of segmenting the automobile market cuts across the lines drawn by the other two modes of segmentation analysis. This involves measuring the relative susceptibility of potential car buyers to changing their choice of make. Consider the buyers of Chevrolet during any one year from the point of view of a competitor:

At one extreme are people whose brand loyalty is so solidly entrenched that no competitor can get home to them. They always buy Chevrolets. They are closed off to change.

At the other extreme are the open-minded and the unprejudiced buyers. They happened to buy a Chevrolet because they preferred its styling that year or because they got a good buy, or because someone talked up the Fisher body to them. They could just as easily have purchased another make.

In the middle of this susceptibility continuum are people who are predisposed to Chevrolet to a greater or lesser degree. They can be persuaded to buy another make, but the persuasion has to be strong enough to break through the Chevrolet predisposition.

The implications of this kind of a susceptibility segmentation are far-reaching. Advertising effectiveness, for example, must be measured against each susceptibility segment, not against the market as a whole. Competitors' advertising should appear in media most likely to break through the Chevrolet predisposition of the middle group. In addition, the wants of those who are not susceptible must be factored out, or they will muddy the picture. Marketing programs persuasive enough to influence the uncommitted may make no difference at all to the single largest group—those who are predisposed to Chevrolet but still open enough to respond to the right stimulus.

If the marketing director of an automobile company does not break down his potential market into segments representing key differences in susceptibility, or does not clearly understand the requirements of each key segment, his company can persevere for years with little or no results because its promotion programs are inadvertently being aimed at the wrong people.

Perfume

A segmentation analysis of the perfume market shows that a useful way to analyze it is by the different *purposes* women have in mind when they buy perfume.

One segment of the market thinks of a perfume as something to be added to what nature has supplied. Another segment believes that the purpose of fragrance products is to help a woman feel cleaner, fresher, and better groomed—to correct or negate what nature has supplied. In the latter instance, the fragrance product is used to *cancel out* natural body odors; in the former, to *add* a new scent. To illustrate this difference in point of view:

> One woman told an interviewer, "I like a woodsy scent like Fabergé. It seems more intense and lingers longer, and doesn't fade away like the sweeter scents."
>
> But another woman said, "I literally loathe Fabergé. It makes me think of a streetcar full of women coming home from work who haven't bathed."

These differences in reaction do not indicate objective differences in the scent of Fabergé. They are subjective differences in women's attitudes; they grow out of each woman's purpose in using a perfume.

Purposive segmentation, as this third mode of analysis might be called, has been of great value to alert marketers. For instance:

A company making a famous line of fragrance products realized that it was selling almost exclusively to a single segment, although it had believed it was competing in the whole market. Management had been misled by its marketing research, which had consistently shown no differences in the demographic characteristics of women buying the company's products and women buying competitors' products.

In the light of this insight, the company decided to allocate certain lines to the underdeveloped segments of the market. This required appropriate changes in the scent of the product and in its package design. A special advertising strategy was also developed, involving a different copy approach for each product line aimed at each segment.

In addition, it was learned that visualizations of the product in use helped to create viewer identification in the segment that used perfume for adding to nature's handiwork, but that more subtle methods of communication produced better results among the more reserved, more modest women in the second segment who want the "canceling out" benefits of perfume. The media susceptibilities of women in the two segments were also found to be different.

Thus, from a single act of resegmentation, the advertising department extracted data critical to its copy platform, communication strategy, and media decisions.

Bathing Soap

A comparable purposive segmentation was found in the closely related bathing soap field. The key split was between women whose chief requirement of soap was that it should clean them adequately and those for whom bathing was a sensuous and enjoyable experience. The company (a new contender in this highly competitive field) focused its sights on the first segment, which had been much neglected in recent years. A new soap was shaped, designed, and packagd to appeal to this segment, a new advertising approach was evolved, and results were very successful.

Hair-Care Market

The Breck-Halo competition in the shampoo market affords an excellent example of another kind of segmentation. For many years, Breck's recognition of the market's individualized segmentation gave the company a very strong position. Its line of individualized shampoos included one for dry hair, another for oily hair, and one for normal hair. This line accurately paralleled the marketing reality that women think of their hair as being dry, oily, or normal, and they do not believe that any one shampoo (such as an all-purpose Halo) can meet their individual requirements. Colgate has finally been obliged, in the past several years, to revise its long-held marketing approach to Halo, and to come out with products for dry hair and for oily hair, as well as for normal hair.

Other companies in the hair-care industry are beginning to recognize other segmentations in this field. For example, some women think of their hair as fine, others as coarse. Each newly discovered key segmentation contains the seeds of a new product, a new marketing approach, and a new opportunity.

Other Packaged Goods

Examples of segmentation analysis in other packaged goods can be selected almost at random. Let us mention a few briefly, to show the breadth of applicability of this method of marketing analysis:

1. In *convenience* foods, for example, we find that the most pragmatic classification is, once again, purposive segmentation. Analysis indicates that "convenience" in foods has many different meanings for women, supporting several different market segments. Women for whom convenience means "easy to use" are reached by products and appeals different from those used to reach women for whom convenience means shortcuts to creativity in cooking.
2. In the market for *cleaning agents,* some women clean preventively, while others clean therapeutically, i.e., only after a mess has been made. The appeals, the product characteristics, and the marketing approach must take into account these different reasons for buying—another example of purposive segmentation.
3. In still another market, some people use *air refresheners* to remove disagreeable odors and others to add an odor. A product like Glade, which is keyed to the second segment, differs from one like Airwick in product concept, packaging, and type of scent.
4. The *beer market* requires segmentation along at least four different axes—reasons for drinking beer (purposive); taste preferences (aesthetic); price/quality (value); and consumption level.

Retail Soft Goods

Although soft-goods manufacturers and retailers are aware that their customers are value conscious, not all of them realize that their markets break down into at least four different segments corresponding to four different conceptions of value held by women.

For some women value means a willingness to pay a little more for quality. For others, value means merchandise on sale. Still other women look for value in terms of the lowest possible price, while others buy seconds or discounted merchandise as representing the best value.

Retailing operations like Sears, Roebuck are highly successful because they project *all* these value concepts, and do so in proportions which closely parallel their distribution in the total population.

Adding Machines

In marketing planning for a major adding machine manufacturer, analysis showed that his product line had little relationship to the segmented needs of the market. Like most manufacturers of this kind of product, he had designed his line by adding features to one or several stripped-down basic models—each addition raising the model price. The lowest priced model could only add; it could not subtract, multiply, divide, or print, and it was operated by hand.

Since there are a great many features in adding machines, the manufacturer had an extremely long product line. When the needs of the market were analyzed, however, it became clear that, despite its length, the line barely met the needs of two out of the three major segments of the market. It had been conceived and planned from a logical point of view rather than from a market-need point of view.

The adding machine market is segmented along lines reflecting sharp differences in value and purpose:

1. One buyer group values accuracy, reliability, and long life above all else. It tends to buy medium-price, full-keyboard, electric machines. There are many banks and other institutions in this group where full-keyboard operations are believed to ensure accuracy.
2. Manufacturing establishments, on the other hand, prefer the ten-key machine. Value, to these people, means the maximum number of labor-saving and time-saving features. They are willing to pay the highest prices for such models.
3. Both these segments contrast sharply with the third group, the small retailer whose major purpose is to find a model at a low purchase price. The small retailer does not think in terms of amortizing his investment over a period of years, and neither labor-saving features nor full-keyboard reliability count for as much as an immediate savings in dollars.

Despite the many models in the company's line, it lacked those demanded by both the manufacturer and small-retailer segments of the market. But, because it had always been most sensitive to the needs of financial institutions, it had developed more models for this segment than happened to be needed. Product, sales, and distribution changes were required to enable the company to compete in the whole market.

Computers

One pragmatic way of segmenting the computer market is to divide potential customers between those who believe they know how to evaluate a computer and those who believe they do not. A few years ago only about 20% of the market was really open to IBM's competitors—the 20% who believed it knew how to evaluate a computer. By default, this left 80% of the market a virtual captive of IBM—the majority who did not have confidence in its own ability to evaluate computers and who leaned on IBM's reputation as a substitute for personal appraisal.

Another segmentation in this market involves differences in prospects' attitudes toward the inevitability of progress. Although this factor has been widely ignored, it is a significant method for qualifying prospects. People who believe that progress is inevitable (i.e., that change is good and that new business methods are constantly evolving) make far better prospects for computers than those who have a less optimistic attitude toward progress in the world of business.

Light Trucks

The market for light trucks affords us another example of segmentation in products bought by industry. As in the computer example, there are both buyers who lack confidence in their ability to choose among competing makes and purchasers who feel they are sophisticated about trucks and can choose knowledgeably. This mode of segmentation unexpectedly turns out to be a key to explaining some important dynamics of the light truck market. Those who do not trust their own judgment in trucks tend to rely very heavily on both the dealer's and the manufacturer's reputation. Once they find a make that gives them reliability and trouble-free operation, they cease to shop other makes and are no longer susceptible to competitive promotion. Nor are they as price-sensitive as the buyer who thinks he is sophisticated about trucks. This buyer tends to look for the best price, to shop extensively, and to be susceptible to the right kind of competitive appeals, because he puts performance before reputation.

These ways of looking at the truck market have far-reaching implications for pricing policy, for product features, and for dealers' sales efforts.

CONCLUSION

To sum up the implications of the preceding analysis, let me stress three points:

1. *We should discard the old, unquestioned assumption that demography is always the best way of looking at markets.*

The demographic premise implies that differences in reasons for buying, in brand choice influences, in frequency of use, or in susceptibility will be reflected in differences in age, sex, income, and geographical location. But this is usually not true. Markets should be scrutinized for important differences in buyer attitudes, motivations, values, usage patterns, aesthetic preferences, or degree of susceptibility. These may have no demographic correlatives. Above all, we must never assume in advance that we know the best way of looking at a market. This is the cardinal rule of segmentation analysis. All ways of segmenting markets must be considered, and *then* we must select out of the various methods available the ones that have the most important implications for action. This process of choosing the strategically most useful mode of segmentation is the essence of the marketing approach espoused in this article.

In considering cases like those described, we must understand that we are not dealing with different types of people, but with differences in people's *values*. A woman who buys a refrigerator because it is the cheapest available may want to buy the most expensive towels. A man who pays extra for his beer may own a cheap watch. A Ford-owning Kellogg's Corn Flakes-eater may be closed off to Chevrolet but susceptible to Post Toasties; he is the same man, but he has had different experiences and holds different values toward each product he purchases. By segmenting markets on the basis of the values, purposes, needs, and attitudes relevant to the product being studied, as in Figure 1, we avoid misleading information derived from attempts to divide people into types.

2. *The strategic choice concept of segmentation broadens the scope of marketing planning to include the positioning of new products as well as of established products.*

It also has implications for brand planning, not just for individual products but for the composition of a line of competing brands where any meaningful segment in the market can possibly support a brand. One explanation of the successful competing brand strategy of companies like Procter & Gamble is that they are based on sensitivity to the many different modes of market segmentation. The brands offered by P & G often appear very similar to the outsider, but small, marginal differences between them appeal to different market segments. It is this rather than intramural competition that supports P & G successes.

3. *Marketing must develop its own interpretive theory, and not borrow a ready-made one from the social sciences.*

Marketing research, as an applied science, is tempted to borrow its theoretical structures from the disciplines from which it derives. The social sciences offer an abundance of such structures, but they are not applicable to marketing in their pure academic form. While the temptation to apply them in that form is great, it should be resisted. From sociology, for example, marketing has frequently borrowed the concept of status. This is a far-reaching concept, but it is not necessarily the most important one in a marketing problem, nor even one of the important ones. Again, early psychoanalytic theory has contributed an understanding of the sexual factor. While this can sometimes be helpful in an analysis of buying behavior in a given situation, some motivation researchers have become oversensitive to the role of sex and, as a result, have made many mistakes. Much the same might be said of the concept of social character, that is, seeing the world as being "inner-directed," "other-directed," "tradition-directed," "autonomous," and so forth.

One of the values of segmentation analysis is that, while it has drawn on the insights of social scientists, it has developed an interpretive theory *within* marketing. It has been home-grown in business. This may explain its ability to impose patterns of meaning on the immense diversity of the market, and to provide the modern marketing director with a systematic method for evolving true marketing objectives.

MARKET MEASUREMENT AND FORECASTING

8

Pinpointing
Prospects for
Industrial Sales

FRANCIS E. HUMMEL
Stanley Hardware

Finding new prospects and new accounts is the "lifeblood" of any expanding industrial concern. Yet many companies approach this problem in a relatively haphazard manner.

Sources of information as to prospective new accounts are commonly found by one or more of the following methods: (1) from requests received directly from industrial prospects; (2) from advertising, trade shows, and other promotion efforts; (3) from "leads" supplied by associates and friends; and (4) from salesmen "cold-turkey" calls on industrial plants in their territory.

Many times these activities result in many wasted sales calls, particularly when salesmen merely follow "smoke-stacks" in an effort to obtain new potential accounts. And often many good prospects are overlooked. Marketing analysis can aid in the search for new prospects by predetermining those industrial firms who afford the greatest probability of using a given industrial product and becoming a new account. This can be accomplished by first determining the industries having use for the product and the relative purchasing requirements of each industrial segment. These data can be used in conjunction with industrial directories, surveys, trade show attendance lists, advertising, and promotional inquiries to determine the probable best sources for sales calls.

Reprinted with permission from *Journal of Marketing*, published by the American Marketing Association, July 1960, pp. 26–31.

DETERMINING THE INDUSTRIAL MARKET

The first step is to classify the firm's industrial market. This serves as a basis for the preliminary research needed to determine potential accounts.

The classification system most widely used is the Standard Industrial Classification System. The S.I.C. is a numerical system set up by the federal government to classify the many different segments of industry. For manufacturing industries the S.I.C. System combines and classifies all manufacturing into twenty major industry groups (designated by a 2-digit code—example: #20, Food and Kindred Products).

Each group then is subdivided into about 150 industry groups (designated by a 3-digit code—example: #202, Dairy Products).

A further breakdown reveals approximately 450 individual industries (designated by a 4-digit code—example: #2021, Creamery Butter). Thus, each industry has a classification number—the more digits, the finer the classification.

This classification is based on the *product produced* or *operation performed*. A few industries have other classification fundamentals. such as materials or processes used. However, in general, establishments involved in similar production operations are grouped together and the product is the major determining factor of classification.

INDUSTRIAL BUYING MOTIVES

The S.I.C. classification system can be viewed in the light of the buying motives of industrial purchasing agents. Purchasing agents buy things that help their concern to solve production, distribution, control, or development problems. For example, the machine-tool firm buys ball bearings to make a better product; the box shop buys automatic gluers to increase production.

The industrial market is made up of manufacturing plants whose problems can be solved through the use of particular products or services, and who buy them as the best solution to *their problems*. If the problems of all industrial plants could be categorized into those that can or cannot be solved through the use of certain products, it could be determined what plants are in a certain market and the exact problems each one faces.

The industrial purchasers' problems stem from the product manufactured or the operations performed. The S.I.C. System is based on these factors. Therefore, if you know the S.I.C. number of a manufacturing plant, you have a good clue to the problems it faces. If you know the size of the plant, you have a good idea of the extent of the problem.

Since plants in the same S.I.C. make essentially the same kind of products and have the same or similar production problems. the first determining factor must be the listing of those industries making up the market for the product. Second. the relative importance of each S.I.C. industry must be determined in relation to each other along with the approximate need of each S.I.C. for your product. Thus, an estimate of the consumption of the product can be made by industries, areas, and specific firms from published S.I.C. data on production.

The various industries (usually 4-digit S.I.C.) can be determined, along with their relative importance for a particular market, by three complementary methods: (1) sales analysis, (2) judgment analysis, and (3) marketing surveys.

1. Sales Analysis

For established products, the first step is to analyze past sales records and assign appropriate 4-digit S.I.C. numbers to the plant of each customer. At the same time other valuable statistical data can be collected regarding dollar sales, models, attachments, etc. from the sales records. Punch-card analysis is essential for large studies.

This analysis yields valuable information *only* about *past* accomplishments by industries; it tells *nothing* of *potential* industries not sold.

2. Judgment Analysis

One or more persons thoroughly familiar with the market for the product can go through the S.I.C. manual and check off the 4-digit classifications which they believe fall into the market. Naturally, accuracy depends upon the experience, ability, and judgment of the persons selected.

3. Marketing Surveys

Inquiries can be solicited through news releases, advertising, and by a widespread sample mail survey. The inquiry returns are tabulated by S.I.C., indicating those companies and industries having use for the product.

This method is particularly applicable to a new product or to any established product about which there is some doubt as to whether or not present customers encompass all the S.I.C.'s in the potential market. The value of this method depends upon receiving an adequate cross-section of the market and reliable respondent information.

Basic Factors

By taking the above steps, preliminary data will be available to determine with a reasonable degree of accuracy the composition of the industrial market for the products under consideration. Three basic factors will be evident:

The industries having use for the product (called S.I.C. Effective Industries).

The proportion of plants within *each* industry that have use for the product (called S.I.C. Percentage).

The relative value of each S.I.C. as a proportion of the total market (called S.I.C. Weight).

For example, the above steps were taken by a manufacturer in analyzing the market for an inspection gauge. Marketing analysis showed that

S.I.C. 3423 (hand-and-edge tool industry) was one of the Effective Industries. And 80 per cent of the plants in S.I.C. 3423 had inspection problems best solved through the use of its product. However, this 80 per cent of the hand-tool industry plants (S.I.C. %) represented only 2.2 per cent of the total market for the product (S.I.C. Weight).

Another Effective Industry, S.I.C. 3722, Aircraft engines and engine parts, was found to be a major user. And 100 per cent of all the plants in S.I.C. 3722 (S.I.C. %) had inspection problems best solved through the use of its products, representing 30 per cent of the total market for the product (S.I.C. Weight).

These data can then be used as the basis for determining prospects. But the S.I.C., even on a 4-digit basis, is not a fine enough classification to assume that all plants in the same S.I.C. have identically the same problems. Therefore, the fact that a sale has been made to *one* plant in any particular S.I.C. does not necessarily mean that *all* the plants in the S.I.C. are potential customers. For example, the S.I.C. does not distinguish between plants that manufacture their own component parts and those that assemble parts made elsewhere.

PINPOINTING PROSPECTS

Once the composition of the industrial market is determined—that is, the industries having use for the product, the number of plants in each industry, and the relative market values of each industry—marketing research can utilize this information to pinpoint those industrial concerns that have a use for the product or that afford the greatest probability of becoming a new account. These prospects must be defined by names and addresses of companies—not merely percentage or dollar figure by areas—so that field salesmen can call for specific follow-up.

There are four major areas where marketing research can determine industrial concerns that have a high probability of becoming new industrial prospects—by use of (1) industrial directories, (2) surveys, (3) trade-show attendance lists, and (4) advertising and promotional inquiries.

1. Industrial Directories

A number of state and regional industrial directories published are by various organizations such as Chambers of Commerce and State Development Commissions that list the industrial plants within their areas.[1] These directories give names and addresses of industrial plants and products produced. Some provide additional data, such as employment and names of executives. Unfortunately they vary in completeness of data given and the method of classifying firms. There are only eighteen directories classifying firms on a 4-digit S.I.C. basis. To utilize the remaining directories most effectively, the listings must be classified into the S.I.C.

[1] For an annotated bibliography of state industrial directories, see: M. J. Reutter and N. R. Kidder, "State Industrial Directories," *Sales Management*, Volume 81, (July 10, 1958). pp. 72–78.

Such industrial directories provide an excellent source for finding new prospects. For each 4-digit S.I.C. making up the market for a product, each firm listed can be checked in relation to the sales and prospect files of the concern. Such an analysis gives a listing of plants by industries that probably are prospects. If the S.I.C. percentages and weights have been predetermined, the probability of any given firm becoming a good prospect is evident.

For example, one machine-tool manufacturer carefully analyzed each industrial directory in the United States. Preliminary research revealed that five S.I.C.'s made up over 75 per cent of the market for its specialized equipment. Only these industries were studied in detail. For each sales territory a master sales-analysis list was developed. The five S.I.C. industries were listed along with the names and addresses of each concern. Employment figures were noted where available. S.I.C. percentages and weights were shown for each industry under study. For each concern it was determined whether it had been sold or contacted previously. If no record of either, it was added to the new-prospect list for contact by a field salesman. In this manner a number of firms were discovered that had use for the equipment and were potential future customers.

Another metal-working concern utilized a similar approach. Personal sales calls were made on firms listed in the directories for four major 4-digit S.I.C. groups which accounted for 60 per cent of the market. The next eight S.I.C. groups, having lower S.I.C. percentages and weights, accounted for only 22 per cent of the market. Therefore, these "new prospects" were first contacted by telephone to determine whether they had a use for the product under study. Personal sales calls were then made on those firms reporting in the affirmative. This procedure resulted in a 25 per cent saving in sales time and expenses.

2. Surveys

A second way of determining new industrial prospects is through the use of market-research surveys. Such surveys made for a given product can provide information whether specific plants are in the market for that product, and the extent to which they are in it.

For example, a New England manufacturing firm had an established product which was sold for years primarily to ball bearing manufacturers. Management felt that the product should have more widespread use in the broad metal-working field. A mail questionnaire was developed to send to many 4-digit S.I.C.'s in the metal-working industry. The questionnaire asked whether the plant used product "X" (product "X" being a type of product made by several firms—not a brand name), the number of production workers in the plant, how product "X" was used, from whom the plant purchased it, the approximate annual dollar value of purchases, the names and titles of the officials responsible for specifying and purchasing this material, and their comments.

Table 1 is a sample of results obtained. The following important information became available from this study:

TABLE 1: SALES-PLANNING-BLUEPRINT[a], SURVEY OF METAL-WORKING PLANTS FOR PRODUCT "X," DAYTON-CINCINNATI AREA.

S.I.C. No. Workers	Plant Surveyed	Plant Uses Product "X" for:	Products in Which "X" Used:	From Whom Purchased	Approximate Value	Comments
3545 215	Cutting Tools, Gages, M.T. Attachments National Tool Co. 123 Fourth Ave. Dayton, Ohio R. L. Henchman, Plant Manager	Seal out dust	Spindles	A.B.C. Co.	$5,000	A.B.C. delivery poor
3621 25	Motors, Generators, Generator Sets G. Biggs, Inc. 456 Seventh Ave. Dayton, Ohio A. J. Israel, Mgr. Manufacturing	Keep lubrication in	Fractional horsepower motors	General National Co.	$ 185	Good price, service Quality high
3729 50	Aircraft Parts & Sub-Assemblies E. J. Walsh Co. Prospect Street Cincinnati, Ohio E. J. Walsh, Gen. Mgr. etc.	Seal out light cushioning	Precision assemblies	Connecticut Superior Co.	$8,500	Good price Need special size for precision parts. Estimated value $5,000 annual. Conn. Superior research facilities-poor for engineering design.

[a]All names and addresses are fictitious, but the information in the Blueprint is drawn from an actual case. The mark Sales-Planning-Blueprint is a service mark owned by Kidder and Company. Unauthorized use of the mark is prohibited. Copyright, Kidder and Company, Cambridge 38, Massachusetts, 1957.

1. The names and addresses of good prospective accounts were learned, and a knowledge of use of product and the competition and annual volume purchased. For example, the National Tool Company, a manufacturer of cutting tools, purchased $5,000 a year of competitor A.B.C. Company's product for use as a component in sealing out dust. Better deliveries were desired.

2. New uses for the product were determined. For example, pressure sealing was the prime discovery.

3. A list of the major disadvantages of Product "X" was compiled. Unfavorable comments regarding Product "X's" performance under cold temperatures resulted in redesign of the brand.

4. Data were obtained which could be further analyzed for use in advertising. For example, a number of concerns reported that they did not use the product because their requirements called for special sizes. The past advertising and sales-promotion brochures of the firm stressed standard lines. Future promotion was then designed to include mention of available engineering services to "tailor-make" the product for special requirements.

3. Trade-Show Attendance Lists

Registration lists of major trade shows can also be helpful in determining new accounts.

Classified registration lists are more frequently being supplied by progressive show managements. The lists are simply compilations of information taken from registration cards filled out by show visitors. The information includes the visitor's name and job title, company name and address, number of production employees, and major products produced by the plant. Such information permits each visitor to be classified by company size, location, and S.I.C. type of product.

These lists provide excellent data for marketing analysis, and obvious sales-promotion advantages. For example, a manufacturer of specialized machinery used the 1955 Machine Tool Show listings as an aid in determining market coverage and building a prospect list, particularly for some of its weaker sales areas. The registration lists were analyzed as follows: (1) The data from all registrants in the areas under study were assembled separately. (2) Only plants within certain 4-digit S.I.C.'s making a market for the machinery were studied; plants were further subdivided by S.I.C. weights and potentials along with plant size. (3) These plants were then compared with present prospect lists, and sales lists to determine specific coverage and possible new accounts. In addition, the company compiled its own list of show visitors to its *booth*. Such concerns not previously contacted were considered prime prospects because their representatives took the time to visit the manufacturer and obviously had an interest in the product.

Another firm used the 1956 Material Handling Institute Exposition data which classified its registration list by twenty-two job titles and forty-five industry classifications. The firm analyzed only industries that were original-equipment users, and carefully compared this list to past sales records. A number of new prospects were discovered by this analysis, and each was contacted subsequently by the field sales force.

One limitation of using trade-show attendance lists is that trade shows pull registrants most heavily from the local surrounding trading area of 200 to 300 miles. This means that distant areas under study must be evaluated accordingly because many plants may not have sent representatives to the show.

4. Advertising and Promotional Inquiries

Finally, a thorough analysis of advertising and promotional inquiries can be made. This method is particularly useful in determining markets for new industrial products. It makes use of the S.I.C. in order to "spot" those industries giving a genuine interest in the product.

For example, one manufacturer developed a high-frequency electric spindle for use on its precision machinery. These high-speed rotational units offered other industrial possibilities among many different industries. Therefore, an analysis of the broad industrial U.S. market was needed to determine specifically what other applications of the product were possible. It was decided that the most economical and efficient approach would be to solicit inquiries from the manufacturing community and to determine from those inquiries received, the industries having a potential use for the product. They would serve as a basis for conducting further research.

A small advertising campaign was conducted in the *Saturday Evening Post* designed to reach a broad section of manufacturing industry. In addition, publicity releases were prepared for twenty selected business publications to cover the broad design and metal-working field.

As inquiries were received as a result of the publicity, the sales department immediately answered them. The appropriate 4-digit S.I.C. number was then assigned to each inquiry, based on the major product produced by the plant. This showed that many plants within the same S.I.C. industry were interested in the product. These industries were then segregated and studied in detail by further surveys—both mail and personal interview. This resulted in a number of new applications and customers.

The use of inquiries derived from advertising and publicity offers many advantages for determining the market for both new and existing products. This approach is particularly applicable where people in the industry are not aware of the new industrial product, and for an industrial product which may have broad industrial usage.

9

Operations Research
in Solving
a Marketing Problem

JAMES S. CROSS
Sun Oil

The Sun Oil Company is an integrated company, performing the functions of producing, refining, transporting, and marketing petroleum and its products. The marketing department serves consumer and industrial markets, both in this country and abroad, with a well-established sales organization.

When occasion demands, management forms task forces to undertake specific projects. These teams consist of company personnel who are able by virtue of their training and experience to contribute to the solution of the problem to be studied.

Several of the marketing problems handled by operations research teams fall into the classical operations research pattern. One of these problems was the question of where to locate a pipe-line terminal to supply ninety-one retail outlets in Michigan. A mathematical model was constructed to represent the distribution costs that would be incurred in supplying these service stations from any possible terminal location. The method used for determining distribution costs was that of measuring mileage, weighted by potential gallonage, from each retail outlet to each possible terminal location. A system of grid squares was superimposed over a map of the area studied.

The question then became: "Which terminal point would minimize

Reprinted with permission from *Journal of Marketing,* published by the American Marketing Association, January 1961, pp. 30–34.

distribution costs?" Using an electronic computer and employing a search technique, or area scanning, this point was established; and management was given the location of the theoretically optimum place to build the terminal.

A recent project arose out of the problem of customer delay at service stations. This research sought to determine the optimum number of service channels that should be provided in any given station. A service channel requires a car position, a pump, and a serviceman. Thus, the number of channels limits the number of cars that can be simultaneously services.

The penalty for providing too many service positions is the loss involved in unused investment, or unearned wages. The penalty for providing too few service positions is the loss of sales due to the fact that customers are unwilling to be delayed. Since these costs are inverse to each other, the optimum solution should balance these factors to achieve the most profitable operation.

Empirical studies of service-station operations have clearly demonstrated that both automobile arrivals and the amount of time that it takes to service an automobile can be described by probability distributions. This justifies the application of queuing or waiting-line theory to a model of service-station operations. A model which is adaptable to Sun's service stations is now being constructed.

THE CUSTOM BLENDING EXPERIMENT

The most ambitious operations research effort undertaken by Sun Oil Company was that which culminated in the adoption of a new gasoline marketing method—the custom blending system. As early as 1953, the executive committee had been concerned with the long-range question of whether Sun's traditional marketing policy for motor fuel could be maintained in the light of then current and possible future market developments. The traditional policy had been to supply one grade of motor fuel of a quality intermediate between regular and premium and selling at regular gasoline price. This single fuel, branded "Blue Sunoco," was designed to satisfy the anti-knock requirements of 90 percent of the cars on the road. The 10 percent not satisfied was composed for the most part of the newer, higher-compression models.

Forecasts of future automobile engines indicated that the trend toward higher compression ratios would continue. In general, the higher the compression ratio of an automobile engine, the higher is its octane appetite. This trend, coupled with the fact that there would still be older cars on the road, pointed to a growing spread in octane requirements within the passenger car fleet. In 1953 there was a spread of about seventeen research octane numbers between the lowest and highest requirement cars. Today this range has increased to as high as twenty-five. It became obvious that to follow the single-grade policy would commit Sun to marketing a higher and higher octane fuel in order to continue to satisfy 90 percent of the drivers on the road.

This policy appeared untenable for several reasons. First, the entire octane pool would have to be elevated. This would waste costly octane numbers on the bulk of the automotive fleet not requiring extraordinarily high quality. Second, the cost of raising octanes would become progressively more expensive as the octane number was increased. In addition, a considerable capital investment would be necessary to provide the refining facilities to manufacture the quality fuel required. From a manufacturing standpoint, it would be difficult to absorb the cost of added pool octanes within the competitive regular price structure. From a marketing point of view, the specter of raising the price above competition was even less attractive. Finally, motivational research suggested that Sun would have difficulty in selling to owners of new, luxury-model cars, even though the bulk of these cars could be satisfied with the single-grade fuel.

An operations research task force, composed of social and physical scientists, together with operating and administrative personnel, was appointed to consider the problem of what Sun's future marketing policy should be.

Possible Courses of Action

Four possibilities were considered by the group: (1) To retain the present policy of marketing only a single grade of gasoline. (2) To market a regular and a premium grade, similar to competition. (3) To market three grades of gasoline: a regular, a premium, and a super premium. (4) To continue marketing the present "Blue Sunoco," but with an "octane concentrate" which could be custom blended at the pump to produce a wide range of fuels; this would permit the individual motorist to select the fuel best fitted to his car.

The concept of blending motor fuels at the pump, first proposed by the chairman of the board, was entirely new. Before this possibility could be considered as a realistic possibility, it was first necessary to determine whether a workable system could be devised. Accordingly, the attention of the operations research group was focused on the engineering aspects of the problem.

Technical Considerations

The practicability of custom blending hinged on two technical questions: (1) Could an octane concentrate be produced in sufficient quantity and within a realistic cost framework? (2) Could a pump be developed that would effectively blend the two basic components?

The concentrate problem was handled by a subgroup composed of representatives of the marketing and research and engineering departments. Any proposed concentrate had to meet several stringent requirements. From a marketing point of view, the various qualities of fuel resulting from the blending process would have to satisfy the operating requirements of a wide range of present and future automobiles. The concentrate would have to possess properties, other than anti-knock, which would be compatible with the base fuel so that any blend would be consistent in terms of such qualities as quick starting, fast warm-up, and good mileage. An additional requirement was to produce a concentrate commercially without incurring prohibitive costs.

The marketing requirements were met and proved out in many tests made on special test engines, and on cars under field operating conditions. At the same time refining techniques for producing these concentrates were developed. The economic evaluation of any proposed concentrate was an interesting operations research problem in its own right.

The operation of a refinery consists essentially of a flow process in which the output of one unit becomes input for other units and so on, until finished products are withdrawn from the system. Altering the operating conditions of any of the units thus affects the flows to the other units and eventually the product mix.

It is common to employ a technique called refinery simulation. This consists of programming the complex operations of a refinery on electronic computers. By supplying the computer with instructions as to the types of feed stock to be run and the operating conditions of each unit, it is possible to obtain the product output of the system. Experiments are conducted by altering the "throughput" or operating conditions or the sequence of unit processing.

By considering the market value of the products together with the operating costs, it is possible to choose an optimum range within which the desired product can be manufactured. After a considerable amount of laboratory, plant, and field research, an octane concentrate which satisfied the marketing and manufacturing requirements was developed.

At the same time another subgroup attacked the problem of producing the blending pump. As in the octane concentrate problem, the group had to "balance" several requirements. The pump not only had to perform the usual operations of dispensing, measuring, and computing, but also had to be equipped with a mechanism which would accurately apportion two product streams so as to produce the exact blend required. In addition, it had to lend itself to mass-production methods, so that its production cost could be kept within reasonable limits. Two years of intensive research resulted in a pump that accomplished these objectives.

Measuring Consumer and Competitive Reactions

After solving these technical problems, the task force turned to the question of how the motoring public would react to an entirely new concept in gasoline retailing. Since the custom blending system was so radically different, it was decided that the only possible way to evaluate consumer and competitive reaction was to perform actual tests at service stations.

Two and one-half years had passed since the inception of the project, and the work had been carried out with utmost secrecy. Only top management and the task-force employees had knowledge of the proposed changes in marketing policy. Although this had the advantage of keeping information from competition, there were two disadvantages: the loss of help that could have been gained from employees not on the task force, and the absence of market information.

An example of the first type of cost resulted when the custom blending pump was demonstrated to the marketing people. It soon became evident that the pricing mechanism was not flexible enough to handle all possible pricing situations. The price computer was subsequently redesigned to correct this deficiency. However, it was the lack of knowledge as to how the system would work in the market that resulted in the decision to conduct a pilot test; and so the cloak of secrecy was removed.

Sun's Southeastern region, encompassing the states of Florida and part of southern Georgia, was selected as the site of the test for two reasons. First, it was an isolated area for the company, with little advertising "spill-over" from other Sun marketing regions. Second, the resort character of the area would expose the custom blending system to a diverse group of individuals and thus secure the reactions of consumers driving a wide variety of cars.

The first phase of the experiment began in February 1956, in Orlando, Florida, and was extended throughout the region in June of the same year. Competitive reactions to the announced custom blending system were soon apparent. Within a short time several competitors were offering three grades of gasoline. Others stepped up their second grades to "super premium" quality and price.

Reactions of consumers to custom blending were highly favorable. Paired stations were set up, allowing comparisons to be made between competitive stations and Sun stations *with* custom blending, and between competitive stations and Sun stations *without* custom blending. By observing traffic through these paired stations, it was found that custom blending increased both the volume of sales and the proportion of sales made to high-priced, high-octane requirement cars at those Sun stations which had the new system.

This case study illustrates an important difference between a purely mathematical operations research approach and one more concerned with a dynamic marketing situation. When a mathematical model is set up, it is possible to perform experiments without altering it or the environment which it represents. However, once an experiment is performed on a system which operates in a social environment, no matter how hard one tries to keep the experiment "pure," the system and the environment in which it operates are usually subject to outside influences.

In the case of custom blending, two things happened. First, competitors altered their basic marketing strategy, for example, by selling three grades, which changed the "rules of the game." Second, they increased marketing pressure in advertising, promotion, and station building. Nonetheless, by careful examination of very small markets, it was possible to minimize considerably the effect of the changed environment.

Evaluation

The final task of the operations research group was to evaluate each of the possible policies. To accomplish this, a model was constructed to evaluate the rate of return on investment for a given sales volume for each system.

The problem was stated as follows: Consider three different alternatives to Sun's traditional single-grade motor fuel system:

1. Custom blending.
2. The two-fuel system.
3. The three-fuel system.

For each system, at what point in sales volume will additional revenue:

a. Equal additional costs?
b. Yield 10, 15, or 20 percent return on investment before taxes?

Measurements were made on an incremental basis. That is, the costs, investment, and revenue for each system were compared with the dollar sales that would have been generated by the traditional single-grade system as it would have been operated in the reference year. Only the incremental amounts were reported.

Detailed estimates of the capital requirements and operating costs for each system were obtained and substituted in the model. The marketing and manufacturing assumptions were varied in order to determine the effect of different sets of operating conditions. For example, separate computations were made for a two-fuel system, one assuming a three-cent retail differential and another assuming a four-cent differential. The expected results of a three-fuel system were calculated, using varying proportions of each grade. For the custom blending system, profitability estimates were made for a range of octane-concentrate ratios.

The final report did not specify an optimum solution, but rather presented management with the return on investment for each possible course of action, with a variety of sales volumes and sets of operating conditions. Management decided in favor of custom blending.

FINAL CONSIDERATIONS

Here are some final considerations, developed during the course of the work on this project.

1. It is not always possible to construct a mathematical model to represent the system under study.
2. At almost every point there are conflicts of interest among functional units of a system. These should not be suppressed, but rather balanced so that an optimum solution for the entire system is achieved.
3. It may not be possible to supply an optimum solution because one or more of the essential variables of the system cannot be evaluated objectively. Under such conditions a plausible range of values may be stated. Within this framework possible values can be specified. The decision-maker may then exercise his subjective judgment as to which is the most probable value, and the solution follows from this selection.

4. Provision should be made to cope with possible changes in conditions that may arise from conducting experiments in the market.

5. If it is desired to maintain a high degree of security over the research operation, the advantages and disadvantages of doing so should be carefully weighed.

6. Final decisions should not be made by the operations research team, but rather by management.

SELECTED BIBLIOGRAPHY
for
PART 2

BAYTON, JAMES. "Motivation, Cognition, Learning—Basic Factors in Consumer Behavior," *Journal of Marketing*. January, 1958, pp. 282–89.

BOYD, HARPER W., JR., and LEVY, SIDNEY J. "New Dimensions in Consumer Analysis," *Harvard Business Review*, November–December, 1963, pp. 129–40.

BRIGHT, JAMES R. "Opportunity and Threat in Technological Change," *Harvard Business Review*. November–December, 1963, pp. 76–86.

BROOKS, JOHN. "Annals of Business: The Edsel," *The New Yorker*. November 26, 1960, and December 3, 1960.

COLEMAN, RICHARD P. "The Significance of Social Stratification in Selling," in Martin Bell, ed., *Marketing: A Mature Discipline*. (Chicago: American Marketing Association, 1961), pp. 171–84.

LEVITT, THEODORE. "The New Markets—Think before You Leap," *Harvard Business Review*. May–June, 1969, pp. 53–67.

LIPSTEIN, BENJAMIN. "The Dynamics of Brand Loyalty and Brand Switching," *Better Measurements of Advertising Effectiveness: The Challenge of the 1960s*. (New York: Advertising Research Foundation, 1959), pp. 101–108.

RITLAND, ROSS W. "New Methods of Estimating and Forecasting Retail Sales—A Microanalytical Approach," *Journal of Retailing*. Fall, 1963, pp. 1–9.

ORGANIZING
FOR
MARKETING

After examining the different marketing opportunities, we now turn to the individual organization and consider how it can be effectively organized for marketing decisions. Two articles consider growth and competitive strategy in marketing. Adler (pp. 120–136) explains and illustrates such competitive strategies as "the end run," "market stretching," and "multibrand entries." Klaw (pp. 137–50) presents a perceptive discussion of the competitive strategies of the large soap manufacturers over a decade. Luck (pp. 151–58) describes the promise and the problems of the product-manager position in the marketing organization. In the area of marketing information systems, management is becoming increasingly aware that information needs to be managed as a valuable resource. McNiven and Hilton (pp. 159–74) reassess the current "state of the art" of marketing information systems. Business Week (pp. 175–86) discusses the growing demand and supply of better information through marketing research. The last article, by Ames (pp. 187–202), shows the contribution of intelligent marketing planning to the performance of industrial companies.

GROWTH AND COMPETITIVE STRATEGY

10

A New Orientation
for Plotting
Marketing Strategy

LEE ADLER
RCA

Since World War II ever intensifying competition and the need for profits have prompted alert companies to forge a number of new and productive marketing strategies, concepts, and tools. Unfortunately, however, there are signs that a grave illness affects many managements, preventing their effective use of these modern marketing instruments. Among the symptoms are:

1. A tendency to engage in bloody, knock-down-drag-out fights with entrenched competitors. Examples abound, especially in the packaged goods industries.
2. Haphazard or sophomoric application of theoretically sound marketing strategies—market segmentation, selection of companies for merger or acquisition and, above all, product differentiation. Products without truly demonstrable points of difference meaningful to the consumer are legion. Ask any advertising agency copywriter.
3. Devoted marriage to an existing business pattern despite evidence that it is in a declining phase. In the beauty aids business, for example, a famous company jealously guarded its department and drug store trade while sales volume in their product categories relentlessly shifted to supermarkets. To make matters worse, this company persisted in holding onto its older customers, despite ample evidence that women under thirty-five are the heavy users and are also becoming a larger proportion of the entire female population.
4. Emotional attachment to products that have outlived their viability. Take the case of the packaged breakfast food. It had been the foundation item in the

Reprinted with permission from *Business Horizons,* Winter, 1964, pp. 37–50. Copyright 1964 by the Foundation for the School of Business at Indiana University.

original line, and, though tastes in breakfast foods had shifted and new products had been successful competitors for years, its manufacturer, like an indulgent parent, could find no fault with it. Or, when pressed to justify its continued existence, the company rationalized that the brand was a symbol for the company and that its old-time trade was still loyal to it.

5. A passion for the cachet conferred by volume without reckoning the cost of attaining that volume. This bit of irrationality leads to a drive for volume for the sake of volume, rather than volume at a profit.

6. Failure to consider alternate routes to profitable volume. Thus, some companies continue to regard the United States as their sole territory while their peers are also vigorously expanding abroad where product potentials are easier to tap. Similarly, some marketers maintain safe advertising-to-sales ratios in fields where advertising makes a powerful contribution to total sales effect. In the meantime, their rivals have learned not to regard advertising as a cost, an inhibiting, negative viewpoint, but rather as an investment that can produce fabulous returns.

MARKETING VISION

What is the nature of this illness that so inhibits creative marketing effort? Levitt called it "marketing myopia."[1] He argued that failure to define a business broadly enough leads to premature senescence. Levitt noted four conditions which tend to foster decay in the midst of apparent bounty: reliance on population growth, confidence in the infallibility of one's current product, reliance on the cost efficiencies of mass production, and "preoccupation with products that lend themselves to carefully controlled scientific experimentation, improvement, and manufacturing cost reduction."[2]

Several other considerations that seem also to interfere with the achievement of marketing breakthroughs can be added to Levitt's discussion. The concern here is not so much with a whole industry as with the growth of individual companies, divisions, and brands.

Trapped in the Square

The problem is basically lack of vision and self-imposed limitations. There is no better analogy than to the nine-dot square, the familiar puzzle requiring the player to connect all nine dots arranged in the form of a square with no more than four lines, without lifting his pencil from the paper.

FIGURE 1: NINE-DOT SQUARE (solution in Figure 2)

---

[1] Theodore Levitt, "Marketing Myopia," *Harvard Business Review*, XXXVIII (July–August 1960), pp. 47–48.

[2] *Ibid.*

Most players do not succeed at first because, even without being told, they think that they have to remain within the square. It's only the bolder and more deeply reasoning who immediately realize that they must go outside the square in order to succeed.

Another factor responsible for this near-sightedness is the overdetailing of objectives. It used to be that if a man was asked what his business goal was he would say, "to make money." More likely, he would not even have been asked the question in the first place. A corporate manager today will give some fancy responses, such as:

—To implement the marketing concept
—To build my share of market by five percentage points by January 1966
—To assure maximum use of our manpower, financial, and productive resources
—To widen our distribution to 90 per cent of all supermarkets
—To achieve an advertising penetration of 62 per cent by the end of the campaign, and so on.

It is vital to have goals. A steady parade of marketing experts are calling for businesses to lay down both broad corporate and divisional goals, and specific marketing objectives. But we should be aware of a danger inherent in setting objectives. To be workable a given objective must be concretized and aimed at a single target. While doing so, however, one tends to block his broader thinking. Thus, the objective of building brand X's share of market from 18 per cent to 23 per cent within two years leaves out such other considerations as, "Maybe we should launch another brand in this market," or "Would franchising help broaden our market, lessen our competitive burden?" or, "Our technical people say they can obsolete our brand and those of our competitors with a radically new idea. Should we market the idea, or suppress it for the time being?"

Although the process of detailing objectives is necessary, it tends at the same time to scatter objectives. The setting of numerous, detailed targets for an existing business bearing on advertising, sales management, sales channels, expense control, and so on may not add up to an integrated system of goals leading to market breakthroughs. On the contrary, this process may perpetuate the status quo because it obscures the need for fresh approaches, because its benchmarks and building blocks all emerge from the existing situation, and because it administratively entangles marketers in today to the neglect of tomorrow.

Two other factors abet this tendency to blind business vision. The first is decentralization. Not decentralization itself, to be sure, for when unit managers are given the freedom and responsibility to operate, the spirit of innovation often flourishes. The trouble is with those managements who cannot keep their hands off the divisional steering wheels and insist that profit responsibility belongs to headquarters. When only lip service is paid to decentralization, both practical and psychological obstacles are raised to the free-thinking of divisional personnel.

The brand manager system, with all its merits, is an even worse offender in this respect. While acceptable in concept, in practice brand managers are often turned into production schedulers, inventory controllers, budget preparers, sales analysts, and expense control clerks. They are so busy with the mechanical details of their jobs that they have no time for its vital aspects—market planning, improving the creativity of their advertising, expanding their brands' domains. The growing roles of marketing consultants, package designers, sales promotion creators, and other outside business services testify to the sterility inside.

This problem is a serious one. It leads to such ill-advised actions as discordant mergers, copy-cat brands, and futile attacks on well-fortified positions. Or it leads to no action at all. The results are failure to grow and to manage change, and increased vulnerability to competition. This is a useless waste when powerful and proven marketing weapons are waiting to be deployed.

Breaking Out the Square

To take advantage of opportunities, management needs a vision of the business.[3] This vision, McKay observes, should be spelled out in terms of (a) customers and markets, (b) products and services, (c) technology and production capability, and (d) corporate personality and character—all geared to the satisfaction of customer wants and needs.

Development of this vision enables a company or a division to apply marketing strategies in an orderly, consistent manner. It helps to plan and program marketing innovation. In a more detailed fashion, it guides the selection and use of each marketing weapon geared to the desired direction, pace, and timing of growth.

Put another way, this vision helps marketers break out of their nine-dot squares. It arises from a wholistic view of a business' raison d'etre, a return to fundamentals. And of all the fundamentals, the most basic is: a company is in business to make money by providing consumer gratifications. Within reason, it does not matter how the company makes money. No law says it must make money with brand A if brand A simply no longer has the capacity to make money. Brand B might do a much better job. Or, similarly, if market C is exhausted, market D may be wide open.

The vision necessary to grasp this fundamental reality has two dimensions. For breadth, according to Levitt,[4] industries should define their spheres broadly enough to assure continuing growth and to head off competition or, at least, to be fully prepared to deal with it. Thus, it is not sufficient for an oil company to conceive of itself as being in the oil business; it is far healthier if it regards itself as being in the fuel or energy business, or in the even broader petro-chemicals business.

The second dimension is depth. Every company has an essential being, a core, the commercial equivalent of a soul. Deep-thinking managers learn

3 Edward S. McKay, "The Marketing and Advertising Role in Managing Change," in an address before the 54th meeting of the Association of National Advertisers, November 10–13, 1963.
4 "Marketing Myopia," *Harvard Business Review*, pp. 52–53.

to look for, identify, and capitalize on the essence of a company—that which gives it vitality and makes the crucial difference in dealing with rivals and making money.

Consider the Coca-Cola Company. It can be described as a manufacturer of a popular soft drink, or, more correctly, as the manufacturer of syrup used as the base of the soft drink. Or, more recently, as the parent of a whole line of soft drinks—Coca-Cola, Tab, Sprite, Fanta. But a definition of the Coca-Cola Company as a remarkable distribution network may be much closer to the truth. The company's great leader, Robert Woodruff, laid down the policy in the 1920s of putting Coca-Cola "within an arm's length of desire." Today, Coca-Cola is distributed in 1,600,000 outlets, more than any other product in the world. Every kind of retail outlet carries the brand. It is put into these outlets by over 1,000 local franchised bottlers in the United States. Because these bottlers, guided by the parent company, have created this extraordinary distribution, it is easier for the company to market new brands. So, with increasing competition on all sides, the heart of this success is the means of achieving widespread availability.

Procter & Gamble Company furnishes another good example. Sure, P&G manufactures soaps and detergents. To define their business in broader terms, as they keep adding products by internal development and by acquisition, P&G is in the household cleaner business, the food business, the health and beauty aids business, or in short, in the personal and household products business—a broad enough definition to keep even P&G going for years.

But P&G can also be viewed as a marketing management philosophy embodying such vital elements as careful market testing, the assurance of genuinely good products, a high order of merchandising skill, and well-supported brand managers. The application of these elements in a determined and unified manner brings marketing success whether the product is a detergent, a dentifrice, or a decaffeinated coffee.

FIGURE 2: SOLUTION TO NINE-DOT SQUARE

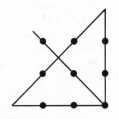

Still another example is the Alberto-Culver Company, a manufacturer of hair preparations that has lately been broadening its line to include a headache remedy, a first-aid item, a dentifrice, and so on. Its president, Leonard Lavin, has said: "If you judge us to be successful (the company went from sales of $400,000 in 1956 to over $80,000,000 in 1963), chalk it up to innovator products, excellent packaging, premium pricing, hard-driving promotions, and heavy TV backing of effective creative commercials."[5] Many marketers have innovator products and excellent packaging, and the rest, but not many have the kind of heavy TV backing Lavin refers to. For in my opinion the essence of Alberto-Culver is really a courageous media investment policy that results in their profit rate outdistancing their sales rate. The company has said as much:

> We have found an astounding fact: the more we invest in advertising, the less our advertising-to-sales ratio becomes. The sales for our established brands are growing at a greater rate than their substantial advertising budgets. Where a million dollars in advertising used to buy for us $1 to $2 million in gross sales, for our leading brands it now buys added millions of dollars worth of sales, and the ceiling hasn't been reached. Our aggressiveness continues with the added incentive that once we get a brand off the ground, its ability to grow and return profits to the company accelerates at a much greater rate than the increased advertising expenditure.[6]

A company's definition of itself is at the root of marketing success. Only the company with unobstructed vision can use the marketing weapons with maximum effect.

MARKETING WEAPONS SYSTEM

There are an even dozen marketing weapons and together they make up a weapons system. They have been isolated by a qualitative analysis of the operations of many firms, mainly in the consumer, nondurable packaged-goods industries. Utilization of one or more of these marketing weapons was found to run as a common thread through the marketing practices of the successful companies in these fields. But these weapons were not used in a vacuum. Rather, an underlying philosophy gave them power and impact. By contrast, haphazard utilization of these weapons consistently characterized the less-able marketers.

The End Run

The purpose of the end run is to avoid unnecessary, costly, time-consuming, or otherwise undesirable battles with entrenched competitors or other nearly insuperable obstacles. The objective is to create the arena rather than uncritically accept one made by the competitor. The following examples show how to do battle in one's own arena.

Those tobacco companies that are outflanking the serious problem of government regulation, public outcries, and negative publicity revolving around the health issue are practicing the end run. A number of possible end runs are available to the industry. Defining oneself as being in the tobacco business, not just the cigarette business, leads to more vigorous activity in cigars and pipe tobaccos, which do not have the serious prob-

[5] Leonard Lavin, in an address before the New York Marketing Executives Association, April, 1962.

[6] John S. Lynch, "Turmoil in Toiletries—the Rise of Alberto-Culver," *Food Business* (November, 1962), p. 19.

lem of cigarettes. The self-definition can refer to a technology-based firm using the tobacco plant as raw material. R. J. Reynolds' development of a fertilizer from tobacco stems is a step in this direction. The next step is to become a chemical processor of other vegetable matter.

Increased overseas marketing to escape or soften the strictures of the U.S. scene is another illustration. So, too, is a tobacco company's viewing itself as an expert in mass distribution rather than as a cigarette manufacturer. Philip Morris exemplifies this approach, as shown in their acquisition of Burma-Vita Company, American Safety Razor Company, and Clark Chewing Gum Company, all different products that rely on the same channels of distribution.

During the late 1940s and early 1950s, Lever Brothers Company made a number of unsuccessful assaults on P&G's solid position in the heavy-duty detergent field.[7] Finally, in 1957, Lever acquired "All" from Monsanto for the automatic washing machine market. In this way, Lever succeeded in outflanking P&G in a high-volume segment of the laundry market.

Not to be outdone, P&G counterattacked "All" frontally with Dash. This tactic worked for a time, but by 1961 "All" had regained its lost ground. Then P&G launched its own end run—Salvo low-sudsing tablets. What P&G could not accomplish directly, it accomplished indirectly. Between Dash and Salvo P&G won half the low-sudsing business in several years. By 1963, P&G was well ahead of Lever with a 16.1 per cent share of the heavy-duty soap and detergent market with two brands as against only 12.7 per cent for Lever's "All" and Vim low-sudser combined.[8]

Thus, acceptance of the boundaries of a marketing battlefront, or of the weapons to be used, does not nurture the development of competitive advantage. But a penetrating vision of one's business strips away these restrictive definitions and leads to refreshing new horizons.

Domination

The principle of domination calls for sufficient concentration of effort, funds, manpower, or creativity (within the limits of one's resources) in one area to "own" that area rather than to spread oneself thin over a wider sector. Application of this principle calls for realistic self-perception. For example, one manufacturer of deodorants recognized that in his field, crowded with multi-million dollar advertisers relying heavily on television, his own modest resources would be insufficient. He, therefore, elected to use a medium then largely ignored by his competitors—radio. Put into radio, his budget was large enough to make him the dominant deodorant brand for radio listeners. This advertiser understood that it was not absolute dollars only that mattered but *share* of dollars too. Moreover, he saw that domination brought not only extra dollar volume but important

---

[7] Spencer Klaw, "The Soap Wars: A Strategic Analysis," *Fortune* (June, 1963), p. 123ff.

[8] *The Gallagher Report*, Vol. 12 (May 13, 1964).

psychological advantages in leadership and in the surety of a solid position, as well as a good jumping-off point to seize another segment of the business.

Market Segmentation

The concept of market segmentation is well known, and need not be discussed here. Its purpose is to identify and concentrate on fractions of a total market capable of yielding a disproportionate volume and profit. The key point of focus is on the skill with which factors that truly divide markets are identified, vital target groups are defined, marketing programs are tailored according to their motivations and needs, and segments harmonizing with a company's own talents are selected.

Some companies in the cosmetic industry, for instance, have developed an almost uncanny skill at grasping the psychology of beauty-conscious American women. The essence of their business is selling beauty rather than certain chemicals made up into cosmetics. "In the factory, we make cosmetics," says Charles Revson, president of Revlon, "in the drugstore, we sell hope." The subtle sale of hope has led to a profitable segmentation of the total cosmetics market.

Other companies have developed a flair for segmenting markets on a price basis. The heart of their business is efficient, low-cost production combined with low-margin marketing effort. Price segmentation also works at the other end of the scale—some firms have the taste for opulence that leads to success in "class" selling.

In this manner, insight into the heart of a business leads to use of the principle of market segmentation in ways that are uniquely right for the individual marketer. Market segmentation is no longer necessarily an unenlightening slicing of populations in terms of demographic and socioeconomic characteristics. It becomes a creative approach to markets that leads to real benefits.[9]

Consider what manufacturers of makeup and skin-care preparations have achieved. Once upon a time there was a simple product called cold cream. Segmenting in terms of specialized consumer needs and desires, manner and occasion of use, age, motivation, and attitude, cold cream manufacturers now market foundation, cleansing, vanishing, nourishing, conditioning, hormone, astringent, lanolin, marrow, and wrinkle creams.

The vision of a business as a money-making operation also helps to secure concentration on key target groups, rather than dissipation of effort over a broad front. And so beauty aids companies zero in on young women, beer marketers direct their attention to young men, laxative and tonic producers to older, lower-income people, soft drink bottlers to teenagers, floor wax makers to suburban housewives, cigarette manufacturers to men, and so on through all the heavy users in each field.

At the same time, this vision of a business reduces the dangers of the

9 Daniel Yankelovich, "New Criteria for Market Segmentation," *Harvard Business Review*, Vol. XLII (March–April 1964), pp. 83–90.

misuse of market segmentation. Three misapplications frequently observed are described below.

Pursuing the wrong segment. One Western brewer, having won a good hold on the heart of the beer market—younger, lower-income male drinkers—aspired to win the favor of a more elegant, upper-income audience. Not only did his effort fail, but he also managed to alienate his original market. Contrast this with the cases of other brewers who appeal to different social class and price segments with different brands. Thus, Anheuser-Busch now offers two premium beers, Michelob and Budweiser, and one popular-priced brand, Busch Bavarian. Schlitz has two regional popular-priced brands, Burgemeister and Old Milwaukee, along with its premium-priced Schlitz.

Oversegmentation. This phenomenon manifests itself in more specialization than the market requires. The deodorant industry is a case in point. Until the mid-1950s, women were the heart of the market and all products were named and promoted with feminine appeal uppermost. Men used women's products. By the early 1960s the female market was saturated and much had been done to evolve brands with a masculine appeal. Gillette's Right Guard was a prominent example. Then Gillette discovered that other family members were using Right Guard, too. Now the brand is being promoted for the whole family. Since men are willing to use "women's" deodorants and women are willing to use "men's" deodorants, one wonders whether segmentation by sex may not be overdone.

Overconcentration. Sometimes companies, indeed whole industries, learn to concentrate too well. The brewery industry, for instance, has concentrated for many years on young men and justifiably so, in light of their heavy usage. But this has led to a sameness in advertising themes and subjects, media, and sports associations, and to near-maximum penetration of the young male market at the expense of other segments worthy of further development. This may help to explain a static per capita level; annual gallons consumed per person were 18.0 in 1946, 16.8 in 1952, and 15.1 in 1962.

In the malt beverage field additional cultivation could include many other segments. The segments suggested in Table 1 are necessarily an incomplete catalog and do not purport to be a set of recommendations to brewers. Rather, they are cited to demonstrate the potential in building new segments where competition is low-key or nonexistent, while not neglecting established segments.

Soundly used, with guidance provided by a vision of the business, market segmentation is a creator of new markets rather than a constrictor of established markets.

Market Stretching

New markets are created in many different fashions; the one a business uses depends on how it identifies itself. For example, it is becoming more common for industrial chemical producers to "go consumer." This can only come about from a redefinition of a business. Dow Chemical Com-

TABLE 1: POSSIBLE MALT BEVERAGE MARKET
SEGMENTS FOR ADDITIONAL CULTIVATION

Upper social class, "snob" appeal	via	Ale, imported beers
"With-meals" market	via	Advertising and store promotions depicting with-meals use
With snack foods	via	Promotion such as Coca-Cola's "Nothing beats a Coke n' Pizza," or "Coke n' Burger" promotions
Women	via	Feminine appeal brand-name, small package sizes, recipes using beer, as the wine industry does*
Those who prefer strong beers	via	Malt liquor, some imports
Draught beer lovers	via	Bottled draught beer (for example, Michelob)

* These measures would be introduced to foster greater consumption of beer by women, in addition to the fact that they buy most of the beer sold in grocery stores (now over 40 per cent of total beer volume—and growing steadily) as their families' purchasing agents.

pany, for example, has broadened its horizon with plastic food wraps, oven cleaners, even Christmas tree decorative materials, among a long list of consumer products. A number of makers of hair care products have gone consumer another way; specialists serving the beauty salon trade, Helene Curtis, Rayette, Ozon, Breck, Clairol, and VO-5, have all made their mark by selling direct to the consumer.

Paradoxically, market segmentation can lead to the broadening of markets. Zealous specialization evokes a countervailing force: a strong desire is born for all-purpose products sold to and used by practically everyone. The detergent industry is ripe for one; now there are specialized products for heavy-duty laundering, fine laundering, manual dishwashing, automatic dishwashing, cleaning floors, kitchens, bathrooms, and so on. As a result, uses for even the most general cleansers are narrowing. The floor wax business is also setting the stage for an all-purpose product with its profusion of pastes, waxes, polishes—including a product that removes the other products. In this context, the recent burgeoning of one-step cleaning and waxing in floor waxes and one-step dusting, waxing, and polishing in furniture waxes may be the industry's way of broadening user segments. Thus, the sharp strategist recognizes when the time has come to throw the gears into reverse and use the tool of product or line simplification.

Multibrand Entries

Underlying this marketing strategy is a basic premise: two brands tend to capture more of the available sales than one. Marketers with a broad conception of their business have learned to overcome their passionate devotion to one brand. Their vision grants them detachment; they can see that their role in life is not to nurture their brand regardless of cost, but rather to maximize profitable volume. They can then also see that there will always be a few contrary consumers who will persist in buying a rival brand. So they reason that the other brand might just as well be theirs too. They know there may be some inroads into sales of the original brand, but that there will be a *net* gain in volume with two brands instead of one.

Many packaged-goods industries provide examples of the application of this strategy. In deodorants, Bristol-Myers has four brands and seven product variants: Ban (roll-on and cream), Mum (including Mum Mist and Mum Mist for Men), Trig, and Discreet. In soaps and detergents and tobacco products, examples of this strategy abound. Alberto-Culver has enunciated multibrand competition as a policy, and has begun to send second brands into markets in which they already compete.

Perhaps the shrewdest extension of this strategy, particularly applicable when a company is first with a truly new product and can realistically anticipate competition, is to lock out rivals by bringing out multiple offerings at the time of product introduction. One food manufacturer used this approach recently in a product category segmented by flavor. Similarly, a housewares producer applied this strategy to preempt the key position with different-features models in a market that segments by price. The cigarette field also furnishes current examples: Philip Morris brought out no less than four new charcoal filter brands virtually at the same time —Philip Morris Multifilter, Galaxy, and Saratoga; and Liggett & Myers introduced two—Lark and Keith.

Brand Extension

Marketers' emotional attachment to products often includes the brand-name. With brand extension strategy, too, a wholesome and realistic view of the business precludes the imposition of artificial and unnecessary limitations on the use of brand-names. There is nothing holy about a brand-name, and if extension of it can bring about marketing good, while not discrediting or cheapening the original product or confusing the consumer, then extension can serve as a potent instrument. Thus, Dristan, first a decongestant tablet, is now a nasal spray, cough formula, and medicated room vaporizer. Lustre Creme, in addition to ignoring the literal meaning of its name and coming out as a liquid and a lotion shampoo, is now also a rinse and conditioner and a spray set. Ivory, as homey and hoary a brand-name as any, is as vital as ever in Ivory Flakes, Ivory Snow, Ivory Soap, and Ivory Liquid.

Product Change

As in the case of market segmentation, the crucial importance of product innovation is so clear and so well understood that it requires no description here. Product change lies at the heart of many market strategies and is capable of application in a marvelous variety of ways. The essential prerequisite is a conception of a business that permits free scope to product change and, indeed, urgently demands ceaseless product change. The exact form and pattern of change will be conditioned by the nature and goals of the individual business.

End-run candidates—and the concomitant avoidance of me-tooism—are evident in the development of essentially new products, such as cold water detergents, hair sprays, electric toothbrushes, low-calorie foods and beverages, sustained-release cold tablets.

Flank attacks are also possible by what might be called extra-benefit innovation, as contrasted with straight innovation. The typical example is in the use of an additive, for instance, lanolin, hexachlorophene, fluoride. The less typical example is the double-duty product; shampoos may also provide a color rinse, suc has Helena Rubinstein's Wash 'n' Tint.

Product differentiation is the usual means of seeking a demonstrable point of difference. Taste, packaging size, and ways of using established products are the customary variations, as in orange-flavored analgesics for children, spray antiseptics, aerosol oven cleaners, liquid aspirin, mint-flavored laxatives, roll-on lipsticks, powdered deodorants, and travel-size packages of dentifrice.

To outflank competition or to carve out new segments, the ultimate in products must come from a policy of deliberate obsolescence. But this policy is applied reluctantly, and as a result, change is forced on companies by bold innovators, or by new competitors who have no vested interest to preserve. P&G changed the detergent industry with the introduction of Tide synthetic detergent in 1946, and thus widened the future of its own soap brands. Armstrong Cork Company entered the consumer field with a one-step floor cleaner and wax and had no compunctions about upsetting the established order. Gillette joined the stainless-steel razor blade fray to protect its enormous franchise; because it was less than enthusiastic about it, the firm also demonstrated the high cost of being late.[10]

Overseas Expansion

Not only can the definition of a business be product-based, saying, "We are in the railroad industry, not the transportation industry," or conceptual in foundation, believing, "The strength of our company lies in the skillful use of media of communication rather than in our experience in this or that segment of the food trade," but the definition may also be geographic. Therefore, the vision of a business can also be liberating in this respect. Most American companies have, until recently, regarded themselves as serving the American market. The foreign market was truly foreign to their thoughts.

In contrast, companies that have the vision to see both the vast potential of the foreign market for basic goods, and their own role in supplying it, have profited enormously. In the case of Colgate-Palmolive, for instance, while its headquarters happens to be in New York, its spirit is global. This self-image is reflected in its sales and profit story. Faced with savage competition in most of its markets in the United States, Colgate has pushed its business abroad. Thus, its 1952 foreign sales were 36 per cent of its worldwide total; by 1962 this ratio had risen to 51 per cent.

[10] Walter Guzzardi, Jr., "Gillette Faces the Stainless Steel Dragon," *Fortune* (July, 1963), p. 159ff.

But the profit contribution from abroad soared from 45 per cent of total earnings in 1952 to a whopping 89 per cent in 1962. True, Colgate's overseas divisions do not have to absorb any of the costs of product development and testing, all of which are borne by the U.S. division. Nonetheless, the disproportionate overseas profit role is eloquent testimony to the benefit of this liberating vision. Another kind of corporate vision is working here in providing the extra margin necessary to overcome cost differentials, tariff barriers, and so forth, permitting overseas business to become feasible.

Investment Philosophy

The packaged-goods world provides a sad, almost daily spectacle of products being sent into ferociously competitive markets by their loving . . . but niggardly parents. To prevent nearly certain slaughter, products, especially new ones, require continued substantial support. But again it takes a certain vision to see beyond the tendency to hold down on spending and seek as rapid as possible a return on investment. The vision includes a financial aspect in seeing the company as investor, not spender, and a temporal aspect in realizing that the company is going to be around for a long time and, if necessary, can wait for its money. It is surely going to have to wait longer as marketing rivalries intensify and greater resources are brought to bear. In the packaged-goods field, a realistic vision is frequently identified by three policies:

Heavy weight in advertising, sales promotion, merchandising, and distribution-building, particularly in the introductory phase

Substantial share of weight in whatever media and segment(s) one competes in

Prolongation of payout periods from a "traditional" three years to four or five years, where necessary, while maintaining a firm hold on future profit by sharp sales forecasting and margin control. (Obviously, this can't be done in fields where product life-cycles are growing shorter.)

To challenge so well established a brand as Listerine is a formidable undertaking. When Johnson & Johnson entered the market with Micrin, their investment in traceable advertising expenditures alone gave evidence of their awareness of these realities of the market place. Similarly, a deodorant brand of fairly recent vintage bought position by both heavy weight and deferment of profit taking to four and one-half years after launching. As the president of Alberto-Culver has observed, very heavy advertising appropriations build volume and market share to the point where, in that rarefied atmosphere where few marketers venture, the return becomes disproportionately higher than dollars invested, and the advertising-to-sales ratio actually drops.[11]

Distribution Breakthroughs

Almost as limiting in its effect on the vision of a business is being

[11] Leonard Lavin, in an address before the New York Marketing Executives Association, April, 1962; and Alberto-Culver's *1963 Annual Report*, p. 4.

wedded to a given distribution system. It is also almost as frequent a manifestation of marketing backwardness because the forces of inertia, tradition, and myopia all exert their pull in the same direction. Helene Curtis' acquiring Studio Girl and Bristol-Myers' acquiring Luzier to tap the rich house-to-house sales channel are positive examples. So, too, is Chock Full o' Nuts' signing up local licensees for door-to-door selling. Cosmetics lines nationally sold to main-line department stores and Class A drug stores that have now extended distribution to grocery stores are also cases in point. (Indeed, one must credit supermarkets more than manufacturers for breaking out of the traditional mold of being only food outlets and creating a vast enterprise in health and beauty aids and in packaged household necessities. Moreover, one must credit retailers in general for the positive effects of scrambled distribution in all manner of goods.) If a national beer brand were to franchise local brewers, taking a leaf from the book of the parent, soft drink companies, they would be acting on this principle.

Merger and Acquisition

The growing tide of mergers and acquisitions testifies to industry's awareness of the potential benefits of corporate marriages. Yet many curious matings raise questions about the vision of the corporations initiating them. This is not to argue against a most unlikely merger of a business whose vision is management talent for buying depressed situations and upgrading them or a business whose core is financial wizardry. But these are special circumstances. For most companies, mergers are a serious drain on manpower, time, and resources. Blind worship at the shrine of the Great God Diversification may hinder or arrest opportunities to blend the benefits of diversification with logical extensions of a business. Sound mergers take sound vision.

Chiclets are quite different from Bromo-Seltzer, Richard Hudnut Shampoo, Anahist, and DuBarry cosmetics, yet the purchase of American Chicle by Warner-Lambert marries dissimilar products with similar characteristics of packaging, rapid purchase-repurchase cycles, channels of merchandising, and advertising response. By the same principles, the subsequent merger of American Chicle with Smith Brothers cough drops is a further logical development of the Warner-Lambert vision.

The merger of Coca-Cola with Minute Maid and Duncan Coffee simultaneously with soft drink line extensions in different flavor categories with Sprite and Fanta and the low-calorie category with Tab represents the application of a two-fold vision of the business. One aspect of the vision has already been noted —an extraordinary distribution skill that Coca-Cola management can contribute to the acquired companies, though outside the bottler network, of course. The second is the definition of the firm as being not in the carbonated cola beverage field, nor even in the soft drink field, but rather in the refreshment business, or indeed, in the beverage business. To these instances of horizontal mergers can be added vertical ones, such as cosmetics companies acquiring chemical interests or, more frequently, chemical and ethical drug producers entering cosmetic and proprietary drug fields. Philip Morris has effected mergers in both directions—

horizontally with shaving cream and razor blades and vertically with Milprint.

Moreover, creativity and imagination in realizing a business' vision can lead to interesting symbiotic relationships. (Here I borrow the concept of symbiosis from biology where it refers to the living together of two dissimilar organisms in a mutually beneficial relationship.) International Breweries, for example, has undertaken to manufacture the product requirements of a small Cleveland brewer at one of International's own plants. The added volume will help amortize a goodly share of plant overhead and, at the same time, the Cleveland firm will become the distributor in that market for International's brands. The two companies remain independent while enjoying the benefits of a merger.

Iconoclasm

One of the hallmarks of practical application of a creative vision of a business is a willingness to depart from customary ways, to seek unorthodox solutions to orthodox problems. This iconoclasm runs as a common thread through the success stories of the period after World War II. Icon-breaking is necessary even in applying the most sophisticated marketing strategies. For example, it is by now axiomatic to concentrate on heavy users; yet this is not always the wisest strategy. In the wine industry, for example, a careful analysis of the characteristics of heavy users reveals a diverse assemblage of consumer segments. Marketing to each segment requires different tools and can be quite costly. Moreover, many confirmed users require only reminder advertising, but it is well worth promoting to the occasional user who can be cultivated to a greater frequency of usage.

To illustrate further, it is customary for national marketers to have advertising agencies serving them nationally. But Carling Breweries chose a quite different method to help bring the company from forty-ninth place to fourth place between 1950 and 1960. Reasoning that much of the beer business is local in character and competition, and that local advertising agencies are best suited to understand local circumstances, Carling worked up a network of eight local agencies, each of which serves the brewer in one of its marketing divisions, and is coordinated by the agency in the home city.

The advantages of marketing vision should be apparent. It is a mind-opening, horizon-stretching way of business life, keeping industries in the growth camp or converting them into growth situations. It fosters industry leadership, enabling companies to bypass competition and to manage change rather than to be managed by it. It helps decentralization to live up to its promise. Moreover, in providing a systematic framework for exploring new profit avenues, marketing vision is especially valuable in fields with built-in limitations. Some industries have trouble in new product development. Dentifrice manufacturers, for example, despite many efforts to give toothpaste companions in powder, liquid, and tablet forms, still find the paste in the collapsible tube owning the business. In their case, marketing vision found its practical expression in additives, including chlorophyll, antienzymes, hexachlorophene, and, most recently, the brilliantly successful fluoride development.

FIGURE 3: MULTIBRAND DEPLOYMENT OF
MARKETING STRATEGIES

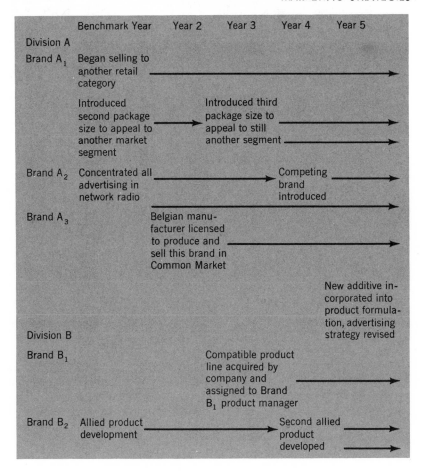

For another field, marketing vision might call for overseas expansion, diversification, or new distribution channels. But for each industry, for each company, for each division, and for each brand or line there is often one success factor that is more appropriate than any other. The utilization of these marketing weapons cannot be generalized. What works well for one business will not work for another; what works well for one set of competitive circumstances will not work for another. Also, what works well at one point in time will not work at another. On the other hand, in some situations, two or more strategies may be applicable concurrently. Thus, a chart depicting various strategies at work in a multi-division, multibrand company might present a most haphazard appearance and yet make sense for each unit and harmonize with overall corporate goals. To exemplify this point, Fig. 3 shows the strategies at work over a recent five-year period for some of the components of one company. Some of these strategies can be developed within a brand management group; others, for example the acquisitions, have been worked out by top management.

It should be evident that these marketing strategies *interlock*. Segmenting a market helps one to dominate it. Product change is often an essential for segmentation. Brand extensions can lead to new distribution channels. And, in the final analysis, all other strategies are end runs, and all break with the rhythm and style of the past. It is this systematic yet bold imposition of a fresh image of a business that provides insurance against decay and a foundation for growth.

11

The Soap Wars: A Strategic Analysis

SPENCER KLAW

Few secrets in American business are more closely guarded than the strategy and tactics of selling soap. It is no secret, of course, that advertising is the ammunition on which the big U.S. soap companies mainly rely in their perpetual wars with one another. Colgate-Palmolive, Lever Brothers, and Procter & Gamble, the three companies that make close to 85 percent of all the soap and synthetic-detergent products consumed in the U.S.—they also make some non-soap products, like shortening and toothpaste—spend approximately $250 million a year to advertise their wares. They spend an additional $150 million or so on sales promotion—e.g., on prize contests, price-off coupons, distributing free samples. But the broad strategies that underlie the firing of all this ammunition are ordinarily invisible to the neutral observer. Such reports as find their way into the pages of the trade press are inaccurate at worst and sketchy at best. One learns that detergent X, which Cleans Everything Washable, has been routed by detergent Y, a similar product that Cleans Like a White Tornado. The maneuvers that led to victory, the enemy weaknesses that were exploited, the cost of the victory, and its effect on the balance of power among the big soap companies—all these remain obscure.

Last January, however, the secrecy surrounding some of the great battles of recent years was at least partially dispelled. The occasion was the trial, in New York, of an antitrust case arising out of a 1957 deal in which

Reprinted with permission from *Fortune*, June, 1963, pp. 123ff.

Lever Brothers obtained from Monsanto Chemical the right to market a product called "All"—a laundry detergent of the variety known as low-sudser, that Monsanto had developed and had been selling in competition with the big soap companies. The government's contention was that the deal tended to lessen competition in the detergent business, and therefore violated Section 7 of the Clayton Act. At the trial Lever made two main arguments in opposing the government's demand that it divest itself of All. One was that All's sales had been falling off in 1957, and that Lever had actually served the cause of competition by taking the product over and marketing it more effectively than Monsanto could. The second argument was that Lever, having recently suffered a series of defeats at the hands of Procter & Gamble, needed a best-selling detergent like All if it was to remain a serious competitor in the laundry-products business.

These arguments evidently impressed the court, and several weeks ago the government's suit against Lever and Monsanto was dismissed. But the record of the trial will stand as a document of extraordinary interest. For days Lever executives testified in rich detail about the strategy of the soap-and-detergent business, and about the humiliations inflicted on them by Procter & Gamble. Moreover, at Lever's request—though over the strong protests of Procter & Gamble's chairman, former Defense Secretary Neil H. McElroy—the court forced P&G to reveal certain facts about *its* operations as well. These included figures showing how much P&G had spent to advertise and promote certain brands, and how much money it had made in certain years from the sale of its laundry soaps and detergents— information that the big soap companies often deny even to their own advertising agencies.

The trial dealt with only one class of soap products: so-called heavy-duty soaps and detergents that are used mainly for washing clothes. The big soap companies also sell toilet soap, shampoos, all-purpose liquid cleaners, light-duty liquid detergents for washing dishes and delicate fabrics, and other kinds of cleaning products. But the heavy-duty products are the heart of the soap business: of the five billion pounds of soap and detergents that Americans will consume this year, well over three billion pounds, costing about $900 million at retail, will be consumed in washing machines, and it is for the privilege of supplying the American housewife with laundry products that the big companies wage their most costly and bitter wars. Last winter's trial not only shed light on the way these wars are fought; it also made clear some of the reasons why they have so consistently been won in recent years by Procter & Gamble.

MIRACULOUS TIDE VS. NO-RINSE SURF

The balance of power among the big soap companies has, in fact, shifted radically in favor of P&G since World War II. The shift began with that company's introduction, in 1946, of a product called Tide, which was billed as a "revolutionary washday miracle." Tide was not a soap, but a synthetic detergent—i.e., it was made by chemical synthesis, not by the simple processing of animal fats. While there had been detergent powders on the market for years, Tide was the first one strong enough for washing clothes as well as dishes. It did such a good job, in fact, that before the end of 1949 one out of every four women was doing her laundry with Tide.

Confronted with this flight from old-fashioned soap powders, both Colgate and Lever Brothers hastily introduced heavy-duty detergents of their own. Colgate's was called Fab, and in time it sold moderately well. But Lever's entry, Surf, did such a mediocre washing job that it was withdrawn from the market. In 1949 a new, reformulated Surf was introduced, which was said to be so efficient that it obviated the need for rinsing clothes after they had been washed. This impressed housewives to such an extent that very soon Procter & Gamble advertisements were proclaiming that Tide, too, "washes clothes so miracle clean NO RINSING NEEDED." The claim was also appropriated by Colgate, and since Tide and Fab were available in almost every grocery store in the U.S., while Surf had up to then been introduced in only a few markets, almost all the benefits of the no-rinse story, as it was known in the trade, accrued to P&G and Colgate. Whether any benefit at all accrued to housewives is another question; the FTC insisted that rinsing *did* make clothes cleaner, even if they had been washed with a detergent, and eventually all three companies agreed not to make any further claims to the contrary.

By the end of 1953, according to evidence given at last winter's trial, about all that Lever had to show for six years of effort on behalf of Surf was a $24-million loss. The company was still bent on having a best-seller in the laundry-detergent field. But the feeling was strong, a Lever executive testified, that "we couldn't make that soufflé [i.e., Surf] come up for a second time," and so a decision was made to start over again and try promoting a new detergent called Rinso Blue instead. Lever's hopes for Rinso Blue were based in part on the results of blind tests, a procedure in which consumers are asked to try two different products, each in an unmarked box, and to say which one they prefer. While Surf appears not to have shown up too well in such tests, a Lever witness testified that housewives seemed to like Rinso Blue just as well as Tide, and even better than a second Procter & Gamble detergent called Cheer.

When one of the big soap companies launches a new product, it must, as a rule, commit itself to a huge outlay for advertising and promotion; otherwise, grocery stores are loath to stock the product. The amount of such investment spending, as it is called, is determined partly by the level of sales the new product is expected to reach after it has been on the market for a few months: the bigger the expected sales volume, of course, the bigger the investment that can be risked. Encouraged by Rinso Blue's showing in blind tests, Lever was confident that its sales would eventually hit at least $70 million a year, at which level the gross profits would amount to between $20 million and $25 million. On this assumption, the company felt justified in investing a very large sum—nearly $22 million— to get Rinso Blue into national distribution as quickly as possible.

When Rinso Blue reached the market, Procter & Gamble reacted with unexpected vigor. In the two areas where the new detergent was first placed on sale—the West Coast and the middle Atlantic states—P&G increased by hundreds of thousands of dollars its local advertising budget for Tide and Cheer. At the same time, it took other and more direct steps to neutralize any effect of Lever's introductory sales campaign. While Lever handed out millions of free sample packages of Rinso Blue, P&G handed out coupons good for the purchase, at reduced prices, of Tide and other P&G products. In Baltimore and Philadelphia, a Lever executive testified, P&G adopted the "highly unusual practice for them of delivering coupons on a door-to-door basis . . . they came in so hard and heavy that as our sampling crews were going up one side of the block, the Procter men were coming down the other side handing out the Tide coupons." P&G also used straight price-off deals to accomplish the classic defensive maneuver known as "loading the customer." Vast quantities of merchandise were put on sale at big price discounts, so that a woman who had tried her free sample of Rinso Blue, and had gone to the supermarket intending to buy a box, would be tempted to load up on Tide or Cheer instead.

Partly as a result of these countermeasures, by the end of 1955 Lever had lost more than $7 million on Rinso Blue, in addition to the $24 million it had already lost on Surf; and in those areas where the new detergent had been introduced, its sales had leveled out, not at 10 percent of the market for detergents, as Lever had hoped, but a little over 4 percent. The J. Walter Thompson agency, to which the Rinso Blue advertising account had just been shifted, studied the situation and reported gloomily that it was unlikely to improve. Tide and Cheer were so profitable, the agency pointed out, and P&G could therefore afford to spend so much money in their defense, that Lever would be able to achieve its sales goal for Rinso Blue only at a ruinous cost. Thompson underlined its conviction that Lever's situation was all but hopeless by gallantly proposing a 60 percent cut in the Rinso Blue advertising budget. The proposal was accepted, and Lever's executives did some painful thinking. "This led to the conclusion," the company's chairman, William H. Burkhart, testified last winter, "that we were facing apparently a hopeless task to get a real entry, a winner, into this field [and] we came to the conclusion that we would give up any further attempt to force our way into a winning position in the heavy-duty field."

The full dimensions of P&G's triumph and Lever's defeat emerged clearly at the trial. Before the war, the two companies had been fairly evenly matched in the laundry-soap business. But between 1940 and 1956, P&G's estimated share of the market rose from 34 percent to nearly 57 percent, while Lever's share fell from 30 percent to 17 percent. (Colgate's share was unchanged at approximately 11 percent.) This shift naturally had a profound effect on the earnings of the big soap companies. From 1951 through 1956, according to figures reluctantly provided by P&G, the sale of Tide and its other laundry soaps and detergents yielded profits totaling about a quarter of a billion dollars before taxes. In the same period, Lever and Colgate were *losing* money in the laundry-products field. P&G's net earnings nearly tripled in the postwar decade, rising to $59 million in 1956 on sales of just over $1 billion. Meanwhile, Colgate's earnings on its domestic business declined from $16 million in 1946 to $5 million ten years after. Lever's record was even worse: in the early 1950's the company barely broke even, and the $3 million that it earned in 1956, on sales of $282 million, was only about a third of what Lever had earned in a good prewar year.

THAT OLD BLUE MAGIC

While the Rinso Blue fiasco had impressed on Lever Brothers the folly of making frontal assaults on entrenched positions, the company's management did not intend simply to abandon the field to P&G. When Lever was given the opportunity to acquire All, and thereby to occupy an entrenched position of its own, it gladly seized the chance. Before turning, however, to the new series of battles into which Lever Brothers was plunged, it may be useful to consider in a general way the evolution of marketing strategy in the soap industry since World War II.

Probably no event in this period has more greatly influenced the strategy of the big companies than the successful launching by Procter & Gamble of its second heavy-duty detergent, Cheer. By 1950, four years after the introduction of Tide, Procter & Gamble had at least two good reasons for wanting to market another laundry detergent. One was that it might appeal to housewives who just didn't like Tide. The other was that it would get P&G a larger share of the limited shelf space in the grocery stores. Often the big soap companies contrive to get additional "facings" for a brand by bringing it out in a variety of different-sized packages. But Tide was already being sold in three sizes—regular, medium, and giant— and there was obviously not much more that could be done along this line.

Although Cheer was not a bad product—in cool water, for instance, it was considered by P&G to perform better in some ways than Tide—the company could not at first get women interested in buying it. Then it tried a scheme for giving Cheer a new and distinctive personality. Like other detergents on the market, Cheer contained an optical bleach—a dye, that is, that made clothes look very white in sunlight by causing them to reflect some of the sun's ultraviolet rays in the form of blue light. The scheme was to add blue coloring matter to Cheer, which had been sold up to then as a white powder, and to make a great point of the "blue whiteness" it imparted to shirts and sheets. This worked so well that by 1953 the new Cheer ("It's New! It's Blue! . . . *only* Cheer has the Blue-Magic Whitener!") was outselling every other brand of laundry soap or detergent except Tide.

IF IT ISN'T "NEW," IT'S "IMPROVED"

The success of Tide had shown the enormous benefits to be reaped from a basic improvement in a soap product. The lesson soap men drew from Cheer was that even what they call a "me-too product"—i.e., one essentially similar to others on the market—can be marketed successfully if it at least *looks* new and different. This discovery has led the big soap companies to put much less emphasis than they did before the war on devising new claims for old products—inventing BO, for example, and announcing that Lifebuoy would cure it, or suggesting that the way to avoid "undie odor" was to use Lux Flakes. The emphasis today is on making constant changes, often of a fairly superficial kind, in the products themselves.

Soap products are constantly being brought out in new colors and new forms, or at least in new containers. Light-duty liquid detergents have successively been marketed in bottles, in cans, and in plastic containers, and they are now sold in three different colors. P&G, for example, offers the housewife her choice of Creamy Pink Thrill, Ivory Liquid ("the gentle white detergent"), and New Sparkling Clear Joy. Elsewhere in the soap-products section, the shopper is confronted with a rich variety of laundry powders and laundry liquids; of all-purpose cleaners with ammonia, and all-purpose cleaners without ammonia; of toilet soaps that contain bacteriostatic additives, and toilet soaps that contain cold cream; of low-sudsers that are "condensed," and low-sudsers that are "fluffy"; of detergents that come in small, soluble packets, and detergents that come in the form of large tablets. Most items are labeled "New!" or "Improved!" As a Colgate executive observed recently, "If the package doesn't say 'New' these days, it better say 'Seven Cents off.' "

The fact that soap companies are putting more stress on product changes does not mean that they are putting any less stress these days on advertising. On the contrary, the rise of the self-service store has caused soap manufacturers to cut back on promotional efforts aimed at storekeepers, and to concentrate even more single-mindedly than in the past on selling the consumer directly. As a group, the big soap companies today spend more money on advertising, in proportion to their total sales, than they did twenty years ago; P&G salesmen are informed when they sign on with the company that "nearly one billion Procter & Gamble messages are delivered to the housewives of America each week."

It is hard to find new things to say about a soap product (apart from the fact that it is "new"), and as a result the advertising claims that are made on behalf of competing brands in any given category of products—e.g., laundry powders—tend to sound a lot alike. In 1953 the Chicago *Tribune* commissioned a study, by a firm called Social Research, Inc., of women's feelings about laundry soaps and detergents, and their feelings about the way these products were advertised. The resulting report listed a number of advertising slogans that were current at the time, and observed, "For a woman to learn to distinguish between product claims like these requires her to become a scholar in the subtle evaluation of textual difference . . . to decide whether a wash is whiter when it is 'whiter *without* a bleach' or when it is 'whiter *than* bleach.' " Most women, the report added, simply stop paying attention to the claims.

PURALIN PLUS AND NEW GERMASEPTIC DREFT

Since 1953, there have been some changes in soap advertising. Humor is in vogue, and soap commercials abound with humorous lady plumbers and humorous washing-machine repairmen; P&G even has a commercial featuring an Oriental houseboy, who says, "Lady know Joy not hurt pretty little hands . . . Joy mild as lotus blossom." But the specific advertising claims sound pretty much the same, and there is evidence that many women find them just as hard to sort out—and to take seriously—as ever. Oxydol "bleaches as it washes," New Super Suds offers "a *brighter* wash, a *whiter* wash than ever before," Dreft is "New Germaseptic Dreft," Cascade has Chloro-Sheen, Lifebuoy has Puralin Plus, Spic-and-Span contains Germ-Fite, Salvo is "the *fortified* detergent," Tide is "New Improved Tide," and offers "the cleanest, freshest smelling wash in Tide history," while Fab has "five extra launderatives" and produces "a wash that's not just detergent clean—but clean right through."

But whatever they think about such advertising claims, housewives seem to have a special confidence in detergents that *are* advertised. One evidence of this is the relatively poor sales record of private-label soaps and detergents. Private-label laundry detergents, which have been found by independent testing organizations to perform, in general, about as well as brands like Fab or Cheer or Tide or Rinso Blue, are now available in most supermarkets. But nine out of ten women prefer to buy a nationally advertised brand, even though it may cost them as much as 40 to 45 percent more.

The big soap companies themselves, it is true, frequently offer their own products at bargain prices. In a particular store, on a particular day, half a dozen different brands of soap products may be on sale in boxes prominently marked "Five Cents Off Regular Price!" Cents-off deals of this kind are initiated by the manufacturer, who offers retailers for a limited time a chance to buy a particular brand at a big price reduction if the retailer will agree to pass the saving on in full to his customers. But the fact that a soap company can resort to this maneuver again and again is in itself proof of the power of advertising, since it is on advertising that the manufacturer mainly relies to persuade housewives that the product they were offered at 27 cents a box last week is still a pretty good value now that it is back at its regular price of 32 cents.

If a new product is to be profitably marketed by one of the big soap companies, it must normally meet certain basic requirements. It must fill a real need—or one that can be demonstrated by advertising to be a real need—and it must work reasonably well. All together, the Big Three are now spending around $30 million a year on efforts to develop such products. In addition, a product must strike consumers as giving good value—although this does not necessarily mean that it must be sold at the same price as similar products already on the market. In 1959, for example, P&G introduced its liquid cleaner Mr. Clean in a twenty-eight-ounce bottle, and charged as much for it as the makers of Lestoil, a similar and very popular product, got for a thirty-two-ounce bottle. However, since Mr. Clean had some inherent advantages (unlike Lestoil, it was noninflammable), and since the Mr. Clean bottle was not only more conveniently shaped than the Lestoil bottle but was cleverly designed so that it looked just as big or even bigger, consumers overlooked the discrepancy, and within two years Mr. Clean was outselling Lestoil two to one.

MUDDYING THE TEST WATERS

But even if a product performs well and seems to offer a good value, it is impossible to tell a priori what the actual demand for it will be. Overestimating its potential sales can cost many millions of dollars, as Lever's experience with Rinso Blue demonstrated, and soap companies ordinarily test the market very carefully before launching a new brand. Colgate, for example, will spend over $16 million this year on market tests.

Putting a product on sale in a test market has one obvious risk, however. While the test may furnish a good line on the potential sales of the product, and on the amount of advertising and promotion that will be required to sustain that volume, it is very hard to keep this information secret. If Lever Brothers puts a new product on sale in, say, Grand Rapids, P&G and Colgate will be among the first to buy it. Often they will not only analyze the product in their laboratories, but try it out on consumer panels in blind tests. Furthermore, by keeping a close watch on what Lever is doing to advertise and promote the new product, and by auditing its sales in a few Grand Rapids grocery stores, Lever's rivals can learn almost as much as Lever does about the product's potentialities.

Actually, market tests in the soap business often more nearly resemble a poker game than a scientific experiment. When player A puts a new product on sale in a certain market, player B, who has a similar product already in national distribution, may raise the stakes—that is, he may triple his advertising of that product in the area where player A is making his test. This confronts player A with a difficult question: Does player B intend to triple his *national* advertising budget if player A puts his new product on sale nationally? Or is player B bluffing? He may only be engaged in what is commonly known as "muddying the test waters."

A classic demonstration of water-muddying was staged some years ago by the Toni Corp., then the leading producer of home-permanent preparations. When Colgate began a market test of a product called Lustre Creme Home Permanent, Toni launched a counteroffensive referred to, in intracompany memoranda, as Operation Snafu. Toni already had three home permanents on the market, Toni, Prom, and Bobbi; in addition to stepping up greatly its local advertising of all three of these brands, the company introduced a fourth brand, called Epic, in the cities Colgate had chosen for its test. The object was to scare Colgate off entirely or, failing that, to make Colgate underestimate the potential sales of its new product, and therefore to launch it with a relatively small advertising and promotion budget—which would, of course, make life easier for Toni. Whether or not Operation Snafu was the deciding factor, Colgate did in fact drop its plans to market Lustre Creme Permanent nationally.

WHY NOBODY WANTED ALL

When Lever Brothers acquired All in 1957, no market test was needed to find out if there was a big demand for it. All had been on the market for more than ten years, and recently it had been selling a lot better than either Rinso Blue or Surf. It was, in fact, outselling every other brand of packaged soap or detergent apart from Tide and Cheer and Colgate's Fab.

All's popularity was doubtless an irritation to the big soap companies. Although they expect stiff competition when marketing toiletry items like shampoos and home permanents, they have, for some forty years, almost completely dominated the market for basic soap products. The only important exception to this rule, apart from Monsanto's success with All, has been Armour's success in marketing Dial soap. For years, the Big Three did not consider the market for a high-priced deodorant soap like Dial big enough to be interesting. Then, when they realized their mistake, Armour was so solidly entrenched in the soap business that not even an all-out offensive by P&G, which is 1958 introduced a deodorant soap of its own, called Zest, was able to dislodge Dial more than temporarily from its position as the best-selling toilet soap on the market.

But if Armour has shown that the big soap companies can be beaten in their own territory, the story of Monsanto's venture shows how great are the dangers that threaten an invader. The history of All goes back to the early 1940's, soon after the development by Westinghouse of a device it called the Laundromat. The Laundromat was an automatic washing machine of the kind known as a front-loader, in which the clothes are washed by being tossed around in a revolving drum. In a washer of this type, the cleaning action is impeded by too many suds, and Westinghouse asked Monsanto if it could develop a synthetic detergent that would wash well without making a lot of foam. In 1945, Monsanto came up with a low-sudsing product, called Sterox, that did the trick, and began looking around for a company that would be interested in putting it on the market.

But very few automatic washers were in use as yet, and none of the companies first approached by Monsanto—they included all three of the big soap manufacturers—was interested in a product for which the demand would presumably be so limited. The deal that Monsanto finally made was with a new company called Detergents, Inc. It had been formed, with the encouragement of Westinghouse, for the specific purpose of buying Sterox in bulk from Monsanto and selling it to consumers under the trade name of All.

In 1946, when All first went on sale, many of the new automatic washers then coming onto the market were of the top-loading variety, in which the clothes were swished around by a mechanical agitator, or paddle. In most such machines there was no harm in having lots of suds; ordinary soap powders, or high-sudsing synthetic detergents like Tide, worked well in them, just as they did in old-fashioned nonautomatic washing machines. Detergents, Inc., however, promoted All as the ideal product to use in *any* automatic washer, not just in front-loaders, and as the number of automatics in use rose into the millions, sales of All grew rapidly. They grew so rapidly, in fact, that Detergents, Inc., soon had more business on its hands than it could cope with. The company had been formed with very little capital, and by 1951 it was strapped for working funds and heavily in debt to Monsanto. Monsanto decided it had better buy out the company's stockholders and market All itself.

For two years everything went beautifully. Then, in 1954, P&G introduced a low-sudsing detergent of its own, called Dash, and Colgate soon followed with a product called Ad. While Colgate's efforts on behalf of Ad were modest, Dash was launched with heavy expenditures for advertising and promotion. Some of the money spent by P&G went into tie-in deals with washing-machine manufacturers. Detergents, Inc., had hit on the notion of promoting All by persuading manufacturers of automatic washers to put a sample box of All in every machine they sold. P&G now offered the manufacturers large amounts of free advertising on its television programs if they would agree to stop packing All in their machines and pack P&G products instead. Specifically, P&G proposed to manufacturers of top-loading machines that they pack Tide, and to manufacturers of front-loaders that they pack Dash. By 1957, every manufacturer had deserted All and gone to Tide or Dash.

THE HORRIFYING AD BUDGET

At first, Monsanto tried slugging it out with P&G. In 1955 the company spent what Monsanto's chairman, Dr. Charles Allen Thomas, described at the trial as the "rather horrifying" sum of $12 million to advertise and promote All. But even so, sales fell off, and Monsanto's Consumer Products Division, which had been organized to market All, reported a $3-million loss for the year.

It was obvious that part of the difficulty arose from the fact that All was the only consumer product Monsanto had. There was talk of adding a conventional, high-sudsing detergent to the company's line. Nothing came of this, however, partly because the big soap companies were good customers of Monsanto—in 1956, they bought some $27 million worth of its phosphates and other chemicals—and the company's management was reluctant to antagonize them. Monsanto also considered buying the Clorox Corp., the largest U.S. producer of household bleach, but nothing came of this either. Monsanto's estimate was that it would take at least $22 million to buy Clorox, and Thomas testified that "being of technical background we thought it rather ridiculous to pay this much money for water to which some chlorine and caustic soda had been added."

Meanwhile, P&G's campaign was continuing to cut into the sales of All, and Monsanto soon concluded that the best thing to do was to sell off the All business before it was too late—that is, to turn the All trademark over to some company that could market the product successfully, and that would therefore be in the market for lots of Sterox. Talks were held with several companies, and for a time a deal with Armour seemed likely. But after several months negotiations broke down—mainly, it appears, over the question of how much Armour should pay for the Sterox.

Then, early in 1957, Monsanto approached Lever Brothers. Two years before, Lever had put a low-sudsing detergent of its own into test markets. But the product had been withdrawn in the face of complaints that it solidified when it was left standing too long, and Lever was delighted at the prospect of acquiring All. It was agreed that for five years Lever would buy the finished product (that is, Sterox) from Monsanto, and that during the same period it would buy an additional $80 million worth of Monsanto chemicals. Monsanto, congratulating itself on having withdrawn from the field in fairly good order and with no serious losses, handed the All trademark over to Lever.

"MAKES WHITE CLOTHES GREENER!"

At the trial Lever witnesses gave a number of explanations for Monsanto's unimpressive showing against P&G. They pointed out that Monsanto had been selling All through food brokers, and allocating 12 to 13 percent of the net sales receipts to direct selling expenses. By contrast, a Lever executive testified, his company (or P&G), having a big sales force of its own, was in a position to do a much better selling job for only about 3 percent of sales. Lever also argued that the ability to get volume discounts in buying network television time gave P&G a significant advantage that was not available to Monsanto. (For very big buyers, like P&G and Lever, these discounts amount to as much as 25 or 30 percent off the card rate.) Thomas Carroll, Lever's vice president of marketing, testified that Monsanto, partly because of inexperience, had in any case made a mistake by concentrating too much of its advertising in newspapers, where, he said, "the delivery of messages to homes is very expensive" compared to television.

Another cause of Monsanto's difficulties, Lever witnesses said, was that All had had some serious deficiencies as a product in the days when Monsanto was marketing it. According to tests made by Lever in 1957, a good many women didn't think it smelled as nice as Dash. More important, All had a tendency to cake, it sometimes left sandlike grains in the bottom of a washing machine, and in cities where the air was badly polluted it was apt to turn white shirts and sheets an apple-green color. "Dash was a superior product," Carroll testified. "It was being introduced with vast quantities of television advertising. . . . Their selling was good. They introduced it with sampling. They would go from door to door, and knock on the door, and ask a woman if she owned an automatic washing machine. And if she did they gave her a sample of Dash . . ." Carroll added, "They followed it up with couponing, price packs, and other very strong promotions. They had a sales force that numbered nearly a thousand men . . . and, in short, they were coming in and it was pretty clear that All was going to suffer the ravages of this warfare."

When Lever took over All, the tide of battle began to turn. The market for low-sudsing detergents was expanding rapidly, and between 1956 and 1959 Lever was able to increase All's sales from $30 million to $44 million. This was brought about, moreover, with an annual outlay for advertising and promotion amounting to only about half of what Monsanto had spent on All in 1955. As a result, profits on All rose to more that $8,500,000 (before taxes) in 1959.

This was the first decent piece of business Lever had done for many years in the laundry-products field. Since 1956, it is true, the company had been making around $4 million a year before taxes on the sale of its four conventional high-sudsing detergents. (Besides Rinso Blue and Surf, they included two other low-volume brands called Breeze and Silver Dust Blue.) But these profits had been made possible only by reducing advertising and promotional expenses so drastically that sales had begun to decline, and Lever's management was unhappily aware that the four brands were gradually being milked dry.

In 1960, Lever introduced "New *Active* All," which smelled nicer than the old All and didn't have the same tendency to cake or to turn shirts green. Up to this time, sales of Dash had been increasing even faster than sales of All. But in 1961, even though P&G appeared to be spending more money (figured on a dollars-per-case basis) to advertise and promote Dash than Lever was spending on All, the trend was reversed. For the first time since the introduction of Dash, its share of the market fell, while All's share rose. Lever's joy at this development was mingled with apprehension, however. A Lever executive recalled at the trial that "we, for once in our life, had a reversal of the classic position . . . and we were observing Procter & Gamble spending on a much higher per-case basis, and it was our conjecture as to just how long they would be willing to play this game . . ."

As it turned out, P&G had already thought up a new game. Lever and P&G had both been testing the market for a low-sudsing detergent to be sold in tablet form, and in 1961 both companies began to put their products into national distribution. P&G, however, appeared to be investing a lot more money in the introduction of its product, Salvo, than Lever felt it could afford to invest in Vim, its own low-sudsing tablet. It was obvious that Procter's strategy was to shift the battle of the low-sudsers to new ground, where Lever would not have the advantage of an entrenched position; by the end of last year, it was also obvious that the strategy was working. While Lever's Vim had captured only 8.5 percent of the total market for low-sudsing detergents, Procter's Salvo had captured 20 percent. Although Dash still lagged behind All, sales of Dash *plus* Salvo were running well ahead of sales of All plus Vim. P&G had thus succeeded, at last, in becoming the leader in the low-sudsing field.

While these facts were being recited to the court by a Lever witness, the trial judge, Archie O. Dawson, broke in impatiently at one point to ask what they all added up to. He added, "I can see that the witness is annoyed with Procter, there is a competitive feeling there, and all that, and this is the poor little boy with the rich relative or rich uncle who's got lots of money to spend, but what has that to do with this case?" In reply, Lever's principal trial attorney, William L. McGovern, said that he assumed the government would contend that Lever, in acquiring All, had acquired the power to lessen competition. He went on to say, "The purpose of this testimony, Your Honor, is to show that not only did we not lessen any competition, but with all of our own talents and skills and funds we have been scarcely able to keep our head above the water."

THE FRUITS OF VICTORY

It can be argued that P&G is not quite so irresistible a force as Lever Brothers made it out to be at the trial. Lever's toilet soaps—Lux, Lifebuoy, Dove, and Praise—have, for instance, been giving P&G's Ivory, Camay, and Zest a very good run for their money. And Colgate's Liquid Ajax has recently replaced P&G's Mr. Clean as the best-selling brand in the $100-million-a-year market for liquid cleaners.

But while P&G may lose now and then, its batting average is still very high. More than half of all the cleaning products sold in the U.S. are manufactured by P&G, and last year, as the following table shows, it made more than three times as much money as its two big competitors made between them; if foreign earnings are excluded, it made seven times as much:

	Net sales	Net income
Procter & Gamble		
Domestic and foreign	$1.619 billion	$109.3 million
Domestic only	N.A.	89.1 million
Lever Brothers	413 million	10.2 million
Colgate		
Domestic and foreign	673.8 million	22.9 million
Domestic only	327.3 million	2.4 million

These figures, coupled with some of the evidence given at last winter's trial, raise an interesting question: Why doesn't P&G go after an even bigger share of the soap-and-detergent business by cutting substantially the price of Tide and of its other heavy-duty detergents? Within the industry, P&G's restraint is sometimes attributed to fear of the Department of Justice's antitrust division. But P&G may well figure that it can make more money by keeping the price of its laundry detergents at a high enough level to assure a copious flow of profits, and by investing a portion of those profits in fields outside the soap-and-detergent business.

ANOTHER SECRET WEAPON: TOOTHPASTE

In any case, P&G in the past ten years has added to its product line such non-soap items as scouring powder, bleaches, facial and toilet tissue, peanut butter, and cake mixes. It has also added toothpaste, and sales of its two brands, Crest and Gleem, now account for almost half of all U.S.

toothpaste sales. Crest and Gleem have benefited P&G in two ways. Besides contributing handsomely to company profits, their success has cut into the profits that Lever and Colgate had been making in the toothpaste business, and has thereby deprived them of money they might have been able to use against P&G in the soap-and-detergent business.

As the evidence at last winter's trial demonstrated, to play the kind of game the big soap companies play takes a lot of money, and the fact that P&G has so much more money than its competitors has certainly been one important reason for its long winning streak. Ever since its early triumphs in the synthetic-detergent field, P&G has been able to invest the kind of money in the launching of a new product—Salvo, for example— that its rivals find it difficult to match.

But it is not just P&G's ability to outspend its rivals that makes it so formidable a competitor. The fact is that it is also an extremely well managed company. At various times since World War II both Lever and Colgate have had difficulty in finding capable top executives. By contrast, P&G's managers have been successful in recruiting and training successors as tough and able as they are themselves, with the same natural flair for poker, and the same willingness to play as a member of a big team. As P&G's president, Howard Morgens, has said, "Everything we do is created, adjusted, and tested by the team." This way of doing business is not everybody's dish of tea, but there is no doubt about the fact that it sells a lot of soap.

MARKETING ORGANIZATION

12

Interfaces
of a Product
Manager

DAVID J. LUCK
*Southern Illinois University
at Edwardsville*

The position of product manager was established over 40 years ago in a prominent marketing organization, that of Procter and Gamble. Despite this long history, scholarly research and writing have seemingly ignored the product management organization. Literature specifically treating product management organization is confined to perhaps three or four monographs or thin volumes which are largely descriptive.[1]

Does this obscurity imply that the product manager is a rare or unimportant functionary in modern business? Evidence points to the contrary. This writer's experience and that of other observers indicates that most large multiproduct companies have initiated the product management plan of organization.

Product managers operate on a horizontal plane, in contrast to the primarily vertical orientation of most marketing personnel. Their specialization is cross functional with primary focus on a specific product line or brand. They have numerous titles such as brand manager, product planning manager, or product marketing manager. These titles frequently denote varying emphases, but do not alter their basic responsibilities. The position of "product manager" is a radical departure in management

Reprinted with permission from *Journal of Marketing*, published by the American Marketing Association, October, 1969, pp. 32–36.

[1] The more thorough analyses of product manager's work are in: Gordon H. Evans, *The Product Manager's Job* (New York: American Management Association, 1964) and Gordon Medcalf, *Marketing and the Brand Manager* (London, England: Pergamon Press, Ltd., 1967).

that is not easily slotted into and absorbed by the existing organization. Consequently, it is not readily defined, staffed, and implemented.

OBJECTIVES OF THE PRODUCT MANAGER

Enthusiasts for product management have envisioned this position to be the answer to the needs of large enterprises to create true profit centers within the organization. This vision has proved generally impracticable.[2] Product managers are seriously hampered by ambiguity of authority in the execution of their plans and decisions, in addition to the problems of a new type of position asserting its intended role. Undefined authority precludes clear-cut, enforceable responsibility. Despite such problems, the main purposes of product managers are seemingly being accomplished. They are:

1. Creation and conceptualization of strategies for improving and marketing the assigned product line or brands.
2. Projection and determination of financial and operating plans for such products.
3. Monitoring execution and results of plans, with possible adaptation of tactics to evolving conditions.

An underlying role of the product manager is that of becoming the information center on the assigned products.

Product management provides integrated planning which is intimately related to the market needs and opportunities of specific products. This contrasts with decisions that formerly were diffused among functional specialists who could not bring to bear comprehensive knowledge and analysis of factors peculiar to a product. The establishment of interfaces between product manager and these functional specialists is necessary in order to insure acquisition of the variety of information which these specialists can contribute. Simultaneously, the product manager needs to maintain interfaces with the functional personnel who execute the strategies and plans that he originates.

This leads us to the product managers as vital organizational loci for the focus of marketing interfaces. The subject of these interfaces and the means whereby they may be efficiently realized thus merits our serious concern.

INTERFACES VITAL TO PRODUCT MANAGERS

Research information obtained during studies of 17 product managers in the course of an advertising decision study[3] and during a current study

2 David J. Luck and Theodore Nowak, "Product Management: Vision Unfilled," *Harvard Business Review*, Vol. 43 (May, 1965), pp. 143–150.

3 This study under sponsorship of the Marketing Science Institute contributed to the volume: P. J. Robinson and D. J. Luck, *Promotional Decision Making* (New York: McGraw-Hill Book Company, 1964).

of eight product managers for pharmaceutical manufacturers indicates that the interfaces which are important to a product manager's work are perhaps the most numerous and varied of any in middle management. They may be placed in the following six categories.

The Buying Public

In ultimate significance to marketing strategy and planning, the buyers and users of the particular product line overshadow all other interfaces. The man who is to conceive product and promotion strategies and prepare competitively viable plans can hardly be too well apprised of how, when, and for what purposes the product is bought and used. Market segments with unique needs may be identified and are often the clue to very effective strategies. Brand images, brand loyalties, consumer profiles, and the reception of advertising and sales promotion campaigns are further examples of the vast information the experienced product manager acquires and studies as he appraises the past and explores future possibilities.

Distributors

Wholesalers and retailers play major roles in the market success of products which they distribute. Relatively small shifts in shelf facings, out-of-stocks, displays, and other dealer support may produce favorable or dangerous trends. A significant portion of the product distribution strategy may be aimed at the distributors themselves to stimulate and maintain their interests through special programs, sales aids, and other trade promotion. Often the product manager's concern includes monitoring the inventories in the pipelines in order to control production rates.

Sales Force

The salesman is a necessary ally of the product manager, although often a very independent one. For most industrial products and for some consumer products, personal selling is the principal force in promoting the product. Since the salesman is frequently selling many products of the firm, product managers often compete with one another in seeking the salesman's support. Product managers are most concerned with the development of selling methods, sales aids, and applications literature. For industrial products, the product manager often makes sales calls with the salesman, particularly where technical expertise is needed.

Advertising Agencies

The degree of involvement with advertising agencies varies widely among product managers. For most industrial products it is of less concern than the sales force. In some consumer goods organizations, product managers are limited by policy to working with the agencies only to the extent of developing advertising strategies, with all other liaison conducted through advertising departments. At the other extreme, there are companies which place virtually all collaborations with the agencies in the hands of product managers. Typically a consumer goods product manager works intimately and continuously with his counterparts in the agency—a relationship that has received some criticism where inexperienced product managers have been troublesome to agencies.[4] Regardless of such views, agency account men tend to work as a team with product managers of major advertisers in developing advertising campaigns and in providing market information and merchandising ideas to the client.

Product Development

The product manager's involvement with new product development is dependent on the firm's organizational structure, the nature of the product itself, and the background of the manager. Where there is a separately designated manager for new products, the managers of current products are usually confined to planning modifications in existing products and packaging. With new products that can be designed relatively quickly, the product manager may maintain a close relationship with all stages of their development; in cases requiring prolonged research and development, product managers tend to have little contact with the emerging products until a market testing stage approaches. Another factor is that, typically, industrial products managers are technically trained and oriented, while the contrary is true in consumer goods. The former naturally have more frequent interface with research and development.

Marketing Research

In their roles of originating and formulating marketing plans and of monitoring the progress and obstacles of products, product managers require substantial marketing research information. Typically, they depend heavily on marketing research personnel to obtain and process this information. Within the enterprise, a marketing researcher may be the closest collaborator with a product manager.

Other Marketing and Corporate Personnel

The product manager's superior within the organization represents the interface most critical to the manager's personal career. Regardless of the superior's title, which will vary from firm to firm, this superior will usually bear the responsibility for marketing planning of a division or corporation. Very commonly these men are themselves former product managers and a high level of empathy tends to exist between these men, as the superior strives to develop the analytical and decision powers of his product managers.

[4] In *Management and Advertising Problems* (New York: Association of National Advertisers, 1965) this problem is discussed on page 53. The study reported in this volume, however, later affirmed the continuous growth of product management, but in more effective relationships with advertising agencies. (p. 92.)

When a product manager interprets his position broadly, he may have many intra-firm interfaces. For example, Scott Paper Company's diagram of its product manager relationships depicts up to 17 interfaces with other departments in the company and its advertising agency, not including the higher management line of responsibility.

SIGNIFICANCE OF PRODUCT MANAGEMENT INTERFACES

One may assert that product managers' interfaces are exceedingly important to effective marketing, at the same time acknowledging the value of involving other corporate personnel. The much more numerous confrontations of salesmen with buyers might be considered of primary importance; yet these are relatively routine and remote from marketing strategy and policy. High echelon marketing executives' interfaces, both internal and external, are quite important since the more comprehensive and far-reaching decisions on goals, allocations, and programs are reached at that level. Regardless, product managers' interfaces are of high importance from each of three viewpoints.

Product Manager Viewpoint

Position descriptions for product managers are aptly couched in terms of "formulating" or "originating" product plans and strategies, or centralizing" information about assigned products. A man placed in a conceptual and informational hub of the organization must personally be an intelligence headquarters. To maintain competitive position and profit of his products, with his performance starkly exposed to higher management, he must strive to be the best informed man about any aspect substantially affecting their future. He must arrange and nurture a number of information interfaces to achieve his functions.

The verb "coordinate" is often and aptly used to describe how a product manager should execute his "responsibilities." His interfaces are used to enthuse others about his plans and to obtain their concurrence and action. To a substantial degree, his success depends upon his effectiveness in motivating others to implement his plans without direct organizational authority.

The Firm's Viewpoint

The properly functioning product manager is the firm's main intelligence center for its product lines. Much more than a repository, he is an action center at which all strategy and plans for his product lines converge. A large company cannot rely on higher executives, functional middle managers, or committees to become sufficiently informed about the situation and opportunities facing an individual product line. Higher executives and committees should be well briefed in order to integrate various product managers' recommendations and make allocations fairly to each program; however, they cannot possess the depth of understanding and analysis of each product manager.

A General Marketing Viewpoint

The marketing institution viewpoint and the consumer or user viewpoint, taken broadly, should coincide in seeking what Paul Mazur considered marketing's goal to deliver a standard of living. This can be accomplished only when marketing interfaces with its buying publics as fully and intelligently as possible. The potential for effectively realizing this goal is enhanced when the information focus and the marketing strategy focus are centered within one position in the firm. This position ideally is that of a product manager who can devote all his powers and attention to his assigned product area. The man who serves as a gatekeeper in the firm at the spot where market needs and opportunities meet the firm's capabilities, objectives, and strategies, is most critical from a socially-aware marketing viewpoint.

OBSTACLES

While the number of interfaces realized by product managers may be adequate, the quality of these relationships tends to fall seriously short of the ideal. Product managers should be of gregarious nature, ready and anxious to meet others, and typically they are. Establishing a wide network of contacts is thus not overly difficult. The deficiency tends to arise from the failure of the product manager to develop the most productive associations in depth. Causes underlying this failure might include the following:

1. Preoccupation with trivial and distracting tasks. Many product managers find their time burdened with correspondence with salesmen and customers about minor problems and adjustments. Many allow themselves to become expediters of deliveries, and of the production and distribution of promotional literature.
2. Lack of assistance. This tends to prevent a product manager from allocating time to the interfaces which are most important. Most product managers have no help beyond a secretary (and some share secretaries). Some have trainees who are only temporary help before being elevated into full production managerships. More companies are providing assistant product managers, but there has not been general recognition of the need.
3. Lack of cooperation with functional departments. This may result in the functional department either passing along to the product manager tasks that the functional department should assume, or conversely, encroaching on the decision sphere of a product manager by making decisions that are rightly his. At the extreme, a functional department may actually balk at cooperating in carrying out product plans.
4. Lack of well-conceived formal position descriptions. Where they exist, such descriptions either tend to assign the product manager too broad a responsibility, or list his duties in unrealistic detail. The interfaces implied for the manager may be too many and too unsystematic to be efficient. Sometimes the number of products and brands assigned a manager are excessive. In one case, for example, the author found a product manager responsible for 17 distinct nationally advertised products.
5. Restriction of the product manager to a single brand or type of a product

with no supplemental participation regarding new products serving the same needs. While specific brand managers are needed where a single brand sells in enormous volume, product managers should not be excluded from the dynamics of product improvement and innovation.

6. Inadequate scheduling of available time. A specific set of priorities should be established and periodically reviewed, particularly for the novice product manager.

7. Inadequate training of product managers. Because the demands of the position are more varied than those of most other middle management jobs, training of product managers is relatively more important. Unfortunately many product managers learn under loose supervision or by trial and error. If each product manager kept explicit records of his planning and decision analyses and of the ensuing results, others could profit from this store of experience. This training technique, however, is often overlooked.

8. Short job tenure. The median in consumer products is about two years. The period is usually somewhat longer for industrial products managers. One product line, aggregating over $20,000,000 annual sales, was observed to have had three product managers in four years. In addition, new product managers appear to have little communication with their predecessors, although they are still working in the company.

9. Last, but very important, is the excessive number of interfaces that most product managers attempt, particularly intra-company. The product manager should be selective in the interfaces he establishes. This positions him to concentrate on decoding and analyzing the inputs he receives from these especially strategic linkages, and where necessary, to direct his communications skills towards them.

SOME RECOMMENDATIONS

There appears to be a gradual shift in the positioning, functioning, and training of product managers as firms which utilize this approach gain experience. The writer has identified four dimensions of development which may promote effective interfacing by product managers.

1. Realignment of product managers' assignments toward a market orientation. The typical assignment is in terms of a particular product or products, and the concentration is on promoting their sales. The result can be a myopic vision of the market in terms of the given product. A more balanced and progressive view is likely when this manager is assigned a specific market or product-use area, in which he works to improve market penetration through innovation while simultaneously formulating the optimal strategy and marketing mix to increase the profitability of his existing products. This should result in a systematic market/product development while also accentuating the entirety of the market interface. Further, involvement with a homogeneous market may be less confusing for the product manager than a strict product alignment which often involves dealing with the heterogeneous uses and markets that a single product may serve.

2. Provision of an improved atmosphere for the serious study by product managers of markets and alternative strategies in product, pricing, promotion, and distribution. Some companies do provide sufficient privacy and, on a smaller scale, some seek to limit the many tasks and other distractions in order to provide product management with adequate time for marketing planning.

FIGURE 1: INTERFACES OF A PRODUCT MANAGER

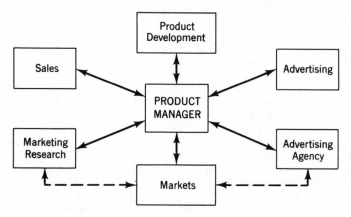

3. Restrictions of the interfaces attempted by product managers to the few that are most productive. This avoids the superficial contacts and fragmentary communications that are much too common. It is suggested that a consumer goods product manager restrict himself within the interfaces shown in Figure 1 and concentrate on those itemized below.

> Marketing research
> Advertising agency
> The market (dealers and buyers)
> Sales management
> Advertising management
> Product development

His relationships should be conducted primarily through one liaison in the four named departments and the advertising agency. This is increasingly common with the market research interface, the chief and constant aid of many product managers. It is further suggested that the time saved by reducing intra-company communication be devoted to more personal interface with markets.

4. Development of complete and realistic job descriptions accompanied by more specific performance evaluation criteria. In addition to removing much of the vagueness that contributes to inefficient product manager work, this would relieve personal frustration and direct the manager's efforts, including those related to interfacing within and outside the firm. In providing a solid basis for extensive job training and manpower development, this procedure can make a long-range contribution to the product manager concept.

CONCLUSION

Product managers are surely here to stay, for it appears that no other organizational arrangement so well promotes efficient marketing planning in the spirit of the marketing concept. Clear recognition of the fundamental role that effective interfaces play, both within the firm and with the external publics who shape the firm's destiny, will be a long first step to realization of the profit potential of the product manager system.

THE MARKETING INFORMATION SYSTEM

13

Reassessing
Marketing Information
Systems

MALCOLM MCNIVEN AND BOB D. HILTON
Coca-Cola Company

Until very recently, it would have been sheer heresy for a management scientist or "up-to-date" businessman to refute or doubt the many claims being made for computerized information systems.

There is mounting evidence that this is no longer true. An article in a recent issue of *Fortune* described the progress that has been made in setting up management information systems in business. It states that "Many corporations are waking up to the fact that they were oversold (on MIS). Now they recognize that the most important business decisions cannot be reduced to neat mathematical terms."

A recent survey by the Research Institute of America of some 2,500 companies disclosed that only half the companies with in-house computers could give an unqualified "yes" to the question of whether they were paying off, and only 28 per cent believed that the machines were doing a good job. According to the survey, the majority of computer users felt they were too precipitous in acquiring their machines.

Roy Ash, president of Litton Industries, contends, "Business has gone through a stage in which it was popular to consider it as a science. Now it is increasingly regarded as an art. For there are no absolute answers, and if there are no answers, how can it be a science?"

In another article entitled "Management Misinformation Systems,"

Reprinted with permission from the *Journal of Advertising Research,* Copyright Advertising Research Foundation (1970).

Professor Russell Ackoff, one of the leading proponents of management information systems, speaks frankly of the weaknesses of existing systems. He says: "Contrary to the impression produced by the growing literature, few computerized management information systems have been put into operation. Of those that I have seen which have been implemented, most have not matched expectations and some have been outright failures."

Other leading figures in the field of management science have expressed disappointment and dismay and, in some cases, indignation at the lack of progress made in implementing computerized decision systems in American business. A distributor of automotive parts recently won a court suit against a division of IBM for failure to fulfill contract obligations in setting up a computerized control system. He was promised an exception-reporting system but he got only stacks of computer printouts and even they were late.

There has been a surprising growth in the use of case study methods in business schools around the world. Those teaching methods, which present judgmental situations with which a businessman may be faced, may be returning to their previous position of strength in the curriculum of some business schools in place of more quantitative techniques.

What does all of this mean? Have we had our fling with computers, with decision theory, and with mathematical models? Have we finally found the type of problems that computers cannot solve? Does the future of executive decision-making lie in well-trained intuition gained from years of experience in the business?

Certainly not! There is no turning back in the rapid development of information systems. It does mean, however, that management is beginning to recover from the dazed shock of having the computer age thrust into its midst. It also means there is a definite need for reassessment of the promise and the reality of management information systems in today's business world.

There is little doubt that decision-making problems in business are much more difficult than originally perceived. In addition, decision-making procedures developed by businesses over the years are not necessarily the best or most efficient procedures. And to try describing these procedures in mathematical terms for the computer is not the answer.

It has become necessary to revise the entire manner in which decisions are made and, in some cases, to change the way a company does business in order to realize the full power of modern management science techniques. To restructure a business in this sense is truly a monumental problem.

A more specific problem is that hardware progress has out-paced that of software, personnel, or concepts. A high percentage of third generation 360's are still operating using 1401 or comparable second generation concepts. Although computers are expensive, only 20 per cent of present computer systems' cost is in hardware. The other 80 per cent is for keypunchers, operators, programmers and other personnel.

Human problems are the key stumbling block in resourceful use of the computer. Programming is still an art. No two programmers would solve a problem the same way; therefore, there are few standards of performance. Good programmers do not necessarily make good systems analysts. Good systems analysts may not make good managers. Management people often tend to regard analysts as either mere technicians or threats to their position. They are unwilling to spend adequate time with the analyst to devise a good system. Equipment manufacturers provide numerous courses for programmers, and it takes only months to train them; however, few courses exist for systems designers, and it may take several years before they are fully competent. This shortage will limit the development of MIS more than any other single factor.

One of the greatest areas of disillusionment has been in marketing. Marketing information systems have not developed as expected. This failure is due to several causes. Marketing decisions as a class are more difficult to model than other business decisions. Many of the methods that have been developed for modeling these decisions don't seem to work when checked with real world results, and it is very hard to measure them. All of these factors together have brought about a series of unproductive attempts to develop marketing information systems, and failure to produce has led to skepticism on the part of marketing management. They (perhaps more so than any other area of business) have continued to rely on traditional, though inefficient, means of decision making.

Presently, marketing systems are made up of six distinct areas of effort, all of which are necessary to some degree.

These are: (1) classification, (2) measurement, (3) analysis, (4) reporting systems, (5) information retrieval systems, and (6) decision models. The last three identify major areas or kinds of systems; the first three are more traditional marketing research areas, and they affect the quality of the overall system's effort (see Figure 1).

The first requirement in a marketing information system is a *Classification* scheme, or a taxonomy of marketing elements. These are carefully selected structural building blocks, or standard units, that make the

FIGURE 1:

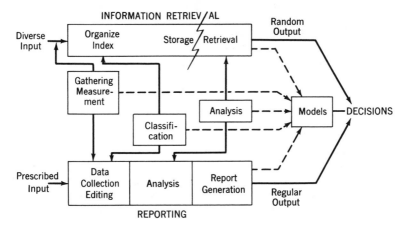

creation of integrated systems possible. They provide important guidelines for operations and reduce the need for programming change and data modification.

One should clearly distinguish between the problem of identification and classification. People, in general, can be "classified" by blood type, whereas they are "identified" by a unique social security number.

Identification coding schemes, such as customer numbering, are tending toward being unique "nonsignificant" numbers. These are grouped and linked together where needed by separate modifiable linking systems. Furthermore, classification should not be integrated within the identification code. For example, all too often the first or last digit of a customer number has some meaning, such as big or little customer, chain or nonchain.

The approach to both these problems is essentially the same, and certainly there is some overlap. A recommended approach is:

1. Identify the important areas of classification and identification (A, B, C, D, etc.). For example, outlet identification, product identification, outlet description, or package description.
2. Within each identification area
   a. determine the maximum size code required.
   b. determine the needs for this code (e.g., billing, sales reporting) and support these needs with a good linking system.
3. Within each classification area delineate the mutually exclusive dimensions, if any (B_1, B_2, B_3, etc.). For example:

B_{1-n} = Outlet description (classification area)
B_1 = Primary business function (dimension)
B_2 = Proprietorship/ownership and control (dimension)
B_3 = Product class handled (dimension)
B_4 = Primary type of consumer service (dimension), etc.

4. Within each classification area dimension, specify a list of terms and associated codes. In dimensions where a single or primary term is required of each classification unit, care must be taken to avoid overlap. For example:

B_1 Primary business function (dimension)
   21 Full-line grocery
   22 Specialty food store
   31 Movie theater (indoor)
   32 Movie theater (outdoor), etc.

In those dimensions where combinations are possible, provide for them. For example:

B_3 Product class handled (dimension)
   1 Soft drinks
   2 Coffee/tea
   3 Soft drinks/coffee/tea

The outcome of this approach is that, within each classification area, any unit to be classified *fully* must be categorized in each of the mutually exclusive dimensions of that classification area. Of course, it will not always be feasible or even desirable to classify a unit (e.g., an outlet) by a given area of classification (e.g., outlet description). Furthermore, even if it is desirable to describe an outlet by certain dimensions (e.g., primary business function), data on other dimensions (e.g., product class handled) may be excluded or ignored. The point is that a standard taxonomy should exist for use where applicable.

The second area is called *Measurement,* or data gathering systems. This area figures heavily in the traditional idea of marketing research. It includes all kinds of sales data, outlet data, consumer surveys, store auditing data, and various testing procedures which are used to measure changes in the marketing environment.

Most market researchers and analysts are aware of the current level of knowledge on measurement factors. A great deal has been written and taught about the pros and cons, what to measure, and how best to measure it. Generally, though, these measures can be divided into two categories: (1) monitoring and (2) problem solving. The monitoring activity refers to measurements regularly taken of basic elements in the marketing systems (for example, sales or advertising awareness) in hopes that they will alert management to problems that exist. The most common marketing reports are merely regular summaries of monitoring measurements. In some companies, marketing information systems are limited to this type of information.

Problem solving procedures are an attempt to develop specific information or measures related to a specific problem that is facing a marketing manager at that time. These measurements are obtained for that specific purpose.

The third area is *Analysis,* and a great deal of progress is being made here. The capabilities of the computer now allow us to use many statistical techniques which have been around for some time but which have not really been feasible due to the large amount of computation required. These include multivariate techniques such as multiregression, factor analysis, and a variety of other techniques which are described in modern textbooks. Most of these statistical and operations research analysis methods are available in the form of several software packages, and they allow detailed inferences from marketing data. The techniques also permit a reduction of massive data down to a few important conclusions. These data reduction techniques must be built into any marketing information system since they reduce the information to a manageable set with which the manager can cope.

So far we've been talking about merely systematizing our information, and being systematic is not being scientific. Science is an attempt to find causal relationships between variables. Once these relationships are established, so that one can make very accurate predictions, it usually can be considered a law or a theory. Many laws of marketing are yet to be discovered, and the best way to set about finding these laws is to undertake a series of controlled measurement studies. (CMS).

In order to conduct CMS, certain marketing variables like advertising, promotions, and price can be manipulated, and the effects of dependent variables, such as sales, profits, or perhaps attitudinal responses, can be observed.

It is surprising that the CMS still has not been widely accepted in the field of marketing. Generally, it is felt that the marketing environment is much too changeable to study these relationships. However, these studies have been done quite successfully by many companies over the last ten years (duPont, Ford, Anheuser-Busch, USDA). It is important to embody a CMS program in any marketing information system.

The most widely used CMS method uses the retail outlet as the measurement unit where certain variables are manipulated within the store. The movement of the product through the store is measured and related to changes in the experimental variable.

For example, a CMS of different package designs was conducted to determine which sold more products. A rational design was used with all test packages appearing at the same time in each outlet. In addition to the three test packages, a control package was included. Therefore, four groups of outlets and four time periods were used. The sales and cost indices are shown in Table 1.

TABLE 1:

Package	Sales Index	Cost Index
1	151	114
2	149	116
3	135	112
Control	100	100

In this case, the higher sales index for package 1, coupled with the slightly higher cost, made package 1 generally the most profitable.

Another CMS technique, with an entire market as a measurement unit, is used when the variables being tested cannot be studied in a retail outlet (e.g., advertising distribution). The variable of interest is changed from market-to-market in a planned way using one of a variety of experimental designs available for this purpose. The response measure is usually some form of sales measurement (e.g., market share change, actual unit sales), and this is compared across markets to estimate the effect of the experimental variable.

The relationships between marketing variables and sales must be measured or estimated if efficient allocation of resources is to be accomplished by a marketing manager. For example, he must know which media are providing the most in sales response to his advertising if he is to allocate funds rationally to these media. This is also true when allocating funds among marketing variables such as advertising, promotion, sales effort, distribution, etc. A CMS program produces information about these relationships which are used as input for marketing models.

REPORTING SYSTEMS

The first of three major areas of Marketing Information Systems is *Reporting Systems*. These are the systems which can easily be thought of as having a beginning, middle, and end. In the beginning, prescribed data are gathered from one or many sources. In the middle, it is processed in a prescribed way. Finally, some prescribed output is emitted. This output may be produced periodically or upon request.

Three points can be made about reporting systems.

First, they should be designed with the user in mind. That is, each management person has a particular form in which he likes to receive information. It may be in charts; it may be in tables of numbers; it may be in written narrative. But whatever the form, output of a reporting system should be designed to help the user interpret it quickly and readily.

Second, it should be as brief as possible. Computers can produce enormous quantities of information very rapidly. This has scared many management people away from making requests because they only receive a huge stack of computer printouts. Exception reporting systems are, of course, a solution to this problem, but they also leave something to be desired since business people want to be able to see everything that is happening, not just those things that the computer selects out for them to see. In this case, an exception reporting system should be backed up by a good on-request program. Then if management wants something other than exceptions, it is available upon request.

Third, the type of reporting system is unlikely to be real-time or on-line reporting. There has been a great deal said about real-time output, instant reporting, and conversational mode. This can only be accomplished by utilizing huge storage capabilities in computers and with a great deal of complex programming. In most cases, it turns out to be unfeasible at the present stage of development. It also has become apparent that most top management people prefer to have someone else talk with the computer. In spite of this, real-time reporting systems will still be the most useful marketing information system for middle management in the near future.

The second of the three major areas is *Information Retrieval Systems*. The distinction for this type of system is neither in the media format, such as documents or microfilm, nor even in the type of information input or output. The distinction is in the type of function it is expected to perform.

The function of an information retrieval system is to accept isolated and significant items of information from many sources and organize, index, and store these data, and to disseminate logical sets of information later upon inquiry from requestors.

NATURAL CLEAVAGE

The marketing information void existing because of the lack of efficient information retrieval systems is astonishing. For example, what per cent of the documents normally passing over an executive's desk are prescribed output from reporting systems compared to the vast amount of other documents, reports, etc.? The latter are potential input to an information retrieval data base, but because there has been no really efficient information retrieval system, this segment of the decision-making process has been effectively programmed out of the pattern. So a typical "rational" decision might be made without even considering related past data or experience.

There is a natural *cleavage* in all information retrieval systems that is not found in other types of systems. This cleavage is between the storage and the output. The human mind acts as an information retrieval system. It gathers information from whatever the source, stores it, and later uses part or all of this knowledge to fulfill some random, unanticipated demand.

It is true that most information retrieval systems to date are non-computer systems. However, this is changing. Many existing computer systems are at least quasi-information retrieval systems. Incidentally, the multidimensional nature of the marketing activity makes this type of system highly desirable.

Within the last few years, information retrieval systems have undergone a revolution with the rise of microfilm, computers, telecommunications, the Uniterm principle, etc. The old versions of files based on subject classification schemes are, or should be, a thing of the past.

For example, the systems currently being built within The Coca-Cola Company utilize the Uniterm or concept-coordination principle. This idea is applicable to any size file from that of an individual to that of a major marketing or technical information center, such as are being built within The Coca-Cola Company.

The basic principle is very simple. The units of information used in the system are called Uniterms. These terms, usually individual words selected directly from the document being indexed, are key words that are descriptive of ideas or concepts embodied in the documents. Although Uniterms are usually single words, they may also be simple combinations of words; and they may even be proper names, dates, or numbers.

FIGURE 2: CONCEPT COORDINATION

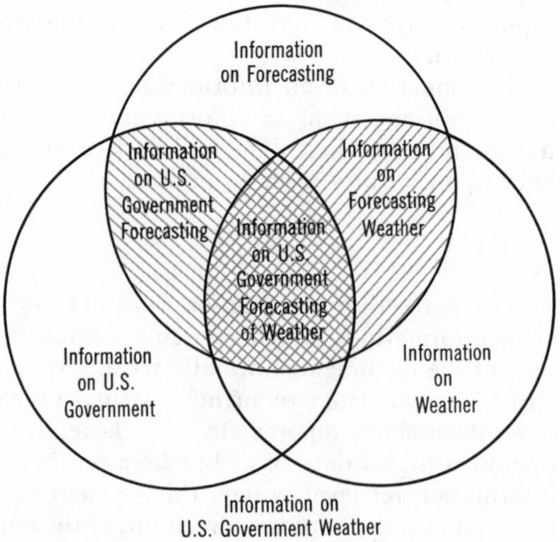

Information on
U.S. Government Weather

Each Uniterm is typed on a separate card, which is then placed in alphabetical order in the card file. A document number (serial) is assigned to each report or document as it is added to the collection. The document number is recorded on all Uniterm cards that pertain to that document.

Typical Uniterms are "plastic," "sleep," "budgeting," and "oxidation." The Uniterm card, "oxidation," for example, contains the document numbers of all documents that pertain to oxidation.

The terms chosen are considered "concepts," and the system operates on the principle of "concept-coordination."

The operation of the system may be illustrated by the following example. Suppose we wish to retrieve all reports that apply to the subject, "U.S. Government Forecasting of Weather." The words, or Uniterms, are "U.S. Government," "Forecasting," and "Weather."

The principle of the search, concept-coordination, is illustrated in Figure 2.

In actual operation, there would be three cards headed "U.S. Government," "Forecasting," and "Weather," respectively. The numerals at the top of each card represent the last digit in the document number. Listing in this manner facilitates comparison of the numbers in the columns on the cards as they are examined for common document numbers. The document number of each report pertaining to these three Uniterms

FIGURE 3: U.S. GOVERNMENT

0	1	2	3	4	5	6	7	8	9
90	41	22	33	104	75	46	57	98	109
370	101	592	103	1194	115	716	157	478	219
	291	1022	493	1574	875	986	307	888	839
	1101	2502	2003		1025	1136	1317	1208	1009
			3203			1446			

FORECASTING

0	1	2	3	4	5	6	7	8	9
370	21	52	73	104	115	56	57	148	109
890	131	1002	953	794	225	286	497	328	789
1300	291	1852	1193	1194	525	816	1197	888	1179
	301	2502	2113	2564	1015	1126	2317	918	1909
	3221		2213	2964	2205		2447		2349
				3004					

WEATHER

0	1	2	3	4	5	6	7	8	9
120	21	702	113	104	15	76	17	88	219
890	131	1492	813	504	125	186	147	178	309
	291	1852	1123	784	305	326	237	528	809
	401	2502	2213	1004	1055	786	1027	888	1019
				2014	2035			1128	

Document numbers 291, 2502, 104, and 888 are found on all three cards. These four documents, therefore, all pertain to U.S. Government, Forecasting or Weather.

would be posted on each card as the report is received. The three cards might then appear as illustrated in Figure 3.

A mechanical version of this system using punched holes in plastic cards is being used within The Coca-Cola Company and is operational and inexpensive to install.

In addition, within Coca-Cola USA's Marketing Intelligence Center, the push is heavily in the direction of microfilm. Over one-half million frames can be stored in a single drawer. Any document can be located on film in a minute or two, and if desired, a hard copy can be made. In addition, with the use of microfiche, one can obtain a postcard-sized duplicate containing as many as 72 pages of data which never has to be returned. Simple, cheap readers are utilized for reading documents.

The most promising and least developed of the six major areas of marketing information systems is *Decision Models*. A model is a mathematical description of the marketing decision-making process which serves as a structure within which marketing information is used. This is an area which has provided the most disillusionment in marketing since much has been promised and little delivered. Nevertheless, models must be built, however crude, to serve as guides to the marketing information required for marketing decisions.

Following is one example of a marketing model that has recently been developed. The purpose of the model is to allocate funds to advertising. It was developed by Management Division Systems of Lincoln, Mass., and it is available on time-sharing terminals. It uses a conversational mode, and a representative problem is shown in Figures 4 and 5. The output is shown in Figure 6. In between, the computer asks a number of questions of the user, and he must provide certain input.

This model, although general, can be made directly applicable to a company's marketing problems, and, over time, it evolves into a far more specific model relating directly to those factors that are important to a company's business. As these models become part of a brand manager's operating procedure, they allow him to start developing a control procedure. As he develops more and more experience with the model, he will be refining the estimates of the effects of different marketing variables. This, in turn, will allow the model to predict the effects of his actions much more accurately.

This brings up a concept called "Adaptive Control Systems," developed by J. D. C. Little, whereby a marketing model is used as a guiding structure, and the relationships among the marketing variables in the model are continuously modified by the results of controlled-measurement studies. The model is always moving closer and closer to a representation of reality as the CMS provide improved input. In this way, the marketing research functions and the computer systems are wedded to produce better estimates of the effects of marketing strategies. These models are crucial and must exist in some form at the early stages of the development of a sophisticated marketing information system.

In building decision models of marketing decisions, it is of utmost importance to realize the existence of directive informational needs, as

FIGURE 4: TRACE OF A USER PUTTING INPUT DATA FOR GROOVY INTO THE COMPUTER

ADBUDG II–A MULTIPERIOD ADVERTISING BUDGETING MODEL
1 COMPUTER ASKS QUESTIONS IN STANDARD FORM
2 COMPUTER ASKS QUESTIONS IN SHORT FORM
ANS-1

1 ENTER NEW DATA
2 USE SAVED DATA
ANS-1

BRAND NAME: GROOVY

NO. OF TIME PERIODS (MAX-8): 4

LENGTH OF PERIOD: QUARTER

NAME OF FIRST PERIOD: 1ST 69

GEOGRAPHIC AREA: US

BRAND DATA FOR REFERENCE CASE. TWO CONSECUTIVE PERIODS, CALLED A & B, WITH SEASONALITY, TREND, OR OTHER NON-ADV. EFFECT REMOVED

MARKET SHARE IN PERIOD A (% OF UNITS): 1.86
ADVERTISING RATE IN PERIOD A (DOLLARS/PERIOD): 486000

MARKET SHARE IN PERIOD B IF ADVERTISING REDUCED TO ZERO IN PERIOD B: 1.77

MARKET SHARE IN PERIOD B IF ADV INCREASED TO SATURATION IN PERIOD B: 2.25

MARKET SHARE IN PERIOD B IF ADV IN PERIOD B INCREASED 50% OVER PERIOD A: 1.95

MARKET SHARE IN LONG RUN IF ADV REDUCED TO ZERO: ?

INDEX OF MEDIA EFFICIENCY (E.G. AVERAGE EFFICIENCY–1.0): 1.0

INDEX OF COPY EFFECTIVENESS (E.G. AVERAGE COPY–1.0): 1.0

UNITS IN WHICH SALES ARE TO BE MEASURED
(TO BE USED FOR BOTH BRAND AND PRODUCT CLASS.
E.G., POUNDS, GALLONS, CASES, THOUSANDS OF DOLLARS, ETC.): HOGSHEADS

CONTRIBUTION PROFIT (EXCLUSIVE OF ADV EXPENSE) EXPRESSED IN DOLLARS/SALES UNIT: .68

AVERAGE BRAND PRICE (DOLLARS/SALES UNIT): 1.812

OTHER BRAND DATA

MARKET SHARE AT START OF PERIOD 1: 1.86

PRODUCT CLASS DATA FOR REFERENCE CASE. TWO CONSECUTIVE TIME PERIODS, A & B WITH SEASONALITY, TREND AND OTHER NON-ADV EFFECTS REMOVED.

NAME OF PRODUCT CLASS: TREACLE

PRODUCT CLASS SALES RATE IN PERIOD A
(UNITS/PERIOD): 290000000

CONSIDER RESPONSE TO PRODUCT CLASS ADV ? NO

AVERAGE PRICE FOR PRODUCT CLASS (DOLLARS/SALES UNIT) : 1.86
TIME VARYING DATA. IF TIME VARIATION NOT SPECIFIED, REFERENCE DATA WILL BE COPIED INTO ALL PERIODS.

PRODUCT CLASS SALES RATE HAS SEASONAL OR OTHER NON-ADV TIME EFFECT ? YES

INDEX OF PRODUCT CLASS SALES (REFERENCE CASE—1.00) FOR PERIOD:
1: .943
2: 1.012
3: 1.065
4: .959

BRAND SHARE HAS A NON-ADV TIME EFFECT ? YES

INDEX OF NON-ADV EFFECTS (REFERENCE CASE—1.00) FOR PERIOD
1: 1.0
2: 1.03
3: 1.0
4: 1.0

MEDIA EFFICIENCY VARIES ? NO

COPY EFFICIENCY VARIES ? NO

CONTRIBUTION VARIES ? NO

AVERAGE BRAND PRICE VARIES ? NO

AVERAGE PRICE FOR PRODUCT VARIES ? NO

BRAND ADV RATE VARIES ? YES

BRAND ADV (DOLLARS/UNIT) IN PERIOD
1: 486000
2: 606000
3: 876000
4: 414000

1 SAVE DATA
2 PRINT DATA
3 CHANGE DATA
4 OUTPUT
5 RESTART
ANS-1
DATA FILE   NAME: GROOVY-69

well as rational informational needs. This means that certain components of a decision-making model must be variable, depending upon the individual who is currently the decision-maker. Since the manager is the key element in the decision-making system, the system should be modeled for him and consider his style of decision-making.

In order to build and use marketing models, a better understanding is needed of the decision-making process. Quantitative decision theory, as it exists today, has very little to do with methods used by managers in making decisions, and it may be worthwhile to consider some of the points made in psychological studies of decision-making.

When a manager is in a decision-making situation, he is trying to obtain information for two purposes: First, information is sought which will help him identify and select the alternative that best meets his decision criteria; second, after having made the decision, he will seek out information to support the decision he has made. His motivation to obtain information is a function of the degree of uncertainty he has in a situation, as well as the importance of the decision that is being made. Of course, individuals differ widely in their levels of uncertainty in a given

FIGURE 6: OUTPUT FOR GROOVY BRAND FOR THE INPUT

#			1	2	3	4
1	OUTPUT FOR		GROOVY			
2	PERIOD LENGTH:		QUARTER			
3	STARTING PERIOD:		1ST 69			
4	AREA:		US			
5	SALES UNIT:		HOGSHEADS			
6	DATA FROM FILE:		/GROOVY–69/			
8	PERIOD		1	2	3	4
9	MARKET SHARE: (% OF UNITS)		1.860	1.961	2.043	2.009
10	PROD. CLASS SALES (UNITS/PER)		273M	293M	309M	278M
11	PROD. CLASS SALES (DOL/PER)		514M	552M	581M	523M
12	BRAND SALES (UNITS/PER)		5.09M	5.76M	6.31M	5.59M
13	BRAND SALES (DOL/PER)		9.22M	10.4M	11.4M	10.1M
14	CONTRIBUTION (DOL/PER)	3.46	3.91M	4.29M	3.80M	
15	BRAND ADV (DOL/PER)	.486M	.606M	.876M	.414M	
16	CONT. AFTER ADV (DOL/PER)	2.97M	3.31M	3.41M	3.39M	
17	CUMULATIVE CONT. AFTER ADV	2.97M	6.28M	9.70M	13.1M	
23	SLOPE	1.634	1.169	.241	.379	
24	BRAND DECAY CONSTANT	.048				
26	BRAND ADV. EXPONENT	2.357				
27	BRAND DEN. CONSTANT	4.333				

decision situation and in their ability to select an alternative, given the appropriate information. Once the decision-maker is motivated to acquire information, then his preference for a source of information is directly related to the uncertainty-reducing properties of that source.

Sources of information generally reduce uncertainty with two kinds of information—either directive information or rational information. Directive information is that type of information which will directly reduce the uncertainty in the situation due to past experience with the source. This may be called irrational or unconscious evaluation of the information source. For instance, women continue to seek the advice of their mothers when making purchases; a government official seeks the opinion of high status university figures; or a businessman uses a consultant as an information source.

Rational information represents that which ought to be considered in making a rational decision—that is, the type of information that we usually include or should include in our decision-making models. There is a great deal of difference between the decisions which might be made based on the information provided by a directive source or a rational source. Generally, directive information incurs less cost and effort than rational information. Because of this and emotional reasons, there is generally a bias in favor of directive information.

Managers' perceived informational needs are evolving rapidly, and as they change, the types of information systems to support them must change. This has resulted in a revolutionary process in the resulting information systems area which has caused some controversy.

There is a logical explanation of why business is in an unsatisfactory position with regard to marketing information systems. The explanation has to do with the inter-relationship between managers' perceived information needs and actual fulfillment of those needs. It also concerns the unusually large amount of skilled manpower required to develop new information systems. Perhaps the following will clarify the situation.

Reporting systems have been around for some time. They are also the easiest to develop. Figure 7 shows that, although most reporting systems take less time to develop than either information retrieval systems or

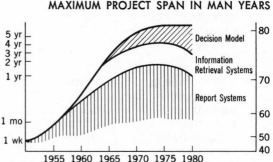

FIGURE 7: INFORMATION SYSTEM DEVELOPMENT
MAXIMUM PROJECT SPAN IN MAN YEARS

FIGURE 8: TYPE OF SYSTEMS OUTPUT AND NEEDS

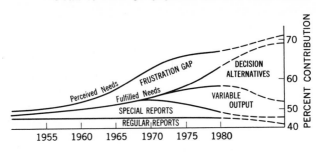

models, the average time for development is still increasing and perhaps will for awhile longer. The reason is the increasing complexity and degree of integration required as a company's systems expand. As a general rule, all types of systems are becoming more complex and time-consuming to develop. However, for any one class of systems, the software support, etc., finally reach a point of efficiency and use to enable the developmental time-curve to actually turn down. For example, much of the sorting, selecting, ranking, cross-taping, etc., normally required in reporting systems can be routinely handled by built-in utility features.

Figure 8 is a pictorial representation of how the specific outputs will change and vary in the relative contribution to management needs over time.

Gradually, the switch will be away from periodic reports into the area of special or exception reporting. This switch is attributable primarily to more sophisticated reporting systems. However, as information retrieval systems begin to come into their own, a new type of random open-end inquiry will be possible, and this is represented by "variable output." Finally, with the utilization of better models, the output will become more intelligent or decision-oriented.

The overstatements on one hand and the problems that have been pointed out on the other hand have widened the gap between perceived needs and fulfilled needs. This is demonstrated by the "fulfilled needs" line in Figure 8, which represents the sum of the output currently available to the manager. The "perceived needs" line represents the manager's desire for information based on the promises and dreams of computer manufacturers and management scientists. As it can be seen, the frustration gap is at its widest point in 1970–1975, but narrows after that as systems design and programming begin to be implemented. As management reassesses the situation and as software and personnel begin to catch up with hardware, this gap should narrow.

The evolution of types of systems in Figure 7 and the evolution of types of output to management in Figure 8 are, of course, directly related as shown in Figure 9. Growing information needs have not been satisfied due to the extensive effort being placed on the development of new reporting systems and a beginning of information retrieval systems. These new systems are not yet operational, except in a few isolated instances (e.g.,

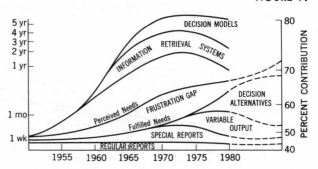

airline and hotel reservation systems). Of course, the frustration gap will continue to be large as management's perceived needs continue to grow faster than the systems' development and increased output.

Marketing information systems have been seriously oversold to marketing management, and most attempts at setting up sophisticated systems have not performed as expected.

Still, a great deal of progress has been made in understanding the problems of marketing and how they should be supported by marketing information. It is possible at this time to set up an interim marketing information system which will be helpful and compatible with future systems when operational.

In summary, a marketing information system which can be implemented at the present time should include the following:

(1) Standard classification of elements, (2) marketing measurement, (3) analytical packages, (4) information retrieval systems, (5) reporting systems, and (6) simple marketing models.

In each of the above areas, there have been significant changes in technology in the last year which make a marketing information system more feasible and efficient.

However, interaction of management information requirements and system planning capability has produced a frustration gap which is not likely to be reduced in the near future.

A general conclusion one can reach is that there is a good deal to be done by most companies to improve their marketing information systems quickly, with a minimum of expenditure. This will not put them into the wonderland of futuristic systems, but it will give them a good, solid base on which to build for the future. In order to achieve this, professional people, either outside or inside the company, must be used extensively to make some of those critical decisions regarding equipment and systems, which can either send the company on the right path for future development or send them down the wrong path to frustration and loss of faith on the part of management.

It is time to stop living in the world of delusion regarding marketing information systems and come back to reality. But then, reality isn't all that bad.

14

Why Business
Is Spending Millions
to Learn How Customers Behave

BUSINESS WEEK

Say you are a manufacturer of perfume. It's a president's business to look ahead. If you take your job seriously—and assume that your subordinates will do the same—there are three fundamental questions that you need to answer:

1. What will women want to smell like five years from now?
2. How much will they be willing to spend to make themselves glamorous—and who besides the perfumers will be competing for a share of that spending?
3. What sort of retail outlets will be doing the bulk of perfume sales? Department stores? Discount houses? Drug stores? Suburban shopping centers? Downtown salons?

These are pertinent questions but broad ones. The brand managers of the different perfumes you sell will have questions of a different sort to answer. Each will want to know:

1. This square bottle my scent comes in—what does it convey to the customer? Is it exotic? Tweedy? Expensive? Sexy? Would we be better off with something slinky in swirls and gold leaf?
2. When do most of my sales take place? I advertise my stuff as a light summer scent, but most of the orders seem to come in around Christmas. Is that the time to be talking about creamy shoulders and drugged summer nights?
3. Would retailers push the brand harder if I sweetened the deal; increased the cooperative advertising allowance, or just gave the clerks more push money?

Reprinted with permission from *Business Week*, April 18, 1964, pp. 90ff.

If you have 12 brands that means your brand managers have 36 questions among them. Add your own three, and like the Church of England with the historic 39 Articles of Religion on which it is founded, you have an equal number of points on which you must take a stand. Unlike the Church of England, however, you cannot take your 39 points as a matter of faith.

So at this stage you buy yourself some market research.

THE FINDER OUTERS

It is you and several thousand manufacturers and marketers like you who have made market research an established part of the U.S. business scene. There are about as many definitions of market research as there are active market researchers today, but they all have one thing in common: Market research is the arm of marketing that finds out things and thereby lays the basis for marketing strategy.

It is concerned with the facts of what people buy, when they buy, where they buy, why they buy.

Altogether, U.S. business spends something more than $200 million a year to support this question-asking. That doesn't seem like much when you compare it with a total of $246 billion retail sales annually. And even the $200 million figure drags in a number of purely statistical, figure-juggling functions, on analysis of warehouse reports, for instance, that have to be assigned to somebody's budget, so why not to the marketing department?

Nevertheless, the market researchers feel that the future is all on their side. The rough and tumble of today's competition makes old-fashioned seat-of-the-pants marketing prohibitively expensive. The unprecedented outpouring of new products in search of a market can make it not only expensive but a breeder of red ink.

The pace at which new products move onto the market is breathtaking. Within a few months, a company such as General Electric may put on store shelves or in dealer showrooms (1) an electric knife, (2) a new 11-in. TV set, (3) an improved caulking compound for sealing windows, and (4) a "self-cleaning" electric oven priced at $575. On a single day, Bristol-Myers Co. offered the American consumer three new products—Score hair cream, Ban cream deodorant, Softique bath oil.

It's a costly process at best. In a two-year introductory period, it can take something like $10 million—not counting development expenses—to put into retail distribution a product retailing for just 49 cents. If the product fails, that's money down the drain.

Yet today four out of five new products fail after launching.

It's to forestall such expensive failures that so many companies have turned to market research. As yet, it's not a bandwagon rush—though you'll find it some places where you might least expect it—and the lure of market research varies from industry to industry.

New York's Seventh Avenue either tests its fashions by inviting buyers to town and waiting for orders, or goes direct to the public. Cosmetics manufacturers don't yet do much market research, but their use of it is growing along with their advertising budgets. All the big food companies, on the other hand, have taken it up as routine procedure—as well they might, since any product on the average supermarket shelf competes with some 6,500 others to get into the housewife's cart.

Detroit is something of a special case. The auto companies run elaborate research programs, but they make up their minds on styling according to their own peculiar logic, which usually revolves around the idea of continuity of design from one year to the next and the continuation of an already defined styling trend. Necessarily the auto stylists have to go on their own judgment, since a $2,500 automobile is hardly an item that can easily be put into text markets—when it's a question of styling, not something radically new like Chrysler's gas turbine engine.

On such matters as what kind of transportation the public will buy— economy, luxury, sport, family, suburban—marketing research has been used heavily by Detroit. General Motor's market research section, which jumped its research budget 75% since 1959, and which does most of its work at the behest of the company's top-level distribution committee, has contributed greatly to the notable success of the divisions in recent years.

It's no accident that Chevrolet's four successive nameplate introductions, from Corvette to Chevelle, have hit their market niche just right— and without taking sales away from the standard, and more profitable, Chevrolet.

For the companies that use market research it is already a way of life; they take it for granted that someday everyone will have to do the same. A big outfit like Procter & Gamble Co., the grand panjandrum of consumer goods selling, will put as much as $4 million a year into its own research and spend another $2 million on outside advice. A smaller marketer will shoot $12,000 a year just to get a report every 60 days on how its product is selling.

As management's purse strings loosen, more and more companies are joining this trend toward serious use of marketing research. A new survey of the field by the American Marketing Association offers some evidence of this dramatic growth:

1. In the five years since AMA's last study, 502 companies responding to the questionnaire formed market research departments. That's more than in the 10 preceding years from 1948 to 1957 combined.
2. Industry's outlay in the field is climbing. The mean annual expenditure for marketing research among consumer goods manufacturers nearly doubled in the five-year period—to $265,000. Four spent more than $1.7 million each. Among industrial goods makers, annual expenditure went up 44%, to $75,000.

As the market research expert finds more takers for his services, his confidence grows. He talks less and less in terms of modest fact-finding. More and more his vision expands to broad "information systems" that can be integrated into day-to-day management.

The market researcher's ambitions reach not only outward but upward. Today, he is not only answering broader and broader marketing questions; he is also taking a hand in framing the questions. He is not bashful, either, about suggesting the conclusions that should be drawn from his findings.

Thus, he is rapidly promoting himself, or being promoted by force of circumstances, to a place in management itself.

The top dog in market research today is the consultant—either on or off the payroll—who frames a theory of marketing, checks it out, pretests it, and watches as it is put into effect. Such a man cannot be classed as a mere technician. He is a strategist, and he is not content with a subordinate role.

WHO DOES WHAT IN THE FACT FACTORIES

The industry that serves the developing corporate appetite for market research is a fragmented affair, an industry of small businesses with only one sizable focus. The 300 or so companies and firms that make up its roster range from tiny (half a dozen employees) to large (5,000 employees). Most of the outfits grew up around a single, strong personality with a dominating idea, and most still retain the personal touch.

Their job is finding out things for marketers—and since there are so many pertinent things to find out and so many possible methods of doing it, it's not surprising that the industry is so split up.

Nor is it surprising that the biggest operator of them all is the one that performs the simplest and most basic function—keeping track of what goods are sold and where. This is the cornerstone of the business—the elemental, indispensable information that any marketer of fast-moving goods must have.

The company that purveys it is A.C. Nielsen Co. of Chicago. Its $45 million annual volume is nearly six times that of its nearest competitor, and a big hunk of the industry's $200 million-plus a year.

Aside from its much-publicized broadcast measurement services—a relatively small part of its business—Nielsen offers a series of so-called Retail Indexes. The two largest measure the movement of goods in food stores and drug outlets though Nielsen also pokes into appliance stores, camera retailers, and, most recently, discounters.

To represent the nation's food retailers, Nielsen uses a sample of 1,600 stores including units of every major grocery chain save A&P, which has always declined to co-operate. Teams of Nielsen field men are constantly in one store or another—counting packages on the shelf and cases in the back room, examining delivery invoices, noting special displays, cents-off deals, two-for-one offers, shelf prices.

Naturally, they count only products of Nielsen clients. Since these include all the top 50 food concerns, they count nearly everything in foods but meat and produce plus a heaping handful of beauty and health aids, such as toothpaste and aspirin.

Every 60 days Nielsen reports. Early in May its account executives will stream out to marketing headquarters of clients, armed with charts and tables of the audit period ended April 15.

In sessions averaging two hours, they will lay out a wealth of data: total inventory of a product as of April 1; February and March sales and cases moved into retail stores during those months; distribution of a product broken down several ways—the maximum number of stores stocking it on date of audit and the number of stores stocking it analyzed by size. Clients get the same kind of information on competing products, lumped together or specified by name, as they wish.

The least you can spend on all this is about $12,000 a year, for a regional report covering about 25% of the national market. Cost for a national marketer averages $50,000 per "subject"—Nielsen's jargon for a single product group. A manufacturer of cold cereals buys one subject; if he wants data on hot cereals, too, that's another subject, and another $50,000. Prices vary as much as $20,000 up or down, depending on the data wanted; and a 10% discount for two or more subjects sweetens things for the multi-line producers.

That's the basic tab; on top of it the extras can really pile up. You can get monthly reports, data analyzed by as many as 20 sales territories, price and package-size differential studies on the effects of pricing under competitors or offering three package sizes instead of one—and so on until the annual tab per subject reaches $100,000. There are clients who shell out $2 million a year on retail indexes alone, before they even start on broadcast measurement.

If Nielsen's reports are the bread and butter of market research, Audits & Surveys Co., Inc., one of its rising competitors, offers bread and butter with a little jam—or perhaps, some say, just margarine. It depends partly on your taste in figures.

Founded by statistician Solomon Dutka with a little money borrowed from his former boss Elmo Roper, A&S has rocketed in 10 years to No. 2 spot in the industry, with close to $8-million a year.

Its technique is to draw up a probability sample of business blocks in cities around the country and audit every store in these blocks. It counts by type of goods, not type of store, thus can pick up sales of razor blades, say, in candy, tobacco, and hardware stores and discount houses as well as in drug stores and supermarkets. This not only gives you a better reading on how goods are selling, Dutka argues, but also tells you how patterns of distribution are shifting.

The actual data clients get from the A&S sample of 5,300 stores are much the same as what Nielsen provides. The A&S service, however, is considerably less expensive. Where Nielsen's charges vary by size of client and number of brands reported, A&S charges a flat fee for each category, but sets a different price for each class. A good average figure is about $35,000 each. Extras can bring it up to $40,000.

Obviously, with such similar services, Nielsen and A&S have few clients in common. Yet, though Gillette Co. is a Nielsen client of long standing, its Paper Mate Div. uses A&S—because of the variety of outlets for pens.

Some find the Nielsen service too costly, or its reporting not broad enough for their distribution. Others criticize the A&S master sample.

Nielsen's sample, heavily weighted toward large chain supermarkets, concentrates on the outlets that produce the high volume; so it gives reliable results for relatively small geographical areas as well as nationally. Critics say the A&S sample lacks this flexibility; if you want the sales of hair spray in a three-state Midwestern area, it may not pick up enough sales volume for an accurate reading.

To get around some of this A&S will over-sample in some market areas where requested. This seems to satisfy clients, because the list is large—and growing.

THE PANEL SHOW

Both Nielsen and A&S confine their counting to retail stores. Other market researchers prefer to count the customers. They do this, of course, by setting up a consumer panel consisting of a group of households, and keeping tabs on what these households buy and when they buy it.

The biggest panel operator, Market Research Corp. of America, uses the mails to keep track of 7,500 families every week. Each family submits a detailed diary of purchases in a broad range of product categories—food, household supplies, drugs, toiletries, and, most recently, textiles and clothing.

For a monthly report, and even more detailed quarterly summaries, MRCA gets anywhere from $25,000 to $60,000 a year per product class. It costs more for a product that's bought every week rather than once a month, more for a class with eight heavily competing brands, half a dozen sizes, and five flavors than for one with two or three brands.

What you get from MRCA looks on the surface much the same as what you get from Nielsen—total sales, share of market nationally and regionally. But the two-thirds of Nielsen's clients who also subscribe to MRCA obviously find something different. A panel taps a dimension of information unavailable to a store audit.

MRCA reports, for example, whether purchases are evenly distributed over the market or concentrated among a relatively small group, the economic level of purchasers, the amount of brand-switching. To a heavy user of advertising, it's apparent that this helps him pinpoint the kind of people who use his product—or are likely to—and to allocate his advertising dollars to the media that reach them best.

But an extra dimension can be tricky. The experts approach panel research with a grain of salt, because it depends on busy housewives remembering to put down everything in a diary and mail it in. A 5% gain or loss in share of market is phenomenal for packaged goods; but a diary sample can be subject to statistical variations up to 20%. When the sample error exceeds the fluctuation being measured, watch out.

The simple facts of who buys how much of what are basic; but to predict which way the customers will jump next you need to know why they make their decisions. If you can't quite rely on the customers themselves to tell you accurately, then what?

HEAD-SHRINKING

That's where the psychologists and sociologists of marketing research rush in, with their bag of clinical tricks with fancy names—projective techniques, depth interviews, semantic differential scales. They operate on the frontier of marketing knowledge, and turn up odd but often useful information.

Take the experience of the Nestle Co., which makes the little semi-sweet chocolate bits that go into toll-house, or chocolate-larded cookies. Nestle proposed to use some bitmaking capacity by fashioning bits of unsweetened chocolate and selling them for baking—so women wouldn't have to break up baking chocolate to melt it.

A little deep-dish research into women's attitudes disclosed that what they objected to wasn't the breaking up but the whole mess of melting. So a semiliquid baking chocolate is in the test markets.

Most of the techniques these researchers apply so assiduously stem, in one form or another, from pioneer work in academic psychology. The "depth interviewing" techniques, in which an individual is allowed to talk himself out for hours, without checklists or leading questions, is basically the tool of the psychoanalysts. People talk about how they feel: What do they think of when smoking? What kind of people do they think smoke cigarettes with filters?

Recently, a tobacco company commissioned just such a study among physicians. The aim: to find out what doctors really think about cigarette smoking and how hard they intend to push patients to give it up.

The so-called projective techniques are lifted intact from diagnostic clinical psychology. One—the semantic differential method—hands the subject a scale of words from good-to-bad, weak-to-masterful, lets him grade his feelings accordingly. This helps researchers measure subtle differences in thinking.

Some of the most striking results come from the thematic apperception tests, which acknowledge similarly that people may not reveal the truth about themselves in answer to direct questions, but often project their feelings onto another person. The classic example is the case of the lagging instant coffee sales, nearly a decade ago, which showed marketers that housewives must have at least the illusion of participation before they will accept convenience products.

Groups of housewives, presented with two shopping lists identical except for ground coffee on one, instant coffee on the other, loudly branded the compiler of the instant coffee list as lazy, neglectful of her family, far less of a housekeeper than the ground coffee buyer.

This basic result accounts for TV commercials advising the housewife to simmer her instant coffee "to bring out the flavor," and for prepared cake mixes requiring a fresh egg and cup of milk (when the powdered variety pre-added at the factory would serve as well).

Burleigh B. Gardner, who left the University of Chicago in 1946 to launch Social Research, Inc. (with backing from Sears, Roebuck & Co.) was a pioneer in another approach, the sociological—examining how people behave in groups and in the mass. He tries to explain—and predict—consumer behavior largely in terms of social class. One study concluded, for example, that women pick department stores that way; a Bloomingdale woman feels Macy's has too much of the common touch and Bergdorf Goodman is above her aspirations.

Study of behavior from a more mechanistic angle—now growing in popularity—derives from the behavioristic experimental psychology of the late John B. Watson. He made his reputation before World War I, then launched a new career in the early 1920s as J. Walter Thompson Co.'s first research director.

Watson's descendants deal with physiological effects of what goes on in the mind. Their "eye-cameras," registering eye movements in reading an advertisement, are a case in point; a slow rate of eye-blink is supposed to indicate aroused interest. A somewhat newer eye-camera, developed by Dr. E. H. Hess of the University of Chicago for an ad agency, records instead pupil dilation. In one experiment, 10 men mostly went wrong in identifying their own cigarette brand in a batch with marks disguised. But the investigator, noting pupil dilation while smoking, matched brand to man nine times in 10.

Though there's a lot of this sort of thing going on, it still doesn't bulk large in dollar totals or, for that matter, in the esteem of most professional researchers; one expert figures that $10 million a year probably overstates what is spent on all psychological and sociological market research. One reason is that the dog still has something of a bad name, from the days a decade ago when "motivational research" seemed a panacea to some, just downright chicanery to others.

Another reason is that it takes less money. The head-shrinkers believe they get good results with few heads. Elaborate reports based on fewer than 200 interviews are common, and you'd be surprised at the edifice that can be erected on only 50. That makes costs a good deal lower than for massive population samplings by the head-counters.

There are signs, though, that the depth interviewers are getting more ambitious—and more expensive. Every company now has its own sociologist or psychologist doing small reports with a few dozen interviews, says Burleigh Gardner, "so our clients are no longer satisfied. We have to get into big samples—maybe 2,000 interviews—and we have to make more sense out of them. We've been pushed into large-scale computer analyses, would you believe it?"

AUTOMATING RESEARCH

Gardner is clearly amazed to find himself in professional relationship with computer technology—and he is not alone. Yet the computer is the market researcher's latest toy; it removes his old limitations of manpower and office space. An IBM 7090, ripping off 15 million computations a minute, can take all the questionnaires you want, break out the social and economic characteristics of the population 16 ways, and come up with enough percentages to snow the analysts under.

But will a print-out the size of the Chicago phone book give you enough statistically valid and meaningful results to be worth it?

To make more significant use of computers, market researchers are beginning to explore a variety of complex mathematical techniques.

There is something called Bayesian decision theory, for example—a method of forecasting actions by manipulating statistical probabilities mathematically. Its special contribution is that probability values can be assigned not only to observable facts but to an executive's seasoned judgment. Instead of multiplying consumer interviews to predict the success of a new product, you can interview an experienced sales executive and add his opinion to the formula.

The rage these days is mathematical model-building, which in theory lets a marketer test the consequences of his decisions without actually committing resources. One research company that has put most of its eggs in that basket is Simulmatics Corp., a rather uneasy alliance of mathematicians, psychologists, and economists.

A well-publicized computer model of the U.S. Presidential electorate, set up with a view toward helping elect the late John F. Kennedy, launched Simulmatics as a commercial venture. Then it went into public opinion and economics, and now marketing models. One of the last is a brand-switching model called Dyna-Mark I. Given the results of a consumer panel of at least 1,000—with demographic data on each, observed for at least three successive purchases of a brand category—plus about $8,000 in cash, Simulmatics says it can:

1. Tell where your new product's market share will likely end up.
2. Show which competing brands are most vulnerable to your ads.
3. Tell you whether your market is made up principally of loyal purchasers or of occasional purchasers.

PIONEERS AND PRIMA DONNAS

Except for Nielsen and Audits & Surveys, the concerns engaged in these many lines of market research seem to stay at annual volumes of $3 million or less—sometimes much less. Some claim the industry remains one of such small units because the long shadow of the one relative "giant"—Nielsen—keeps the sun off everyone else.

There are other reasons, though. Aside from Nielsen, A&S, and the biggest panel operators such as Market Research Corp. of America, research services are mostly hired for custom work—single studies or groups of related studies. This generates a relatively low volume.

Market researchers, too, are by and large prima donnas. The head men are fundamentally intellectuals whose chief joy in life is finding ways to get people to tell them interesting things; they shun administration, tend to fear size. The men they hire are also prima donnas, and this breeds conflict of personalities. The tendency is for talented employees to strike out on their own.

So it happens that Louis Harris and Solomon Dutka once worked for Roper; Willard Simmons and Lester Frankel came from Politz.

Politz is generally regarded as one of the super-salesmen of the research business. He has a faculty for putting complex concepts into clear language, an original turn of mind, and the ability—common to the best of the research fraternity—to look at problems from an odd angle, with deceptively simple results.

But what would happen to his business if Politz had to retire? Nothing, he says; it's not just a man, but an organization. To his colleagues in the field, it looks more like an organization tied to a man. Sometimes the strings break. In recent weeks, at least half a dozen of Politz' top people have left to set up a new research unit at an ad agency.

Most other research services are also extensions of one or maybe two personalities. Of the famous firms, only Opinion Research Corp., founded by the late Claude E. Robinson, and Crossley S-D Surveys, Inc., by the now-retired Archibald M. Crossley, are still significant factors though the top man is gone.

Most of the founders, however, are still active, or influential, though growing older. The business is so young that its pioneer generation is still around. Marketing research of even the most primitive kind is little older than the formation in 1911 by Charles C. Parlin, a Wisconsin school teacher, of a research department for Curtis Publishing Co. Until the late 1920s research simply meant analysis—juggling government statistics.

It was not until Crossley founded Crossley, Inc., in 1926 that modern methods of opinion sampling really got rolling. Elmo Roper set out on his own in 1933, George Gallup formed his own business in 1935.

These men are all positive personalities. They are also all pragmatists, who entered the business because someone had an urgent need to find out something specific about a market. The pioneers' reputations depended on personalities and results, not technique. The methodology—this kind of sample or that kind of questionnaire—developed along the way, empirically.

MOVING IN ON MANAGEMENT

The individualism of the research pioneers has permeated the business right up to the present. In recent years, however, the center of gravity in marketing research has been moving from the research services and the ad agencies—which formed the first research departments and offered the earliest support to the independent research practitioners—to client headquarters. That's because marketing research is becoming less and less a one-shot affair aimed at a specific problem, and is beginning to achieve status as a legitimate business activity conducted on a continuing basis. As with any such activity, management wants it in the house, where it can be controlled.

A typical consumer goods company with about $50-million sales will spend about $100,000 a year on market research—half on staff payroll, half on outside services. An industrial goods maker of similar size will spend approximately half that total.

As you might expect, the bulk of the internal research budget—salaries—is spent on activities with only a tenuous connection with market research. To organization chartists, a market research section looks like a perfect place to dump a lot of figure-churning activities that have roosted for decades in other departments—economic analysis of government statistics, warehousing studies, analysis of district sales reports.

Though valuable, these are not really what modern marketing research is about. The crucial distinction is that they are fundamentally desk-bound, while marketing research, to its modern practitioners, is a field activity. To find out things, you sally out and ask people.

Yet these older statistical disciplines often pay the freight. One research department manager says economic analyses—which chew up two-thirds of his staff's time—yield enough savings in sales-force allocation studies, warehouse sitting, and such, to cover his whole budget.

How well the research department uses its opportunities depends almost entirely on the quality of the man who runs it. Time was, notes one research man wryly, when a number of research directors were just "superannuated salesmen."

Today, many top company research directors possess the restless, probing minds, the impatience with pat answers always characteristic of the best research men. Respected by management, they have been able to get marketing research accepted on its own not as an adjunct to advertising or sales. In short, research is a tool of management.

This attitude will have to become far more widespread, though, if market research is ever really to mature. In all the long chain of marketing intelligence, from consumer through interviewer, tabulator, report writer, and research director to client management, the most tenuous link is the last. It boils down to a question of belief: Does the company president trust his research man's figures?

The automobile business provides the most dramatic example, simply because serious miscalculation there is at once the most public and the most expensive. Ford, building the Falcon, sought a car that could compete with the burgeoning foreign-car market; it mounted a massive fact-finding drive to discover exactly what the consumer wanted. His wants and needs were translated minutely into the finished design, down to a curb weight within pounds of what the market said it wanted.

Purely from a research viewpoint, the car was right on target; Ford sold 500,000 in 1960, the Falcon's first year. But Ford, clinging to a notion that the car would have limited appeal—as something in the nature of a "schoolteacher's car"—ignored some clear signals from the consumer research data. One research report, pointing to a wider market, said: "The idea of an economy car seemed to appeal more to the higher-income, college-educated, multi-car younger families."

To the researchers, at least, it was clear that the Falcon had an appeal far broader than Ford thought. And so it did. The market was broad enough to cut heavily into sales of the standard Ford and seriously affect the company's profits.

This helps to explain why, more and more often, research professionals are rejecting a passive role as an instrument of management, and are clamoring for a louder and more active voice in the corporate councils where research findings are acted on.

Many marketing researchers are content now to leave the physical assembly of data to mammoth fact-gatherers like Nielsen and to piece-work interviewers and tabulators—if they can control the research process at an earlier and more meaningful level. As outside consultants, they seek a permanent relationship with clients that plugs them in to day-in, day-out decision making. Inside research directors mount a parallel drive to increase their role in management. Both talk in terms of complete information systems, and a role in corporate strategy.

Like other technicians before them—from public relations men to marketing specialists—researchers look toward the day when their particular angle of vision will influence the way that management sees things.

MARKETING PLANNING

15

Marketing Planning
for Industrial
Products

B. CHARLES AMES
McKinsey and Company

Corporate life would be a lot easier if management could forget or wish away the whole idea of formal marketing planning. For no one yet has been able to figure out how to get marketing plans into written form without a lot of hard work. But, if anything, this process is likely to become a more important management tool in the future as companies continue their scramble to add new products and markets to their base.

Consumer goods companies have relied increasingly on a formal marketing planning approach to focus and coordinate product strategies, and to map the tactics for sales and profit growth. Going through this discipline helps avoid the dumbbell mistakes that are bound to occur when one tries to ad lib his way to the marketplace with a complex product line.

Not surprisingly, many industrial goods companies have tried to follow suit. If marketing planning can sell more products to housewives, it ought to sell more tractors, more chemicals, or more electronic components to industrial customers. So reasoning, makers of industrial goods have set up sophisticated planning systems designed to gear their business more closely to the requirements of the marketplace.

Yet many—and perhaps even most—of these companies have found that this approach, which works so well for consumer goods makers, somehow loses its magic in the industrial marketing context. Too often, their top

Reprinted with permission from *Harvard Business Review*, September–October, 1968, pp. 100–111. © by the President and Fellows of Harvard College.

executives are sadly disappointed in the results of costly and time-consuming planning efforts. The comment of one vice-president is typical:

"We knock ourselves out every year with a major time commitment and massive paper flow to put a plan for the business together that is heavily based on marketing input. But we can't really point to any substantive benefits that are directly traceable to all the extra effort. As I see it, our marketing group has not done the planning job it should. If it had, we'd have a lot stronger edge in the marketplace. At this point I am not sure whether it is something important that we ought to do better or whether it is just a fad that we ought to get rid of."

Why should his reaction be the rule rather than the exception? Why should the concepts that work so well in consumer goods companies be so difficult to apply successfully in the industrial field? Is is really fair to blame the marketing function when planning results fall short of expectations? Most important, what lessons can be learned from the experience of those few industrial companies which can honestly point to concrete results from their marketing planning activities?

These are the questions that a project team from McKinsey & Company recently set out to answer through a study of the planning practices and their effectiveness in 50 industrial companies. The names of these companies cannot be disclosed, but since they are all large, multidivision businesses listed in *Fortune*'s "500," they can be presumed to have all the necessary skills and sophistication to do an effective planning job. In carrying out this project, the team worked directly with general managers and marketing executives of each of the participating companies to get a comprehensive picture of where marketing planning fits into the management process, what approaches are being followed, which are working, and which are not.

PRACTITIONERS' PITFALLS

Ignorance of planning theory or mechanics is not the cause of the disappointments so many companies are experiencing. Most of the executives we talked to—in both line and staff positions—were well aware that effective planning (a) depends on market and economic facts, (b) focuses on points of leverage, and (c) results in operating programs, not just budgets. Few executives appeared to be at all mystified by formal planning concepts. These concepts have of course received their share of emphasis in business literature and the academic world over the past few years, and apparently most executives have learned their lessons well.[1]

Yet major problems crop up when companies set about putting these

[1] See, for example, Victor Buell, "Guides to Marketing Planning," *HBR*, July–August, 1960, p. 37; W. I. Little, "The Integrated Management Approach to Marketing," *Journal of Marketing*, April, 1967, p. 32; Leon Winer, "Are You Really Planning Your Marketing?" *Journal of Marketing*, January, 1965, p. 1; John Brion, "Decisions, Organization Planning, and the Marketing Concept," *Management Bulletin #47* (New York, American Management Association, 1964) and Lee Adler, "Phasing Research Into the Marketing Plan," *HBR*, May–June, 1960, p. 113.

concepts into practice. Our study findings strongly suggest that these problems fall into three categories:

- Failure of fit the concept to the industrial context.
- Overemphasis on the system at the expense of content.
- Nonrecognition of alternative strategies.

Let us examine each of the problem categories a bit more closely before moving on to see what vital steps have been taken by those participating companies which have successfully applied marketing planning in the industrial context.

Failure to Fit Concept

To a large extent, the disappointing results encountered by industrial companies reflect their failure to realize that the concept of marketing planning cannot be borrowed intact from consumer goods companies and applied successfully to their particular situation. Large industrial companies have two distinguishing characteristics that set them apart and dictate the need for a different planning approach.

The first is the multiplicity of markets and channels in which they operate, each requiring a discrete marketing strategy. A consumer goods company typically markets its several brands through one or two channels, but a multiproduct industrial manufacturer is likely to sell in a wide range of different markets through a variety of channels. For example, one electrical equipment company which participated in our study sold one of its major product lines in 30 distinct markets through several different channels. The company had been trying to cover this complex network of markets and channels with a single marketing plan; what is actually needed was 30 separate marketing plans.

Juggling a large number of markets and channels is not the only feat an industrial marketing department must perform. The second distinguishing characteristic is that the marketing department must also plan around the constraints imposed by other functions, since marketing simply does not control the factors that make or break performance in the marketplace. In the industrial world, marketing success depends largely on the activities of other functions, such as engineering, manufacturing, and technical service. This means, in turn, that changes in marketing strategy are likely to be based on product design, cost, or service innovations. Contrast this with a consumer goods company, where advertising, promotion, and merchandising are generally the core elements of the marketing plan.

Since the success of marketing plans is dependent on activities in other functional areas and on the share of total company resources each product/market business receives, it is unrealistic to expect product managers, market managers, or even the head of marketing to handle the job without the full participation of corporate and operating managers throughout the process.

Thus the role of the marketing planner in an industrial company is significantly different from that of his counterpart in consumer goods.

Rather than developing self-contained marketing plans, he analyzes and interprets market requirements so that top and operating management can decide how best to respond.

Obvious as this point might seem, it is frequently overlooked in industrial companies. Having embraced formal marketing planning as a sophisticated way of running the business, many executives try to implement the concept by turning the entire job over to marketing. After a couple of years of frustration, they are ready to write off marketing planning as a monumental waste of time. The real cause of their disappointment lies not in the concept, however, but in the way it has been applied.

For example, one major chemical company added a group of six industry planning managers to its marketing organization. Once on board, each was given a marketing planning format to follow and was told to develop a written plan for achieving a stronger and more profitable position in his assigned markets. All six men, eager to earn their spurs, embarked on a massive fact-gathering and writing effort. After several months, hundreds of pages of plans and supporting documentation had been written, but no one in top management was much impressed. The president put it this way:

"I'm being generous when I say the end products are only slightly better than useless. Admittedly, we have some better market facts now, but the plans are based on a lot of ideas for product and market development that just aren't in line with my idea of the direction this business should take. On top of that, they've left out a lot of technical and capital considerations that really count. I've concluded that our industry managers are simply too far out of the mainstream of the business to do an intelligent job of planning for us."

Not surprisingly, the industry managers felt that they too had good cause for complaint. As one of them put it:

"The first month of effort was worthwhile. We were putting a fact base together that is essential for intelligent planning. But after that we were flying blind. We never had any idea from top management on the kind of business the company wanted or didn't want, the minimal return it expected, or the kind of support it would be willing to throw into various markets. Worse still, we had no cooperation from the development group or the plants, where decisions are made that really control the business. The planning we did was bound to be a bust."

Unfortunately, this kind of situation has occurred in a great many otherwise well-managed companies. And instead of building marketing planning solidly into the management process, far too much of it is carried on as a parallel activity that gets plenty of lip service but little real attention from the decision makers.

Overemphasis on System

During the past several years, makers of industrial goods have put more and more effort into committing plans to writing for their various product/market businesses. Many companies have developed comprehensive planning systems that lay out formats and procedures in great detail.

Although some of this structure is unquestionably necessary, we saw a number of cases where the system was so detailed and so highly structured that it acted as a hindrance rather than a help to the planning process. In effect, the system serves as the end product rather than the means to an end.

Of all the problems described to us, this one drew the most vehement reactions from executives. They recognize that good planning is hard work and cannot be done without a certain amount of pencil pushing. But they bitterly resent demands for excessive writing that serves no practical business purpose. A product manager for an electronic equipment manufacturer voiced this complaint:

> "As part of my planning responsibility, I have to follow a format prescribed by the corporate planning group that calls for a point-by-point discussion of history and a laundry list of problems and opportunities. I'm 'gigged' if I don't cover every point in the format, and there's no way to do it in less than 10 pages of text. That takes a lot of time—mostly wasted time. All the product managers are sore about it. Much of what we have to write is a rehash of the same old things year after year. In effect, we're being discouraged from concentrating on the aspects of the business that are really critical. What they want to see, apparently, is a nice, neat set of plans that all look alike. It just doesn't make sense."

The study team encountered a great number of similar situations and comments. As a rule, someone or some group had designed an overstructured and overdetailed planning system that was out of phase with the realities of the business. Typically, the resulting paper work chewed up great blocks of precious time without producing anything more than a codification of what would have been done anyway.

Nonrecognition of Alternatives

In company after company, when we compared the plans that were developed for a particular product or market over several years, we were surprised to see how many planners had tunnel vision in thinking about how the business should be run. In fact, so many plans were based on nothing more than straight-line extrapolation of the past and on repetition of prior programs that they seemed hardly worth the paper they were written on.

This tendency to base current plans on past programs was forced into the open in one company when each planner was asked by top management to outline alternative strategies for developing his assigned market area and to summarize the commitments (e.g., financial, manpower, facilities) required and the payoff expected (sales, profits, ROI). The request drew a complete blank. The planners were so locked into their accustomed way of thinking about their markets that they could not conceive of a different approach that made any commercial sense at all.

Insufficient or less-than-candid analysis is a prime cause of unimaginative planning. Many planners either misjudge or fail to understand the underlying economics of the business or the changes going on in the marketplace (e.g., competitive moves, shifts in usage or demand patterns) that call for alternative strategies. Many planners also appear reluctant to face up to unpleasant truths about their competitive situation—such as high price, low product quality, or poor service—that place the company in an untenable marketing position. Without a thorough, candid appraisal of the business climate, the need for fresh ways of running the business goes unrecognized. Thus, instead of getting a choice among alternatives, top management has to content itself with a single recommendation which usually calls for the continuation of stale or imitative strategies.

IMAGINATIVE INSIGHTS

Considering that the whole purpose of formal planning is to conceive more imaginative ways of developing the business, the record so far is pretty dismal. Yet the experience of the handful of participating companies which have successfully applied marketing planning in the industrial context provides some encouragement and some useful insights. Without exception, these companies have taken the necessary steps to avoid the pitfalls just described. And they are now concentrating on developing marketing-oriented plans for their businesses that are part and parcel of the management process of each company. Our study indicates that they have reached this level of sophistication primarily because of three factors:

- Better definition and direction from the top.
- Development of fact-founded product/market strategies.
- Superior programming for strategy implementation.

The balance of this article will consider each of these vital factors and how they can lead to better ways of doing things and to improved results when applied in the industrial marketing context.

Better Definition & Direction

The marketing planning done in leader companies produces results because it is carried out with full recognition of the multiplicity of products, markets, and channels, and the need for a technical, rather than a sales or merchandising, orientation. As one president in our survey commented:

"It took me three years to realize that our marketing people couldn't come up with the kind of plans I wanted for our products and markets unless I worked closely with them. They have always been able to develop a picture of where our markets are heading, identify the opportunities that exist, and interpret what we have to do to build the business. But so many considerations and options require a general management perspective that marketing can't be expected to come up with recommendations that make sense from my point of view. Unless I set the basic direction for our business, specify who is to plan what, see to it that engineering and manufacturing really work with marketing to provide what is needed, and then challenge and contribute any ideas I can on how our business can be developed, the whole planning effort is nothing more than a paper-work exercise."

Let us look at this comment more closely, for it underscores the four ways in which top management must participate in marketing planning to make it pay off.

1. *Specify corporate objectives:* Throughout our study, inadequate direction from the top was a common complaint from planners. "If only top management would tell me what they want!" I am sure we heard a hundred variations on this theme. A few of these men no doubt would like top management to spell everything out for them in detail, and they are using its failure to do so as an excuse for their own inability to do the planning job.

Nevertheless, top management guidelines that spell out the rules of the game are unquestionably a necessity for anyone who holds a marketing planning responsibility. At a minimum, these guidelines should include definite long-range growth targets or a statement of corporate objectives that expresses in specific terms how fast top management wants the business to grow, what products and markets should be emphasized, what kinds of businesses should be avoided, and what profit returns are acceptable. These guidelines do not have to be expressed with precision, and they are certainly not immutable. But without some definition like this, product/market planners will be working in a vacuum, and they will almost inevitably come up with marketing plans that are out of phase with top management's interests and objectives.

2. *Determine organization arrangements:* It is an important step in any company to determine organization arrangements, but it is particularly vital in a large-scale industrial complex with its numerous product/market businesses. Since marketing planning requirements vary so widely from business to business, there is no one organization that is valid for all companies. Nor is the same oragnization necessarily valid for all time. Leader companies understand the importance of appraising and reappraising organization arrangements to make sure that the planners have the right focus and that their roles are clearly understood by everyone in the organization.

For example, the marketing organization in a capital goods company had traditionally been structured around products—that is, the product managers were responsible for planning the growth and profits of each of their major product lines (see left column in *Exhibit I*). Obliged to sell to three distinct markets, each product manager was spread so thin that he could not do a thorough job of planning for any one of them. Also, since his focus was on his product lines, he was blinded to the broader needs of the individual markets.

Management soon recognized that this traditional organization arrangement greatly restricted the company's ability to plan for development of the total market. Therefore, to provide the market orientation it wanted, the company restructured its organization around the market managers, who were responsible for identifying and planning to meet all the needs of their assigned markets (see right column in *Exhibit I*).

This example is not meant to suggest that market managers will do a better job of planning for a company than product managers. But it does demonstrate how important it is for top management to think through the planning objectives and requirements for each business, and then to design an organization structure that will provide the right focus.

3. *Provide interfunctional coordination:* Even the most carefully conceived marketing organization structure will fail unless the marketing planners (a) work effectively with the other functions that influence the performance of a business in the marketplace, and (b) command the respect of their functional counterparts. And all concerned must have a clear understanding of how they are expected to work together. This is especially important in industrial companies, for without interfunctional coordination the planners do not stand a chance.

A manufacturer in the building products field set up a product planning group in its marketing organization to spearhead the marketing planning for each product area. During the first two years of the group's existence, the plans developed fell far short of everyone's expectations, and there was much friction between the planning group and other functions.

One of the product planning managers put his finger on the problem when he pointed out the many functions other than marketing and sales he had to work with to do a good planning job. Much of the difficulty he encountered, he said, stemmed from misunderstanding on the part of many functions managers about how the marketing planning job was to be done. Even the product planning managers themselves, he added, were unsure about their responsibilities.

Recognizing the need to put the product planning group on a more sound footing for dealing with other functions, the marketing vice-president took three steps. He decided first to replace four of the five product planning managers, who were basically sales-oriented, with men who had stronger technical backgrounds and better grasp of the business as a whole. He then eliminated the position of group product planning managers—putting the product planning managers on an organization par with their major contacts in other functional areas. Since they had a broader understanding of the business, they were able to communicate more effectively. Even more important, as a result of the reorganization, they now reported directly to the head of marketing and, therefore, were in close touch with top management thinking.

Finally, the marketing head persuaded the president of the company to hold a meeting with the executives of all major functions to explain what the product planning managers were trying to accomplish and how the different functions should work with them. At this meeting, the president made it clear that he was looking to the product planning managers to develop plans geared to the characteristics and requirements of the marketplace:

"We are going to bank everything on their interpretation of where the market is heading and what we must do internally to respond to market needs.

EXHIBIT I: ORGANIZATION SHIFT TO PROVIDE CAPITAL
GOODS COMPANY WITH BETTER PLANNING FOCUS

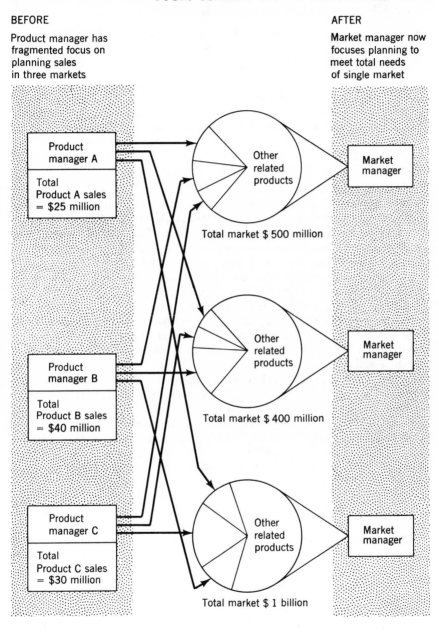

BEFORE

Product manager has
fragmented focus on
planning sales
in three markets

AFTER

Market manager now
focuses planning to
meet total needs
of single market

Product
manager A

Total
Product A sales
= $25 million

Other
related
products

Total market $ 500 million

Market
manager

Product
manager B

Total
Product B sales
= $40 million

Other
related
products

Total market $ 400 million

Market
manager

Product
manager C

Total
Product C sales
= $30 million

Other
related
products

Total market $ 1 billion

Market
manager

I expect all functions to cooperate with our marketing planners and follow their lead completely. If we don't operate along these lines, all of our talk about being a market-oriented company is just a lot of hot air."

This no-nonsense statement on the role of marketing cleared away any misconceptions blocking effective interaction between the product planning managers and other functions.

4. *Contribute to marketing plans:* If top management truly wants to find ways of improving profits and growth, it must actively participate in the development of marketing plans by challenging their underlying assumptions and by contributing alternative ideas on strategy and programs. To be sure, most top executives try to do this; but the way they do it often stifles rather than encourages new ideas. They must take pains to avoid any atmosphere of an inquisition and, instead, must stimulate open exchange of ideas and opinions.

In such an environment one idea leads to another, and the management team soon finds itself exploring new and imaginative ways of developing the business. An interfunctional give-and-take discussion like this led a heavy machinery manufacturer to adopt a new market strategy that gave its parts operation a chance for survival. Consider:

In this company, as in many others, parts sales had traditionally been a major source of profits. Now management was concerned because "parts pirates" (local parts producers) were cutting sharply into their business. Asked to develop a marketing strategy that would reverse the trend, the parts manager first came up with a plan that called for adding three salesmen and cutting prices on a large number of parts to be more competitive. As he acknowledged, his plan was essentially no more than a holding action.

During the planning review session in which all functions took part, the company president encouraged everyone to take an entrepreneurial look at the parts business and to try to think of ways to preserve or even enlarge it. Predictably, fresh ideas were hard to come by in a business that had been run the same way for years. But eventually three embryonic ideas emerged that were considered worthwhile: (1) Build a service organization and sell contracts for maintenance service instead of just parts; (2) decentralize the parts business and set up local parts and repair shops to compete head to head with local competitors; and (3) start to buy and sell parts for other manufactureers' equipment in order to spread overhead costs.

The parts manager was naturally somewhat reluctant to do any of these things, since they would revolutionize his end of the business. But with top management backing and encouragement, he did the required analytical work and came back with alternative strategies, based on the first two ideas, that offered a much more attractive outlook.

Of course, to think that this process always leads to a more viable product/market strategy would be a foolhardy assumption. It is not always possible to overcome the scarcity of fresh ideas characteristic of a business run the same way for years. Moreover, alternative strategies are

EXHIBIT II. FORCES LIKELY TO AFFECT INDUSTRIAL COMPANY'S MARKET POSITION AND OUTLOOK

A. Identifying Points of Leverage

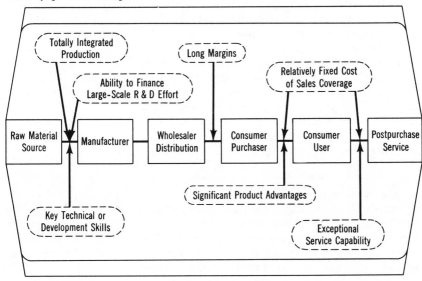

B. Identifying Points of Vulnerability

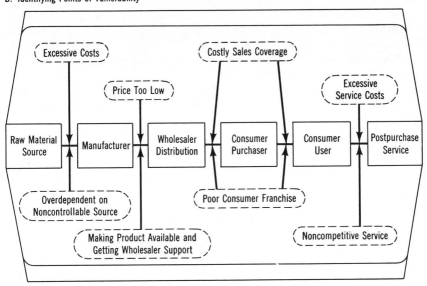

not always available. But the more successful companies insist that their planners seek out alternative strategies and avoid getting locked into a self-defeating "business as usual" pattern of thinking.

This kind of give-and-take among marketing, top management, and other functions is really the heart of the planning process. For it is during these discussions that marketing presents the requirements of the market-place and the other functions discuss feasible ways of responding to them. With all the opportunities and constraints out in the open, top management has a good basis for deciding how to allocate corporate resources. Once the best combination of ideas is agreed on, the various functions are then in a position to make commitments on the timing and costs of the alternative actions that underlie the marketing plan. Leader company executives insist this is the best vehicle for triggering fresh ideas and ensuring interfunctional coordination.

Fact-founded Strategies

The marketing planning done by leader companies is aimed at the development of strategies for each product/market business realistically tied to market and economic facts. Once developed, these strategies point the way for each present business, serve as underpinning for overall corporate long-range planning, and provide direction for programming key activities and projects in all functional areas.

Strategy development is an art few companies have mastered. Those that have this expertise stress the need for comprehensive knowledge of the economics of the business and the trends of the market. More specifically, this means that planners need to know the economics of their competitors as well as of their own businesses—that is, where value is added, how costs behave with changes in volume, where assets are committed, and so on. To complete their understanding, planners must also know how the market is structured and what forces are likely to affect the company's market position and outlook.

With this understanding, planners can recognize points of leverage where the company can exercise an advantage, as well as points where the company might be vulnerable to competitive thrusts. *Exhibit II* illustrates what some of these points of leverage or vulnerability might be in a typical industrial operation.

One outstanding company built a marketing strategy for its major product line on just this sort of understanding. The planners in this company, which I shall call Company A, recognized that they were operating in a slow-growth business, offering a commodity product for which demand was highly inelastic. They therefore concluded that (a) it would not make sense to sacrifice short-term profits to build a larger share position, since the value of a share point would not increase enough to pay off such an investment, and (b) although price is an important consideration in market share, it would not influence total demand.

This market analysis brought a further important trend to light: Company A was losing market position to the strong second-place factor in the industry, Company B. As no other important shifts in market share

EXHIBIT III: COMPARATIVE ANALYSIS OF TWO COMPETITIVE COMPANIES
(Dollar figures in millions)

Economic indicators	Companies A	Companies B	Conclusions
Current dollar sales	$403	$146	A's sales volume is roughly twice B's
Breakeven point	$217	$121	B's breakeven point is lower, but B is operating much closer to breakeven than A
Contribution margin rate (sales dollars less variable costs)	48%	45%	Contribution margin rates are about the same
Contribution loss from 5 percentage point drop in unit margin	$20	$7.3	However, because of differences in dollar volume, Company A stands to lose far more marginal income than B by lowering unit margin
Volume gain to offset 5 percentage point drop in unit margin	$46.5	$18.2	Thus, the volume needed to offset a 5 percentage point drop in unit margin would be much greater for Company A
Equivalent share point gain	7.0 pts.	2.8 pts.	

had occurred, Company A concluded that its marketing strategy should be aimed first and foremost at reversing its losses to Company B.

Next, the planners at Company A compared their own profit structure with that of Company B to find the weaknesses and strengths of the two companies. Their analysis produced the information shown in *Exhibit III*. (Admittedly, obtaining information of this sort about competitors is unquestionably tough. No one is going to hand it to you, and it is not likely to be available in published material. But bits of data on competitor sales and capacity levels can be pieced together from annual reports, newspaper articles, and trade and government publications. By combining such data with one's own experience, conservative assumptions can be made about competitor costs and efficiency to complete the picture.)

By the time the planners in Company A had completed this comparative analysis, they were in a position to predict what Company B's strategy was likely to be. This is what they thought Company B would do, assuming that B knew its own market and economic position:

- Cut prices on the products competitive with Company A's highest volume products to upset price stability and to force Company A to retaliate or give up volume.
- Add new industrial distributors by giving larger discounts, and go after Company A's distributors in prime markets.
- Emphasize development of lower-cost products, thereby gaining more flexibility to compete on a price basis.

Starting from these assumptions, the planners in Company A proceeded to develop a counterstrategy. These were its key points:

- Avoid going for volume on a price basis or by adding to unit costs.
- Hold a firm price line with distributors—even at the risk of losing share in the most price-sensitive markets.
- Build the marketing program around the changes in costs which are non-variable with volume—e.g., upgrading and enlarging the sales force, strengthening distributor programs, and improving the physical distribution and warehousing network.

A superficial review of the situation would undoubtedly have led the planners to come up with quite a different strategy. For, in view of the high contribution rate and apparent profit leverage on volume, the most obvious strategy would have been to cut price to counteract any aggressive pricing actions of Company B. Instead, Company A planners decided to avoid price concessions or any actions that would raise unit costs. They recommended concentrating on marketing programs where costs could be amortized over their much larger unit volume and on other programs that would reduce their cost base. Management agreed, reasoning that this strategy would enable the company to lead from strength rather than play into the hands of its major competitor.

The details of Company A's strategy may be open to dispute. In themselves, however, they are not important. The purpose of the example is to show how a penetrating analysis of market and economic facts can provide a reasoned basis for strategy development. This is the process by which sophisticated planners are gaining significant advantages over their competitors, and it is easy to see the three reasons why:

1. Planners can help focus management attention on actions that really count in the marketplace and make sure that these are based on facts and judgment, not hunch or opinion.
2. They can adopt an aggressive posture instead of having to rely on retaliation or defensive maneuvers.
3. They can minimize the impact of surprise competitive moves by developing alternative contingency plans.

Superior Programming

Everybody goes through the motions of programming, but leader companies follow three ground rules that enable them to do a superior job of strategy implementation.

First, management will approve no major program or project that is not inextricably linked to a product/market strategy. This approach may sound a little stuffy, but it makes eminently good sense, for there is really no way to evaluate a program's usefulness without the background of a product/market strategy. Moreover, the linkage keeps the functional areas of a business working together for a common purpose and prevents them from being sidetracked on functionally interesting activities that lack commercial relevance.

Second, management makes some sort of organization provision for follow-through on major programs, particularly those that cut across functional lines. In some cases, they have enlarged the role of their product managers. In others, they have set up a task force with responsibility for following a program through to completion.

Take, for example, the case of an industrial controls producer we surveyed. When it became clear that the company's product line had slipped behind competitors', the management team saw that holding market position would require a complete redesign of the product line, both to improve performance characteristics and to take out cost.

Even though the bulk of the actual work had to be done by engineering and manufacturing, the president pulled the responsible product manager out of the marketing department, placed him directly under his wing, and made him fully accountable for coordinating and pushing the program through to completion. As the president told us:

"This program can make or break us in the marketplace. It's so vital to us I'd watch over it myself if I could let some other things slip. Since I can't, I want someone to do it for me, and the product manager is the logical one to do it. I know I'm stretching his role somewhat in giving him this assignment, and I know some noses are going to be out of joint in engineering and manufacturing, but the job is too important not to have a full-time program manager."

This is one way of shepherding a crucial program. As discussed, there are others; but the objective is always to ensure interfunctional coordination for all major programs and to break through any obstacles to successful completion.

Third, leader companies see to it that the detailed steps involved in major programs are mapped out in such a way that performance can be measured against these individual steps. For some time, of course, companies in the aerospace, military electronics, construction, and other industries have been using network scheduling techniques (e.g., PERT, RAMPS) to control large and complex projects. Now, however, a few industrial goods makers are applying similar techniques to ensure interfunctional coordination on a wide variety of programs that affect market performance, since they permit management to flag potential problem areas and initiate corrective action before the program slips or gets off track.

In one company, the program for introducing a new line of flow meters was broken down into 25 steps over an 18-month span. The first step was a kick-off meeting between R&D, engineering, manufacturing, and marketing to define performance and cost requirements. Subsequent steps tracked the new product idea through development, manufacture, and market launching. Each week management received a report showing whether scheduled steps had been completed and, if not, where the bottleneck was. This feedback made it much easier to trace problems to their source for corrective action. Said the president: "The program is too important to us to rely for control on typical accounting reports. They simply tell us after the fact whether we won or lost. They're no help when it comes to making sure the program doesn't collapse."

It would be absurd to structure every program in so much detail. But detailed planning is essential for effective control over major programs that involve many functions and require tight scheduling and careful adherence in order to achieve profit and market objectives.

IN SUMMARY

Formal marketing planning can undoubtedly make a real contribution to the performance of any industrial company, just as it has in consumer goods companies. But if marketing planning is to have real impact on the industrial side, it will have to be adapted much more closely to the particular requirements of the business. This demands much less emphasis on the system—that is, format, sophisticated techniques, and lengthy writing assignments. Instead, the whole focus must be on achieving substantive improvements in thinking and actions through tough-minded analysis, continual interchange between marketing and technical executives, and more top management inputs. This is the only approach that can really lead to better ways of doing things and to improved results, thus making the formal marketing planning process something more than a costly facade.

SELECTED BIBLIOGRAPHY
for
PART 3

ANSOFF, H. IGOR. "Strategies for Diversification," *Harvard Business Review.* September–October, 1957, pp. 113–24.

BLANKENSHIP, A. B. "Creativity in Consumer Research," *Journal of Marketing.* October, 1961, pp. 34–38.

CASSADY, RALPH, JR. "The Price Skirmish—a Distinctive Pattern of Competitive Behavior," *California Management Review.* Winter, 1964, pp. 11–16.

COX, DONALD F., and GOOD, ROBERT. "How to Build a Market Information System," *Harvard Business Review.* May–June, 1967, pp. 145–54.

EVANS, GORDON H. *The Product Manager's Job.* Research Study 69 (American Management Association, 1964), pp. 49–62.

LUCK, DAVID, and NOWAK, THEODORE. "Product Management—Vision Unfilled," *Harvard Business Review.* May–June, 1965, pp. 143–54.

MINDAK, WILLIAM A. "Fitting the Semantic Differential to the Marketing Problems," *Journal of Marketing.* April, 1961, 28–33.

PHILLIPS, JOHN. "The End-Run," in Lee Adler, ed., *Plotting Marketing Strategy.* (New York: Simon and Schuster, 1967), pp. 43–55.

WINER, LEON. "Are You Really Planning Your Marketing?," *Journal of Marketing.* January, 1965, pp. 1–8.

PLANNING
THE MARKETING
PROGRAM

In planning the marketing program, marketing managers need to examine the controllable variables that are relevant in marketing. The four controllable variables in the "marketing mix" are product, price, distribution, and communication.

Four articles relate to product decisions. Levitt (pp. 204–24) demonstrates through many examples how marketing executives may extend the life cycle of a product. Murray (pp. 225–32) illustrates the advantages of a systems approach to developing full lines of compatible products in the industrial area. Learner (pp. 233–49) treats new product planning as a sequential decision process, while Reynolds (pp. 250–58) documents the case history of one of the major new-product failures in recent years.

Two articles relate to price decisions. Oxenfeldt (pp. 259–73) shows how pricing policies can be logically determined through a series of planning stages. Green (pp. 274–88) presents an extended example of how the Bayesian approach can aid a seller in determining whether or not to cut his price.

Three articles relate to distribution decisions. McCammon (pp. 289–99) examines several significant changes in channels of distribution, while Mallen (pp. 300–16) looks at forces leading to conflict and cooperation within marketing channels. Business Week (pp. 317–28) describes how the physical-distribution concept is changing traditional transportation, warehousing, and customer-service policies.

Finally, three articles relate to communication decisions. The role of advertising and personal selling in the total marketing effort is contrasted by Cash and Crissy (pp. 329–38). Levitt (pp. 339–50) investigates the importance of company reputation and salesmen effect in industrial marketing. Lastly, Britt (pp. 351–62) questions if advertising agencies really know whether or not their campaigns are successful.

PRODUCT DECISIONS

16

Exploit
the Product
Life Cycle

THEODORE LEVITT
Harvard University

Most alert and thoughtful senior marketing executives are by now familiar with the concept of the product life cycle. Even a handful of uniquely cosmopolitan and up-to-date corporate presidents have familiarized themselves with this tantalizing concept. Yet a recent survey I took of such executives found none who used the concept in any strategic way whatever, and pitifully few who used it in any kind of tactical way. It has remained—as have so many fascinating theories in economies, physics, and sex—a remarkably durable but almost totally unemployed and seemingly unemployable piece of professional baggage whose presence in the rhetoric of professional discussions adds a much coveted but apparently unattainable legitimacy to the idea that marketing management is somehow a profession. There is, furthermore, a persistent feeling that the life cycle concept adds luster and believability to the insistent claim in certain circles that marketing is close to being some sort of science.[1]

The concept of the product life cycle is today at about the stage that the Copernican view of the universe was 300 years ago: a lot of people knew about it, but hardly anybody seemed to use it in any effective or productive way.

Reprinted with permission from *Harvard Business Review*, November–December, 1965, pp. 81–94. © by the President and Fellows of Harvard College.

[1] For discussions of the scientific claims or potentials of marketing, see George Schwartz, *Development of Marketing Theory* (Cincinnati, Ohio: South-Western Publishing Co., 1963); and Reavis Cox, Wroe Alderson, and Stanley J. Shapiro, editors, *Theory in Marketing* (Homewood, Illinois: Richard D. Irwin, Inc., Second Series, 1964).

EXHIBIT I: PRODUCT LIFE CYCLE—ENTIRE INDUSTRY

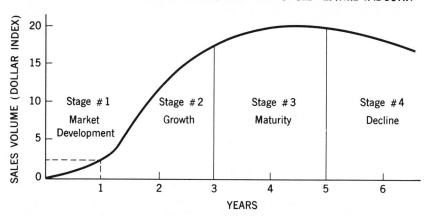

Now that so many people know and in some fashion understand the product life cycle, it seems time to put it to work. The object of this article is to suggest some ways of using the concept effectively and of turning the knowledge of its existence into a managerial instrument of competitive power.

Since the concept has been presented somewhat differently by different authors and for different audiences, it is useful to review it briefly here so that every reader has the same background for the discussion which follows later in this article.

HISTORICAL PATTERN

The life story of most successful products is a history of their passing through certain recognizable stages. These are shown in Exhibit i and occur in the following order:

Stage 1. Market Development—This is when a new product is first brought to market, before there is a proved demand for it, and often before it has been fully proved out technically in all respects. Sales are low and creep along slowly.

Stage 2. Market Growth—Demand begins to accelerate and the size of the total market expands rapidly. It might also be called the "Takeoff Stage."

Stage 3. Market Maturity—Demand levels off and grows, for the most part, only at the replacement and new family-formation rate.

Stage 4. Market Decline—The product begins to lose consumer appeal and sales drift downward, such as when buggy whips lost out with the advent of automobiles and when silk lost out to nylon.

Three operating questions will quickly occur to the alert executive:

- Given a proposed new product or service, how and to what extent can the shape and duration of each stage be predicted?
- Given an existing product, how can one determine what stage it is in?
- Given all this knowledge, how can it be effectively used?

A brief further elaboration of each stage will be useful before dealing with these questions in detail.

Development Stage

Bringing a new product to market is fraught with unknowns, uncertainties, and frequently unknowable risks. Generally, demand has to be "created" during the product's initial *market development stage*. How long this takes depends on the product's complexity, its degree of newness, its fit into consumer needs, and the presence of competitive substitutes of one form or another. A proved cancer cure would require virtually no market development; it would get immediate massive support. An alleged superior substitute for the lost-wax process of sculpture casting would take lots longer.

While it has been demonstrated time after time that properly customer-oriented new product development is one of the primary conditions of sales and profit growth, what have been demonstrated even more conclusively are the ravaging costs and frequent fatalities associated with launching new products. Nothing seems to take more time, cost more money, involve more pitfalls, cause more anguish, or break more careers than do sincere and well-conceived new product programs. The fact is, most new products don't have any sort of classical life cycle curve at all. They have instead from the very outset an infinitely descending curve. The product not only doesn't get off the ground; it goes quickly under ground—six feet under.

It is little wonder, therefore, that some disillusioned and badly burned companies have recently adopted a more conservative policy—what I call the "used apple policy." Instead of aspiring to be the first company to see and seize an opportunity, they systematically avoid being first. They let others take the first bite of the supposedly juicy apple that tantalizes them. They let others do the pioneering. If the idea works, they quickly follow suit. They say, in effect, "The trouble with being a pioneer is that the pioneers get killed by the Indians." Hence, they say (thoroughly mixing their metaphors), "We don't have to get the first bite of the apple. The second one is good enough." They are willing to eat off a used apple, but they try to be alert enough to make sure it is only slightly used—that they at least get the second big bite, not the tenth skimpy one.

Growth Stage

The usual characteristic of a successful new product is a gradual rise in its sales curve during the market development stage. At some point in this rise a marked increase in consumer demand occurs and sales take off. The boom is on. This is the beginning of Stage 2—the *market growth stage*. At this point potential competitors who have been watching developments during Stage 1 jump into the fray. The first ones to get in are generally those with an exceptionally effective "used apple policy." Some enter the market with carbon-copies of the originator's product. Others make functional and design improvements. And at this point product and brand differentiation begin to develop.

The ensuing fight for the consumer's patronage poses to the originating producer an entirely new set of problems. Instead of seeking ways of getting consumers to *try the product*, the originator now faces the more compelling problem of getting them to *prefer his brand*. This generally requires important changes in marketing strategies and methods. But the policies and tactics now adopted will be neither freely the sole choice of the originating producer, nor as experimental as they might have been during Stage 1. The presence of competitors both dictates and limits what can easily be tried—such as, for example, testing what is the best price level or the best channel of distribution.

As the rate of consumer acceptance accelerates, it generally becomes increasingly easy to open new distribution channels and retail outlets. The consequent filling of distribution pipelines generally causes the entire industry's factory sales to rise more rapidly than store sales. This creates an exaggerated impression of profit opportunity which, in turn, attracts more competitors. Some of these will begin to charge lower prices because of later advances in technology, production shortcuts, the need to take lower margins in order to get distribution, and the like. All this in time inescapably moves the industry to the threshold of a new stage of competition.

Maturity Stage

This new stage is the *market maturity stage*. The first sign of its advent is evidence of market saturation. This means that most consumer companies or households that are sales prospects will be owning or using the product. Sales now grow about on a par with population. No more distribution pipelines need be filled. Price competition now becomes intense. Competitive attempts to achieve and hold brand preference now involve making finer and finer differentiations in the product, in customer services, and in the promotional practices and claims made for the product.

Typically, the market maturity stage forces the producer to concentrate on holding his distribution outlets, retaining his shelf space, and, in the end, trying to secure even more intensive distribution. Whereas during the market development stage the originator depended heavily on the positive efforts of his retailers and distributors to help sell his product, retailers and distributors will now frequently have been reduced largely to being merchandise-displayers and order-takers. In the case of branded products in particular, the originator must now, more than ever, communicate directly with the consumer.

The market maturity stage typically calls for a new kind of emphasis on competing more effectively. The originator is increasingly forced to appeal to the consumer on the basis of price, marginal product differences, or both. Depending on the product, services and deals offered in connection with it are often the clearest and most effective forms of differentiation. Beyond these, there will be attempts to create and promote fine product distinctions through packaging and advertising, and to appeal to special market segments. The market maturity stage can be passed through rapidly, as in the case of most women's fashion fads, or it can persist for generations with per capita consumption neither rising nor falling, as in the case of such staples as men's shoes and industrial fasteners. Or maturity can persist, but in a state of gradual but steady per capita decline, as in the case of beer and steel.

Decline Stage

When market maturity tapers off and consequently comes to an end, the product enters Stage 4—*market decline*. In all cases of maturity and decline the industry is transformed. Few companies are able to weather the competitive storm. As demand declines, the overcapacity that was already apparent during the period of maturity now becomes endemic. Some producers see the handwriting implacably on the wall but feel that with proper management and cunning they will be one of the survivors after the industry-wide deluge they so clearly foresee. To hasten their competitors' eclipse directly, or to frighten them into early voluntary withdrawal from the industry, they initiate a variety of aggressively depressive tactics, propose mergers or buy-outs, and generally engage in activities that make life thanklessly burdensome for all firms, and make death the inevitable consequence for most of them. A few companies do indeed weather the storm, sustaining life through the constant descent that now clearly characterizes the industry. Production gets concentrated into fewer hands. Prices and margins get depressed. Consumers get bored. The only cases where there is any relief from this boredom and gradual euthanasia are where styling and fashion play some constantly revivifying role.

PREPLANNING IMPORTANCE

Knowing that the lives of successful products and services are generally characterized by something like the pattern illustrated in Exhibit i can become the basis for important life-giving policies and practices. One of the greatest values of the life cycle concept is for managers about to launch a new product. The first step for them is to try to foresee the profile of the proposed product's cycle.

As with so many things in business, and perhaps uniquely in marketing, it is almost impossible to make universally useful suggestions regarding how to manage one's affairs. It is certainly particularly difficult to provide widely useful advice on how to foresee or predict the slope and duration of a product's life. Indeed, it is precisely because so little specific day-to-day guidance is possible in anything, and because no checklist has ever by itself been very useful to anybody for very long, that business management will probably never be a science—always an art—and will pay exceptional rewards to managers with rare talent, enormous energy, iron nerve, great capacity for assuming responsibility and bearing accountability.

But this does not mean that useful efforts cannot or should not be made to try to foresee the slope and duration of a new product's life. Time spent in attempting this kind of foresight not only helps assure that a more rational approach is brought to product planning and merchandising; also, as will be shown later, it can help create valuable lead time for important strategic and tactical moves after the product is brought to market. Specifically, it can be a great help in developing an orderly series of competitive moves, in expanding or stretching out the life of a product, in maintaining a clean product line, and in purposely phasing out dying and costly old products.[2]

Failure Possibilties . . .

As pointed out above, the length and slope of the market development stage depend on the product's complexity, its degree of newness, its fit into customer needs, and the presence of competitive substitutes.

The more unique or distinctive the newness of the product, the longer it generally takes to get it successfully off the ground. The world does not automatically beat a path to the man with the better mousetrap.[3] The world has to be told, coddled, enticed, romanced, and even bribed (as with, for example, coupons, samples, free application aids, and the like). When the product's newness is distinctive and the job it is designed to do is unique, the public will generally be less quick to perceive it as something it clearly needs or wants.

This makes life particularly difficult for the innovator. He will have more than the usual difficulties of identifying those characteristics of his product and those supporting communications themes or devices which imply value to the consumer. As a consequence, the more distinctive the newness, the greater the risk of failure resulting either from insufficient working capital to sustain a long and frustrating period of creating enough solvent customers to make the proposition pay, or from the inability to convince investors and bankers that they should put up more money.

In any particular situation the more people who will be involved in making a single purchasing decision for a new product, the more drawn out Stage 1 will be. Thus in the highly fragmented construction materials industry, for example, success takes an exceptionally long time to catch hold; and having once caught hold, it tends to hold tenaciously for a long time—often too long. On the other hand, fashion items clearly catch on fastest and last shortest. But because fashion is so powerful, recently some companies in what often seem the least fashion-influenced of industries (machine tools, for example) have shortened the market

2 See Philip Kotler, "Phasing Out Weak Products," *HBR* (March–April 1965), p. 107.

3 For perhaps the ultimate example of how the world does *not* beat such a path, see the example of the man who actually, and to his painful regret, made a "better" mousetrap, in John B. Matthews, Jr., R. D. Buzzell, Theodore Levitt, and Ronald E. Frank, *Marketing: An Introductory Analysis* (New York: McGraw-Hill Book Company, Inc., 1964), p. 4.

development stage by introducing elements of design and packaging fashion to their products.

What factors tend to prolong the market development stage and therefore raise the risk of failure? The more complex the product, the more distinctive its newness, the less influenced by fashion, the greater the number of persons influencing a single buying decision, the more costly, and the greater the required shift in the customer's usual way of doing things—these are the conditions most likely to slow things up and create problems.

. . . vs. Success Chances

But problems also create opportunities to control the forces arrayed against new product success. For example, the newer the product, the more important it becomes for the customers to have a favorable first experience with it. Newness creates a certain special visibility for the product, with a certain number of people standing on the sidelines to see how the first customers get on with it. If their first experience is unfavorable in some crucial way, this may have repercussions far out of proportion to the actual extent of the underfulfillment of the customers' expectations. But a favorable first experience or application will, for the same reason, get a lot of disproportionately favorable publicity.

The possibility of exaggerated disillusionment with a poor first experience can raise vital questions regarding the appropriate channels of distribution for a new product. On the one hand, getting the product successfully launched may require having—as in the case of, say, the early days of home washing machines—many retailers who can give consumers considerable help in the product's correct utilization and thus help assure a favorable first experience for those buyers. On the other hand, channels that provide this kind of help (such as small neighborhood appliance stores in the case of washing machines) during the market development stage may not be the ones best able to merchandise the product most successfully later when help in creating and personally reassuring customers is less important than wide product distribution. To the extent that channel decisions during this first stage sacrifice some of the requirements of the market development stage to some of the requirements of later stages, the rate of the product's acceptance by consumers at the outset may be delayed.

In entering the market development stage pricing decisions are often particularly hard for the producer to make. Should he set an initially high price to recoup his investment quickly—i.e., "skim the cream"—or should he set a low price to discourage potential competition—i.e., "exclusion"? The answer depends on the innovator's estimate of the probable length of the product's life cycle, the degree of patent protection the product is likely to enjoy, the amount of capital needed to get the product off the ground, the elasticity of demand during the early life of the product, and many other factors. The decision that is finally made may affect not just the rate at which the product catches on at the beginning, but even the duration of its total life. Thus some products that are priced too low at the outset (particularly fashion goods, such as the chemise, or sack, a few years ago) may catch on so quickly that they become short-lived fads. A slower rate of consumer acceptance might often extend their life cycles and raise the total profits they yield.

The actual slope, or rate of the growth stage, depends on some of the same things as does success or failure in Stage 1. But the extent to which patent exclusiveness can play a critical role is sometimes inexplicably forgotten. More frequently than one might offhand expect, holders of strong patent positions fail to recognize either the market-development virtue of making their patents available to competitors or the market-destroying possibilities of failing to control more effectively their competitors' use of such products.

Generally speaking, the more producers there are of a new product, the more effort goes into developing a market for it. The net result is very likely to be more rapid and steeper growth of the total market. The originator's market share may fall, but his total sales and profits may rise more rapidly. Certainly this has been the case in recent years of color television; RCA's eagerness to make its tubes available to competitors reflects its recognition of the power of numbers over the power of monopoly.

On the other hand, the failure to set and enforce appropriate quality standards in the early days of polystyrene and polyethylene drinking glasses and cups produced such sloppy, inferior goods that it took years to recover the consumer's confidence and revive the growth pattern.

But to try to see in advance what a product's growth pattern might be is not very useful if one fails to distinguish between the industry pattern and the pattern of the single firm—for its particular brand. The industry's cycle will almost certainly be different from the cycle of individual firms. Moreover, the life cycle of a given product may be different for different companies in the same industry at the same point in time, and it certainly affects different companies in the same industry differently.

ORIGINATOR'S BURDENS

The company with most at stake is the original producer—the company that launches an entirely new product. This company generally bears most of the costs, the tribulations, and certainly the risks of developing both the product and the market.

Competitive Pressure

Once the innovator demonstrates during the market development stage that a solid demand exists, armies of imitators rush in to capitalize on and help create the boom that becomes the market growth, or takeoff, stage. As a result, while exceedingly rapid growth will now characterize the product's total demand, for the originating company its growth stage paradoxically now becomes truncated. It has to share the boom with new competitors. Hence the potential rate of acceleration of its own takeoff is

EXHIBIT II: PRODUCT LIFE CYCLE—ORIGINATING COMPANY

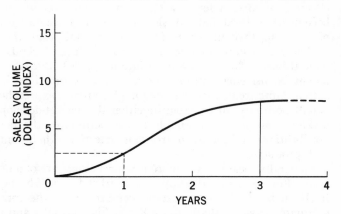

diminished and, indeed, may actually fail to last as long as the industry's. This occurs not only because there are so many competitors, but, as we noted earlier, also because competitors often come in with product improvments and lower prices. While these developments generally help keep the market expanding, they greatly restrict the originating company's rate of growth and the length of its takeoff stage.

All this can be illustrated by comparing the curve in EXHIBIT II with that in EXHIBIT I, which shows the life cycle for a product. During Stage 1 in EXHIBIT I there is generally only one company—the originator—even though the whole exhibit represents the entire industry. In Stage 1 the originator is the entire industry. But by Stage 2 he shares the industry with many competitors. Hence, while EXHIBIT I is an industry curve, its Stage 1 represents only a single company's sales.

EXHIBIT II shows the life cycle of the originator's brand—his own sales curve, not that of the industry. It can be seen that between Year 1 and Year 2 his sales are rising about as rapidly as the industry's. But after Year 2, while industry sales in EXHIBIT I are still in vigorous expansion, the originator's sales curve in EXHIBIT II has begun to slow its ascent. He is now sharing the boom with a great many competitors, some of whom are much better positioned now than he is.

Profit Squeeze

In the process the originator may begin to encounter a serious squeeze on his profit margins. EXHIBIT III, which traces the profits per unit of the originator's sales, illustrates this point. During the market development stage his per-unit profits are negative. Sales volume is too low at existing prices. However, during the market growth stage unit profits boom as output rises and unit production costs fall. Total profits rise enormously. It is the presence of such lush profits that both attracts and ultimately destroys competitors.

EXHIBIT III: UNIT PROFIT CONTRIBUTION LIFE CYCLE—
ORIGINATING COMPANY

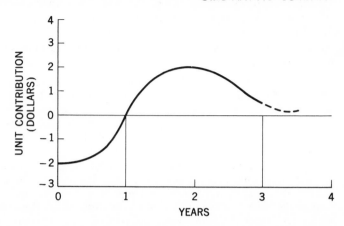

Consequently, while (1) industry sales may still be rising nicely (as at the Year 3 point in EXHIBIT I), and (2) while the originating company's sales may at the same point of time have begun to slow down noticeably (as in EXHIBIT II), and (3) while at this point the originator's total profits may still be rising because his volume of sales is huge and on a slight upward trend, his profits per unit will often have taken a drastic downward course. Indeed, they will often have done so long before the sales curve flattened. They will have topped out and begun to decline perhaps around the Year 2 point (as in EXHIBIT III). By the time the originator's sales begin to flatten out (as at the Year 3 point in EXHIBIT II), unit profits may actually be approaching zero (as in EXHIBIT III).

At this point more competitors are in the industry, the rate of industry demand growth has slowed somewhat, and competitors are cutting prices. Some of them do this in order to get business, and others do it because their costs are lower owing to the fact that their equipment is more modern and productive.

The industry's Stage 3—maturity—generally lasts as long as there are no important competitive substitutes (such as, for example, aluminum for steel in "tin" cans), no drastic shifts in influential value systems (such as the end of female modesty in the 1920's and the consequent destruction of the market for veils), no major changes in dominant fashions (such as the hour-glass female form and the end of waist cinchers), no changes in the demand for primary products which use the product in question (such as the effect of the decline of new railroad expansion on the demand for railroad ties), and no changes either in the rate of obsolescence of the product or in the character or introductory rate of product modifications.

Maturity can last for a long time, or it can actually never be attained. Fashion goods and fad items sometimes surge to sudden heights, hesitate momentarily at an uneasy peak, and then quickly drop off into total obscurity.

Stage Recognition

The various characteristics of the stages described above will help one to recognize the stage a particular product occupies at any given time. But hindsight will always be more accurate than current sight. Perhaps the best way of seeing one's current stage is to try to foresee the next stage and work backwards. This approach has several virtues:

¶ It forces one to look ahead, constantly to try to reforesee his future and competitive environment. This will have its own rewards. As Charles F. Kettering, perhaps the last of Detroit's primitive inventors and probably the greatest of all its inventors, was fond of saying, "We should all be concerned about the future because that's where we'll have to spend the rest of our lives." By looking at the future one can better assess the state of the present.

¶ Looking ahead gives more perspective to the present than looking at the present alone. Most people know more about the present than is good for them. It is neither healthy nor helpful to know the present too well, for our perception of the present is too often too heavily distorted by the urgent pressures of day-to-day events. To know where the present is in the continuum of competitive time and events, it often makes more sense to try to know what the future will bring, and when it will bring it, than to try to know what the present itself actually contains.

¶ Finally, the value of knowing what stage a product occupies at any given time resides only in the way that fact is used. But its use is always in the future. Hence a prediction of the future environment in which the information will be used is often more functional for the effective capitalization on knowledge about the present than knowledge about the present itself.

SEQUENTIAL ACTIONS

The life cycle concept can be effectively employed in the strategy of both existing and new products. For purposes of continuity and clarity, the remainder of this article will describe some of the uses of the concept from the early stages of new product planning through the later stages of keeping the product profitably alive. The chief discussion will focus on what I call a policy of "life extension" or "market stretching."[4]

To the extent that Exhibits ii and iii outline the classical patterns of successful new products, one of the constant aims of the originating producer should be to avoid the severe discipline imposed by an early profit squeeze in the market growth stage, and to avoid the wear and waste so typical of the market maturity stage. Hence the following proposition would seem reasonable: when a company develops a new product or service, it should try to plan at the very outset a series of actions to be employed at various subsequent stages in the product's existence so that its sales and profit curves are constantly sustained rather than following their usual declining slope.

---

[4] For related ideas on discerning opportunities for product revivification, see Lee Adler, "A New Orientation for Plotting a Marketing Strategy," *Business Horizons* (Winter 1964), p. 37. [See pp. 120–36.]

In other words, advance planning should be directed at extending, or stretching out, the life of the product. It is this idea of *planning in advance* of the actual launching of a new product to take specific actions later in its life cycle—actions designed to sustain its growth and profitability—which appears to have great potential as an instrument of long-term product strategy.

Nylon's Life

How this might work for a product can be illustrated by looking at the history of nylon. The way in which nylon's booming sales life has been repeatedly and systematically extended and stretched can serve as a model for other products. What has happened in nylon may not have been purposely planned that way at the outset, but the results are quite as if they had been planned.

The first nylon end-uses were primarily military—parachutes, thread, rope. This was followed by nylon's entry into the circular knit market and its consequent domination of the women's hosiery business. Here it developed the kind of steadily rising growth and profit curves that every executive dreams about. After some years these curves began to flatten out. But before they flattened very noticeably, Du Pont had already developed measures designed to revitalize sales and profits. It did several things, each of which is demonstrated graphically in Exhibit iv. This exhibit and the explanation which follows take some liberties with the actual facts of the nylon situation in order to highlight the points I wish to make. But they take no liberties with the essential requisites of product strategy.

Point A of Exhibit iv shows the hypothetical point at which the nylon

EXHIBIT IV: HYPOTHETICAL LIFE CYCLE—NYLON

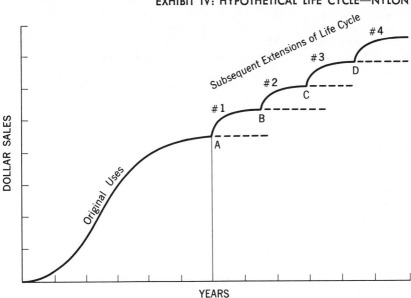

curve (dominated at this point by hosiery) flattened out. If nothing further had been done, the sales curve would have continued along the flattened pace indicated by the dotted line at Point A. This is also the hypothetical point at which the first systematic effort was made to extend the product's life. Du Pont, in effect, took certain "actions" which pushed hosiery sales upward rather than continuing the path implied by the dotted line extension of the curve at Point A. At Point A action #1 pushed an otherwise flat curve upward.

At points B, C, and D still other new sales and profit expansion "actions" (#2, #3, #4, and so forth) were taken. What were these actions? Or, more usefully, what was their strategic content? What did they try to do? They involved strategies that tried to expand sales via four different routes:

1. Promoting more frequent usage of the product among current users.
2. Developing more varied usage of the product among current users.
3. Creating new users for the product by expanding the market.
4. Finding new uses for the basic material.

Frequent Usage. Du Pont studies had shown an increasing trend toward "bareleggedness" among women. This was coincident with the trend toward more casual living and a declining perception among teenagers of what might be called the "social necessity" of wearing stockings. In the light of those findings, one approach to propping up the flattening sales curves might have been to reiterate the social necessity of wearing stockings at all times. That would have been a sales-building action, though obviously difficult and exceedingly costly. But it could clearly have fulfilled the strategy of promoting more frequent usage among current users as a means of extending the product's life.

Varied Usage. For Du Pont, this strategy took the form of an attempt to promote the "fashion smartness" of tinted hose and later of patterned and highly textured hosiery. The idea was to raise each woman's inventory of hosiery by obsolescing the perception of hosiery as a fashion staple that came only in a narrow range of browns and pinks. Hosiery was to be converted from a "neutral" accessory to a central ingredient of fashion, with a "suitable" tint and pattern for each outer garment in the lady's wardrobe.

This not only would raise sales by expanding women's hosiery wardrobes and stores' inventories, but would open the door for annual tint and pattern obsolescence much the same as there is an annual color obsolescence in outer garments. Beyond that, the use of color and pattern to focus attention on the leg would help arrest the decline of the leg as an element of sex appeal—a trend which some researchers had discerned and which, they claimed, damaged hosiery sales.

New Users. Creating new users for nylon hosiery might conceivably have taken the form of attempting to legitimize the necessity of wearing hosiery among early teenagers and subteenagers. Advertising, public relations, and merchandising of youthful social and style leaders would have been called for.

New Uses. For nylon, this tactic has had many triumphs—from varied types of hosiery, such as stretch stockings and stretch socks, to new uses, such as rugs, tires, bearings, and so forth. Indeed, if there had been no further product innovations designed to create new uses for nylon after the original military, miscellaneous, and circular knit uses, nylon consumption in 1962 would have reached a saturation level at approximately 50 million pounds annually.

Instead, in 1962 consumption exceeded 500 million pounds. Exhibit v demonstrates how the continuous development of new uses for the basic material constantly produced new waves of sales. The exhibit shows that in spite of the growth of the women's stocking market, the cumulative result of the military, circular knit, and miscellaneous grouping would have been a fflattened sales curve by 1958. (Nylon's entry into the broadwoven market in 1944 substantially raised sales above what they would have been. Even so, the sales of broadwoven, circular knit, and military and miscellaneous groupings peaked in 1957.)

Had it not been for the addition of new uses for the same basic material—such as warp knits in 1945, tire cord in 1948, textured yarns in 1955, carpet yarns in 1959, and so forth—nylon would not have had the spectacularly rising consumption curve it has so clearly had. At various stages it would have exhausted its existing markets or been forced into decline by competing materials. The systematic search for new uses for the basic (and improved) material extended and stretched the product's life.

Other Examples

Few companies seem to employ in any systematic or planned way the four product lifestretching steps described above. Yet the successful application of this kind of stretching strategy has characterized the history of such well-known products as General Foods Corporation's "Jell-O" and Minnesota Mining & Manufacturing Co.'s "Scotch" tape.[5]

Jell-O was a pioneer in the easy-to-prepare gelatin dessert field. The soundness of the product concept and the excellence of its early marketing activities gave it beautifully ascending sales and profit curves almost from the start. But after some years these curves predictably began to flatten out. Scotch tape was also a pioneer product in its field. Once perfected, the product gained rapid market acceptance because of a sound product concept and an aggressive sales organization. But, again, in time the sales and profit curves began to flatten out. Before they flattened out very much, however, 3M, like General Foods, had already developed measures to sustain the early pace of sales and profits.

Both of these companies extended their products' lives by, in effect, doing all four of the things Du Pont did with nylon—creating more frequent usage among current users, more varied usage among current users, new users, and new uses for the basic "materials":

---

[5] I am indebted to my colleague, Dr. Derek A. Newton, for these examples and other helpful suggestions.

218

EXHIBIT V: INNOVATION OF NEW PRODUCTS POSTPONES THE TIME OF TOTAL MATURITY—NYLON INDUSTRY

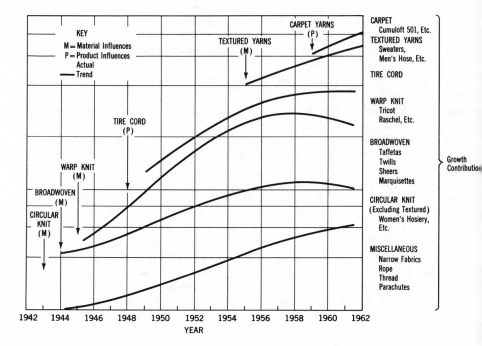

SOURCE: *Modern Textiles Magazine,* February, 1964, p. 33. © 1962 by Jordan P. Yale.

(1) The General Foods approach to increasing the frequency of serving Jell-O among current users was, essentially, to increase the number of flavors. From Don Wilson's famous "six delicious flavors," Jell-O moved up to over a dozen. On the other hand, 3M helped raise sales among its current users by developing a variety of handy Scotch tape dispensers which made the product easier to use.

(2) Creation of more varied usage of Jell-O among current dessert users involved its promotion as a base for salads and the facilitation of this usage by the development of a variety of vegetable flavored Jell-O's. Similarly, 3M developed a line of colored, patterned, waterproof, invisible, and write-on Scotch tapes which have enjoyed considerable success as sealing and decorating items for holiday and gift wrapping.

(3) Jell-O sought to create new users by pinpointing people who could not accept Jell-O as a popular dessert or salad product. Hence during the Metrecal boom Jell-O employed an advertising theme that successfully affixed to the product a fashion-oriented weight control appeal. Similarly, 3M introduced "Rocket" tape, a product much like Scotch tape but lower in price, and also developed a line of commercial cellophane tapes of various widths, lengths, and strengths. These actions broadened product use in commercial and industrial markets.

(4) Both Jell-O and 3M have sought out new uses for the basic material. It is known, for example, that women consumers use powdered gelatin dissolved in liquids as a means of strengthening their fingernails. Both men and women use it in the same way as a bone-building agent. Hence Jell-O introduced a "completely flavorless" Jell-O for just these purposes. 3M has also developed new uses for the basic material—from "double-coated" tape (adhesive on both sides) which competes with ordinary liquid adhesives, to the reflecting tape which festoons countless automobile bumpers, to marker strips which compete with paint.

Extension Strategies

The existence of the kinds of product life cycles illustrated in EXHIBITS I and II and the unit profit cycle in EXHIBIT III suggests that there may be considerable value for people involved in new product work to begin planning for the extension of the lives of their products even before these products are formally launched. To plan for new life-extending infusions of effort (as in EXHIBIT IV) at this preintroduction stage can be extremely useful in three profoundly important ways.

1. *It generates an active rather than a reactive product policy.*

It systematically structures a company's long-term marketing and product development efforts in advance, rather than each effort or activity being merely a stop-gap response to the urgent pressures of repeated competitive thrusts and declining profits. The life-extension view of product policy enforces thinking and planning ahead—thinking in some systematic way about the moves likely to be made by potential competitors, about possible changes in consumer reactions to the product, and the required selling activities which best take advantage of these conditional events.

2. *It lays out a long-term plan designed to infuse new life into the product at the right time, with the right degree of care, and with the right amount of effort.*

Many activities designed to raise the sales and profits of existing products or materials are often undertaken without regard to their relationship to each other or to timing—the optimum point of consumer readiness for such activities or the point of optimum competitive effectiveness. Careful advance planning, long before the need for such activity arises, can help assure that the timing, the care, and the efforts are appropriate to the situation.

For example, it appears extremely doubtful that the boom in women's hair coloring and hair tinting products would have been as spectacular if vigorous efforts to sell these products had preceded the boom in hair sprays and chemical hair fixers. The latter helped create a powerful consumer consciousness of hair fashions because they made it relatively easy to create and wear fashionable hair styles. Once it became easy for women to have fashionable hair styles, the resulting fashion consciousness helped open the door for hair colors and tints. It could not have happened the other way around, with colors and tints first creating fashion consciousness and thus raising the sales of sprays and fixers. Because understanding the reason for this precise order of events is essential for appreciating the importance of early pre-introduction life-extension planning, it is useful to go into a bit of detail. Consider:

For women, setting their hair has been a perennial problem for centuries. First, the length and treatment of their hair is one of the most obvious ways in which they distinguish themselves from men. Hence to be attractive in that distinction becomes crucial. Second, hair frames and highlights the face, much like an attractive wooden border frames and highlights a beautiful painting. Thus hair styling is an important element in accentuating the appearance of a woman's facial features. Third, since the hair is long and soft, it is hard to hold in an attractive arrangement. It gets mussed in sleep, wind, damp weather, sporting activities, and so forth.

Therefore, the effective *arrangement* of a woman's hair is understandably her first priority in hair care. An unkempt brunette would gain nothing from making herself into a blond. Indeed, in a country where blonds are in the minority, the switch from being an unkempt brunette to being an unkempt blond would simply draw attention to her sloppiness. But once the problem of arrangement became easily "solved" by sprays and fixers, colors and tints could become big business, especially among women whose hair was beginning to turn gray.

The same order of priorities applies in industrial products. For example, it seems quite inconceivable that many manufacturing plants would easily have accepted the replacement of the old single-spindle, constantly man-tended screw machine by a computerized tape-tended, multiple-spindle machine. The mechanical tending of the multiple-spindle machine was a necessary intermediate step, if for no other reason than that it required a lesser work-flow change, and certainly a lesser conceptual leap for the companies and the machine-tending workers involved.

For Jell-O, it is unlikely that vegetable flavors would have been very successful before the idea of gelatin as a salad base had been pretty well accepted. Similarly, the promotion of colored and patterned Scotch tape as a gift and decorative seal might not have been as successful if department stores had not, as the result of their drive to compete more effectively with mass merchandisers by offering more customer services, previously demonstrated to the consumer what could be done to wrap and decorate gifts.

3. *Perhaps the most important benefit of engaging in advance, pre-introduction planning for sales-extending, market-stretching activities later in the product's life is that this practice forces a company to adopt a wider view of the nature of the product it is dealing with.*

Indeed, it may even force the adoption of a wider view of the company's business. Take the case of Jell-O. What is its product? Over the years Jell-O has become the brand umbrella for a wide range of dessert products, including cornstarch-base puddings, pie fillings, and the new "Whip'n Chill," a light dessert product similar to a Bavarian Creme or French Mousse. On the basis of these products, it might be said that the Jell-O Division of General Foods is in the "dessert technology" business.

In the case of tape, perhaps 3M has gone even further in this technological approach to its business. It has a particular expertise (technology) on which it has built a constantly expanding business. This expertise can be said to be that of bonding things (adhesives in the case of Scotch tape) to other things, particularly to thin materials. Hence we see 3M developing scores of profitable items, including electronic recording tape (bonding electron-sensitive materals to tape), and "Thermo-Fax" duplicating equipment and supplies (bonding heat reactive materials to paper).

CONCLUSION

For companies interested in continued growth and profits, successful new product strategy should be viewed as a planned totality that looks ahead over some years. For its own good, new product strategy should try to predict in some measure the likelihood, character, and timing of competitive and market events. While prediction is always hazardous and seldom very accurate, it is undoubtedly far better than not trying to predict at all. In fact, every product strategy and every business decision inescapably involves making a prediction about the future, about the market, and about competitors. To be more systematically aware of the predictions one is making so that one acts on them in an offensive rather than a defensive or reactive fashion—this is the real virtue of preplanning for market stretching and product life extension. The result will be a product strategy that includes some sort of *plan for a timed sequence of conditional moves*.

Even before entering the market development stage, the originator should make a judgment regarding the probable length of the product's normal life, taking into account the possibilities of expanding its uses and users. This judgment will also help determine many things—for example, whether to price the product on a skimming or a penetration basis, or what kind of relationship the company should develop with its resellers.

These considerations are important because at each stage in a product's life cycle each management decision must consider the competitive requirements of the next stage. Thus a decision to establish a strong branding policy during the market growth stage might help to insulate the brand against strong price competition later; a decision to establish a policy of "protected" dealers in the market development stage might facilitate point-of-sale promotions during the market growth state, and so on. In short, having a clear idea of future product development possibilities and market development opportunities should reduce the likelihood of becoming locked into forms of merchandising that might possibly prove undesirable.

This kind of advance thinking about new product strategy helps management avoid other pitfalls. For instance, advertising campaigns that look successful from a short-term view may hurt in the next stage of the life cycle. Thus at the outset Metrecal advertising used a strong medical theme. Sales boomed until imitative competitors successfully emphasized fashionable slimness. Metrecal had projected itself as the dietary for the overweight consumer, an image that proved far less appealing than that of being the dietary for people who were fashion-smart. But Metrecal's

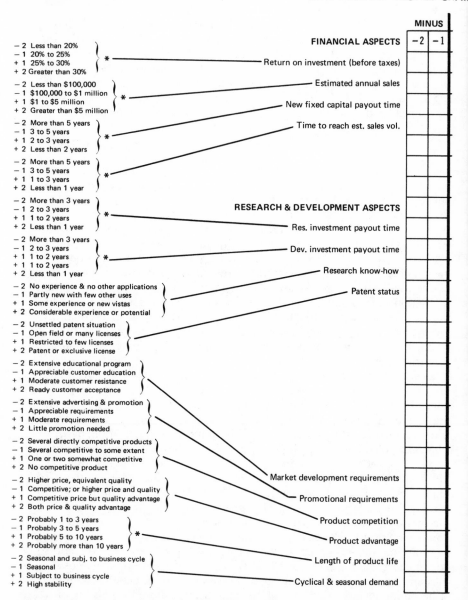

MINUS

FINANCIAL ASPECTS

-2 Less than 20%
-1 20% to 25%
+1 25% to 30%
+2 Greater than 30%
Return on investment (before taxes)

-2 Less than $100,000
-1 $100,000 to $1 million
+1 $1 to $5 million
+2 Greater than $5 million
Estimated annual sales
New fixed capital payout time

-2 More than 5 years
-1 3 to 5 years
+1 2 to 3 years
+2 Less than 2 years
Time to reach est. sales vol.

-2 More than 5 years
-1 3 to 5 years
+1 1 to 3 years
+2 Less than 1 year

-2 More than 3 years
-1 2 to 3 years
+1 1 to 2 years
+2 Less than 1 year
RESEARCH & DEVELOPMENT ASPECTS
Res. investment payout time

-2 More than 3 years
-1 2 to 3 years
+1 1 to 2 years
+1 1 to 2 years
+2 Less than 1 year
Dev. investment payout time
Research know-how

-2 No experience & no other applications
-1 Partly new with few other uses
+1 Some experience or new vistas
+2 Considerable experience or potential
Patent status

-2 Unsettled patent situation
-1 Open field or many licenses
+1 Restricted to few licenses
+2 Patent or exclusive license

-2 Extensive educational program
-1 Appreciable customer education
+1 Moderate customer resistance
+2 Ready customer acceptance

-2 Extensive advertising & promotion
-1 Appreciable requirements
+1 Moderate requirements
+2 Little promotion needed

-2 Several directly competitive products
-1 Several competitive to some extent
+1 One or two somewhat competitive
+2 No competitive product

-2 Higher price, equivalent quality
-1 Competitive; or higher price and quality
+1 Competitive price but quality advantage
+2 Both price & quality advantage
Market development requirements

-2 Probably 1 to 3 years
-1 Probably 3 to 5 years
+1 Probably 5 to 10 years
+2 Probably more than 10 years
Promotional requirements
Product competition
Product advantage

-2 Seasonal and subj. to business cycle
-1 Seasonal
+1 Subject to business cycle
+2 High stability
Length of product life
Cyclical & seasonal demand

-2 | -1

*The ratings for this aspect will depend on the individual company's type of business, accounting methods, and financial objectives. The values shown above are estimated on the basis of various published information to bracket the averages for large chemical companies

original appeal had been so strong and so well made that it was a formidable task later on to change people's impressions about the product. Obviously, with more careful long-range planning at the outset, a product's image can be more carefully positioned and advertising can have more clearly defined objectives.

Recognizing the importance of an orderly series of steps in the intro-

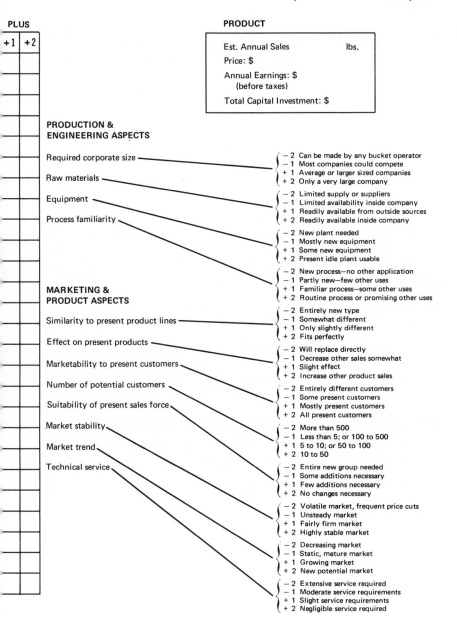

PLUS

+1	+2

PRODUCT

Est. Annual Sales   lbs.

Price: $

Annual Earnings: $
(before taxes)

Total Capital Investment: $

PRODUCTION &
ENGINEERING ASPECTS

Required corporate size

Raw materials

Equipment

Process familiarity

− 2 Can be made by any bucket operator
− 1 Most companies could compete
+ 1 Average or larger sized companies
+ 2 Only a very large company

− 2 Limited supply or suppliers
− 1 Limited availability inside company
+ 1 Readily available from outside sources
+ 2 Readily available inside company

− 2 New plant needed
− 1 Mostly new equipment
+ 1 Some new equipment
+ 2 Present idle plant usable

− 2 New process—no other application
− 1 Partly new—few other uses
+ 1 Familiar process—some other uses
+ 2 Routine process or promising other uses

MARKETING &
PRODUCT ASPECTS

Similarity to present product lines

Effect on present products

Marketability to present customers

Number of potential customers

Suitability of present sales force

Market stability

Market trend

Technical service

− 2 Entirely new type
− 1 Somewhat different
+ 1 Only slightly different
+ 2 Fits perfectly

− 2 Will replace directly
− 1 Decrease other sales somewhat
+ 1 Slight effect
+ 2 Increase other product sales

− 2 Entirely different customers
− 1 Some present customers
+ 1 Mostly present customers
+ 2 All present customers

− 2 More than 500
− 1 Less than 5; or 100 to 500
+ 1 5 to 10; or 50 to 100
+ 2 10 to 50

− 2 Entire new group needed
− 1 Some additions necessary
+ 1 Few additions necessary
+ 2 No changes necessary

− 2 Volatile market, frequent price cuts
− 1 Unsteady market
+ 1 Fairly firm market
+ 2 Highly stable market

− 2 Decreasing market
− 1 Static, mature market
+ 1 Growing market
+ 2 New potential market

− 2 Extensive service required
− 1 Moderate service requirements
+ 1 Slight service requirements
+ 2 Negligible service required

duction of sales-building "actions" for new products should be a central ingredient of long-term product planning. A carefully preplanned program for market expansion, even before a new product is introduced, can have powerful virtues. The establishment of a rational plan for the future can also help to guide the direction and pace of the on-going technical research in support of the product. Although departures from such a plan will surely have to be made to accommodate unexpected events and revised judgments, the plan puts the company in a better position to *make* things happen rather than constantly having to react to things that *are* happening.

It is important that the originator does *not* delay this long-term planning until after the product's introduction. How the product should be introduced and the many uses for which it might be promoted at the outset should be a function of a careful consideration of the optimum sequence of suggested product appeals and product uses. Consideration must focus not just on optimum things to do, but as importantly on their optimum *sequence*—for instance, what the order of use of various appeals should be and what the order of suggested product uses should be. If Jell-O's first suggested use had been as a diet food, its chances of later making a big and easy impact in the gelatin dessert market undoubtedly would have been greatly diminished. Similarly, if nylon hosiery had been promoted at the outset as a functional daytime-wear hosiery, its ability to replace silk as the acceptable high-fashion hosiery would have been greatly diminished.

To illustrate the virtue of pre-introduction planning for a product's later life, suppose a company has developed a nonpatentable new product —say, an ordinary kitchen salt shaker. Suppose that nobody now has any kind of shaker. One might say, before launching it, that (1) it has a potential market of "x" million household, institutional, and commercial consumers, (2) in two years market maturity will set in, and (3) in one year profit margins will fall because of the entry of competition. Hence one might lay out the following plan:

I. *End of first year: expand market among current users*
Ideas—new designs, such as sterling shaker for formal use, "masculine" shaker for barbecue use, antique shaker for "Early American" households, miniature shaker for each table place setting, moisture-proof design for beach picnics.

II. *End of second year: expand market to new users*
Ideas—designs for children, quaffer design for beer drinkers in bars, design for sadists to rub salt into open wounds.

III. *End of third year: find new uses*
Ideas—make identical product for use as a pepper shaker, as decorative garlic salt shaker, shaker for household scouring powder, shaker to sprinkle silicon dust on parts being machined in machine shops, and so forth.

This effort to prethink methods of reactivating a flattening sales curve far in advance of its becoming flat enables product planners to assign priorities to each task, and to plan future production expansion and capital and marketing requirements in a systematic fashion. It prevents one's trying to do too many things as once, results in priorities being determined rationally instead of as accidental consequences of the timing of new ideas, and disciplines both the product development effort that is launched in support of a product's growth and the marketing effort that is required for its continued success.

17

Systems Selling: Industrial Marketing's New Tool

THOMAS J. MURRAY

When C. Ray Harmon was brought in as assistant to the president of Los Angeles' Electronic Specialty Co. in 1955, he found the firm floundering along with a few components on its production lines, a meager $1.6 million in sales and only $72,000 in profits. The company had just gone public after an erratic eleven-year existence, and its growth prospects in the electronics market were not particularly bright. Harmon, however, came armed with a reputation as a "hatchet man" whose specialty was chopping off operating inefficiencies. More important, he brought with him a plan to change the entire profile of the concern.

In just nine years, Harmon's idea has transformed a sluggish outfit into a thriving operation. Sales are expected to top $85 million this year, and earnings will probably exceed $1.6 million. And what was Harmon's plan? It was to develop full lines of compatible products and services that could be tied together and marketed in packages called "systems." His method: spin off all unrelated items and build a full "systems" capability for the firm through acquisitions.

Electronic Specialty's experience, while unusually successful, is by no means an isolated case. The systems approach to industrial marketing has sent a quiet revolution rippling through the ranks of American business. Scores of companies have placed their marketing emphasis on selling systems, or, as they are often described, combinations of products and ser-vices designed to perform a complete function for the customer. The upshot is a dimming of the traditional role of many suppliers as mere vendors of off-the-shelf items and a concomitant growth in their ambitions to act as project contractors who move in and solve problems.

Big firms such as Allis-Chalmers, Honeywell and General Precision, as well as medium-sized and small concerns, such as Dorr-Oliver, Taylor Instrument, Ajax Magnethermic, Hobart Manufacturing and Rohr Corp. to name but a few, are trying to become all things to their customers. From their wide range of goods and services, these companies are now providing start-to-finish systems designed, engineered and packaged to perform integrated functions ranging from manufacturing to material handling and from data processing to distribution.

Among the more complex systems are General Precision's fully auto-matic pressure pumping and inventory measuring system for huge petro-leum tank farms and Ajax Magnethermic's fully integrated continuous-casting system for the processing of nonferrous metals from raw materials to finished product. Somewhat simpler systems include the total power propulsion package engineered for and installed in commercial jet trans-port by Rohr Corp. and the full refrigeration, heating, ventilating and air-conditioning package designed and sold by Hussmann Refrigeration to supermarkets.

For most of these firms, the big push toward systems selling in the industrial market is of very recent vintage and in many cases involves some of the same corporate integration achieved at Electronic Specialty. Thus, with companies such as Allis-Chalmers, which began its drive about four years ago through the acquisition of a joint interest in a systems company, or with General Precision, which combined two hardware com-panies in 1962 to enhance its systems capability, or with Ajax, which bought two concerns with compatible product lines in 1958, the shift to this has involved a step-by-step development of their capabilities. Says William Terry, general manager of Allis-Chalmers' electrical apparatus and systems division: "Every expansion of our plants is geared in some way to further development of this systems concept."

Why is everybody getting on the systems-selling bandwagon? For the most part, it is due to an emerging awareness among marketing men that industrial buyers are searching for greater value for every purchasing dollar. Says Conrad Jones, vice president at the well-known management consulting firm Booz, Allen & Hamilton: "In the future, you'll find more customers thinking in terms of doing more business with fewer suppliers. You can't satisfy a customer with just a product. We think selling a total package of satisfaction is the way of the future."

More specifically, the reasons for the upsurge of interest in this market-ing strategy range over the full spectrum of recent industrial develop-ments:

● Intensifying competition has caused suppliers to search out new ways to mar-ket their goods, hence the accent on selling whole packages of products and services with its promise of more sales, fuller use of capacity and greater turn-over.

- An increasing awareness on the part of industrial firms that the machinery and techniques required for a modern plant are so complex, they can rarely under-stand all their own needs, much less buy and install the equipment on their own.
- The need for greater reliability of technical machinery and processes is forcing industrial buyers to lean heavily on the quality of equipment purchased, hence the demand for greater supplier responsibility.
- The realization of small industrial firms, caught in a competitive squeeze, that they can no longer afford to think in terms of individual components.

Spurred on by these developments, vendors have been promoting, advertising and selling this systems concept with ever-widening emphasis. And yet, for all the hoopla surrounding the trend, there is really nothing new about it at all. Its origins can probably be found in the approach of the Bell System more than fifty years ago when American Telephone & Telegraph President Theodore Vail looked upon the telephone not as a product to be sold but as a total communications system with a variety of integrated services. Similarly, heavy-equipment manufacturers such as General Electric and Allis-Chalmers decades ago were putting together combinations of their equipment and services to perform complete cycles on production lines.

What is new, however, is the increasing integration of automation with manufacturing and processing functions and all the allied operations of a contemporary industrial facility. Suppliers view the possibilities of apply-ing some form of automation to their products as virtually endless. "In ten years," says George W. Downs, director of systems sales at General Telephone's Automatic Electric Co., "it will be fantastic. Soon all pro-cesses will be automated."

Moreover, applications of the systems approach in the military market have provided a powerful impetus to its growth in the industrial field. The skills, advanced technology and marketing ability acquired in servic-ing defense contracts have begun to give many companies new outlets to the commercial market. "In one case about two years ago," points out Electronic Specialty President William H. Burgess, "we discovered that a system we had been building for a defense contract was applicable to the industrial area."

But for all the emphasis on the term *systems*, there is considerable objection in some quarters to the glibness with which it is used. To Harold A. Wolff of Booz, Allen & Hamilton, the packages being sold by most suppliers are not, despite their claims, systems. "They're just selling related products," insists Wolff. "There's nothing new about that. It's just fundamental marketing know-how."

And certainly there is no unanimity among suppliers themselves on a precise definition of the term they have begun to use so freely. In fact, at a seminar organized by the American Management Association, represen-tatives of several leading manufacturers found themselves at odds about what systems selling is. Finally, after much wrangling, says Lester M.

Gottlieb, manager of marketing plans for IBM's data-processing division, a consensus was reached. The definition: "It is marketing based on the consideration of a customer or prospect's needs together with a proposal of a solution for his problem," relates Gottlieb. "This is opposed to coming in with a product and creating a need for it. Or to put it simply, it's really just problem-solving." Nevertheless, until a more precise term is coined, the prevailing trend among suppliers is to describe the concept they are using as systems selling.

WHITHER OBJECTIVITY?

There is, of course, some question about whether a company selling its own equipment in the design and installation of a system can be truly objective in its solution to a customer problem. "The nub of this thing is objectivity," asserts President Allan Harvey of Dasol Corp., New York management consultant firm. "There is a fundamental conflict of interest here and a question of whether a firm has developed the best solution to a client's problem."

By way of answering this charge, most firms assert that they are staking far too much of their reputation on such sales to chance such a risk. To George F. Lambeth, Dorr-Oliver marketing manager, for example, project responsibility means that the firm can insure the quality and performance of its product and thus enhance its prestige. Moreover, management likes the fuller corporate identity that goes with the sale of a system rather than a mere product, and regards its installations as a showcase to spur further sales.

The advantages accruing from this marketing tool do not stop there. Right off the top is the obvious boost it gives to sales. "Ours have grown by one-third," claims Ralph L. Shapcott, president of General Precision's industrial controls division. Adds Donald T. Gregg, manager of Taylor Instrument Co.'s contract and construction division: "Over several years now it has added an appreciable portion to our volume, perhaps as much as 10%." And reports Nathaniel T. Holzer, vice president of marketing at Los Angeles' Redcor Corp.: "You might say that our climb from just $300,000 in sales just two years ago to over $4.5 million this year is largely a result of this approach."

Equally heart-warming to its practitioners is the broader line of products the systems approach can spawn. A vendor's capabilities can be stretched to produce new items for integration in more elaborate systems or in further improvements to an original installation. Also, the competitive edge it gives a firm is so compelling, it is almost sufficient reason in itself for switching to a systems approach. Since sale of a total system involves a long-term marriage between vendor and buyer, the supplier is virtually assured of being the one continuing source of parts and service. Says one marketing executive, with an almost diabolical grin: "It's positively Machiavellian, isn't it?"

For all firms marketing such packaged programs, the one enduring benefit is an overall improvement in customer relations. The intimate relationship that develops between both parties, together with the solution that a supplier brings (hopefully) to his client's problems, molds a special tie that is unlike anything in more conventional vendor-customer relationships.

Organizing a company for the systems approach to marketing involves, in many cases, a thoroughgoing overhaul of its operations—from management outlook to sales procedures in the field. At Electronic Specialty, the basic decision started at the very top and was predicated on the belief that an acquisition program was the essential route to building up the required product lines. The firm has since picked up some twenty firms with compatible products, including a complete marketing organization for its selling, and has developed a full engineering capability to handle its design and application programs.

One major problem that can trouble the multidivisional company getting into the systems business is coordinating the various activities of each division. This problem has been solved at Electronic Specialty by the creation of a position called system project manager, an outgrowth of military and aerospace marketing practices. Notes IBM's Lester Gottlieb: "This is a fairly prevalent solution among systems companies. Making him [the system project manager] responsible for the whole project is one of the most efficient ways to coordinate the activities of each group and to optimize the total corporate point of view."

The actual selling process also calls for a radically different approach. For one thing, sales personnel must completely revamp their thinking away from the traditional product orientation. Says Taylor Instrument's Donald Gregg: "You're working on higher echelons, perhaps even with corporate officials. You rarely discuss the comparative merits of your hardware. You focus on your competence, your reputation and your ability to perform."

For most companies this has meant the establishment of special training programs for sales personnel. At Allis-Chalmers, says William Terry, sales people are brought into headquarters four times a year for special seminars that continuously build up their technical competence and familiarity with new developments.

But not every company agrees with the training approach. At Dorr-Oliver, for example, an official says the company does not contemplate any special training for its salesmen. "For those still oriented in their thinking toward equipment rather than a process," he explains, "we have to convince them to change their approach themselves. It won't happen overnight, of course, but they just have to learn to educate themselves."

Still another development is the increasing use of team selling. Involving as it does in most cases a very high price tag and a relatively complex package of equipment, a systems sale calls for presentation by at least a systems engineer in addition to the regular sales personnel. At Ajax Magnethermic, says marketing manager Marvin E. Hackstedde, the field sales people, all of whom are graduate engineers, are backed up by specialized inside salesmen who follow through on an assigned product area all the way from the initial approach to the prospect to the final installation of a complete continuous-casting system.

But, as more than one observer has pointed out, the systems approach is still so relatively new in its expanded use that there is really no genuinely adequate training ground for systems engineers. "There is an extreme lack of qualification in this field and it is dangerous," warns John W. Field, director of the management information services department for The Diebold Group, a leading management consultant specializing in automation problems. "Words can be sold, but not performance. An intimate knowledge of many disciplines is required for this kind of work, but the demand for trained people hasn't been gratified with adequately trained personnel. What we need are analytical generalists."

In at least one case, that of General Precision's industrial controls division, a likely spawning ground for this new breed of technician is in the customer's own engineering department. According to one General Precision spokesman, the division has found that the man in an equipment user's engineering department who has already been responsible for putting together machinery to solve problems and is familiar with all the functions of the firm's technical operations is, in effect, a systems engineer. "Getting him on our side, however, is the problem," said the official.

IDENTIFY THE PROBLEM!

While this problem is certainly a knotty one for suppliers, an even more critical one is the very heart of any system sale: identifying the problem to be solved for a customer. In many cases, prospects are not even aware of the exact trouble they are having and throw the full responsibility on the supplier. Depending on the relative complexity of the problem, sales engineers steeped in the lore of production and technology may be able to-pinpoint the trouble at an initial session. Or, as in most of today's highly complex situations, the customer will have to provide the supplier with all the knowledge about his process for a full study and evaluation. "When you go into a customer's plant, you have to know every step of his process," says Allis-Chalmers' Terry. "You can't apply computers and controls until you have an intimate knowledge of the whole process."

To most suppliers, this initial step is the most crucial moment in a potential sale. Embroiled as they are in bidding for many contracts, they feel that an early foothold in determining a customer's requirements is absolutely imperative; otherwise, as some vendors complain, they may spend thousands doing the groundwork only to find the prospect using someone else's specifications and purchasing the equipment from a competitor. "We have met situations," claims a Dorr-Oliver official, "where our preliminary engineering for a proposal was taken by the prospect and used to purchase equipment elsewhere."

To minimize the chance of such occurrences, systems sellers must carefully size up each prospect. At Allis-Chalmers, for example, where proposal costs run from $10,000 to as much as $50,000, marketing people calculate their risks very carefully. Says Terry: "We have to decide if we have a reasonable chance of getting the contract. This is very selective selling." Agrees IBM's Gottlieb: "To stay profitable, there is one over-riding guideline: propose only when there is a reasonable chance of getting the order."

If proposals have proven costly to some firms, so too has the develop-ment of the systems themselves. Notes Taylor Instrument's Gregg: "This is high-risk stuff. Many of these things have never been done before, and it's awfully difficult to cost them out. We've been too prone to base prices on customer intent; yet this has been too obscure in many cases." Adds David P. Wilkinson, Electronic Associates vice president of planning: "If you can sell some stock solution over and over again via a system, then it's possible to make a profit out of this systems business. Otherwise, a systems company really has a tough time of it."

No less pressing a problem is the need to educate the customer in the limits and potentials of his system. Lack of comprehension has frequently led to misuse of an installation and consequent complaints to the sup-plier about the quality and performance of his equipment. "Many clients simply don't understand what their system is, what it does and what it can do," laments Redcor's Nat Holzer. "We have launched a customer education program and are beefing it up with a continuing documenta-tion program. As far as we are concerned, it's becoming more and more the responsibility of the manufacturer to teach the customer completely about his system."

One further ramification of this education process, says George M. Muschamp, vice president for engineering at Honeywell's industrial prod-ucts group, is fully informing the customer that if he is to take on a com-plete system he may have to accept some reorganization that goes deep into company operations.

Obviously, then, systems selling is not in any way a simple undertaking. For, as one marketing executive points out with almost painful memory: "It usually takes about three years of hard, hard work to convert fully to the systems approach to selling. Moreover, it calls for an unlimited amount of patience, conviction and perseverance."

Left unsaid in that statement are many obstacles. Among them: the enormous task of pulling together products and services that relate; the costly job of gearing production to meet neatly dovetailed schedules; the tough problem of finding or training adequate engineering and sales forces; the backbreaking effort of coordinating autonomous divisional activities; and the continuing task of keeping customers satisfied with a full line of services.

Despite these obstacles, the trend to systems selling is gathering strength and spreading. In fact, some marketing authorities, such as Roger Ball of Chicago's Roger Ball & Associates and Booz, Allen's Conrad Jones, predict that it will eventually move into the consumer market. Ball envisions companies selling housewives complete storage and maintenance systems for their households. Jones points to the upcoming S. C. Johnson & Son (Johnson Wax) nationwide car-wash chain, with its complete wash and wax capability, as a variation on the systems-selling theme.

But it is to the industrial market that most companies look for the most advanced strides. Just getting off the ground as it is in most cases, the systems approach has already endowed its practitioners with a rewarding glimpse of what can be done for a host of industries, from chemicals to transportation. More important, as Automatic Electric's George Downs puts it: "This is really the infancy of something new in industry. Its future will be fabulous."

18

DEMON
New Product Planning:
A Case History

DAVID B. LEARNER
Applied Devices Corporation

INTRODUCTION

The motivation for a corporation to introduce new products may be to increase its net earnings or market share; to utilize excess capacity or by-products; as a defensive manoeuvre; or some combination of these.[1] Whatever its motives, American business does an appallingly poor job of achieving success in new product introductions.

The measure of this failure varies, depending upon the expert. The generally accepted figure of merit (or more accurately demerit) is that only two out of ten consumer products that emerge from Research and Development become commercial successes.[2] When we reflect that the development of new products is essential to sound growth, and that at least 80% of new products fail—in spite of the market research that is carried on—the prospects are grim indeed.

For those who achieve success in new product ventures the rewards more than compensate the risks. The degree to which annual sales depend upon relatively new products (less than 4 years old) ranges from 5 to 30%, with an average, across industry, of 14%.[3] In essence, one out of every

Reprinted with permission from *Commentary: The Journal of the Marketing Research Society*, October, 1965, pp. 243–61.

[1] Leonard Silk, *The Research Revolution* (New York: McGraw-Hill), 1960.
[2] Booz, Allen & Hamilton, *Management of New Products* (New York, 1960).
[3] *Business Week*, April 29, 1961. pp. 33–34.

seven sales dollars is likely to come from products that didn't exist five years ago. Thus the incentives are great, the pitfalls are clear, yet management persists in using new product planning methods that virtually ensure that 80% of the entries will be unsuccessful.

In the simplest terms, new product planning is supposed to yield the largest return, consistent with market place risks and corporate contraints.

The fact of the matter is that traditional new product marketing methods can handle neither risks or constraints, and are not oriented toward providing maximum return. In alleviating this problem the key ingredients of improved new product marketing are organization and flexibility. Organization is the way in which pertinent information is dealt with. Flexibility is the examination of many alternative marketing plans prior to implementing one.

More than three years have elapsed since a program to develop improved management planning and decision methods for new product marketing along these lines was undertaken. The program, now called DEMON, began by reviewing the methods used by marketing management to introduce new consumer packaged goods products. This review, a great variety of marketing data, and newly developed (for this purpose) mathematics, are the origins of the revolution taking place in new product marketing.

CONCEPTS

Typical of any management system, DEMON is composed of a *planning* and a *decision* function. The planning function required the development of a *planning* system. Planning is defined as the systematic development of a variety of new product marketing program alternatives. A system for evaluating these programs by ranking them from the most to the least profitable is also required. Whether this ranking is on the basis of profit or some other financial criterion—such as return on investment or net cash flow or discount rate—is quite immaterial. Attention is focused upon profit and not share of market, simply because we do not go to the bank with market share points.

In the planning system a wide variety of alternative marketing programs for the new product are developed, each one composed of different values for the same marketing elements: elements such as advertising expenditures, levels of distribution, levels of advertising awareness, performance of the product and so on. The value of each element is determined such that the total effectiveness, measured by profits, is as large as it can possibly be. Now it is quite one thing to put values on these elements, such as requiring advertising content, after three years, to have cumulative awareness of 60%. However, it is quite another issue to develop the copy content and execution in order to achieve that 60% objective. Market research results verify whether the actual performance of each element in the marketing program has achieved, to some reasonable degree, the performance objective set for it. A wide variety of values may be examined for each marketing element, thus providing many alternative plans to choose among on the basis of which is likely to make the most money. These plan alternatives require a framework for evaluation, for making the decision of which plan to implement. This framework is the *decision* system. The decision is reached by relating the way in which the plan is likely to perform with the ground rules management uses for making decisions and the way in which the world is behaving. All three factors are taken into consideration, the plan, the company's internal environment and the external environment in the market place. These three elements are inter-related and must be considered simultaneously, the way in which they normally behave in the world.

These three kinds of information, lead to a decision to *GO* national, say *NO-GO* and scrub the entire effort, or continue *ON* with program development to provide improvement in profit while at the same time reducing the risk or uncertainty about the market place. This rather clear cut and unequivocal three-alternative decision and planning system is described in Figure 1, which illustrates a *GO, NO-GO* Network.

FIGURE 1:

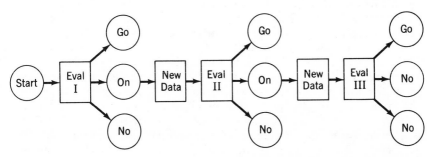

A CASE HISTORY ILLUSTRATION

Although the concepts in the preceding paragraphs are straightforward, they need a great deal of clarification to amplify their meaning and draw a contrast with conventional new product introduction. The best manner of illustrating the use and usefulness of DEMON is to describe one of its earliest applications.

Let us consider the case of a corporation that desires to introduce a new brand into a drug product category. After receiving appropriate approvals for new drugs from the Food and Drug Administration, management initiated development of its marketing program via DEMON.

To the initial surprise of the product group it was unnecessary to compile the usual volumes of market statistics prior to developing the first marketing estimates. Quite to the contrary, since DEMON is founded, in part, upon the way various marketing elements perform, it is straightforward to link these performance ratios so that the result is the most likely response for a new brand in the product category. This response (profit) can then be related to Corporate policies that bear on marketing the new brand. Thus these three sets of data: (1) Management Policies;

(2) Product category description: and (3) Marketing performance ratios, form the starting point for DEMON'S first evaluation.

The Management Policy data are summarized in Table 1, and explained in detail.

TABLE 1: MANAGEMENT POLICIES

Planning Period	5 years
Payout Period	3.5 years
Minimum Acceptable Profit	$4,000,000
Profit Required to GO National	$6,400,000
Marketing Research Budget	$500,000
Profit per Unit	$ .04 per oz.
Management Decision Confidence	70%

The *planning* period serves as the basic time frame of reference for all programs developed by the system. It is an arbitrary planning horizon whose length is established by management practice. The planning period commences when the decision to put the product into national distribution is made. Since its length is arbitrary, management in this case set the planning period at five years to coincide with their normal production and financial planning estimates.

The period during which investments in national marketing will be recovered is called the *Payout Period*. In this example the break-even point for recovering these marketing costs can be *no greater than* three and a half years. This policy statement on payout is quite in contrast with conventional marketing practice that states payout as an objective of marketing, rather than the more flexible and realistic statement of payout as a constraint, or upper limit, on the investment risk management is willing to assume. For that matter, in all of the break-even literature, achievement of payout is stated, and used, as an objective of the plan. Management's real concern with payout is to control risk. DEMON now provides the vehicle for use of payout as a management control rather than as an objective of marketing. Controlling investment risk through payout (at any time *up to* three and a half years), but always pointed toward the objective of delivering maximum profit provides great flexibility in marketing program development.

The *minimum acceptable* profit is the figure below which management would not continue the venture. If no more than a $4,000,000 profit, over the five-year planning period can be expected with some reasonable degree of assurance, then management would elect *No*; i.e. decide to discontinue commercial development. This, of course, is an initial estimate and may be changed from time to time to reflect the way in which the world is changing and management's changes in point of view.

Conversely, when $6,400,000 in profit over the five-year planning period can be achieved, with some reasonable degree of assurance, management would decide to *GO* national. This figure is the threshold above which a *GO* decision is warranted. But the DEMON planning system always seeks the *maximum* profit plan, which might be far greater than the threshold.

The *GO* threshold prevents settling for a maximum profit that would be *below* the acceptable *GO* level. Matching the maximum likely achievement with minimum acceptable management requirements is a unique capability of DEMON planning that forms the heretofore missing link between management's desires and market place realities.

Since DEMON is a decision system the acquisition of new market information that can verify the likely performance of one or more elements of the marketing program is critical. Market research that measures the performance of advertising, promotion, distribution, product performance, or any combination of these and other marketing elements is pivotal for revising the program in order to improve its performance. The $500,000 five-year budget for market research plays a significant role in improving the marketing program. This occurs because when market research appropriations increase, so do the varieties of market programs that may be tested, and as program alternatives increase so does the likelihood of uncovering a better program. Hence larger market research appropriations allow verification of more program alternatives. Without verification, changes in the marketing program simply increase the risk of the entire venture.

The profit per unit of $ .04/oz. represents a target that corporate management established. It is quite possible, indeed probable, that this unit profit target will be modified during program development as price-volume relationships become clearer as a result of tests and measurements. For this reason unit profit ought not be treated as a policy, but as one more marketing program element. In contrast to this reasoning, the product group management elected to fix the unit profit as a policy, and at a later date examine the likely effects of altering that policy.

The final policy statement, attempts to define in meaningful terms the phrase "with a reasonable degree of assurance," appended to both the minimum acceptable profit and the profit required to go national. Management decision confidence is a statement of the surety management requires that the *GO* or *NO* decision will, in fact, be correct. Simply put, this figure is the answer to the question: "How sure am I, that this is the right decision?" In this case, management agreed that they wanted *at least* 70% confidence in either a *GO* or *NO* decision. Greater confidence in one or the other of these decisions might be more desirable. In that event, the management decision confidence for the *GO* and *NO* decisions would be different. In this case, the values were arrived at as a consensus of the product group, and reflect its entrepreneurial spirit; since 50% is like coin flipping and 90% represents 9 put of 10 chances of being right.

Any one of these management policies may be changed from time to time and others may be added. This initial set of policies always serves as a baseline for alterations and additions, thus indicating how policy revisions may affect the marketing program and its likely accomplishments.

PRODUCT CATEGORY DESCRIPTION

Information that describes the product category into which the new brand would enter are compiled in Table 2.

The product category description defines the way in which the world behaves, in much the same way policy statements reflect the way the company behaves.

TABLE 2: PRODUCT CATEGORY DESCRIPTION

Product Class Average Market Share	22.1%
Product Class Variability	±12.3%
Market Size during Five-Year Planning Period	$576,100,000
Cost of Going National	$1,500,000

The product class average market share of 22.1% is based upon a summary of ten years of bi-monthly retail sales audits of brands in the product category. All brands, new, sustaining, and dying, were counted. The class average, and its companion figure product class variability (±12.3%) were arrived at by counting, among all brands over all time periods, the number of times each share of market (from 1 to 100 in 1% steps) occurred. It is quite likely that in another case ten years of data would not be available. Whatever data are available would be used just as is the case if DEMON were not available. With DEMON, in such cases we have the additional advantage of examining the extent to which poor data may affect our conclusions.

Figure 2 shows a typical distribution of the frequency with which each market share was observed.

FIGURE 2: MARKET SHARE FREQUENCY DISTRIBUTION

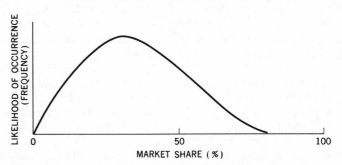

The most likely market share is represented by the greatest frequency, 22.1%. This is a very pertinent number, but it is not sufficient because one other aspect of this distribution is immediately striking: its range of variation. The next figure, Product Class Variability, is ±12.3%. This variability describes the range of the distribution and is a means of interpreting the risk or opportunity represented in any product category. If we consider average as a dividing line, below average market shares represent risk.

Market shares that are above average represent opportunity. In this distribution with large variability, there is a high probability of a low share of market—a risky situation. Similarly, there is high probability of high share of market—great opportunity. The variability of the market

FIGURE 3: RISK—OPPORTUNITY OF PRODUCT CATEGORY

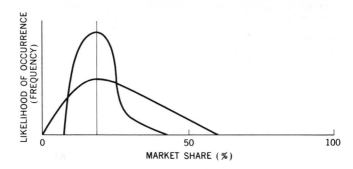

share distribution measures the risk and opportunity inherent in each product category.

We might speculate about a different product category that has precisely the same average—22.1% but a very small range of variability as in Figure 3. The part of the distribution below average is risk, the part above average is opportunity. Low chance of a small market share, very little risk. Virtually no chance of a high market share, little opportunity. This description makes sense in terms of the way in which our economic system is put together. Where there are big risks there ought to be big opportunities. Where there are small risks there ought to be small opportunities. The notion of risk and opportunity may be an interesting way of differentiating among managements: whether they are really entrepreneurs, represented by selecting product categories of big risks and big opportunities or whether they are conservative—choosing small risks with similarly small opportunity.

The forecast of the total dollar volume of the product category over the length of the planning period is $576,100,000. This forecast must be revised as planning moves on by replacing time consumed in the early years of the forecast with projections for additional years at the end. In this fashion we always maintain a forecast that coincides with the planning period.

The $1,500,000 cost of going national represents one-time fixed costs associated with plant expansion, inventory accumulation, sales training, capital costs, and all other non-advertising and promotion expenses associated with putting the brand into national distribution.

These two classes of information: (a) management policies that describe company behavior, and (b) product category description and market behavior were accumulated over a number of weeks, during which regular contact was maintained with the marketing director and his product group. These data were available for the initial marketing program development to help set target values for each marketing element.

PLANNING SYSTEM

The planning component of DEMON is based on certain useful relationships among the elements that make up a marketing program. These relationships identify critical ratios between factors such as advertising expenditures, copy content, product performance, price, distribution and so forth. Of course some of these relationships are specific to each product category but a number of them are sufficiently general to hold over a wide range of product categories. Figure 4 describes in simplified form, a representation of these relationships.

FIGURE 4: DEMON PLANNING SYSTEM

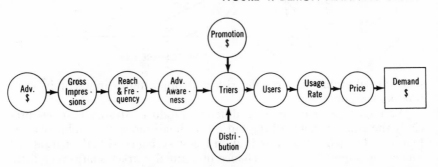

The linkage between the marketing performance ratios (between price and usage, awareness and triers, triers and users and so forth) has been developed from a wide variety of historic performance data. Figure 5 is an illustration of the relationship between advertising awareness, the fraction of the audience that can recall the brand advertising, and brand trial, the fraction of product users who bought the new brand once. The band represents 200 or so case histories of this simultaneous measurement of advertising awareness and brand trial. The solid line is the best summary of those data. If ad awareness is measured by a copy test, the likely trial level resulting from that awareness can be determined using this relationship. There are at least 16 different product categories such as soft drinks, beer, foods, cosmetics, toiletries, and drugs represented in this relationship, but there was no clustering of similar products in any one part of the range.

A similar relationship between trial, (first time brand purchase), and usage, (second time brand purchase) was uncovered. Again the typical band of data can be summarized by a line indicating, for example, that measured trial of 40% is expected to result in usage of 24%. The performance ratio between awareness and trial and the ratio of trial and usage can be linked mathematically to generate the ratio of awareness to usage. This can be done with the relationship between each of the other marketing elements as well.

In this fashion if advertising expenditures are known, estimates of gross rating points, and reach and frequency can be made. Linking all these performance ratios provides the likely result of the expenditure, the media plan, and the copy in terms of consumer awareness of brand advertising. Thus, relationships for each pair of marketing elements provide, for any set of values of these elements, the likely consumer sales of the brand.

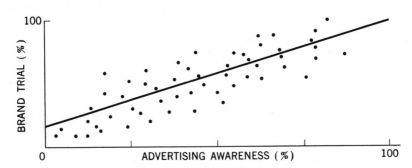

FIGURE 5:

Similarly, if the likely consumer sales required to achieve certain profit levels are known, the values for each element of the marketing program can be estimated. Thus the performance ratios can be used in reverse, moving from right to left through Figure 4.

The program planning component of DEMON relates the data describing the product category (Table 2) to the marketing elements (Figure 4) in such a way that specific values for each element are selected on the basis of making the profits accrued over the five-year planning period maximum. Of course, for the initial program the values are derived by using as a benchmark the likely result of applying the performance ratios to what is known about the product category. In subsequent plan improvements, the verified performance values for each element result from market research, and the initial program bench marks are modified to reflect actual consumer response to the specific advertising, promotion, product, etc., under evaluation.

EVALUATION 1—DECISION

In the case history illustration of DEMON planning, Table 3 illustrates the optimum, or best marketing plan when the product category description is combined with the planning relationships for a first evaluation. Also appended to Table 3 are the management decision implications resulting from simultaneous interaction of the program with management's new product policies. This latter step is accomplished by translating the likely best sales result of the program ($127,000,000) into its profit equivalent ($10,200,000), combining it with risk, the likelihood of achieving that level of profit ($6,200,000), and relating these profit and risk figures to the previously stated management policies. This relationship is illustrated in Figure 6.

The values of each item in Table 3 refer to the most likely response over the five-year planning period. For example, the five-year advertising expenditure of twenty-three million dollars would be most likely to accumulate 69% advertising awareness, and result in the most likely maximum profit of slightly in excess of ten million dollars. Other figures on the program for promotion expenditures and distribution levels were com-

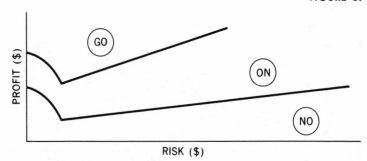

RISK ($)

puted, but for brevity of presentation are omitted here. (See below for Table 3).

Any combination of elements in this marketing program may be examined to determine alternative results in terms of the likely profit. For example, Figure 7 demonstrates the likely profit response to various advertising expenditures ranging from ten million to forty million dollars. It is apparent that the greatest profit occurs at $23,000,000 expenditure; this is the value that is part of the optimum marketing program in Table 3. In similar manner the other elements of the program may be examined illustrating the profit sensitivity of each component of the program.

The *ON* decision occurred for two obvious reasons and one subtle reason. Table 3 shows that the payout control of 3.5 years was exceeded by 1.3 years, even under conditions of the best program possible. Obviously, the best profit could not recover the investment in less than fifty-eight months, because profit will accumulate slowly. The control policy has been exceeded and thus warrants an *ON* decision, setting the stage for improving the marketing program.

In a more subtle manner the risk estimate, or the likelihood of achieving the stated profit also results in the *ON* decision. Risk is composed of

TABLE 3: OPTIMUM MARKETING PROGRAM
AND DECISION GUIDELINES

		Policies
Advertising Expenditures	$23,00,000	
Media Gross Impressions	14.8 billion	
Virtual Reach of Media	146%	
Advertising Awareness	69%	
Product Trial (1st Purchase)	42%	
Product Usage (Re-purchase)	18%	
Price	$.09/oz.	
Total Consumer Demand	$127,000,000	
Profit	$10,200,000	$6,400,000
Risk	6,300,000	
Decision	*ON*	
Decision Confidence	67%	70%
Payout Period	4.8 years	3.5 years

FIGURE 7: PROFIT–AD EXPENDITURE TRADE OFF

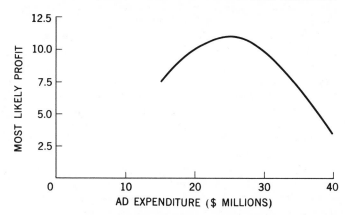

two parts. The first arises from the risk (or opportunity) inherent in the product category; that is, the likelihood of achieving any specified share of market (Figure 2). The second source of risk is the uncertainty arising due to inaccuracies in our data about the way the world behaves. This latter notion accounts for biases in market research, as well as uncertainties arising from estimates of the performance ratios that link the elements in the marketing program. Risk, then, indicates how the product category and the way we view the world may affect our maximum profit expectations.

Obviously, changes in the market share distribution and market research results can change the risk estimate. The first evaluation of the marketing program established this combined risk, or uncertainty, at $6,300,000, relative to the maximum likely profit of $10,200,000. This means that it is almost as likely to achieve $3,900,000 as $16,500,000. Since $3,900,000 is below the $4,000,000 figure established as the NO-boundary, this is equivalent to saying that there is some, although small, chance that the correct decision is NO.

The third reason for an ON decision results because management wanted 70% confidence in a GO decision, but only 67% was achieved considering all risk and policies.

The most obvious policy changes would be to reduce the required GO decision confidence from 70% to 67% and increase the payout control policy from 3.5 years to 4.8 years. The immediate result would be to achieve a GO decision. It is most crucial to point out, however, that management's policies and decisions may be changed, but the maximum likely profit will still be $10,200,000. As one member of the management team expressed it, "This is what we would normally do, get enthusiastic about the product, change our ground rules, and make up our minds to go national with a program that won't excite any more enthusiasm among consumers than we had originally thought."

Although the best course of action might be to continue ON, this must be accomplished in the best possible way. Herein lies another aspect of the management planning role of DEMON. It brings into focus the notion that the system is not merely evaluative, but more importantly it provides the framework for evolving an improved marketing program.

The manner in which the evaluation of the marketing program occurs has two objectives, both of which must be satisfied simultaneously. The product group observed that the marketing program at the conclusion of the first evaluation was likely to generate $10,200,000 in profit with a risk of $6,300,000. Two obvious ways of improving this program would be to produce greater profit with less risk. The profit depends, in part, upon the actual performance of each element in the marketing program. The risk depends, in part, upon the accuracy with which we are able to measure that performance. The selection of one or more elements of the marketing program for improvement must be based on the likelihood of providing the greatest profit increase for the program. Similarly, the surety of that increase must be measured by the market research most likely to reduce uncertainty and risk. Of course, both these objectives should be accomplished in the least costly fashion. The biggest increase in profit coupled with the greatest reduction in risk, considering the cost-effectiveness of each alternative marketing element-research verification combinations determines the manner of continuing *ON*.

FIGURE 8: ON DECISION ALTERNATIVES

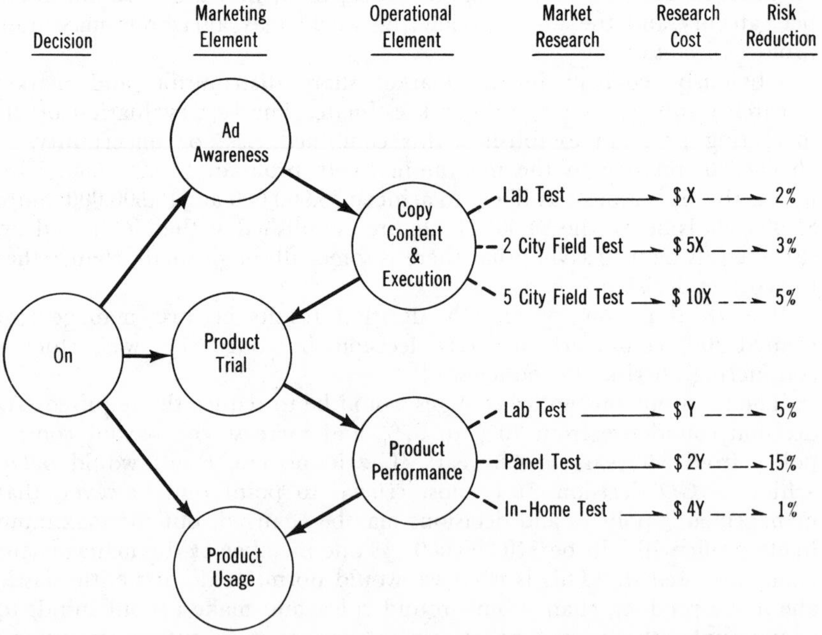

| Decision | Marketing Element | Operational Element | Market Research | Research Cost | Risk Reduction |

These notions can be illustrated by referring to Figure 8 as an example. The *ON* decision alternative has been specified and one or more of the three marketing elements illustrated may be selected as most appropriate for improvement. In each case the conversion of consumers from one element to another is accounted for by some element of the marketing program. Thus the conversion of consumers from being aware of the brand advertising to trying the brand is accomplished by the effectiveness of the copy content and execution of the advertising. The conversion of consumers from triers (first purchase) to users (second purchase) depends upon the product's functional performance. Obviously, then, it is the market performance of the element we wish to improve, and verify such improvement through market research results. There are clearly a variety of ways to measure the performance of each element. Market research tools vary both in accuracy and in cost. The inaccuracy of the research contributes to risk; the performance of the marketing element contributes to profit potential. The choice of the marketing program element for revision is based upon the likely extent of improvement and the resulting increase in profitability of the entire program. The choice of the research tool depends upon the ratio of risk reduction to the cost of the research to reduce the risk.

In the case of this drug product the *ON* analysis indicated that both elements shown in Figure 8 copy content and execution and product performance, were selected to be improved and tested in parallel, thus providing the basis for a second evaluation. Both elements were selected for simultaneous development and testing because their risk reduction per research dollar were virtually equivalent. The creative personnel at the advertising agency developed specific copy and ads in the most professional manner guided by previously collected consumer research. It was the performance of this advertising for magazines and television that was tested to determine what proportion of those who viewed the medium could recall the specific advertising message (awareness) for each of three alternative advertising approaches.

While this creative development and research was completed, the product group arranged an in-home product use test of two alternative product formulations. This project was undertaken to determine the proportion of the sample who purchased the brand after having used each formulation (usage).

In this manner, then, both the performance of the advertising and the performance of the product were measured under realistic conditions. The proportions for both *awareness* and *usage* were then used as up-to-date indications of the performance of these two elements of the marketing program. In conducting the second program evaluation these current values replaced those that were based simply on historic new product performance expectations. Table 4 illustrates the optimum marketing program values and decision resulting from the second evaluation. The asterisks indicate the measured values for the two newly developed marketing program elements.

Comparing Tables 3 and 4 the results of the program improvement are readily apparent. The same level of advertising expenditures provides comparable results up to the point of substituting the actual performance results of the tested advertising. It is apparent that the performance of this advertising is superior to the achievements of the advertising assumed at the first evaluation.

The improved advertising will in all likelihood generate greater trial (47% as compared to 42%). This higher trial augmented by the product performance results achieved a usage figure double (18% compared with 36%) that of the first evaluation. This conversion ratio (trial to usage) indicates that product performance is superior since three out of four triers are likely to re-purchase the brand.

TABLE 4: OPTIMUM MARKETING PROGRAM AND DECISION GUIDELINES

Evaluation 2	
Advertising Expenditures	$23,000,000
Media Gross Impressions	14.8 billion
Virtual Reach of Media	146%
Advertising Awareness	79%
Product Trial (1st Purchase)	47%
Product Usage (Re-purchase)	36%
Price	$.09/oz.
Total Consumer Demand	$257,000,000
Profit	$60,500,000
Decision	GO
Decision Confidence	82%
Payout Period	15 months

Thus with the two verified marketing elements, the program is likely to achieve $257,000,000 in sales over the five-year planning period. These sales result in $60,500,000 of profit with a risk of ±1,600,000. Thus by developing advertising and testing it along with product performance the most likely result is greater profit with reduced risk, in comparison to the initial marketing program. A GO decision is warranted, with 82% confidence that this is the correct decision.

The rate at which this program is likely to generate revenue, compared to expenditures determines the payout period or break-even point of 15 months, well below the management requirement of 42 months. Thus we can see illustrated, once more, the notion of driving towards a maximum profit program and then comparing the likely results to established management policies to determine whether such policies have been satisfied.

It was pointed out to the product group that they had this flexibility in policy examination and they were encouraged to examine the likely consequences of making policy changes. Since the Decision Confidence had been exceeded they speculated what might occur if they settled for the 70% confidence they initially established, rather than the 82% provided by the most recent program. They were very quickly able to see the results in Table 5.

By revising the Decision Confidence downward to the original policy level, two other simultaneous changes resulted. The revised evaluation indicates less confidence (70%) of making more profit ($110 million), thus

TABLE 5: PROFIT–CONFIDENCE PAYOUT TRADE OFF

	Evaluation II	Evaluation II (Revised)
Profit	$60.5 millions	$110 millions
Confidence	82%	70%
Payout Period	15 months	5 months

paying out in a much shorter (5 months) time. This revision shows how closely management policies are related to each other, as well as how they directly effect the marketing program and its objectives.

The marketing program as outlined represented a *GO* decision. The management team was prepared to initiate plans to implement this program and place the brand in the national market, when a review of the in-home use test turned up errors in the data processing. These errors reduced the product usage from 36% to 28%. Rather than three out of four re-purchasers, there were, in fact, only three out of five.

This reduced Trial-to-Usage conversion curtailed likely Consumer Demand to $199,000,000 from $257,000,000 and similarly affected profits from $60,500,000 to $38,400,000. Even with this reduced maximum profit the decision was *GO*, although Decision Confidence dropped to 75% and payout increased to thirty months. Considering Table 5 as well as these new results it was possible to plot a Profit–Payout Period relationship, as in Figure 9.

It is quite apparent that as profit increased the payout period decreases, although not in a directly proportional manner. This is a graphic illustration of the notion that had we chosen a single payout as is conventionally done, we would not even have examined the maximum profit opportunities represented by the short payout periods. Moreover, to expect a market planner to compute a controversial payout plan using a different time period for each is quite preposterous. Nor would automating this task alleviate the basic payout computation assumption of directly proportional marketing expenditures and sales volume. This assumption clearly does not hold, as is so vividly portrayed by the decreasing rate of profit return shown in Figure 9.

FIGURE 9: PROFIT–PAYOUT RELATIONS

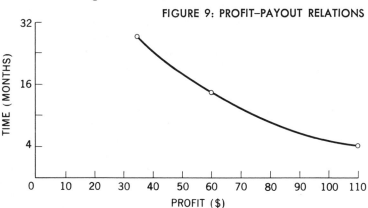

At this point the product group perceived the handicaps they had faced using traditional new product planning approaches. As they were ready to wrap up the program development phase of this product's introduction, one of the product R and D liaison men made a most significant observation. In reviewing the product use test, he pointed out that a 75% conversion from trial to usage would describe a better product than a 60% trial–usage conversion. In this case the two different conversion ratios resulted from research errors. He suggested that had we in fact measured the 60% conversion we could have also examined the likely consequences of 75% conversion just as we had examined ranges for other marketing elements. The \$22,100,000 difference between the likely profit returns of the two product conversions (\$60,500,000 @ 75% = \$38,400,000 @ 60%) represents the likely incremental profit from a better product. One that can convert more triers to users. He continued to point out that the £22.1 million represents what he could afford to spend in R and D toward developing a better product. He quickly went on to say that he did not advocate such a course, but that for the first time, to his knowledge, some reasonable criteria could be expressed to suggest R and D budgets and their target results.

On this insightful note the DEMON product management group disbanded so that the product group could devote its time to implementing the program that had been developed. A number of non-marketing road blocks appeared to frustrate their plans to go national. Production and legal difficulties beset the brand and management was forced to elect the non-optimal strategy of regional introduction. DEMON's planning results were consistent for even in this case they were, unfortunately for their peace of mind, always aware of the likely profits they could have made had other management functions been attended to as carefully as the marketing role.

CONCLUSION

In this case history we have tried to show, in some reasonable detail, the ingredients and results that can be achieved through DEMON new product management planning. We have not extensively contrasted DEMON planning with traditional approaches, although such a comparison is in order. The list is only a partial statement of difference, Table 5.

Two factors can extend this list of contrasts. The first is the reader's grasp of both methods of new product introduction. The second, and more significant results from extended and expanded use of DEMON. The nature of any systematic, organized method focuses our attention upon the collection of certain information.

As these data accumulate, they provide the seed bed for the growth of new insights, in much the same manner as the R and D liaison made his contribution. Thus, continuous improvement is an inherent part of DEMON's use. Imagine the profitability to today's new product introductions, had we had systematic guidelines fifteen years ago. In addition to the short range operational benefits, this is the long range promise of

TABLE 6: NEW PRODUCT PROGRAM
PLANNING CONTRASTS

DEMON	TRADITIONAL
Profit Maximization Objective	Arbitrary Market Share Objective
Relates management policies to likely profits	No policy evaluation available
States decision confidence	Assumes "all or nothing" decisions
Systematically weighs the quality of data needed and used	Intuitive judgment of data quality
Considers profit and risk simultaneously	No risk estimate available
Systematic marketing program development	Trial-and-error market research
Payout period is a maximum limit	Payout period is a fixed point objective
Assumes "all factors varying together"	Assumes "all other things being equal"
Examines alternative plans flexibly	Alternate plan examination is tedious
Unfamiliar method	Comfortable, familiar method
Unproved record	Proven record of failure

DEMON. In examining this promise, one question is most pertinent. How valid is the system?

Any answer must examine validity at three different levels. Does it make sense; so-called face validity? The opinions of people who have worked with it do indicate that it makes sense. It provides reasonable marketing programs, worthwhile insights, and it is, in their judgment, a sound way of making decisions. The component validity of the performance ratios between pairs of marketing elements has been established by making predictions to other cases with a maximum error of $\pm4\%$. The third level of validity concerns the overall system. The evidence is insufficient to answer with any degree of confidence. However, the face validity combined with component validity is more positive verification than has been achieved by any method of introducing new products. At the very minimum DEMON has not established an 8 out of 10 failure rate.

19

The Edsel
Ten Years Later

Wayne State University

It has been almost exactly ten years since the introduction of the Edsel automobile.

There have been more costly new product failures than the Edsel, failures that have been more disastrous from the standpoint of a firm's future, and failures stemming from more egregious mistakes.

The Edsel, nevertheless, is one of the most conspicuous new product failures in business history. The events leading up to the tragedy (or down to the comedy) are examined in this account. It can be argued that the decision to introduce the Edsel was one of the wisest decisions ever made by Ford Motor Company. This extreme position is the one defended. The story is one of a firm proceeding carefully and methodically, working within the context of an elaborate marketing plan, doing most things right—and ending up with a total disaster.[1]

The story begins in 1946, when young Henry Ford, after the death of his father and grandfather, has just taken over management of the com-

---

Reprinted with permission from *Business Horizons,* Fall, 1967, pp. 39–46. Copyright, 1967 by the Foundation for the School of Business at Indiana University.

[1] There are several excellent references on the Edsel, the best of which is "The Fate of the Edsel and Other Business Adventures," by John Brooks (New York: Harper & Row, publishers, 1966). The present account is by way of a personal memoir. While not directly involved in the Edsel—it is hard nowadays to find anyone who was—I held jobs with Ford during the middle fifties, which made it possible for me to have a fair idea of what was going on and to meet personally most of the principal persons involved.

pany. The major problem facing him was a serious need for top level management personnel. This problem was met in two ways, by pirating General Motors and by capitalizing on the fortuitous appearance of the so-called "Whiz Kids."

One of the exclusives pirated from General Motors was Lewis Crusoe, who is—depending on the point of view—either the hero or the villain of this article. Ernest Beech, later chairman of the board of directors, also had been a General Motors executive. The Whiz Kids were several young Air Force officers who had worked together on Air Force logistics and whom Ford hired as a group after World War II. The group was headed by C. B. Thornton, now president of Litton Industries, and included Robert S. McNamara, later president of Ford and eventually Secretary of Defense, and soon to be president of the World Bank, and Arjay Miller, also later president of Ford. Other Whiz Kids who will figure to some degree in this article are F. C. Reith, Ben Mills, and J. O. Wright.

Ford Motor Company, under the first Henry Ford and his confidant Harry Bennett, had fallen far behind most major American industries in sound and modern management practices.

The General Motors alumni and the Whiz Kids quickly remedied this situation. The company was reorganized on a decentralized basis, with operating divisions having almost full profit responsibility. Controllers manuals, procedures manuals, and organization manuals were published. Cost controls were instituted. In effect, in about five years, the company was made over from the equivalent of a feudal barony into the image of a modern corporation. (Thornton left during this time.)

Partly because of this infusion of management talent and subsequent reorganization, Ford made giant strides in the postwar period both in market penetration and profit position.

It should be noted, however, that Ford had some other factors working in its favor. One was that Ford, alone in the automobile industry, operated its own steel mills, an important competitive advantage during the steel shortage following World War II. Another was Fords' excellent cash position, which made it possible for sizeable amounts of money to be poured into new plants and facilities.

A third factor—and perhaps the most important—was the tremendous impact of the styling of the 1949 Ford, which established an entirely new fashion in automobile design. It was the first car—although Studebaker might argue—that had a flat rear deck and hood with the passenger compartment amidships. For its time, the car had a low, rakish look, which made it an immediate styling hit.

A MARKETING PLAN DRAWN

By 1954, Ford had a young, ambitious, and reasonably experienced management team; new and modern facilities; a revitalized group of dealers; money in the bank; and a solid consumer franchise in the low price field. (Ford came very close to beating Chevrolet in sales in 1954.) This combination of circumstances led Ford to decide to expand its share of the market.

The marketing plan that was developed took the form of a head-on assault upon the General Motors car lines. Ford intended to bring General Motors to its knees. At that time, roughly speaking, the Ford car had about 25% of the market, the Chevrolet another 25%, the Buick-Oldsmobile-Pontiac (or "B-O-P") cars a third share 25%, with the final 25% shared by all other makes. It seemed apparent that any gain in Ford Motor Company sales would have to be at the expense of the B-O-P's.

Crusoe, as much as anyone else, was responsible for Ford's plan of battle, although it was Reith, who worked for Crusoe, who actually presented the plan to management. Crusoe had gone from corporate finance to become vice-president and general manager of the Ford division (where he had scored notable successes), and from there to executive vice-president—car and truck divisions. McNamara, under Crusoe, became general manager of the Ford division. Richard Krafve, later to head the Edsel division, was general manager of the Lincoln-Mercury division.

Crusoe, a small dapper man, could inspire personal loyalty and hard work from subordinates. Many Ford executives still refer affectionately to the great days of "Uncle Louie." He was a man with enormous merchandising flair. The two-passenger Thunderbird was Crusoe's car; someone once commented that no one except him would have thought that a combination of the discomfort of a sports car and the performance of a family sedan would be irresistibly appealing.

Crusoe realized that tackling General Motors successfully would not be easy; consequently, his plan was many-faceted. Incidently, no one with Ford thought General Motors would be easy to take, and, for this reason, inordinate effort was put into the attempt; this effort made the final failure conspicuously majestic. Crusoe's product plans went something like this:

1. The 1957 and 1958 Fords cars (longer, wider, and more highly styled than any car ever introduced in the low price field, and with two separate body shells) were to attack the Chevrolet at the low end of the GM line.
2. The Mark II Continental (priced at $10,000) and the 1958 Lincoln (a huge dramatically styled automobile) were to take on the Cadillac at the high end of the GM line.
3. Three entries were planned against the B-O-P cars. One of these was the 1958 four-passenger Thunderbird. A second was a massive, restyled Mercury line, with a special model called the Turnpike Cruiser. The third was the Edsel.

The plan thus envisaged a car-for-car attack, with the principal effort in the middle against the B-O-P's. One is reminded of Pickett's charge at Gettysburg. Nevertheless, the rationale behind the plan was compelling— and remains compelling in retrospect.

First, Ford looked at trends in sales by car lines. It was clear in the middle fifties that the sales of medium price cars were increasing as a percentage of the total market while the sales of lower price cars were declining. Buick was third in sales in 1955. The Mercury, Ford's only medium price entry, had never done particularly well. If the trend continued, Ford saw itself almost out of business in a few years.

Second, the trend to higher price cars was confirmed by the fact that even low
price cars were increasingly sold "loaded"; also, more expensive cars in
lower price lines were selling better than those at the bottom of the line.
Third, with incomes rising, the number of people in the income groups that
bought low price cars was declining. In comparison, the number of people
in the income groups that bought medium price cars was increasing.
Fourth, people who bought Ford cars when they were young tended to trade
them in on B-O-P's when they became more affluent. To retain these owners,
strong entries in the medium price field were essential.

The reasoning was sound then, and is sound now. Ford's principal weakness in the automobile market at the present time, ten years after the Edsel,
is that it does not have a car that can compete vigorously with the Buick,
Oldsmobile, and Pontiac. It needed a car that could do this in 1958, and it
still needs one today. The decision to introduce the Edsel was wise. Its
execution was faulty and plagued by bad luck.

PLAN PUT IN MOTION

Realistic appraisal of the magnitude of the task was the reason for
almost everything done wrong by Ford in its assault on General Motors.
For instance, Crusoe, and others, felt that the new entries would stand a
better chance if handled by independent, divisional profit centers. It was
believed that the Edsel should be merchandised by a separate Edsel division, aggressively concerned with its fate rather than as a separate and
second entry by the Ford or Lincoln-Mercury division. The company
thought that the new Lincoln and the Continental Mark II should be
merchandised similarly.

This marketing scheme led to the establishment of five car divisions—
Ford, Mercury, Continental, Lincoln, and Edsel—in place of the original
Ford and Lincoln-Mercury divisions.

Suddenly, there were five divisional controllers instead of two, five divisional industrial relations managers instead of two, five marketing managers instead of two, and so forth.

It was a time of wild excitement over personal careers. Promotions
came quickly and easily, and morale was high. McNamara was left with
Ford division, Reith given the Mercury, Mills the Lincoln, William Clay
Ford the Continental, and Krafve the Edsel. Establishment of separate
divisions was probably the first, and perhaps the most serious, mistake
made. The divisions were expensive, and raised break-even points impos-
sibly high, and Ford simply did not have the management personnel to
staff them adequately. Talent was spread too thinly, with young and eager
but inexperienced managers handling important and responsible jobs.[2]

It was also believed that separate dealerships for each car line would
be necessary. There was no question that Ford dealers would continue to
handle the Thunderbird; efforts to set up separate dealerships for the

---

[2] I was involved in building a new office building and plant for the new Lincoln
division. The building was depopulated when the Lincoln division was discontinued
in 1957 and was still half-vacant in the early sixties. Some of my friends call it "Reynolds' folly." I was one of the inexperienced managers mentioned in the text.

Lincoln were blocked by the outcries of Mercury dealers. A network of new dealerships, however, was established for the Edsel. These new dealers tended to be under-financed, and many of them were not skilled traders. The company had assumed that a Ford dealer handling the Edsel, if he encountered price resistance, would steer the customer to a Ford. In retrospect, it seems probable that Ford or Mercury dealers could have done a better job than the hastily assembled Edsel dealers.

As part of the push behind the Edsel, the car was introduced in four series and a multitude of models, backed by enormous advertising weight. Such extensive promotion increased expenses, and it is possible that the advertising caused the public to expect too much of the car.

Another mistake from the same root source—realistic recognition of the size of the job—was a decision to try to get as many Edsels as possible on the road immediately after introduction. Ford wanted people to see the car, and to look upon it as an established make. A failure to adhere to quality standards resulted. Many cars that should not have been released from assembly lines without extensive rework were sent to dealers. The Edsel acquired very early the reputation of a poorly constructed car. Most of the "bugs" in the Edsel were ironed out fairly quickly, but not until after the damage had been done.

Finally, the styling of the Edsel turned out to be a grievous error. One cannot attach too much blame to Ford executives for this. For security and other reasons, no automobile manufacturer before the Edsel used consumer research to test the appeal of advanced models prior to introduction. Instead, designers and executives relied on judgment. The styling of the Edsel may have failed because the judgment of the designers and executives who approved it was too well-informed.

For instance, the vertical grille on the Edsel was compared by some executives to the classic cars of the thirties, the LaSalle and the Pierce Arrow. Others were reminded of European sports cars with vertical grilles, the Alfa-Romeo and the Bugatti. At least one executive thought that the Edsel grille resembled the front of the Navy Grumman fighter plane.

None of these associations was clear to the car-buying public. Few remembered the LaSalle and the Pierce Arrow; even fewer were familiar with the Alfa-Romeo and Bugatti. The grille was considered peculiar looking and became the subject of countless jokes. On the other hand, the people responsible for the design of the Edsel wanted the car to look distinctive and different. It is possible that they would have welcomed a research finding that the car did not look like other cars.

MARKETING MISTAKES ALLEGED

Three alleged mistakes in the marketing plan of the Edsel legitimately should not be laid at Ford's door. The target market for the car was reasonably well delineated, the marketing research conducted was of high quality, and the name—while not good—is not likely to have been much of a factor in the Edsel's failure.

Ford was primarily concerned about the market represented by the upward trend in trading from a Ford to one of the B-O-P's. This market could be identified with a high degree of precision; registration lists plus a screening procedure made it easy to single out for further interviewing persons who had left Ford for a GM middle price make. One could then investigate the customers' preferences in automobile design and write advertising themes accordingly.

It was found that people in this market wanted their cars to be elegant and luxurious to communicate their rising status. At the same time, since they were still relatively young, they wanted cars sporty in appearance and high in performance. To reach this market, the stylists working on the Edsel tried to make its design reflect a combination of elegance and youthfulness. Advertising copy stressed the same two points.

The B-O-P's of the middle fifties were all somewhat stodgy cars. The Buick was looked upon as a conservative "doctor's car"; the Pontiac still had its silver streak and was often called an "old maid's car." The Oldsmobile was considered more experimental, but had the same body shell as the other two cars, and resembled them. All three were solid, respectable cars, but none was either elegant or particularly youthful. They appeared vulnerable to the approach taken with the Edsel.

As it turned out, the Edsel failed to accomplish the objectives established for it; nevertheless, the plan itself was probably sound. Less than three years after the introduction of the Edsel, Semon Knudsen set almost identical objectives for the Pontiac and was phenomenally successful.

Moreover, the research done by the Edsel division cannot be faulted. If one goes through the bound volumes of Edsel research reports in the Ford archives, one is struck—after a somewhat eerie feeling is overcome— by the sophistication of the techniques used and the perspicacity of the findings. No styling research was conducted, but, as noted at that time, no one in the industry was doing such research. Otherwise, the research was comprehensive in the areas of market delineation, product characteristics and image, competition, copy strategy, and other aspects of the marketing plan.

Finally, the name "Edsel" was questionably bad, with few associations and those mostly unfavorable. But other brands with equally unfortunate names have been successful. "Buick" is perhaps the ugliest word in the language. (Repeat it aloud to yourself two or three times to become convinced of the truth of this observation.) The name "Oldsmobile" is simply silly; imagine a car called the "Sloanmobile" or the "Fordmobile." The name of the Edsel certainly did not help, but it is unlikely that it had much to do with the failure of the car.

BAD LUCK ENCOUNTERED

In addition to mistakes, real and alleged, the Edsel encountered incredibly bad luck. Unfortunately, it was introduced at the beginning of the 1958 recession. Few cars sold well in 1958; few middle price cars sold; even fewer Edsels sold. It is not argued that timing was the only problem, or that the Edsel would have been successful if introduced earlier or later.

It was a combination of factors that hurt the Edsel, and any one might have been enough.

A less well-known piece of bad luck was the agreement against racing and the advertising of power and performance signed by the members of the Automobile Manufacturers Association in 1957. Firms in the industry that actively supported stock car racing in the middle fifties ran into criticism from the National Safety Council and other bodies. Also, the support of racing was very expensive, and every manufacturer lived in fear of a serious accident involving one of his cars. The result was the 1957 agreement.

The Edsel had been designed to be the "hottest" car on the American road. High performance was one of the central elements in the sporty, youthful image the car was to project. The 1957 agreement knocked the pins out from under this major selling point. Instead of advertising "Sweet, hot, and sassy," as Chevrolet did in 1956, Edsel copy on engine horsepower had to use diffident words and numbers in small type that minimized racing success. Ironically, the Pontiac of three years later entered and won races, thus establishing itself quickly as a high performance automobile. Inability to compete as a "fast" car frustrated Edsel management.

The third piece of bad luck is more nebulous, but for some reason a rash of "Hate Detroit" articles and books began to flood the market at about the time the Edsel was introduced. John Keats published his *Insolent Chariots*, with drawings by Osborn, and the poet Robert Lowell wrote a line referring to our "tailfin culture."

One public relations man at Ford almost filled a file drawer between 1957 and 1960 with clippings of articles critical of "Detroit Iron." The tide slacked off for a while, but the current safety issue has probably produced enough material to fill several more file drawers. The articles may have been the result of a snow-balling process that began with the increasing popularity of foreign cars. At any rate, young men customizing their cars began to remove chrome, take out grilles, take off wheel covers, and perform surgery on tail fin sheet metal. The flashy Edsel was utterly out of tune with this trend in taste.

It might be charged that Ford management should have anticipated this trend. To a certain extent, it did. As early as 1952 Ford began studies of a small domestic car similar to foreign imports. But no one really anticipated the radical change in taste that took place. It is hard to see how anyone could, given the kind of car market that existed in 1955 and 1956, when most of the crucial decisions were made.

FINALLY, FAILURE

The Edsel's failure has been widely noted. Less well publicized is the fact that the Mark II Continental, the 1958 Lincoln, the 1958 Mercury, and the 1958 Ford were also product failures. The 1958 four-passenger Thunderbird was a success. Except for it, Ford's assault on General Motors failed across the board.

It was apparent a month or so after introduction that the Edsel was unlikely to achieve the share of market necessary for it to be successful. Ford management took steps immediately to cut losses. The Edsel division was discontinued and combined with Mercury in a new organization called the "M-E-L division," for Mercury-Edsel-Lincoln. (The Continental division had already been absorbed by Lincoln.)

Suddenly, instead of five divisional controllers, there were once more only two, the same was true of divisional industrial relations managers and marketing managers. Many members of Ford middle-management were laid off or reduced in rank or pay. Higher ranks also suffered. Cause-and-effect cannot be ascertained positively, but it is nevertheless a fact that Breech, Crusoe, Krafve, and Reith all left the company shortly after the debacle. McNamara, at Ford division, was less involved and moved up to Crusoe's spot. Jim Wright, another Whiz Kid, took McNamara's place.

The damage to morale was devastating. Young Ford executives became convinced that their superiors regarded them more as expensive head-count than as members of the management team. Jim Nance, formerly of Studebaker and Hotpoint, was put in charge of the M-E-L division. One of his first acts was to issue a general letter saying that layoffs were pending but that every man's record would be carefully considered. One manager commented, "The letter says to feel good if you get fired, because it means that a better man got your job." "Gallows" humor became common in executive dining rooms.

As an opinion, it is suggested that Ford management experienced a failure of nerve that made major product innovations—other than the pedestrian Falcon and Fairlane—impossible for almost a decade. For instance, Ford retained the push-button vent window, the so-called "knuckle-buster," long after other firms had gone to crank vents. Ford also retained the lift-gate on its station wagons until after most firms had adopted roll-down windows. The Falcon was introduced with a dial radio instead of push buttons, which aroused criticism from a safety point of view. Management was not in a mood for change.

The Edsel itself was kept alive by heroic measures through two model changes and was finally allowed to die early in the 1960 model year. In the meantime, it lost its vertical grille and adopted a grille resembling that of the Pontiac.

The real tragedy was suffered by the Edsel dealers, many of whom lost their life savings when the car went under. Most of the Ford executives and managers who were released went on to other, and in many cases, better jobs. Some were kept on until they found these jobs, and did not experience even the briefest unemployment. The Edsel dealers, as risk-taking entrepreneurs, lost real cash.

When the smoke cleared away, the Ford car had 25% of the market, the Chevrolet 25%, the B-O-P's 25%, and other makes 25%.

A failure, properly understood, can make a man—or a corporation—wiser, stronger, and more effective. It can also enfeeble a man or a corporation. For a time, after the Edsel, it appeared that the latter was true of Ford. Ford cars became dull and undistinguished. Chevrolet and Pontiac captured the image of performance, high styling, and youthfulness that Ford had held since the advent of the V-8 in the early thirties.

Ford market penetration declined year by year. Ford management wondered why, and initiated study after study. It was obvious all the time that General Motors cars had a genuine edge regardless of the features a prospective buyer wanted in a car—performance, trade-in value, styling, prestige, or whatever.

In the meantime, the lessons of the Edsel were slowly and painfully being absorbed. One lesson was organizational. Ford has not tried to establish any new automotive divisions or dealership networks. The Falcon, Fairlane, and Mustang have all been merchandised through established institutions. The company learned that effective management organizations and dealership networks cannot be set up by fiat, and that distribution is a central consideration in new product introduction.

Second, Ford learned to use marketing research. In part, this was a consequence of fear. Ford managers, if a mistake were made, wanted to be able to point to the research that had caused it. Ford researchers underwent the curious experience of a management that placed more confidence in research findings than the researchers did themselves. The result, however, was healthy. Ford management, partly because of the lack of confidence caused by the Edsel, is immunized against believing that their own preferences are identical to those of the public.

Third, the massive rigidities of brand shares came to be respected. One cannot destroy an established brand simply by offering what one conceives to be a better version of the same item. The strategy of indirection is imperative. One must look for unprotected flanks or undefended weak points. General Motors had no car like the four-passenger Thunderbird or the Mustang when these two highly successful cars were introduced.

While these lessons were being learned, new managers and executives, not infected by the Edsel malaise, were hired or moved up from junior to senior positions. Lee Iococca is an example. Now vice-president—car and truck divisions—he was largely concerned with truck sales at the time of the general defeat. Unaffected himself, he has moved forward boldly to reestablish Ford's image for styling and performance. (He was instrumental in Ford's repudiation of the 1957 agreement and Ford's re-entry into racing.)

Ford is beginning to take chances again. Perhaps the principal lesson to be learned from the Edsel is that a company must be careful of youthful overconfidence and youthful inability to accept occasional failures as inevitable. The introduction of the Edsel was reasonably wise; the reluctance to accept its failure was not.

PRICE DECISIONS

20

Multi-Stage Approach
to Pricing

ALFRED R. OXENFELDT
Columbia University

Of all the areas of executive decision, pricing is perhaps the most fuzzy. Whenever a price problem is discussed by a committee, divergent figures are likely to be recommended without a semblance of consensus. Although unanimity in marketing decisions is a custom more remarkable in its occurrence than in its absence, agreement in pricing decisions is even more rare.

This article accordingly presents a long-run, policy-oriented approach to pricing which should reduce the range of prices considered in specific situations and consequently improve the decisions which result. This approach, which to the best of my knowledge is new, calls for the price decision to be made in six successive steps, each one narrowing the alternatives to be considered at the next step.

Is this method just another mechanical pricing formula? Hardly, for it is my conviction that the quest for mechanical pricing methods is unduly optimistic, if not downright naive. Nevertheless, many businessmen consistently employ almost mechanical formulas for pricing. They do this even though they scoff at the claim that there are reliable fixed formulas for handling personal problems or making advertising or capital outlay decisions. Certainly, experience has not produced recipes that guarantee correct decisions in any sphere of business. The best of them

Reprinted with permission from *Harvard Business Review*, July–August, 1960, pp. 125–33. © by the President and Fellows of Harvard College.

only apply under normal conditions, and it is most rare indeed that conditions resembling normalcy prevail.

On the other hand, many discussions of pricing present a long list of factors to be "taken into account," carefully weighed and balanced, and then subjected to a process called "judgment." While a specific price is thus arrived at, this does not alter the fact that intelligent and experienced business executives using the method will arrive at widely different price decisions—all based on the same information.

Yet, even if mechanical pricing formulas are the hope of the optimistic, it would be excessively pessimistic to resign ourselves to a *formless* consideration of all the relevant factors and to a random exercise of judgment. Many things are known about the subject that would be extremely helpful to those responsible for making such decisions.

SEQUENTIAL STAGES

In order to organize the various pieces of information and considerations that bear on price decisions, a multi-stage approach to pricing can be a very helpful tool. This method sorts the major elements in a pricing decision into six successive stages:

1. Selecting market targets.
2. Choosing a brand-image.
3. Composing a marketing mix.
4. Selecting a pricing policy.
5. Determining a pricing strategy.
6. Arriving at a specific price.

The sequence of the stages is an essential part of the method, for each step is calculated to simplify the succeeding stage and to reduce the likelihood of error. One might say that this method divides the price decision into manageable parts, each one logically antecedent to the next. In this way, the decision at each stage facilitates all subsequent decisions. This approach might also be regarded as a process of selective search, where the number of alternatives deserving close consideration is reduced drastically by making the decision in successive stages. Of course, one could arrive at the same result by simultaneously considering all the factors mentioned—but it might require a computer to do so.

While it appears that this approach is applicable over a broad range of industry and trade, the great diversity of business situations precludes the possibility of its being a universally applicable method. No rigid approach, and certainly not the one presented here, offers a guarantee of reaching the best—or even a satisfactory—price decision. It must be adapted to prevailing circumstances; consequently, information, experience, and the application of rigorous logic are required for its optimum utilization.

MARKET TARGETS

A going concern is "committed," confined, and tied down by several important circumstances which can be altered only over a considerable period of time. It must live with many conditions, even while it may attempt to alter them. Also, an operating business possesses specified resources on which it will strive to capitalize in achieving its objectives. For example, a firm will have:

- A fixed production location, given physical facilities, and a particular production and sales labor force.
- A set of distribution arrangements through which the firm generally sells, including particular distributors with whom it has established relationships.
- Contracts with suppliers, customers, laborers, and lenders of funds.
- A portfolio of customers who have a definite opinion of the firm's reliability, and the quality of its offerings and service.

These commitments and resources of a firm contain pricing implications. Mainly, they determine the type of product that it can make, the type of service it can render, and its probable costs of operation. What is more, these circumstances form the basis for the most fundamental pricing decision that management should make—namely, the types of customers, or market segments, it will attempt to cultivate.

By virtue of its fixed commitments, then, a firm is limited to the several market segments it can reasonably hope to capture. It has customer connections on which it can capitalize, and it has a variety of strengths and weaknesses that limit its choice among potential submarkets for intensive cultivation.

Two examples drawn from the TV-set industry will help to clarify this crucial first stage. Certainly, no two firms could possibly exemplify all situations, nor is it possible for an outsider to explain satisfactorily why specific decisions were made in specific cases. However, these illustrations are intended to indicate what factors management must consider if it is to apply the multi-stage approach. They do *not* describe how management reasoned or what would have been the best decision under the circumstances.

Zenith Radio

First, consider the pricing problem of the Zenith Radio Corporation at the time it started to produce TV sets in 1948:

This company, which is one of the two largest TV-set producers now, dropped out of the automobile radio business in order to manufacture television sets. (At that time, it was the largest single producer of automobile radios, but this business was not very profitable.) Zenith possessed these resources and was subject to these commitments and limitations that could have influenced its selection of market targets in the TV business—

- It had production facilities in Chicago that had been designed for and used in radio production for many years; its labor force and supervisory personnel were familiar with the electronics business. The firm had substantial manufacturing skills in electronics because of its work for the military during and after World War II. Zenith could assess its manufacturing capabilities as very substantial, but not outstanding.

● Financially, Zenith was also in a very strong and liquid position and could readily have undertaken heavy expenditures at this time.

● But Zenith's outstanding resource was a distributor and dealer organization that was as good as that possessed by any other firm in the nation. Its dealers commanded strong loyalty among their clientele not only in small communities but also in large cities—a most vital fact in view of the technical character of TV and the great power that retailers wield over consumer choices of such products. Here Zenith was helped by the fact that it had acquired an excellent reputation for quality products in radios; for many years, it was the Cadillac of the radio industry. Zenith management, like all other radio manufacturers who entered the television business, decided to sell its sets through the distributor organization it had already created; its distributors, in turn, would sell them mainly to dealers already buying Zenith radios.

● There were also several other peripheral advantages. Zenith was closely identified, in the minds of many consumers, with hearing aids which were widely advertised as much on grounds of moderate price as in terms of high quality. Further, Zenith started to telecast, experimentally, in the Chicago market even before World War II and had some local identification as a telecaster, as well as a manufacturer. Its products were strongly favored in the Chicago market.

In summary, Zenith Radio could count on its strong distributor and retail organizations as its outstanding resource, while recognizing that it did not possess any particular advantage in costs of manufacture or quality of product and, in fact, that its behavior in the television business was necessarily circumscribed by its radio and hearing-aid business. Zenith's management would have required very strong reasons to choose as its market targets customers who were very different from those who bought its radios and hearing aids.

Under these circumstances, Zenith management might have decided to attempt to reach customers at almost all levels of income. Partly, it could do this by including "low-end" and promotional models in its line; partly because television sets were sold on installment credit involving modest monthly charges; and partly because, at least in the early years, television purchases were spread rather evenly over all income groups.

On the other hand, Zenith management, as its first step, might well expect to cultivate particularly those consumers who were conservative and quality-conscious, who felt a strong loyalty to particular appliance retailers, and who were located mainly in small cities and towns. On this basis, the Zenith customer targets would not include "snobs" who, at that time, favored the Dumont brand and, to a lesser degree, the RCA set. Also they would not include bargain hunters. Rather Zenith's customers would be the kind of people who feel that "you get what you pay for." (Zenith would presumably capitalize on its strong position in the Chicago area by special measures aimed at that market.)

Columbia Broadcasting

Now contrast Zenith's position with that of Columbia Broadcasting System, Inc. when it started to produce and sell TV sets under its own brand name in 1953.

CBS resources and commitments were altogether different from those possessed by Zenith, with the result that the two companies could have been expected to cultivate different market targets, Specifically, in the case of Columbia Broadcasting—

- CBS executives were primarily familiar with the management of entertainment talent and the creation and servicing of a network of stations. Although its phonograph record and Hi-Fi phonograph business did involve a type of production and distribution experience, CBS was completely new to major appliance manufacturing and possessed no suitable distribution facilities whatsoever for appliances.

- In addition, CBS acquired production facilities when it entered the TV business that were of relatively poor quality. The size, location, equipment, plant layout, and employee facilities of the Air King firm, which CBS acquired, were widely recognized as mediocre or below. Many people familiar with that company and with the TV industry strongly doubted that Air King's management was capable of establishing a prestige national brand and producing the high-quality product needed to support a quality reputation.

- On the other hand, CBS had some genuine pluses in its favor. Its radio and television networks were the largest, and enjoyed great prestige at the time CBS entered the TV-set business. Also, by virtue of its telecasting facilities, it could advertise its sets during unsponsored programs at virtually no out-of-pocket cost. It could, moreover, get the advertising support—mainly through testimonials from outstanding personalities such as Arthur Godfrey, Edward R. Murrow, Jack Benny, and others—for little or no cost.

To what kinds of customers could a firm with these resources and limitations appeal?

One way that CBS might have adjusted to its particular combination of resources and weaknesses would have been to select as its chief consumer-market target the metropolitan customer who is anxious to be associated with prestigeful figures, vulnerable to advertising over radio and TV, prepared to pay a premium price, and relatively unfamiliar with or insensitive to technical performance features. But this market target would hardly have been very large in the first instance; moreover, CBS management must have recognized that many other firms were cultivating this type of customer.

It would appear, then, that CBS was compelled to select its market targets mainly in terms of distributors and retailers, rather than ultimate consumers. Whereas Zenith already possessed a strong distributor and dealer organization, CBS had to construct one. Only after it secured representation on the market could it hope to sell to consumers.

CBS management must have realized that whatever it did in an effort to win distributors and dealers would also influence the kind of customers it could hope to attract. For example, if it had to extend big markups to distributors and retailers to get them to handle its sets (combined with the fact that its production facilities were mediocre), CBS would be compelled to charge a relatively high retail price for its sets. In turn, it would have to rely on intensive advertising to persuade customers to pay these higher prices and find methods of making its sets appear luxurious and worth the high price.

In addition to having to accept the fact of a relatively high-price product, CBS would feel pressure to concentrate on customers in the large metropolitan centers, because of the need to build large sales volume rapidly in order to get its production costs in line with those of its competitors. Even as early as 1953, the large metropolitan markets were pervaded by severe price competition among set manufacturers and relatively little emphasis on quality and brand loyalty on the part of retailers. Independent distributors were leaving the business because of great manufacturer pressure to gain heavy sales volume. Hence CBS could not have much hope of obtaining strong independent distributors for its line in most metropolitan markets, but would have to look ahead to a considerable period during which it "supported" both distributors and key retailers to obtain an organization that would distribute its sets.

Other Cases

Zenith and CBS have been cited as companies that would have been justified in placing relatively little weight on price in their selection of target submarkets. These companies mainly had to avoid alienating customers by charging prices that were far out of line with other companies' prices. Not all TV-set manufacturers could have taken this approach, however. Thus:

Companies like Admiral, Emerson, and producers of private brands were under pressure to cultivate customers who place heavy emphasis on price. Why? Because in some cases they lacked the personnel and financial resources to sustain a claim of quality and style superiority; or, because their experience in the major appliance business before adding a line of TV receivers could have indicated that they had won acceptance mainly among customers who want moderate quality at prices below the average; or, finally, because their chief asset was a very efficient manufacturing organization that could imitate the products of their more progressive rivals at low cost.

Other industries offer clear examples of firms that selected as market targets persons who were not particularly interested in high intrinsic quality or style. Specifically:

A fairly obvious example is the Scripto pencil, which offers satisfactory performance at minimum cost. Apparently the customers Scripto selected for intensive cultivation were those who would want a pencil to write with and not for display, a pencil they could afford to lose or misplace.

Some producers of private brands of aspirin likewise have selected as market targets those persons who know of the fundamental similarity of aspirin quality and who actively desire to minimize their outlays for this product.

These examples illustrate a point that may not have been particularly clear in the discussion of the Zenith and CBS example: *one important criterion in the selection of market targets is customer awareness of and sensitivity to price.*

BRAND-IMAGE

Once management has defined the submarkets it wishes to cultivate most actively, it must select the methods it will use to achieve its goal.

Success in the market place for more and more products seems to depend on creating a favorable general image (often vague and formless) of the product or company among prospective customers. The selection and development of this image become of prime importance and have a direct bearing on price, as will be explained subsequently. A favorable image is especially important when one sells consumers' goods, but only rarely is it completely unimportant even in the sales of producers' goods. Buyers' very perceptions are affected by their prior attitudes, the actions and opinions of others, first impressions, and early associations. It is a rare firm that can ignore the total impression its potential customers have of it and of what it is selling.

The firm's selection of its company and brand-image should be dictated by the types of customers it is trying to attract. Submarkets may be likened to targets at which the seller is firing, and images are powerful weapons that can be used to hit the targets.

Almost every going concern has invested—often very heavily—in the creation of a favorable image. Most businesses know what image they wish to achieve and are concerned lest they or their products fail to have a favorable "meaning" to potential customers. At the very minimum, almost every management knows there are certain images that customers might have of it and its product that would prove disastrous.

The type of image a firm can create of itself and its wares depends to a considerable degree, again, on its fixed commitments and resources. With its physical and personnel resources, there is a limit to what it can do to alter the prevailing opinions—for they reflect all that the company was and did in the past. In that sense, the basic commitments limit the type of image a firm can establish, how much time it will require to establish it, and the cost. Even as brand-image is frequently an effective weapon in cultivating particular submarkets, price helps to create the brand-image. It is for this reason that the selection of brand-image which is consistent with the firm's market targets implies particular forms of price behavior.

Let us carry our original examples a little further. Given the market targets that they might have selected, as explained earlier, what brand-image could Zenith and CBS try to create?

Alternative Qualities

As in the selecting of market targets, every firm has only a few *reasonable* alternatives from which to choose its desired image. For example:

Zenith already possessed a brand-image that contributed strongly to its success in the radio and hearing-aid business. Even if another image might have been advantageous for its television business, Zenith's management could hardly afford to injure the bird already in hand. Consequently,

Zenith would be obliged to perpetuate for its TV line the brand-image it had already established in its other activities. As it happened, that image was altogether suitable for its TV-set business.

To implement this line of thinking, Zenith would be obliged to establish the image of a "premium" product and of a company that was old-time, conservative, and mainly concerned with quality and craftsmanship. Above all, it would seek to avoid high-pressure selling, emphasis on price, and shoddiness of product. In styling, it could pursue a safe policy of including a wide variety of styles, while being especially careful not to alienate its conservative small-town customers with models too far in the vanguard of modern design.

CBS faced a very different choice with regard to brand-image. It, too, could not afford to jeopardize its eminent position in the radio- and TV-network field, for those activities were very profitable and would always remain its major sources of income. Except for this limitation, CBS had a relatively free choice of brand-images.

CBS could well undertake to be the style leader in the industry. This image would be consistent with relatively inefficient manufacturing facilities, concentration on selling in the metropolitan market, and the necessity of charging a high retail price. It would appear that few brand-images other than for advanced styling and for gimmicks would have been consistent with the resources and limitations on CBS at this time.

In contrast to Zenith and CBS, other TV-set producers sought a brand-image that did have an important price ingredient. Again, most producers of private brands, Admiral, Emerson, and others, often featured price in their advertising and apparently sought to sensitize prospective customers to price. They could purposely become identified as firms that were not afraid to discuss price and that seemed confident they offered better values than their competitors.

Many firms outside the TV-set industry attempt to establish a brand-image that has a heavy price ingredient. Among producers, one finds Caron boasting that its Joy perfume is the most expensive, and Chock-Full-o-Nuts implying much the same thing about its coffee. Without being explicit, some retailers seem to claim that no stores charge more than they—and, strangely, this image is a source of strength. The retail world is full of stores that claim that they are never knowingly undersold; on the other hand, it is difficult to name manufacturers who claim that their product is the cheapest on the market—probably because of the implication that their is also the brand of lowest quality. (Automobile manufacturers occasionally claim to be the "cheapest of the low-price three," but none has occupied that position long.)

MARKETING MIX

The third stage in multi-stage pricing calls for the selection of a combination of sales promotion devices that will create and re-enforce the desired company and product brand-image and achieve maximum sales for the planned level of dollar outlays. In this stage, a role must be assigned to price. The role in which price is cast should be selected only after assessment is made as to the relative effectiveness and appropriateness of each sales-promotion device that might be employed. The short-term gains of certain sales-promotion devices may entail injury to the image objectives of the firm. Conflicts of such a nature must be resolved at this stage.

Then, too, a firm might achieve precisely the *desired* image and still find customers very hard to get. It is not enough to establish the desired image; it must be an *effective* image. Furthermore, even though a firm may establish highly favorable impressions of itself and its wares, the company and its products must live up to the image they foster. Not only must its product be "within reach" in price, but it must be accessible by being offered through convenient channels of distribution, and must be sold in outlets where customers like to buy.

The third stage builds directly upon the second. The need to conform to the prior decision about company and brand-image greatly limits the number of price alternatives that a price setter can reasonably consider.

The marketing-mix decision at this stage need not be translated into specific dollars and cents amounts to be devoted to each sales-promotion device; however, it does at least call for crude answers to the following questions:

- How heavily to advertise?
- How much for salesmen?
- How much for product improvement?
- How much of an assortment to carry?
- How large an inventory to hold?
- How best to provide speedy delivery?
- How much emphasis on price appeal?

The composition of a marketing mix (arrived at by answering the type of questions just listed) is admittedly very difficult and highly subjective. But the job is facilitated greatly when answers are subjected to the test of conforming to the desired company and brand-image and to the firm's fixed commitments.

Few firms can afford to switch "images," usually because they have invested heavily in them in prior years and should, therefore, not abandon them lightly. Moreover, past images persist and blur any future attempts at image-building. Although it cannot easily scrap its brand-image, a firm can vary its marketing mix within moderate limits and remain consistent with the image it seeks to create. Thus, the selection of an image sets limits and gives direction to the decision about the elements to be included in the marketing mix. In that way, it facilitates the decision and also increases the likelihood that it will be correct. However, it does not isolate a single marketing mix as the only correct one.

Marketing the Image

How might have Zenith, CBS, and other TV-set manufacturers composed a marketing mix, if they had reasoned about market targets and brand-image along the lines of the foregoing discussion? Let us see:

In Zenith's case, price clearly would have have to be subordinated as a sales appeal. The company could have placed major emphasis on quality of product, subdued advertising, and reliable service, while placing its product with retailers who would enhance the reputation of the brand. By these measures, Zenith could have re-enforced the image of a high-quality and reliable producer.

In the case of CBS, the role of price in the marketing mix would not have been subject to much control. As explained, it might have been forced to charge a high price; if so, most of its other actions would have been dictated by that fact. It could have relied very heavily on radio and TV advertising to generate consumer preference, and justified its high price by adding externals to the set—particularly attractive styling, an expensive furniture appearance, or special features of some sort. It could not have reasonably hoped to get very much support from retailers who commanded strong loyalty among their patrons.

Other TV-set producers adopted quite different market mixes from those that Zenith and CBS would have selected if they had reasoned along these lines. Some, however, apparently had no conscious marketing-mix philosophy and, therefore, seemed to improvise and stumble from one crisis to another. Nevertheless, in their bids for patronage, some TV-set producers apparently placed relatively heavy reliance on advertising (including mainly RCA, General Electric, Westinghouse, and Sylvania). Others made strong quality claims (like Dumont and Andrea). Still others placed chief emphasis on styling (Magnavox).

DETERMINING POLICY

The fourth stage in multi-stage pricing calls for the selection of a pricing policy. But before a pricing policy can be determined, answers to the following questions must be obtained:

How should our price compare with "average" prices in the industry? Specifically, should we be 2 per cent above or 4 per cent below the average? And, when we speak of the average, which firms' prices are we going to include in the computation?

● How fast will we meet price reductions or increases by rivals?
● How frequently will it be advisable to vary price? To what extent is stability of price advantageous?
● Should the firm make use of fair-trade price maintenance?
● How frequently should the firm run price promotions?

These are simply illustrative of the aspects of a pricing policy which management can and should spell out—in proper sequence. By virtue of having made the evaluations and decisions called for in the first three stages, management will find itself limited in the number of choices on these points.

In addition, each company must take account of the valuations placed on its product-service "package" as well as the valuations of rival products by the market segments it is most anxious to cultivate. On the basis of such considerations, plus its target market segments and marketing mix, it will decide whether it can afford to charge much more or less than its rivals.

"Bracketing" the Price

Before proceeding further, let us summarize, Surely, a price setter would be some distance from a specific price decision even after completing the fourth step. We must ask ourselves whether he would not also has covered considerable distance toward a price decision. By taking account of the firm's basic commitments and resources, the images it desires to establish, its decision about marketing mix, and the selection of a detailed pricing policy, has not the price setter reached the point where he is very strongly circumscribed in the price decision he will ultimately make? To illustrate step four, let us carry our two main examples—Zenith and CBS —about as far as they can be taken and see what pricing policy these companies might have adopted:

If the Zenith management had selected the market targets set forth here and made the same decisions regarding brand-image and marketing mix, it would have had little trouble in selecting a pricing policy. It would have felt obliged to charge a price somewhat above the average in the market and to minimize emphasis on price in its advertising. Moreover, it could have varied price relatively infrequently to the consumer— except possibly in some of the large metropolitan markets where neither consumers nor retailers are loyal to anything or anyone, except their own pecuniary interests.

In Zenith's pricing policy, the preservation of distributor and retailer loyalty would have figured very prominently in its thinking. It would be compelled to sacrifice long-term price advantages in order to protect its distributors and retailers from financial loss owing to price change.

CBS, on the other hand, need not have concerned itself much with dealer and retailer loyalty. It had none and must have realized that it would not have been able to create a loyal distribution structure unless it were willing to make very large financial outlays. If it had reconciled itself to a not-too-loyal distributor and dealer organization, CBS could have conducted sales promotions and varied price frequently and by large amounts. It could have emphasized price in these promotions, but presumably only when combined with strong emphasis on alleged high quality and superior styling. CBS need not have felt obliged to match the prices charged by its competitors, but it could not have afforded to have its retailers' margins be out of line on the low side.

Since it commanded no loyalty from its retailers, CBS was, in fact, compelled to buy their sales support. This it could do, primarily by offering a higher than average margin. (CBS could also have attempted to solve its distribution problem by granting exclusive privileges to a small number of retail outlets. In the case of the TV industry, such a policy has been used successfully by Magnavox. However, this company had already sewed up the strong quality retailers who were capable of producing large volume. As a result, CBS was shut out of this pattern of distribution.)

Although Zenith and CBS apparently would have been obliged to charge more than the average by the foregoing line of thinking, other TV producers were wise to take a very different tack, mainly because of their different resources and commitments. For example, Admiral and Emerson have tended to charge somewhat less than average, while General Electric has not adopted a very consistent price position.

PRICING STRATEGY

It is difficult to draw a sharp line between policy and strategy, but it is possible and useful to make some sort of distinction between them. Policy is formulated to deal with anticipated and foreseeable situations of a recurrent type. However, markets frequently are beset and dominated by *special* situations that basic policy was not designed to meet. For example:

- A Congressional committee might threaten to investigate the company's or the industry's pricing arrangements.
- A sizable firm may have fallen into a desperate financial situation so that it was forced to raise cash through a liquidation of its inventories.
- A large new firm may have entered the market.
- Business may have fallen off precipitately for the entire industry or economy.
- The company may have introduced a model that is either a "dud" or a "sure winner."

Special situations like these ordinarily require an adjustment in price —and the formulation of a strategy to guide management in setting price *during the time that the special* situation endures.

There generally are several strategies which would be compatible with the firm's basic commitments and resources, its market targets, its image objectives, its convictions about the relative emphasis to attach to various elements in the marketing mix, and its specific pricing policies. Others would be incompatible with earlier decisions and, therefore, might endanger precious values. A threat to one's very survival might justify a scrapping of these, but impetuousness, shortsightedness, or avarice would not. Explicit recognition of these earlier stages of the pricing decision should prevent hasty short-run actions that are painful, but quite common.

No effort will be made to discuss the Zenith and CBS examples in connection with the formulation of a pricing strategy. They have already been stretched far enough to illustrate the application of the multi-stage approach to pricing—especially in the most difficult stages. The reader might, however, speculate about how, within the framework of the approach outlined here, both Zenith and CBS management could have responded to a great pricing crisis in the TV-set industry. This occurred in the fall of 1953 when Westinghouse suddenly reduced its TV sets by approximately 20 per cent during the very heart of the selling season. We may speculate that adherence to decisions regarding market targets, brand-image, marketing mix, and price policy would have prevented both Zenith and CBS from reducing their prices to the levels set by Westinghouse Electric Corporation.

SPECIFIC PRICE

Here is the final step—the selection of a specific price. At this point, the price setter will usually find himself sharply circumscribed in the specific sums he can charge. Nevertheless, he usually will have some range of price possibilities that are consistent with the decisions made in the preceding five stages of the price decision. How may he best select among the alternatives?

To the extent that he is able, he should be guided by the arithmetic of pricing—that is, by a comparison of the costs and revenues of the alternative prices within the zone delimited by the prior stages of his pricing decision. Once he has taken into account his market targets, brand-image, marketing mix, pricing policy, and strategy, he can afford to ignore everything but the calculations of costs and revenues. *The first five stages of decision are designed to take account of the business considerations which may be ignored if one selects price solely on the basis of prevailing cost and revenue conditions.*

It often is impossible to obtain reliable information about sales at different prices; this difficulty is present whatever method of pricing one employs. But the multi-stage policy approach facilitates research and experimentation into demand conditions by limiting the number of alternatives to be considered.

The price that would be established under this multi-stage policy approach would rarely be the same as that set by balancing marginal cost and marginal revenue. The former probably would exclude, as incompatible with the firm's basic commitments and resources, desired brand-image, and so on, the prices that would be most profitable in the very short term.

THE ADVANTAGES

First, this approach breaks up the pricing decision into six relatively manageable pieces.

In that way, it introduces order into the weighing of the many considerations bearing on price. This approach, therefore, should increase the likelihood that all major factors will be taken into account and that there large number will not overwhelm the price setter.

Second, this method of pricing reduces the risk that the price setter will destroy the firm's valuable investments in corporate and brand images.

Also, it requires the price setter to determine and take into account the limitation on the firm's freedom of decision. In that way, it would discourage the pricing executive from undertaking what he is powerless to accomplish. Similarly, the multi-stage policy approach should militate against a short-run policy of opportunism that would sacrifice long-term values.

Third, the multi-stage policy approach to pricing should be valuable to those executives who are compelled to delegate pricing responsibilities.

In the first place, high-level executives are virtually required by the method to make the decisions for several stages, which thus limits their dependence on their subordinates. In the second place, as explained, it simplifies the making of a price decision so that greater success can be expected. Then, too, its use should make it easier for subordinates to raise questions and obtain advice from their superiors should they be unable to reach a decision.

Fourth, this approach to pricing puts considerable emphasis on the intangibles that are involved in pricing—particularly on the total impression that customers have of the vendor and of the things he sells.

Price is far more than a rationing device that determines which potential customers will be able to afford to make a purchase. Generally it is one of the most important actions in creating an impression of the firm among potential customers. Especially as tangible differences among rival products shrink, these intangibles will grow in significance for marketing success.

THE LIMITATIONS

This approach does not indicate all the considerations that should be taken into account at each stage in the pricing decision. In other words, the price setter is compelled to isolate the significant factors operating at each stage and weigh them for himself.

Second, this approach does not indicate what price to charge in any specific situation. The most that can be claimed for it is that it narrows down the zone of possible prices to the point where it may be matter a great deal which particular price is selected. As stated at the outset, one must beware of any pricing method that does lead to a single price, for such a method could not possibly take into account all of the special circumstances which are relevant to a price decision and which vary so greatly from market to market and from time to time.

Third, this method does not guide price setters in recognizing the factors that dominate the market at any time and in knowing when to switch basic strategies. Also, there may well be more than one dominant condition which must be considered in selecting a basic strategy.

On balance, then, the multi-stage approach to pricing at best only takes an executive fairly close to his ultimate destination. Although the multi-stage policy approach does not do the whole job of pricing, the part of the job that is left is relatively easy to finish in many cases. Where this is not so, one can only assume that the task would be almost hopeless without the assistance of a method that reduces the pricing decision to a series of relatively manageable steps in a prescribed sequence.

CONCLUSION

The multi-stage policy approach outlined here differs from usual approaches to pricing in two major respects. First, it demands a long-range view of price by emphasizing the enduring effects of most price actions on company and brand-image. One might say this approach constructs a policy framework for the price decision. And, second, it allows the price decision to be made in stages, rather than requiring a simultaneous solution of the entire price problem.

21

Bayesian Decision Theory
in Pricing Strategy

PAUL E. GREEN

University of Pennsylvania

Since the publication of Robert Schlaifer's pioneering work, *Probability and Statistics for Business Decisions*,[1] the Bayesian approach to decision-making under uncertainty has received much comment, pro and con, by theoretical and applied statisticians alike.

However, in contrast to the large number of theoretical contributions being made to decision theory in general and Bayesian statistics in particular, reported applications of these procedures to real-world problem situations have been rather meager. Applications appear especially lacking in the marketing field.

In highly oversimplified terms, the Bayesian approach to decision-making under uncertainty provides a framework for explicitly working with the economic costs of alternative courses of action, the prior knowledge or judgments of the decision maker, and formal modification of these judgments as additional data are introduced into the problem.

In the Du Pont Company, the decision theory approach, often augmented by computer simulation, has been used experimentally over the

Reprinted with permission from *Journal of Marketing*, published by the American Marketing Association, January, 1963, pp. 5–14.

[1] Robert Schlaifer, *Probability and Statistics for Business Decisions* (New York: McGraw-Hill Book Company, 1959). In addition two excellent general articles dealing with the Bayesian approach are: Harry V. Roberts, "The New Business Statistics," *Journal of Business*, vol. 33 (January, 1960), pp. 21–30 and Jack Hirshleifer, "The Bayesian Approach to Statistical Decision—An Exposition," *Journal of Business*, vol. 31, October, 1961, pp. 471–489.

past few years in a variety of market planning applications, ranging from capacity expansion problems to questions concerning the introduction of new products and long-range price and promotional strategy. The application to follow concerns the use of Bayesian theory in the selection of a "best" pricing policy for a firm in an oligopolistic industry where such factors as demand elasticity, competitive retaliation, threat of future price weakness, and potential entry of new competitors influence the effectiveness of the firm's courses of action. Although the content of this case is apocryphal, its structure has been compounded from actual situations.

No attempt will be made to describe even superficially all of the many facets of the Bayesian approach to decision-making under uncertainty. The content of this article is focused on only two main considerations.

First, in dealing with actual marketing situations, for example, pricing problems, the opportunity to obtain field information may be non-existent. Second, in dealing with actual marketing problems, the complexity of the situation may force the analyst to develop a problem structure in much greater detail than has been described in the literature.

AN ILLUSTRATIVE APPLICATION

Since early 1955, the Everclear Plastics Company had been producing a resin called Kromel, basically designed for certain industrial markets. In addition to Everclear, three other firms were producing Kromel resin. Prices among all four suppliers (called here the Kromel industry) were identical: and product quality and service among producers were comparable. Everclear's current share of Kromel industry sales amounted to 10 per cent.

Four industrial end uses comprised the principal marketing area for the Kromel industry. These market segments will be labeled A, B, C, and D. Three of the four segments (B, C, and D) were functionally dependent on segment A in the sense that Kromel's *ultimate* market position and rate of approach to this level in each of these three segments was predicated on the resin's making substantial inroads in segment A.

The Kromel industry's only competition in these four segments consisted of another resin called Verlon, which was produced by six other firms. Shares of the total Verlon-Kromel market (weighted sums over all four segments) currently stood at 70 per cent Verlon industry, and 30 per cent Kromel industry. Since its introduction in 1955, the superior functional characteristics per dollar cost of Kromel had enabled this newer product to displace fairly large poundages of Verlon in market segments B, C, and D.

On the other hand, the functional superiority per dollar cost of Kromel had not been sufficiently high to interest segment A consumers. While past price decreases in Kromel had been made, the cumulative effect of these reductions had still been insufficient to accomplish Kromel sales penetration in segment A. (Sales penetration is defined as a market share exceeding zero.)

In the early fall of 1960, it appeared to Everclear's management that future weakness in Kromel price might be in the offing. The anticipated capacity increases on the part of the firm's Kromel competitors suggested that in the next year or two potential industry supply of this resin might significantly exceed demand, if no substantial market participation for the Kromel industry were established in segment A. In addition, it appeared likely that potential Kromel competitors might enter the business, thus adding to the threat of oversupply in later years.

Segment A, of course, constituted the key factor. If substantial inroads could be made in this segment, it appeared likely that Kromel industry sales growth in the other segments not only could be speeded up, but that ultimate market share levels for this resin could be markedly increased from those anticipated in the absence of segment A penetration. To Everclear's sales management, a price reduction in Kromel still appeared to represent a feasible means to achieve this objective, and (even assuming similar price reductions on the part of Kromel competitors) perhaps could still be profitable to Everclear.

However, a large degree of uncertainty surrounded both the overall attractiveness of this alternative, and under this alternative the amount of the price reduction which would enable Kromel to penetrate market segment A.

PROBLEM STRUCTURING AND DEVELOPMENT OF THE MODEL

Formulation of the problem required a certain amount of artistry and compromise toward achieving a reasonably adequate description of the problem. But it was also necessary to keep the structure simple enough so that the nature of each input would be comprehensible to the personnel responsible for supplying data for the study.

Problem components had to be formulated, such as:

1. length of planning period;
2. number and nature of courses of action;
3. payoff functions; and
4. states of nature covering future growth of the total Verlon-Kromel market, inter-industry (Kromel vs. Verlon) and intra-Kromel industry effects of a Kromel price change, implications on Everclear's share of the total Kromel industry, and Everclear's production costs.

Initial discussions with sales management indicated that a planning period of five years should be considered in the study. While the selection of five years was somewhat arbitrary, sales personnel believed that some repercussions of a current price reduction might well extend over several years into the future.

A search for possible courses of action indicated that four pricing alternatives covered the range of actions under consideration:

1. maintenance of status quo on Kromel price, which was $1.00 per pound;
2. a price reduction to $.93 per pound within the next three months;
3. a price reduction to $.85 per pound within the next three months;
4. a price reduction to $.80 per pound within the next three months.

Inasmuch as each price action would be expected to produce a different time pattern in the flow of revenues and costs, and since no added investment in production facilities was contemplated, it was agreed that cumulative, compounded net profits over the five-year planning period would constitute a relevant payoff function. In the absence of any unanimity as to the "correct" opportunity cost of capital, it was decided to use two interest rates of 6 and 10 per cent annually in order to test the sensitivity of outcomes to the cost of the capital variable.

Another consideration came to light during initial problem discussions. Total market growth (for the Kromel or Verlon industry) over the next five years in each market segment constituted a "state of nature" which could impinge on Everclear's profit position. Accordingly, it was agreed to consider three separate forecasts of total market growth, a "most probable," "optimistic," and "pessimistic" forecast.

From these assumptions a base case was then formulated. This main case would first consider the pricing problem under the most probable forecast of total Verlon-Kromel year-by-year sales potential in each segment, using an opportunity cost of capital of 6 per cent annually. The two other total market forecasts and the other cost of capital were then to be treated as subcases, in order to test the sensitivity of the base case outcomes to variations in these particular states of nature.

However, inter- and intra-industry alternative states of nature literally abounded in the Kromel resin problem. Sales management at Everclear had to consider such factors as:

1. The possibility that Kromel resin could effect penetration of market segment A if no price decrease were made;
2. If a price decrease were made, the extent of Verlon retaliation to be anticipated;
3. Given a particular type of Verlon price retaliation, its possible impact on Kromel's penetration of segment A;
4. If segment A were penetrated, the possible market share which the Kromel industry could gain in segment A;
5. If segment A were penetrated, the possible side effects of this event on speeding up Kromel's participation in market segments B, C, and D;
6. If segment A were not penetrated, the impact which the price reduction could still have on speeding up Kromel's participation in segments B, C, and D;
7. If segment A were not penetrated, the possibility that existing Kromel competitors would initiate price reductions a year hence;
8. The possible impact of a current Kromel price reduction on the decisions of existing or potential Kromel producers to increase capacity or enter the industry.

While courses of action, length of planning period, and the payoff measure (cumulative, compounded net profits) for the base case had been fairly quickly agreed upon, the large number of inter- and intra-Kromel industry states of nature deemed relevant to the problem would require rather lengthy discussion with Everclear's sales personnel.

Accordingly, introductory sessions were held with Everclear's sales management, in order to develop a set of states of nature large enough to represent an adequate description of the real problem, yet small enough to be comprehended by the participating sales personnel. Next, separate interview sessions were held with two groups of Everclear's sales personnel; subjective probabilities regarding the occurrence of alternative states of nature under each course of action were developed in these sessions. A final session was held with all contributing personnel in attendance; each projection and/or subjective probability was gone over in detail, and a final set of ground rules for the study was agreed upon. A description of these ground rules appears in Table I.

USE OF TREE DIAGRAMS

The large number of alternative states of nature which were associated with inter- and intra-industry factors necessitated the construction of "tree diagrams" for each pricing alternative. These diagrams enabled sales management to trace the implications of their assumptions. Figure 1 shows a portion of one such tree diagram.

A word of explanation concerning interpretation of the probability tree is in order. The two principal branches underneath the *$1.00 case* refer to the event of whether or not Kromel penetrates segment A in the first year of the planning period. Sales personnel felt that a 5 per cent chance existed for penetration, hence the figure .05000 under A.

However, if A were penetrated, four market participations were deemed possible: 25, 50, 75 and 100 per cent carrying the conditional probabilities of .15, .35, .40 and .10 respectively.

TABLE 1: SUBJECTIVE PROBABILITIES AND DATA ESTIMATES ASSOCIATED WITH EVERCLEAR'S PRICING PROBLEM

1. If Kromel price remained at $1.00/pound and market segment A were not penetrated, what market share pattern for Kromel industry sales pounds would obtain in segments B, C, and D?

| | Base assumptions—Kromel industry share | | |
	Segment B	Segment C	Segment D
1961	57.0%	40.0%	42.0%
1962	65.0	50.0	44.0
1963	75.0	80.0	46.0
1964	76.0	84.0	48.0
1965	76.0	84.0	50.0

2. If Kromel price remained at $1.00/pound, what is the probability that Kromel would still penetrate market segment A?

	Probability of penetration—segment A
1961	.05
1962	.10
1963	.20
1964	.25
1965	.40

3. Under price strategies $.93/pound, $.85/pound, and $.80/pound, what is the probability of Verlon industry price retaliation; and given the particular retaliation (shown below), what is the probability that Kromel would still penetrate market segment A?

Pricing case (entries are probabilities)

Verlon industry retaliation	$.93 case	$.85 case	$.80 case
Full match of Kromel price reduction	.05	.15	.38
Half match of Kromel price reduction	.60	.75	.60
Stand pat on price	.35	.10	.02

Given a particular Verlon retaliatory action, the probability that Kromel would still penetrate segment A

	$.93 case			$.85 case			$.80 case		
	Full match	half match	Stand pat	Full match	half match	Stand pat	Full match	half match	Stand pat
1961	.15	.20	.35	.20	.40	.80	.75	.80	.90
1962	.25	.30	.60	.30	.60	.90	.80	.85	.95
1963	.35	.40	.65	.40	.65	.95	.85	.90	1.00
1964	.60	.65	.75	.70	.75	.98	.90	.95	1.00
1965	.65	.70	.80	.75	.80	.98	.95	.98	1.00

4. If penetration in market segment A were effected, what is the probability that Kromel would obtain the specific share of this segment (a) during the first year of penetration, and (b) during the second year of participation?

Share	First year	Second year
25%	.15	.00
50	.35	.00
75	.40	.00
100	.10	1.00

5. If Kromel penetration of market segment A were effected, what impact would this event have on speeding up Kromel industry participation in segments B, C, and D?

Segment B—Would speed up market participation one year from base assumption shown under point 1 of this Table.

Segment C—Would speed up market participation one year from base assumption shown under point 1 of this Table.

Segment D—Kromel would move up to 85% of the market in the following year, and would obtain 100% of the market in the second year following penetration of segment A.

6. Under the price reduction strategies, if Kromel penetration of market segment A were not accomplished, what is the probability that Kromel industry participation in segments B, C, and D (considered as a group) would still be speeded up one year from the base assumption shown under point 1 of this Table?

Probability of speedup	
$.93 case	.45
$.85 case	.60
$.80 case	.80

7. If Kromel price at the end of any given year were $1.00/pound, $.93/pound, $.85/pound, or $.80/pound respectively, and if market segment A were not penetrated, what is the probability that present competitive Kromel producers would take the specific price action shown below?

If Kromel price	Action	Probability
@ $1.00/pound	$1.00/pound	.15
	.93	.80
	.85	.05
	.80	.00
@ $.93/pound	.93	.80
	.85	.20
	.80	.00
@ $.85/pound	.85	1.00
	.80	.00
@ $.80/pound	.80	1.00

8. Under each of the four price strategies, what is the probability that competitive (present or potential) Kromel producers would add to or initiate capacity (as related to the price prevailing in mid-1961) in the years 1963 and 1964? (No capacity changes were assumed in 1965.)

Competitor	$1.00/pound	$.93/pound	$.85/pound	$.80/pound
R	.50	.20	.05	.00
S	.90	.75	.50	.20
T	.40	.10	.05	.00
U	.70	.50	.25	.00
V	.70	.50	.25	.00

Timing and amount available beginning of year

Competitor	1963	1964
R	10 million pounds	20 million pounds
S	12	20
T	12	20
U	6	12
V	6	6

Multiplication of each conditional probability, in turn, by the .05 marginal probability leads to the four joint probabilities noted in the upper left portion of the chart.

Next, if Kromel did not penetrate segment A during the first year, a probability of .80 was attached to the event that competitive Kromel producers would reduce price to $.93 per pound. Multilying the conditional probability of .80 by .95 results in the .76000 probability assigned to the joint event, "did not penetrate segment A and Kromel price was reduced to $.93 per pound."

However, if Kromel price were reduced to $.93 per pound, Verlon retaliation had to be considered, leading to the joint probabilities assigned to the next set of tree branches. In this way probabilities were built up for each of the over-400 possible outcomes of the study by appropriate application of the ground rules noted in Table 1.

A mathematical model was next constructed for determining the expected value of Everclear's cumulative, compounded net profits under each price strategy. See Table 2.

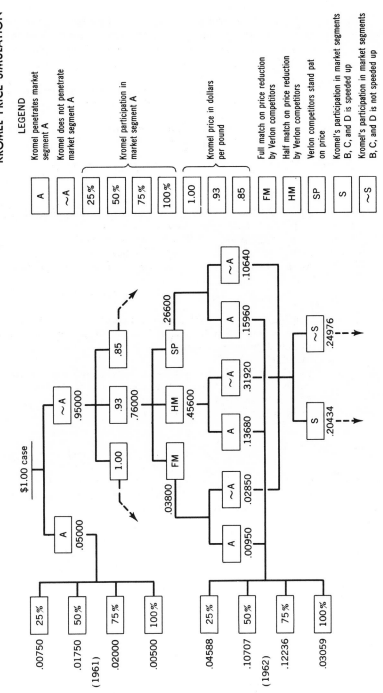

FIGURE 1: PORTION OF A "TREE DIAGRAM";
KROMEL PRICE SIMULATION

LEGEND

| A | Kromel penetrates market segment A |
| ~A | Kromel does not penetrate market segment A |

Kromel participation in market segment A
25%	
50%	
75%	
100%	

Kromel price in dollars per pound
1.00	
.93	
.85	

FM	Full match on price reduction by Verlon competitors
HM	Half match on price reduction by Verlon competitors
SP	Verlon competitors stand pat on price
S	Kromel's participation in market segments B, C, and D is speeded up
~S	Kromel's participation in market segments B, C, and D is not speeded up

This model was then programmed for an electronic computer. The simulation was first carried out for the base case assumptions regarding total Verlon-Kromel market growth and cost of capital. Additional runs were made in which these assumptions were varied.

TABLE 2: KROMEL MODEL—EXPECTED VALUE OF CUMULATIVE, COMPOUNDED NET PROFITS

The mathematical model used to determine the expected values of Everclear's cumulative, compounded net profits was as follows:

$$CCN(X_k) = \sum_{j=1}^{n} pj \cdot \sum_{i=1}^{m} [(1 + r)^{m-i}T\{(D_{ij} - Z_{ij})(K_{ij}M_{ij})\}]$$

$$Z_{ij} = \phi(K_{ij}M_{ij})$$

$CCN(X_k) =$ Expected value of Everclear's cumulative, compounded net profits under each X_k price strategy ($k = 1, \ldots, 4$).

pj $=$ Probability assigned to the j-th outcome ($j = 1, 2, \ldots, n$).

r $=$ Interest rate per annum, expressed decimally.

T $=$ Ratio of net to gross profits of Everclear's Kromel operation (assumed constant in the study).

$D_{ij} =$ Kromel price in \$/pound in the i-th year ($i = 1, 2, \ldots, m$) for the j-th outcome.

$Z_{ij} =$ Cost in \$/pound of Everclear's Kromel resin in the i-th year for the j-th outcome. (This cost is a function of the amount of Kromel pounds sold by Everclear.)

$\phi =$ Function of.

$K_{ij} =$ Everclear's overall market share of Kromel Industry sales (in pounds) in the i-th year for the j-th outcome (expressed decimally).

$M_{ij} =$ Kromel Industry poundage (summed over all four market segments) in the i-th year for the jth outcome.

RESULTS OF THE COMPUTER SIMULATIONS

The computer run for the base case showed some interesting results for the relevant variables affecting Everclear's cumulative, compounded net profits position at the end of the planning period. These results are portrayed in Figures 2 through 4.

Figure 2 summarizes the cumulative probability of Kromel's penetration of market segment A (the critical factor in the study) as a function of time, under each pricing strategy. As would be expected, the lowest price strategy, the *\$.80 case*, carried the highest probability of market penetration. However, the cumulative probability approached 1, that *all* price strategies would eventually effect penetration of market segment A by the end of the simulation period. This behavior stems from the impact of price decreases assumed to be initiated by Kromel *competitors* (if penetration were not initially effected under the original price strategies) which in turn changed the probability of Kromel's penetration of segment A in later years, since this probability was related to price.

Figure 3 shows the expected incremental sales dollars (obtained by subtracting the expected outcomes of the *\$1.00 case*, used as a reference base,

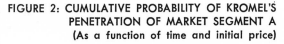

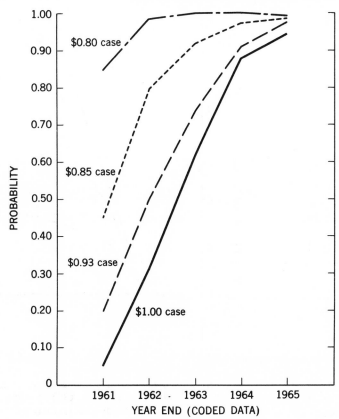

FIGURE 2: CUMULATIVE PROBABILITY OF KROMEL'S
PENETRATION OF MARKET SEGMENT A
(As a function of time and initial price)

from the expected outcomes of each of the other three cases respectively)
generated for Everclear under each price strategy. While some tapering
off in average sales dollars generated from the price reduction cases compared to the *$1.00 case* can be noted near the end of the simulation
period, this tapering off is less pronounced than that which would be
experienced by the total Kromel industry.

The reason for this different pattern is that the price reduction strategies (by reducing the probability of future capacity expansion on the part
of existing and potential Kromel competitors) led to gains in Everclear's
market share, relative to market share under the *$1.00 case*. These
increases in Everclear's market share, under the price reduction strategies,
partially offset the decline in incremental sales dollar gains (experienced
by the Kromel industry near the end of the period) and thus explain the
difference in sales patterns that would be observed between Everclear and
the Kromel industry.

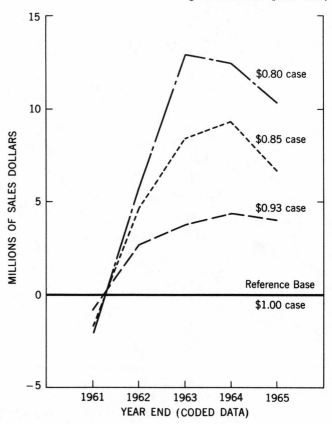

FIGURE 3: KROMEL SALES VOLUME—EVERCLEAR PLASTICS CO. (Incremental sales dollars generated over $1.00 case)

Figure 4 summarizes the behavior of Everclear's average, year-by-year (compounded) net profits performance again on an incremental basis compared to the *$1.00 case*. As would be expected, time lags in the penetration of segment A, under the price reduction strategies, result in an early profit penalty compared to the *$1.00 case*. This penalty is later over-

TABLE 3: CUMULATIVE, COMPOUNDED NET PROFITS—EVERCLEAR PLASTICS CO. (1961–65)

Price strategy	End of period profit position
$1.00 case	$26.5 million
.93 case	30.3 million
.85 case	33.9 million
.80 case	34.9 million

FIGURE 4: COMPOUNDED YEAR-BY-YEAR NET PROFITS
OF EVERCLEAR PLASTICS CO.
(Compound rate equals 6% annually)

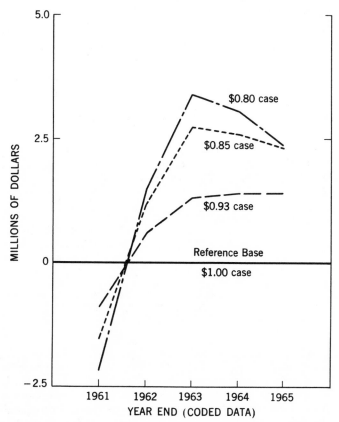

balanced by the additional sales dollars accruing from earlier (on the average) penetration of segment A under the price reduction strategies versus the *status quo* price case.

The overall performance of each pricing strategy on Everclear's cumulative, compounded net profits position (expected value basis) at the *end* of the five-year planning period is shown in Table 3. These values were obtained by application of the formula shown in Table 2.

Table 3 shows that all of the price reduction strategies yield expected payoffs which exceed the *$1.00 case*. These additional profits stem from two principal sources:

1. the higher profits generated in the middle portion of the planning period, as a function of the increased probability of effecting penetration of market segment A, and its associated effect on Kromel industry sales in market segments B, C, and D; and

2. the higher market share for Everclear, resulting from the influence of the price reduction strategies on lowering the probability of capacity expansion

and/or entry by Kromel competitors (existing or potential). These combined factors overbalance the lower profit margins per pound associated with the price reduction strategies compared to the *$1.00 case.*

However, a relevant question arose concerning the influence of the more favorable market share factor (under the price reduction cases) on the outcomes of these strategies vs. the *$1.00 case.* Suppose that no favorable difference in market share were obtained under the price reduction strategies compared to the no-price reduction case. That is, suppose the probability that lower Kromel price would discourage future competitive expansion of Kromel industry capacity in the 1963–64 period were zero. How would this affect Everclear's profit position?

In order to test the impact of this variable on Everclear's cumulative, compounded net profits, the market share factor was held constant at the trend level estimated under the no-price reduction, or *$1.00 case* over the simulation period. This analysis resulted in the information given in Table 4.

TABLE 4: PROFIT POSITION—MARKET SHARE
HELP CONSTANT (Everclear's cumulative,
compounded net profits; 1961–65)

Price strategy	End of period profit position
$1.00 case	$26.5 million
.93 case	26.9 million
.85 case	27.4 million
.80 case	25.2 million

It is clear from Table 4 that the market share factor is important in producing Everclear's higher profit position as associated with the price reduction alternatives noted in Table 3. If increased share for Everclear were *not* obtained in the 1963–65 period (relative to the share expected under the *$1.00 case*), all strategies would yield close to equal payoffs. That is, over the planning period, the increased sales volume resulting from earlier (on the average) penetration of segment A under the price reduction strategies just about balances the less favorable profit margins associated with these strategies.

However, beyond the planning period, all strategies have for all practical purposes accomplished penetration of segment A. The impact of *higher market share* for Everclear thus assumes an important role toward maintaining higher payoffs for the price reduction cases versus the *$1.00 case.*

When computer run results were analyzed for the sub-cases (varying the total market forecast and cost of capital variables), it was found that the study outcomes were not sensitive to these factors. Although the absolute levels of all payoffs changed, no appreciable change was noted in their relative standing.

In Summary. This illustration has shown two principal findings regarding the expected payoffs associated with the alternative courses of action formulated by Everclear:

1. All price reduction strategies result in higher expected payoffs than that associated with the *status quo* pricing case and of these, the *$.80 case* leads to the largest expected value.
2. The higher payoffs associated with the price reduction strategies are quite sensitive to the assumption that Everclear's future market share would be favorably influenced by reductions in Kromel price.

Everclear's management is now at least in a position to appraise the *financial implications* of its marketing assumptions in order to arrive at a reasoned selection among alternative choices.

IMPLICATIONS

The preceding illustration indicates the extent of problem detail which can be (and frequently must be) introduced to reflect adequately the characteristics of real market situations. Nevertheless, this illustration omits some important features of Bayesian decision theory.

First, payoffs were expressed in monetary terms (cumulative, compounded net profits) rather than utility, in the von Neumann-Morgenstern sense, as discussed by Schlaifer.[2] One assumes implicitly, then, that utility is linear with money. As tempting as this assumption may be, some small-scale studies at Du Pont in which attempts were made to construct empirical utility functions raise some questions regarding the assumption of linearity. However, this feature of the Bayesian approach may well take many years of further education and development before it may find regular application on the industrial scene.

Second, while a plethora of Bayesian prior probabilities were used in this problem, no mention was made of analyzing sample data and calculating *posterior* probabilities. How does one investigate states of nature in problems of this type? Certainly the problems of conducting meaningful experiments are hardly trivial in pricing problems, or the general area of market planning.

Third, just how detailed a structure can be warranted, particularly when the inputs to the problem are largely subjective in character? One may obviously over-structure as well as under-structure a problem. This *caveat*, however, applies to all model building. While sensitivity analysis may be used to shed light on which variables "make a difference," the fact remains that the model-building process is still based largely on the builder's intuitive grasp of problem essentials and the interplay between analyst and decision-maker. The structure of the problem discussed in this article turned out to be complex precisely because the variables included *were* deemed important by the decision-maker(s). And part of the analyst's job is thus to examine the impact of supposedly important

---

2 Schlaifer, *op. cit.*, chap. 2.

variables on the relevant payoff junction and then feed back his findings to the decision-maker.

Finally, in conducting this study, realistic problems have a way of generating quite a lot of arithmetic detail, for example, a multi-stage set of alternative states of nature and payoffs. Implementation of the Bayesian approach must, therefore, frequently be aided by recourse to a high-speed computing device. Moreover, a computer model also facilitates the task of running sensitivity analyses concerning either changes in the payoff values related to any particular combination of state of nature and course of action.

Our experience has indicated that the Bayesian approach, even coupled with the ancillary techniques of computer simulation and sensitivity analysis, does not offer any foolproof procedure for "solving" market planning problems. Still, it would seem that this method *does* offer definite advantage over the more traditional techniques usually associated with market planning. Traditional techniques rarely consider *alternative* states of nature, let alone assigning prior probabilities to their occurrence. Moreover, traditional market planning techniques seldom provide for testing the sensitivity of the study's outcomes to departures in the basic assumptions.

At the very least, the Bayesian model forces a more rigorous approach to market planning problems and offers a useful device for quickly finding the financial implications of assumptions about the occurrence of alternative states of nature. In time, this procedure coupled with a more sophisticated approach to the design, collection, and interpretation of field data appears capable of providing an up-to-date and flexible means to meet the more stringent demands of dynamic decision situations, so typical in the problems faced by the marketing manager.

DISTRIBUTION DECISIONS

22

Alternative Explanations
of Institutional Change
and Channel Evolution

BERT C. McCAMMON, JR.
Center for Advanced Studies in Distribution

Marketing channels and institutions must adapt continuously to their environment in order to avoid "economic obsolescence." Most of the required adaptations are tactical in nature. Channel alignments, for example, can usually be maintained over an extended period of time by effecting a series of minor, though necessary, revisions in marketing practices. Individual firms, under normal conditions, can also maintain their competitive position without significantly altering prevailing policies and procedures. Thus, institutional change in marketing tends to be a process in which firms and channels maneuver for short-run advantage and in which they adapt almost imperceptibly to environmental disturbances.

Periodically, however, a firm's or channel's existence is threatened by a *major* change in marketing practices. The sudden appearance of new products, new methods of distribution, new types of competitors, and new sales approaches, may imperil existing institutional relationships. These abrupt departures from the *status quo* can disrupt prevailing patterns of competition, alter cost–price relationships, and "enforce a distinctive process of adaptation"[1] on the part of threatened organizations.

Schumpeter earlier, Barnet and Levitt later, argue that this type of competition, usually called innovative competition, is a prerequisite for

Reprinted with permission from *Toward Scientific Marketing*, ed. S. A. Greyser (Chicago: American Marketing Association, December 1963), pp. 477–90.
[1] Joseph Schumpeter, *Business Cycles* (New York: McGraw-Hill, 1939), p. 10.

289

economic growth.[2] Despite general acceptance of this position, very little is known about the innovative process in marketing. More specifically, we lack a body of theory that explains how new marketing practices are originated and diffused throughout the structure of distribution.

The emergence and acceptance of new practices is a complex process which has been analyzed extensively in the agricultural sector of our economy,[3] and in the medical profession.[4] For example:

> The farmers participating in the diffusion process are relatively easy to identify. Beal and Rogers have classified such participants as innovators (the developers or initial accepters of new ideas), early adopters, majority adopters, and laggards. "Indirect" participants, who occupy important positions in the communications network, are classified as key communicators, influentials, and skeptics. Each of these decision makers has a distinctive socio-economic profile and a differentiated mode of behavior. Researchers, by analyzing interaction patterns, can predict the rate at which a new farm practice will be accepted, and they can forecast the probable impact of this innovation on non-adopters.[5]

Unfortunately, comparable analysis has not been undertaken in retailing or wholesaling. The distinguishing characteristics of innovators, early adopters, and other participants in the diffusion process have not been identified, nor have the factors which inhibit or encourage change been isolated. Consequently, the explanation and prediction of institutional change in marketing tends to be a tenuous intellectual exercise.

The diffusion process in marketing is more complex than it is in agriculture because the counter strategies of non-adopters have to be considered as well as the spread of the innovation itself. The phenomenon of transient and selective adoption has to be recognized too. Individual firms may emulate an innovator in the short-run while devising long-run strategies, or alternatively these firms may adopt new practices on a limited or modified basis. Conventional department stores, for example, have recently emulated the discounter by opening self-service branches. This may be an interim strategy in the sense that the branches may change over time so that they eventually bear little resemblance to the original innovation. With respect to selective adoption of new practices, many supermarkets prepack meat but not produce, and numerous department stores operate self-service drug and toy departments while merchandising other lines on a full-service basis. Consequently, it appears that a complex model is needed to analyze the emergence and diffusion of new practices in the marketing structure.

2 Joseph Schumpeter, *Capitalism, Socialism, and Democracy* (New York: Harper and Brothers, 1947); Edward M. Barnet, *Innovate or Perish* (New York: Columbia University, 1954); and Theodore Levitt, *Innovation in Marketing* (New York: McGraw-Hill, 1962).

3 See for example, E. M. Rogers and G. M. Beal, *Reference Group Influence in The Adoption of Agricultural Technology* (Ames: Iowa State University, 1958).

4 See for example, J. Coleman, E. Katz, and H. Menzel, "The Diffusion of an Innovation among Physicians," *Sociometry* (December, 1957), pp. 253–270.

5 S. C. Dodd, "Diffusion is Predictable: Testing Probability Models for Laws of Interaction," *American Sociological Review* (August, 1955), pp. 392–401.

The purposes of this paper are (1) to explore the barriers to change in the marketing structure, (2) to evaluate the sources of innovation within the structure, and (3) to suggest some hypotheses about the factors which determine the rate at which new practices are accepted.

BARRIERS TO CHANGE WITHIN THE MARKETING STRUCTURE

Conventional economic analysis provides a useful frame of reference for explaining institutional change. The firm, in economic theory, attempts to maximize its profits and thus accepts technological improvements as soon as they appear. Innovations under these circumstances are absorbed quickly and the diffusion process is completed in a relatively short period of time. Shifts in channel alignments are also susceptible to economic analysis. Client firms utilize intermediaries because the latter can perform specific functions (in a given location) at a lower cost per unit than can the former. Intermediaries, in this context, are sources of external economies to their clientele. Such economies are possible because intermediaries, by aggregating user requirements, can perform the designated function(s) at an optimum scale, or alternatively, intermediaries, by aggregating user requirements, can more fully utilize existing (though non-optimum) facilities.[6]

As output expands or as *technology changes*, the client firms reach a point at which they can perform the delegated functions at an optimum scale. When this point is reached, functions tend to be reabsorbed, and the channel becomes more completely integrated. This process of reintegration is not necessarily frictionless. The intermediary attempts to avoid being "integrated out" of the channel by changing his method of operation so that it more closely conforms to the client's requirements. Manufacturer's agents in the electronics field, for example, have retained their principals by carrying inventory, and building supply wholesalers continue to sell to large developers by offering goods on a cash and carry basis.

Economic analysis of institutional change can be and has been carried much further.[7] This type of analysis, however modified, inevitably assumes that the firm's behavior is determined by cost/revenue considerations, and thus it leaves unanswered some or all of the following questions:

---

6 The latter source of economies is often called the "blending principle."

7 See, for example, R. H. Coase, "The Nature of The Firm," *Economica*, New Series, Volume IV (1937), pp. 386–405; George J. Stigler, "The Division of Labor is Limited by the Extent of The Market," *The Journal of Political Economy* (June, 1951), pp. 185–193; R. Artle and S. Berglund, "A Note on Manufacturers' Choice of Distribution Channel," *Management Science* (July, 1959), pp. 460–471; Edward H. Bowman, "Scale of Operations: An Empirical Study," *Operations Research* (May–June, 1958), pp. 320–328; Louis B. Bucklin, "The Economic Structure of Channels of Distribution," *Marketing: A Maturing Discipline*, ed. Martin Bell (Chicago: American Marketing Association, 1960), pp. 379–385; and F. E. Balderston, "Theories of Marketing Structure and Channels," *Proceedings, Conference of Marketing Teachers from Far Western States* (Berkeley: University of California, 1958), pp. 134–145.

Why is change resisted by marketing institutions even though it appears to offer economic advantages?

Why do "uneconomic channels of distribution" persist over extended periods of time?

Why do some firms accept change rapidly, while others lag in their adaptation or refuse to change at all?

Answers to these and related questions depend upon an analysis of sociological and psychological barriers to change, some of which are discussed below.

Reseller Solidarity[8]

Resellers in many lines of trade often function as a highly cohesive group, bargaining with suppliers and adjusting to their environment collectively as well as individually. Resellers "organized" on this basis must maintain internal harmony and a workable consensus. Consequently, they tend to support traditional trade practices and long established institutional relationships.

Several factors are apparently conducive to group action. Resellers tend to act as a unit when the firms involved are relatively homogeneous. Each of the entrepreneurs in this situation tends to be confronted by similar problems and has comparable expectations. Thus he identifies with other members of the trade and is willing to work cooperatively with them.

Resellers also tend to engage in collective action when the entrepreneurs have common backgrounds. The owner-managers of drugstores, for example, are often "highly organized" because most of them are pharmacists and are often alumni of the same universities. Business conditions affect reseller solidarity too. There is likely to be more group action during periods of adverse business conditions than during periods of prosperity. Finally, the degree of reseller solidarity that prevails is conditioned by the intensity and complexity of competition. A line of trade, confronted by unusually aggressive competition from outside sources, is more likely to engage in group action than would be the case if this threat did not exist.

The presence of a strong professional or trade association tends to reinforce conservative group behavior. Retail druggists, as an illustration, support long established professional associations which defend existing trade practices. Carpet retailers, on the other hand, are not represented by a trade association, and for this reason, as well as others, their industry is characterized by unstable retail prices and by constantly changing institutional arrangements.

To summarize, the presence of group solidarity within the structure of marketing tends to inhibit the rate at which innovation is accepted and thus slows down the diffusion process.

[8] The discussion in this section is based on the analyses contained in J. C. Palamountain, Jr., *The Politics of Distribution* (Cambridge, Massachusetts: Harvard University Press, 1955), and in E. T. Grether, "Solidarity in the Distribution Trades," *Law and Contemporary Problems* (June, 1937), pp. 376–391.

Entrepreneurial Values

The entrepreneur's reaction to change is conditioned by his value hierarchy. Large resellers, as a group, are growth oriented and their decisions are based upon economic criteria. Innovations that promote growth are regarded as being desirable, and technological alternatives are evaluated on the basis of "profitability" analysis.[9] Consequently, the large reseller, given sufficient time to adjust, tends to be responsive to innovation and will either accept it or otherwise react to it on the basis of cost–revenue relationships.

Small resellers often have a markedly different set of values. Wittreich, on the basis of his research, argues that small retailers tend to have relatively static expectations.[10] That is, they are interested in reaching and *maintaining* a given scale of operation, and reject opportunities for growth beyond this point. Such retailers tend to view their demand curve as being relatively fixed. Thus, they are inclined to resist innovation because it presumably cannot improve their position and could conceivably disrupt a reasonably attractive *status quo.*

Vidich and Bensman, in their study of life in a small community, reach essentially the same conclusions about the small merchant's behavior.[11] Furthermore, they argue that small retailers are extremely reluctant to invest additional funds in their businesses, almost irrespective of the profits involved. Instead they prefer "secure" investment outlets such as real estate and securities. The small retailers studied by Vidich and Bensman also believed that they had suffered a decline in status during the past three decades, and they resisted any institutional arrangements that would further depress their relative position within the community. This latter condition may partially explain why voluntary and cooperative groups have not been more successful. Retailers participating in these programs sacrifice some of their autonomy, and the loss of this autonomy may be perceived as a loss of status. Wroe Alderson, in another context, has argued that a behavior system will survive as long as it fulfills the status expectations of its participants.[12] Since the small retailer's status is a function of "being in business for himself," the desire to maintain independence may partially explain both the rejection of contractual integration and the persistence of "uneconomic channels."

To summarize, recent research indicates that the small retailer (and presumably other small businessmen) will resist innovation, because they

[9] See Bert C. McCammon, Jr. and Donald H. Granbois, *Profit Contribution: A Criterion for Display Decisions* (New York: Point-of-Purchase Advertising Institute, Inc., 1963).

[10] Warren J. Wittreich, "Misunderstanding the Retailer," *Harvard Business Review* (May–June, 1962), pp. 147–159.

[11] Arthur J. Vidich and Joseph Bensman, *Small Town in Mass Society* (Garden City, N.Y.: Doubleday and Company, Inc., 1960), pp. 73 and 91–93.

[12] Wroe Alderson, "Survival and Adjustment in Behavior Systems," *Theory in Marketing* (Edited by Reavis Cox and Wroe Alderson) (Homewood, Illinois: Richard D. Irwin, Inc., 1950), p. 80.

"value" stability more highly than growth.[13] They will also resist innovations that require a substantial investment of funds or that result in a perceived loss of status.

Organizational Rigidity

A well established firm is an historical entity with deeply entrenched patterns of behavior. The members of the organization may resist change because it violates group norms, creates uncertainty, and results in loss of status. Customers may also resent change and threaten to withdraw their patronage. Furthermore the firm has "sunk" costs in training programs, in office systems, and in equipment which it prefers to recover before instituting major revisions in its procedures. Consequently most firms absorb innovation gradually, or react to innovative competition through a series of incremental adjustments.[14] Because of these factors, the diffusion of an innovation through an industry and the distinctive pattern of adaptation it enforces takes considerable time.

The firm's reaction to change is also a function of the extent to which the innovator has penetrated the firm's core market. Most firms appeal to a specific group of customers who are uniquely loyal. These customers may patronize the firm for a variety of reasons, but the attraction is such that their patronage is virtually assured. As long as this core market remains intact, the firm can usually maintain sufficient sales to continue operations until it matures strategies to counteract the innovator.[15] If the core market is infringed, however, the firm must either emulate the innovator or develop immediate counterstrategies.

To summarize, a firm, because of organizational rigidities, prefers to respond incrementally to innovation. It will gradually imitate the innovating firm or develop counterstrategies over an extended period of time. If the innovator has penetrated the firm's core market, however, it must respond quickly to this challenge in order to ensure continued operation.

The Firm's Channel Position[16]

There is a dominant channel of distribution for most lines of merchandise. This channel, as compared with other institutional alignments, has the greatest prestige and often handles the bulk of the industry's output. Behavior within the channel is regulated by an occupational code which "controls" pricing policies, sales promotion practices, and other

[13] For additional confirmation of this hypothesis, see Louis Kriesberg, "The Retail Furrier, Concepts of Security and Success," *American Journal of Sociology* (March, 1952).

[14] For an interesting discussion of incremental adjustments to innovation, see Alton F. Doody, "Historical Patterns of Marketing Innovation," *Emerging Concepts in Marketing,* ed. William S. Decker (Chicago: American Marketing Association, 1962), pp. 245–253.

[15] Alderson, *op. cit.,* p. 81.

[16] The discussion in this section is based on the analysis that appears in Louis Kriesberg, "Occupational Controls Among Steel Distributors," *The American Journal of Sociology* (November, 1955), pp. 203–212.

related activities. Deviation from the code's prescriptions are punished in a variety of ways, ranging from colleague ostracism to economic sanctions.

Individual firms can be classified in terms of their relationship to the dominant channel of distribution and in terms of their adherence to the occupational code. The *insiders* are members of the dominant channel. They have continuous access to preferred sources of supply, and their relatively high status in the trade is a byproduct of channel membership. The insiders, as a group, prescribe the contents of the occupational code and enforce it. They are desirous of the respect of their colleagues, and recognize the interdependency of the firms in the system. In short, the insider has made an emotional and financial commitment to the dominant channel and is interested in perpetuating it.

The *strivers* are firms located outside the dominant channel who want to become a part of the system. These firms have discontinuous access to preferred resources, and during periods of short supply, they may be "short ordered" or not shipped at all. The striver, since he wants to become a member of the system, is responsive to the occupational code and will not engage in deviate behavior under normal economic conditions. Thus he utilizes the same marketing practices as the insider.

The *complementors* are not part of the dominant channel, nor do they desire to obtain membership. As their title suggests, these firms complement the activities undertaken by members of the dominant channel. That is, the complementors perform functions that are not normally performed by other channel members, or serve customers whose patronage is normally not solicited, or handle qualities of merchandise the dominant channel doesn't carry. Thus the complementors are marginally affiliated with the dominant channel and want to see it survive. Their expectations are of a long-run nature and they respect the occupational code.

The *transients* also occupy a position outside the dominant channel and do not seek membership in it. Many transients are mobile entrepreneurs who move from one line of trade to another; other transients are firms that owe their allegiance elsewhere, i.e., they consider themselves to be members of a channel other than the one in question. Therefore they utilize the latter channel's product as an "in and out" item or as a loss leader, since it is not their market "that is being spoiled" by such activity. All of the transients have short-run expectations and the occupational code is not an effective constraint.

Classification of firms into these four categories explains some of the competitive patterns which have emerged in the ready-to-wear field, in the toy industry, and in the TBA market. Transient firms, in all of these merchandise lines, have disrupted the *status quo* by engaging in deviate competitive behavior. Significantly, none of the four types of firms described above are likely to introduce major marketing innovations. The insiders and the strivers are primarily interested in maintaining existing institutional arrangements. The complementors also have a vested interest in the *status quo*, and the transients are not sufficiently dependent on the product line to develop an entirely new method of distribution. Thus the above analysis suggests that a firm completely outside the system will introduce basic innovations, and historically this has often been the case. Consequently, a fifth category for *outside innovators* is required to explain major structural realignments.

Market Segmentation

As market segments emerge and/or as they are recognized by entrepreneurs, firms that formerly competed directly with each other begin to compete in a more marginal sense. That is, former rivals begin to appeal to different types of customers, and as a result the tactics adopted by one firm may have a negligible potential impact on other firms. Competition, under these circumstances, becomes more fragmented, and the compulsion to accept or react to innovation declines—a condition that slows down the diffusion process.

The discount supermarket, for example, has not increased in importance as rapidly as many of its proponents initially believed, and the bantam supermarket has experienced much the same fate. It appears that these innovative methods of operation appeal to a limited number of market segments, and conventional supermarkets, appealing to other market segments, have not been compelled to react to these new forms of competition.

SOURCES OF INNOVATIVE ACTIVITY

The Channel Administrator

An individual firm usually controls a given marketing channel in the sense that it directs the allocation of resources for all channel members. Manufacturers, farm marketing cooperatives, voluntary groups, and chain store buying offices are illustrations of organizations that direct the activities of other channel members. These decision makers do not set goals for the other firms in the channel, but they do decide what kind of firms shall be combined to form the distribution network for the systems they organize.[17]

The channel administrator often is an innovator, particularly when a new product is being marketed. Manufacturers of new fabricated materials, for example, often have to develop unique institutional arrangements to distribute their products,[18] and the Singer Sewing Machine Company pioneered the use of a franchise agency system and installment credit when it began to market sewing machines during the 1850's.[19]

[17] For a more complete discussion of the channel administrator concept, see George Fisk, "The General Systems Approach to the Study of Marketing," *The Social Responsibilities of Marketing*, ed. William D. Stevens (Chicago: American Marketing Association, 1961), pp. 207–211.

[18] See E. Raymond Corey, *The Development of Markets for New Materials*, Division of Research, Graduate School of Business Administration (Boston: Harvard University, 1956).

[19] Andrew B. Jack, "The Channels of Distribution for an Innovation: The Sewing-Machine Industry in America, 1860–1865," *Explorations in Entrepreneurial History* (February, 1957), pp. 113–141.

Furthermore channel administrators can be quite responsive to *procedural* innovations. During the last decade, channel administrators have taken the initiative in developing new physical distribution techniques, and they have accepted rather rapidly such innovations as merchandise management accounting, PERT cost analysis, stockless purchasing arrangements, and value analysis.

Channel administrators, however, tend to be well established firms, and thus they are subject to the organizational constraints described above. More specifically, they tend to resist an innovation that involves a major restructuring of the firm's relationship with its customers, since they have the most to lose by such restructuring and the least to gain.

Large firms can overcome their tendency to maintain the *status quo* by underwriting *elite* activities. The elite members of an organization engage in projects that have problematic, long-run payouts rather than certain, short-run yields. The ratio of professional personnel to high status administrators is a rough measure of the use of elite personnel within an organization. The higher the proportion of professional personnel to proprietors, managers, and officials, the more likely is the existence of staff departments preserving long-run interests against the pressure of immediate problems. Stinchcombe, and Hill and Harbison have analyzed the relationship between innovation and the proportion of elite personnel employed.[20] Their findings indicate that innovating industries employ proportionately more professionals than do non-innovating industries.

Furthermore, within a given industry, the firms with proportionately more professionals innovate more rapidly than those with fewer. Significantly, wholesaling and retailing are classified as "stagnant" industries, and the payrolls of these types of firms contain significantly fewer professional employees per hundred administrators than is the case in "progressive" industries. Admittedly, the definitions of "progressiveness" and "stagnation" can be somewhat arbitrary, as can the definition of a "professional" employee. Consequently, the data just cited should be regarded as being suggestive rather than definitive, but the suggestion is unambiguous —retailers and wholesalers could effect economies and develop more productive institutional arrangements if they engaged in additional research and underwrote more elite activities.

The "Outsider"

Institutional innovation, particularly in retailing, has historically occurred *outside* of the established power structure. The retail innovator, in fact, has tended to resemble Eric Hoffer's "The True Believer."[21] J. C. Penney, Richard Sears, King Cullen, and others were discontented "outsiders" who believed that they had discovered a technique of irresistible

[20] Arthur L. Stinchcombe, "The Sociology of Organization and The Theory of the Firm," *The Pacific Sociological Review* (Fall, 1960), pp. 75–82. Samuel E. Hill and Frederick Harbison, *Manpower and Innovation in American Industry* (Princeton University Press, 1959), pp. 16–27.

[21] Eric Hoffer, *The True Believer* (New York: New American Library, 1951), pp. 13–20.

power. They had an extravagant conception of the potentialities of the future, minimized the problems of managing a large enterprise, and promulgated their merchandising doctrines with an almost evangelical fervor. The premise that the institutional innovator is likely to come from outside the established power structure is also inherent in the wheel of retailing concept which is the most comprehensive theory of innovation yet developed in marketing.[22] Silk and Stern, in their recent study, also conclude that the marketing innovator has traditionally been an "outsider," but they additionally argue that recent innovators have tended to be much more deliberate in their choice processes and much more methodical in their analyses than were their predecessors of several decades ago.[23] In any case, if we accept the assumption that significant innovation tends to occur outside the existing system, then it is important from a social point of view to create a marketing environment in which entry is relatively easy.

ANALYZING INSTITUTIONAL CHANGE

There is a tendency in marketing to refine analysis beyond the point of maximum usefulness, and this is particularly true when the phenomena under investigation are relatively complex. Quite obviously, many of the changes that have occurred in the structure of distribution during the past 50 years can be explained in terms of a relatively simple challenge and response model. The emergence and rapid growth of voluntary and cooperative groups in the food field is a logical response to the expansion of corporate vertical integration, and the rise of the cash and carry wholesaler in the building supply industry is a natural response to the growing importance of the large developer. Thus, if the marketplace is viewed as an arena in which firms constantly search for differential advantage and/or react to it, much of what appears to be rather complex behavior can be reduced to fairly simple terms.

Hypotheses

Systems theorists and sociologists have selectively investigated the diffusion of new ideas and practices. The hypotheses that have emerged from this research serve as useful points of origin for subsequent exploration in marketing. More specifically, *marketing analysts should consider the following hypotheses when attempting to explain institutional change*:

1. The rate of diffusion depends upon the innovation itself. Innovations that involve a substantial capital investment, a major restructuring of the firm's relationship with its customers, and a sizable number of internal realignments are more likely to be accepted slowly than those that involve relatively minor intra- or inter-firm changes.

22 For a careful analysis of the wheel of retailing concept, see Stanley C. Hollander, "The Wheel of Retailing," *Journal of Marketing* (July, 1960), pp. 37–42.

23 Alvin J. Silk and Louis William Stern, "The Changing Nature of Innovation in Marketing: A Study of Selected Business Leaders, 1852–1958," *Business History Review* (Fall, 1963), pp. 182–199.

2. The innovator is likely to be an "outsider" in the sense that he occupies a marginal role in a given line of trade and is on the outskirts of the prevailing sociometric network. Such individuals are interested in innovation because they have the most to gain and the least to lose by disrupting the *status quo*.

3. A firm will respond incrementally to innovation unless its core market is threatened. If the latter is the case, the response to innovation will proceed swiftly. That is, the firm will parry the innovator's thrust by developing a counterstrategy or it will emulate the innovator on a partial or total basis.

4. The higher the entrepreneur's aspirations, the more likely he is to initiate or accept innovation. Alternatively, the lower the entrepreneur's aspirations, the less likely he is to accept innovation, particularly when such acceptance conflicts with his other values.

5. The acceptance of innovation is not always permanent. A firm may emulate an innovator as a part of a transitional strategy. When the firm develops an ultimate strategy, the emulating features of its behavior will be discarded.

6. Innovation will be accepted most rapidly when it can be fitted into existing decision-making habits. Innovations which involve an understanding of alien relationships or which involve new conceptual approaches tend to be resisted. Many small retailers, for example, have difficulty in accepting the supermarket concept, because it involves a fairly sophisticated understanding of cost–volume relationships.

7. Influentials and innovators are not always the same firms. Institutional innovators, since they tend to be "outsiders," have relatively little influence among their entrepreneurial colleagues. Other firms, occupying central positions in a given line of trade, possess considerable influence, and an innovation will not be adopted widely until these influential firms accept it.

8. Greater energy is required to transmit an innovation from one channel to another than is required to transmit it within a channel. The diffusion of innovation therefore tends to be confined to a given line of trade, before it is adopted by another. The supermarket, as an illustration, became dominant in the food field, before this method of operation was employed by ready-to-wear retailers.

The above hypotheses represent only a small sampling of those developed in other fields. They deserve careful consideration by researchers interested in explaining and predicting institutional change in marketing.

23

Conflict and Cooperation
in Marketing Channels

BRUCE MALLEN
Sir George Williams University

The purpose of this paper is to advance the hypotheses that between member firms of a marketing channel there exists a dynamic field of conflicting and cooperating objectives; that if the conflicting objectives outweigh the cooperating ones, the effectiveness of the channel will be reduced and efficient distribution impeded; and that implementation of certain methods of cooperation will lead to increased channel efficiency.

DEFINITION OF CHANNEL

The concept of a marketing channel is slightly more involved than expected on initial study. One author in a recent paper[1] has identified "trading" channels, "non-trading" channels, "type" channels, "enterprise" channels, and "business-unit" channels. Another source[2] refers to channels as all the flows extending from the producer to the user. These include the flows of physical possession, ownership, promotion, negotiation, financing, risking, ordering, and payment.

Reprinted with permission from *Reflections on Progress in Marketing*, ed. L. George Smith, published by the American Marketing Association, December, 1964, pp. 65–85.

[1] Ralph F. Breyer, "Some Observations on Structural Formation and the Growth of Marketing Channels," in *Theory in Marketing*, Reavis Cox, Wroe Alderson, Stanley J. Shapiro, editors. (Homewood, Ill.: Richard D. Irwin, 1964), pp. 163–175.

[2] Ronald S. Vaile, E. T. Grether, and Reavis Cox, *Marketing in the American Economy* (New York: Ronald Press, 1952), pp. 121 and 124.

The concept of channels to be used here involves only two of the above-mentioned flows: ownership and negotiation. The first draws merchants, both wholesalers and retailers, into the channel definition, and the second draws in agent middlemen. Both, of course, include producers and consumers. This definition roughly corresponds to Professor Breyer's "trading channel," though the latter does not restrict (nor will this paper) the definition to actual flows, but to "flow-capacity." "A trading channel is formed when trading relations, making possible the passage of title and/or possession (usually both) of goods from the producer to the ultimate consumer, is consummated by the component trading concerns of the system."[3] In addition, this paper will deal with trading channels in the broadest manner and so will be concentrating on "type-trading" channels rather than "enterprise" or "business-unit" channels. This means that there will be little discussion of problems peculiar to integrated or semi-integrated channels, or peculiar to specific channels and firms.

CONFLICT

Palamountain isolated three forms of distributive conflict.[4]

1. Horizontal competition—this is competition between middlemen of the same type; for example, discount store *versus* discount store.
2. Intertype competition—this is competition between middlemen of different types in the same channel sector; for example, discount store *versus* department store.
3. Vertical conflict—this is conflict between channel members of different levels; for example, discount store *versus* *manufacturer*.

The first form, horizontal competition, is well covered in traditional economic analysis and is usually referred to simply as "competition." However, both intertype competition and vertical conflict, particularly the latter, are neglected in the usual micro-economic discussions.

The concepts of "intertype competition" and "distributive innovation" are closely related and require some discussion. Intertype competition will be divided into two categories, (a) "traditional intertype competition" and (b) "innovative intertype competition." The first category includes the usual price and promotional competition between two or more different types of channel members at the same channel level. The second category involves the action on the part of traditional channel members to prevent channel innovators from establishing themselves. For example, in Canada there is a strong campaign, on the part of traditional department stores, to prevent the discount operation from taking a firm hold on the Canadian market.[5]

Distributive innovation will also be divided into two categories; (a) "intrafirm innovative conflict" and (b) "innovative intertype competi-

3 Breyer, *op. cit.*, p. 165.

4 Joseph C. Palamountain, *The Politics of Distribution* (Cambridge: Harvard University Press, 1955).

5 Isaiah A. Litvak and Bruce E. Mallen, *Marketing: Canada* (Toronto: McGraw-Hill of Canada, Limited, 1964), pp. 196–197.

tion." The first category involves the action of channel member firms to prevent sweeping changes within their own companies. The second category, "innovative intertype competition," is identical to the second category of intertype competition.

Thus the concepts of intertype competition and distributive innovation give rise to three forms of conflict, the second of which is a combination of both: *1.* traditional intertype competition, *2.* innovative intertype competition, and *3.* intrafirm innovative conflict.

It is to this second form that this paper now turns before going on to vertical conflict.

Innovative Intertype Competition

Professor McCammon has identified several sources, both intrafirm and intertype, of innovative conflict in distribution, i.e., where there are barriers to change within the marketing structure.[6]

Traditional members of a channel have several motives for maintaining the channel status quo against outside innovators. The traditional members are particularly strong in this conflict when they can ban together in some formal or informal manner—when there is strong reseller solidarity.

Both entrepreneurs and professional managers may resist outside innovators, not only for economic reasons, but because change "violates group norms, creates uncertainty, and results in a loss of status." The traditional channel members (the insiders) and their affiliated members (the strivers and complementors) are emotionally and financially committed to the dominant channel and are interested in perpetuating it against the minor irritations of the "transient" channel members and the major attacks of the "outside innovators."

Thus, against a background of horizontal and intertype channel conflict, this paper now moves to its area of major concern; vertical conflict and cooperation.

Vertical Conflict—Price

The Exchange Act. The act of exchange is composed of two elements: a sale and a purchase. It is to the advantage of the seller to obtain the highest return possible from such an exchange and the exact opposite is the desire of the buyer. This exchange act takes place between any kind of buyer and seller. If the consumer is the buyer, then that side of the act is termed shopping; if the manufacturer, purchasing; if the government, procurement; and if a retailer, buying. Thus, between each level in the channel an exchange will take place (except if a channel member is an agent rather than a merchant).

---

6 This section is based on Bert C. McCammon, Jr., "Alternative Explanations of Institutional Change and Channel Evolution," in *Toward Scientific Marketing,* Stephen A. Greyser, editor (Chicago: American Marketing Association, 1963), pp. 477–490. [See p. 289.]

One must look to the process of the exchange act for the basic source of conflict between channel members. This is not to say the exchange act itself is a conflict. Indeed, the act or transaction is a sign that the element of price conflict has been resolved to the mutual satisfaction of both principals. Only along the road to this mutual satisfaction point or exchange price do the principals have opposing interests. This is no less true even if they work out the exchange price together, as in mass retailers' specification-buying programs.

It is quite natural for the selling member in an exchange to want a higher price than the buying member. The conflict is subdued through persuasion or force by one member over the other, or it is subdued by the fact that the exchange act or transaction does not take place, or finally, as mentioned above, it is eliminated if the act does take place.

Suppliers may emphasize the customer aspect of a reseller rather than the channel member aspect. As a customer the reseller is somebody to persuade, manipulate, or even fool. Conversely, under the marketing concept, the view of the reseller as a customer or channel member is identical. Under this philosophy he is somebody to aid, help, and serve. However, it is by no means certain that even a large minority of suppliers have accepted the marketing concept.

To view the reseller as simply the opposing principal in the act of exchange may be channel myopia, but this view exists. On the other hand, failure to recognize this basic opposing interest is also a conceptual fault.

When the opposite principals in an exchange act are of unequal strength, the stronger is very likely to force or persuade the weaker to adhere to the former's desires. However, when they are of equal strength, the basic conflict cannot so easily be resolved. Hence, the growth of big retailers who can match the power of big producers has possibly led to greater open conflict between channel members, not only with regard to exchange, but also to other conflict sources.

There are other sources of conflict within the pricing area outside of the basic one discussed above.

A supplier may force a product onto its resellers, who dare not oppose, but who retaliate in other ways, such as using it as a loss leader. Large manufacturers may try to dictate the resale price of their merchandise; this may be less or more than the price at which resellers wish to sell it. Occasionally, a local market may be more competitive for a reseller than is true nationally. The manufacturer may not recognize the difference in competition and refuse to help this channel member.

Resellers complain of manufacturers' special price concessions to competitors and rebel at the attempt of manufacturers to control resale prices. Manufacturers complain of resellers' deceptive and misleading price advertising, nonadherence to resale price suggestions, bootlegging to unauthorized outlets, seeking special price concessions by unfair methods, and misrepresenting offers by competitive suppliers.

Other points of price conflict are the paperwork aspects of pricing. Resellers complain of delays in price change notices and complicated price sheets.

Price Theory. If one looks upon a channel as a series of markets or as the vertical exchange mechanism between buyers and sellers, one can adapt several theories and concepts to the channel situation which can aid marketing theory in this important area of channel conflict.[7]

Vertical Conflict—Non-Price

Channel conflict not only finds its source in the exchange act and pricing, but it permeates all areas of marketing. Thus, a manufacturer may wish to promote a product in one manner or to a certain degree while his resellers oppose this. Another manufacturer may wish to get information from his resellers on a certain aspect relating to his product, but his resellers may refuse to provide this information. A producer may want to distribute his product extensively, but his resellers may demand exclusives.

There is also conflict because of the tendency for both manufacturers and retailers to want the elimination of the wholesaler.

One very basic source of channel conflict is the possible difference in the primary business philosophy of channel members. Writing in the *Harvard Business Review*, Wittreich says:

In essence, then, the key to understanding management's problem of crossed purpose is the recognition that the fundamental (philosophy) in life of the high-level corporate manager and the typical (small) retailer dealer in the distribution system are quite different. The former's (philosophy) can be characterized as being essentially dynamic in nature, continuously evolving and emerging; the latter, which are in sharp contrast, can be characterized as being essentially static in nature, reaching a point and leveling off into a continuously satisfying plateau.[8]

While the big members of the channel may want growth, the small retail members may be satisfied with stability and a "good living."

ANARCHY[9]

The channel can adjust to its conflicting-cooperating environment in three distinct ways. *First,* it can have a leader (one of the channel members) who "forces" members to cooperate; this is an autocratic relationship. *Second,* it can have a leader who "helps" members to cooperate, creating a democratic relationship. *Finally,* it can do nothing, and so have an anarchistic relationship. Lewis B. Sappington and C. G. Browne, writing on the problems of internal company organizations, state:

The first classification may be called "autocracy." In this approach to the group the leader determines the policy and dictates or assigns the work tasks. There are no group deliberations, no group decisions. . . .

[7] Bruce Mallen, "Introducing The Marketing Channel To Price Theory," *Journal of Marketing,* July, 1964, pp. 29–33.

[8] Warren J. Wittreich, "Misunderstanding The Retailer," *Harvard Business Review,* May–June, 1962, p. 149.

[9] The term "anarchy" as used in this paper connotes "no leadership" and nothing more.

The second classification may be called "democracy." In this approach the leader allows all policies to be decided by the group with his participation. The group members work with each other as they wish. The group determines the division and assignment of tasks. . . .

The third classification may be called "anarchy." In anarchy there is complete freedom of the group or the individual regarding policies or task assignments, without leader participation.[10]

Advanced in this paper is the hypothesis that if anarchy exists, there is a great chance of the conflicting dynamics destroying the channel. If autocracy exists, there is less chance of this happening. However, the latter method creates a state of cooperation based on power and control. This controlled cooperation is really subdued conflict and makes for a more unstable equilibrium than does voluntary democratic cooperation.

CONTROLLED COOPERATION

The usual pattern in the establishment of channel relationships is that there is a leader, an initiator who puts structure into this relationship and who holds it together. This leader controls, whether through command or cooperation, i.e., through an autocratic or a democratic system.

Too often it is automatically assumed that the manufacturer or producer will be the channel leader and that the middlemen will be the channel followers. This has not always been so, nor will it necessarily be so in the future. The growth of mass retailers is increasingly challenging the manufacturer for channel leadership, as the manufacturer challenged the wholesaler in the early part of this century.

The following historical discussion will concentrate on the three-ring struggle between manufacturer, wholesaler, and retailer rather than on the changing patterns of distribution within a channel sector, i.e., between service wholesaler and agent middleman or discount and department store. This will lay the necessary background for a discussion of the present-day manufacturer-dominated *versus* retailer-dominated struggle.

Early History

The simple distribution system of Colonial days gave way to a more complex one. Among the forces of change were the growth of population, the long distances involved, the increasing complexity of new products, the increase of wealth, and the increase of consumption.

The United States was ready for specialists to provide a growing and widely dispersed populace with the many new goods and services required. The more primitive methods of public markets and barter could not sufficiently handle the situation. This type of system required short distances, few products, and a small population, to operate properly.

---

[10] Lewis B. Sappington and C. G. Browne, "The Skills of Creative Leadership," in *Managerial Marketing*, rev. ed., William Lazar and Eugene J. Kelley, editors (Homewood, Ill.: Richard D. Irwin, 1962), p. 350.

19th Century History

In the same period that this older system was dissolving, the retailer was still a very small merchant who, especially in the West, lived in relative isolation from his supply sources. Aside from being small, he further diminished his power position by spreading himself thin over many merchandise lines. The retailer certainly was no specialist but was as general as a general store can be. His opposite channel member, the manufacturer, was also a small businessman, too concerned with production and financial problems to fuss with marketing.

Obviously, both these channel members were in no position to assume leadership. However, somebody had to perform all the various marketing functions between production and retailing if the economy was to function. The wholesaler filled this vacuum and became the channel leader of the 19th century.

The wholesaler became the selling force of the manufacturer and the latter's link to the widely scattered retailers over the nation. He became the retailer's life line to these distant domestic and even more important foreign sources of supply.

These wholesalers carried any type of product from any manufacturer and sold any type of product to the general retailers. They can be described as general merchandise wholesalers. They were concentrated at those transportation points in the country which gave them access to both the interior and its retailers, and the exterior and its foreign suppliers.

Early 20th Century

The end of the century saw the wholesaler's power on the decline. The manufacturer had grown larger and more financially secure with the shift from a foreign-oriented economy to a domestic-oriented one. He could now finance his marketing in a manner impossible to him in early times. His thoughts shifted to some extent from production problems to marketing problems.

Prodding the manufacturer on was the increased rivalry of his other domestic competitors. The increased investment in capital and inventory made it necessary that he maintain volume. He tended to locate himself in the larger market areas, and thus, did not have great distances to travel to see his retail customers. In addition, he started to produce various products; and because of his new multiproduct production, he could reach—even more efficiently—these already more accessible markets.

The advent of the automobile and highways almost clinched the manufacturer's bid for power. For now he could reach a much vaster market (and they could reach him) and reap the benefits of economics of scale.

The branding of his products projected him to the channel leadership. No longer did he have as great a need for a specialist in reaching widely dispersed customers, nor did he need them to the same extent for their contacts. The market knew where the product came from. The age of wholesaler dominance declined. That of manufacturer dominance emerged.

Is it still here? What is its future? How strong is the challenge by retailers? Is one "better" than the other? These are the questions of the next section.

Disagreement among Scholars

No topic seems to generate so much heat and bias in marketing as the question of who should be the channel leader, and more strangely, who is the channel leader. Depending on where the author sits, he can give numerous reasons why his particular choice should take the channel initiative.

Authors of sales management and general marketing books say the manufacturer is and should be the chief institution in the channel. Retailing authors feel the same way about retailers, and wholesaling authors (as few as there are), though not blinded to the fact that wholesaling is not "captain," still imply that they should be, and talk about the coming resurrection of wholesalers. Yet a final and compromising view is put forth by those who believe that a balance of power, rather than a general and prolonged dominance of any channel member, is best.

The truth is that an immediate reaction would set in against any temporary dominance by a channel member. In that sense, there is a constant tendency toward the equilibrium of market forces. The present view is that public interest is served by a balance of power rather than by a general and prolonged predominance of any one level in marketing channels.[11]

John Kenneth Galbraith's concept of countervailing power also holds to this last view.

For the retailer:

> In the opinion of the writer, "retailer-dominated marketing" has yielded, and will continue to yield in the future greater net benefits to consumers than "manufacturer-dominated marketing," as the central-buying mass distributor continues to play a role of ever-increasing importance in the marketing of goods in our economy. . . .
>
> . . . In the years to come, as more and more large-scale multiple-unit retailers follow the central buying patterns set by Sears and Penney's, as leaders in their respective fields (hard lines and soft goods), ever-greater benefits should flow to consumers in the way of more goods better adjusted to their demands, at lower prices.[12]
>
> . . . In a long-run buyer's market, such as we probably face in this country, the retailers have the inherent advantage of economy in distribution and will, therefore, become increasingly important.[13]

---

[11] Wroe Alderson, "Factors Governing The Development of Marketing Channels," in *Marketing Channels For Manufactured Products,* Richard M. Clewett, editor (Homewood, Ill.: Richard D. Irwin, 1954), p. 30.

[12] Arnold Corbin, *Central Buying in Relation To The Merchandising of Multiple Retail Units* (New York, Unpublished Doctoral Dissertation at New York University, 1954), pp. 708–709.

[13] David Craig and Werner Gabler, "The Competitive Struggle for Market Control," in *Readings in Marketing*, Howard J. Westing, editor (New York: Prentice-Hall, 1953), p. 46.

The retailer cannot be the selling agent of the manufacturer because he holds a higher commission; he is the purchasing agent for the public.[14]

For the wholesaler:

The wholesaling sector is, first of all, the most significant part of the entire marketing organization.[15]

. . . The orthodox wholesaler and affiliated types have had a resurgence to previous 1929 levels of sales importance.[16]

. . . Wholesalers have since made a comeback.[17] This revival of wholesaling has resulted from infusion of new management blood and the adoption of new techniques.[18]

For the manufacturer:

. . . the final decision in channel selection rests with the seller manufacturer and will continue to rest with him as long as he has the legal right to choose to sell to some potential customers and refuse to sell to others.[19]

These channel decisions are primarily problems for the manufacturer. They rarely arise for general wholesalers. . . .[20]

Of all the historical tendencies in the field of marketing, no other so distinctly apparent as the tendency for the manufacturer to assume greater control over the distribution of his product. . . .[21]

. . . Marketing policies at other levels can be viewed as extensions of policies established by marketing managers in manufacturing firms; and, furthermore, . . . the nature and function can adequately be surveyed by looking at the relationship to manufacturers.[22]

Pro-Manufacture

The argument for manufacturer leadership is production-oriented. It claims that they must assure themselves of increasing volume. This is needed to derive the benefits of production scale economies, to spread their overhead over many units, to meet increasingly stiff competition, and to justify the investment risk they, not the retailers, are taking. Since retailers will not do this job for them properly, the manufacturer must control the channel.

---

[14] Lew Hahn, *Stores, Merchants and Customers* (New York: Fairchild Publications, 1952), p. 12.

[15] David A. Revzan, *Wholesaling in Marketing Organization* (New York: John Wiley & Sons, 1961), p. 606.

[16] *Ibid.,* p. 202.

[17] E. Jerome McCarthy, *Basic Marketing* (Homewood, Ill.: Richard D. Irwin, 1960), p. 419.

[18] *Ibid.,* p. 420.

[19] Eli P. Cox, *Federal Quantity Discount Limitations and Its Possible Effects on Distribution Channel Dynamics* (Unpublished Doctoral Dissertation, University of Texas, 1956), p. 12.

[20] Milton Brown, Wilbur B. England, John B. Matthews, Jr., *Problems in Marketing,* 3rd ed. (New York: McGraw-Hill, 1961), p. 239.

[21] Maynard D. Phelps and Howard J. Westing, *Marketing Management,* Revised Edition (Homewood, Ill.: Richard D. Irwin, 1960), p. 11.

[22] Kenneth Davis, *Marketing Management* (New York: Ronald Press, 1961), p. 131.

Another major argumentative point for manufacturer dominance is that neither the public nor retailers can create new products even under a market-oriented system. The most the public can do is to select and choose among those that manufacturers have developed. They cannot select products that they cannot conceive. This argument would say that it is of no use to ask consumers and retailers what they want because they cannot articulate abstract needs into tangible goods; indeed, the need can be created by the goods rather than vice-versa.

This argument may hold well when applied to consumers, but a study of the specification-buying programs of the mass retailers will show that the latter can indeed create new products, and need not be relegated to simply selecting among alternatives.

Pro-Retailer

This writer sees the mass retailer as the natural leader of the channel for consumer goods under the marketing concept. The retailer stands closest to the consumer; he feels the pulse of consumer wants and needs day in and day out. The retailer can easily undertake consumer research right on his own premises and can best interpret what is wanted, how much is wanted, and when it is wanted.

An equilibrium in the channel conflict may come about when small retailers join forces with big manufacturers in a manufacturer leadership channel to compete with a small manufacturer big retailer leadership channel.

Pro-Wholesaler

It would seem that the wholesaler has a choice in this domination problem as well. Unlike the manufacturer and retailer though, his method is not mainly through a power struggle. This problem is almost settled for him once he chooses the type of wholesaling business he wishes to enter. A manufacturers' agent and purchasing agent are manufacturer-dominated, a sales agent dominates the manufacturer. A resident buyer and voluntary group wholesaler are retail-dominated.

Methods of Manufacturer Domination

How does a channel leader dominate his fellow members? What are his tools in this channel power struggle? A manufacturer has many domination weapons at his disposal. His arsenal can be divided into promotional, legal, negative, suggestive, and, ironically, voluntary cooperative compartments.

Promotional. Probably the major method that the manufacturer has used is the building of a consumer franchise through advertising, sales promotion, and packaging of his branded products. When he has developed some degree of consumer loyalty, the other channel members must bow to his leadership. The more successful this identification through the promotion process, the more assured is the manufacturer of his leadership.

Legal. The legal weapon has also been a poignant force for the manufacturer. It can take many forms, such as, where permissible, resale price maintenance. Other contractual methods are franchises, where the channel members may become mere shells of legal entities. Through this weapon the automobile manufacturers have achieved an almost absolute dominance over their dealers.

Even more absolute is resort to legal ownership of channel members, called forward vertical integration. Vertical integration is the ultimate in manufacturer dominance of the channel. Another legal weapon is the use of consignment sales. Under this method the channel members must by law sell the goods as designated by the owner (manufacturer). Consignment selling is in a sense vertical integration; it is keeping legal ownership of the goods until they reach the consumer, rather than keeping legal ownership of the institutions which are involved in the process.

Negative Methods. Among the "negative" methods of dominance are refusal to sell to possibly uncooperative retailers or refusal to concentrate a large percentage of one's volume with any one customer.

A spreading of sales makes for a concentrating of manufacturer power, while a concentrating of sales may make for a thinning of manufacturer power. Of course, if a manufacturer is one of the few resources available and if there are many available retailers, then a concentrating of sales will also make for a concentrating of power.

The avoidance and refusal tactics, of course, eliminate the possibility of opposing dominating institutions.

Suggestives. A rather weak group of dominating weapons are the "suggestives." Thus, a manufacturer can issue price sheets and discounts, preticket and premark resale prices on goods, recommend, suggest, and advertise resale prices.

These methods are not powerful unless supplemented by promotional, legal, and/or negative weapons. It is common for these methods to boomerang. Thus a manufacturer pretickets or advertises resale prices, and a retailer cuts this price, pointing with pride to the manufacturer's suggested retail price.

Voluntary Cooperative Devices. There is one more group of dominating weapons, and these are really all the voluntary cooperating weapons to be mentioned later. The promise to provide these, or to withdraw, can have a "whip and carrot" effect on the channel members.

Retailer's Dominating Weapons

Retailers also have numerous dominating weapons at their disposal. As with manufacturers, their strongest weapon is the building of a consumer franchise through advertising, sales promotion, and branding. The growth of private brands is the growth of retail dominance.

Attempts at concentrating a retailer's purchasing power are a further group of weapons and are analogous to a manufacturer's attempts to disperse his volume. The more a retailer can concentrate his purchasing, the more dominating he can become; the more he spreads his purchasing, the more dominated he becomes. Again, if the resource is one of only a few, this generalization reverses itself.

Such legal contracts as specification buying, vertical integration (or the threat), and entry into manufacturing can also be effective. Even semiproduction, such as the packaging of goods received in bulk by the supermarket can be a weapon of dominance.

Retailers can dilute the dominance of manufacturers by patronizing those with excess capacity and those who are "hungry" for the extra volume. There is also the subtlety, which retailers may recognize, that a strong manufacturer may concede to their wishes just to avoid an open conflict with a customer.

VOLUNTARY COOPERATION

But despite some of the conflict dynamics and forced cooperation, channel members usually have more harmonious and common interests than conflicting ones. A team effort to market a producer's product will probably help all involved. All members have a common interest in selling the product; only in the division of total channel profits are they in conflict. They have a singular goal to reach, and here they are allies. If any one of them fails in the team effort, this weak link in the chain can destroy them all. As such, all members are concerned with one another's welfare (unless a member can be easily replaced).

Organizational Extension Concept

This emphasis on the cooperating, rather than the conflicting objectives of channel members, has led to the concept of the channel as simply an extension of one's own internal organization. Conflict in such a system is to be expected even as it is to be expected within an organization. However, it is the common or "macro-objective" that is the center of concentration. Members are to sacrifice their selfish "micro-objectives" to this cause. By increasing the profit pie they will all be better off than squabbling over pieces of a smaller one. The goal is to minimize conflict and maximize cooperation. This view has been expounded in various articles by Peter Drucker, Ralph Alexander, and Valentine Ridgeway.

Together, the manufacturer with his suppliers and/or dealers comprise a system in which the manufacturer may be designated the primary organization and the dealers and suppliers designated as secondary organizations. This system is in competition with similar systems in the economy; and in order for the system to operate effectively as an integrated whole, there must be some administration of the system as a whole, not merely administration of the separate organizations with in that system.[23]

Peter Drucker[24] has pleaded against the conceptual blindness that the idea of the legal entity generates. A legal entity is not a marketing entity. Since often half of the cost to the consumer is added on after the product leaves the producer, the latter should think of his channel members as

23 Valentine F. Ridgeway, "Administration of Manufacturer-Dealer Systems," in *Managerial Marketing*, rev. ed., William Lazer and Eugene J. Kelley, editors (Homewood, Ill.: Richard D. Irwin, 1962), p. 480.
24 Peter Drucker, "The Economy's Dark Continent," *Fortune*, April, 1962, pp. 103ff.

part of his firm. General Motors is an example of an organization which does this.

Both businessmen and students of marketing often define too narrowly the problem of marketing channels. Many of them tend to define the term channels of distribution as a complex of relationships between the firm on the one hand, and marketing establishments exterior to the firm by which the products of the firm are moved to market, on the other. . . . A much broader more constructive concept embraces the relationships with external agents or units as part of the marketing organization of the company. From this viewpoint, the complex of external relationships may be regarded as merely an extension of the marketing organization of the firm. When we look at the problem in this way, we are much less likely to lose sight of the interdependence of the two structures and more likely to be constantly aware that they are closely related parts of the marketing machine. The fact that the internal organization structure is linked together by a system of employment contracts, while the external one is set up and maintained by a series of transactions, contracts of purphase and sale, tends to obscure their common purpose and close relationship.[25]

Cooperation Methods

But how does a supplier project its organization into the channel? How does it make organization and channel into one? It accomplishes this by doing many things for its resellers that it does for its own organization. It sells, advertises, trains, plans, and promotes for these firms. A brief elaboration of these methods follows.

Missionary salesmen aid the sales of channel members, as well as bolster the whole system's level of activity and selling effort. Training of resellers' salesmen and executives is an effective weapon of cooperation. The channels operate more efficiently when all are educated in the promotional techniques and uses of the products involved.

Involvement in the planning functions of its channel members could be another poignant weapon of the supplier. Helping resellers to set quotas for their customers, studying the market potential for them. forecasting a member's sales volume, inventory planning and protection, etc., are all aspects of this latter method.

Aid in promotion through the provision of advertising materials (mats, displays, commercials, literature, direct-mail pieces), ideas, funds (cooperative advertising), sales contest, store layout designs, push money (PM's or spiffs), is another form of cooperation.

The big supplier can act as management consultant to the members, dispensing advice in all areas of their business, including accounting, personnel, planning, control, finance, buying, paper systems or office procedure, and site selection. Aid in financing may include extended credit terms, consignment selling, and loans.

By no means do these methods of coordination take a one-way route. All members of the channel, including supplier and reseller, see their own organizations meshing with the others, and so provide coordinating

[25] Ralph S. Alexander, James S. Cross, Ross M. Cunningham, *Industrial Marketing*, rev. ed. (Homewood, Ill.: Richard D. Irwin, 1961), p. 266.

TABLE 1: METHODS OF COOPERATION AS LISTED[26]

1. Cooperative advertising allowances
2. Payments for interior displays including shelf-extenders, dump displays, "A" locations, aisle displays, etc.
3. P.M.'s for salespeople
4. Contests for buyers, salespeople, etc.
5. Allowances for a variety of warehousing functions
6. Payments for window display space, plus installation costs
7. Detail men who check inventory, put up stock, set up complete promotions, etc.
8. Demonstrators
9. On certain canned food, a "swell" allowance
10. Label allowance
11. Coupon handling allowance
12. Free goods
13. Guaranteed sales
14. In-store and window display material
15. Local research work
16. Mail-in premium offers to consumer
17. Preticketing
18. Automatic reorder systems
19. Delivery costs to individual stores of large retailers
20. Studies of innumerable types, such as studies of merchandise management accounting
21. Payments for mailings to store lists
22. Liberal return privileges
23. Contributions to favorite charities of store personnel
24. Contributions to special store anniversaries
25. Prizes, etc., to store buyers when visiting showrooms—plus entertainment, of course
26. Training retail salespeople
27. Payments for store fixtures
28. Payments for new store costs, for more improvements, including painting
29. An infinite variety of promotion allowances
31. Payments of part of salary of retail salespeople
32. Deals of innumerable types
33. Time spent in actual selling floor by manufacturer, salesmen
34. Inventory price adjustments
35. Store name mention in manufacturer's advertising

weapons in accordance with their ability. Thus, the manufacturer would undertake a marketing research project for his channel, and also expect his resellers to keep records and vital information for the manufacturer's use. A supplier may also expect his channel members to service the product after the sale.

A useful device for fostering cooperation is a channel advisory council composed of the supplier and his resellers.

Finally, a manufacturer or reseller can avoid associations with potentially uncooperative channel members. Thus, a price-conservative manufacturer may avoid linking to a price-cutting retailer.

E. B. Weiss has developed an impressive, though admittedly incomplete list of cooperation methods (Table 1). Paradoxically, many of these instruments of cooperation are also weapons of control (forced cooperation) to be used by both middlemen and manufacturers. However, this is not so strange if one keeps in mind that control is subdued conflict and a form of cooperation—even though perhaps involuntary cooperation.

[26] Edward B. Weiss, "How Much of a Retailer Is the Manufacturer," in *Advertising Age,* July 21, 1958, p. 68.

Extension Concept Is the Marketing Concept

The philosophy of cooperation is described in the following quote:

The essence of the marketing concept is of course customer orientation at all levels of distribution. It is particularly important that customer orientation motivate all relations between a manufacturer and his customer—both immediate and ultimate. It must permeate his entire channels-of-distribution policy.[27]

This quote synthesizes the extension-of-the-organization system concept of channels with the marketing concept. Indeed, it shows that the former is, in essence, "the" marketing concept applied to the channel area in marketing. To continue:

The characteristics of the highly competitive markets of today naturally put a distinct premium on harmonious manufacturer–distributor relationships. Their very mutuality of interest demands that the manufacturer base his distribution program not only on what he would like from distributors, but perhaps more importantly, on what they would like from him. In order to get the cooperation of the best distributors, and thus maximum exposure for his line among the various market segments, he must adjust his policies to serve their best interest and, thereby, his own. In other words, he must put the principles of the marketing concept to work for him. By so doing, he will inspire in his customers a feeling of mutual interest and trust and will help convince them that they are essential members of his marketing team."[28]

SUMMARY

Figure 1 summarizes this whole paper. Each person within each department will cooperate, control, and conflict with each other (notice arrows). Together they form a department (notice department box contains person boxes) which will be best off when cooperating (or cooperation through control) forces weigh heavier than conflicting forces. Now each department cooperates, controls, and conflicts with each other. Departments together also form a higher level organization—the firm (manufacturer, wholesaler, and retailer). Again, the firm will be better off if department cooperation is maximized and conflict minimized. Finally, firms standing vertically to each other cooperate, control, and conflict. Together they form a distribution channel that will be best off under conditions of optimum cooperation leading to consumer and profit satisfaction.

CONCLUSIONS AND HYPOTHESES

1. Channel relationships are set against a background of cooperation and conflict; horizontal, intertype, and vertical.
2. An autocratic relationship exists when one channel member controls conflict and forces the others to cooperate. A democratic relationship exists when all

---

[27] Hector Lazo and Arnold Corbin, *Management in Marketing* (New York: McGraw-Hill, 1961), p. 379.
[28] Lazo and Corbin, *loc. cit.*

FIGURE 1: ORGANIZATIONAL

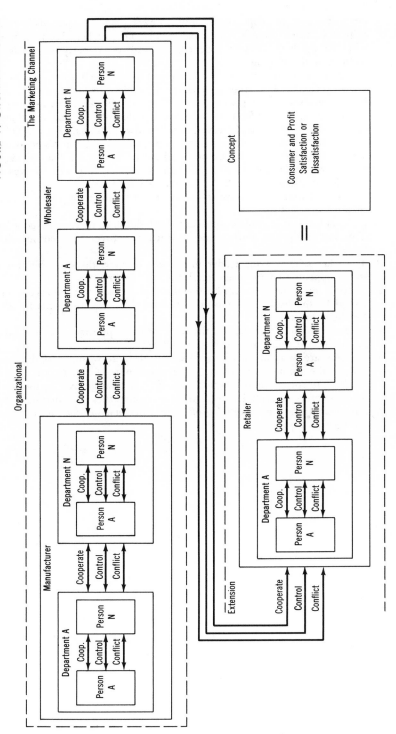

members agree to cooperate without a power play. An anarchistic relationship exists when there is open conflict, with no member able to impose his will on the others. This last form could destroy or seriously reduce the effectiveness of the channel.

3. The process of the exchange act where one member is a seller and the other is a buyer is the basic source of channel conflict. Economic theory can aid in comprehending this phenomenon. There are, however, many other areas of conflict, such as differences in business philosophy or primary objectives.

4. Reasons for cooperation, however, usually outweigh reasons for conflict. This has led to the concept of the channel as an extension of a firm's organization.

5. This concept drops the facade of "legal entity" and treats channel members as one great organization with the leader providing each with various forms of assistance. These are called cooperating weapons.

6. It is argued that this concept is actually the marketing concept adapted to a channel situation.

7. In an autocratic or democratic channel relationship, there must be a leader. This leadership has shifted and is shifting between the various channel levels.

8. The wholesaler was the leader in the last century, the manufacturer now, and it appears that the mass retailer is next in line.

9. There is much disagreement on the above point, however, especially on who should be the leader. Various authors have differing arguments to advance for their choice.

10. In the opinion of this writer, the mass retailer appears to be best adapted for leadership under the marketing concept.

11. As there are weapons of cooperation, so are there weapons of domination. Indeed the former paradoxically are one group of the latter. The other groups are promotional, legal, negative, and suggestive methods. Both manufacturers and retailers have at their disposal these dominating weapons.

12. *For maximization of channel profits and consumer satisfaction, the channel must act as a unit.*

24

New Strategies
to Move Goods

BUSINESS WEEK

In most modern factories today, everything is beautifully organized. Components flow together in a purposeful and orderly manner with little waste motion or material.

Then the finished product reaches the shipping dock. And chaos begins.

In many cases, the product moves by inappropriate means of transportation, often in undesired quantities. It may well be protected by the wrong kind of package. It is almost sure to be picked up and put down needlessly. It is stored in warehouses that may be badly located for today's shifting markets or not needed at all. And it is likely to be controlled by the wrong kind of paperwork.

Cost Battle

Moving and storing goods on their way from mine and mill through various subassemblies and assemblies to their final markets costs anywhere from $50 billion to $75 billion a year—$100 billion if paperwork costs are included.

This is now the third highest cost in doing business, trailing only the payout for materials and labor. Factory automation has proceeded so far that now there's little that can obviously be done to reduce the cost of these two. But with profit margins always under pressure, a new attack has to be launched somewhere.

Reprinted with permission from *Business Week*, September 24 ,1966, pp. 112ff.

That's why distribution is the next—some say possibly the last—place where truly significant savings can be achieved.

A New Concept

Smart, far-sighted companies are already going after those savings by attacking antiquated methods and high costs of distribution. These companies are applying the order and system that prevail inside the factory to the shipment of finished goods. As the movement spreads, a new era of sophisticated distribution techniques is dawning.

This new revolution is made possible by new tools and techniques in transportation, materials handling, packaging, order processing and inventory control. It grows out of such things as jet cargo planes, larger and more versatile freight cars, container ships, broad interstate highways, and—perhaps most of all—high-speed computers with an insatiable capacity.

But the revolution is far more than the sum of all these. It is an intellectual rather than mechanical revolution.

And a New Job

Management for the first time is learning how to use all these gadgets as part of one huge, interrelated system. A new kind of executive position at the policymaking level is appearing alongside sales, production, and finance.

The fact that this new responsibility must be carved out of other executives' empires is the cause of much friction in the changeover. Nevertheless, for most companies, it is becoming inevitable.

Increasingly, one man is being handed the responsibility for getting the proper amount of the right kind of a product to a place where demand for it exists, at the time it exists, and at minimum cost. That is the true import of the revolution in what some people call physical distribution and others call business logistics.

The specific responsibilities usually combined in the new department are: traffic and transportation (that is, deciding among trucks, rail, water, or air, and the rates and routes most suitable); warehousing; materials handling; protective packaging; order processing; production planning; inventory control; customer service; market forecasting; and plant and warehouse site selection.

Many into One

Formerly, everything that occurred in most of these areas was so helplessly detailed and complex that the human brain simply couldn't comprehend it all as one single system. Each area was set apart and left to a specialist often in lower middle management who was looked upon by top management with some respect, but whose chances of promotion to higher levels were not the best.

Order processing was part of sales, warehousing was part of production, transportation was autonomous, and so on. Costs were kept separately and often allocated to the wrong place. Each fragment was interested in keeping its own cost down, little realizing or caring that higher costs in its activity could result in lower total costs.

Though the human brain still can't take in all the detail and paperwork involved in treating physical distribution as one system, computers can. That is one of the extraordinary things happening today. The need for doing an incredibly complex job becomes unmistakably apparent just at the moment management has developed the tools that enable it to perform the job.

New Basis for Decisions

Now companies can feed the intricate detail of purchase orders, shipping instructions, freight charges, damage claims, insurance, invoices, inventory costs, stock levels, customer complaints, and everything else into a machine so that, at last, total distribution costs can be understood.

With this new information, management has for the first time an intelligent basis for deciding where to make trade-offs:

- Whether to reduce warehouses and go to air freight.
- Whether to hire more clerical people, speed up order processing, and then take advantage of slower, cheaper transportation.
- Whether to hold back and combine shipments to take advantage of lower truckload and carload rates at the risk of decreasing customer service.
- Whether to switch products from one factory to another to fill otherwise empty company-owned trucks.

The list of possible variations is endless.

So new, in fact, so big and mysterious is the whole idea that one of its major prophets, George C. Smith, distribution manager of Du Pont's Fabrics & Finishes Department, likes to describe it as the "witchery of physical distribution."

Explosive Impact

Witchery or science, its effects will be explosive. Once a company puts into operation a sophisticated physical distribution program, its costs can plummet so abruptly and its customer service improve so rapidly that it gains a significant edge over its competition. Since no one else can allow a competitor to keep such an advantage, the physical distribution concept is bound to spread like a prairie fire.

Already, some Wall Street analysts are taking it into account, and are including in their study of any company an investigation into its distribution philosophy and methods.

As the concept spreads, companies that for decades have sat secure in geographical areas other producers couldn't economically reach will find their territories invaded by competitors from halfway around the world. By the same token, they can push their own markets into their competitors' backyard.

New Ballgame

Certainly, different kinds of transportation companies will have to tailor their services to fit into the total distribution concept. For them, it will be practically a new experience. The ancient advantages held by railroads, truckers, water carriers, and airlines can often be upset by new equipment and tighter, more customer-oriented service.

By and large, there will be less need in distribution for the independent middleman, if all he does is provide intermediate halts in the flow of goods to market. But for those who can speed products on their way while cutting distribution costs, the future is assured.

The need for salesmen will be greater than ever—but they will have to know more about their own products and their customers' needs. In short, they will have to sell. The function of order taking will be fulfilled by computers talking to each other.

Most important, the distribution revolution will free capital for more profitable uses than inventory carrying. For the long run, the implications of this are enormous. Thanks to a greater control of inventories at every step in the distribution line and a faster reaction time when inventories do get out of line, both companies individually and the economy as a whole will run a smoother course.

THE ROAD IS DIFFICULT BUT THE PAYOFF BIG

Everyone caught up in the excitement of the physical distribution revolution agrees on one thing: Its purpose is to increase profits. But agreement ends there. The distribution roads leading to this objective can be many and diverse, often taking off in opposite directions.

Today, with money expensive and hard to get, most retailers and wholesalers don't want to carry any larger inventories than they have to. A manufacturer finding a way to make fast, dependable deliveries can thus gain a big competitive edge. Many manufacturers are gaining that edge—and boosting sales and profits or winning new markets—by a total overhaul of their distribution systems.

Paradoxical

For a company like Norge Division of Borg-Warner Corp., in the highly competitive consumer products field, a key consideration was to improve dealer service. U.S. retailers can choose among many kitchen appliance makers, so the manufacturer that provides the retailer with the greatest profit margins will have his appliances displayed and pushed.

Norge found that the somewhat paradoxical way to greater profits was to increase its own warehousing costs—because this led to more-than-offsetting increases in sales, as well as to lower dealer inventories.

In general, what Norge did is representative of the thinking of many consumer products companies with relatively high-cost products.

In a completely different field Hammond Valve Corp., a small company in the Chicago area that makes bronze valves, took a similar road.

Hammond, which used to distribute its line through jobbers, discovered five years ago that it could boost profits by improving its service to its ultimate consumers. So it opened six regional warehouses. Now it takes two days to service a customer's order, instead of six weeks.

The results parallel Norge's. "Our sales have more than doubled in the last five years," says Morris R. Beschloss, Hammond's youthful president. Greatly increased volume and lower unit production costs, he says, have far outweighed the added costs of operating warehouses.

Paperwork

This doesn't mean that for manufacturers the blueprint for the distribution revolution is more warehouses.

For some, on the contrary, it means fewer warehouses. It can mean going to air freight as innumerable manufacturers, such as Raytheon Co. and American Optical Co., have done. Or it can mean using a truck or boxcar as a rolling warehouse if the transportation company can be relied upon for dependable deliveries.

The Gillette Co., maker of the world's largest-selling brand of double-edge razor blades and safety razors, was faced by a staggering assortment of changes in its business: diversification into a broad range of toiletry products, a shift of its main distribution channels from drug and tobacco chains to grocery chains, introduction of stainless steel blades by competitors.

Gillette took to air freight to rush its own new blades to market, but this added to costs, cut profit margins. Finally, by way of a management study group and a computer model of the distribution system, Gillette found its answer: a total revamping of paperwork. By cutting down the number of days it took to process an order, the company could return to low-cost surface freight for routine shipments, yet keep up delivery schedules. In a sense, the transportation pipeline took on a part of the function of a warehouse.

It All Depends

Johnson & Johnson, maker of bandages and surgical supplies, also came up with faster order-handling procedures, rather than speedier shipment, as the solution to its problems. "We used to ship to every part of the country every day of the week," says John F. Varley, director of sales and distribution services. Now J&J holds back shipments to take advantage of full truckload rates, as against costlier LTL (less-than-truck-load-lot) charges.

Even so, it finds service just as fast. By shipping a whole truckload at a time, J&J avoids repeated intermediate handlings that might cause soiling, delay, or loss. "Everything was rushed before," says Varley. "Now everything is on a scheduled basis, and when we have a true emergency we can handle it efficiently."

But it all depends in the complicated world of physical distribution, one man's meat is another's poison. Singer Co., the sewing machine maker, took off in exactly the opposite direction from J&J.

Singer, which used to ship its machines once a month, has lately upped this to four times a month. "We pay higher LTL rates, but this is more than offset by lower inventories in stores," says George L. Cwik, assistant manager in the transportation services department. Since most of Singer's 1,600 sewing centers are in high-rent districts, low inventories are a gain even if they mean high freight rates.

Counting up the Payoff

If the solutions to the distribution problems are often opposite to each other, there's no doubt where they all aim—to greater profitability through such sales increases as Hammond Valve's doubling in five years, or such savings as the 30% cut in five years in distribution costs that Singer has set as its goal.

Xerox Corp., which switched to a comprehensive distribution organization in May, 1963, tots up some massive gains. Xerox needs to maintain a huge amount of supplies for its office copying machines. Formerly, it worked out of 40 sales branches, each with its own inventories of paper, chemicals and machine parts.

Then a small group of officers, making a study of this setup, found it extremely wasteful; the group discovered that 80% of the items in the inventories were slow movers, and that many could be stored at one location and air-freighted as needed. In the end, the group determined that 92% of the company's customers could be served adequately from just seven distribution centers in the U.S. and Canada.

As a result, supplies in the distribution pipeline were cut in half. "In May, 1963, we were processing 1,000 orders a day," says Andrew Price, manager of corporate distribution; "now we're processing 4,000 and we're still shipping 92% of today's orders today."

One inside estimate of what the new distribution organization has meant to Xerox—even though the payroll in the department has grown from nothing to more than 3,000—is that it has added $9 million to net profits in three years.

Fertilizer

It's not only in high-cost, high-value manufactured goods that innovations in physical distribution build a big payoff. Very often it is in the field of low-cost bulk commodities that more efficient distribution gives a real competitive edge.

Take fertilizer as a good example. "The price of a ton of phosphate rock at the mine is about $7, while the costs of warehousing, shipping, and handling frequently total an additional $11," says Anthony E. Cascino, vice-president for the Agricultural Products Marketing Group at International Minerals & Chemicals Corp. "If we're not aggressive, innovative, imaginative, and resourceful, and one of our competitors is, and discovers a way to cut his distribution costs by $3—we're dead."

IMC uses long-term deals to cut costs and invade new markets. It mines phosphate rock in Florida, potash in Canada. Through a long-term lease of 4,000 hopper cars and a long-term ship charter, it can now sell phosphate in Canada and potash on the U.S. East Coast, two markets it never served before.

Another long-term deal—with the Rice Growers' Assn. of California, a farmers' cooperative—lets it ship Florida phosphate to California as a return cargo in a ship whose primary job is carrying California rice to Puerto Rico. And it can sell the phosphate in California at $2 a ton less than when Idaho phosphate producers had that market tied up.

But, says Cascino, citing the $14 million to $16 million commitment in hopper cars and ship charters: "You've got to have a lot of courage mixed in with your innovation."

ON THE RETAIL END, THE COMPUTER IS KING

Sweeping changes and innovations in physical distribution are by no means confined to industrial and manufacturing companies. Most marketing companies in the retail field have an even greater need to streamline their distribution setups.

But if manufacturing companies must each chart a laborious road through the distribution tangle, the miraculous computer offers to those in the retail field a ready-made key to the future. The computer bids fair to turn retail distribution inside out.

Inventory by Computer

Using computers as tools, Walgreen Co., led by its director of physical distribution, Robert G. Smith, with the wholehearted backing of top management has instituted one of the most advanced warehouse inventory control systems anywhere.

Walgreen, the nation's largest retail drug chain, has nearly 500 supermarket-type drug stores in 36 states and Puerto Rico, each containing something like 20,000 items; it has a chain of discount stores and junior department stores in the South; and it services about 1,900 franchised "agency" stores.

Just one of the things its electronic data processing system does is to analyze once a week the stock status of each item in all of Walgreen's stores and warehouses. If the inventory of an item reaches what the computer has previously determined is a reorder level, out comes a requisition card. All these cards then go back into the equipment. Then, the computer can search out other items from the same source that might be ordered at the same time for volume discounts or lower freight rates, even though their levels aren't yet critical.

The computers give Walgreen so much information about every single product going through its stores that vendors are often embarrassed to find Walgreen knows more about a product's acceptance than they do.

Crosstalk

Computers are not only mines of information; they can tell each other what they know. One of the most exciting prospects in distribution comes from the possibility of two companies' computers talking to each other.

California Packing Corp. is currently teaming up with a pair of large grocery chains in two "direct ordering tests." The idea, says F. H. Bergtholdt, Calpak director of distribution, is to try out "computer-managed inventories and direct wire communications between customer and manufacturer."

"The customer's computer determines what, how much, and when to buy," explains Bergtholdt, "and the order is transmitted from the customer's data processing center to Calpak's data processing center."

All the Way

Several other food processors, too, are trying out computer-to-computer systems. If the tests succeed, the next step may well be to tie in a third computer, the transportation company's.

As stocks in a supermarket chain's warehouse neared a predetermined reorder level, the chain's computer would not only alert the producer, it would also alert the railroad or trucker to have equipment ready at the loading dock.

Then, the computers would follow the boxcar or trailer across the country, making nightly reports on its whereabouts. If and when such a system reaches perfection, big grocery chains could even do without warehouses, shipping directly to stores. Only shelf space and a back room in each store would be needed. Already, some venturesome chains are experimenting in this direction, though still on a primitive basis.

If there's one thing clear from the experience of companies in the distribution revolution, it's this: Building the complex elements of physical distribution into a "total system" is an intricate job.

Computers may offer retail marketers an indispensable tool, but they provide no ready-made construction chart. Just dumping responsibility for distribution on one man or department isn't enough, either.

When a corporation president decides his company needs an integrated distribution system, how does he go about the job?

Companies have undertaken it in a number of different ways. At Xerox, a thorough study of the company's distribution was made by a small group of officers. At Singer Co., President Donald P. Kircher called key executives from all over the world to New York in October, 1963, for a redistribution seminar to set cost-reduction goals. International Minerals & Chemicals put its corporate imagination to work. Norge and others turned to management consultants for guidance.

HOW A COMPANY BLAZES THE NEW TRAIL

When a company decides to overhaul its distribution system, though, the first thing most executives do is to set up a mathematical model of the company. Hard and expensive as this is, it's easier and cheaper than getting locked into an unworkable system.

To be complete, believes Wendell M. Stewart of the management consulting firm of A. T. Kearney & Co., such a model must show more than shipping and storage charges, packaging and order processing costs.

"It must go all the way into the marketplace," he says, "and find what products are hot sellers, what the demands are and where they originate. It must also go back into the factories and find which are the most efficient production lines for each product."

When the model is completed—and this can take a year or more—the next step is to set management objectives. It is possible, for example, to give every customer one-day service on every item—but the cost may be prohibitive. Within limits that can be programmed into the model, the best service at the lowest cost can be determined by varying such factors as number, size, and location of factories and warehouses, and speeds and rates of different kinds of transportation.

It's also important for companies to remember that transportation rates are not fixed. They can often be lowered by negotiation or threats. Building existing rates into a model, therefore, can destroy the value of the whole exercise.

A model that's correctly formulated can bring to light warehouses serving wrong territories or territories with wrong boundaries, and can suggest that some products are being made in the wrong plants. It can keep a company from adopting a distribution system its customers can't use; if a customer can't store a whole barge load of a product, there's no point in building a distribution system around barges.

Not in a Day

Once the model is built and the computer begins to turn out the trade-offs and compromises that will most nearly achieve a company's long-term objectives, the company can start moving.

According to Robert S. Reebie, former New York Central vice-president and now an independent consultant, it's best to make the move to a comprehensive physical distribution program in a series of short steps. Trying to get there all at once, he feels, is sure to ruffle too many feathers, upset too much existing capital investment, and multiply the chances for mistakes, endangering the success of the whole thing.

Repeat Engagement

When the long-range objective is finally attained and the distribution system is churning out better service to customers at lower cost, many a company finds it's time to start over again. For there's one law of the new distribution revolution that can't be repealed: Physical distribution needs constant attention and renewal.

Fundamental changes are coming so fast in every phase of distribution that no system, however good, can be permanent; a competitor may be already working on a better one. Besides, no wide-awake company's business stands still, and growth can upset even the best-designed program.

Inundated

Rapid growth is sending a flock of major companies to Arthur D. Little, Inc., for a total distribution blueprint, according to David Boodman, a senior staff member at the management consultant company. "In just the last half year," he says, "we have been inundated."

Boodman feels many of these companies have grown so fast that such things as inventory control got out of hand; one company had grown four times over in eight years. Inventory control is Boodman's forte—and fixing optimum inventory levels and maintaining them is one of the most difficult yet essential parts of the distribution revolution.

Changes in products or outlets, diversification, and acquisitions can also upset a previously smooth flow—as Gillette found—or provide a spur to seek new patterns. Anti-freeze, to cite another example, formerly sold primarily at filling stations, now goes mostly through supermarket checkouts, changing the manufacturers' distribution patterns.

Sometimes a change can bring a distribution bonus. When Singer acquired Friden, Inc., the San Leandro (Calif.) maker of calculating machines, it discovered that a private truck fleet would pay off. Now Singer trucks carry sewing machines to California and calculating machines back to the East. With its own trucks, protective packaging requirements are less.

TRANSPORTATION STRIPS DOWN FOR THE RACE

The spur that is driving industrial and marketing companies to the new concept of distribution comes not only from internal change. It comes also from the technological upheaval that is transforming the means of distribution. Nowhere are the effects of the revolution in physical distribution more evident than in transportation—and the rapidity of change in this area is speeding up the entire process.

The changes affect truck, rail, ship, and air alike—and they all point to faster, more efficient, less expensive delivery of goods.

Bigger and Cheaper

For truckers, the substantial completion of the interstate highway program within five years will mean sharp reductions in maintenance cost as trucks get free of tangled traffic. Reduced costs could mean lower rates.

Bigger and heavier trailers will be allowed—again permitting reduced costs and rates. The so-called double-bottom rig, in which a tractor hauls a semitrailer and full trailer, is being legalized in more and more states. Even a triple-bottom rig is now under test.

With superhighways crisscrossing the map, with bigger, faster trucks manned by teams of drivers who alternate driving and sleeping, the average rig will be able to double the distance it travels in a night. This means manufacturers can double their marketing area—or cut inventories and storage space in existing areas.

Look, No Wheels

The larger, so-called "damage free' freight car which is posing a challenge to distribution specialists and making over entire industries is only one example of railroad modernization.

In coming years the rails will develop containerization to higher degrees of efficiency. Dramatic as the story of piggybacking and its 20% annual growth has been, leaving the wheels off trailers and carrying only the big boxes will make things still cheaper and faster. Each flatcar will hold more than two containers, and a lower center of gravity will permit more speed. For shippers, again, this means wider distribution, or reduced inventories.

So-called unit trains—semi-permanently coupled trains that shuttle back and forth between one shipper and one consignee—will have an even broader impact as their use spreads among shippers of bulk commodities, particularly coal and grain. By avoiding intermediate freight yards, these trains improve dependability and cut costs.

As their use grows, intermediate storage facilities, notably for grains, may no longer be needed, or may be needed in different spots. And as rates on heavy, bulk materials come down, it may prove desirable to move plants away from raw material sources, closer to markets.

On the Water

Even more dramatic changes will flow from continuing improvements on inland waterways. Central Oklahoma, for example, is to have a 9-ft. deep canal. Old locks on existing canals will be enlarged. Dallas and Fort Worth will be connected to the Gulf of Mexico.

Bulk materials will flow along these waterways at ultra low costs. Industries needing coal, ores, oil, and chemicals at cheap prices, or the low-cost electricity made possible by water-borne coal, will flock to canal and river banks. New communities built for their workers will create new distribution patterns.

On the ocean, container ships are about to become significant in international commerce. Ocean containerization is still hesitant and riddled with problems, but in coming years it will be fast, frequent, and efficient. Shipping, packaging, and insurance costs will plummet. Many domestic producers will find overseas markets opening up—but overseas producers will also find more U.S. markets feasible.

World Shrinkers

Perhaps most sweeping will be the changes in air cargo. The short- and medium-range jets that are already crowding the skies have a limited passenger appeal late at night. Any flight that takes off after 10 p.m. is apt to arrive at an unsalable hour. So, many of these planes are being made convertible for night cargo duty.

This huge increase in air freight capacity will drive down air freight rates—and as some rates descend close to those of surface carriers, the industry will grow at rocket speed.

Most short-range planes will feature cargo pallets interchangeable with those of long-range cargo jets. A pallet loaded in, say, Terre Haute can be flown to Chicago, put intact on a big jet for Frankfurt, Germany, arrive there next morning.

Within six or seven years airlines will be flying truly huge cargo planes similar to the Boeing 747 and the Air Force's C-5A, capable of lifting up to 110 tons per plane, up from about 45 tons today. Says the economist Eliot Janeway: "It behooves every corporation in America now making commitments for new plant and warehouse capacity around the world to keep a sharp eye on the job the C-5A will be doing by the time today's commitments go on stream."

COMMUNICATION DECISIONS

25

Comparison
of Advertising
and Selling

HAROLD C. CASH AND W.J.E. CRISSY

Personnel Development Associates
Michigan State University

Advertising, like selling, plays a major role in the total marketing effort of the firm. The degree to which each is important depends upon the nature of the goods and the market being cultivated. In the industrial product field, personal selling is generally the major force. Here the nature of the goods often requires specific application information that is best presented in person by the salesman. The dollar value of the order generally makes it economically feasible to finance this more effective and expensive method of presentation. Comparable effort to sell a box of soap powder to the housewife would be a ridiculous extravagance. On the other hand, it is likely that personal selling will be used to get this consumer product into the channels of distribution—through the wholesaler or chain store buying organization.

The person-to-person two-way communication of personal selling makes it a superior means of selling every time. Advertising by contrast is only a one-way communication system and is necessarily generalized to fit the needs of many people. Where the unit value of the sale is small, however, advertising is more economical. For example, a full page advertisement in an issue of *Life* magazine, which costs upward of $30,000 will deliver the message at a rate of less than $\frac{1}{2}$ cent per copy. And since, on an average, about 4 persons read each copy, message exposure per reader is in the neighborhood of $\frac{1}{8}$ cent per copy-reader. A full-color page advertisement

Reprinted with permission from *The Psychology of Selling,* published by Personnel Development Associates (Box 36–Station A, Flushing, New York 11358), 1965.

329

provides exposure for about $\frac{1}{6}$ cent per copy-reader. Of course, not every reader is likely to see a particular advertisement but even if only 25% of the exposures capture attention, the cost is minute. Comparable costs of message delivery apply to radio, T.V. and other mass media. Recent figures indicate a total of $31.31 as the cost of a typical sales call when all expenses are considered.

The worth of the sales call and an advertising impression is not likely to be equal. If the prospect is serious and has sincere interest in the proposal, the sales call is definitely worthwhile. If, on the other hand, the prospect is not nearly ready to place an order, a reminder of the existence of the product or services in the form of an advertisement would have been more economical.

Generally speaking, advertising needs additional support, either through personal selling or through promotional activities, to effect the sale. In most cases, its basic function is in the demand-cultivation area. Hence it is more significant in the pretransactional phase of marketing. There are, of course, instances where advertising alone makes the sale, as in the case of mail-order selling. This channel, however, represents only a very small volume of total sales in any year. To a lesser extent, advertising can help in the posttransactional area of demand-fulfillment by providing a rationalization to the purchaser after the buying decision has been made.

Advertising can be thought of in many ways. Perhaps, however, the most useful perspective to take is in terms of primary objectives. Most advertising is aimed at inducing purchase of a particular brand of product. Sometimes this is referred to as preselling since the aim is to lead the person to the transactional stage, even though the transaction itself is not accomplished. This type of advertising is essentially competitive.

There are many things that can be accomplished through advertising. Perhaps the most obvious is to create an awareness of, an interest in, or demand for a product. When fluoride was added to toothpaste, large-scale advertising was conducted to let customers know that the product was available. Concurrently, the sales organization obtained distribution in retail outlets so that customers could acquire the product. It is doubtful that many sales could be accomplished without the advertising program. The alternative to advertising would be to have retail store personnel personally sell the toothpaste to customers. This is not feasible because the unit sale is too low to support the salary and expense of a sales person. In this sense, advertising paves the way for the salesman because, without the promise of a huge advertising and promotion campaign, retailers would not cooperate in finding display space. It has been said "Salesmen put products on shelves and advertising takes them off."

Less frequently, advertising is used to introduce an entirely new idea. The educational effort may be underwritten by a single company or, where there are a number of producers in the field, it may be the cooperative effort of the industry. Here the advertising is designed to win for the industry a share of the consumer's dollar. Again it is a preselling activity. Such advertising is often called "pioneering" as contrasted with "competitive" advertising.

Many advertisements are aimed at reinforcing the product name or brand in the minds of the buying public. This may be considered as reminder advertising. It is normally used when a product has a dominant share of the market and cannot expect to attain any marked increase in volume within the economic limits of the extra promotional cost.

Some advertisements are primarily designed to convey a favorable image of the company as a good firm with which to do business. This institutional or public relations advertising is used by public utilities and major corporations which have an important stake in gaining a favorable public acceptance.

It is not unusual for a single advertisement to attempt to achieve a combination of these objectives.

As was noted before, generally speaking, advertising plays a more significant role in the marketing of consumer goods than it does in the case of industrial products. This is particularly true with respect to contact with the end users. However, even consumer goods depend to a significant extent on personal selling to move them through the channels.

When the item represents a substantial outlay and when there are complexities to be explained to the prospect, obviously, personal contact is both practical and necessary. Advertising for such goods, however, is often used in specialized media for the purpose of generating leads for the field sales force.

When goods flow through indirect channels, advertising grows in complexity. It may be used to cultivate demand on the part of the ultimate users through nationally distributed media. It may also be used in selected specialized media to encourage the various intermediaries to stock the merchandise.

When advertising is used with industrial products, it has different functions. As mentioned above, one function is to generate leads for salesmen. It is common for the advertisement to carry a coupon. When the coupon is received at the home office, it is relayed to the salesman covering that territory who then makes a sales call.

A second function of the advertising of industrial products is to keep the name of the company and product before the customers between sales calls. Good advertising also reassures a customer that he is buying from a good supplier. The advertising adds prestige to the product, the company, and the salesman, especially when it equals or excels that of competitors.

When a company has a substantial advertising program, salesmen can use tear sheets of the advertisements to good advantage. These can appropriately be shown to both prospects and customers. With prospects, consideration should be given to leaving copies of the advertisements as they create a feeling of stability and solidity with regard to the supplier. When prospects see advertisements, normally in the trade press, this paves the way for salesmen.

In a well organized and disciplined industrial sales force, there will be a similarity between the content of the advertisement and the sales presentation. Thus the advertisement and the sales call reinforce each other.

Many products must be used in a certain way to produce the desired results. Complaints arise when the product does not fulfill the salesman's claims. Advertising can carry instructions on using the product. This will help to insure satisfactory performance. If the product has already been used inappropriately, the advertising may cause the customer to understand the poor performance and give it another chance. In this way, it holds customers that might otherwise be lost.

SIMILARITIES AND DIFFERENCES BETWEEN ADVERTISING AND SELLING

From the viewpoint of communications, advertising and selling have much in common. Both must meet four criteria. They need to be *understandable, interesting, believable,* and *persuasive* if they are to achieve their purpose. There are, however, some noteworthy differences. Communication through advertising is one-way. In contrast, selling is uniquely two-way. There is an inherent weakness in advertising—*"noise."* This is likely to be present in greater amounts in advertising than in the case of the sales interview where misunderstandings can be cleared up on the spot. Whatever the medium being used, advertising must compete with other messages. For example, in a magazine the ad competes with surrounding editorial copy. The message conveyed by the salesman does not compete with other messages, at least at the time of the presentation.

Advertising may be used to generate either primary or selective demand; for example, an industry group may collaborate on its advertising with a view to enlarging the total market. In contrast, selling is aimed invariably at selective demand, that is, preference for the products and services being sold by the particular company over those available from competitors.

From the standpoint of persuasion, a sales message is far more flexible, personal, and powerful than an advertisement. An advertisement is normally prepared by persons having minimal personal contact with customers. The message is designed to appeal to a large number of persons. By contrast, the message in a good sales presentation is not determined in advance. The salesman has a tremendous store of knowledge about his product or service and selects appropriate items as the interview progresses. Thus the salesman can adapt his message to the thinking and needs of the customer or prospect *at the time of the sales call.* Furthermore, as objections arise and are voiced by the buyer, the salesman can treat the objections in an appropriate manner. This is not possible in advertising.

Company control over the advertising message is more complete than over a sales presentation. When an advertisement is prepared, it is submitted for the approval of all interested executives before it is released to the media. Thus there is little likelihood of any discrepancy between company policy and the content of the advertisement. In theory, salesmen receive training so that they understand the product or service and company policy. With the best possible training program, there are two possible sources of error or bases for deviation from company doctrine. One is loss of memory. Salesmen just cannot remember everything they are told. Also, they may meet situations that are unforeseen, and their reaction may not be identical with what the company management would specify if the problem were referred to them.

There is little a prospect can do to avoid a well planned advertising campaign. With the number of media available, he is almost certain to be exposed to one or more advertising messages. Buyers can refuse to see salesmen. When the salesman arrives at the premises of the buyer's company, he is subject to the will of the buyer as to whether he enjoys an interview. Thus, over a period of time, advertising will bring the product to the attention of persons who would be missed by salesmen.

Perceptual Similarities and Differences

In terms of perceptual process, there are also similarities. Both must penetrate the sensory mechanisms of the customer or prospect if they are to be effective. With both, careful selection of the stimuli to be presented is important. However, significant differences do exist from the standpoint of perception.

In selling, it may be possible to enlist not only the senses of vision and audition, but taste, smell, and the tactual senses as well. Time and space restraints on advertising limit the number and array of stimuli that can be presented. In selling, it is possible to vary the stimuli and to apply them as the salesman deems appropriate. Actual time duration of an ad generally limits the opportunity to summate and reinforce the message. In contrast, during the sales interview, frequent repetition and reinforcement are possible. In most instances, advertising commands less full attention than does selling. This limits the number of concepts that can be conveyed and places a high premium on careful construction of the ad copy and selection of the illustrations. In the case of the "commercial" on radio or television, few opportunities for reinforcement are possible within the ad itself. The salesman, too, must have a well planned presentation. However, it can be varied and adjusted as the sales interview progresses. Further, the salesman on the spot is able to re-arrest attention when he detects it is waning. This is not possible with an advertisement.

Cognitive Similarities and Differences

In terms of cognitive process, both advertising and selling are designed to induce favorable thoughts toward the company, its products and services, and its people. Both are aimed at conveying an image of *different* and *better vis-à-vis* competition. Advertising is far more limited than selling in influencing thought process. A relatively small number of ideas can be conveyed by an ad. There is no way to check on understanding. In the sales interview, the ideas and concepts can be tailored to the understanding of the prospect or customer. Because advertising employs mass media, the message must often be geared to the less sophisticated segment of the readership or audience. In contrast, the salesman who is effective gears his message to the sophistication of the person with whom he is conversing. Only to a limited extent can advertising carry the person exposed to the message through a reasoning process about the product or service. Instead, suggestion must be utilized.

In contrast, the salesman is able to employ suggestion or reasoning as the sales interview progresses, depending upon the perception of his message on the part of the customer or prospect. In the case of relatively complex products and services, the most that can be hoped for from advertising is a whetting of the prospect's appetite for more information. Questions can be raised but relatively few answers can be provided. In the case of those same goods and services, the salesman is able to cope with problems and questions at first hand. In fact, in some instances he plays an important role as a problem-solver for the prospective customer.

Feeling State Similarities and Differences

Advertising and selling both try to induce favorable feelings. In the case of selling the salesman himself becomes an important determiner of the customer's feeling state by the manner in which he conducts himself while he is with him. In advertising, too, it is important to induce a favorable feeling state or mood in order to provide more favorable receptivity to the message itself. This may be attempted directly within the ad by means of pleasant illustrations, anticipatory enjoyment attending the use of the product, emotional words, phrases, analogies and comparisons. This is accomplished less directly, where the medium permits it, by the entertainment bonus preceding and following the ad, as in the case of a television show or a radio program. In the case of printed media, the surrounding editorial copy may be employed to set the mood. Even with these direct and indirect efforts, it is unlikely that any advertisement meets the objective of emotional reinforcement with all those who are exposed to the message. In fact, what may please one person may annoy another. Paradoxically, there is some research evidence from the radio field that if an ad doesn't please the person it is next best to have it annoy him rather than to leave him in a neutral feeling state.

Selling, in contrast, has a tremendous advantage in the domain of feelings. The salesman in the first few seconds of face-to-face contact gauges the mood of the other person and adjusts his own behavior accordingly. Further, if he detects an unfavorable feeling state he may provide the other individual the opportunity to vent his feelings, or he may, in an extreme case, decide to withdraw and call on a more favorable occasion. This option is not open to the advertiser.

Advertising permits the firm far less control over the ultimate buying decision than does selling. The person exposed to the ad may turn the page or spin the dial, or walk out of the room. In contrast, once a salesman has gained entry, if he is effective, he is likely to be able to make a reasonably full presentation of the sales message.

Transactional Similarities and Differences

If the market is viewed as having the three phases . . . , *pretransactional, transactional,* and *posttransactional,* it is evident that advertis-

FIGURE 1: RELATIVE IMPORTANCE OF ADVERTISING AND
SELLING MARKET PHASE

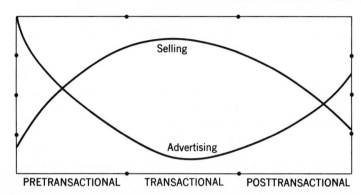

PRETRANSACTIONAL   TRANSACTIONAL   POSTTRANSACTIONAL

ing fits mainly in the pretransactional phase as a market cultivating force. It may also enter into the posttransactional phase by providing a rationalization to the purchaser. Only in rare instances does it accomplish the transaction itself. In contrast, selling is of importance in all three phases. (Figure 1.)

Advertising may be viewed as readying the market for the salesman's personal efforts. Even with carefully selected media and well-conceived advertising, the strategy employed must be relatively general. In the case of selling, not only can strategy be formulated for each account and each decision maker in the account, but tactical adjustments can be made on the spot in order to influence those accounts.

SALESMAN'S USE OF ADVERTISING

Even though the salesman may not be directly involved in planning and formulating the advertising campaign of his firm, he certainly must be aware of the company's advertising plans, the media in which the advertisements are appearing, and the objectives that are being sought. If this information is not being furnished to him, it is legitimate for the salesman to request it. It can be very embarrassing to have a customer or prospect refer to an ad of which the salesman is unaware. The astute salesman is not only aware of his own company's ads, but he is also observant of the advertising done by competitors. The latter is often an important input for his own selling strategy. . . .

Certainly if the demand cultivation of the company is to be coordinated, there must be a congruency between the content of the advertising and the salesman's presentations to customers and prospects. If this is accomplished, the summation principle discussed in Volume 2 can be effectively utilized. Temporally, the exposure to the advertisements plus the periodic sales calls combine to reinforce the message. From a spatial summation standpoint the ads plus the sales messages bring to bear a varied array of stimuli on the customer and prospect.

Many companies accomplish this mutual reinforcement of advertising and selling by furnishing the sales force with selling aids, reprints and tear sheets of advertisements from printed media. If this is done, the salesman has a direct means of reinforcing his oral presentation with advertising copy. Further, he is able to leave copies of ads as reminders to the persons called on.

When such ads are taken from prestige media they contribute to the building of a favorable image of the salesman's company. Sometimes local spot advertisements on radio and television make specific references such as "advertised in *Life* (or *Time*, or some other medium)" as an attempt to build up the prestige of the product and the company. The salesman accomplishes the same result with effective use of reprints and tear sheets.

The salesman is in a prime position to gauge the effectiveness of advertising. He is able to determine by inquiry how many of his customers and prospects have actually seen or heard the ad. By judicious questioning he also can learn of their reactions to the ads. This provides management useful feedback. He also may be able to suggest changes that will render the advertising more effective.

If suggestions are to be meaningful to management and the personnel who work on the advertising program, they must be in sufficient detail so that they can understand the reasoning of the salesman who submits them. They should include the following kinds of information:

1. Specific reasons why the campaign was not maximally successful. This should be supported by comments or behavior of customers and other interested parties, not merely an opinion of the salesman.
2. Sales figures which are directly related to the advertising campaign. If advertising mats are supplied, a comparison of the relative use of mats with those of other campaigns may be appropriate.
3. Comparisons can be made with competitive advertisers in the local area. In this case, samples of the competitive advertising should be submitted along with comments.

The foregoing observations should relate primarily to large scale print or broadcast media. In the case of dealer aids and point-of-purchase materials, the salesman is in an even stronger position to offer sound criticism. He can give first-hand reports of the ease with which display stands could be erected. He can report dealers' reactions to the materials and, even better, tally the actual use of the materials. When the materials have not been well received, he can inquire into the reasons for the poor reception and pass the information through the proper channels. It is perfectly proper for a salesman to state his opinion as well as the data he has collected, but to preserve his intellectual honesty and make his ideas more useful to management and advertising personnel, he should indicate which ideas are his own and which are opinions or behavior of dealers and customers.

Salesmen who wish to have their ideas considered should find out when advertising campaigns are in a formative stage and submit their ideas so that they can be considered before the final ideas have been selected for development.

Lead Generators

Advertising containing a coupon or a request to write to a box number or to phone may be a useful lead generating device for the salesmen. An important caution: Such leads must be carefully screened before an appreciable investment of time and effort is made. A recent study of leads generated through reader service cards in a trade magazine indicated that only ten to twelve per cent were bona fide prospects for the goods offered. The remainder were curiosity seekers, literature collectors, and high school students.

In some sales situations, an added value expected by the reseller is assistance from the salesman with his own advertising. In such instances, the salesman must be knowledgeable on the actual principles, methods and techniques of advertising. Usually, however, if this is a job duty, his firm furnishes instructional materials and specimen ads for use directly or with some modification. To the extent that the salesman can convince the customer of the worthwhileness of advertising, he is likely to generate increased profitable business for himself. Some firms encourage their intermediaries to advertise by sharing the costs. When this is the policy, it becomes even more imperative for the salesman to be astute in his recommendations. He is investing his company's money in the suggestions he makes. Ideas expected of him may range from choice of media, size of advertisement, frequency of insert, optimum time, to co-ordination of the advertising with other promotional efforts.

Where indirect channels are employed, the salesman may be able to use his firm's national advertising program as a potent force in his sales presentation. He can demonstrate as a *value-added* that his company is applying a powerful, demand generating force on the ultimate user which will develop increased business for all intermediaries. This is the "push–pull" effect. In this connection, if the salesman has information concerning an impending campaign, this can become a means of creating increased business in anticipation of likely demand. Inadequate inventory or "stock-out" can be translated into a loss of profit for the reseller as well as an attendant loss of good-will by not having the merchandise available when the customer wants it.

SALESMEN'S ATTITUDES TOWARD ADVERTISING

A company's emphasis on advertising will vary depending on the nature of the product, the price, and the distribution of its customers. Salesmen's attitudes will vary with the relative importance of selling and advertising in the promotional mix. One common finding, however, is that salesmen tend to become critical of their own company's advertising.

In some instances, salesmen, especially those handling industrial goods, feel too much money is spent on advertising. There is no point in discussing this problem, except in a specific instance. It can be pointed out that a salesman in his territory seldom has all the facts necessary to decide on the proper ratio of advertising and selling. It may be that he is entitled to more facts but that is an internal management decision, not one for outsiders. The best assumption for a salesman to make is that his company has established sound marketing objectives and has selected the right tools to achieve them. If the salesman feels differently, he should offer constructive criticism or, in the extreme case, consider seeking other employment. (Few salesmen have any idea of the cost of advertising per prospect. While the figures cited earlier in this chapter apply to consumer mass media, the cost per reader of industrial media is not too much greater.)

The content of advertising messages is often criticized by salesmen. As salesmen are face to face with customers and prospects every day, they are in a good position to gauge the impact of the firm's advertising. This does not mean they should compose the advertising because, as in the case of the amount of advertising, the company may have some objectives not known to the salesmen. It may wish to use part of the budget to promote what the salesmen feel is a minor rather than a major product in the line. This could very well happen if the salesmen are not informed on the profitability of each item in the line. In any event, each salesman should back up the company advertising because, however little immediate value he sees in it, he is in a stronger position supporting the advertising than opposing it.

Another area of possible disagreement between salesmen and management may be the media used. When the number of available advertising and promotional media is considered (T.V., radio, magazines [general and trade], newspapers, direct mail, transportation [car cards], outdoor, point of purchase, and sampling), it is not surprising that there may be disagreement. Indeed, there have probably been prolonged and exhaustive discussions within the management group before the media decision was reached. There are specialists in advertising agencies to help in selecting appropriate media. The likelihood of salesmen making constructive suggestions in this area of advertising is minimal except for some local conditions which may not have come to the attention of those making the final decision.

SUMMARY

Advertising and selling play major roles in the total marketing effort of the firm. Advertising, however, focuses mainly on market cultivation, though it sometimes plays a part in the actual transaction, and with some frequency, in the posttransactional aspect of the marketing program. The most useful way for the salesman to view advertising is in terms of its three key objectives—to induce an intention to purchase, to keep the product or brand in conscious awareness in the market place, and to project a favorable image of the firm. Similarites and differences between advertising and selling are discussed in terms of communication, perception, thought-process, feelings, and degree of control. Specific suggestions are made for effective use of advertising by the salesman, as well as ways and means the salesman can employ for apprising his management of the impact of the company's advertising efforts and for suggesting ways of improving them.

26

Communications
and Industrial Selling

THEODORE LEVITT
Harvard University

—Does corporate or institutional advertising by industrial-product companies pay?

—Do the salesmen of well-known industrial-products companies have an automatic edge over the salesmen of little-known or unknown companies?

—Is it better for an industrial-product company to spend its limited funds on aggressive advertising of its general competence or on more careful selection and training of its salesmen?

—Are the decisions of prospective buyers of new industrial products affected by the amount of personal risk these decisions expose them to?

—Are the buying decisions of practicing purchasing agents affected more by the reputation of a vendor-company than are the decisions of practicing engineers and scientists?

—Does the effect of a company's reputation on a customer's buying decision hold up over time, or does it erode as time passes?

These are some of the questions that have been investigated in a study recently completed at the Harvard Graduate School of Business Administration. Specifically, the questions focused on the extent to which an industrial-product company's generalized reputation affects its ability to launch new products. The accelerating flood of new and often complex industrial products, coupled with the continuing shortage of capable salesmen and the rising costs of advertising make the above questions particularly timely.

Reprinted with permission from *Journal of Marketing*, published by the American Marketing Association, April, 1967, pp. 15–21.

"Source Effect"

This timeliness is further enhanced by studies by Harvard Business School Professor Raymond A. Bauer, which have suggested that business communicators have been inadequately aware of the extent to which their audiences influence the communicators, rather than the usual one-way preoccupation with how the communicators (or advertisers) influence their audiences.[1] To illustrate:

Research shows that a newspaper editorial identified to one group of Americans as emanating, say, from *The New York Times* and to a similar group of Americans as emanating, say, from *Pravda* would lead one to expect that a change in audience opinion in the direction advocated by the editorial would be greater for those who believed it was a *New York Times* editorial than those who believed it to be a *Pravda* editorial. In other words, the audience's feelings about the credibility of the message source help determine the persuasive effectiveness of the message itself. The greater the prestige or the more believable the message source, the more likely that it will influence the audience in the direction advocated by the message. The less prestigeful or believable the source, the less likely that it will influence the audience in the direction advocated by the message.

This phenomenon is now generally referred to as "source effect." Obviously what source effect amounts to is some sort of independent judgment by the audience such that it is either more or less affected by the message. The audience takes a form of initiative, independent of the message, which affects its susceptibility to the message.[2]

If in their private lives people such as businessmen and scientists exhibit source effect and audience initiative in response to political communications and propaganda, there is the question of whether they do this same thing in their business lives in response to advertising and direct sales presentations. McGraw-Hill expresses its belief that source effect works powerfully in industrial selling in its famous advertisement of a stern-looking purchasing agent facing the reader (salesman) from behind his desk and saying:

> I don't know who you are.
> I don't know your company.
> I don't know your company's product.
> I don't know what your company stands for.
> I don't know your company's customers.
> I don't know your company's record.
> I don't know your company's reputation.

[1] Bauer, "The Obstinate Audience," *American Psychologist,* Vol. 19 (May, 1964), pp. 319–328, and "Communication as a Transaction," *Public Opinion Quarterly,* Vol. 27 (Spring, 1963), pp. 83–86.

[2] For the seminal research in this area, see Carl I. Hovland and Walter Weiss, "The Influence of Source Credibility on Communication Effectiveness," *Public Opinion Quarterly,* Vol. 15 (Winter, 1951–1952), pp. 635–650, and Carl I. Hovland, A. A. Lumsdaine, and Fred D. Sheffield, *Experiments in Mass Communication* (Princeton: Princeton University Press, 1949).

Now—what was it you wanted to sell me?

MORAL: Sales start before your salesman calls—with business publication advertising.

To test this and a variety of related hypotheses, an elaborate communications simulation was devised and administered. Participants included 113 practicing purchasing agents from a wide variety of companies, 130 engineers and scientists, and 131 business school graduate students. (For simplifying purposes, the engineers and scientists are in this article referred to as "chemist.") This article is a report on the results of this simulation. But while it is a "report," it is not a simple document. As will be seen, it is full of moderating qualifications and carefully phrased conclusions. It cannot be read with easy speed or casual comfort. The more complex a subject, the more involuted its rhetoric. In the present case, the reader must be prepared to go slow along an agonizing path.

Methodology

Basically what was done in the research was to divide each audience group (purchasing agents, chemists, and students) into six separate subgroups and then to expose each subgroup to a ten-minute filmed sales presentation for a new, but fictitious, technical product for use as an ingredient in making paint. Each audience member was put into the position of assuming he was listening to the presentation as it would be given by a salesman sitting across his desk. Some groups were asked to assume they were purchasing agents for a paint firm and some were asked to assume they were chemists. The film presentation technique and audience setup were created to make conditions as realistic as possible, with great care taken to prevent communications between subgroups and to create realistic and thoughtful responses by the subjects. All saw what was basically the same ten-minute film with the same actors. However, some subgroups saw a relatively good presentation and some a relatively poor one; for some the selling company was identified in the film as a relatively high-credibility company (the Monsanto Company), for other subgroups it was identified as a relatively lower-credibility and less well-known company (the Denver Chemical Company), and for still others the company identity was kept anonymous. Immediately after the film was run, and then again in five weeks, each respondent filled out a detailed questionnaire.[3]

RESULTS

Let us now take up each of the question areas posed at the outset of this article, and see how our findings respond to them.

[3] The details of the research mechanism are spelled out in Theodore Levitt, *Industrial Purchasing Behavior: A Study in Communications Effects* (Boston, Massachusetts: Division of Research, Harvard Business School, 1965).

1. Does Corporate or Institutional Advertising by Industrial-Product Companies Pay?

For complex industrial products or materials, a company's generalized reputation does indeed have an important bearing on how its sales prospects make buying decisions. While the research did not specifically investigate the influence of corporate or institutional advertising, the results show that to the extent that such advertising helps in building a company's reputation it clearly helps in making sales. Whether such advertising specifically helps build a reputation is, however, a separate question. But the presumption is that mere visibility of a company is in some way helpful and reassuring, provided that the impressions that are created are not negative.

Generally speaking, the better a company's reputation, the better are its chances (1) of getting a favorable *first hearing* for a new product among customer prospects, and (2) of getting early *adoption* of that product. Vendor reputation influences buyers, decision makers, and the decision-making process. But since industrial products, and particularly new products, generally require direct calls by salesmen, does the value of company reputation automatically give an edge to the salesman from a well-known company over the salesman from a less well-known or anonymous one?

2. Do Well-Known Company Salesmen Have an Edge over the Salesmen of Other Companies?

The answer is "yes," but it is a more complex answer than one might offhand suspect. Just because his company is favorably well known and to this extent puts the customer in a more favorable frame of mind toward that company, does not give the salesman a simple and automatic leg up over the salesman of a less-known company. The fact seems to be that customers *expect* more, or at least a better sales-presentation job, from well-known company salesmen. Hence they judge their performance somewhat differently from the way they judge the performance of other salesmen. Indeed there is some indication that some types of customers (or "audiences" of sales presentations) almost unconsciously "help" the salesmen of lesser-known companies by lowering their expectations in order to encourage competition between vendors. Thus, when they eventually make buying decisions, while these customers tend clearly to favor the better-known companies, they seem to give disproportionate encouragement to the salesmen of the less well-known companies.

Still, everyone knows from experience that a good sales presentation is always better than a poor one, regardless of company reputation. A vital question that therefore arises is whether it is generally better for an industrial-products company to spend its limited funds on more aggressive or effective advertising of its general competence, or on more careful selection and training of its salesmen?

3. Is It Better To Advertise More or To Select and Train Salesmen Better?

As would be expected, the research found that the quality of a sales-man's presentation in support of a technically complex new product is an important variable in obtaining a favorable customer reaction. In other words, there is a "presentation effect" in favor of the product supported by a well-done sales presentation.

When the influences of source effect and presentation effect are com-bined, the research suggests that when a relatively unknown or anony-mous company makes a good direct sales presentation, it may be just as effective in getting a favorable first hearing for a complex new industrial material as a well-known company making a poor presentation. Thus a well-known company loses the advantage of its reputation if its direct sales presentation is clearly inferior to that of an unknown or little-known company. Against a good sales presentation by a little-known company, a well-known one must also have a good presentation if the customer-getting value of its reputation is to be realized. Conversely, a little-known company, by concentrating strongly on training its salesmen to make good presentations, may be able to make considerable progress toward over-coming the liability of its relative anonymity.

Combining this with the finding that certain buyers apparently want to favor less well-known companies and expect more of better-known companies, even though they are strongly attracted to the latter, the con-clusion seems to be that the lesser-known company—particularly when its resources are limited—can do an unexpectedly effective job for itself through more careful salesman selection and training.

On the other hand, everyone knows that every buying decision for a new product, and some for an established product, involves a certain amount of risk for the buyer. Moreover, the buyer's personal risk (as opposed to the risk for his company) varies as between whether he has sole personal responsibility for the buying (or, indeed, the "rejection") decision or whether it is a shared or committee decision. To what extent does the degree of the decision maker's personal risk affect the importance of vendor reputation and quality of a sales presentation in the buyer's decision process?

4. The Role of Personal Risk in Buying Decisions

The amount of personal risk to which the individual decision maker is exposed in a buying or rejection decision proves to be a vital factor in his decisions. And it is vital in the extent to which source effect is influ-ential. Company reputation clearly results in a higher proportion of high-risk decisions in favor of the well-known company. Presentation quality tends substantially to strengthen the position of the less well-known com-pany in high-risk buying situations, but not as much in low-risk buying situations. While careful attention to salesman selection and training can be said to help equalize greatly the competitive position of lesser-known firms, these help it more to get a foot in the door than help it get an immediate adoption for its product. When it comes to the most important and most risky of customer actions—actually deciding to buy or reject a new product—assuming the various suppliers' products to be equal in all respects, source credibility exerts a dominant influence over other considerations.

But this still leaves unanswered the question of whether and to what extent all of these influences are equal among customers with varying degrees of technical competencies. Do they apply equally, for example, to purchasing agents and technically trained personnel such as chemists?

5. The Influence of Customer "Competence"

The research found that the power of source effect (company reputation for credibility) varies by the character and "competence" of the recipient of a sales message. Thus, there is some indication that, in the case of complex industrial materials, purchasing agents, who are usually highly competent as professional buyers, may be less influenced by a company's generalized reputation than are technical personnel, who are presumably less competent as buyers but more competent as judges of a complex product's merits. In first appraising complex new materials on the basis of sales presentations made directly to them, technically sophisticated personnel seem to be influenced by the seller's reputation to a point that is unexpectedly higher than the influence of that reputation on such technically less sophisticated personnel as purchasing agents. In short, technical personnel are probably influenced far more by company reputation than has been widely assumed, and certainly more than such technically less sophisticated people as purchasing agents.

While all audiences seem to be influenced by the quality of the sales presentation, important differences apparently exist between purchasing agents and technical personnel. In the lower-risk decision situation of whether to give a newly presented complex new product a further hearing, technical personnel are more powerfully influenced by the quality of a direct sales presentation than are purchasing agents. Put differently, on low-risk purchasing decisions, the technically less sophisticated purchasing agents seem to rely less heavily on the quality of the sales presentation than do the technically more sophisticated personnel in making their decision. But on high-risk decisions (whether actually to buy the product) the reverse is true: that is, the greater the risk, the more favorably purchasing agents are influenced by good sales presentations, and the less favorably technical personnel are influenced by such presentations. The greater the risk, the more likely technical personnel are to rely on their technical judgments about a new product's virtues rather than on the quality of the sales presentation in favor of that product. But purchasing agents, being technically less sophisticated, seem forced, in high-risk situations, to rely more heavily on the seller-s presentation.

6. The Durability of Vendor Reputation on
Buying Decisions

Philip Wrigley, of the chewing gum empire, is alleged to have answered a query about why his company continues to spend so much on advertising now that it is successful with this observation: "Once you get a plane up in the air you don't turn off the engines." For industrial-product companies, a related question concerns the durability of buying inclinations (and even of buying decisions) that sales prospects exhibit immediately after hearing a sales presentation. Since few new industrial products are immediately purchased on the making of a sales presentation to a customer—since, for many reasons, there is generally a time lag before a decision is made—the question is: Does source effect hold up over time? For example, with the passage of time does the prospect forget the source of a new product presentation, remembering only the facts and the claimed product performance, such that when the actual buying decision is made at some later time the vendor's reputation plays little or no role? Similarly, does the importance of quality of the sales presentation hold up over time?

The present research indicates that there is in industrial purchasing a phenomenon which communications researchers call the "sleeper effect." The favorable influence of a company's generalized good reputation (source effect) does indeed erode with the passage of time. But the conditions under which this happens appear to be quite special. Based on what the present research was able to test, what can be said is that this erosion occurs specifically when there is no intervening reinforcement or reinstatement of the identity of the source. Put differently, in the absence of repeated sales call-backs or advertisements to reinstate the identity of the source, the seller tends, over time, to lose the favorable impact of his good reputation on the attitudes and actions of his sales prospects.

But the declining power of source effect over time on audience decision-making works *in opposite directions* for the well-known company than for the lesser-known company. Sleeper effect, in a manner of speaking, hurts the well-known company but helps the lesser-known company. In the case of the former, as the sales prospect forgets the well-known source his originally favorable attitude toward the product declines; and in the case of the latter, as he forgets the lesser-known source his originally less-favorable attitude toward the product also declines. That is, the likelihood of his buying from the high-credibility company declines while the likelihood of his buying from the low-credibility company rises—even though the high-credibility company is still likely to get more customers in absolute terms.

IMPLICATIONS AND RESERVATIONS

The implications of the present research for industrial products companies are numerous, but so also are the reservations and qualifications which must be attached to the research findings. While the research sought to simulate reality as carefully as possible, it still remains only a simulation. Moreover, individual competitive situations, product characteristics, and a vast variety of other conditions can greatly affect the value of these findings in specific cases. But in the absence of better information and research, the present findings may be viewed as at least a beginning toward unravelling some age-old mysteries.

Reputation and Presentation

From the point of view of a producer of industrial materials or components, it seems safe to conclude that the cultivation of a good reputation among potential customers will have some payoff in the sense that it will help his salesmen to get "a foot in the door" of a prospect. But the value of cultivating a good reputation seems to be considerably less when it comes to its effect on the likelihood of the prospect's *actually buying* a new product on being first exposed to it. A good reputation always helps, but it helps less as the riskiness of the customer's decision rises and as he has something else to rely on draw on.

Hence it seems safe also to suggest that a producer of technically advanced products which are used as components or as ingredients by other manufacturers would be wise systematically to cultivate for himself a strongly favorable generalized reputation among technical personnel of prospective manufacturing customers. In other words, in trying to sell such products to technically trained personnel it may not be wise to rely so extensively, as many such companies do, on the product's inherent virtues and on making strong technical product presentations. Technical personnel are not human computers whose purchasing and product-specification decisions are based on cold calculations and devoid of less rigorously rational influences. They do indeed seem to be influenced by the seller's general reputation.

However, as might have been expected, the quality of a salesman's presentation in support of a product is an important variable in obtaining favorable buyer reactions, regardless of the technical or purchasing competence of the audience. A good direct sales presentation is generally more effective than a poor one. There is a "presentation effect" in favor of the product supported by a well-done sales presentation. But, as in the case of source effect, the research indicates that a good sales presentation is generally more useful in getting a favorable first hearing for a new product (that is, in what is, for the prospect, a low-risk decision) than it is in getting a favorable buying decision (that is, a high-risk decision). A good sales presentation is definitely better than a poor one in getting product adoption, but it has even more leverage than a poor one in getting a favorable first hearing for a product.

All this indicates that both the reputation of a vendor company and the quality of its direct sales presentations are important elements in sales success, but that the way the importance of these elements varies as between audiences and between types of audience decision-situations greatly affects how a vendor might wish to shape his marketing tactics.

"Sleeper Effect"

The findings on "sleeper effect" are particularly interesting in that, contrary to the other findings, they suggest that some policies appropriate for the well-known company may not be appropriate for the lesser-known company. Thus, repeat advertising and sales call-backs reinstate the well-known company's identity and therefore influence the prospect in its favor. But since the sales prospect tends to forget the source over time and therefore makes a more "objective" decision, reinstating the identity of the lesser-known company could actually tend to hurt that company. All other things being equal, the lesser-known company may find it better to leave well enough alone. But whether "all other things" are equal is highly doubtful, and in any case varies by the situation. The most that can be said here is that there can conceivably be circumstances in which sleeper effect can work to the advantage of the lesser-known company.

However, the research also found that the passage of time has different consequences for source effect than for presentation effect. A good sales presentation is more effective over time than a good reputation. Moreover, the better the original sales presentation, the greater the durability of its influence over the audience with the passage of time. That is, regardless of the presence of sleeper effect (the declining influences of source credibility with the passage of time), if the original sales presentation was relatively good, the prospects tend more strongly to favor the product in question at a later date than if that presentation had been poor. The originally favorable influence of the highly credible source declined less, and the originally unfavorable influence of the less-credible source hurt less, as the original sales presentation was better. A good sales presentation has greater durability than a good company reputation. Company reputation, in order to work for that company, has to be more regularly reinforced (possibly through advertising repetition) than does the effect of a good sales presentation.

A related finding on the dynamics of sleeper effect involves the strength of a sales prospect's reaction to a sales presentation. Thus, there is some evidence that the more self-confidently a prospect refuses at the outset to permit a new product to be viewed and reviewed by others in his firm, the greater the likelihood later that he will change his mind and give such permission. That is, a strong outright refusal for a further hearing at the time of the first sales call may suggest greater probability of getting permission later than does a weak and vacillating original refusal. Hence the very vigor with which a new product is at first rejected by a prospect may, instead of signaling that it is a lost cause, actually signal that a later repeat call is likely to get a good hearing.

High Risk Situations

But this refers only to relatively low-risk decisions—decisions in which the prospect is asked merely to give the product serious consideration, not actually to buy it at that time. In high-risk decision situations the findings were different. The research confirms the common-sense expectation that the greater the personal risk to the responding sales prospect, the more persuasion it takes to get him to switch from a product he is currently using. Moreover, once a prospect has made a decision in a high-risk situation, the seller will generally have considerable difficulty both in getting the negative respondent subsequently to change his mind and in keeping the affirmative respondent from changing his mind. This means that, especially in high-risk situations, it pays to try to get a favorable customer decision at the outset. Once he has rejected a product, it appears to be extremely difficult to get the prospect to be willing to reopen the discussions. Similarly, once he has accepted a new product under high-risk conditions, the customer appears to suffer from considerable self-doubt about whether he has made the right decision. He is probably very susceptible to being "unsold" by a competitor. This suggests the need for continuous followup by the original seller to reassure the customer and thus keep him sold.

Salesman or Company?

It has already been pointed out that, generally speaking, the more credible the source the more likely it is that its message will get a favorable reception. But the question arises as to who "the" source is: Is it the salesman who makes the sales call, or is it the company he represents? Do customers perceive this "source" as being one and the same or different? The present research indicates that they think of them as being two different sources. The salesman is not automatically thought of as being the company. When asked to rank the trustworthiness of the salesman on the one hand and then the trustworthiness of the company he represented, respondents consistently scored the salesman lower than his company.

While this might reflect the relatively low esteem with which salesmen are generally held, paradoxically, in our highly sales-dependent society, a closer look at the results suggests a great deal more. It was found, for example, that respondents are more likely to favor the products of salesmen whom they rank low in trustworthiness when these salesmen represent well-known companies than they are to favor the products of salesmen whom they rank relatively high in trustworthiness but who represent unknown companies. A similar result occurred in connection with respondents' feelings about how well informed and competent the salesmen from high-vs.-low-credibility companies are. Thus, offhand it would seem that favorably well-known companies operate at the distinct advantage of being able to afford to have less "trustworthy" and less "competent" salesmen, at least in the short run, than little-known or anonymous companies. But close examination suggests something else. It suggests that source effect is such a uniquely powerful force that for respondents to favor well-known companies, their need to trust the salesmen of these companies and to think highly of their competence is much less urgent than it is in order for them to favor less well-known and anonymous companies. In other words, the favorably well-known company does indeed have an advantage over its less well-known competitor in that its salesmen need to *seem* less trustworthy and competent in order to be effective. Well-known companies need not be as scrupulous in their hiring and training of salesmen. Source effect seems almost to conquer everything.

But not entirely everything. As noted above, presentation quality and quality of the message can overcome some of the disadvantages of being relatively anonymous. So can, of course, trust in the salesman. What is it then that makes for an appearance of salesman trustworthiness? First of all, the results of the present research suggest that trustworthiness of the communicator (such as, for example, a salesman, television announcer, etc.) is not as clearly related to the audience's feeling about his knowledge or understanding of the product he is selling as might be expected. While there is some relationship, trust is much more closely related to the over-all quality or character of the salesman's sales presentation. Poor presentations in particular reduce trust in the message transmitter (salesman). They also reduce trust in the message source (the salesman's company). The better the presentation the more trustworthy both the company and the salesman are perceived to be. To say this, and what has been said before, is equivalent to saying that there is obvious merit in making sure that salesmen have quality sales presentations, and this holds true particularly for less well-known companies.

It is interesting to note from the research that there was only a very modest, certainly not a clear, connecting between audience ratings of a salesman's trustworthiness and their judgments regarding the extent of his product competence. An audience's willingness either to recommend or adopt a product was not clearly related to its judgment about a salesman's product knowledge. Nor was it related, in the short run, to how much of the information which the salesman gave out was actually retained by the audience.

All this suggests that in making his adoption decisions the customer is influenced by more than what the salesman specifically says about the product or even how effectively he communicates product facts. It seems very probable that the communicator's personality and what he says about things other than the product in question play a vital role in influencing his audience. The effective transmission of product facts seems to be more important in the long run than in the short run. With the passage of time since the date of the original sales presentation, persons who retained more product information right after that presentation were more likely to make and hold decisions favorable to the source. Hence the importance of the effective transmission of product facts during the original presentation seems to increase as the product-adoption decision is delayed. But it is not clear that detailed recall of product facts ever becomes a paramount ingredient in obtaining favorable buying decisions.

SUMMARY

It seems clear that company reputation is a powerful factor in the industrial purchasing process, but its importance varies with the technical competence and sophistication of the customer. The quality of a sales message and the way it is presented are capable of moderating the influence of this source effect, but again it varies by audience. Generally speaking, it pays for a company to be favorably well known, and perhaps especially among customers having some degree of technical sophistication, such as engineers and scientists. But superior sales messages and well-trained salesmen can help less well-known companies to overcome some of the disadvantages of their relative anonymity. A well-planned and well-executed direct sales presentation can be an especially strong competitive weapon for the less well-known company. Moreover, the greater the riskiness of the purchasing decision the customer is asked to make, the more likely it is that a good sales presentation will produce a customer decision in favor of the direction advocated by the source.

27

Are So-called
Successful Advertising Campaigns
Really Successful?

STEUART H. BRITT
Northwestern University

To what extent do advertising agencies know whether their advertising campaigns are successful? Even more to the point, to what extent do agencies really set specific objectives for their campaigns? And in attempting to judge the success of a campaign, are the "proofs of success" relevant to the objectives stated?

For the first time, public statements by advertising agencies of campaign objectives and "proofs of success" of various campaigns have been set forth publicly in a form that permits systematic investigation of this question. The United States Trade Center for Scandinavia held an exhibition in Stockholm, Sweden, during May 1967, that featured advertisements from successful American advertising campaigns. One Swedish advertising agency, Annonsbyrå, prepared and distributed a special booklet that contained descriptions of 135 "successful advertising campaigns" created by 40 American advertising agencies.

The statements of campaign success in this booklet are presented in a consistent form. For each of the 135 campaigns, the agency states its "campaign objectives" and also the prooft of success." A knowledge of what is said about both of these variables is essential in order to evaluate objectively the criteria by which each agency determines the success of its campaigns.

Reprinted with permission from the *Journal of Advertising Research,* Copyright Advertising Research Foundation (1969).

Although it would be extremely difficult to determine the extent to which the sample of 135 campaigns by the 40 agencies is a representive sample, the campaigns are indicative of what many American advertising agencies say they do in attempting to measure the success of their campaigns.

In the present study, statements of named agencies about particular campaigns are quoted and sometimes found to be lacking in specificity of objectives or relevance of proofs of success, or both.

Each of the 40 agencies had submitted materials to be printed in the booklet, describing what they considered to be representative of their most successful campaigns. Although some agencies listed all major clients, most did not.

The format for each campaign described was:

Agency
Client
Length of service
Market situation
CAMPAIGN OBJECTIVES (of special importance in the present investigation
Individuals responsible
Media plan
PROOF OF SUCCESS (of special importance in the present investigation)

As an example, here is the description by Papert Koenig Lois for Wesson Oil:

"Client:
Hunt-Wesson Foods
Wesson Oil Campaign

"Length of service: two years

"Market situation:
Wesson Oil, the cooking oil leader, has been steadily losing share of market to Procter & Gamble's Crisco oil. Wesson's share has declined from a high of 36 per cent to below 32 per cent when the campaign started.

"Campaign objectives:
To first arrest, then reverse the trend. In terms of creative objectives, the advertising was to say that Wesson's high heat tolerance made it desirable for frying (the largest cooking oil in use), specifically, that it was better than competition for making fried foods crisp.

"Individuals responsible:
This was a group effort, no individuals can be cited.

"Media plan:
The magazine ads ran in McCall's, Reader's Digest, Good Housekeeping; the television commercials were largely in eight week waves in the prime time shows "My Three Sons," and spot daytime locations, throughout 1966.

"Proof of success:
Although details are confidential, three months after the campaign started, Wesson showed its first month-to-month share increase. Procter & Gamble's

Crisco oil showed a sharp decline, and that trend seems to have been maintained."

THREE QUESTIONS

The following is a summary of an analysis of each of the 135 different campaigns, based on answers to the following three questions:

A. Did the agency set *specific objectives* for the campaign, that is, objectives specific enough to be measured?

B. Did the agency attempt to measure the effectiveness of the campaign by clearly stating *how the campaign fulfilled the previously-set objectives?*

C. Were there any differences in the results . . . in either specificity of the objectives or in fulfillment of objectives in terms of (a) *size of agency* or (b) *product classification?*

Specific Objectives

A. *Did the agency set specific objectives for the campaign, that is, objectives specific enough to be measured?*

As a basis for analysis, an *operational definition* for a specific objective was established. An operational definition entails defining a term by stating the procedures (or operations) employed in distinguishing the item referred to from others.

Four points were established as the criteria of a specific objective. All four of these had to be given in the stated objective for it to be considered a specific type of objective. Thus, the statement of the advertising objective had to make it clear:

1. *What basic message* was to be delivered . . .
2. *to what audience* . . .
3. *with what intended effect(s)* . . .
4. and as to *what specific criteria* were going to be used later on to measure the success of the campaign.

Analysis of the stated campaign objectives in the present instance showed that a majority—87 of the 135, or 64 per cent—fulfilled the first three of the four criteria of the operational definition of a specific objective. *But in only two campaigns—less than one per cent of the 135 campaigns—were all four criteria met as to having specific objectives.*

Doyle, Dane, Bernbach is an example of the group that utilized three criteria as to the campaign objectives for their Polaroid Swinger campaign:

"*Campaign objectives:*
To create awareness of a Polaroid Camera for the fantastically low price of $19.95, particularly among teenage and young adult groups."

In other words, the *basic message* is the "fantastically low" price of $19.95 for the Polaroid Swinger. The *audience* is primarily teenage and young adult groups. The *intended effect* is awareness.

The following objectives of Campbell-Ewald for its Marathon Oil campaign apparently met the four criteria of the operational definition of a specific objective:

"Campaign objectives:

To increase awareness of the Marathon brand and instill confidence in it.

To introduce the Marathon guarantee and convince motorists that it was a legitimate offer, completely backed by the company.

To increase the number of persons who regarded Marathon as a major oil company.

To increase the number of persons who regarded Marathon's gasoline and oil products as being of the highest quality."

Although the specific awareness goal of 60 per cent is not mentioned in the statement of objectives but only in the statement about success, presumably this specific goal must have been an essential element in the original statement of the campaign objective.

Deficiencies in Statements of Objectives

The major deficiencies of the stated campaign objectives are of four kinds:

1. Failure to state the objective(s) in quantifiable terms
2. Apparent failure to realize that the results of the advertising could not be measured in sales
3. Failure to identify the advertising audience
4. Use of superlatives (which are unmeasurable).

1. *Failure to state the objective(s) in quantifiable terms*—in 133 instances, or 99 per cent of the 135 campaigns. Quantification of an objective should be a standard method of setting up benchmarks or criteria, scarcely represented by the two instances only in which this was done.

2. *Apparent failure to realize that the results of the advertising could not be measured in sales*—33 instances, or 24 per cent of the 135 campaigns. Too many other variables affect the buying decision—price, competition, relative newness of the product, and so on—that it is not logical to indicate that sales will be used as the measure of advertising effectiveness.[1] In rare instances it has been found possible to relate advertising and communications goals to sales by a strict control of extraneous variables such as price and point-of-purchase efforts. But without controlled experimentation, a direct cause–effect relationship between advertising and sales cannot be accepted as a defensible proof of advertising success. This means that an advertising objective involving the assumption of direct cause–effect relationship between advertising and sales is not adequate.

3. *Failure to identify the advertising audience*—21 instances, or 16 per cent of the total number of campaigns. In 12 of the stated objectives, the

---

[1] Darrell B. Lucas and Steuart Henderson Britt, *Measuring Advertising Effectiveness* (New York: McGraw-Hill, 1963), pp. 180–187.

fact that the campaign had any intended audience at all is not even indicated. Carl Ally in the following statement of campaign objectives delineates what is going to be said, but never mentions an audience:

> *"Campaign objectives:*
> To demonstrate Corning Ware's unique versatility (top-of-stove, oven, and serving).
> To visually depict the attractive appearance of Corning Ware—again, a characteristic competitors could not match."

4. *Use of superlatives* (which are unmeasurable)—three instances, or 2 per cent of the total number of campaigns. J. Walter Thompson's campaign objective for the American Red Cross, "To obtain *maximum* public support and voluntary contributions for the American Red Cross" (italics added) is an example. Instead of the use of the superlative "maximum," what was probably meant was "more" public support and voluntary contributions.

Fulfillment of Objectives

B. *Did the agency attempt to measure the effectiveness of the campaign by clearly stating how the campaign fulfilled the previously-set objectives?*

In 93 instances of the 135—69 per cent of the cases—proofs of success were not directly related to the previously-stated campaign objectives. Only in 42, or 31 per cent, of the cases were proofs of success related directly to the objectives the agency set.

Here is an example of a logical statement by Redmond, Marcus & Shure, in that the proof of success is given in terms of the previously-stated campaign objectives:

> *"Campaign objectives:*
> To establish awareness of Crystallose in a highly competitive field, using a very small budget and small space. A 10 cent trial offer was placed in the advertisement in order to obtain a check on reading; the assumption being that many trial users would then go to their drug stores to make a full size purchase."

> *"Proof of success:*
> The objective evidence of effectiveness is the number of dimes which were sent in for trial samples. These have varied from several hundred to over a thousand per insertion, and have in every case exceeded all previous advertising for the product."

The objective was awareness of the product to be measured by the number of replies to the trial offer received. In the discussion of proof of success, the number of replies is mentioned, a direct follow-up on the criterion that was established in the campaign objectives.

But compare this example of logic with the following statement from Richard K. Manhoff for Welch's Grape Juice, in which the statement of proof of success does not relate logically to the statement of campaign objectives:

"Campaign objectives:

To convince mothers that Welch's Grape Juice is the best fruit drink they can serve their children: (a) Because it is good for them; (b) Because it is the best-tasting of all fruit drinks."

"Proof of success:

Despite the aggressive competition from the scores of competitive brands of fruit drinks, Welch's has not only held its position but shown consistent improvement in sales year after year."

Although this campaign purportedly was intended to convince mothers of the quality of Welch's Grape Juice as a drink for children, the statement of proof of success indicates no attempt to measure any awareness of the product on the part of mothers. Instead, sales were cited as proof of success of the advertising—whereas any number of other factors, including increased enthusiasm for the product, at the dealer level, may have been responsible.

Deficiencies in Statement of Objectives

Careful analysis showed that deficiencies of the agencies in relating proofs of success to stated campaign objectives were of three principal kinds:

a. With the objective of *awareness,* success stated in sales.

b. With the objective of a *new image,* success stated in terms of readership or inquiries.

c. With *more than one objective* set forth, success stated only in relation to one of these, with the others ignored.

a. With the objective of awareness in 56 instances, 38 proofs of success, or 68 per cent, were stated in terms of sales.

As mentioned above, increasing sales *could* be one indication of successful advertising; but many, many other variables also could account for the sales increase.

Yet Knox Reeves Advertising in a campaign plan for Betty Crocker Au Gratin and Scalloped Potatoes cited sales increases as proof that advertising had been successful in getting women to "see how Betty Crocker Au Gratin and Scalloped Potatoes can help make meals more varied and interesting." But increased sales must have been dependent on the successful operation of many phases of the total marketing mix.

"Campaign objectives:

The objective of the advertising has been to help women see how Betty Crocker Au Gratin and Scalloped Potatoes can help them make meals more varied and interesting. We know most American women plan their evening meals, starting with meat. Therefore, we set out to show the reader how these products can 'dress up' the most frequently-served meats. We have attempted to do this by showing popular cuts of meat with our products, and suggesting them with fresh, interrupting copy."

"Proof of success:
These products have captured over 50 per cent of the total specialty instant potato market, in the face of strong competition from both price brands and other quality brands."

Compare the above example with the logical way in which Campbell-Ewald followed through with a stated objective of awareness by showing an increase of awareness of the product advertised by inquiries that came as a direct result of the advertising campaign. This was for the Aero Commander Division of the Rockwell-Standard Corporation:

"Campaign objectives:
To increase awareness and establish Aero Commander as the leading producer of a complete line of durable, quality aircraft."

"Proof of success:
The first ad was published in January, 1967. Campaign will continue for nine months. Within four weeks after the first ad ran, Aero Commander received 1,330 inquiries answering the simple 'more information' offer mentioned in the copy. More impressive still, many of the letters were inquiries about the Jet Commander: a $750,000 product."

b. With the objective stated in terms of a new image in 20 instances, the statements of proof of success, or 35 per cent, were defined in terms of increased advertisement-readership or inquiries about the product as a result of the advertisement.

Although both readership and inquiries may be indicative of consumer attention and awareness, it cannot be demonstrated that a change in image necessarily results.

In the following statement for Burny Bros., Inc., no evidence is cited by Draper Daniels, Inc., to show a change in the public concept of Burny Bros. Although readership might be indicative of product awareness, this does not indicate what the public think of Burny Bros. as a direct result of the advertising campaign:

"Campaign objectives:
To stress freshness, quality and individuality not ordinarily associated with mass production; to do so in a fresh and friendly way without resorting to the usual exaggerated manufacturer's claims; to feature weekly price specials and yet maintain a quality image."

"Proof of success:
Sales increased by five per cent in the face of much heavier expenditures by national advertisers of both fresh and frozen baked goods. *Consumer interviews revealed that ads were well read and enjoyed despite their length."* (Italics added.)

By contrast, only two agencies indicated the difficulties faced in trying to measure the results of a campaign that seeks to change an image. As one example, Liller, Neal, Battle & Lindsey included the following in their campaign objectives for Rich's department store: "It's difficult to determine to what extent image advertising is successful; it's a cumulative effect rather than specific . . . [We must give] much credit to the store itself in living up to all advertising." A statement by the J. Walter Thompson Company also indicated the difficulties involved in measuring a change in image.

c. With more than one objective stated in 37 instances, in only 20 cases was each of the objectives discussed. J. Walter Thompson's statement for the Institute of Life Insurance is an example of failure to discuss each of the objectives stated:

"Campaign objectives:
Long-Term: To promote the generic product—life insurance—by conditioning people of all ages to the idea that life insurance is an essential element in their financial planning and one that should be reviewed and updated as often as financial circumstances change.

Short-Term:
1. To strengthen public awareness of the unique ability of life insurance to provide for:
   —immediate family security
   —a lifetime income for beneficiaries
   —funds to pay the mortgage
2. To increase appreciation of the professional stature of life insurance agents and their ability to help policy holders use the unique advantages of life insurance in family financial planning."

"Proof of success:
As noted above, sales are not an objective of the Institute or this campaign. Based upon the response and support from the insurance companies supporting the Institute, it is genuinely felt by both these companies and their agents that this campaign has helped significantly to soften the resistance many people hold against increasing their insurance coverage. The commercials themselves have scored *very* high impact and recall scores in viewer tests."

In this example the first objective, awareness, is discussed in the proof of success; but no direct statement is made with regard to the second objective, the professional stature of life insurance agents.

By contrast, the following is a thoroughly logical statement by Cunningham & Walsh Inc., interrelating their proofs of success for the St. Regis Paper Company with the stated campaign objectives:

"Campaign objectives:
1. Create greater awareness of St. Regis and its products.
2. Establish St. Regis' stature and progressiveness as a leader in the forest product industry.
3. Communicate St. Regis' depth of manufacturing coverage and competence.
4. Reiterate St. Regis' dedication to the concept of intelligent management of its major resources, the forest."

"Proof of success:
1. More than 3,500 letters from interested readers commenting favorably on the advertising or requesting more information.
2. Requests for more than 130,000 color reprints of the advertisements.
3. Recognition in Saturday Review's annual competition for advertising in the public interest by finishing among the top four companies selected.
4. Among the business audience, the first nine advertisements that appeared in Business Week ranked in the top five of all ads in the issue in which these ads appeared, as measured by Starch Readership studies.
5. Among the consumers reading Time Magazine, the ads also received high noting scores as measured by Starch. One of the ads in the series (July 22, 1966 issue) was the highest ranked advertisement in the issue."

SIZE OF AGENCY AND PRODUCT CLASSIFICATION

C. *Were there any differences in the results in either specificity of the objectives or in fulfillment of objectives in terms of (a) size of agency or (b) product classification?*

Of the 135 campaigns, 62 represented campaigns of agencies billing over $20 million. As Table 1 shows, there is a trend toward the larger agencies stating specific objectives, and a fairly significant trend toward the larger agencies using the terms of the objective to state proofs of success.

TABLE 1: RELATION OF SIZE OF ADVERTISING AGENCY
TO SPECIFICITY OF CAMPAIGN OBJECTIVES
AND FULFILLMENT OF OBJECTIVES

Campaign	*Agencies billing over $20 million*	*Agencies billing under $20 million*
Number of campaigns represented	62	73
Campaign described as having specific objective	44	43
Proof of campaign success stated in terms of campaign objective	25	17

Insofar as a trend being apparent in terms of product class and specificity and fulfillment of campaign objectives, the present investigation is hindered by the diversity of products represented by the 135 campaigns. That is to say, 51 of the product classes listed in *The Standard Directory of Advertisers* are represented in these campaigns; and thus no significant trend is apparent.

1. A specific advertising objective must include a statement as to what basic message is to be delivered, to what audience, with what intended effect, and what specific criteria are going to be used later on to measure the success of the campaign. Sixty-four per cent of the campaigns met the first three of these criteria, but *less than one per cent of the campaigns met all four criteria.*

In addition to not meeting these criteria, the most frequent deficiencies in the statements of the objectives were in:

   a. Not stating the objectives in quantifiable terms—99 per cent.
   b. Not recognizing that the results of advertising cannot be measured by sales—24 per cent.
   c. Not identifying the advertising audience—16 per cent.
   d. Using superlatives, which are unmeasurable, in stating the campaign objectives—two per cent.

2. Sixty-nine per cent of the campaign statements did *not* relate proofs of success of the advertising campaign to the stated objective of the campaign. The deficiencies were of three different kinds:

   a. Objective stated to be awareness, but success stated in sales.
   b. Objective stated to be a new image, but success stated in terms of readership or inquiries.
   c. More than one objective stated, but success given only in relation to one of these objectives and the others ignored.

3. As to those advertising agencies that did give specific statements of campaign objectives and also specific proofs of success related to these objectives, there were more campaigns (71 per cent) with stated specific objectives among the agencies billing over $20 million than among those campaigns (59 per cent) from agencies billing under $20 million.

Also, more of the agencies of over $20 million (40 per cent) stated more proofs of success in the same terms as campaign objectives than did the agencies of under $20 million (23 per cent).

4. Finally, as to differences in product classifications, no trend was indicated.

IMPLICATIONS

Advertising of a product or service must prove its success as advertising by *setting specific objectives.* Such general statements of objectives as "introduce the product to the market," "raise sales," and "maintain brand share" are not objectives for advertising. Instead, they are the objectives of the entire marketing program. And even when considered as marketing goals, such statements still are too general and broad to be used to determine the extent of a plan's success or failure.

Advertising Goals

Advertising goals should indicate 1. what basic message is to be delivered, 2. to what audience, 3. with what intended effect, and 4. what specific criteria are going to be used to measure the success of the campaign.

When the advertising campaign is over, the advertiser can best judge the results by comparing them with the intended results, as expressed in the campaign objective. Only when he knows what he is intending to do can he know when and if he has accomplished it.

The present analysis shows the need for emphasis on the setting of specific objectives in advertising campaigns, and an even greater need for agencies to use their campaign objectives as means of measuring campaign success or failure.

Why does a business firm or organization spend money on advertising without knowing exactly what is supposed to be achieved by the advertising?

When a business firm purchases a new line of production equipment, management is quite sure of the adventages to be gained for the price paid. But why has management not consistently established the same types of objectives and results with respect to advertising expenditures?

When asked for a statement as to company advertising goals and objectives, many companies can supply such a statement only after the advertising has run.[2] Actually management ought to decide exactly what advertising is expected to achieve, and then at that time develop the necessary plans to test, so as to find out how successful the advertising was in terms of the expected results.

Precise, specified goals and objectives ought to be set and measured for advertising as advertising. Perhaps the agencies represented in the Annonsbyrå AB book actually are doing so; but their publicly-stated objectives for successful campaigns indicate that the majority are *not* doing this, at least in the campaigns discussed.

Successful Campaign?

What is the answer to the central question posed at the outset: "To what extent do advertising agencies know whether or not their campaigns are successful?"

The answer is that most of the advertising agencies do *not* know whether their campaigns are successful or not. In the majority of the 135 campaigns analyzed here, the agencies did *not* prove or demonstrate the success of the campaigns which they themselves had publicly stated were successes.

There is even a further implication. That is that most of the advertising agencies did *not* state (and possibly did not know) what the objectives

2 Harry Deane Wolfe, James K. Brown, and G. Clark Thompson, *Measuring Advertising Results* (New York: National Industrial Conference Board, 1962).

for determining success were for a particular campaign, and consequently they could not possibly demonstrate whether a "successful" campaign was actually a success.

Advertising may consist of doing something right or of doing something wrong. But do most advertisers and advertising agencies actually know just what that "something" is?

SELECTED BIBLIOGRAPHY
for
PART 4

DEANS, JOEL. "Does Advertising Belong in the Capital Budget?," *Journal of Marketing*. October, 1966, pp. 15–21.

EVANS, FRANKLIN B. "Selling as a Dyadic Relationship—A New Approach," *The American Behavioral Scientist*. May, 1963, pp. 76–79.

HANAH, MARK. "Corporate Growth through Venture Management," *Harvard Business Review*. January–February, 1969, pp. 43–61.

LALONDE, BERNARD J. "Locational Strategy as an Element in the Design of Marketing Systems," in Raymond Haas, ed., *Science, Technology and Marketing*. (Chicago: American Marketing Association, 1966), pp. 403–411.

MCDONALD, A. L. JR. "Do Your Distribution Channels Need Refreshing?," *Business Horizons*. Summer, 1964, pp. 29–38.

MIRACLE, GORDON. "Product Characteristics and Marketing Strategy," *Journal of Marketing*. January, 1965, pp. 18–24.

MYERS, JAMES H., and REYNOLDS, WILLIAM H. *Consumer Behavior and Marketing Management*. (Boston: Houghton Mifflin Company, 1967), pp. 263–76.

SHAPIRO, BENSON. "The Psychology of Pricing," *Harvard Business Review*. July–August, 1968, pp. 14–16.

WELSH, STEPHEN J. "A Planning Approach to New Product Pricing," in *Pricing: The Critical Decision*. Research Study 66 (American Management Association, 1961), pp. 45–57.

YOUNG, ROBERT W. "Multibrand Entries," in Lee Adler, ed., *Plotting Marketing Strategy*. (New York: Simon and Schuster Inc., 1967), pp. 143–64.

CONTROLLING THE MARKETING EFFORT

Regardless of how well a company organizes and plans its marketing program, unforeseen developments outside the control of marketing decision makers will probably occur. Thus, marketing planning needs to be supplemented by controls to insure that the marketing goals are achieved.

One method of control in marketing is the use of sales quotas. Rich (pp. 364–372) shows how the sales quota is gaining acceptance as a planning and control device. Shuchman (pp. 373–381) suggests that organizations should take periodic marketing audits, providing a comprehensive appraisal of all marketing activities. Taylor (pp. 382–387) demonstrates how the computer is transforming sales analysis into an efficient marketing-control tool. The last article, by Hudig (pp. 388–397), points out that marketing should be as much concerned with costs, profits, and return on investment as with sales.

MARKETING CONTROL

28

The Controversy
in Sales Quotas

LESLIE RICH

The sales quota, traditional enemy of salesmen, is stronger and more widespread than ever in American industry. But it often has such a sophisticated, disarming face that salesmen no longer fear it.

In fact, the quota today is usually part of a comprehensive marketing system involving constant research and delicately attenuated compensation plans. Quotas are also being extended to distributors and retail dealers; and even companies whose salesmen are on straight salary without commission are finding new use for the quota as a planning device.

"I don't see how you can have any semblance of long-range planning without quotas," says John C. Emery Jr., executive vice president of Emery Air Freight Corp. "We have to know how much profit will be available at the end of 1966 or, for that matter, in 1970. The only way to make any reasonable estimate is by carefully using short- and long-term sales quotas."

But marketing managers are far from agreed on how to set up and administer a quota system, and a few still hold out against quotas altogether. Some of the questions frequently asked are:

- How, in the first place, do you arrive at a fair quota for any individual?
- Should a salesman's quota be higher than you actually expect him to produce? If so, how much higher?

- How can you keep quotas from interfering with the development and service calls so necessary to most companies?
- Should quotas be set in product units, dollars, according to profits—or how?
- Should quotas be the same for everybody, or different according to territory potential, experience, ability, and so forth?
- What relation should quotas have to salary?
- How can you "sell" salesmen on quotas?
- What do you do when a salesman fails to meet his quota?

In older, simpler days, small groups of salesmen often would sit down with the manager and work out equitable quotas for themselves, gaining an invaluable "consent-of-the-governed" factor. But in today's complex markets, this is rarely possible. The planning must come from a nerve center at company headquarters.

One strong proponent of quotas is Ralph J. Weiger, who last October joined the Signal-Stat Co., a division of Lehigh Valley Industries, Inc., as executive vice president and chief operating officer. He found a company whose sales had been growing rapidly for several years, but whose management controls had fallen behind. The Brooklyn-based manufacturer of automotive signals, flashers and safety devices was in a good position to profit greatly when some of these devices became standard equipment on 1967 model automobiles.

"Looking into past records, I saw that profits had been going up and expenses had been held down," says Weiger. "Things were going well, with a new plant on the drawing boards. Why, then, did I want to set up a system of rigid quotas?

"Because we needed *control.* Growing so fast, we were headed for trouble unless we knew what we would be selling in each product category and, more important, what the profits would be."

Weiger and his lieutenants quickly made up a forecast of 1966 operations, setting somewhat arbitrary figures for profits, sales, return on sales and investment. They also made long-range studies that showed it was possible for Signal-Stat to have around 50% of some automobile markets by 1970.

The problem was to convey these plans down to the front line of sales, in this case to the fifty manufacturers' agents who sell Signal-Stat products to the "after market" of jobbers, garages, fleets and gasoline stations. (Orignal-equipment manufacturers sales were less of a problem since they are handled directly by the company's three regional managers.)

"Relying heavily on past performance," says Weiger, "we gave each agent a dollar quota for each of six product categories. To head off complaints, we started selling the idea of the new system right away."

Weiger hired an experienced promotion man who began to spice up packaging of the "Flarestat," an emergency signal with consumer appeal. Advertising was stepped up, and agents were offered more help. Individual agents in territories with high potential were singled out for special attention, such as raising quotas substantially and paying higher commissions for sales above quota.

At the same time, Signal-Stat formed a Merchandising Advisory Board

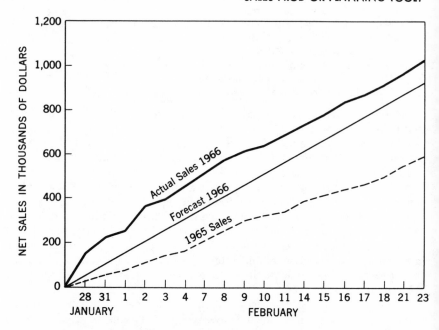

The sales quota, long a headache for salesmen, is gaining new acceptance as a planning and control device. Signal-Stat Co. recently instituted a rigid quota system, even though its sales were already outstanding, as a means of exercising needed control and keeping tabs on daily performance. The cumulative results are charted above.

of four experienced agents to make recommendations on product changes, advertising policy, and so forth. This group gave the Brooklyn head-quarters some of the feedback it had lacked by not having factory salesmen.

"Then at the annual meeting of agents we formed our Dollar Club," says Weiger. "Through a complicated mathematical process, it comes out that when an agent is doing an exceptionally good job for us, his sales are roughly $1 for every vehicle registered in his state. So we set this extra quota—well above the regular one—and formed an exclusive club of top producers."

As the new marketing system took hold, Weiger found sales running about 110% of quota, with all but a handful of agents meeting their individual quotas. The short-term outlook for sales is so promising that Signal-Stat is rushing to complete a new plant. "We apparently made close guesses on the quotas," says Weiger, "and it's very important that quotas be realistic. They also must be easily explainable, so that every man knows exactly where he stands at all times."

For many companies, a reasonable estimate of sales on which quotas can be set involves analysis of masses of data, the weighing of market factors and indices on both national and local scales.

ANALYSIS & GUESSWORK

In the plumbing and heating division of American-Standard Corp., for example, quotas are tied directly to a budget based on yearly market forecasts. Starting in October, the ten-man marketing research department begins to assemble data for each of the thirteen geographical sales districts. The analysts talk to company people in each district, go over economic bulletins from local banks and building and loan associations, and compare this with national predictions on housing. They try to judge the type of building planned (multiple or single dwelling, for example), the possibility of American-Standard penetration into competitive markets and the historic comparison of one region's housing with the nation as a whole.

"From all this, we make our considered guess on next year's sales for each of our twenty major products in each district," says Jerome A. Cleveland, division manager of marketing research. "And 'guess' is the correct word."

However, after years of refinement, Cleveland's department now regularly comes within a few percentage points of actual sales each year. Bathtubs are used as cornerstones of the forecast, since other plumbing products can be related to sales of this product.

Cleveland takes his forecasts to the division's general sales manager, who suggests revisions according to his knowledge of local situations and personnel. Then, during the December meeting of district managers, the general sales manager and Cleveland meet with each district manager individually to agree on the budget, and thus the quota, for that district. Prior to this meeting, each district manager is exposed to a complete review of new products and programs planned for the coming year.

The figures then become official, and the data is placed in the company's computer in New Brunswick, New Jersey. With a program developed by American-Standard, the computer produces monthly unit and dollar quotas for each district. Anticipated changes in price and product mix for each area are programmed, but after a first stage Cleveland reviews a print-out and makes hand adjustments for outside factors, such as the March inventory tax in California.

Use of the computer for detailed quotas saves an estimated twelve man-weeks of analysis. In fact, the company has experimented with a process known as "expodential smoothing," in which the entire market forecast is handled by computer, but to date has found it unreliable.

As the year progresses, American-Standard checks its quotas against a short-term indicator, the F. W. Dodge statistics on contract awards, as well as against actual sales results. Partly because the products are not subject to quick changes caused by advertising and promotion, the quotas have checked out very closely.

"But there are always unexpected developments," says Cleveland. "Last year building in Los Angeles went into a severe 30% slump, and everybody was hard hit. In a situation like that, we look for other areas where we might be able to make up the lost revenue. If housing is unusually strong in another area, the sales manager might try to get more results there even if the district is running ahead of quota."

It is up to each district manager to divide his quota into sales territories and individual quotas for wholesale distributors. Each manager uses his own method, within limits, and it is this last stage—setting quotas for individuals—that often causes the most agonizing headaches. "Establishing potential is a refined science, but assigning sales quotas equitably is a painful art," says Cleveland.

Realistically, each salesman should have a different quota based on conditions within his territory, and many companies operate this way. But this makes for great confusion when the territories change hands or must be split, especially if the salesmen are being paid bonuses or extra commissions for beating the quota. There are great advantages in setting some sort of uniform quota "so we can speak to all as one," as one sales manager puts it.

SIMPLEX' POINT SYSTEM

Another problem is whether to rate the quota to profitability. This has been solved by the Simplex Wire & Cable Co. in Cambridge, Massachusetts through a point system for products.

Each product is given a point value from one to five, according to its contribution to profits, and each salesman is given a point total to achieve. When he reaches his total, it is understood that he has earned his salary, and he begins to collect extra compensation.

Since he can earn this quota by any arrangement of points he wishes, his goal is still mainly gross dollar volume. But the company has rated the products so that the salesman's volume efforts have the effect of emphasizing profitability. "This has worked very well for us," says Marshall A. Williams, vice president for corporate marketing in the power and control division. "We think quotas are essential to schedule production, control product mix, predict capital equipment needs, give us a basis for incentive programs and generally stabilize planning."

Other companies have tried different kinds of quotas to meet supposedly special needs. One popular idea has been to give each man a quota of "face-to-face" selling time, so many hours per week in which he is actually on calls, as opposed to nonselling duties. The theory, of course, is that salesmen often spend too many hours in nonproductive work, either through poor planning or procrastination. "I recall a time at another company when we gave a big award to the salesman who had the greatest number of calls per month," says Signal-Stat's Weiger. "Unfortunately, the winner was one of the worst men on the force. He made lots of calls but very few sales."

Of the companies that eschew quotas altogether, many simply do not have enough control over the people who sell their products. The Knapp Bros. Shoe Manufacturing Corp. of Brockton, Massachusetts has franchised some 11,000 "shoe counselors" to sell its products. "To set quotas for these independent businessmen would be unthinkable," comments

John W. Learnard, vice president for sales. However, Knapp counselors do get awards for beating "specific totals."

And in some industries the principle of quotas is being extended to nonemployees in ingenious ways. The All-State Welding Alloys Co. of White Plains, New York, for example, uses a simple but effective quota system for its 800 distributors, many of whom sell not only other products but competing lines.

The distributors can be in any of three categories—non-stocking, which means they have no quota and get no discount; stocking, with a quota of $500 worth of products to be bought a month, at a discount; and special plan, with a quota of $2,500 along with an inventory of $10,000, and the allocation of one salesman to sell only All-State products. The company's own fifteen salesmen (called regional managers) constantly work to upgrade distributors, and records are checked every six months to see if any distributor has stepped up or slid back.

Recently, All-State increased its efforts to help distributors by offering sales courses taught with films and a 71-page manual written by the company's marketing staff. The manual emphasizes All-State products but attempts to teach methods of selling any welding product.

Meanwhile, the fifteen salesmen have been meeting their own 20% quota increase each year for more than a decade. "That may seem high," says Charles Brown, sales manager, "but it's based on past experience. The fact is that for years sales have been going up an average of 25%, so we know the 20% is realistic. If our growth slows down, we'll have to think about making adjustments in the quota." All-State also sets special quotas on certain alloys and pays special commissions for beating them.

PLENTY OF PROSPECTS

The Muzak division of Wrather Corp., the background music service and a newcomer to the quota system, is also in a growth situation, with plentiful prospects in every territory. Operating mostly through franchises, it had never used quotas for salesmen until three years ago, when they were imposed in company-owned operations in New York City and suburbs, San Francisco, Chicago and Bridgeport, Connecticut.

"Every man has the same monthly dollar quota for new billings. It's written into his contract," says J. R. H. Wilson, vice president for company-owned operations. "It began as a 'seat of the breeches' quota— a figure that we knew a reasonably good salesman could make by getting four or five new accounts a month, depending on the size of the installations."

In Muzak's salary-commission-bonus system, the salesmen are paid $45 for each $1 over quota on new billings. And some of the payments are quite large, because sales have continued to climb since the quotas were set. "We thought about increasing quotas," says Wilson, "but so far we've decided against it. We would rather the quotas be looked on as an absolute minimum, something it would be disgraceful not to beat. If a man falls down a month or two, however, we usually say nothing because the other men razz him enough." Wilson adds: "We prefer to create additional incentives by giving each man an informal but definite goal, usually tailored just for him."

The Muzak quota is for new business only, although the salesman also gets commissions for renewals and sale of equipment. Each office has a customer relations department, which is supposed to take care of most service, leaving salesmen free to get new customers. "But a good salesman makes some service calls anyway," says Wilson. "If a bank has the service only in its key punch area, for example, the salesman might use a service call as an opportunity to get Muzak extended to other areas. He gets more commission for the extension, of course—and quota credit.

"We know our quotas are low at this point," Wilson adds. "But we've got such a 'gung-ho' spirit among our men that we hesitate to upset anything."

If Muzak errs on the side of low quotas, many other companies have been guilty of setting goals that are unrealistically high. "I've seen this happen many times, and it produces nothing but trouble," says Francis D. Whiting, marketing manager of the copier division of the Dennison Manufacturing Co. in Framingham, Massachusetts.

"You can't fool salesmen," says Whiting. "All they have to do is look about them and note how many service men are being hired, and so forth. If the company is giving them a quota much above what the budget counts on, they know it's unrealistic and tend to shrug off the whole thing. We think there should be only a budget quota, to plan production and predict service expenses. Higher field quotas should be used only for special contests."

At Dennison, a newly hired copier salesman has no quota for the first month, half quota for the next three months. After that all men have the same quota—a certain number of machine units. Of the 100 salesmen, most derive about two-thirds of their income from commissions.

"We also have a supply quota," says Whiting, "but that's just to make sure the salesman services the account. When a new machine is installed, sales of supplies are sure to follow as long as someone calls."

Dennison also has imposed quotas on dealers of its equipment. If a dealer misses his quota repeatedly, Dennison asks for a conference to recheck the quota and see that it is fair. If the dealer still does not make it, he is given thirty days' notice that he will lose the franchise.

Some companies have not set quotas because it is difficult to assign credit for sales. In the airline industry, for example, who can say whether a salesman's presentation six weeks before was the reason why a businessman or vacation group chose his flight? Comments Edwin W. Breed, vice president for traffic and sales of Northeast Airlines: "We don't believe in sales quotas as such. Our industry is fast-growing, and we have all we can do to keep up with the pace of Americans who want to fly."

However, Eastern Air Lines, as part of a dramatic overhaul of its marketing system, is working on a plan to bring quotas down to the individual. Details are undisclosed, but this would be a distinct innovation for the industry.

Currently Eastern's 210 salesmen (on straight salary) are in the midst of a retraining program based on a series of programmed instruction manuals. Turning from the specialist system, Eastern is equipping each man to call on all customers in a geographic territory—travel agents, commercial accounts, freight prospects, hotel and convention prospects, and so forth.

Quotas are set on a national level by the market research department, which uses government statistics and other sources to estimate traffic between "city pairs" for the coming year, then sets a goal for Eastern's share of the business on each of its routes. At the same time, each of the company's regional offices checks its own sources and makes up its own quota. "The figures were so close this year that the field quotas for each region were adopted as the national quota," says Russell G. Collins, regional sales manager in New York. "So each region has a quota, which is then divided into the 36 district offices." Adds Collins: "We would like to break down the quota further, for individual salesmen. But every new service we offer, such as ticketing facilities within companies, makes it more difficult to assign individual credit for a sale."

Nevertheless, Eastern hopes to come up with some kind of quota system for salesmen through "closer checking of sources." If the system is successful, the compensation plan could be changed to include commissions and other incentives. (Last year, Eastern used an unusual incentive system for all company employees. Everyone, from the president to the last clerk, received exactly 25,000 trading stamps because the company met its revenue quota for every month of the year.)

In a related industry, Emery Air Freight Corp. has less difficulty assigning quotas since passengers are not involved. According to John C. Emery Jr., executive vice president, the company uses "revenue per salesman per day" as the basis of its planning, counting only working days without regard to months. This year Emery is aiming for an average of $1,300 a day (the average single sale is only $25), although individual quotas vary from about $800 to $2,000. "We think quotas are a measuring device," says Emery. "If sales are way above quota in one office, we know it's time to add more men there. On the other hand, we also know when a local manager is not getting the most out of his territory."

Every salesman has a computer code number, and records of any sale show at a glance who is responsible, both on the sending and receiving ends. The company's computer at Scranton, Pennsylvania receives records so that the company knows immediately how it is doing in each of its nine regions and eighty station offices.

"Our men, on straight salary, accept quotas as a fact of life," says Emery, "although I don't suppose any salesman likes them. We raise quotas frequently, sometimes in the middle of the year, but we emphasize that beating them is one quick road to promotion, and we're opening new stations all the time. Also, we have a profit-sharing plan that includes salesmen. This is somewhat unusual, and it gives our salesmen an unusual incentive."

As a final example of the insistent spread of the quota system, the Maytag Co. of Newton, Iowa this year began to impose quotas on its retail dealers, who, of course, also sell competitive machines. "We believe in quotas very, very strongly," says G. E. Ankeny, sales manager. "We appraise the performance of dealers in other ways, such as advertising and promotion, but the quotas are an important factor. We even give each dealer a little desk calendar with his quota for each month plainly marked."

Ankeny points out that all other reports common in marketing come "after the fact." Only quotas can be used for planning. For years, they have been a way of life for Maytag salesmen. The company believes its quotas are unusually equitable because they are based on local conditions.

From its examinations of business forecasts, Maytag's market research department produces a quota for each county in the United States. The quota is based on industry climate and what Maytag feels should be its share in each county according to the competitive situation. Then the county quotas are added up to produce quotas for each of the company's 23 geographic branches. The branch manager cannot change his quota, but he may make changes in the "blocks" to allow for differences in personnel or other conditions. Each of the company's 225 salesmen then gets a quota in writing. And so do the dealers.

"As in any quota system, there is a certain amount of grumbling," says Ankeny. "But we call directly on dealers, not through distributors, and we feel the dealer is our partner. We compete for his attention, and we would never give a quota without also bringing a complete merchandising plan to help the dealer—and the salesman—meet that quota and surpass it."

29

The Marketing Audit:
Its Nature, Purposes,
and Problems

ABE SHUCHMAN
Columbia University

The notion of an audit—a periodic review and appraisal of a business activity—is familiar to all executives. In most companies, financial audits to establish the adequacy and accuracy of accounting and financial operations are accepted practice. Periodic inventories for the evaluation of physical assets are also commonplace. In addition, many firms today make periodic reviews of the records and achievements of all employees, and there is evidence that such "personnel audits" are fast becoming standard practice.

In recent years there has been increasing awareness that the future growth—indeed, the very survival—of most companies depends primarily upon the success of their marketing operations. There has been widespread recognition of the central and critical role of marketing activities in the shaping of a firm's destiny. It has not, however, been generally recognized that, because marketing operations are of such crucial importance, it is necessary to apply to these operations a type of stock-taking analogous to that currently applied to financial and personnel activities. Very few firms have yet come to realize that a *marketing audit* is as essential as an audit of the company's books, physical assets, or employees.

Reprinted by permission of the publisher from Management Report No. 32, *Analyzing and Improving Marketing Performance*. © 1959 by the American Management Association, Inc.

Most marketing executives would probably deny indignantly that they do not recognize the need for auditing the operations which are their responsibility. They would insist, in fact, that they are *constantly* evaluating these operations—and they would probably be right. Within every modern marketing organization, evaluations of many different kinds *are* constantly being made. It is important to recognize, however, that not every marketing evaluation is a marketing audit. Neither, except very rarely, does the sum of all the evaluations currently being made equal a marketing audit.

Some Distinguishing Characteristics

There are a number of reasons for asserting that current appraisals do not, either singly or as a group, constitute a marketing audit. The principal reason, however, is that they are far too limited in scope. Executives review and appraise the effectiveness of the field sales force, the advertising program, the company's product mix, and the like, but they evaluate each of these elements at different times, and in no planned or coherent pattern. They do not, within a specified interval, examine each and every facet of the *total* operation. There is no integrated, coordinated, comprehensive appraisal encompassing all marketing activities and executed systematically in accord with a planned program and schedule. Yet the principal characteristic of the marketing audit is that it *is* such a systematic and comprehensive survey and evaluation of the total marketing operation—a programed appraisal of *all* of the activities included within the marketing function.

Current appraisals are much more limited than the marketing audit in another respect. They are, in general, confined to the review and evaluation of performance, methods and procedures, and personnel, concentrating on the manpower and tactics used and the results achieved within a given framework of objectives and policies. Rarely is the framework itself subjected to systematic and critical analysis and appraisal.

Now a marketing audit is, to be sure, an appraisal of performance and tactics—of methods, procedures, personnel, and organization. Beyond this, however, it is a great deal more. In fact, its principal focus is on those elements of the marketing function which are almost never subjected to careful, regular, and orderly scrutiny but which are of fundamental importance because they comprise the base from which methods, procedures, and organization are derived. In short, the marketing audit is primarily a re-examination and evaluation of marketing objectives and policies—an appraisal not only of a company's marketing program but also of the framework which has given the program its direction, structure, and shape.

The preoccupation of the marketing audit with objectives and policies is one of its most salient and distinguishing characteristics, for it implies that, unlike other appraisals, the audit is a searching inquiry into the character and validity of the fundamental premises underlying a company's marketing operations. It is a review and evaluation of the assumptions, conceptions, and expectations that guide executives in their planning and operating decisions. It is a planned effort to test and assess executive beliefs and opinions about the character of the market, the company's position in the market, the company's objectives and capabilities, and the effectiveness of the various policies, methods, personnel, and organizational structures which are or might be employed.

As Wroe Alderson of Alderson Associates, Inc. has observed:

> *The marketing executive may be visualized as operating on the basis of a sort of map. There are boundaries or limits marking off the class of customers he is trying to reach or the trade channels through which he is willing to sell. There are routes over which he can move in attaining his objectives which experience or investigation has indicated are better than other routes. This map may have to be brought up to date by a validation or a revision of operating assumptions. . . .[1]*

In this context, the marketing audit becomes essentially an effort to step back and take a penetrating look at the basic ideas which are the ultimate source of a company's marketing programs. It is an attempt explicitly to define and verify these ideas about the company, the market, and methods of reaching the market by testing them against current and accurate information.

The Basic Purposes

The marketing audit may thus be defined as a *systematic, critical, and impartial review and appraisal of the total marketing operation: of the basic objectives and policies of the operation and the assumptions which underlie them as well as of the methods, procedures, personnel, and organization employed to implement the policies and achieve the objectives.* This definition, however, is not complete. It conveys no sense of the purpose of the audit, as it should, for it is important to understand that the audit is a prognostic as well as a diagnostic tool—a search for opportunity as well as for malfunction.

Too many executives take a static view of appraisals. In examining the marketing operation or one of its component activities, they are concerned almost exclusively with the here and now. They are intent on identifying *existing* problems or weaknesses and discovering their causes, so that appropriate remedies can be applied. A marketing audit, too, aims at locating existing weaknesses, at pinpointing current problems and their sources. Like other types of evaluations, therefore, the audit too is a diagnostic tool. But diagnosis is not the only, or even the most important, purpose of the marketing audit. It is concerned as much with the future as with the present. It is a search not only for weaknesses that clearly exist but also for those that may arise. It is aimed at identifying current problems and determining their causes, but at the same time it probes for

---

[1] Wroe Alderson, *Marketing Behavior and Executive Action* (Homewood, Ill.: Richard D. Irwin, Inc., 1957), p. 419.

incipient problems—those just beginning or likely to emerge. This is what we mean when we say that the marketing audit is a prognostic as well as a diagnostic tool.

Executives tend also to conceive of audits almost exclusively as means for locating and defining problems. The identification of problems and possible remedies is, however, only one of the purposes of the marketing audit. The audit is, in addition, concerned with identifying the particular strengths of the marketing operation. It is a search for opportunities, existing and potential, to apply the factors which create strength in one marketing activity to others. And it is a search for opportunities in the market which had previously been overlooked or which have only recently emerged.

Thus, the marketing audit has several purposes. It is intended to reveal potential as well as existing strengths and weaknesses in a company's marketing operation, and it is intended also to bring into sharp focus possibilities for capitalizing on the strengths and eliminating the weaknesses. In consequence, the marketing audit is a tool that can be of tremendous value not only to the less successful, crisis-ridden company but also to the highly successful and profitable industry leader. No marketing operation is ever so good that it cannot be improved. Even the best can be made better. In fact, even the best *must* be made better, for few if any marketing operations can remain successful over the years by maintaining the status quo. Continued success requires continual adaptation to a constantly changing environment. It requires, therefore, continual scrutiny of the environment and of the firm's relationship to the environment, with the aim of spotting the cues which indicate both a need for modifying the firm's marketing program and the direction such modification should take. It requires an unremitting search for emerging opportunities that can and must be exploited if the marketing operation is to remain highly successful. The marketing audit, therefore, is not only a prescription for the sick firm but also preventive medicine for the currently healthy and successful firm.

A Total View

To summarize, then, the most prominent characteristics and most important purposes of the marketing audit are these:

It is a carefully programed appraisal of the total marketing operation.

It is centered on an evaluation of objectives and policies and of the assumptions which underlie them.

Its aim is prognosis as well as diagnosis.

It is a search for opportunities and means for exploiting them as well as for weaknesses and means for their elimination.

It is the practice of preventive as well as curative marketing medicine.

WHY AUDIT—AND WHEN?

Every marketing executive recognizes that he operates in a highly fluid environment. He is fully aware that unceasing change is the most salient characteristic of his company's marketing situation. He knows that there is constant and continuous—sometimes even abrupt and dramatic—change in the size, composition, and geographic distribution of the population; in the size and distribution of incomes; in tastes, preferences, and habits; and in technology. He has, in short, absorbed the truth that has so often escaped other executives: The modern market is highly dynamic.

Keeping Abreast of the Times

Unfortunately, recognition of the dynamic quality of the market has not led marketing executives to recognition of all its implications. Many executives have not yet fully realized that continual flux in the market signifies continual alteration of the relationship of a company to its market and of the competitive relationships between companies, and that such constant and widespread change in the environment makes some facet of almost every existing marketing operation obsolete. As Arthur Felton has described the situation in the *Harvard Business Review:*

> There is probably no marketing plan in industry today that is not out of date. . . . The reason is that there are so many constantly changing factors in any company's marketing situation that it is practically impossible to keep revising a plan so rapidly and so accurately that there is no lag in it. The factors that keep a plan dated are not only those of the "changing American market" which Fortune and other publications have discussed—suburbia, the new middle class, the Negro market, and so forth. The dating factors have also to do with changing selling problems growing out of the major upheavals—shifts in consumer psychology that necessitate different kinds of advertising and packaging, trends in distribution that affect the company's relations with wholesalers and jobbers, changes in the "customer mix" that affect the efficiency of the sales organization, and so on.[2]

The significance of market dynamism, then, is that a firm's marketing operation tends continually to fall out of phase with current conditions and incipient trends. Elements of every marketing program are always losing their effectiveness. Methods, procedures, and organizational structures rapidly become outmoded, and objectives and policies become inappropriate as the validity of the assumptions on which they are based is destroyed. The continual change in a company's marketing situation means, in fact, that no marketing program is ever completely and precisely adapted to the environment in which it is executed; indeed, it means that every program becomes ever more poorly adapted with the passage of time. This is evidenced by the fact that, almost from the moment a marketing program takes effect, a drift away from the program commences which accelerates as time goes by. This drift arises from the efforts of managers and their subordinates to cope with the many specific problems engendered by the lack of adjustment between the marketing program and the changing marketing environment. It is symptomatic of the inability to be always in perfect tune with the times. It is also dan-

---

2 Arthur P. Felton, "Conditions of Marketing Leadership," *Harvard Business Review,* March–April, 1956, p. 119.

gerous if not arrested, for the drift implies that the planned marketing operation is degenerating into a patchwork of opportunistic and expedient actions. It implies that confusion and even chaos increasingly supplant the originally integrated and coherent plan for the application of marketing effort. In time, therefore, unless the marketing operation is revamped —unless objectives, policies, methods, procedures, personnel, and organization are once again combined in a carefully articulated plan which is better adapted to the company's current marketing situation—the drift and its accompanying confusion will almost certainly precipitate a company crisis.

Thus, the dynamic quality of the market implies a need for constant vigilance on the part of marketing executives. It compels recognition of the need for awareness of the nature of the changes taking place within and without the firm, and of the directions in which the marketing organization and program can be and must be modified in order to adapt to these changes. It emphasizes the need for improvement-consciousness, and thus for a continual search for new cost-reduction possibilities and new sales opportunities. In other words, the rapid pace of change in our modes of living and the continually accelerating technological revolution in industry make it imperative that the marketing executive appraise and reappraise every element of his operations and organization. Moreover, if the executive wants the best results from these appraisals he must *plan* them, for only a systematic, careful, and orderly program of appraisal can assure that no activity or element of the marketing operation is neglected or subjected to only the most cursory examination. It follows, therefore, that the marketing audit is a necessary and important tool which can provide a marketing manager with the knowledge required to keep his operations abreast of the times and thus in a strong competitive position.

Auditing under Crisis Conditions

Many executives who recognize the effectiveness of a marketing audit seem to believe that it is needed primarily by companies which are problem-ridden and which face a deteriorating market and profit position. They regard the audit as an effective remedy for a marketing operation which is in critical condition. Such a conception of the audit is entirely erroneous, however, for, as we have already noted, the audit is preventive as well as curative marketing medicine. Nevertheless, this conception of the audit is so widespread that it may be worthwhile to give some reasons for believing that it is wrong.

Executives who conceive of the marketing audit as being unnecessary for a smoothly functioning, highly successful marketing operation have really failed to understand fully its nature and purposes. They fail to see, therefore, that appraisals made in an atmosphere of crisis are unlikely to have the character of a marketing audit. This is true for two reasons:

1. In a crisis situation there exists a compulsion to do something quickly which will resuscitate the marketing operation before it reaches a point of no return. Under crisis conditions, therefore, the aim of an appraisal must be to find an

appropriate stimulant rather than a basic therapy. As a result, such an appraisal inevitably assumes the nature of a rapid scanning rather than a penetrating look at the marketing operation; and even this scanning is limited to those facets of the operation which experience and intuition indicate are most likely both to require attention and to respond quickly to treatment.

2. Since a crisis in a company's marketing operation often means that the company is experiencing financial difficulty, any appraisal undertaken at such a time will almost surely be allotted far less money than is required to do the job properly.

Thus, both for financial reasons and because of the need for haste, an appraisal under crisis conditions is likely to be far more superficial, far more limted in both scope and depth, than a true marketing audit.

Auditing the Successful Operation

The smoothly running and successful marketing operation can, therefore, be more effectively audited than a sick operation. More important, however, is the fact that it *needs* to be audited. Success tends to foster complacency, laxity, and carelessness. It permits tradition and habit to become the dominant shapers of marketing programs. It allows dry rot and excessive costs to develop and spread. It leads some marketing executives to become so deeply involved with existing policies and methods that they never bother to examine the possibility of performing the marketing task in other ways—ways which, although once inappropriate, may now be more closely attuned to the company's needs. Yet none of these well-known concomitants of success may be immediately apparent. A successful operation can move along well, for a time at least, propelled by the momentum which has been generated in the past. The growing waste of marketing effort and the increasing frequency of failures to pioneer innovations are not reflected at once in shrinking profits and market share. Their effect is delayed, for marketing wastes and failures erode rather than shatter the company's market position. Sooner or later, however, the erosion of market position must find expression in reduced volume and profits—and, when it does, the "healthy" marketing operation appears suddenly to have contracted a very severe illness.

The dangers of success clearly suggest that in marketing as in home maintenance the time to fix the roof is when the sun is shining. They point clearly to the need for continual, systematic, critical, and objective appraisal of even the most successful marketing operation *while it is successful*. The negligence and waste, the complacency and blind obedience to tradition and habit which breed so easily in the culture of success, can become extremely noxious viruses if permitted to develop unchecked. They can appear anywhere in a marketing organization, and they can in time sap the strength of the most vigorous marketing operation. The maintenance of health and vigor in the operation requires, therefore, that such factors be identified and eliminated just as soon as they appear. The marketing audit serves this end. It is, consequently, of considerable importance to the successful marketing organization, for it constitutes a kind of insurance against subversion by success.

The dynamism of the market and the awareness that continued success may have undesirable by-products point to a general need for marketing audits. They strongly suggest that every marketing operation can be improved through a systematic and comprehensive program of evaluation. Such a program of evaluation is not likely, however, to be executed without difficulty. It may be helpful, therefore, to indicate the nature of some of the more important difficulties that are likely to be encountered.

Some of the problems that will arise as an executive seeks to inaugurate and execute a marketing audit are of such moment that they have been treated more fully than is possible here by other contributors to this volume. The problem of defining appropriate standards or criteria for each marketing activity and each element of each activity which are valid and operational measures of effectiveness is an example. Other problems, such as that of obtaining the funds needed to pay for a full-scale audit, are so obvious that they require little more than mention. In addition to these problems, however, there are three others which merit attention. These involve: (1) the selection of auditors; (2) the scheduling of the audit; and (3) the impact of the audit on marketing personnel.

Selecting the Auditors

No audit can be better than the people who make it. Consequently, no audit will yield the benefits that it is possible to obtain unless it is made by the right kind of people. As is implied by the definition of the audit, such people must be not only critical and impartial but also knowledgeable and creative. They must not be so involved with or "married" to existing policies and procedures that they cannot really be critical and objective in their assessments. In addition, they must possess the experience, know-how, and creative imagination needed to recognize problems and opportunities that are just beginning to appear on the horizon of the company's marketing situation and to define feasible courses of action for solving the problems and exploiting the opportunities. Finding enough such people to staff the audit can be a tall order. Few companies have an abundance of men with these characteristics. The quality of the audit is, nevertheless, determined largely by the extent to which the auditors possess these characteristics, and successful solution of the staffing problem is, therefore, of singular importance.

Scheduling the Audit

Since the marketing audit is an evaluation of the total marketing operation, it cannot be properly executed in a matter of days or weeks; it must be a relatively long-term project. And, as in any long-term project, there is always the danger that distractions may intervene to delay execution or that interest in the audit may be dissipated, with the result that the audit drags on and on. If the audit is permitted to drag on, however, conditions within and without the firm may change to such a degree that the findings when reported describe the marketing situation as it *was* rather than as it *is*. Any modification of the marketing operation on the basis of such findings could, of course, impair rather than improve the operation. Clearly then, the audit, if it is to yield accurate information about the company's current marketing situation, must be executed in accord with an established timetable. Preventing the many deviations from the timetable which can easily be rationalized is a central problem of any marketing audit.

Impact upon Marketing Personnel

The success of a marketing audit requires the full cooperation of all marketing personnel, from the chief executive and department heads to the salesmen in the field. The evaluation of an activity for which one is responsible, however, is often regarded by those carrying on the activity as a personal evaluation. These people often perceive in the audit a threat to their status and aspirations, and they therefore tend to resist it. They do not necessarily refuse to cooperate, but they may attempt to sabotage the audit wherever they feel it is possible to do so with impunity. Their resistance may make it extremely difficult—if not, in fact, impossible—to obtain accurate information. Moreover, the feeling that they are being threatened may impair their moral and reduce their effectiveness on the job.

It is extremely important to be aware of these possible side-effects of the audit so that pains are taken to obviate them through precautionary measures. Every effort must be made to create a genuine appreciation of the fact that the audit is not a fault-finding expedition but a search for ideas and tools that will enable everyone to do a better job. Marketing personnel must be educated to the fact that the audit is a management tool used to "help us help you" and not a device for "getting" anybody. They must be convinced that the audit is a full-scale effort to provide everyone in the marketing organization with important information that could not possibly be obtained through normal channels and routines. Before inaugurating a marketing audit, therefore, the possibilities of resistance and lowered morale must be dealt with through an educational campaign within the marketing organization.

SALES, COST, AND PROFIT ANALYSIS

30

Sales Analysis

THAYER C. TAYLOR

Each morning, when president Marion Sadler arrives on the seventh floor of American Airlines' Manhattan headquarters at 633 Third Ave., he goes directly from the elevator to the "war room." There, several large-scale, wall-mounted charts and numerical tables give him a fast, comprehensive briefing on American's standing in the highly competitive air carrier business. One chart he studies intently capsules passenger and air freight volume for the previous day, the current month, and the year to date—all compared with forecast goals. Others show on-time record, cancelled flights, and load factors. A glass-topped table, running halfway down the middle of the room, is piled with back-up statistical material. American's fortunes and misfortunes are charted right up to the previous day. Overnight, the company's battery of computers ingest, process, and update a stream of data from all over the airline's far-flung network.

What Sadler sees each morning before heading for his office is a system-wide sales analysis. Concurrently, however, the electronic marvels are churning out more detailed sales analyses for other levels of marketing management. Thus, Marshall D. Kochman, vice-president—freight, can tell you soon after the start of his working day which salesmen in Boston are behind quota, that a sudden spurt in shipments of transistorized TV sets from San Francisco to Cincinnati put that run 20% ahead of forecast, and how the volume of electronic parts out of Dallas is slackening. With

 Reprinted with permission from *Sales Management*, March 4, 1966, pp. 49–56.

this fresh information in hand, management can act fast while the facts are still fresh. The Boston sales manager is asked whether the lagging salesmen are having personal problems or have been given territories too large for them; San Francisco is queried as to whether the TV business is a one-short deal or the start of a new type of business; Dallas is asked what other industries in the area can take up the slack.

For Sadler and Kochman, as well as their counterparts in a raft of other companies, the computer is taking sales analysis away from the laborious study of musty records and shaping it into an efficient, responsive marketing tool. For the Sadlers, the electronic wizard updates what top management must know about the over-all state of the business; for the Kochmans, it fleshes out the skeletal running checks with in-depth details that point to opportunities and troubles ahead. For both men, it dramatically speeds up the time-cycle of sales analysis so that exploitative or corrective action is possible well before the opportunities have slipped away.

LOOKING BENEATH THE SURFACE

Profitable sales are the alpha and omega of a company's marketing strategy, and as volume grows and product lines expand, the need for something more detailed than a summary figure intensifies. Company-wide totals take on an iceberg-like deceptivity—what isn't shown may be more important than what is. A seemingly healthy situation of company sales 10% ahead of last year's becomes just the opposite when more intensive digging shows that the most profitable product group is actually down 10%.

As a performance check, sales analysis is carried out on a multitude of levels—by product, territory, salesman, time period, customer, market, class of trade, and so on; and for a variety of purposes—such as detecting trends, keeping abreast of changing relationships between company and customer and company and competitors, spotting opportunities for new products, uncovering areas of possible cost reductions.

Each management level has its own sales analysis needs. For example, says Alan Gepfert, McKinsey & Co. consultant, "Top management uses sales analysis for investment and deployment of funds—things like advertising budgets and size of the sales force. At the lower level, individual heads of the sales organization are mainly concerned with finding the differences between performances of salesmen by territories, compensation and incentives, and with detailed planning on how the sales force is to be used next year."

A National Industrial Conference Board report, "Sales Analysis," notes that the sales manager is helped three ways: (1) He can seek out the gaps between actual and planned performance and take counteraction, such as improving account servicing, concentrating the sales force on certain products, or counseling those men who are falling behind; (2) If it's apparent that despite such steps, goals won't be met, he can adjust his sales plans and supporting tactics, and (3) He can determine salary increases, bonuses, and staff promotions. The salesman himself looks to sales analysis for clues on how to improve his own selling efforts.

ENTER THE COMPUTER

Both the changing nature of sales analysis and the capabilities of the computer itself have made the mechanized brains a powerful tool in this area of marketing. With competitive marketing increasing, product life cycles shortening, and business conditions changing rapidly—and a concomitant change in the man in sales—management problems have become more complex, the pressure for faster decision-making more intense. Responding to this, sales analysis becomes more penetrating, more reactive to shifting trends. The computer's ability to perform lightning calculations on vast masses of data and to sift the meaningful from the useless becomes essential. And that computers are broadly used is indicated by a recent American Management Association study, "Managing With EDP," by M. Valliant Higginson. When 288 companies were asked how they are using computer information, the two most frequent responses were "measuring performance," cited by 236, and "evaluating progress," 231. Even more startling, when it came to applications, "sales analysis" was cited by 235 companies, topped only by "payroll," listed by 247. In fact, "sales analysis" was mentioned more frequently than "billing and invoicing" and "general accounting," long considered to be the most widespread computer applications.

The electronic wizard's prodigious speed in processing data is an obvious asset in sales analysis. Typical is the account given by Paul S. O'Brien, manager of electronic data processing, U.S. Rubber Co., at a recent meeting of the Chemical Marketing Research Association: "[Before EDP] it was normal for us to furnish our chemical division marketing people historical statistics on sales of any given month by the 20th to the 25th of the subsequent month. We have closed this time-cycle to once a week. Through the combination of computer speed and our communications network, we now produce sales reports every Monday morning for marketing management, by commodity line (involving 4,000–5,000 active products) and by district. These reports bring the manager up to date through the previous Friday on all of U.S. Rubber's sales activities.

"This puts him right on top of current activities of each salesman. A secondary benefit: It is not necessary for the salesman, district office manager, or commodity manager to maintain the kind of book records or historical knowledge they previously kept to perform their normal functions of forecasting. We now let the computer do it for them."

Besides giving management faster, more complete performance checks, the computer makes sales analysis a more effective input for planning ahead. David Savidge, technical assistant to the vice-president for marketing, Univac Division of Sperry Rand Corp., stresses that "Sales analysis is the foundation of the sales forecast. The computer makes the future and present more tightly linked. It makes the sales analysis more reactive —that is, by spotting trends that differ from the forecast, the analysis reacts more quickly to what's going on. You no longer have to wait for the present to become past history to learn from its lessons; you're on to your mistakes much faster."

Obviously, this is especially true for those increasing numbers of companies who, in addition to the annual look-ahead, now forecast by the month, week and even by the day. A case in point is Reliance Electric & Engineering Co., maker of such electrical and electronic products as AC/DC and gear motors, variable speed drives, and engineered systems. In what is a continuous accounting process, each booking that comes in is fed into a Control Data 3100 computer, where the information is classified according to type of product and dollar value. Each month, a print-out of the stored data allows for an analysis of the six major product groups, plus the three subdivisions in each category, which is then matched against the forecasted product mix. This enables management to adjust future production runs at its seven manufacturing plants, if need be, as well as show the marketing department if present profit objectives for each product group are being met. This is especially important because management wants to be sure that the company is retaining its share of the more profitable product business as an offset to the less profitable lines.

THE BIG LOOK

Sales analysis is being given much broader scope by the computer's dexterity in tracing hard-to-see relationships between complex data. V. J. Bannan, manager of the systems application development at Radio Corp. of America, says that "you can now take a total approach to sales analysis by analyzing a region's sales to find a correlation between monthly business and such standardized measures as population or value added by manufacturing. Application of these factors makes comparisons of sales between regions more 'honest' and more meaningful. When sales are 'weighted' in this way, you can respond with facts when a regional manager tries to explain away low sales as owing to a lack of potential."

This kind of market index approach is being tried out by L. C. Forbes Co., a big distributor of pipe and steel products. Beginning with its Atlanta region, the company will make a complete breakdown of the four-digit SIC (Standard Industrial Classification) industries served by each of the three district offices to find out where the sales go. Inputs for the computerized index will go beyond such benchmarks as population and manufacturing employment, says Milton Porter, executive vice-president, and will focus on more pertinent indicators, such as miles of pipeline in the area or number of gas meters installed.

"The index," Porter says, "will enable us to make more effective comparisons between territories and to analyze performance against potential. It will also help evaluate expansion into new districts. State A may look pretty good against State B on the surface, but when you apply the index factors you learn that State B has a much bigger potential and will be more profitable for the long haul."

The use of indexes and the like in sales analysis points up another of the computer's contributions: It encourages the user to go in for more experimentation. This is something that's not so easily pulled off with the analyst's traditional working tools, the slide rule and the desk-top calculating machine. In this respect, statistical techniques that lend themselves to computer programming are used to "clean up" raw data as well as pinpoint the sensitive linkages between sales and the external factors that are a part of sales. The NICB report cited earlier notes that computerized sales analysis at Sun Oil includes: (1) A seasonal adjustment program, which transforms raw data into adjusted totals and provides projected adjustment factors as required; (2) A regression analysis program, which estimates the underlying trend of company and industry sales, validates the trend estimate statistically, and provides an empirical basis for trend projection, and (3) a trend-cycle analysis program, which identifies the underlying trend and cyclical movement by seasonal elements and by smoothing random occurrences in reported sales data. The main purpose of these analyses, NICB observes, "is to help management keep abreast of movements in company sales in the context of the economic and competitive climate in which the sales are made."

FOCUS ON PROFITS

The nimble mathematical machines also encourage experimentation in the reshuffling of standard accounting figures for more meaningful insights into the vital cost and profit aspects of sales. McKinsey's Alan Gepfert points to the growing use of profitability accounting, which is nursed along by the computer's ability to recast, in different forms or structures, the detailed cost and revenue data behind the annual financial report. Here, the focus is put on profit contribution by delineating those variable cost factors on which management can take action. An oversimplified approach would find data segregated by such categories as net revenue, variable cost of production, variable cost of distribution (warehouse and shipping), selling and advertising expenses. The breakout can be done on the basis of individual accounts in a given area, individual products (which requires a bigger geographical area), or class of trade (wholesale druggists, for example).

A typical profitability accounting breakout, based on a big customer, say, would proceed thus: From net revenue you deduct laid-down product costs (which include such variable production items as material and direct labor plus in-transit inventory carrying cost) and laid-down branch freight costs. The resulting figure is profit contribution over the laid-down costs. From this you further deduct distribution costs (warehousing) and customer freight. This gives you revenue contribution over delivered costs which, Gepfert says, "is probably the most significant figure because it shows the account's contribution to the remaining variable costs (primarily in sales and distribution services, selling expense, and marketing). The final measure of customer merit should be this figure adjusted for other variables, especially selling costs." With this kind of information,

Gepfert believes, it's easier to get answers to such puzzlers as: Should I stick with small customers, raise my minimum order level, or shift from direct selling to wholesalers?

Profitability studies at Reliance Electric & Engineering go hand-in-hand with sales analysis. Profit objectives for each of six major product groups are based on expected divisional costs (materials, labor, direct line management) which are applied to general and administrative overhead factors (including sales and promotion outlays). The bookings that go into the computer continuously are supplemented by a running summary of division costs according to the major product groups. Each month, as the computer calculates profits to date, this figure is compared with objectives.

"If a product's profit is down," says R. A. Geuder, Reliance marketing vice-president, "we must analyze whether costs are rising or income is falling. If the price of copper is rising, say, we can't do anything about it. So we ask for an engineering redesign which would cut down on the amount of that metal. If less income is the culprit, we have to analyze why and explore for positive steps."

LOOKING AHEAD

Impressive as the advances have been to date, the mind boggles at some of the prospects held our for future sales analysis. Charles L. Keenoy, vice-president—marketing of National Cash Register, draws a tantalizing picture of the day of "instant sales analysis." Here, all consumer goods will be tagged by the manufacturer with a code indicating the product's size, style, color, price, and so on. When Mrs. John Doe buys a shirt for her husband, the checkout clerk rings up the product's code number along with the sale, and at the same time adds a store code showing location of the outlet, type of neighborhood it's in, whether the product was advertised on TV or in *Life* magazine that week, and so on. A communications network flashes the data from the cash register to the manufacturer's computer center, which immediately updates its memory bank. Thus, the shirtmaker knows by the minute where he stands on sales, stocks, what sizes are selling best, whether an ad is pulling customers. Keenoy says the hardware for such a setup is available today, but costs remain an obstacle.

Possibilities of this kind promise a new dimension for sales analysis. Rather than providing a look at the past, sales analysis will be telling you what action to take today and tomorrow. Such prospects are heady, but there are some who recoil before them. As computer power grows, and users become more sophisticated in reducing everything you can think of to numerical symbols, critics point out, there's a danger of management succumbing to a "tyranny of numbers." But such critics miss the point that the numbers are meaningless until marketing people bring their human judgment and evaluation to them. And marketers will have more time for creative evaluation and planning because the computer will remove more and more of the dronelike chores in management's never-ending quest to make "facts from figures."

31

Marketing Costs
and Their Control

JOHN HUDIG

There has been a major shift and departure from the traditional concept of sales to the concept of marketing. In principle, the sales function is concerned with moving merchandise through conventional channels of distribution to the market place; marketing has undertaken the task of determining what goods are needed for the market, their selling prices, and when and under what conditions the goods are to be delivered.

Marketing is as much concerned with costs, profits and returns on investment as with sales alone. Sales is concerned with volume; marketing is deeply concerned with profits. On the basis of total industry performance, profit margins have gone down from six per cent of sales a few years ago to a present level of a little over three per cent of sales. Three cents on the dollar is not much to work on. The companies that are going to survive present and future economic and competitive pressures must sharpen all the tools at their disposal and exploit the full potential of cost-saving actions. In the plant, we frequently fight for pennies or even fractions of pennies. The cost of marketing still represents an average of somewhat over 50 per cent of the total price the consumer pays. Many opportunities for cost savings have hardly been scratched. For instance, it is a common error to base controls and comparisons of expenditure effectiveness on historical records and reports. Instead, controls must be based on goals and objectives and not on records of past error.

 Reprinted with permission from *Financial Executive*, July, 1963, pp. 16–20.

Too many managements are still confused about strategies and tactics. Strategy is developed to win a war; tactics to win a battle. Managements put out brush fires and concern themselves with tactics, but too frequently do not take time out to develop strategies, goals and objectives based on systematic, critical and objective appraisal of all the factors that influence their business. Many wars have been lost and many businesses have failed because the development of adequate strategy was overlooked.

Another common error is that we just *ex*pect to reach our goals. Too frequently, we fail to recognize that the success of our corporate programs relates directly to what is *in*spected, not *ex*pected. Controllers have too frequently failed to provide leadership in:

1. Insisting on judicious planning.
2. Cajoling managers to set realistic targets and objectives, both short-range and long-range.
3. Devising adequate and systematic bench marks, controls and systems to monitor progress or failure.
4. Reporting attainment or failure when they find out about it.

A lot of lip service is given to "training," "management development" and other terms that have the ring of a modern and dynamic business climate. Nevertheless, the odds are more than ten to one that managements of companies in which these words are used the most, do not know with certainty in which areas they are relatively strong or weak. Consequently, they cannot pinpoint the areas in which training and strengthening are the most needed. Much of the marketing action takes place far from the plant and office, where conjecture, hope and wishful thinking can have an even more damaging effect than they can in corporate functions closer to home base.

MONITOR THE FIELD ACTIVITIES FOR PROFIT LEAKS

One of the principal reasons so many financial executives know so little about marketing effectiveness and control of marketing activities is that they are not spending enough time in the field. Guidance and surveillance of the field effort are not the sole responsibility of the marketing people. The chairman of the board, the president, the treasurer, the controller, the chief engineer, and other nonmarketing men should all spend some time in the field. After all, these executives nearly always spend at least some time in the manufacturing plant, and the "plant" of the marketing man is the field.

Few marketing men have the education, experience or inclination to initiate and administer a systematic profit program. This is where the financial executive should come in. He can bring his experience to bear on profit planning and help marketing men establish long-range and short-range objectives, ground rules for control and inspection, and the means to monitor progress and isolate weak points.

We recently did some work for a company whose direct salesmen cost increased over the past four years from four per cent of sales to seven per cent of sales. This was an increase in cost of 75 per cent; however, it was not offset by either an increase in profits or in sales.

Accountants can diagnose the situation quickly. The trade literature has been full of what we commonly call "profit anemia," "the profit squeeze," or "profit erosion": sales remain essentially stagnant while costs increase. Much of the discussion in trade journals about the profit squeeze points to alibiing and lack of dynamic innovation on the part of management. Management has quite a number of profit and sales increase opportunities in its arsenal.

IDENTIFY PROFITABLE ORDERS

For the purpose of this discussion, we are interested in new profit opportunities in the area of marketing. It is here that accountants should undertake much more leadership than they have in the past.

Not so long ago the president, the treasurer, the vice president of sales and the controller of a company met. Two big orders were pending. Word came that a $100,000 order was booked, and later that a $50,000 order was booked. The president and the vice president of sales were quite pleased, but kidded the man who booked the $50,000 order that he had not sold a really good order as the other salesman had. Nobody present was aware that the smaller order was three times as profitable as the very large order.

On another day the same company accepted 150 orders averaging $100 each, at a gross margin of 25 per cent, but rejected a $1 million order with a gross margin of one per cent. The cost of handle paperwork, packing and processing in the warehouse for the small orders was high, and subsequent analysis showed that the small orders represented in the aggregate a loss. The order for $1 million at one per cent gross margin—or $10,000—required only the writing of one order and one invoice and would have been highly profitable. This may appear obvious to many, but there are relatively few companies that really know which of their orders are profitable.

As another example, a manufacturer had 13 regional distribution centers. Analysis of customer needs, transportation, administrative requirements, inventory needs, inventory turnover frequencies and distribution costs helped to bring about a very different plan of distribution. Of the original 13 regional installations, each with an inventory of from 20,000 to 30,000 items and large administrative staffs, only five were retained. In addition, the planning provided for 26 districts, each located in centers of consumer potential and each carried an inventory of from 4,000 to 5,000 much-used items. Under the new plan, regional locations were selected so that 95 per cent of all orders could be delivered within 24 hours.

The advantages of this system of distribution were several:

1. Total inventory carried was smaller, thus increasing turnover.
2. The total number of administrative personnel was substantially reduced.

3. The number of back orders was also substantially reduced.
4. The number of consumer exposure points was doubled under the plan.

PROFIT AS A LEADING INDICATOR OF SALES

You have probably heard or read about the concept of product life cycles. Figure 1 shows the importance of the impact of product life cycles on profit and sales. The nature of the product has, of course, a lot to do with the length and the degree of incline and decline of product life cycles. For instance, basic materials such as chemicals and alloys generally have very long cycles. Machine tools and fasteners have much longer cycles than, say, women's fashions.

FIGURE 1: PRODUCT LIFE CYCLES

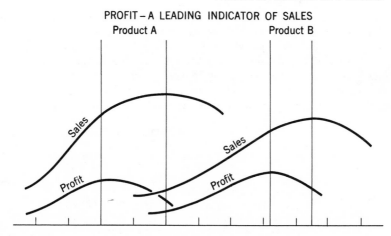

PROFIT – A LEADING INDICATOR OF SALES
Product A   Product B

A major factor governing the length and the incline of profit and sales life cycles is competition. When competition is severe and products are similar in quality and general customer appeal, price will invariably be the principal competitive weapon, and profit will be poor. The figure shows that as a successful new product is introduced, sales and profits rise relatively sharply. But, as the product matures, it becomes more difficult to maintain the rate of sales increase; selling and promotional costs tend to rise; and profits will level off and start to decline.

One very important phenomenon is that profits nearly always reach their peak before sales volume reaches its peak. Profits, therefore, are a leading indicator of sales. The time interval between profit and the sales peaks depends, of course, on many factors. But the point is that when the controller spots a leveling off or a dip in product profits, he should alert the marketing group and instruct them to analyze whether the cause is a matter of an economic trend or of product maturity. Once the cause of a trend is known, it is frequently possible to take action to counteract it. When sales decline, profits decline even faster.

The significance of these remarks is that the controller should have the machinery and the comprehension to spot product profit declines.

Apparently, few controllers are aware of the importance of their function as a watchdog over the well-being of their company's product lines.

MEASURE YOUR SELLING EFFECTIVENESS

As long as there are salesmen there will be substantial differences in their philosophies and approaches to selling. Effective salesmen are nearly always individualists who consider recognition, pride and self-respect more important than security. Salesmen are generally the most important link between customers and their companies. The effectiveness of their calls means the difference between orders and lack of orders. It therefore follows that increasing the effectiveness of salesmen will have an important bearing on sales and thereby on profits.

Figure 2 shows how seemingly justified differences in work habits can accumulate to a variance of 50 per cent in sales call effectiveness. To this variance should be added several intangibles. Salesmen who plan their calls normally make more calls than those who do not plan them. Salesmen who plan their route and the number of calls nearly always also plan the content of their calls. Of course, there are exception, but as a general rule, skill of salesmanship is directly related to ability to plan.

FIGURE 2: SALESMEN'S TIME UTILIZATION

	Salesman A	Salesman B
Average number of dealer calls per day	2	$2\frac{1}{2}$
Number of days on road per year	180	220
Number of dealer calls per year	360	550

It is difficult to make salesmen responsive to company profit objectives. However, those who work on an incentive compensation plan are very responsive to what can help them make more money. A good incentive compensation plan for salesmen, therefore, must reflect product profitability. By tying in corporate profit objectives to salesmen's compensation, the company makes money when the salesmen make money. This may seem like a reverse approach; nevertheless, it is easier to influence salesmen in terms of their own earnings than it is to instill in them the impersonal concept of corporate profitability objectives.

WEED OUT LOSS ACCOUNTS

There are two ways to approach the problem of small sales accounts, namely:

1. Devise methods to determine *accurately* the precise profits or losses for all sales accounts.
2. Devise *rule-of-thumb* estimates of sales account profit or loss contributions.

Most companies should face the fact that 50 per cent or more of their customers contribute in the strict sense to losses rather than profits; in

FIGURE 3: BREAK-EVEN SALES ACCOUNT

Annual's salesman cost (Earnings & travel)	$16,000
Cost per day on road (220 road days)	$ 73
Cost per sales call (Avg. Calls per day)	$ 18
Salesman's commission As % of sales	5%
Break-even sales volume	$ 2,500
(Calls per year on an account)	$\dfrac{7 \times 18 \times 100}{5}$

FIGURE 4: SALES ACCOUNT PROFITABILITY

	Sales Account A	Sales Account B
Annual sales volume	$1,600	$4,800
No. sales calls per year	6	8
Cost per call	$18	$18
Total call cost	$108	$144
Commission rate (incl. travel exp.)	5%	5%
Commission	$80	$240
Account profit—(loss)	$(28)	$96

fact, the average is frequently somewhat in excess of 75 per cent. Rough estimates are frequently good enough to discover the most conspicuous loss producers among the sales accounts. These should be resolved before a more complete and accurate system is developed. Figure 3 shows a rule-of-thumb method of estimating a break-even type of account. This simple method is more than most companies now use.

Figure 4 shows two accounts and a simple way to determine profit and loss contributions, predicated on the premise that salesman compensation is based on company profit objectives.

Many, if not most, salesmen live by a dual standard. Experience has shown that the average salesman spends part of his time—maybe 10 to 20 per cent—on highly remunerative business, and works the balance of his time at half pay or even less. Almost every salesman has what we like to call "old Joe" accounts. He has probably known his old Joes for many years; the old Joes always have a warm handshake and are nearly always able to think up a small order of sorts. I traveled some time ago with a key salesman who earned a gross income of about $35,000 per year. His cost per call amounted to approximately $35 and his commission amounted to five per cent. Consequently, his break-even sales volume per call amounted to $700. Even so, he introduced me to one of his old Joes on whom he had been calling for many years. This old Joe contributed about $1,500 per year in sales and about $75 per year in commissions. The salesman made 40 calls per year on old Joe at the cost of 40×$35 or $1,400.

His return was $75, and his loss on this single account was about $1,325 per year. In fact, if the old Joe account had represented an average type of account, that salesman's annual income would be not more than $5,000. He would have saved money if he had walked in once a week on old Joe, dropped a $25 bill on the table and said, "Sorry, Joe, I love you, but I am busy." Of course, these data are based on the assumption that salesmen have the opportunity to develop more profitable accounts and to spend their time more efficiently and effectively. This assumption is nearly always correct for companies that have developed 50 per cent or less of their available sales potentials.

ESTABLISH REGIONAL INDICES

In marketing, it is not always possible to measure with a scale of which we know the precise length. For instance, we may not know the exact size of the market, or be able to make a numerical estimate of competitive pressures. Nevertheless, it is frequently possible to compare. We can compare the performance of salesmen, or customers, in terms of profit contribution and sales. We can compare numbers and sizes of sale accounts and the working habits of the men who service them.

One company I have worked with had 12 large regional branches, but was unable to compare their sales potentials or to establish realistic manpower requirements. Nevertheless, there were factors that could be measured and compared. Known factors were population, buying power, gross margin contribution, sales, and operating expenses. We determined different weights for each of these factors in conference with the client. We then called average performance 100 per cent or par and established indices for each regional branch. Figure 5 shows the performance indices that resulted. A picture such as this is a lot simpler to absorb than the three or four spread sheets from which the data were developed.

Management was amazed, reappraised the assigned weights of the factors, found that they were fair and equitable and that the facts were as presented. The next step was to find out the whys of the high scores and low scores. When these were known, management decided on and offered the assistance necessary to upgrade the below-average performers. The interesting thing about this approach is that as branches are strengthened, the average performance moves up and the process of upgrading can start all over again.

LEARN TO PRICE FOR PROFIT

Up to this point we have discussed a few examples of areas in which profit improvement in marketing operations is frequently possible. The last area of potential profit improvement is the subject of pricing for profit. This is also the most difficult, the most complex, and most contro-

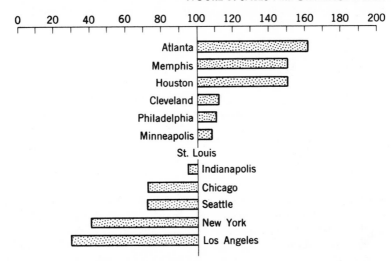

FIGURE 5: SALES PERFORMANCE INDEX

versial aspect of profit planning. In addition, it is the most difficult subject about which to be specific.

Most companies have or should have unique pricing policies. Producers of milk, cigarettes, and gasoline have pricing problems very different from manufacturers of products such as radios, fashion wear, machine tools or paint. When a lady needs a pair of stockings, or a man a pair of socks, the retail clerk can generally convince the customer to buy in multiples. Canned soups, beverages, etc., are frequently packaged and priced for multiple-unit sales. However, when a contractor needs ten "I" beams, chances are that he will not buy a dozen, even if offered a special price.

Take the case of a manufacturer who makes special high-speed, auto-mated assembly machines and had prices that were based on a formula. The salesmen birddogged possible applications for the machine, deter-mined specifications and requested quotations from their plant. The estimators and engineers prepared basic machine layouts and quotations on a cost-plus basis. Out of every seven quotations, one became an order. Much time and expense would have been saved, and, in many cases, higher prices could have been negotiated, if salesmen had made value analyses before asking for engineering layouts and cost estimates. When potential savings are $100,000 per year, it does not make too much differ-ence if the price of a machine is $30,000 or $40,000. However, if potential annual savings are only $10,000, the difference in machine costs is very important.

A five-tube radio is a five-tube radio. Nevertheless, five-tube radios are retailed anywhere between $12.95 and $34.95. More beautiful cabinets, the size of the loud-speaker, and the addition of other features make the difference. When merchandise appeals to us, we are frequently prepared to pay a premium price. But when we compare punch presses or refrigera-tors that are near carbon copies of each other, the matter of price will normally be the deciding factor. When our products are too similar to those manufactured by competitors, we leave ourselves wide open to price-fighting, we destroy our ability to research and develop new products, and we permit our profits to erode.

When pricing a new product, place a prototype model of the new product between comparable competitive items, compare the values from the user point of view and assign a tentative price. After the tentative price has been set it must be compared with factory costs to determine whether the margin will permit a reasonable profit. It is always amazing how frequently products are *under*priced.

A company which manufactures and markets shoes had been selling a popular pattern at $6.95 in the stores. Subsequently, the design and the reliability of the product was improved and the client was considering retailing the new shoes at his normal mark-up for $5.95. (His "normal" mark-up was close to a break-even price.) It was suggested that he offer the new shoe to the trade at the full price of $6.95 with possibly only a slightly higher trade discount as added buying inducement.

When selling cars and appliances, most retail salesmen would rather start talking about price than features, benefits and service. This becomes quite evident when one starts to haggle with suppliers. Many people do not haggle because they believe the price is too high, but because they know that many sales people will lower prices needlessly. On the other hand, some salesmen are adroit at changing the subject of price back to customer benefits and product values, and I am happy to report that this type of salesman is on the increase again.

The toughest part of product pricing concerns products that look alike and act alike. Gasoline is an example. Price was break out as soon as one dealer lowers the price by as little as one cent. Other service station operators get so mad they cut their prices two cents; and so on, nearly ad infinitum. The only one who benefits is the consumer, who did not pressure for a price concession and will not even increase his consumption. The moral of the story is that the fight for volume by cutting prices is frequently self-defeating because competition will follow the price-cutter.

When working with companies, one of my first acts is to take a hard look at products and product prices. In many cases, I can cull unprofitable items, or at least shift sales emphasis from such items to more profitable ones, and quite frequently can suggest price increases. In still other cases, I suggest adding inexpensive features to upgrade products to more salable and more profitable levels. And sometimes I suggest entirely new products. If companies continue to product the old to cater to their own convenience, instead of seeking innovation and improvement to cater to the needs of their customers, they are bound to lose money.

Let me cite another example. The manufacturer in question had 96 items in the product line. Of these 96, only 37 contributed in some degree to profits. More than 60 per cent of the product line contributed to losses rather than profits. It took many days to dig out this information, which should have been available as a matter of course. The controller of this company was more interested in balancing the figures in his journals than in the life and blood of his company.

Grasp the Whole Marketing Concept. Financial executives, in general, should acquire a better grasp of the types of decisions that marketing people have to make, and of the facts and other information needed to provide them with the background for making them. Only when financial executives have a good grasp of marketing problems can they be of any help to marketing people. Accounting is charged with determining profit; marketing with generating profits.

Financial executives can and should participate with more understanding in marketing areas, such as sales quotas, forecasting, product profitability, field sales controls, sales and marketing budgets, pricing, incentive compensation for salesmen, and monitoring marketing results.

There are many things in marketing that may seem strange to the accountant because they do not appear in the ledgers. Nevertheless, such criteria as these are just as important as those that do appear in the ledgers: The value of people; the value of ideas; the value of what is unique and different; the value of the intangible; the value of a market; the value of filling customer needs; and the value of timing.

The days are over—if ever there were such days—when salesmen just sell, accountants just account, and factories just produce. Corporate functions are interrelated, and all executives must have as their principal objective the desire to contribute to that last figure at the end of the right-hand page. And as a final word, let's compete by being creative, not by robbing our own till. Innovation on the part of all functions of a commercial enterprise is the antidote for profit anemia. When financial and marketing executives understand better what each can contribute toward improving marketing controls and marketing effectiveness, company profits are bound to benefit.

SELECTED BIBLIOGRAPHY
for
PART 5

"It'll Take the Fuzz off the Sales Pitch," *Grocery Manufacturer*. December, 1968, pp. 10–13.

GOODMAN, SAM R. *Techniques of Profitability Analysis*. (New York: John Wiley & Sons, Inc., 1970), pp. 28–44.

KOLTUN, ALLEN B. "The Profit Approach to Budgeting," *Management Services*. September–October, 1965, pp. 54–59.

McGANN, THOMAS J. "Cost Analysis—Finding Marketing Weaknesses," *Industrial Marketing*. March, 1959, pp. 54–57.

MYERS, JAMES H., and SAMLI, A. COSKUN. "Management Control of Marketing Research," *Journal of Marketing Research*. August, 1969, pp. 267–77.

STASCH, STANLEY F. "Systems Analysis for Controlling and Improving Marketing Performance," *Journal of Marketing*. April, 1969, pp. 12–19.

BROADENING
THE MARKETING IDEA

In this last part of the reader, a number of articles focus upon social, legal, and ethical issues in marketing. Pollay (pp. 400–13) discusses deceptive advertising from the viewpoint of consumer behavior. Goodman (pp. 414–30) describes the "deviant marketing system" at work in low-income areas. Under this system, low-income consumers frequently fail to benefit from the product and service offerings available to the more affluent consumer. The article by Crawford (pp. 431–42) reports reactions of research directors and line managers to ethical problems in marketing research.

In examining international marketing strategies, Keegan (pp. 443–50) identifies strategic marketing alternatives for multinational product planning. Matlin (pp. 451–56), in a highly creative and imaginative article, describes how he would use marketing methods to slow excessive population growth in India.

SOCIAL, LEGAL, AND ETHICAL
ISSUES IN MARKETING

32

Deceptive Advertising
and Consumer Behavior:
A Case for Legislative
and Judicial Reform

RICHARD W. POLLAY
University of Kansas

I. INTRODUCTION

The recent resurgence of interest in consumerism and consumer protection is of such magnitude that expansion of regulatory activities seems inevitable. Many foresee the creation of a post at the cabinet level for a Secretary of Consumer Affairs to co-ordinate all such activities. The exposures of independent investigators like Ralph Nader, coupled with a more sophisticated view of the marketplace environment that is faced by the poverty classes, are causing legislators and members of the executive branches of government to further increase their efforts to institute and reinforce programs designed to protect and assist the consumer. While the growth of these programs clearly provides an opportunity for necessary real accomplishments, it should also be recognized that such growth, particularly if rapid, can also lead to disorganization, confusion, and ill-formed legislation. Unlike the suggestions of many of the lobby groups resisting consumer legislation, it is not the contention here that progress should be retarded or that nothing should be done lest mistakes be made. Rather, it is suggested that, using our present state of knowledge in various areas, careful examination of current legislation and practices be undertaken in order that we may learn from our experience and thereby

Reprinted with permission from *Kansas Law Review,* University of Kansas, June, 1969, pp. 625–37.

improve the effectiveness of future activities. It is the purpose of this article to discuss deceptive advertising from the viewpoint of students of consumer behavior as a part of this endeavor.

Being the most visible of all marketing activities, advertising naturally invites attention. The size of the industry; its central role in today's economy; its crucial role in the mass media, our culture disseminators; and its general pervasiveness all dictate that advertising be one of the first areas considered in any attempt to deal in consumer protection. This is especially the case when one realizes the ability of a major advertiser by a single mispractice to cause a large amount of social cost. Given the historical roots of contemporary advertising in the promotion of patent medicines at the turn of the century and the continuing examples of questionable practices, some doubt can be attached to the idea that the advertising industry can effectively police itself. It seems appropriate, therefore, for advertising to be analyzed and for legislative and judicial standards to be set which control potential abuses while preserving the advertiser's rights to communicate to the public.

Writing in the area of deceptive advertising makes one sensitive to the complexities of communication and the ability of readers to misinterpret the content of any communication. To help avoid misperception of the intent of this article, a more explicit introduction may be required. This article will not discuss the economic role of advertising, with its effect on prices, sales, and mass production. Similarly, value contentions about advertising, such as advertising's vulgarity, creation of "false" values, and its molding of men's minds, will not be discussed. Because others have done so with competence,[1] a legal history or review also will not be included. What the article does attempt to do is to use knowledge of consumer behavior to shed light on the validity of criteria employed in the attempt to operationally define deceptive advertising and to suggest changes in procedures for identifying such advertising.

II. THE ATTEMPT TO DEFINE DECEPTION

An operational definition of deceptive advertising has been an elusive goal. While outlandishly fraudulent practices are easily recognized, the differences between flagrant misrepresentation and more typical advertising are often difficult to isolate. The techniques of the old snake-oil salesman with his pitch delivered off the back of a wagon and those of many of today's writers of advertising copy are extremely similar. Both carefully choose words to create impressions and expectations on the part of the consumer which are at least in part discrepant with the product's true characteristics. Both create an image of the product in the consumer's mind that is not totally substantiated by the product's true performance. The only major distinction is the subtlety of the techniques used, since today's copy writers avoid clearly false statements. They tend instead to use "those less obvious forms of falsehood which in casuistry and law are

---

[1] G. Alexander, *Honesty and Competition* (1967).

called *suppressio veri* and *suggestio falsi,* concealing a truth and hinting a lie, methods which certain types of advertising have carried to pitch of skill and success that leaves us breathless."[2]

Even without using these methods, a skilled writer can effectively create a total impression which is misleading by careful phrasing and presentation of statements which may be quite literally true when considered individually. This phenomenon, which is called a *Gestalt* effect, occurs commonly in the interpretation of many perceptual stimuli. The meaning a person attaches to a total package of stimuli is often something different from the simple cumulation of the meaning attached to the stimuli individually. This effect usually results from either the sequencing or the omission of some stimuli. In the advertising case, the reader fills in the missing phrase, reads between the lines, or completes the logical argument, adding something to what is literally stated and thereby creating his own deception (albeit with the help of the copy writer). Jurists have recognized that the problem of deceptive advertising does not have the simple solution of merely demanding that statements be literally true. The frustration that arises with recognition that the obvious criterion of "truth" is inapplicable becomes compounded with the pragmatic realization that "intent," the other intuitively acceptable criterion, is virtually impossible for a prosecutor to demonstrate.

Another difficulty arises from the unwillingness to make a seller completely honest. It has been deemed appropriate for a seller to engage in "puffing," an overly enthusiastic, perhaps exaggerated, and clearly biased presentation of his product. The unwillingness to curtail puffing, even when exaggerated, makes it difficult to set any criterion for detecting deception since puffing and deception are so similar from an observer's viewpoint. It is no easier for the advertiser who conscientiously wants to follow the spirit of the law. One commentator, writing for marketing men, has said:

> The principle of capacity or tendency to deceive faces the marketers of goods with a difficult test. . . . Puffing in itself is not illegal. A line has to be drawn somewhere between permissible puffing and that which is not. It boils down to a matter of how far the puffing or expression of opinion is from actual fact. This determination in itself requires personal judgment combined with reference to whatever established standards may be available.[3]

He might also have added that few established standards are available for most advertisers.

Business men and jurists are not alone in being unable to define deception. Consumers too have only vague and inconsistent ideas of what constitutes a deceptive advertisement. A study using three subject pools of students, housewives, and retailers found support for the hypothesis that there was low agreement within any group as to what constituted deceptive advertising.[4] Each subject evaluated ten printed ads as misleading or

[2] D. Masters, *The Intelligent Buyers' Guide to Sellers* (1965).

[3] M. Howard, *Legal Aspects of Marketing* (New York: McGraw-Hill, 1964).

[4] J. Kottman, "A Semantic Evaluation of Misleading Advertising," *Journal of Communications* (1964).

not. It was concluded that "while it is quite likely that persons are as opposed to misleading advertising as they are to sin, it is equally likely that they have vastly different notions as to what constitutes misleading advertising."[5]

In the search for criteria which would allow for the effective prosecution of cases of actual deception, two concepts have evolved. The validity and implication of both deserve discussion. The first is the concept of the "wayfaring fool," a portrayal of the characteristics of the consumer being protected from deception. The one overriding characteristic of the "wayfaring fool" is stupidity, but

> general stupidity is not the only attribute of the beneficiary of FTC policy. He also has a short attention span; he does not read all that is to be read   .   .   . has marginal eyesight, and is frightened by dunning letters when he has not paid his bills. Most of all he is thoroughly avaricious. Fortunately, while he is always around in substantial numbers, in his worst condition he does not represent the major portion of the consuming public.[6]

This, surprisingly, may be a reasonable portrayal of the behavior of a vast majority of consumers at some time or another. Even the most intelligent and thoughtful consumer may make a purchase, particularly if it involves small dollar amounts, without attention, analysis or consideration of the alternatives. This average consumer may even make a major decision such as the purchase of an automobile largely on faith, with little knowledge at least compared to what he might have and as the result of a particularly effective sales presentation, part of which he did not fully comprehend. Although the model used by the FTC is sometimes exaggerated, it is difficult to find major fault with a model of man as less than a perfect acquirer, assimilator, and analyst of relevant information. The simple constraint of available time forces consumers to make decisions with less than perfect information. The additional constraint on technological expertise prohibits much meaningful processing of information pertinent to many contemporary products even if the consumer is so motivated.

The central judgment in cases of deceptive advertising involves not so much the characteristics of the consumer but the characteristics of the advertisement itself. The evolution of thought has eliminated the necessity of showing intent to deceive and has even removed the necessity of demonstrating that somone in fact has been deceived. The current criterion is the "capacity or tendency to deceive." All that seems necessary for a judgment of deception is for an advertisement to have potential for being perceived by some consumers in a way that is discrepant with the true offering by the advertiser.[7] The likelihood of such a perception does not seem to be in question. In order to evaluate the impact of the "capacity to deceive" criterion, let us examine some behavioral research findings concerning factors that influence consumer perception.

5 Ibid., p. 154.

6 G. Alexander, supra, note 2 at 8.

7 *Giant Food, Inc.* vs. *FTC*, 322F.2d977 (D.C. Cir. 1963), *cert. dismissed,* 376 U.S. 967 (1964).

III. COMPLEXITIES IN PERCEPTION AND PERSUASION

Reference to any current work in the behavioral aspects of communications or even a text in social psychology will convince the reader that the components of communication, perception, and persuasion are many and complex. Synthesis of all the research done on the determinants of effectiveness of communications is difficult and the result of an attempt to do so, especially in an article of this length, could be readily criticized for its superficiality. If we narrowly focus our attention solely on studies published in the last five years which deal explicitly with the effectiveness of commercial advertisements, we would find research pointing to the significance of the following factors: length and position of an advertisement,[8] the use of color vs. black and white,[9] the size of the issue (for newspapers),[10] the print style,[11] the size of the advertisement,[12] the believability of the copy premise,[13] the amount of blank space surrounding the advertisement,[14] the prestige (or image) of the media,[15] the editorial or program context,[16] the race of the viewer,[17] the presence of distractions,[18] and factors of motivation and personality.[19]

Focusing just on studies dealing explicitly with responses to advertising is much too narrow a perspective, however. There is a long history of research pertinent to our problem in the areas of perception, persuasion, and attitude organization and change. The aggregation of that research indicates that there is an almost infinite list of factors which can influence

[8] A. Gruber, "Position Effects and Starch Viewer Impression Studies," *Journal of Advertising Research* (September 1966), pp. 14–17; D. M. New, "Further Comments on the Effects of Commercial Positions," *Journal of Advertisnig Research* (September 1966), pp. 18–20; J. Wheatley, "Influence of Commercial's Length and Position," *Journal of Marketing Research* (May 1968), pp. 199–202.

[9] B. Gardner and Y. Cohen, "ROP Color and Its Effect on Newspaper Advertising," *Journal of Marketing Research* (May 1964), pp. 68–70.

[10] Carter, "Newspaper Advertising Readership: Thick vs. Thin Issues," *Journal of Advertising Research* (September 1968).

[11] H. Assael, "Advertising Performance as a Function of Print Ad Characteristics," *Journal of Advertising Research* (June 1967), pp. 20–26.

[12] E. Robinson, "How an Advertisement's Size Affects Responses to It," *Journal of Advertising Research* (December 1963), pp. 16–24.

[13] R. Ferber, Interpretation of Interest in Pharmaceutical Advertisements, *Journal of Advertising Research* (September 1966), pp. 8–13; J. Maloney, "Curiosity vs. Disbelief in Advertising," *Journal of Advertising Research* (June 1962), pp. 2–8.

[14] L. Bogart and S. Tolley, "The Impact of Blank Space: An Experiment in Advertising Readership," *Journal of Advertising Research* (June 1964), pp. 21–27.

[15] D. Fuchs, "Two Source Effects in Magazine Advertising, *Journal of Marketing Research* (August 1964), pp. 59–62; C. Winick, "Three Measures of the Advertising Value of Media Content," *Journal of Advertising Research* (June 1962), pp. 28–33.

[16] L. E. Crane, "How Product, Appeal, and Program Affect Attitudes toward Commercials," *Journal of Advertising Research* (March 1964), pp. 15–18.

[17] A. Barban and E. Cundiff, "Negro and White Response to Advertising Stimuli," *Journal of Marketing Research* (November 1964), pp. 53–56.

[18] M. Venkatesan and G. Haaland, "Divided Attention and Television Commercials: An Experimental Study," *Journal of Marketing Research* (May 1968), pp. 203–205.

[19] R. Bauer, "The Initiative of the Audience," *Journal of Advertising Research* (June 1963), pp. 2–7.

how a consumer perceives and assimilates a persuasive message. Fortunately, however, it seems reasonable to group all of these possible sources of communication distortion into four major groups.

The first group of factors are those concerned directly with the communication message itself. This group has received the most attention in previous analyses of what constitutes a deceptive advertisement. Factors in this cluster include the semantics of the words selected, the omission of pertinent materials, the inclusion of distracting irrelevancies, the organization and logical construction of persuasive arguments, sequencing of the pro and con arguments, the repetition of arguments, the use of emotional or threat appeals, and the statement of the conclusion vs. leaving the conclusion implicit. Other factors which have effects on how individuals perceive focus on the non-verbal aspects of the advertisement and include the relative sizes and styles of type used, the use of color, the use of illustrations, the amount of blank space (or dead air time), the quality of the art work, and the quality of the reproduction of the advertisement.

Often ignored in the attempt to identify deceptive ads are the strong effects that fall into a second cluster. This second group of factors are concerned with the context in which the attempt at persuasive communication takes place, or the perceptual "surround" of the advertisement. These are often strong enough to swamp any effects which would otherwise occur as the result of use of different type styles, for example. Consumers will interpret an advertisement as a function of factors such as the prestige of the media; the editorial or program content preceding and following the advertisement; the perception of the source of the persuasive message, *e.g.*, whether they perceive the message as a paid advertisement or not, or how they perceive the purported speaker in testimonials; and, in general, all experiences closely preceding and following the exposure to the message. This last factor may be important in judging an advertisement's capacity to deceive. Almost any experience from idle daydreams to a traumatic interruption may affect how a consumer interprets an advertisement, *i.e.*, the consumer's peculiar phenomenological state may change the context to something dramatically different from that suggested by the natural embedment of the advertisement in some program or media. Thus, even the most innocuous promotion may have the capacity to deceive in certain peculiar situations, situations which are relevant in assessing how the ad *might* be perceived.

The third group of factors might be labelled the social factors. The cultural and ethnic origins of a consumer, the extent of reinforcement of message credibility by friends and acquaintances, interactions with members of a family unit, membership in a social class, or the presence of appropriate reference groups[20] may all affect the consumer's evaluation of the message. Some of these factors, like ethnic origins, will have their strongest effect in distorting the meaning attached to certain words or phrases. Other social factors, like the presence of reference groups, may

---

[20] The reference group concept is sufficiently complex to prohibit effective discussion in this paper. The interested reader is referred to T. Shibutani, "Reference Groups as Perspectives," *American Journal of Sociology* (1955).

determine whether the individual perceives it to be appropriate for a person of his position in life to respond to a particular type of persuasion or to purchase a particular type of product.

The importance of a consumer's self-perception in determining how he interprets and responds to advertisements introduces the last commonly identified group of factors affecting communication, the individual factors. It has been said that no two people perceive the world in exactly the same fashion, for all people are unique in the experiences they have had. This uniqueness, the evidence of which we commonly label as personality, clearly has a strong effect on how each consumer interprets and responds to an advertisement. Each individual has characteristic ways of perceiving and reacting to all sorts of stimuli, including advertising. In addition to the personality factors, which are normally thought of as long-term behavioral predispositions, perceptions are very strongly influenced by motivational states. Individuals in aroused motivational states have a strong tendency to have perceptions oriented toward satisfaction of their motivational goals. Conversely, individuals in a state of arousal tend to be blind to events which have no relevance to their immediate goals. These phenomena seem valid whether the motivation is a simple biological drive like hunger, or a higher level need like achievement motivation or the need for social acceptance. Arousal of any need makes an individual particularly sensitive to communications offering satisfaction of that need and probably less critical of the validity of the persuasive argument proffered.

Thus far the process by which misperception occurs has not been discussed. Although it can be conceptually partitioned in a more complex manner, it seems sufficient to specify two basic processes determining the consumer's perception and response to advertisements. The consumer would be simply inundated without some avoidance of a substantial portion of the advertising existing in today's commercial milieu. One process, the relatively conscious avoidance of persuasive messages, is known generally as selective exposure. A review of the literature on this process permits the following generalization: "Persuasion that contradicts or otherwise is inconsistent with the attitudinal predispositions of those for whom it is intended is likely to provoke a reaction of selective exposure whereby non-acceptable messages are avoided."[21]

The second process, perhaps more appropriate in the context of this article, is the process of selective distortion. This process, which is less under the consumer's conscious control, is such that "once exposed to the message, the individual may perceive and interpret it in a manner consistent with his predispositions toward that topic, and appeals which deviate substantially from these predispositions are likely to be distorted or otherwise interpreted in a manner not intended."[22] The predispositions referred to may stem from a number of sources such as personality traits, motivational states, previous experience with the product class advertised, the media employed, the appeal used, or the advertiser.

[21] J. Engel, D. Kollat, and R. Blackwell, *Consumer Behavior* (New York: Holt; Rinehart and Winston, 1968).
[22] Ibid., p. 181.

With recognition of the complexities of communication and perception, one begins to get the uncomfortable feeling that nothing is certain and that the potential for misperception of any advertisement is virtually infinite. This feeling is not totally unwarranted, especially when one considers the high degree of variability among people's personality dimensions and the additional variability resulting from confounding factors like motivations and previous experiences. Almost everything that makes an individual unique has some role in determining his interpretation of the persuasive message, making all sorts of reactions to advertising, even the seemingly far-fetched ones, extremely possible and perhaps even likely. Given this potential for misperception and message distortion, it seems reasonable to conclude that any advertisement has the capacity to deceive.

It is interesting to note, at this point, the role played by the recipient of the communication in his own deception. Consumers, as the result of their peculiar personalities and motivations, are complicit partners in deception, and in some cases may be almost solely the cause for any misperceptions that occur. This raises an interesting question of whether the advertiser has the responsibility for protecting the consumer from his own capacity to misperceive. This is a particularly difficult problem since many advertisers are able to take advantage of the consumer's readiness to misperceive, as in the case where ads are deceptive despite the literal truthfulness of each statement.

IV. THE CAPACITY TO DECEIVE AND PROSECUTIONAL DISCRETION

The existence of the "capacity to deceive" notion gives the illusion that there are real standards by which an advertisement can be classified as non-deceptive; but, in fact, all ads *could* be effectively attacked on the basis of their capacity to deceive. Of course, attempts to prosecute seemingly innocuous advertisements would make the inappropriateness of the "capacity to deceive" criterion transparent and probably cause the courts to find a new modified set of criteria. As it now stands, though, employment of the "capacity to deceive" notion gives the FTC the ability to prosecute almost any advertiser and makes the guilt of the defendant almost a foregone conclusion, more the result of selective prosecution than of adjudication.

It has been stated that:

Through the miracle of prosecutional discretion—a device central to the operation of the legal system . . . criminality can, and is, produced or ignored virtually at will by the law enforcement officials.[23]

Since the law could have been used either to acquit or convict, the only relevant question is whether it was just that the law be used to convict. It is no easy task to make lawyers peek out from behind that supposedly value-free facade, the "law," and begin to talk about unjust laws and unjust administration of the law; but they must come out and face the reality of prosecutional and judicial discretion.[24]

23 Sax, "Civil Disobedience: The Law is Never Blind," *Saturday Review* (1968).
24 Ibid., p. 24.

Substitution of "ignore" for "acquit" in the second quote would make it an appropriate description of the current situation of deceptive advertising. With the power of the FTC to prosecute at will, it is perhaps fortunate for many advertisers that its budget and sense of justice has constrained the FTC to pursuing only a limited number of cases, most of which entail a fairly clear violation of the spirit of the law. Nonetheless, some discomfort results from the realization that the present criteria give the FTC substantial power relative to the defendants and even, in some sense, relative to the courts. Reform is called for.

It is often suggested, particularly by those anxious to leave the advertisers as much latitude of action as possible, that we need not bother with any vigorous policing of deception. This call for inactivity is natural in the light of the consumer image that they contend is valid. Their contention is that today's consumer, by virtue of the educational process and experience, is sophisticated and knowledgeable, able to rationally evaluate products and advertisements, and protect himself without the assistance of any legislation. This model of the consumer errs in at least two major respects: (1) in the assumption of sophistication and knowledge and (2) in the assumption of "rationality."

Consumers simply lack the required technical knowledge and capabilities to make the necessary comparisons between most contemporary products. Few consumers, for example, possess the expertise that would be required to make an independent assessment of the qualities of a product as commonplace as a toothpaste, much less items more technologically complex. As a result, consumers must make purchase decisions largely on the basis of faith, primarily in the quality of the product attributes claimed in advertisements. Consumers have imperfect information in another important respect as well, since they have limited experience to assist them in evaluating product offerings. In most product classes it is not possible for a consumer to evaluate all the alternatives through a process of search or trial and error. Even when the consumer benefits from the experiences of friends or professional evaluation organizations like the Consumers Union, he is operating with less than perfect knowledge. Similarly, the consumer may have even less experience and information appropriate to the evaluation of a particular seller. This lack becomes especially pronounced in an economy where the number of products and sellers is enormous and where the dynamics of the marketplace lead to constantly changing product offerings and identity of sellers. Living in a complex economy, typified also by a remoteness of the seller from the ultimate consumer, one feels sympathy for the following: "Only a *caveat venditor* philosophy fits the reality of the second half of the 20th century. For a buyer cannot be required to beware if he has no way (or at least no adequate way) of knowing what to beware of. It is the seller who has (or has access to) that knowledge now."[25]

The other assumption, that of "rationality," also seems in error, although "rationality" is such an elusive and variously employed concept that its usage is somewhat ambiguous. While it is true that "today's

[25] Masters, op. cit., p. 182.

economic citizen may be more sophisticated in many ways than yesterday's. . . . There is no reason, however, to believe that he is less gullible. For he is still credulous, and still looking for bargains and cure-alls."[26] Studying the specific response of consumers to advertising, "there seems to be no reason to believe that Americans are particularly more, or less, critical of advertising today than they have been in the past."[27]

V. CONSUMER REACTION TO DECEPTION

The stauncher supporters of a laissez-faire economic system will argue that the system is self-corrective, *i.e.*, that word of mouth relaying of deception experiences will expose and drive out firms and practices which are socially undesirable. A sample of only one case, the lengthy and checkered history of the Holland Furnace Company,[28] stands as good evidence against the validity of this argument. In that case not even word of mouth communication abetted by publicity stemming from prosecutional activities had the effect of delimiting the firm's continued activity. In a society as large as ours, it would be naïve to think that word of mouth communications would be sufficiently effective to control deceptive practices. One becomes more pessimistic about self-correction of deceptive practices after investigating how consumers are likely to react to deception experiences.

Although there are no studies dealing directly with consumer reaction to experiences of deception, there are several studies indicating how individuals react to other failure experiences.[29] Summarizing briefly, it has been found that individuals having a low need for achievement tend to repress failure experiences,[30] that individuals with high needs for social desirability react to failure with expressive rather than repressive modes of defense,[31] and that, in general, individuals with positive self-evaluations are more able to assimilate negative experiences.[32] Even more pertinent to assessing the validity of the word of mouth notion is the finding that individuals whose self-concepts are threatened adopt low risk strategies for presentation of self.[33]

[26] Howard, op. cit., p. 128.

[27] S. Greyser and R. Bauer, "Americans and Advertising: Thirty Years of Public Opinion," *Public Opinion Quarterly* (1960).

[28] 24 FTC 1413–14 (1936); *Holland Furnace Co.*, 55 FTC 55 (1958); *Holland Furnace Co. v. FTC*, 269 F.2d 203 (7th Cir. 1959), *cert. denied*, 361 U.S. 932 (1960); *Holland Furnace Co. v. FTC*, 295 F.2d 302 (7th Cir. 1961) and *In re Holland Furnace Co.*, 341 F.2d 548 (7th Cir.), *cert. denied*, 381 U.S. 924 (1965).

[29] For a general discussion of adaptation of failure that is both competent and enjoyable see Goffman, "On Cooling the Mark Out: Some Aspects of Adaptation to Failure," *Psychiatry: A Journal for the Study of Interpersonal Relations* (1952).

[30] Caron and Wallach, "Personality Determinants of Repressive and Obsessive Reactions to Failure-Stress," *Journal of Abnormal & Social Psychology* (1959).

[31] Ford and Hersch, "Need Approval, Defensive Denial, and Direction of Aggression in a Failure-Frustration Situation," *Journal of Personality & Social Psychology* (1967).

[32] A. Combs and D. Snygg, *Individual Behavior: A Perceptual Approach to Behavior* (1959).

[33] David J. Schneider, "Self-Presentation as a Function of Prior Success or Failure and Expectation of Feedback of Created Impression," Ph.D. Dissertation, Stanford University, 1966.

Thus, it seems that the individuals least likely to recognize, assimilate, and relay their experiences of being deceived are those whose self-concepts are threatened and who have a generally low self-evaluation and low need for achievement. This type of individual is most likely to be found in the poverty classes. Consequently, the class of consumers most likely to be exposed to many deceptive practices is the group least likely to recognize deception and least able to publicly admit to it and, therefore, the least able to protect itself by "spreading the word."

VI. ON "RATIONAL" ADVERTISING

At the opposite extreme of those arguing for inactivity are those who suggest that only technical and rational aspects of a product be allowed in advertisements and that non-rational motivational appeals be disallowed. "It would be proper," states George Alexander, "for the commission to take the position that an ad which promotes a product without providing a rational basis for its preference is an unfair method of competition."[34] Two major drawbacks prevent even this approach from effectively eliminating the capacity to deceive. Short of requiring such complete technical information that would make all advertising prohibitively expensive and ineffective, the consumer will still be faced with only partial information carefully selected by the seller. In addition, considering the mediating determinants specified above, and given the individual's insufficient technological capability of processing this kind of information, the consumer is still likely to misperceive the true characteristics of product offering.

Even more damning is the recognition that such a rule of thumb would force the assumption of a highly normative position of what constitutes rationality. One gets the feeling that critics of advertising, in using the term rational, are distinguishing between descriptions of technical product performance characteristics and appeals directed toward human motivations. These writers seem to be disturbed by the fact that people purchase products, not with solely pragmatic technical performance criteria, but because they believe that product ownership will help them satisfy some personal or social motivation. But who can say that the value such a "non-rational" consumer derives from the product purchase is any more or less meritorious than the enjoyed by the "economic" consumer? Attempts to draw distinctions between rational and emotional reasons for any behavior are essentially meaningless.

Recalling the model of man assumed by critics supporting the plea for "rationality" and the effects that such a law would have on the human character raises Orwellian images. The presumption that man should be motivated only by the most pragmatic of considerations yields a picture of an automaton, a computer-like evaluator of alternatives, making decisions based solely on some sterile functional benefit that products would

---

34 "Call for More Truth, Less 'Motivations' in Ads," *Marketing Insights* (1968). The quote is taken from a speech delivered to the Student Bar Association at the University of Buffalo.

yield. Denial of the fact that people do, and should, behave so as to enhance their self-esteem, to enhance the way others view them, or, in general, to satisfy any particular motivation, is a denial of the essence of the human condition. Distinctions, therefore, between rational and emotional appeals and reasons for behavior are not only meaningless, but dangerous. Implementation of rules based upon such a distinction would, at best, lead to the existence of advertising irrelevant to the life styles of today's citizens and, at worst, play a part in creating a future generation of citizens devoid of humanity.

VII. A MODEST SUGGESTION

After having criticized the standard for deception in current use, and having also critically commented on the two extreme alternatives of prohibiting nothing and, effectively, prohibiting nearly everything, a suggestion for what the criteria for deception should be seems in order. The principal flaw in the employment of the capacity to deceive standard is that it calls for the FTC and the courts to make hypothetical suppositions about how consumers might interpret an advertisement, an analytic procedure which, given the complexities of the communication process, ought always to lead to a judgment of the advertisement's capacity to deceive. It seems much more reasonable to ask, instead of how consumers *might* interpret an advertisement, how potential consumers in fact *do* interpret an advertisement.[35] Judgment based upon actual rather than hypothetical misinterpretations seems to be in accord with our sense of justice since it serves to protect the innocent advertiser while allowing him the greatest freedom and latitude of action. Not only would the FTC and the courts have greater certainty that their prosecution and judgments were warranted, but the advertiser would be able, if he so desired, to make a valid independent assessment of whether his advertisements were deceptive. Adoption of criteria focusing on actual consumer interpretation of advertisements would reduce the ambiguities intrinsic in the current standard. This procedure would, however, have the disadvantages of judging each case separately, but would at the same time have the advantages of simple flexibility and the absence of the loopholes resulting from the lack of any generally applicable specific standards.

This would not preclude the simultaneous specification of certain more specific standards. Just as we might assess how consumers interpret whole ads, we might also determine how consumers interpret specific words, although doing so from any meaningful context might be misleading. Determining the semantics of words like "safe," "fireproof," "unbreakable," and "free" would permit the establishment of some criteria for when such words could be used with minimal deception potential. Standards for usage of many such words are, of course, already in exist-

---

35 Note that this is *not* a suggestion that it be demonstrated that some consumer has in fact been deceived. Rather it is a suggestion that research be undertaken to demonstrate how typical consumers interpret the advertisement, knowledge which is obviously a key to the determination of the likelihood of deception.

ence but might be improved if based upon actual semantic interpretations by the consumer. As we learn more about how consumers actually do interpret and misinterpret various types of advertisements it should be possible to establish some general guidelines to indicate the kinds of advertisements which are likely to be misinterpreted and, therefore, deceptive.

While the concept for using actual rather than hypothetical evidence of misinterpretation of an advertisement is simple enough, implementation would not be without its difficulties. First, and perhaps foremost, scientifically rigorous and appropriate research methodologies would have to be selected. Fortunately, however, psychologists have been concerned with similar problems and several potential methodologies are already in existence.[36] Included within the methodological considerations would be the problem of determining the size and composition of the sample to be deemed representative of the consuming public for any particular product. The methodological problems, with the assistance of competent psychologists, all seem solvable with the present state of knowledge.

A second set of problems, with probably more elusive solutions, involves the establishment of criteria for assessment of such research evidence. Not only will the quality of the research methodology need assessment, but judgment will also be needed to determine what constitutes sufficient misinterpretation to justify classifying an advertisement as potentially deceptive. Both the proportion of consumers misperceiving and the magnitude and consequences of their misperception will have to be assessed. The final judgment will eventually be the difficult problem of striking a balance between the potential social cost resulting from the misperceptions of some consumers and the potential social gain resulting from effective undistorted communication of information from the advertiser to the balance of the consumers.

The cost of the research, of course, presents other difficulties, although the type of appropriate research does not seem to be of an extraordinarily expensive variety. It might be possible for the burden of proof, and therefore the cost of the research, to be shifted to the defendant, perhaps after some initial warning that his advertising is suspect. The advertiser could then have the option of continuing the advertisement if he is also willing to demonstrate that it is not misperceived and deceptive. Evidence resulting from research conducted at the defendant's initiative ought to be carefully reviewed. Also, it is probably preferable to require that this research be conducted by an independent agent.

An additional problem, which may be a substantial one, will occur in the attempt to convince individuals with legal training to accept these research results. Some evidence and convincing arguments suggest that lawyers and psychologists operate with distinct, and perhaps irreconcilable, orientations and methods.[37] Also, the courts may have been reluctant

---

[36] C. Osgood, G. Suci, and P. Tannebaum, *The Measurement of Meaning* (Urbana: University of Illinois Press, 1957).

[37] Tapp, "Psychology and the Law: The Dilemma," *Psychology Today* (1969).

to place weight on psychological research.[38] But while only a mutual educational process may permit effective rapprochement of psychology and law for the control of deceptive advertising, the benefits from such a program are worth the efforts involved.

Adoption of criteria resulting from psychological research into the actual meaning of advertisement would facilitate truth in advertising in that the interpretation placed on the advertisement by the consumer would be valid. Use of any other definition of truth creates the possibility, hopefully remote, that any activities which result in nothing but "truthful" advertising might also have the result of condemning the advertiser to the fate of the mythological Cassandra, condemned by Apollo to always tell the truth, but never to be believed.

[38] *Bantam Books, Inc.* vs. *FTC,* 275 F.2d 680 (2d Cir. 1960).

33

Whither the Marketing System in Low-income Areas?

CHARLES S. GOODMAN
University of Pennsylvania

The social crisis has focused interest on a long neglected area—the performance of the marketing system, not as a whole but as it serves particular groups. This crisis has led concerned observers and marketing scholars at long last to inquire not how well the marketing system performs in general but how it serves particular groups, especially disadvantaged groups. Even a cursory examination reveals serious shortcomings.

This article will examine several facets of the performance of the marketing system serving low-income, especially low-income minority-group, consumers. Part I will review some of the specific complaints and charges which have been made and review the evidence bearing on their validity. It will also suggest some additional ways in which the marketing system serving low-income minority group consumers has been less than fully adequate. Part II will examine a number of remedies which have been proposed.

I. THE PROBLEM

Although critics have concentrated their fire on allegations of high prices for standard or inferior merchandise and, to some extent, on the issue of consumer frauds, system deficiencies are not confined to these areas. The limited evidence which we have suggests that there may be serious deficiencies in the adequacy and quality of marketing services available to the poor in many areas. Such deficiencies not only deprive the underprivileged of fair access to the marketplace but may in turn contribute to the incidence of the complained practices.

Prices

That some consumers pay more than others for some goods and services goes without saying. That this situation exists among all income groups and all ethnic groups is also evident from the diverse purchasing patterns of consumers and the wide range of stores patronized. But do the poor or certain minority groups pay more, as a class, than other consumers, either by choice or from necessity?

The available evidence suggests that for some classes of goods, important numbers of low-income consumers do pay more than well-to-do consumers for similar merchandise. It is also clear however, that the poor do *not* pay more for *all* classes of goods and services. Moreover, all poor people do *not* pay more.

Evidence of higher prices to low-income groups is strongest in the case of consumer durables such as appliances and furniture—types of goods in which installment selling and high-pressure tactics are widespread. Caplovitz' pioneering study of furniture and appliance retailing in low-income areas of New York City documented the extensive use by low-income consumers of suppliers with exorbitant finance charges and often high initial price tags. The more recent study by the Federal Trade Commission of pricing, financing, and sales practices of District of Columbia retailers adds further evidence that at least some retailers in the low-income neighborhoods often have prices which are substantially above those charged by what the commission referred to as "general market" merchants.[1]

As will be examined below, only a portion of these differences reflect differences in the services which merchants render to consumers. The F.T.C. study, like most studies of this type, examined the practices of merchants in low-income and other areas. It did not undertake to determine which stores were in fact patronized by different consumers and their reasons for patronizing them.

In the case of food, whether low-income consumers pay more depends on the stores which they patronize. A large number of studies by government agencies, scholars, and community groups all suggest that if poor minority-group consumers are able and willing to patronize competitive stores available to them they can expect to pay the same prices as paid by middle- and upper-income consumers. That supermarket chains, for example, charge the same prices in low- and higher-income neighborhoods has been well documented in studies by the Bureau of Labor Statistics, the Department of Agriculture, the Baltimore Community Relations Commission and by scholars such as Dixon and McLaughlin. Whether such stores

---

[1] Federal Trade Commission, *Economic Report on Installment Credit and Retail Sales Practices of District of Columbia Retailers* (1968).

are available to many consumers from disadvantaged groups is, however, quite another matter.

Hard data in areas other than food and consumer durables is sparse or nonexistent. There is good reason to suspect, however, that low-income consumers obtain medical and possibly other services at prices no higher, and quite possibly, somewhat lower, than those paid by others.

It is probably fair to state that at least for some classes of goods, the institutional mix in many low-income areas works to the disadvantage of the poor consumer. In short, there is likely to be in those areas a high proportion of older type, high-cost, high-price outlets and a relative scarcity of modern, low-cost, low-price units.

Frauds

The success of frauds and shady schemes generally depends on a combination of gullibility and inadequate information. In addition, in order to be profitable the intended victims must have sufficient purchasing power to make the game attractive to the perpetrator. Some of the more common frauds are misrepresentation of goods, phony promotions on overpriced goods (e.g. the suede shoe home improvement deal that purports to be offering a special price for promotion while in fact charging inflated regular prices); passing off; bait and switch tactics.

Frauds are not confined to low-income or minority group areas. Indeed the very lowest-income strata provide a less fertile field for the fraud to cultivate than working class families and those moving up from poverty. Frauds tend to prosper also where the individual consumers buy only infrequently; the seller does not expect repeat business or favorable word of mouth but expects to mine new bodies of suckers to sustain his operation.

It is because many of the urban poor are moving up from the marginal starvation of their immediate urban or rural past that they present an attractive target to the sharp operator. The first home owner in his family is the most likely candidate for home improvement racket. The first worker to attain some income beyond food and rent money is the most likely target of the shady freezer, appliance, television or wig scheme. *As the urban poor gain increased incomes, the fraud problem is very likely to become more, rather than less, serious.*

The problem of frauds perpetrated on the disadvantaged is doubly serious not only because they are less able to suffer the loss but, at least equally importantly, because they are likely to be unable to avail themselves of the remedies which may be open to persons further up the economic scale.

The poor are likely to be unacquainted with their legal rights and in any case are unlikely to be able to afford the costs of seeking private legal redress. Particularly in states such as Pennsylvania in which the plaintiff in a civil action cannot recover his attorney's fees or even the costs of witnesses even if he wins the case, the legal system favors the seller generally and the fraud in particular. The widespread use of judgment notes, garnishment, and the assignment of contracts deprives buyers of the most readily available remedy; refusal to pay.

Public agencies to which informed persons might complain are likely to be miles away in city hall or the state house. Moreover, the victim whose only contact with the legal system may be the unhappy experience of garnishment or foreclosure proceedings is, to say the least, hesitant about using the legal system for redress. In addition, enforcement agencies are often indifferent to consumer frauds in part because of lack of funds but also because they have "bigger fish to fry." Moreover, effective action may be difficult or impossible because the complaint is supported by only fragmentary evidence; sometimes none at all.

Notorious frauds suffer heavily from the light of publicity and even from word-of-mouth communication among consumers. But consumers are generally hesitant to admit their gullibility to their peers—especially so if they feel insecure in their social setting, as is so often true in poorer communities. Thus the fraud, like the blackmailer, can often count on silence to keep his past victims from warning the next in line.

Other Deficiencies

Prices and frauds are by no means the only facets of the marketing system which serve low-income consumers poorly. The West Mill Creek Study noted that small stores in the study area were notoriously thin on assortments and that many would be unable to provide a reasonable market basket without extensive substitutions.[2] Discussions with residents of the North Philadelphia "ghetto" revealed that some consumers traveled to distant stores in order to obtain desired items, even in such "convenience" type items as meat and produce. While our evidence in this area is fragmentary, it does suggest that the ambient retailers may not have adjusted well to the changing wants of the market which they should be serving.

THE CAUSES

Alan Andreasen suggests three hypotheses currently in vogue to explain the unfavorable situation in which at least some poor consumers find themselves in the marketplace.

The exploitation hypothesis—The problem is with the people who operate the system. The disadvantaged pay more for their needs because too many merchants, credit companies, salesmen, et cetera, use unethical practices—excessive markups, deception, usurious interest to gouge the disadvantaged.

The consumer ignorance hypothesis—Even if the system functioned effectively and those running it behaved ethically, disadvantaged consumers would still achieve unequal treatment because of their inability

² Charles S. Goodman "Do the Poor Pay More," *Journal of Marketing* (January, 1968). For detailed results see Charles S. Goodman, *Do the Poor Pay More: A Study of the Food Purchasing Practices of Low-Income Consumers* (Mimeo., 1967).

to use the system effectively because of lower education, lower inter-area mobility, and general marketing inexperience attributable to their small-town, Southern rural, or non-American upbringings.

The structural hypothesis—Because of low incomes and minimal mobility, disadvantaged consumers tend to buy low-margin staple items in small quantities at nearby stores. Such buying behavior and the generally higher operating costs (insurance, pilferage) found in disadvantaged areas does not permit many large-scale, low-price retailers to operate there profitably. The resulting market therefore contains a disproportionate number of small, inefficient, high-priced stores which the disadvantaged are forced to patronize.[3]

While each of these hypotheses contains some germ of truth, there has been much more heat in advocating one or the other as the sole source of the problems of the low-income consumer than there has been systematic research to determine their relative importance. Moreover, speechmakers —and to some extent researchers—tend to substitute their view of consumers problems and *their* standards of values, (including their standards of which services are "worth the consumers' money") for those of the low-income consumer.

The evidence bearing upon each of these hypotheses will be examined in two areas which have been the subject of considerable study and widespread discussion: food and consumer durables.

TWO AREAS EXAMINED

A. *Food*—Supporters of the *exploitation* hypothesis advance one or more of the following contentions: (1) chain stores discriminate in both prices and quality between moderate and low-income areas, (2) chain stores raise prices temporarily when welfare checks are due and then remark merchandise back to regular prices after they have taken full advantage of the welfare check recipient, (3) overage perishables are transferred from other stores to low-income, minority-group areas as part of a systematic form of discrimination, and (4) small independent stores charge higher prices in low-income areas and make exploitive profits thereby.

Are these Charges Valid

The price-discrimination-by-area charge is of long standing. Quite possibly it is the successor to the word-of-mouth campaigns directed against the chain stores a generation ago in which they were charged with widespread short-changing of customers, a practice against which, so consumers were told, protection could be obtained only by avoiding chain stores and patronizing the independent merchant.

The discrimination-by-area charge was of sufficient import to warrant the attention of the National Commission on Food Marketing which arranged with the Bureau of Labor Statistics to make a comparative study of prices of chain and independent stores in lower- and higher-income

[3] Unpublished manuscript.

areas. Studies were conducted in six cities (Atlanta, Chicago, Houston, Los Angeles, New York, and Washington) and covered 18 commodities important in the expenditure patterns of low-income consumers.

The Bureau found that "there did not appear to be any basis for the allegation that the chains often charge more for the same item in low-income areas than in higher income areas."[4] In fact, for each of the six cities and for each of the two quality levels studied, the median of relatives for the chain stores turned out to be 100.

In the case of independents there was some variation. The average prices of large independents in low-income areas ranged among the cities from 2½% below to 2½% above those in higher-income areas in the same cities for items of similar quality. In the case of small independents, prices were up to 2% higher in two cities; in the other four cities they were up to 6¼% lower than the average prices of small stores in the higher-income areas of the same cities.[5]

A number of other studies of the discrimination issue have produced similar conclusions. Dixon and McLaughlin, after examining the prices charged by stores in the North Philadelphia Inner Core, reported that the market basket cost in supermarkets in that area was not higher than in the sample of higher income supermarkets.[6] Moreover, prices in small stores in the inner city averaged 4.3% below those charged by small stores in higher-income areas. Dixon and McLaughlin also report that their data do not support the hypothesis that prices rise after the distribution of welfare checks.

A study by the Baltimore Community Relations Commission also found that "stores within a chain located in the inner city do not charge higher prices than stores in the suburbs."[7] A study in New York City produced similar results.[8]

Following testimony by housewives before a congressional committee alleging that discriminatory practices did exist, the Department of Agriculture undertook a new study of chain store prices and quality in February 1968. Two leading chains in each of six cities were selected for study without the knowledge of either chain or store management. February 8 and 9 were selected as survey dates in the expectation that on those dates there would be a relatively high redemption of Food Stamps and issuance of welfare assistance checks.

The stores to be examined within each chain were selected by first dividing all stores of a chain into two groups. Those with high Food Stamp redemption rates and in, or bordering on, poverty areas were placed in the group, "low-income area stores"; those with low or zero

[4] "Retail Food Prices in Low- and Higher-income Areas" in *Special Studies in Food Marketing* (National Commission on Food Marketing, Technical Study No. 10), p. 129.

[5] *Ibid.*

[6] Donald F. Dixon and Daniel J. McLaughlin, "Do the Inner City Poor Pay More for Food?" *Temple University Economic and Business Bulletin* (Spring, 1968), pp. 6–12.

[7] "Findings of the Supermarket Pricing Survey," Baltimore Community Relations Commission (Mimeo., 1968).

[8] *New York Times,* November 25, 1967, cited by Dixon et al., p. 7.

redemption rates located outside poverty areas were assigned to the group "high-income area stores." Stores selected for study were then selected, with one exception, on a random basis within each group. Purchases of 17 items were made by buyers and brought to a central location. In addition to prices, the quality of frankfurters, ground beef, and pork chops was evaluated on the basis of laboratory tests. The results are summarized by the Department of Agriculture:

> Data collected during a survey of prices charged for food items pur-
> chased in stores of two chains in each of six cities showed no identifiable
> pattern of differences between sample stores of the same chain operating
> in high- and low-income areas. Though uniform prices were the rule,
> there was some variation from store to store in prices of individual items.
> Such differences were largely random. An analysis of selected factors asso-
> ciated with quality for a limited number of meat products showed con-
> siderable variation among stores of a chain but no definite pattern by
> income areas of the city.[9]

The overwhelming weight of the evidence suggests that the exploitation hypothesis, as it applies to food, has not been proved.

Supporters of the *structural* hypothesis contend that the poor pay more for food because of the types of stores found in the low-income areas. They point to the "common observation" of large numbers of small, often unkempt, stores in the poorer areas and the dearth of modern super-market units. As prices in small stores tend to be higher than those in supermarkets, it is argued that the residents of the low-income areas are thus paying higher prices for food.

Evaluation of this hypothesis requires both a determination of whether such an unfavorable store mix does in fact exist and also of the extent to which such stores are in fact used by area residents as their principal sources of food supply. Most retailing students would concede that the more modern outlets are likely to locate in areas of established potential. One can also point to the closing of chain outlets in the lower-income areas and their expansion in the growth areas.[10]

Low-income families do appear to make more use of independent stores. Alexis, Simon, and Smith, for example, found that 34% of the low-income (under $5,000) families in their Rochester, N.Y., study used independent stores for their major food shopping, while only 14% of the middle- and upper-income residents used them for this purpose. That this is at least in part the result of the locations of available stores and the immobility of the low-income consumer is suggested by their finding that only 29% of the low-income shoppers travelled more than 3/4 mile to their major food source while 61% of the middle-income and 75% of the upper-income families travelled at least that far. Yet this observation should be kept in perspective. More than three out of five low-income families did

[9] U.S. Department of Agriculture, *Comparison of Prices Paid for Selected Foods in Chain Stores in High- and Low-income Areas of Six Cities* (1968).
[10] The reasons for this behavior by retailers are examined *infra*.

use a chain or discount store as its major food source.[11]

Where such stores are not too remote, low-income residents do make use of them. In a West Philadelphia redevelopment area with no supermarket of its own, over 90% of the residents went outside the area to patronize chain supermarkets or competitively priced independents. Less than 6% drew their main food supplies from local stores of the type found by the survey to have prices higher than those of the supermarket chains.[12] Fortunately competitive outlets were available within ¾ mile of nearly all of the homes.

We may say tentatively that the store population of the low-income areas commonly contains large numbers of small stores selling some food products (although in many cases, not selling a full line) and that such stores may be major sources of supply for some families. At the same time, the evidence which we do have suggests that most poor families are *not* dependent on such stores, nor do they do most of their food shopping in them.

The claim that the poor pay more for food rests largely on the premise that they are often forced by circumstances to patronize the smaller, independent stores and that these stores as a class tend to have higher prices. Such stores because of lower turnover, poorer facilities or the characteristics of the market (as perceived by the merchant) may also offer lower quality.[13]

Less attention has been devoted to what may be an even more important deficiency of small food stores in low-income areas—the thinness of assortments. It may well be that much of the travel to stores outside low-income areas stems from a desire to obtain merchandise not available in local stores. The marketing system serves its customers poorly if it falls down in this respect fully as much as if it offers higher prices.

Supporters of the *consumer ignorance* hypothesis argue that the poor are poor buyers and that lower education and marketing experience both serve to make them more susceptible to sharp practices and less able to make good buys even when afforded the opportunity. Illustrations of poor buymanship are sometimes cited, but it is not clear that poor buymanship is associated with low-income or minority-group status. Indeed the common experience of poor European immigrants would seem to have been an ability in frugal household management.

The limited evidence bearing on the food shopper casts doubt on the validity of the hypothesis, at least as it applies to low-income Negro con-

[11] Marcus Alexis, Leonard Simon, and Kenneth Smith, "Some Determinants of Food Buying Behavior" (ms. University of Rochester, nd), pp. 5, 7, 1966.

[12] Charles S. Goodman, "Do the Poor Pay More," *Journal of Marketing* (January, 1968), pp. 20–21.

[13] The quality problem is a difficult one for several reasons; (a) tastes differ so that attributes desired by one group of consumers may be considered undesirable by others (e.g. Mexican-Americans prefer lean, unmarbled meat); (b) quality of perishables received by the store will differ from the quality purchased by the consumer depending on turnover and the conditions of storage. Thus two grocers purchasing identical cases of lettuce, in the produce market may in fact be offering quite different products to their customers.

sumers. Alexis, *et al.* noted that a much higher proportion of Negroes than of whites reported the use of more than one major food source.[14] Our West Mill Creek study (cited earlier) being based entirely on Negro families, could not make such a comparison, although it noted widespread use of a second supermarket by Negro families. When respondents, after identifying their principal source of supply were asked to identify other stores sometimes patronized, 45% mentioned a supermarket first. Such markets were generally used as alternative stores for weekly shopping, the reason being commonly attributed to specials or prices. They were only rarely used for fill-ins.

In addition, the West Mill Creek study sought to determine consumers' perceptions of the prices in stores:

Respondents were first asked whether there were differences in prices among stores in the area. No comparison of specific stores was requested, though stores were often named. The 439 (85%) who indicated that differences did exist were then asked to indicate the store(s) that had higher and lower prices.

Most respondents (266 cases) consider supermarket prices to be lower than those of other stores. In 21 cases, on the other hand, independent stores were believed to offer lower prices than supermarkets. In 12 of these 21, the lower-priced store named was one of the three stores priced which, according to our price study, had lower prices than A&P.

Respondents who made comparisons among specific independents most often indicated as the low-priced store Max & Jeanne's, Eddie's or Litt's; these are stores which were found to be competitively priced. Twenty-four of the 31 respondents comparing independents named one of these three as the lower-priced store.

In the cases in which respondents compared prices of two supermarkets covered in our pricing survey and showing price differences in excess of 1%, their opinions agreed with those of our pricing survey in 24 cases and disagreed in five cases.

It seems clear that both in their shopping behavior and in their responses to questions shoppers perceive significant price differences quite well.[15]

We need to know much more about the knowledge states and purchasing behavior of low-income consumers, especially those in minority groups. What we do have seems to suggest that those who are unfortunate enough to be poor, cannot on this basis be classified as stupid or ignorant buyers of food products.

B. *Furniture and appliances*—Both Caplovitz' pioneering study[16] and the comprehensive Federal Trade Commission study *Installment Credit and Retail Sales Practices of District of Columbia Retailers* (1968) attest to the plight of the low-income consumer in the purchase of furniture and appliances. The latter study is the most comprehensive study of retailing practices by kind of area which has been published thus far. The 59

---

[14] Alexis, et al., *op. cit.,* p. 9.

[15] Goodman, "Do the Poor Pay More," *Journal of Marketing* (January, 1968), p. 23.

[16] David Caplovitz, *The Poor Pay More* (Free Press of Glencoe, 1963).

retailers of furniture and home furnishings, 31 appliance stores, and 6 department stores embraced in the study were estimated to represent about 85% of the sales of stores of these types in the District of Columbia.[17] Stores which were (a) located in or adjacent to low-income areas *and* (b) did not engage in significant city-wide advertising were classified as "low-income market retailers." Eighteen retailers met these criteria, fourteen of these were "furniture stores," two were "appliance stores" and two were described as "miscellaneous merchandise" stores.[18] All other retailers were classified as "general market retailers." Stores with sales of less than $100,000 were among those not included.

Prices charged by the low-income market retailers and their operating methods lend support to the exploitation hypothesis. Such stores did the bulk of their business on installment credit, and although their explicit finance charges were not significantly different from those of general market retailers, prices of merchandise were substantially higher. Gross margin for low-income market retailers in 1966 was 60.8% of sales, compared with 41.2% for general market furniture and home furnishings stores and 30.2% for general market appliance, radio and television stores. The additional gross margin did not, however, accrue to the owners as an exploitive rent. A statement analysis by the Commission of 10 low-income market retailers and 10 general market retailers of comparable size and merchandise mix revealed that the net return on equity of the low-income retailers was only 10.1% as compared with 17.6% for general market furniture and home furnishings stores and 20.3% for general market appliance, radio, and television shops.[19]

The higher gross margins obtained by low-income retailers were largely dissipated in higher personal selling costs (28.2% of sales v. 17.8%), drastically higher bad debt losses (6.7% v. 0.3%), higher legal expenses, insurance, and interest charges. While some of these expenses may fairly be said to reflect matters beyond the retailers' direct control (e.g. bad debts, insurance), others (e.g. sales expenses reflecting the high cost of door-to-door canvassing and pressure tactics) are within the retailer's control and thus not inconsistent with the exploitation hypothesis.

Other studies suggest that these practices are not confined to the District of Columbia.[20] The practices of these retailers appear to be exploitive in the sense of their effects on consumers even though they do not yield exploitive benefits to the practitioners.

The F.T.C. study being a study of retailers' selling rather than of consumers' buying leaves unanswered the question of the extent to which most low-income consumers rely on such stores, and offers only conjectures as to the reasons these stores are patronized by those consumers who have other alternative open to them. Answers to these questions are needed before we can determine whether the F.T.C. study should be inter-

---

17 F.T.C., *op. cit.*, p. 1.

18 *Ibid.*, p. 1.

19 *Ibid.*, p. 53.

20 Cf. Sturdivant, "Business and Mexican-American Relations in East Los Angeles" (unpublished paper), 1967; Caplovitz, *op. cit.*

TABLE 1: NET SALES (1966) OF DISTRICT OF COLUMBIA
RETAILERS COVERED IN F.T.C. STUDY

Kind of retailer	Sales (000)	Percent
General market retailers:		
Furniture, home furnishings stores	$43,969	
Appliance, radio, television stores	29,105	
Department stores	144,864	
Total, general market retailers	$217,938	96.51%
Low-income retailers	7,874	3.49%
	$225,812	100.00%

Source: Calculated from data in F.T.C., *Installment Credit and Retail Sales Practices of District of Columbia Retailers*, pp. 16, 23.

preted as indicative of the plight of a consumer group or merely a recital of the operations of a group of merchants. This question is particularly significant in view of the fact that the 18 low-income market retailers represented less than $3\frac{1}{2}\%$ of the sales volume of the 96 stores covered in the study (See Table 1).

As 16.6% of District of Columbia families had disposable incomes below $3,000 in 1966 and 32.2% had disposable incomes of less than $5,000,[21] it should be clear that low-income area retailers, for all their faults, do not represent the sole source of supply for low-income families. The Commission estimates that the low-income families represented about an $18 million dollar market for furniture and appliances and that the low-income retailers obtained about 35% of this business.[22]

In the absence of data on consumers buying practices and decisions, it is impossible to evaluate the *structural* hypothesis. Surely, it is possible that low-income consumers are trapped by immobility and forced to patronize high-cost, high-priced stores. On the other hand, the infrequent nature of purchases of durables, the availability of public transportation to other parts of the District and of delivery suggest that patronage of such stores rests on some degree of choice. This position is reinforced by the fact that, according to the Commission's estimate, two-thirds of low-income families' purchases of appliances and furniture are made from "general market" as opposed to "low-income market" retailers. In these circumstances, it seems more plausible to advance the view that high pressure sales tactics, including door-to-door canvassing, emphasis on the need to keep up with the neighbors, and the lure of small weekly payments, with little or perhaps no reference to the total price, serve to lure the gullible consumer.

Thus, consideration turns to the third hypothesis, that of poor consumer buymanship.

It is clear that low-income consumers, taken as a class, often have alter-

[21] Based on *Sales Management* Magazine estimates, as cited in F.T.C., *op. cit.*, p. 24.
[22] *Ibid.* p. 25.

natives beyond the high-priced, installment credit store. To what extent are these alternatives used? If they are not used, why not?

It has been shown that two-thirds of the low-income consumer market for appliances and furniture goes to general market retailers. Does the other third go to "low-income market retailers" because of ignorance of choices by the poor, because their credit standing makes them unattractive to other suppliers from whom their neighbors buy, or because slick sales tactics of sellers find their mark in the gullibility of the poor? All of these factors operate to some degree.[23] Unlike the situation in the case of food, durables are purchased infrequently. The buyer lacks experience both in buying the type of product and with the various available sellers. This lack is likely to be especially marked among groups moving up from the bare subsistence level and lacking prior experience in the purchasing of durables.

The problem is likely to be aggravated by social pressures to possess certain durables and sometimes by a failure to order one's priorities and budget resources. Because of the status implications, some low-income consumers hesitate to ask advice of friends or neighbors and tend to withhold unsatisfactory experiences from them, thus serving as a cover for the unscrupulous merchant, much as it does for the common swindler. At best the buyer finds himself uninformed that alternative buying opportunities exist. At worst he becomes easy prey for the slick house-to-house canvasser who can convince him that social acceptance demands that he have a particular product *now* and assuring him that it will be provided promptly if he will only sign.

SUMMARY OF PROBLEM

The failure of the marketing system to serve low-income consumers as well as it might involves many factors, some of which are structural, some the result of merchant practices, and some the result of the manner in which the poor make their decisions. In the food area, the principal problem appears to be structural—the provision of adequate numbers of fully competitive institutions to meet the needs of consumers. In the case of durables the presence of sharp practice by some merchants suggests that the exploitation hypothesis may have some validity. On the other hand, the fact that most low-income buyers avoid such stores and patronize general market retailers suggests again that structural and consumer education deficiencies may be more significant. The remainder of this paper will deal with various proposals which have been advanced to improve the marketing system in the low-income areas and in particular in those areas populated by so-called minority groups.

II. IMPROVING THE SYSTEM

It is clear that substantial changes in the marketing system which serves low-income consumers are urgently needed. The nature of the changes

[23] Cf. Caplovitz, *op. cit., passim.*

which would best serve low-income consumers is less clear. Examining a number of proposals which have been offered and briefly evaluating them in terms of their probable effect on the consumer, we center attention on the black, low-income consumer because many current proposals are directed at this group. Low-income consumers in other groups (Mexican Americans, Indians, whites) have similar problems which also require attention.

Suppression of Consumer Frauds

The need to suppress consumer frauds is urgent, not only because fraudulent practices are frequently directed against the poor, but because the fraud problem is likely to become more severe as various programs increase the disposable incomes of the lowest economic levels. In addition to more stringent enforcement of existing laws, there is an important need to reform the procedures through which consumers secure redress.[24]

Overcoming Consumer Ignorance

Low-income consumers, especially those recently migrating from rural areas of the South, Puerto Rico, or Mexico need education to improve their buying practices, even in such elementary matters as allocating resources, comparing prices, and the costs of "take it even if you can't pay for it." Extensive programs are needed.

Improvement of Marketing Structure

The deficiencies of the marketing system which serves low-income consumers go beyond instances of fraud and the consequences of consumer ignorance and involve the structure through which commercial services are provided in these areas. Structural changes are therefore needed in many areas if marketing performance is to be significantly improved. A variety of proposals have been advanced to provide such changes.

Consumer Cooperatives

The case for consumer cooperatives rests on the usual argument that the businessman's profit would accrue to the consumer, thus providing him with his goods at a lower net cost. It rests on the dubious premise that such cooperatives would operate with the same efficiency as privately-managed businesses.

Consumer cooperatives in foods are an old retailing form. Their performance has been spotty; generally they have been successful only where private business firms have been noncompetitive in spirit and high cost in operation, for example in England before the advent of modern chain stores. Co-ops have found it difficult to offer consumers competitive values in environments where competitive forms operate on low net profits.

[24] See the author's statement at the Federal Trade Commission hearing on Consumer Protection, November 21, 1968.

As the more competitive food chains in the U.S. earn a pretax profit of only about 2% of sales, there is little opportunity for lower efficiency without wiping out the profit—and thus the dividend to consumers—entirely. If consumer cooperatives were willing to pay for and could obtain management equal in capability to that of the food chains and could perform as well, consumers might well obtain a dividend on the order of 2% of their purchases. Would such a small dividend result in further disillusionment among those who anticipated that a substantial reduction in their food bills would occur?

A somewhat different argument is offered by some promoters of cooperatives. This is that the modern supermarket offers an entirely "unnecessary" range of brand and product choice and thus stores require more land than the planners believe that they should use in high-density areas. They see the cooperative as the means through which the number of brands made available to consumers can be restricted and costs and space requirements thereby lowered.[25]

Black Entrepreneurship

The development of substantially more black entrepreneurship is suggested as a means of furthering the interest of the black consumer. Whatever may be said in favor of encouraging black entrepreneurship on other grounds—and this author believes strongly that such entrepreneurship *must* be developed as a major element in meeting the problems of the black portion of American society—it is by no means clear that blackness will per se provide better institutions for black consumers. Observation of the extensive black entrepreneurship and black control in the segregated rural and urban slum areas of the South provides little comfort to the beleaguered consumer. If the consumer is to benefit, the performance of the institutions which serve him must become attuned to modern concepts of service to the consumer. Merely changing the skin color of the owner or manager is in itself unlikely to accomplish this.

Monopoly Corporations

The most striking program recently advocated is the black monopoly corporation. Legislation to authorize and subsidize such corporations has been introduced in the Congress. These corporations, to be known as Community Development Corporations, would be granted a monopoly of commercial rights in their respective areas in much the same way as the East India Company, the Mozambique Company and other development companies of the colonial era. As originally proposed, these firms would be granted territorial monopolies by the federal government so that they

25 At one dialogue session, an Office of Economic Opportunities advocate of this view stated that two brands of tuna fish were enough for a store to carry and that providing additional brands was unnecessary. That this proposal to substitute planner fiat for consumer choice would meet the approval of low-income consumers seems doubtful. The ramifications of such a policy on the ability of low-income consumers to enjoy access to new products or new brands and of the access of new competitors to the markets are also severe.

would not need to compete with "outside" firms. It has been suggested that the proposal might be amended to permit the operation within black communities of "selected" competitive businesses, subject to the consent of the monopoly corporation in each case. In order to protect its own position, one could expect that the monopoly corporation would approve only those firms which did not offer a real competitive threat—i.e. did not offer consumers better values than the monopoly corporation.

Improvement of Structure Through the Introduction of More Competitive Stores

In the final analysis, protection of the consumer in low-income areas, as in other areas of the community, rests on the availability to the consumer of *viable alternatives* in the way he can obtain the goods which he wants. The revolution in general market retailing which has occurred since World War II is largely the story of new types of arrangements which offered something different in the way of services (different assortments, convenient hours, parking, highway locations, self-selection) to attract patronage. Consumers through their choices in the marketplace caused some of these innovations to succeed, some to fail. The successful ones forced established merchants to change their operations in order to survive.

To the extent that the plight of the low-income consumer derives from the institutions available to him, the more promising remedy would appear to be the development of more, rather than less, viable competition into the so-called "ghettos." Hopefully, this competition could serve the black consumer and at the same time provide opportunities for the extensive development of entrepreneurial capability.

Impediments to Viable Competition in Low-income Areas

It has been noted that low-income areas frequently lack sufficient numbers of the more competitive enterprises. If consumers in these areas are to benefit from the competitive process we must first learn why the more competitive firms have eschewed these areas. A number of factors appear to be operating, although their relative importance is largely unexplored.

1. *Superior opportunities elsewhere*—Food chains and other mass merchandisers have tended to locate new stores in areas of established or growing potential; the low-income areas have not generally been so regarded. Moreover with comparable prices and gross margins and higher operating costs, stores in low-income areas tend to be less profitable or to operate at a loss.[26] As a result old stores are not modernized and locations are vacated as leases expire.

2. *Zoning and redevelopment hazards*—In their emphasis on housing, redevelopment programs have sometimes tended to make no provision for commercial services or to limit provision to a single store of each type, thus limiting consumer choice. Zoning has also been used to restrict modernization. For example, efforts of a Philadelphia supermarket operator to modernize a store in a

[26] See National Commission of Food Marketing *Technical Study No. 7*, pp. 339–341 and *Technical Study No. 10*, p. 122.

low-income area were thwarted by the owner's inability to secure approval for sufficient land to provide needed parking and tail-gate-height unloading facilities.

3. *Inadequate public services*—Low-income areas are often short-changed in police and fire protection and sanitation services. Thus costs are higher for all merchants in these areas but the *impact is greatest on those operating on low margins*. The belief of some merchants that the communities may be expected to tolerate riots and property destruction and the refusal of federal agencies to consider riot-torn areas as disaster areas, thereby enabling the merchants to obtain low-cost reconstruction loans, must also give pause to prospective entrepreneurs and investors, black and white. Again the impact is greatest on the low-margin operator.

4. *Incorrect perceptions of the market*—It is alleged that some retailing organizations fail to recognize the potential of the low-income areas or have misguided or incorrect impressions of the purchasing power, credit standing, or wants of consumers in those areas. Thus they avoid the areas.

5. *Insufficient numbers of able, motivated personnel in the minority groups*—It is argued that there is an insufficient number of prospective employees and store manager talent in the affected areas.

ACTION REQUIRED

It seems unlikely that the plight of the low-income consumer can be resolved by placing him at the mercy of a local monopoly, no matter how well intentioned. If the disadvantaged consumer is to enjoy the benefits available to the rest of the market, the marketing structure in the low-income areas must be modernized. To accomplish this, it is imperative that the interests of other groups, important as they are in their own spheres, be subordinated to the paramount right of the consumer to a free choice of what the market has to offer. To this end, the "ghettos" must be opened up as areas of opportunity for all legitimate businessmen, including particularly black business enterprises developed from the indigenous population. If such a goal is to be more than a pious wish, action along a number of lines is required.

1. *Training of black managers and entrepreneurs*—It is generally recognized that there is a crying need for substantial programs to motivate and train many more members of the black community for commercial activities, including much more widespread participation in entrepreneurial and responsible managerial positions. A number of programs have been developed through universities and such organizations as the Opportunities Industrial Centers and the Philadelphia Enterprise Development Corporation. If such programs are to achieve their full benefit for either the prospective businessman or the consumer, they must be geared to real competitive markets rather than protected ones.

The Rev. Leon Sullivan's Progress Plaza in North Philadelphia may prove a landmark, not so much because it provides a black-owned, black-managed shopping center in a low-income black area, but because of its recognition (a) that service to the consumer must come before the interests of the businessman —hence outlets of white-owned corporations are welcomed where such would provide a center of greater value to consumers than would have been provided by a "blacks only" rule, and (b) that if it is to serve as a training ground for black management and ownership and a place in which black-owned firms may test their mettle, it must provide a truly competitive rather than a "protected market" environment.

2. *Improving operating environments in "ghetto" areas.* Neither black-owned nor white establishments can offer competitive values to consumers unless adequate public services are provided. In particular fire and police protection, sanitary services, and equitable protection under the law are required. In addition, merchants in these areas, regardless of color, require equal access to the resources of their trade: merchandise lines, franchises, financial resources, insurance, leases.[27]

3. *Improvement of merchants' perceptions of consumers*—Merchants need more accurate knowledge of the market potential of low-income areas and of the product and related service wants of consumers. Unfortunately these areas are largely under-researched.

4. *Combatting misinformation*—Consumers, like merchants, may be expected to act on the basis of what they perceive to be true, rather than the truth itself. Thus the widespread circulation of misinformation—e.g. fictitious stories about price discrimination—not only harms consumers but discourages the legitimate businessman, black or white, from serving the area.

CONCLUSION

The consumer in the low-income areas frequently fails to benefit from the product and service offerings available to the more affluent consumer. The reasons for this condition are complex and in many cases not fully understood.

Whether the poor consumer, and especially the black resident of a low-income area, will fare better in the years to come may well depend on whether we succeed in bringing the competitive market to him or whether he will become the pawn of those who would use him as their protected preserve. The critical question for public policy remains: Will the low-income consumer secure the benefits of the competitive market or will his choices become further restricted?

[27] Serious wide-spread efforts to deal with these problems are, unfortunately, rather recent. Many date from about the time of the Vice-President's Conference on Equal Opportunity in Business, held in Washington in October, 1965. Access to franchises was of particular concern at that meeting.

34

Attitudes of Marketing Executives toward Ethics in Marketing Research

C. MERLE CRAWFORD
University of Michigan

American society today is in a period of deep and serious soul searching, with activity on many fronts designed to spotlight unethical or dishonest practices. Marketing is a popular focal point, and marketing executives watch such activities closely. They are working as perhaps never before to anticipate both legislative and public outcries.

But, with rare exceptions, criticisms of marketing have targeted on the basic tools of demand stimulation, while ignoring marketing research. Marketing researchers, from their vantage point of relative *safety*, have often joined the critics, especially as various issues are debated within the firm.

Are some marketing research practices unethical? Do marketing researchers have an obligation within the firm to "guard the facts"? Are there, in other words, some practices which society might not approve, were they fully disclosed?

Such were the questions that prompted a study in November, 1968, the results of which can now be reported. This study, conducted through cooperation of the Bureau of Business Research in The University of Michigan Graduate School of Business, consisted of posing a series of "action" situations to a national sample of marketing research directors and vice-presidents or directors of marketing.

Reprinted with permission from *Journal of Marketing,* published by the American Marketing Association, April, 1970, pp. 46–52.

Each respondent was presented with 20 instances where the marketing research director of Company X had taken some specific action; the essential question was "Do you approve or disapprove of the action taken?" The situations were not organized as in this report, and they had no descriptive titles. Six situations concerned actions by the director which are of general business applicability, and thus are not reported here. Space was provided for explanatory comments.

The response was somewhat surprising. Of the total sample of 700 individuals, responses came from 401, or 57.3%. The 412 research directors responded at a 62.9% rate, and the 288 marketing line executives at a 49.3% rate. This response on a six-page mail questionnaire, coupled with the extensive array of comments, would seem to indicate more than just a passing interest in ethics.

One note of caution, however. There is no way of being certain that what respondents *said* is what they truly *believe*. Ethics questions tend to produce conditioned responses or "acceptable" behavior patterns, and the results of this study must be interpreted accordingly.

FINDINGS

The situations covered in this report span several categories of action. Six situations covered potentially disputable research techniques, ranging from ultraviolet ink to a price exchange program. Three situations concentrated on the role of the marketing research director as a keeper of the facts, and possibly as a marketing conscience. Five situations concerned social matters of some importance today.

Selected Research Techniques

1. *Ultraviolet Ink*

"A project director recently came in to request permission to use ultraviolet ink in pre-coding questionnaires on a mail survey. He pointed out that the letter referred to an anonymous survey, but he said he needed respondent identification to permit adequate cross tabulations of the data. The M. R. Director gave his approval."

	Approve	Disapprove
Research Directors	29%	70%
Line Marketers	22	77

The feeling generally was that the appraisal turns on two issues. (1) How does one define "anonymous" as used in the letter? Some held that the ink technique violates nothing; others said it means what it says, and the ink constitutes obvious deception. (2) At a more generalized level, the issue seemed to be whether this was intended deception or not, and respondents generally assumed it was: For example, "Obviously this is deception, and I want none of it."

Note that research directors were more lenient than were line executives; although the difference was small, it is meaningful on this and the following situation.

2. Hidden Tape Recorders

"In a study intended to probe rather deeply into the buying motivations of a group of wholesale customers by use of a semi-structured personal interview form, the M. R. Director authorized the use of the department's special attache cases equipped with hidden tape recorders."

	Approve	Disapprove
Research Directors	33%	67%
Line Marketers	26	71

Reaction here was slightly more favorable than with the use of ultraviolet ink. Still the survey forms were liberally sprinkled with phrases like "Similar to wire tapping," "Isn't this a federal offense?" "This is patently dishonest." In general, respondents felt this constituted a deliberate attempt to deceive, which they could not condone even if the tapes were used solely within the research department at intended.

Many respondents waved the ethical question aside saying that such deception isn't necessary—recorders need not be hidden. Others approved on the premise that research is better this way, and no one gets hurt. As with the ultraviolet ink, however, cautions were frequent that absolutely no sales use of the information should be allowed.

This is pertinent advice. The legality of this action is open to question, partly because no cases exist covering this particular type of situation, and partly because of the chaotic state of affairs right now in the entire area of personal privacy, at both federal and state levels. It is most likely that the recording would not be actionable, but extra-research use of the tapes would probably reverse this.[1]

3. One-Way Mirrors

"One product of the X Company is brassieres, and the firm has recently been having difficulty making some decisions on a new line. Information was critically needed concerning the manner in which women put on their brassieres. So the M. R. Director designed a study in which two local stores cooperated in putting one-way mirrors in their foundations dressing rooms. Observers behind these mirrors successfully gathered the necessary information."

	Approve	Disapprove
Research Directors	20%	78%
Line Marketers	18	82

Three ideas ran through the comments section on this question. First, many persons, especially research directors, said the technique was entirely

[1] See Alan F. Weston, *Privacy and Freedom* (New York: Atheneum, Publishers, 1967), for a complete discussion of this matter.

unnecessary—that female observers in the dressing rooms could have gathered the same information.

But, far more overwhelmingly, respondents pointed out "Invasion of Privacy." In fact, one respondent put it quite bluntly: "What if your wife was one of the customers in the store that day?" Some even suggested that the responses would be far more negative if the company were one making men's underwear, and a similar technique were used. The legality of such an approach was also questioned, since there is ample case law to indicate that courts would not condone this type of *research*. A comparable case does not seem to exist, but other use of one-way mirrors in retail dressing rooms has been judged a tort and has resulted in fines and damages.

On the other hand, some respondents assumed that the observers were female, in which case they felt that the moral question was insignificant relative to the need for the information. Another said, "The women don't know they've been observed, and thus can suffer no mental anguish."

4. *Fake Long Distance Calls*

"Some of X Company's customers are busy executives, hard to reach by normal interviewing methods. Accordingly, the market research department recently conducted a study in which interviewers called 'long distance' from near-by cities. They were successful in getting through to busy executives in almost every instance."

	Approve	*Disapprove*
Research Directors	88%	10%
Line Marketers	84	16

Note the complete reversal from the three earlier situations. Why? Partly because the situation was not completely deceptive—the calls were actually long distance. But more commonly, if executives want to interrupt their busy day to receive long distance calls, that is their decision.

The small number of disapprovers felt that this technique is deceptive, and should not be used. They would counsel that actions should be judged by their character in the absolute sense, not on a scale of "badness" against a scale of gain.

5. *Fake Research Firm*

"In another study, this one concerning magazine reading habits, the M. R. Director decided to contact a sample of consumers under the name of Media Research Institute. This fictitious company name successfully camouflaged the identity of the sponsor of the study."

	Approve	*Disapprove*
Research Directors	84%	13%
Line Marketers	83	16

The basis for approval on this time-honored practice can perhaps best be summed by the following typical response:

"Most marketing research studies hide the identity of the sponsor. Why should a corporation have to purchase outside services for this privilege? Respondents generally know that research has a commercial purpose and is intended for a sponsor."

Most of the disapprovals involved complaints about the nature of the deception, rather than the deception itself: "Use your agency name instead"; "Better be sure to notify the BBB or Chambers of Commerce"; "Dangerous unless you check carefully to see that some local research firm somewhere doesn't already have this name in use"; and so on. Hiding the name of the sponsor was virtually never criticized.

6. *Exchange of Price Data*

"X Company belongs to a trade association which includes an active marketing research sub-group. At the meetings of this subgroup, the M. R. Director regularly exchanges confidential price information. In turn, he gives the competitive information to the X Company sales department, but is careful not to let the marketing vice-president know about it. Profits are substantially enhanced, and top management is protected from charges of collusion."

	Approve	Disapprove
Research Directors	8%	89%
Line Marketers	14	82

Why did respondents so quickly and completely disapprove of this technique? Simple, it is against the law. Most price collusion is illegal, most price exchanges are suspect, the trade association is no place to *informally* exchange information on price, and keeping top management in the dark is no longer an excuse.

Interestingly, very few respondents said they saw this as an ethical question: "This is a legal matter, and should not have been put on a questionnaire purportedly studying ethics in marketing research." This thinking suggests that illegality removes an act from ethical consideration, and that law and ethics are as unrelated as some critics of marketing claim. Critics say that marketers will readily charge through the gray area of ethics right up to the black wall of illegality. The results here would tend to support this criticism, since (1) respondents apparently made their decisions on legal, not ethical, grounds, and (2) the act was rather commonly condemned as unintelligent.

The Role of the Marketing Research Director

A research director is responsible for seeing that his management gets hard facts where possible, knowing when they are not, preventing mistaken interpretations of research data, and in general seeing that the research function is conducted in a competent and professional manner. The next three situations presented instances where such responsibility was at issue.

1. Advertising and Product Misuse

"Some recent research showed that many customers of X Company are misusing Product B. There's no danger; they are simply wasting their money by using too much of it at a time. But yesterday, the M. R. Director saw final comps on Product B's new ad campaign, and the ads not only ignore the problem of misuse, but actually seem to encourage it. He quietly referred the advertising manager to the research results, well known to all people on B's advertising, and let it go at that."

	Approve	Disapprove
Research Directors	41%	58%
Line Marketers	33	66

Those respondents approving the action generally claimed that whether the misuse should be attacked, supported, or ignored in the advertising, is irrelevant here. . . . The research man discharged his responsibilities, and that is the end of it.

The majority would not let it stop at that, for two different reasons. First, many said the researcher was negligent and that he should have brought the matter to the attention of the head of marketing. Others said such advertising is simply not profitable; that product misuse opens the door to competition; the researcher should have protested along this line.

When those who approved the action are added to those who objected on grounds of strategy, one finds only a minority who actually claimed to condemn the action on ethical grounds. For example, here are several typical disapprovals:

"He should pursue the matter. Ultimately, a competitive product will undercut Product B on cost of usage."

"The decision is the advertising manager's to make. One would hope, however, that the M. R. Director would point out that the decision to encourage misuse is not an ethical decision but a pragmatic profit-and-loss decision."

"Maybe customer prefers to use it that way. Maybe the company has an inaccurate view of value perceived by customer. Would advocate accurate instructions for use—not unusually strong measures to change customer and reduce revenue."

There were, of course, a number of respondents who echoed one man's comment: "Disapprove—and I would be *loud*."

Line marketing executives were more concerned than were researchers. Some accused the marketing research director of being a "gutless wonder." But, in general, if a marketing head disapproved the action and explained his thinking, he said something like this: "He should have passed the word up the line, just to be sure the advertising man's boss knew the facts. But that's the end of it for him."

2. Distortions by Marketing Vice-President

"In the trial run of a major presentation to the Board of Directors, the marketing vice-president deliberately distorted some recent research findings. After some thought, the M. R. Director decided to ignore the matter, since the marketing head obviously knew what he was doing."

	Approve	*Disapprove*
Research Directors	12%	87%
Line Marketers	12	86

Those who approved the action said either: (1) "What else could he do?" or (2) "The boss might have had some good reason or information which the M. R. Director didn't know about."

Disapprovals, however, took a much more complex form. The first, and probably the largest, group felt that some action was called for . . . a private talk, a memo, and in a few cases, an end run. The action should not be dramatic, and if it produced no results, the matter should be dropped.

A smaller, though much more vocal, group demanded strong action. They stood on principle, and stated that if an appeal were lost, the director should either resign on the spot, or move quickly to find a company with a different class of executives.

Perhaps a few quotes will indicate the spread in opinion on this issue:

"It's not the M. R. Director's moral obligation to force his superior to be honest."

"Decision depends on the reasons for the distortion."

"I would drop a written memo to the VP, pointing to distortions. Suggest presentation be changed."

"I would resign my position."

Most situations in this study, however, did not strike this deeply into the confrontation between economic security and moral values.

3. *Possible Conflict of Interest*

"A market testing firm, to which X Company gives most of its business, recently went public. The M. R. Director had been looking for a good investment and proceeded to buy some $20,000 of their stock. The firm continues as X Company's leading supplier for testing."

	Approve	*Disapprove*
Research Directors	40%	57%
Line Marketers	58	38

This situation is difficult to interpret. As one respondent put it, "There's some danger here that he might try to protect his investment!" Yet, almost half of the total respondents approved. It should not be inferred that they were unaware of the potential conflict of interest. Even those approving the action often added that the director must obtain the approval of his supervisor, or that he must be careful to remain objective.

The answer seems to lie in the amount of the investment. If the testing firm in question were A. C. Nielsen, a $20,000 investment would not be the determining factor. In smaller firms, however, a director would realize the direct relationship between his purchase of testing service and the profits of the firm performing the work.

Beyond those who passed the matter on to higher management, it would seem that respondents' answers were a function of their evaluation of the importance of $20,000.

Line marketers as a group actually approved the action. Unfortunately, there was nothing in the comments to explain this difference. It could be the result of confidence that management has acquired for the integrity of researchers, or it is possible that $20,000 has much less significance in their customary dollar frame of reference.

Today's Social Concerns

In the area of social concerns, action situations were to probe the matter of possible conflicts between a firm's self-interest and the natural desire of its marketing people to help their fellow men. Question areas were approached carefully since the strong differences of opinion were known. After some pretesting, it became apparent that most respondents were willing to accept all of the proposed areas of interest as having at least some ethical overtones. Not all did, however, and a few comments came back to the effect, "Don't know why you put this situation in a study of ethics—it has nothing to do with ethics."

1. *General Trade Data to Ghetto Group*

"The marketing research department of X Company frequently makes extensive studies of their retail customers. A federally supported Negro group, working to get a shopping center in their ghetto area, wanted to know if they could have access to this trade information. But since the M. R. Director had always refused to share this information with trade organizations, he declined the request."

	Approve	*Disapprove*
Research Directors	64%	34%
Line Marketers	74	25

Votes of two-to-one and three-to-one are rather overwhelming, and many respondents voiced strong opinions. "What's good for one is good for all." "Everyone must play by the same rules." "Federal or ghetto has nothing to do with it." The consensus was that out of respect to retailers cooperating in past studies or in terms of company profits, the decision was correct; consistency demands that the data not be shared.

Dissenters were divided into two groups. The first group cited the opinion that this is really a top management decision; the research director should not have attempted to make a judgment on his own. But the second group was more direct: "Assuming that the shopping center could improve the situation in the ghetto area, the director has an obligation to the group that transcends the normally ethical business position." "No—this is silly secrecy." "I strongly disapprove—we need to do everything in our power to assist Negroes in their attempt at economic self-improvement." Whether correct or not, those favoring the release of such information constituted a minority.

2. *NMAC Request for Recent Price Study*

"The National Marketing Advisory Council (formed of top marketing executives and marketing educators to advise the Commerce Department) has a task force studying ghetto prices. The head of this study recently called to ask if they could have a copy of a recent X Company study which he understood showed that ghetto appliance prices are significantly higher than in suburban areas. Since X Company sells appliances to these ghetto merchants, the M. R. Director felt compelled to refuse the request."

	Approve	Disapprove
Research Directors	56%	39%
Line Marketers	46	51

Compared to the previous question, the approval rate declined, and line marketing executives actually moved to a point of disapproval. Respondents who felt that ghetto prices should not be higher, or at least not that much higher, were quick to say that social good overrides a loyalty to customers. As one respondent put it: "What's best for the public should have much greater weight than protecting their customers, especially when such customers are engaged in wrong practices." Another respondent went a bit further: "Protecting good and fair customers is one thing—protecting carpetbaggers is another."

These are ethical reasons for disapproval, but many were simply pragmatic: The study could be replicated—NMAC could obtain their own data—so what would be gained by refusing to cooperate?

Those approving the action did so usually on the basis that the company's first obligation is to its customers and to its profits. On the assumption that NMAC would stimulate some action contrary to the best interest of the ghetto merchants, the company would be neither economically wise nor ethically fair to its customers by revealing the data.

3. *Assigning Man to a Ghetto Planning Group*

"A local Office of Economic Opportunity group recently called to ask that the M. R. Director assign one of his men to the planning group working on the ghetto shopping center mentioned earlier. Since one result of such a center would be to force a good number of ghetto retailers out of business, and since some of these retailers were presently customers of X Company, the M. R. Director refused the request."

	Approve	Disapprove
Research Directors	41%	51%
Line Marketers	39	57

Similar reasoning supported approval here. Why should the research director be expected to act contrary to short-term profits and to the interests of present customers? These respondents saw no overriding ethical consideration and felt simply that the director should be a businessman, not a social worker.

Some dissenters stressed the social angle: "Assuming that the shopping center has been thoroughly considered and felt to be good for the community as a whole, Company X should help it." Others were pragmatic, saying that Company X would be of greatest service to these ghetto customers if it had a man involved in the planning—a man who could bring back progress reports and perhaps try to protect the ghetto merchants' interests in the shopping center planning.

4. *Negro Account Executive*

"The President of an interviewing firm which had been doing most of the field work for X Company wrote to say that a new account executive had been assigned to X. The new man was capable, personable, and black. The M. R. Director wrote back to say that there were no Negroes in the department at the moment, and that he felt it would be better all around if a different account man were assigned to X Company."

	Approve	*Disapprove*
Research Directors	5%	94%
Line Marketers	7	92

Little explanation is needed here. Comments ranged from, "This has got to stop—God help us if it doesn't," to "This is total bigotry." Respondents were adamant, underlining words, adding exclamation points, and in many cases berating the author for including this situation as an issue.

In fairness to reportorial accuracy, however, there were some approvals, the thought being that the research director knows his location and his people. If he is in a part of the country where feelings tend to run against this action, perhaps department morale demands a refusal on his part.

That the situation is not entirely unrealistic was underscored by one comment: "Give it a chance—it worked for us."

5. *Hiring Jewish Marketing Analyst*

"When interviewing applicants for a newly created analyst position, the M. R. Director was impressed with one man in particular. But he didn't offer him the job, since the applicant referred to himself as Jewish, and it was well known that X Company wanted no Jewish marketing people."

	Approve	*Disapprove*
Research Directors	26%	71%
Line Marketers	20	77

This situation was included in the study partly to test the times, and partly to compare with the preceding one on the Negro. Respondents were sometimes quite indignant and disapproval was still quite overwhelming, but a significant minority approved, for two reasons. The first reason was the matter of company policy, and the second was the question of practicality. Is it wise to encourage a man of the Jewish faith to enter an environment where he would face personal abuse, and would find it difficult to work to his capacity?

Those disapproving the action cited the obvious reasons, and with frequent vehemence.

Other Ethical Problems in Marketing Research

A final section of the questionnaire invited respondents to list any other situations found in the field of marketing research which might be questioned from an ethical point of view. Of the many situations given, here are the ones thought to be of greatest interest, though none had more than a scattering of mentions:

1. Performing "research" work, either internally or as a consultant, which is specifically geared to gain conclusions sought by higher management.
2. The solicitation of research proposals from several firms, and then combining the best features of each into the one actually performed by the low bidder.
3. Long technical appendices in a study, or use of technical jargon in written or oral presentations, the intent being to delude the reader or listener regarding the thoroughness of the job or the competence of the researcher.
4. The pretense of survey research by firms selling products door to door or over the telephone.
5. Obtaining information by falsely implying that a respondent's superior has given his approval for disclosure.
6. Continuing a study to completion, after finding out late in the game that major errors have been made, the intention being to hide from management or client that costly backtracking should be undertaken.
7. Raising the payment to a research vendor for an upcoming job to make up for loss on last job, when costs were actually higher than expected.
8. A firm that is in the business of compiling cross-classified mailing lists using a fake survey form to obtain the necessary information.
9. The promising of a report of completed results, in order to gain respondent cooperation, but with intention not to follow through.
10. The failure to use techniques purported to be used particularly in the case of probability sampling.
11. The use of purported new techniques as a selling technique by marketing research firms and workers.

CONCLUSIONS

This study was not designed to yield definitive statements covering the ethics of marketers, or even marketing researchers, and any such conclusions at this point are entirely unwarranted. The study was designed to answer the question: Are there ethical matters within the field of marketing research which might be further investigated and discussed? The answer must be affirmative, since there are substantial areas of disagreement and disapproval.

Specifically, respondents disapproved of the use of ultraviolet ink, hidden tape recorders, and one-way mirrors (in a given situation), a particular price exchange program, an action relating to product misuse, the ignoring of executive distortions, conflicts of interest, the refusal of assigning a man to a ghetto business project, and personnel situations involving racial and religious discrimination. Yet very few veteran marketing researchers would claim they have not encountered such or similar situations.

Except in areas involving at best questionable law, nothing but one's conscience operates to inhibit these practices. There is no broadly applicable code, no board of investigation, no licensing authority, and no federal statement of research practice guidelines.

Thus, a situation seems to prevail where objectionable practices occur at least occasionally, if not frequently, without formal resistance. Under stimulation from the vehemence of attack displayed by respondents in this survey and to forestall investigative action by a marketing researcher like Ralph Nader, the following future actions would seem to be in order (current activities in areas of credit investigations, data banks, and census questionnaires suggest there might not be much time):

1. Organize formal discussions of debatable practices, at the national level, via AMA task force.
2. Seriously investigate again the American Marketing Association Code of Ethics and appropriate enforcement procedures.
3. Develop, from these investigations, whatever program of activities appears necessary to markedly reduce the incidence of unethical research practices within the field of marketing. At a minimum, honest researchers deserve a public statement of their beliefs and convictions.

The survey also brought out clearly the evidence that top marketing managers have a set of ethical standards very close to that of researchers. The responses were amazingly similar, with management being only slightly less critical and differing significantly only on the matters of possible conflict of interest and the supplying of data to the National Marketing Advisory Council. It would appear that management would support efforts to reduce the incidence of questionable practices.

One might ask whether persons at the other end of the responsibility spectrum (business students) feel the same. Preliminary research here at The University of Michigan would indicate that they do, but this will not be known for certain until further research, currently under way and using the same forms, is concluded.

INTERNATIONAL MARKETS

35

Multinational
Product Planning:
Strategic Alternatives

WARREN J. KEEGAN
Columbia University

Inadequate product planning is a major factor inhibiting growth and profitability in international business operations today. The purpose of this article is to identify five strategic alternatives available to international marketers, and to identify the factors which determine the strategy which a company should use. Table 1 summarizes the proposed strategic alternatives.

STRATEGY ONE: ONE PRODUCT,
ONE MESSAGE, WORLDWIDE

When PepsiCo extends its operations internationally, it employs the easiest and in many cases the most profitable marketing strategy—that of product extension. In every country in which it operates, PepsiCo sells exactly the same product, and does it with the same advertising and promotional themes and appeals that it uses in the United States. PepsiCo's outstanding international performance is perhaps the most eloquent and persuasive justification of this practice.

Unfortunately, PepsiCo's approach does not work for all products. When Campbell soup tried to sell its U.S. tomato soup formulation to the British, it discovered, after considerable losses, that the English prefer

Reprinted with permission from *Journal of Marketing,* published by the American Marketing Association, January, 1969, pp. 58–62.

a more bitter taste. Another U.S. company spent several million dollars in an unsuccessful effort to capture the British cake mix market with U.S.-style fancy frosting and cake mixes only to discover that Britons consume their cake at tea time, and that the cake they prefer is dry, spongy, and suitable to being picked up with the left hand while the right manages a cup of tea. Another U.S. company that asked a panel of British housewives to bake their favorite cakes discovered this important fact and has since acquired a major share of the British cake mix market with a dry, spongy cake mix.

Closer to home, Philip Morris attempted to take advantage of U.S. television advertising campaigns which have a sizable Canadian audience in border areas. The Canadian cigarette market is a Virginia or straight tobacco market in contrast to the U.S. market, which is a blended tobacco market. Philip Morris officials decided to ignore market research evidence which indicated that Canadians would not accept a blended cigarette, and went ahead with programs which achieved retail distribution of U.S.-blended brands in the Canadian border areas served by U.S. television. Unfortunately, the Canadian preference for the straight cigarette remained unchanged. American-style cigarettes sold right up to the border but no further. Philip Morris had to withdraw its U.S. brands.

The unfortunate experience of discovering consumer preferences that do not favor a product is not confined to U.S. products in foreign markets. Corn Products Company discovered this in an abortive attempt to popularize Knorr dry soups in the United States. Dry soups dominate the soup market in Europe, and Corn Products tried to transfer some of this success to the United States. Corn Products based its decision to push ahead with Knorr on reports of taste panel comparison of Knorr dry soups with popular liquid soups. The results of these panel tests strongly favored the Knorr product. Unfortunately these taste panel tests did not simulate the actual market environment for soup which includes not only eating but also preparation. Dry soups require 15 to 20 minutes cooking, whereas liquid soups are ready to serve as soon as heated. This difference is apparently a critical factor in the soup buyer's choice, and it was the reason for another failure of the extension strategy.

The product-communications extension strategy has an enormous appeal to most multinational companies because of the cost savings associated with this approach. Two sources of savings, manufacturing economies of scale and elimination of product R and D costs, are well known and understood. Less well known, but still important, are the substantial economies associated with the standardization of marketing communications. For a company with worldwide operations, the cost of preparing separate print and TV-cinema films for each market would be enormous. PepsiCo international marketers have estimated, for example, that production costs for specially prepared advertising for foreign markets would cost them $8 million per annum, which is considerably more than the amounts now spent by PepsiCo International for advertising production in these markets. Although these cost savings are important, they should not distract executives from the more important objective of

TABLE 1: MULTINATIONAL PRODUCT-COMMUNICATIONS
MIX: STRATEGIC ALTERNATIVES

Strat- egy	Product Function or Need Satisfied	Conditions of Product Use	Ability to Buy Product	Recom- mended Product Strategy	Recom- mended Communi- cations Strategy	Relative Cost of Adjust ments	Product Examples
1	Same	Same	Yes	Extension	Extension	1	Soft drinks
2	Different	Same	Yes	Extension	Adaptation	2	Bicycles, Motor- scooters
3	Same	Different	Yes	Adaptation	Extension	3	Gasoline, Detergents
4	Different	Different	Yes	Adaptation	Adaptation	4	Clothing, Greeting Cards
5	Same	. . . . . .	No	Invention	Develop New Com- munications	5	Hand- powered Washing Machine

maximum profit performance, which may require the use of an adjust-ment or invention strategy. As shown above, product extension in spite of its immediate cost savings may in fact prove to be a financially disas-trous undertaking.

STRATEGY TWO: PRODUCT EXTENSION— COMMUNICATIONS ADAPTATION

When a product fills a different need or serves a different function under use conditions identical or similar to those in the domestic market, the only adjustment required is in marketing communications. Bicycles and motorscooters are illustrations of products in this category. They satisfy needs mainly for recreation in the United States but provide basic transportation in many foreign countries. Outboard motors are sold pri-marily to a recreation market in the United States, while the same motors in many foreign countries are sold mainly to fishing and transportation fleets.

In effect, when this approach is pursued (or, as is often the case, when it is stumbled upon quite by accident), a product transformation occurs. The same physical product ends up serving a different function or use than that for which it was originally designed. An actual example of a very successful transformation is provided by a U.S. farm machinery com-pany which decided to market its U.S. line of suburban lawn and garden power equipment as agricultural implements in less-developed countries. The company's line of garden equipment was ideally suited to the farm-ing task in many less-developed countries, and, most importantly, it was priced at almost a third less than competing equipment especially designed for small acreage farming offered by various foreign manufacturers.

There are many examples of food product transformation. Many dry soup powders, for example, are sold mainly as soups in Europe but as sauces or cocktail dips in the United States. The products are identical; the only change is in marketing communications. In this case, the main communications adjustment is in the labeling of the powder. In Europe, the label illustrates and describes how to make soup out of the powder. In the United States, the label illustrates and describes how to make sauce and dip as well as soup.

The appeal of the product extension communications adaptation strategy is its relatively low cost of implementation. Since the product in this strategy is unchanged, R and D, tooling, manufacturing setup, and inventory costs associated with additions to the product line are avoided. The only costs of this approach are in identifying different product functions and reformulating marketing communications (advertising, sales promotion, point-of-sale material, and so on) around the newly identified function.

STRATEGY THREE: PRODUCT ADAPTATION— COMMUNICATIONS EXTENSION

A third approach to international product planning is to extend without change the basic communications strategy developed for the U.S. or home market, but to adapt the U.S. or home product to local use conditions. The product adaptation-communications extension strategy assumes that the product will serve the same function in foreign markets under different use conditions.

Esso followed this approach when it adapted its gasoline formulations to meet the weather conditions prevailing in foreign market areas, but employed without change its basic communications appeal, "Put a Tiger in Your Tank." There are many other examples of products that have been adjusted to perform the same function internationally under different environmental conditions. International soap and detergent manufacturers have adjusted their product formulations to meet local water conditions and the characteristics of washing equipment with no change in their basic communications approach. Agricultural chemicals have been adjusted to meet different soil conditions as well as different types and levels of insect resistance. Household appliances have been scaled to sizes appropriate to different use environments, and clothing has been adapted to meet fashion criteria.

STRATEGY FOUR: DUAL ADAPTATION

Market conditions indicate a strategy of adaptation of both the product and communications when differences exist in environmental conditions of use and in the function which a product serves. In essence, this is a combination of the market conditions of strategies two and three. U.S. greeting card manufacturers have faced these circumstances in Europe where the conditions under which greeting cards are purchased are different than in the United States. In Europe, the function of a greeting card is to provide a space for the sender to write his own message in contrast to the U.S. card which contains a prepared message or what is known in the greeting card industry as "sentiment." European greeting cards are cellophane wrapped, necessitating a product alteration by American greeting card manufacturers selling in the European market. American manufacturers pursuing an adjustment strategy have changed both their product and their marketing communications in response to this set of environmental differences.

STRATEGY FIVE: PRODUCT INVENTION

The adaptation and adjustment strategies are effective approaches to international marketing when potential customers have the ability, or purchasing power, to buy the product. When potential customers cannot afford a product, the strategy indicated is invention or the development of an entirely new product designed to satisfy the identified need or function at a price within reach of the potential customer. This is a demanding but, if product development costs are not excessive, a potentially rewarding product strategy for the mass markets in the middle and less-developed countries of the world.

Although potential opportunities for the utilization of the invention strategy in international marketing are legion, the number of instances where companies have responded is disappointingly small. For example, there are an estimated 600 million women in the world who still scrub their clothes by hand. These women have been served by multinational soap and detergent companies for decades, yet until this year not one of these companies had attempted to develop an inexpensive manual washing device.

Robert Young, Vice President of Marketing-Worldwide of Colgate-Palmolive, has shown what can be done when product development efforts are focused upon market needs. He asked the leading inventor of modern mechanical washing processes to consider "inventing backwards"—to apply his knowledge not to a better mechanical washing device, but to a much better manual device. The device developed by the inventor is an inexpensive (under $10), all-plastic, hand-powered washer that has the tumbling action of a modern automatic machine. The response to this washer in a Mexican test market is reported to be enthusiastic.

HOW TO CHOOSE A STRATEGY

The best product strategy is one which optimizes company profits over the long term, or, stated more precisely, it is one which maximizes the present value of cash flows associated with business operations. Which strategy for international markets best achieves this goal? There is, unfortunately, no general answer to this question. Rather, the answer depends upon the specific product-market-company mix.

Some products demand adaptation, others lend themselves to adaptation, and others are best left unchanged. The same is true of markets. Some are so similar to the U.S. markets as to require little adaptation. No country's markets, however, are exactly like the U.S., Canada's included. Indeed, even within the United States, for some products regional and ethnic differences are sufficiently important to require product adaptation. Other markets are moderately different and lend themselves to adaptation, and still others are so different as to require adaptation of the majority of products. Finally, companies differ not only in their manufacturing costs, but also in their capability to identify and produce profitable product adaptations.

PRODUCT-MARKET ANALYSIS

The first step in formulating international product policy is to apply the systems analysis technique to each product in question. How is the product used? Does it require power sources, linkage to other systems, maintenance, preparation, style matching, and so on? Examples of almost mandatory adaptation situations are products designed for 60-cycle power going into 50-cycle markets, products calibrated in inches going to metric markets, products which require maintenance going into markets where maintenance standards and practices differ from the original design market, and products which might be used under different conditions than those for which they were originally designed. Renault discovered this latter factor too late with the ill-fated Dauphine which acquired a notorious reputation for breakdown, frequency in the United States. Renault executives attribute the frequent mechanical failure of the Dauphine in the United States to the high-speed turnpike driving and relatively infrequent U.S. maintenance. These turned out to be critical differences for the product, which was designed for the roads of France and the almost daily maintenance which a Frenchman lavishes upon his car.

Even more difficult are the product adaptations which are clearly not mandatory, but which are of critical importance in determining whether the product will appeal to a narrow market segment rather than a broad mass market. The most frequent offender in this category is price. Too often, U.S. companies believe they have adequately adapted their international product offering by making adaptations to the physical features of products (for example, converting 120 volts to 220 volts) but they extend U.S. prices. The effect of such practice in most markets of the world where average incomes are lower than those in the United States is to put the U.S. product in a specialty market for the relatively wealthy consumers rather than in the mass market. An extreme case of this occurs when the product for the foreign market is exported from the United States and undergoes the often substantial price escalation that occurs when products are sold via multi-layer export channels and exposed to import duties. When price constraints are considered in international marketing, the result can range from margin reduction and feature elimination to the "inventing backwards" approach used by Colgate.

Company Analysis

Even if product-market analysis indicates an adaptation opportunity, each company must examine its own product/communication development and manufacturing costs. Clearly, any product or communication adaptation strategy must survive the test of profit effectiveness. The often-repeated exhortation that in international marketing a company should always adapt its products' advertising and promotion is clearly superficial, for it does not take into account the cost of adjusting or adapting products and communications programs.

What are Adaptation Costs?

They fall under two broad categories—development and production. Development costs will vary depending on the cost effectiveness of product/communications development groups within the company. The range in costs from company to company and product to product is great. Often, the company with international product development facilities has a strategic cost advantage. The vice-president of a leading U.S. machinery company told recently of an example of this kind of advantage:

> We have a machinery development group both here in the States and also in Europe. I tried to get our U.S. group to develop a machine for making the elliptical cigars that dominate the European market. At first they said "who would want an elliptical cigar machine?" Then they gradually admitted that they could produce such a machine for $500,000. I went to our Italian product development group with the same proposal, and they developed the machine I wanted for $50,000. The differences were partly relative wage costs but very importantly they were psychological. The Europeans see elliptical cigars every day, and they do not find the elliptical cigar unusual. Our American engineers were negative on elliptical cigars at the outset and I think this affected their overall response.

Analysis of a company's manufacturing costs is essentially a matter of identifying potential opportunity losses. If a company is reaping economies of scale from large-scale production of a single product, then any shift to variations of the single product will raise manufacturing costs. In general, the more decentralized a company's manufacturing setup, the smaller the manufacturing cost of producing different versions of the basic product. Indeed, in the company with local manufacturing facilities for each international market, the additional *manufacturing* cost of producing an adapted product for each market is zero.

A more fundamental form of company analysis occurs when a firm is considering in general whether or not to pursue explicitly a strategy of product adaptation. At this level, analysis must focus not only on the manufacturing cost structure of the firm, but also on the basic capability of the firm to identify product adaptation opportunities and to convert these perceptions into profitable products. The ability to identify preferences will depend to an important degree on the creativity of people in the organization and the effectiveness of information systems in this organization. The latter capability is as important as the former. For example, the existence of salesmen who are creative in identifying profitable product adaptation opportunities is no assurance that their ideas will be translated into reality by the organization. Information, in the form of their ideas and perceptions, must move through the organization to those who are involved in the product development decision-making process; and this movement, as any student of information systems in organizations will attest, is not automatic. Companies which lack perceptual and information system capabilities are not well equipped to pursue a product adaptation strategy, and should either concentrate on products which can be extended or should develop these capabilities before turning to a product adaptation strategy.

SUMMARY

The choice of product and communications strategy in international marketing is a function of three key factors: (1) the product itself defined in terms of the function or need it serves; (2) the market defined in terms of the conditions under which the product is used, including the preferences of potential customers and the ability to buy the products in question; and (3) the costs of adaptation and manufacture to the company considering these product-communications approaches. Only after analysis of the product-market fit and of company capabilities and costs can executives choose the most profitable international strategy.

METAMARKETING: THE FURTHERING OF ORGANIZATIONS, PERSONS, PLACES, AND CAUSES

36

The Outlandish Idea: How a Marketing Man Would Save India

NATHANIEL MATLIN
The Matlin Company

Notwithstanding their reputation for foresight, government planners find it as difficult as the next man to think new thoughts in new ways. Only on this basis does it seem possible to explain their neglect of marketing techniques in large-scale social and economic planning, for the intelligent application of such techniques offers new hope of solving otherwise intractable problems.

A case in point is the use of marketing methods to slow excessive population growth in India. This has more than academic importance. For on the success of India's decelerating its population growth rests its ability to feed its people and maintain political integrity. And with the People's Republic of China just over the mountains, the peace of the entire world hinges on India's not becoming a political vacuum.

All the solutions thus far attempted have failed. Providing more food, for example, has only exacerbated the problem. Witness how the good 1967 harvest has led to feelings of unwarranted optimism and a blunting of the urgency of birth control programs.

Grasshoppermindedness aside, however, even measures born of despair during the past five years did not work. Why?

I am convinced that it was because men as able and impatient as Sripati Chandrasekhar, the Minister of Health and Family Planning, did not trouble to understand marketing.

Reprinted with permission from *Marketing Communications*, March, 1968, pp. 54–60. **451**

Selling birth control is as much a marketing job as selling any other consumer product. And where no manufacturer would contemplate developing and introducing a new product without a thorough understanding of the variables of the market, planners in the highest circles of Indian government have blithely gone ahead without understanding that marketing principles must determine the character of any campaign of voluntary control.

The Indians have done only the poorest research. They have mismanaged distribution of contraceptive devices. They have ignored the importance of "customer service." They have proceeded with grossly inadequate undertrained staffs; they have been blind to the importance of promotion and advertising.

In choosing the intrauterine contraceptive device—the IUD or "loop" —as their main instrument of reducing births for some years, the government planners did not recognize that the voluntary implantation of such a device calls for an outlook on life and a degree of belief in one's own ability to shape one's life that is not possessed even by many Western women. Yet they tried it in India where the philosophy of *karma*—of "what will be, will be"—permeates every economic and social stratum, and where the women who most need the loop are the poorest, the least educated and sophisticated, and the most tradition-bound of the country.

In a nation constantly beset by internecine quarrels among at least 14 major cultures, the planners used appeals to patriotism, common sense and intellect. Theirs has been a cardinal sin of marketing communications: Because such appeals have force with the planners themselves, they assumed they would offer a positive motivational basis for rural women.

The failure of the loops led to trial of male sterilization—ligation of the vas deferens—as the preferred method of contraception. This did nothing but shift the burden of belief from women to men. Again the planners failed and couldn't understand why.

Their latest effort is to disseminate condoms among the village people, educate them in their use and again hope for the best. Early reports have it that J. Walter Thompson Co. is to be retained to develop a promotional campaign. The only salutary aspect of this is that the planners are at last beginning to recognize that an expertise is needed that they themselves lack.

The choice of the particular means of contraception is an unhappy one, however, for it has had no historic record of success with other poor, orthodox and largely illiterate populations. Any commercial development man will apprehend that whatever product is chosen must be acceptable both on physical and emotional grounds. A product that is good from a medical, mechanical and logistic viewpoint but that is not psychosocially suitable is a bad product. A review of the past 15 years of socially oriented technological experiments in India suggests that there is a better product. It is in fact two products: a "package," including the loop and the solar cooker.

The solar cooker is a small paraboloidal reflector that can concentrate the rays of the sun in a bright climate so that a woman may use it to cook without fuel. Its introduction in India in the past was precluded by its prohibitive cost. It would have to sell for the equivalent of $5 to $15.

If a free solar cooker were used as an inducement for a woman to allow fitting a loop, the combination would be acceptable, as I shall attempt to show, physically, emotionally and economically.

First let us consider whether women would respond more enthusiastically to the loop and cooker combination than to the loop alone. (In the first two years of fitting loops, about 2 million devices were implanted. This was a shortfall of catastrophic proportions, for 9 million births must be prevented each year if the Indian birthrate is to decline from 40 per thousand women of childbearing age to an acceptable 25.)

Aside from the benefits of better health, greater longevity, more comely appearance and increased leisure that a loop offers to a woman, the combination of loop and cooker would have an important benefit for her husband. And her husband is the greatest single influence in her life. For if a man's wife and children need not engage in the inordinately great effort of gathering fuel as is now the case, their time can be better employed in remunerative work. Combining the solar cooker with the loop would do much towards supplanting the deep-rooted belief in agrarian societies that more hands in the family mean more food in the pot.

The husband's acceptance may be solicited in another way too, outlandish though it may seem at first. Many Indian families carry around their entire wealth on the neck of the wife. As loops can be made in part of precious metals as well as plastics, would a part silver loop be considered as much jewelry as a necklace of gold coins? Would it enhance the husband's prestige?

Whatever the case, it seems obvious that appealing to village people with statistics, common sense and patriotism is nugatory. Appeals to personal beauty and pecuniary gain that offer a positive emotional basis for women—and men—to desire the fitting of loops are the only ones that can reasonably be expected to succeed in the Indian market.

This is not to say that intellectual appeals can find no place in this scheme. It is simply that they must be directed where they can do the most good. In the present case, this could be India's female physicians. Of the roughly 10,000 women doctors in India, only a tenth were recruited into fitting loops. This failure limited the entire loop program to begin with, for Indian rural women, being extremely modest, will permit a gynecological examination only by another woman.

Intellectually oriented appeals may also be well directed to the hundreds of thousands of midwives who must be enrolled in any program of loop fitting. Campaigns based on professional as well as economic and emotional factors have helped bring large numbers of midwives into modern family health service in the Soviet Union, Latin America, the African countries and our own deep South. They could do the same in India.

Once enthusiasm has been aroused among the village women and men, and among the physicians and midwives, then enthusiasm must be maintained. The government has found out how disastrous the consequences of ignoring this can be, for a great deal of adverse publicity has sprung up about the loop. Up to 20% of any group of normal women of childbearing age either expel loops involuntarily or experience discomfort in their use. With India so short of gynecologically trained personnel, teams have entered villages, fitted women, and departed immediately, leaving a certain proportion of the women bleeding, frightened and articulate. Rumors of irreversible sterilization and electrical shocks given to sexual partners have become rife. More than anything else, this bad press was responsible for the Ministry of Health and Family Planning deemphasizing loops and trying vasectomy.

To Americans who know that hard goods cannot successfully be marketed by coming to town, selling and leaving immediately, letting the customers worry on their own about where to get service, the failure of the Indians must appear inevitable. But to the Indians who had not even an elementary knowledge of marketing and did not appreciate that loops are indeed hard goods, the failure was all the more painful because it seemed inexplicable.

Having outlined reasons for believing that the cooker-loop combination would find ready acceptance in the Indian marketplace, I must now indicate why it could find similar acceptance with the "marketer." The stumbling block, of course, is money—enormous amounts of money.

Obviously the money must come from the governments of the developed nations. But what arguments will make them part with funds they would much rather spend on military appropriations? Duress of some sort seems necessary.

In our own country the State and Agricultural departments and other executive branch bureaus well know the practical sense of helping India limit her population and are willing to back their belief with funds. But the people who control the funds and who must pass the unpopular tax laws that will generate them are generally unwilling to make their chances for reelection precarious by voting for measures that will immediately benefit only people halfway around the earth.

At some point, of course, it will become apparent to their constituents that continued charity in the form of Public Law 480 wheat shipments is economically unacceptable. American farmers already know it, for continued aid in the form of grain to India rests on long-term agreements and on surpluses from which to ship. This means increased government intervention into the free play of the open agricultural commodity market.

But aside from matters of an open market, rising bread prices, and the friendliness of our friends abroad, it will at last be acknowledged that giving or growing more food does not solve the problem, but only makes it more refractory. I have a little personal knowledge of this, for one of my clients who builds pulp and paper mills around the world (two in India) found that in each case in that country the influx of capital as wages paid to local labor went mainly into higher expenditures for food. And in India as elsewhere, the good life is conducive to larger families. (The only offsetting feature in one village was the introduction of electric lights which helped slow the accelerating birthrate somewhat.)

Ultimately, therefore, it will be economic arguments that will force the United States and other governments to tithe themselves to support a program of birth control in India. This assumption leads to the question of how the funds will best be used.

As one who believes that the American appliance industry is second to none, I suggest that our country is the logical one to produce solar cookers. With development work already done in the universities and research institutes, what will be needed is product engineering à la Louisville to turn out inexpensive, sturdy, good-looking solar cookers in the very best GE style.

If the Russians were gracious, they could volunteer to produce the loops. They have no George Meaneys. Besides, their medical industry seems to be most advanced in the world. And if a bit of precious metal were to be incorporated into each loop, the Russian primary metals industry could supply gold, silver and metals of the platinum family more abundantly and economically than producers in other lands.

To some of the smaller and less wealthy nations could fall the task of preparing and implementing programs for training midwives. Israel has troubles enough of her own, but perhaps she could spare some of her personnel to teach paramedical workers for India. Switzerland, Italy, Germany, and especially France could provide talent to mount the broadside poster campaigns that are necessary to communicate to a largely uneducated and even illiterate market. Three-sheet posters of the sort that command the eye in the passages of the Paris Métro are just what is needed for the walls of Indian village houses.

Is there any question as to who should take responsibility for creating short animated films and live puppet and marionette shows for point-of-purchase promotion? The magnificent achievements of the Czechs at Expo 67 give us the answer. Their efforts and those of the Poles could be channeled into both consumer and "dealer" advertising.

In discussing what talents must be drawn on—those for research, copy, art, production, sales, distribution, auditing—we must not forget those of the bureaucrat. For however much one dislikes him with his feet of clay, he is absolutely necessary for any scheme as ambitious as this. Luckily India has bureaucrats in excellent supply. Not that a few well chosen ones from England and Sweden would not be useful with their extensive experience in socially regulated medicine. Their presence would hopefully prevent the same mistakes being made in Mysore that once were made in Manchester and Malmöe.

Now, up to this point I have been conveying the impression that the marketing man is the central figure in the plan. I must, of course, admit what every marketing man sometime in his life admits—that any marketing plan, no matter how sound, can succeed only if it has a base of responsible fiscal management.

Such management is needed here. It can be found probably only in two areas: in some supranational organization as, for example, an arm of the World Health Organization or in a private profit-making group like

Litton Industries or Arthur D. Little, each of whom has proven competence in systems management. While I have the greatest admiration for the people of the WHO, I would feel easier with a business-oriented group, for only the strictest adherence to principles of profit accountability will enable the plan to succeed.

We must not forget in all this intellectual pot smoking that India herself must place the final imprimatur on the plan, and that it must be Indians themselves who make up the "sales force." In a nation that suffers from the most flagitious problems of color, creed and caste, it is only men and women who speak the local dialect, possess the local complexion and wear the local costume who will obtain consumer acceptance in the village marketplace.

All that I have so far outlined is a plan based on elementary principles of good marketing: Find a need, develop a product to satisfy it, draw up a coherent plan for distributing, selling and servicing the product, get a budget, hire good salesmen who "know the territory," and promote like hell. If it all seems preposterous it is only because of the unfamiliar magnitude of the task.

This article appears in the pages of Marketing/Communications because it is precisely people engaged in marketing communications—those so aptly called "paid propagandists" by Howard Gossage—who must initiate such a plan. No other group in our society has the audacity, the imagination and the acumen to do it. With men like Emerson Foote, Leo Burnett, Chester Bowles and others who have accomplished all that there is to accomplish in commercial propaganda, we have the leaders to shape and clothe the concept delineated in this article. And with the men and women who staff our advertising agencies and departments, we have a reservoir of talent to back them. Whether advertisers and agencies will allow their best people to take a sabbatical for getting the plan underway is, of course, a moot question.

Even if they do, though, these bright, talented and dedicated people might not be willing to accept such a challenge. For they will undoubtedly be called crackpots. They will be told to stick to their typewriters and T-squares and tables of marketing statistics. They will be admonished to let people better qualified than they are do the serious thinking of the world.

But if we let the politicians and columnists and clerics and other traditional preceptors of right thinking do our thinking for us, there may not be much of the world left to do any serious thinking about. Because if India collapses from hunger it will mean the end of things as we know them from Canton in Kwantung to Canton in Ohio.

When all is black and parched and popping with high energy gamma radiation, there will be little need for parliaments or newspapers or churches—much less for advertising departments and agencies.

Who is going to join me in the outrageously sensible attempt to apply marketing methods where they are most needed today?

SELECTED BIBLIOGRAPHY
for
PART 6

DICHTER, ERNEST. "The World Customer," *Harvard Business Review.* July–August, 1962, pp. 113–22.

KIRSTEIN, GEORGE G. "The Day the Ads Stopped," *The Nation.* June 1, 1964, pp. 555–57.

MAYER, MARTIN. "Planned Obsolescence: RX for Tired Markets," *Dun's Review.* February, 1950, p. 40 and pp. 70–74.

McGINNESS, JOE. "The Selling of the President," *Harper's.* August, 1969.

NARVER, JOHN C. "Marketing and the Controversy over Conglomerate Mergers," *Journal of Marketing.* July, 1967, pp. 6–10.

RATHMELL, JOHN M. "What Is Meant by Services?," *Journal of Marketing.* October, 1966, pp. 32–36.

SIMON, JULIAN. "A Huge Marketing Research Task—Birth Control," *Journal of Marketing Research.* February, 1968, pp. 21–27.

STERN, LOUIS L. "Consumer Protection Via Increased Information," *Journal of Marketing.* April, 1967, pp. 48–52.

STURDIVANT, FREDERICK, and WILHELM, WALTER. "Poverty, Minorities, and Consumer Exploitation," *Social Science Quarterly.* December, 1968, pp. 643–50.

YOSHINO, MICHAEL Y. "Marketing Orientation in International Business," *Business Topics.* Summer, 1965, pp. 58–64.